VERTIGO

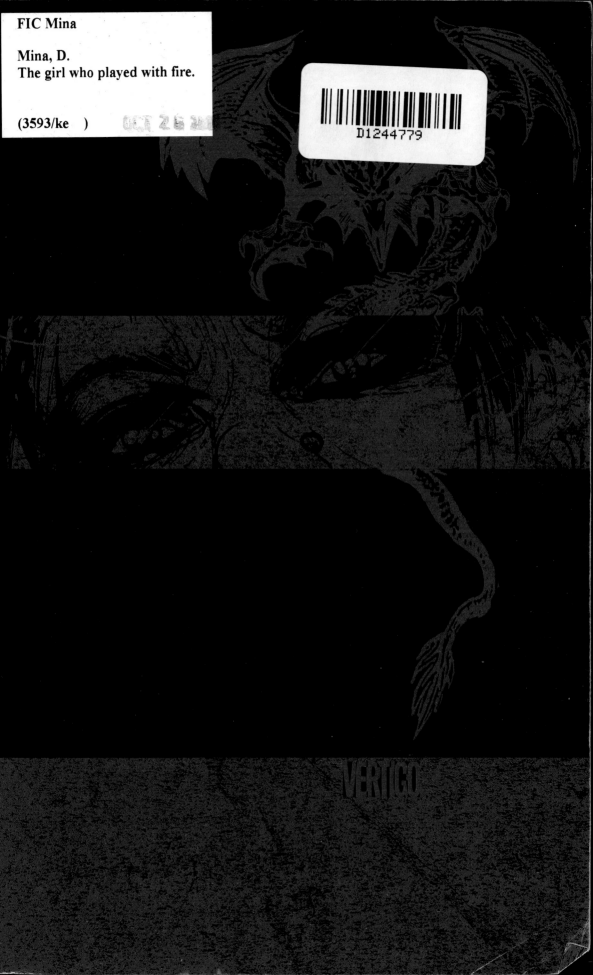

THE GIR
PLAYED W

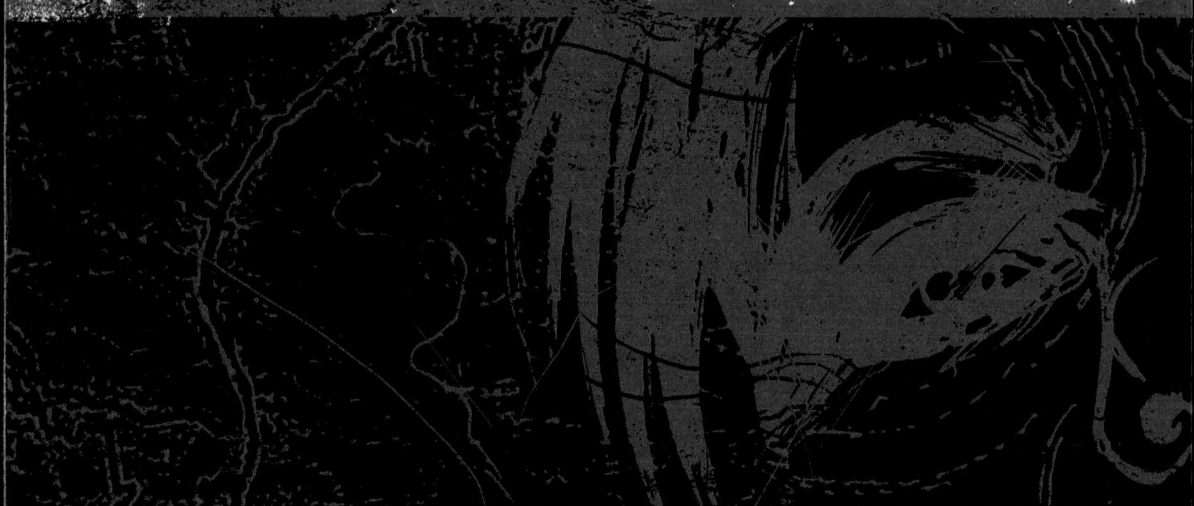

ADAPTED BY DENISE MINA

ART BY ANDREA MUTTI, ANTONIO

COLORS BY GIULIA BRUSCO, PATRICIA

LETTERS BY STEVE WANDS

BASED ON THE NOVEL THE GIRL WHO PLAYED

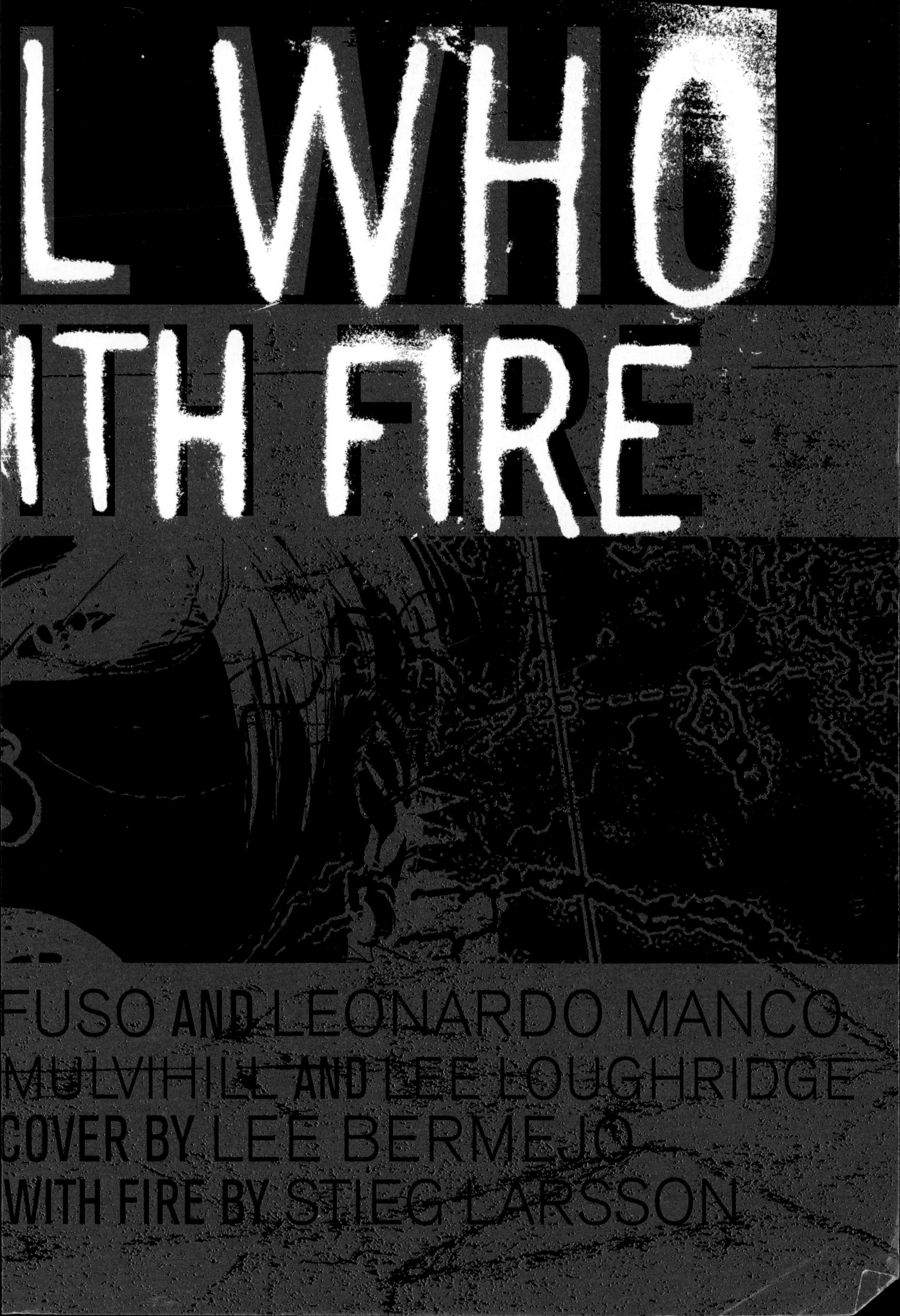
L WHO
ITH FIRE
FUSO AND LEONARDO MANCO
MULVIHILL AND LEE LOUGHRIDGE
COVER BY LEE BERMEJO
WITH FIRE BY STIEG LARSSON

Will Dennis Editor   Greg Lockard Associate Editor   Sara Miller Assistant Editor   Robbin Brosterman Design Director – Books
Louis Prandi Publication Design   Shelly Bond Executive Editor – Vertigo   Hank Kanalz Senior VP – Vertigo & Integrated Publishing

Diane Nelson President   Dan DiDio and Jim Lee Co-Publishers   Geoff Johns Chief Creative Officer   Amit Desai Senior VP – Marketing & Franchise Management
Amy Genkins Senior VP – Business & Legal Affairs   Nairi Gardiner Senior VP – Finance   Jeff Boison VP – Publishing Planning   Mark Chiarello VP – Art Direction & Design
John Cunningham VP – Marketing   Terri Cunningham VP – Editorial Administration   Larry Ganem VP – Talent Relations & Services   Alison Gill Senior VP – Manufacturing & Operations
Jay Kogan VP – Business & Legal Affairs, Publishing   Jack Mahan VP – Business Affairs, Talent   Nick Napolitano VP – Manufacturing Administration   Sue Pohja VP – Book Sales
Fred Ruiz VP – Manufacturing Operations   Courtney Simmons Senior VP – Publicity   Bob Wayne Senior VP – Sales

Library of Congress Cataloging-in-Publication Data

Mina, Denise, author.
The girl who played with fire / Denise Mina ; illustrated by Leonardo Manco ; illustrated by Andrea Mutti.
pages cm
ISBN 978-1-4012-5550-3 (softcover)
1. Crime—Sweden—Comic books, strips, etc. 2. Murder—Investigation—Comic books, strips, etc. 3. Graphic novels. I. Manco, Leonardo, illustrator. II. Mutti, Andrea, 1973- illustrator. III. Larsson, Stieg, 1954-2004. Girl who
played with fire. IV. Title.
PN6737.M57656 2014
741.5'942—dc23
2014008589

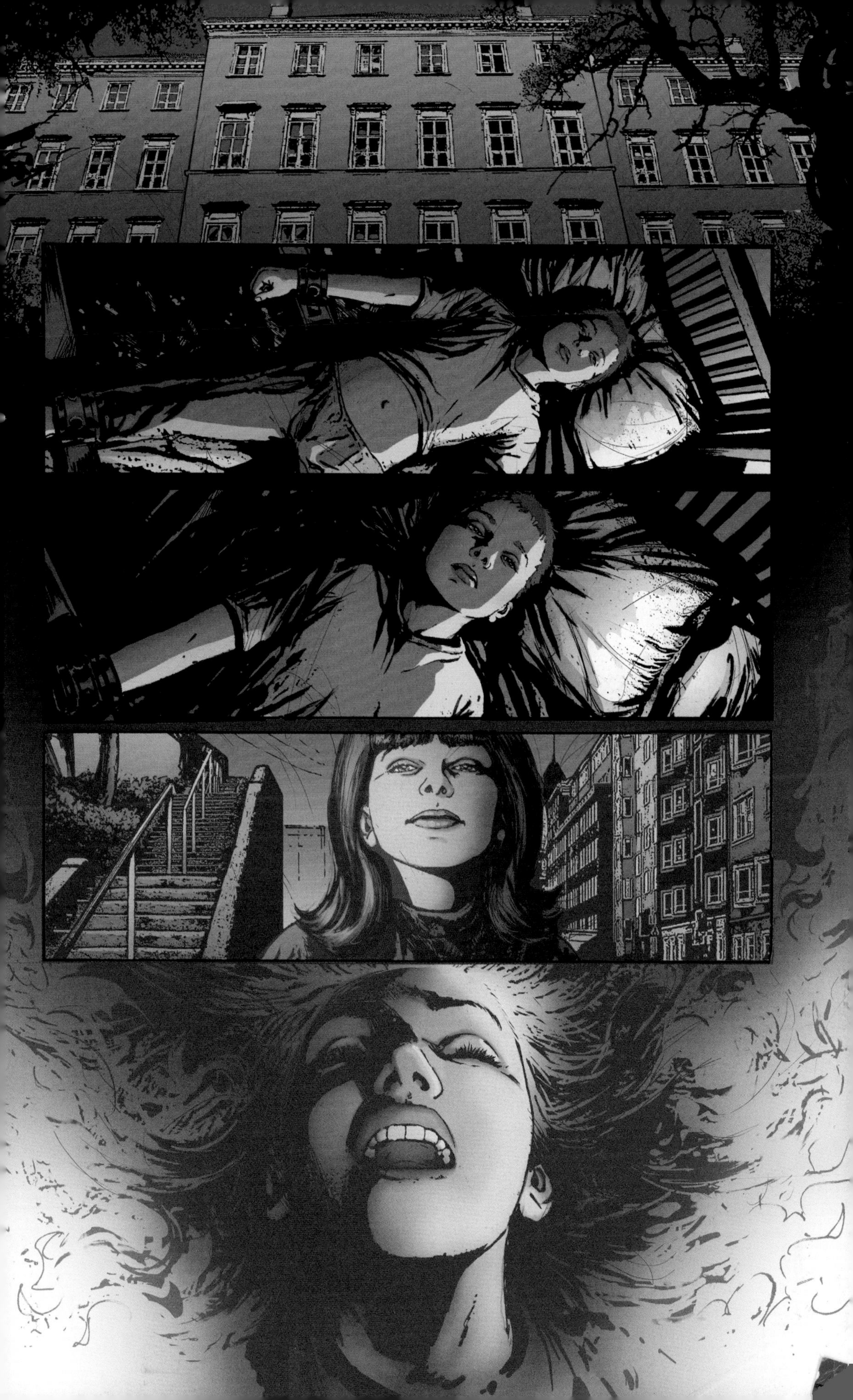

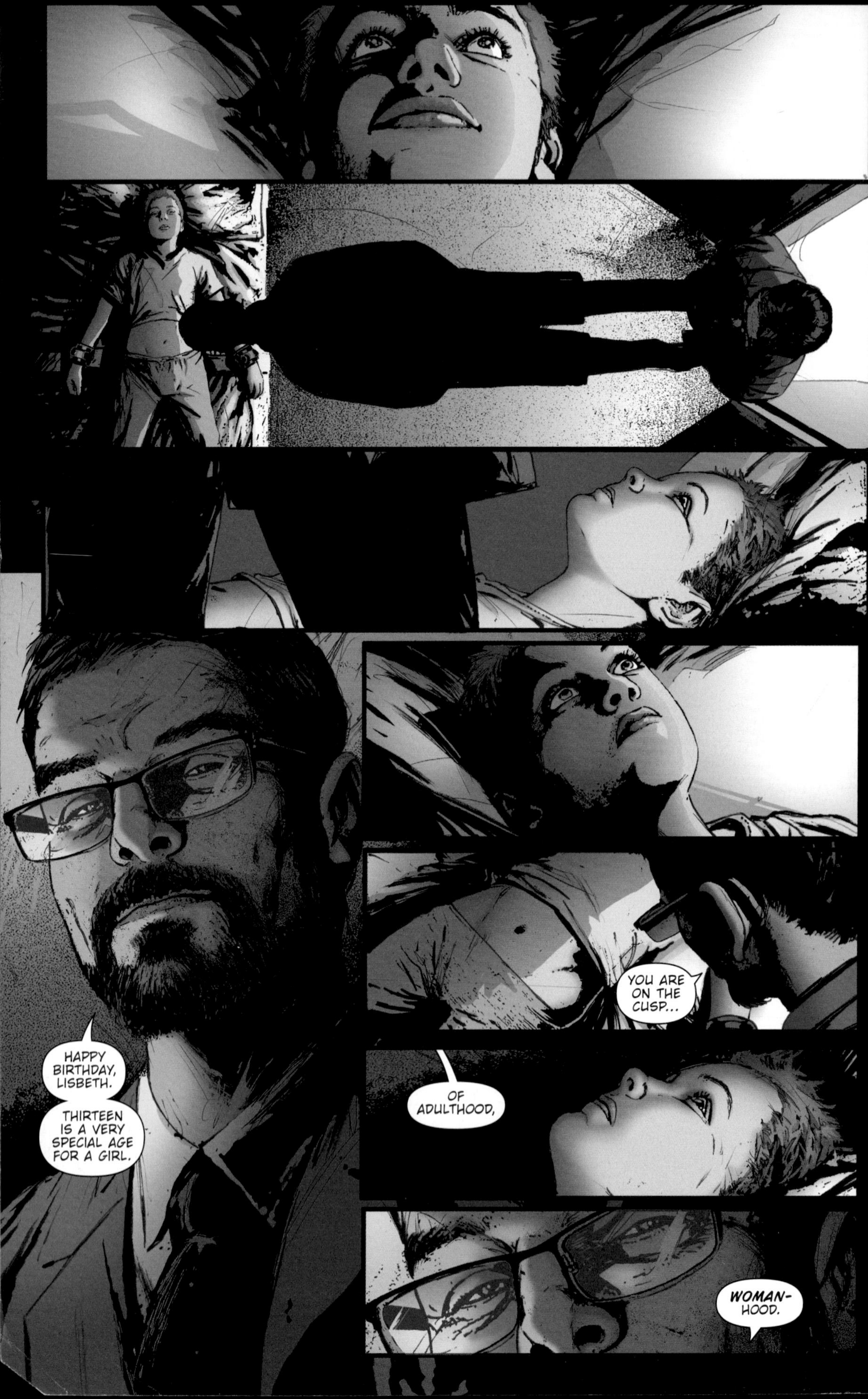
HAPPY BIRTHDAY, LISBETH.
THIRTEEN IS A VERY SPECIAL AGE FOR A GIRL.
YOU ARE ON THE CUSP...
OF ADULTHOOD,
WOMAN-HOOD.

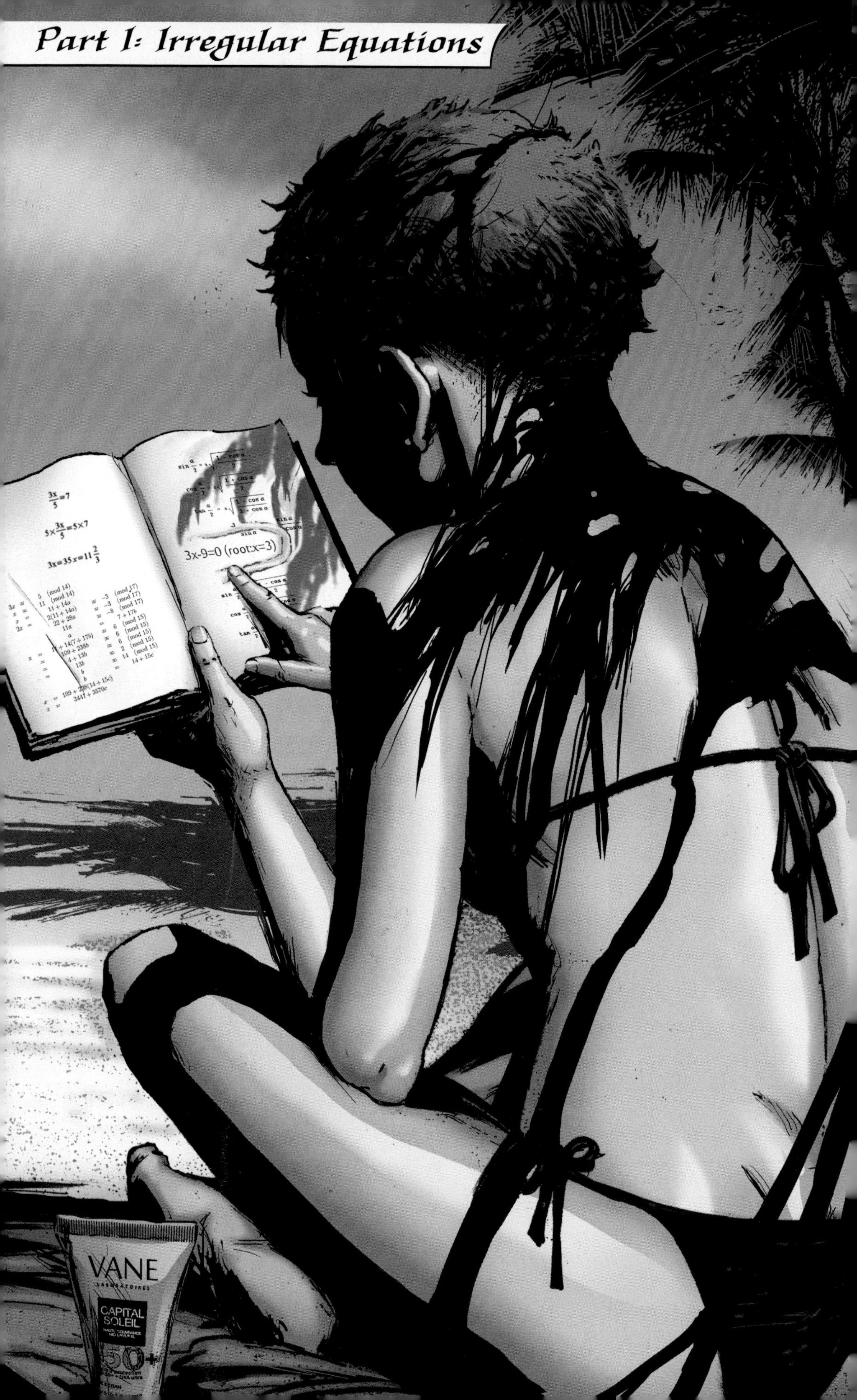
Part 1: Irregular Equations
3x-9=0 (root:x=3)
VANE
CAPITAL
SOLEIL

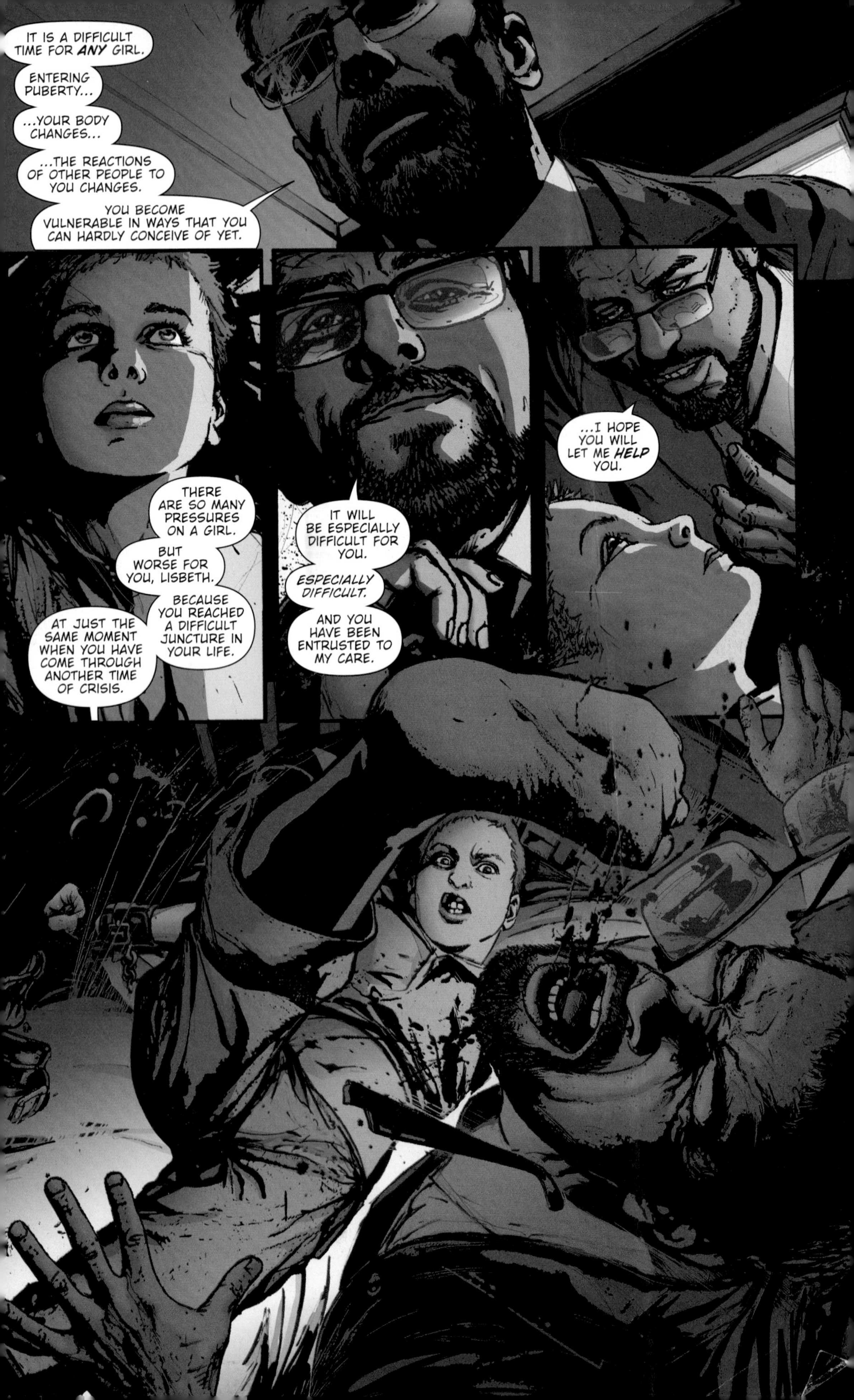

IT IS A DIFFICULT TIME FOR ANY GIRL.
ENTERING PUBERTY...
...YOUR BODY CHANGES...
...THE REACTIONS OF OTHER PEOPLE TO YOU CHANGES.
YOU BECOME VULNERABLE IN WAYS THAT YOU CAN HARDLY CONCEIVE OF YET.
THERE ARE SO MANY PRESSURES ON A GIRL.
BUT WORSE FOR YOU, LISBETH.
BECAUSE YOU REACHED A DIFFICULT JUNCTURE IN YOUR LIFE.
AT JUST THE SAME MOMENT WHEN YOU HAVE COME THROUGH ANOTHER TIME OF CRISIS.
IT WILL BE ESPECIALLY DIFFICULT FOR YOU.
ESPECIALLY DIFFICULT.
AND YOU HAVE BEEN ENTRUSTED TO MY CARE.
...I HOPE YOU WILL LET ME HELP YOU.

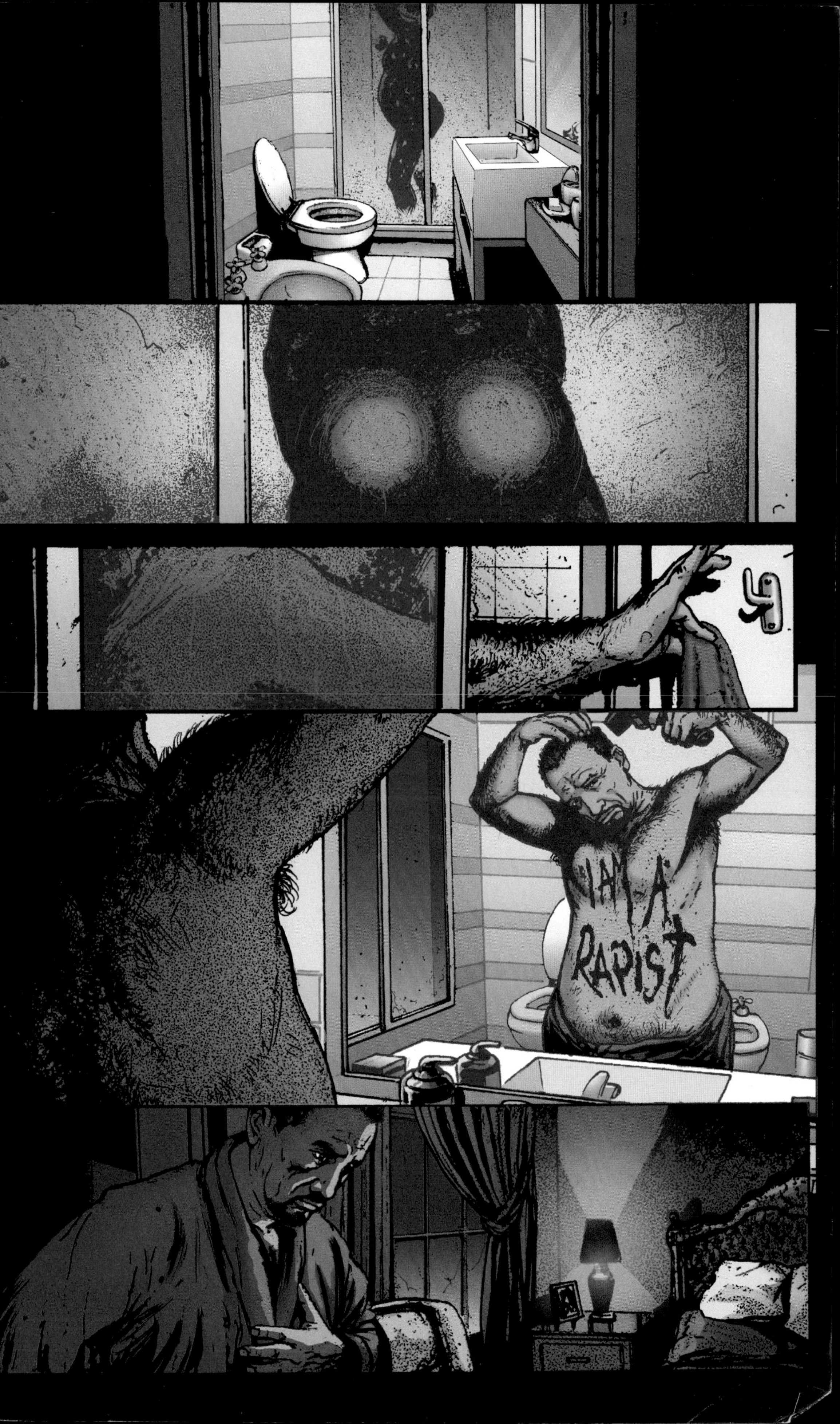
I AM A RAPIST

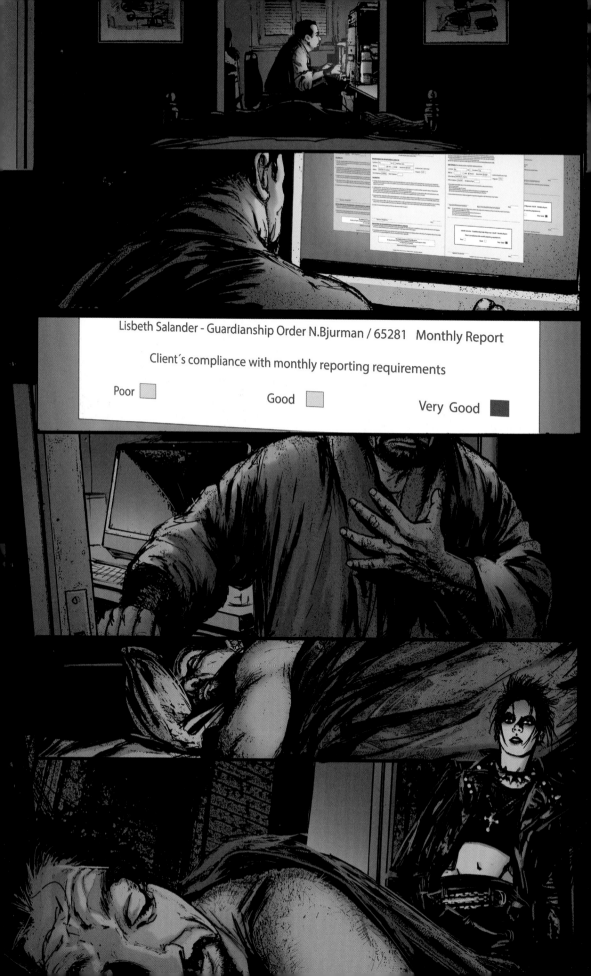

Lisbeth Salander - Guardianship Order N.Bjurman / 65281   Monthly Report

Client´s compliance with monthly reporting requirements

Poor   Good   Very Good

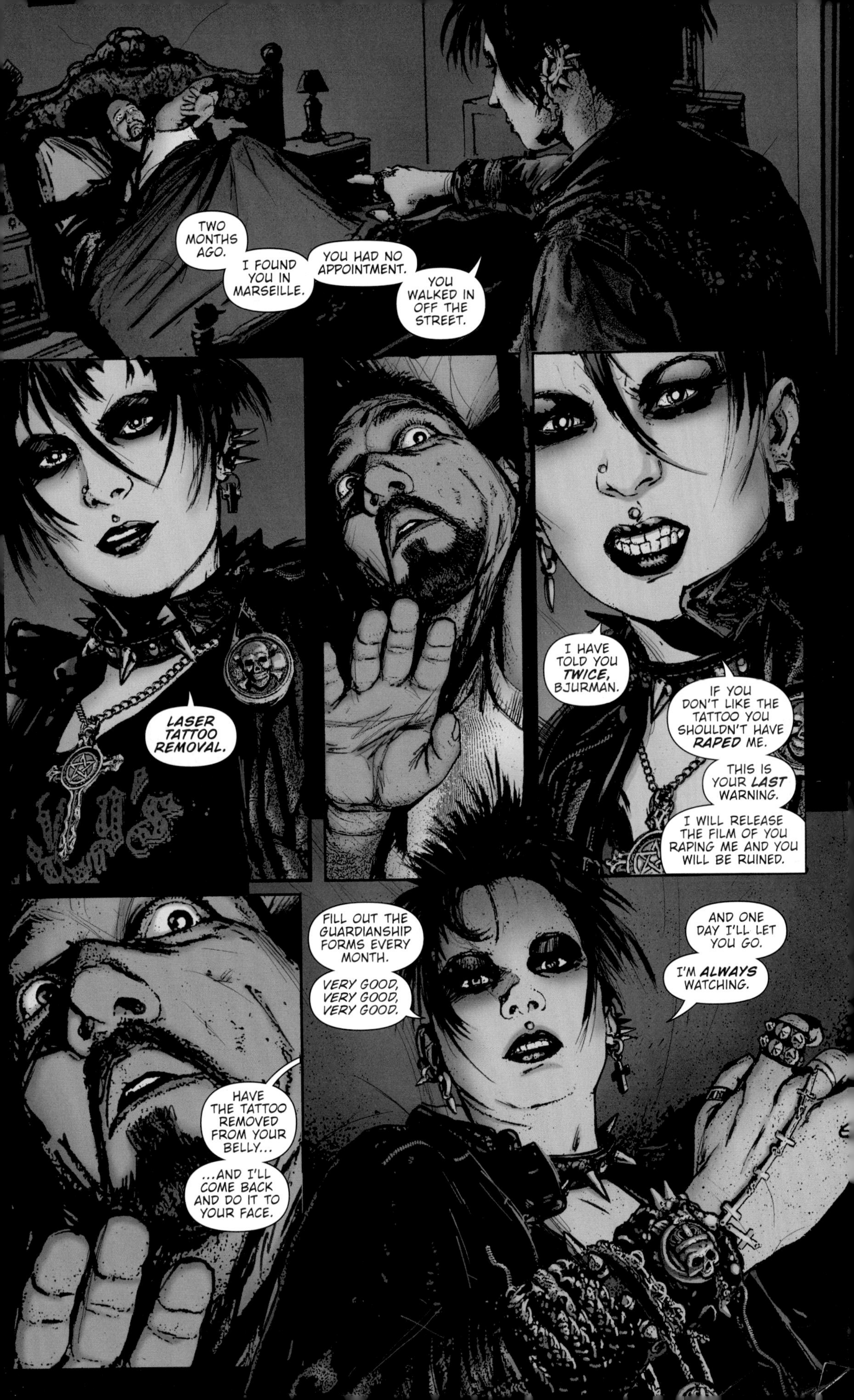

TWO MONTHS AGO.
I FOUND YOU IN MARSEILLE.
YOU HAD NO APPOINTMENT.
YOU WALKED IN OFF THE STREET.
LASER TATTOO REMOVAL.
I HAVE TOLD YOU TWICE, BJURMAN.
IF YOU DON'T LIKE THE TATTOO YOU SHOULDN'T HAVE RAPED ME.
THIS IS YOUR LAST WARNING.
I WILL RELEASE THE FILM OF YOU RAPING ME AND YOU WILL BE RUINED.
HAVE THE TATTOO REMOVED FROM YOUR BELLY...
...AND I'LL COME BACK AND DO IT TO YOUR FACE.
FILL OUT THE GUARDIANSHIP FORMS EVERY MONTH.
VERY GOOD, VERY GOOD, VERY GOOD.
AND ONE DAY I'LL LET YOU GO.
I'M ALWAYS WATCHING.

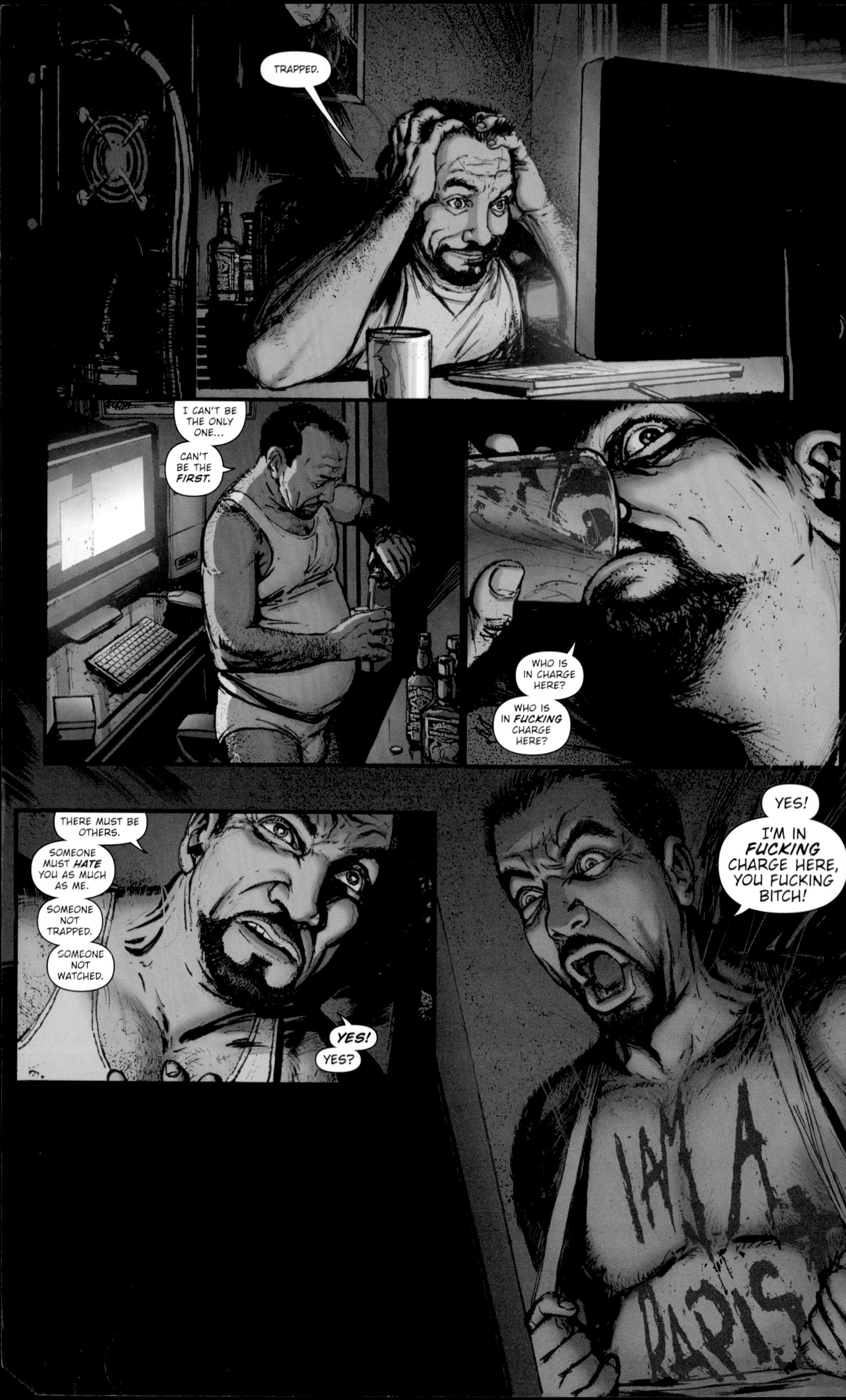
TRAPPED.
I CAN'T BE THE ONLY ONE...
CAN'T BE THE ***FIRST.***
WHO IS IN CHARGE HERE?
WHO IS IN ***FUCKING*** CHARGE HERE?
THERE MUST BE OTHERS.
SOMEONE MUST ***HATE*** YOU AS MUCH AS ME.
SOMEONE NOT TRAPPED.
SOMEONE NOT WATCHED.
YES!
YES?
YES!
I'M IN ***FUCKING*** CHARGE HERE, YOU FUCKING BITCH!

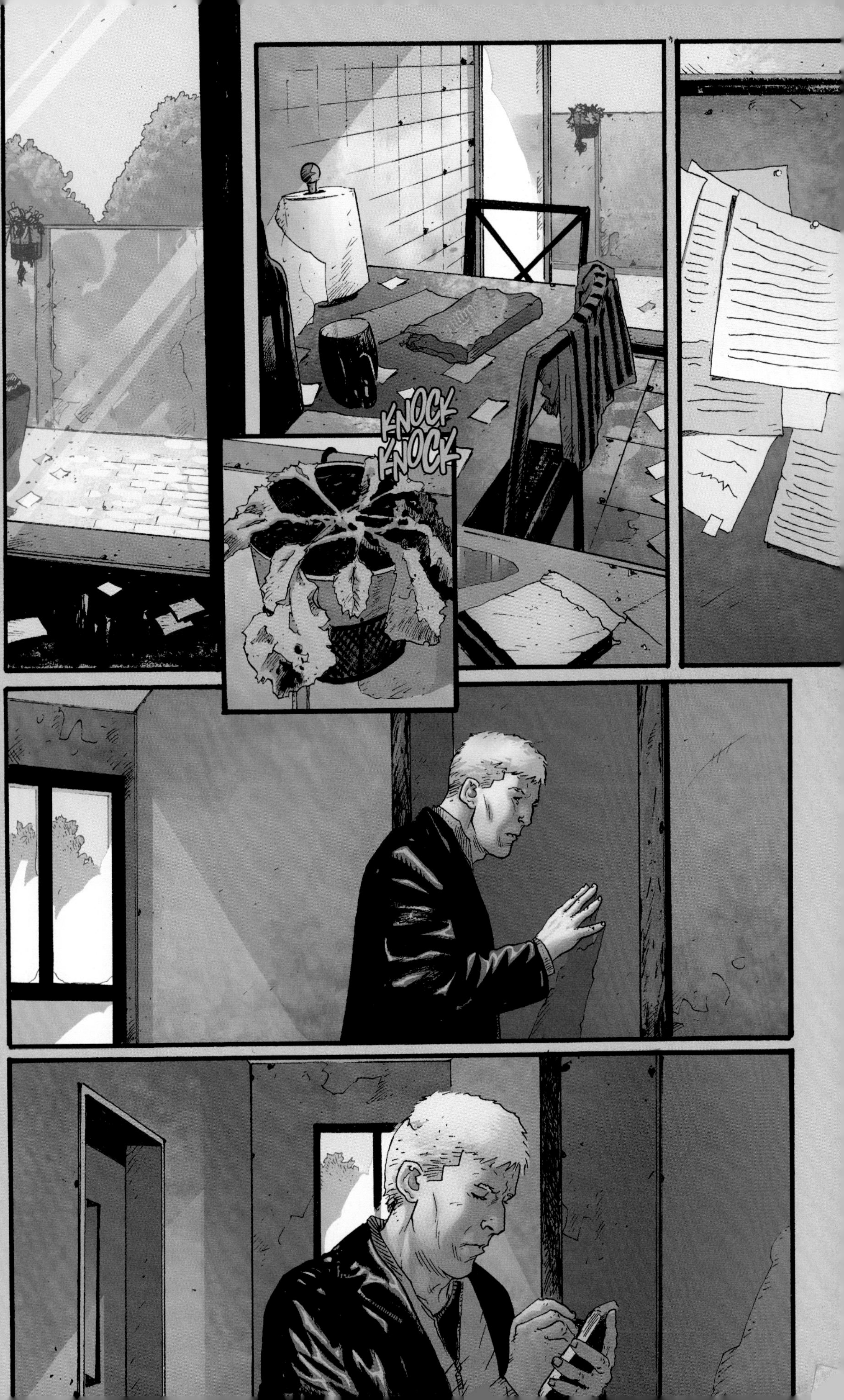
KNOCK
KNOCK

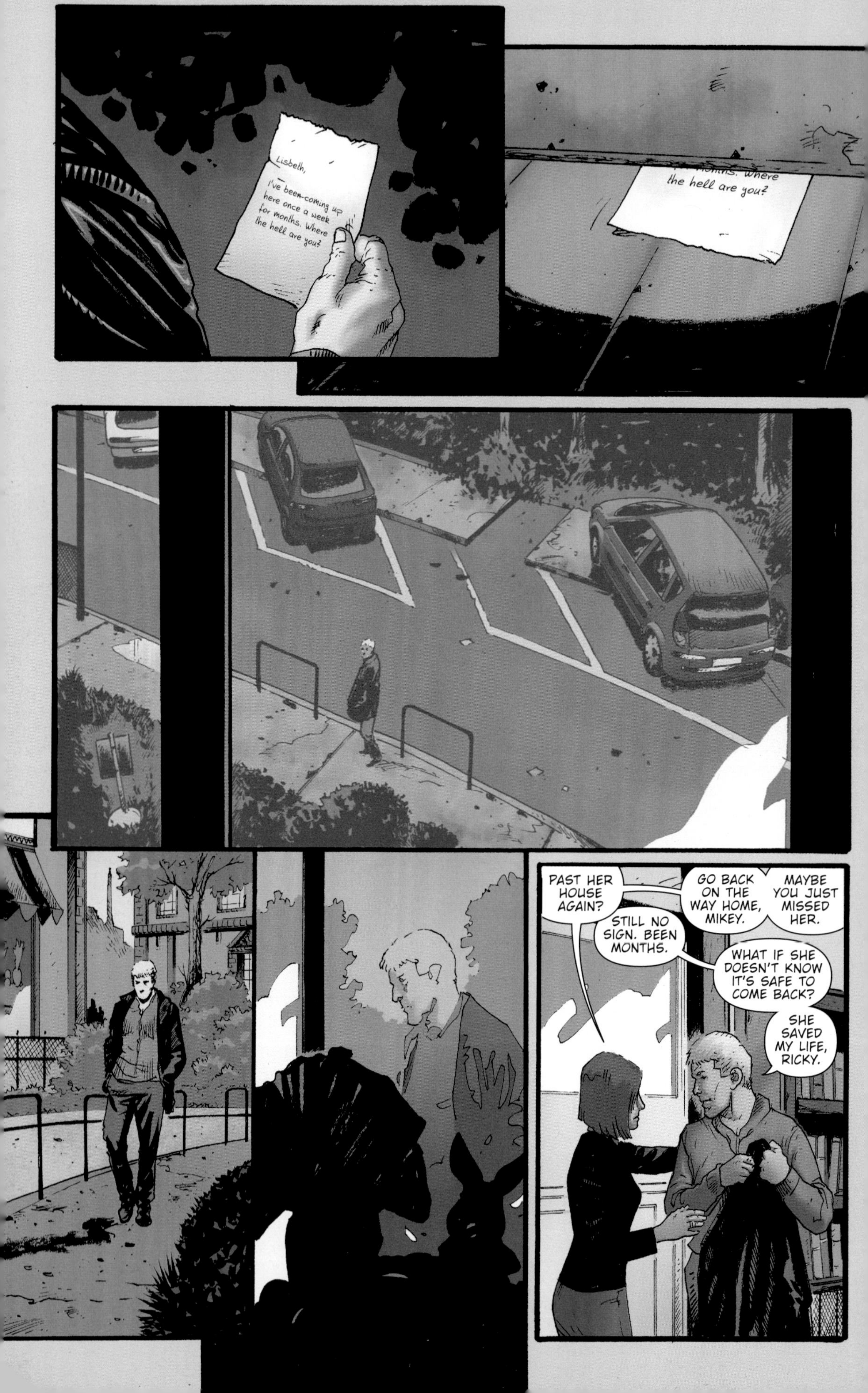
Lisbeth,
I've been coming up here once a week for months. Where the hell are you?
months. Where the hell are you?
PAST HER HOUSE AGAIN?
STILL NO SIGN. BEEN MONTHS.
GO BACK ON THE WAY HOME, MIKEY.
MAYBE YOU JUST MISSED HER.
WHAT IF SHE DOESN'T KNOW IT'S SAFE TO COME BACK?
SHE SAVED MY LIFE, RICKY.

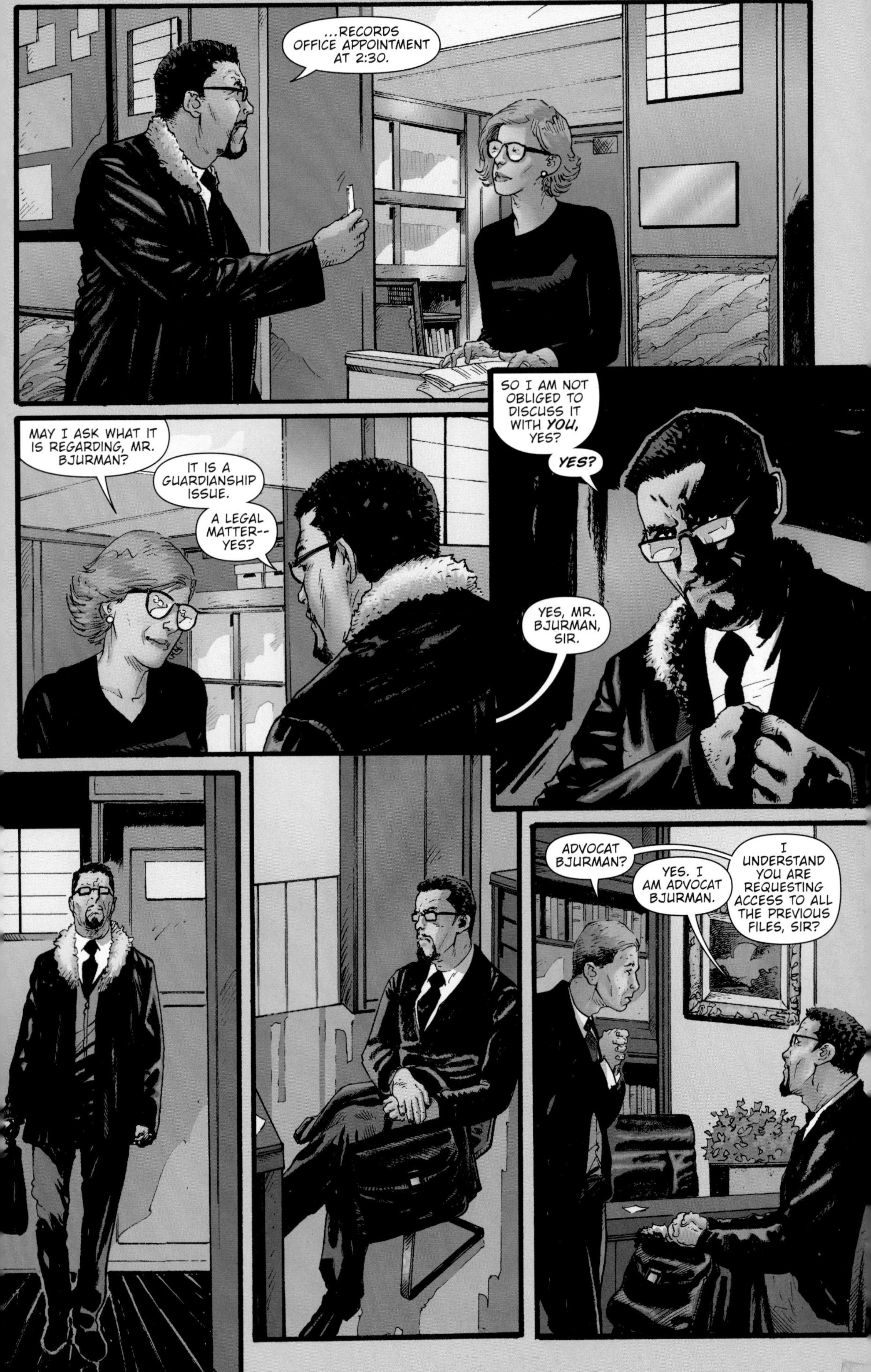
...RECORDS OFFICE APPOINTMENT AT 2:30.
MAY I ASK WHAT IT IS REGARDING, MR. BJURMAN?
IT IS A GUARDIANSHIP ISSUE.
A LEGAL MATTER--YES?
SO I AM NOT OBLIGED TO DISCUSS IT WITH *YOU,* YES?
YES?
YES, MR. BJURMAN, SIR.
ADVOCAT BJURMAN?
YES. I AM ADVOCAT BJURMAN.
I UNDERSTAND YOU ARE REQUESTING ACCESS TO ALL THE PREVIOUS FILES, SIR?

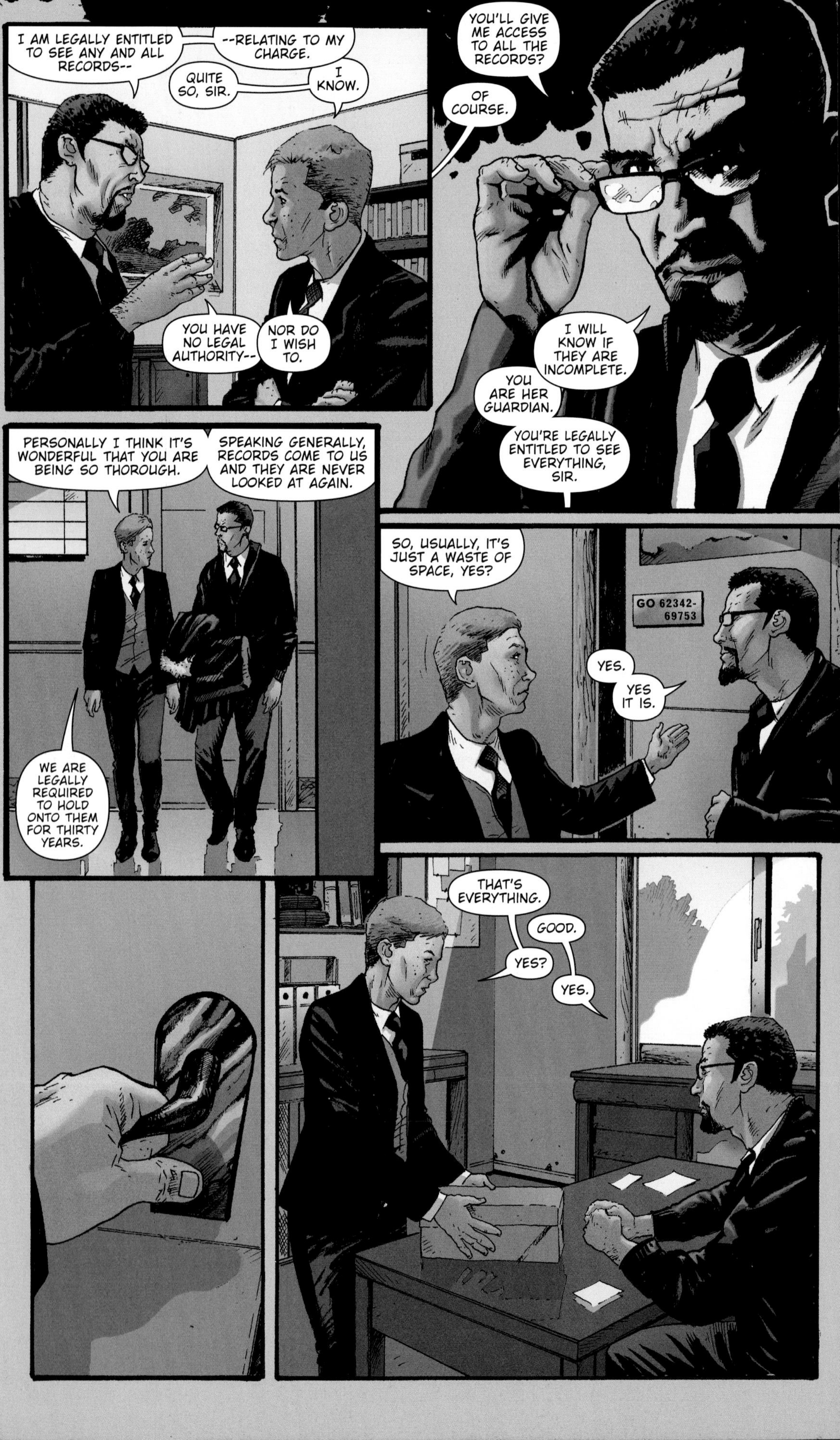
I AM LEGALLY ENTITLED TO SEE ANY AND ALL RECORDS--
--RELATING TO MY CHARGE.
QUITE SO, SIR.
I KNOW.
YOU HAVE NO LEGAL AUTHORITY--
NOR DO I WISH TO.
YOU'LL GIVE ME ACCESS TO ALL THE RECORDS?
OF COURSE.
I WILL KNOW IF THEY ARE INCOMPLETE.
YOU ARE HER GUARDIAN.
YOU'RE LEGALLY ENTITLED TO SEE EVERYTHING, SIR.
PERSONALLY I THINK IT'S WONDERFUL THAT YOU ARE BEING SO THOROUGH.
SPEAKING GENERALLY, RECORDS COME TO US AND THEY ARE NEVER LOOKED AT AGAIN.
WE ARE LEGALLY REQUIRED TO HOLD ONTO THEM FOR THIRTY YEARS.
SO, USUALLY, IT'S JUST A WASTE OF SPACE, YES?
GO 62342-69753
YES.
YES IT IS.
THAT'S EVERYTHING.
GOOD.
YES?
YES.

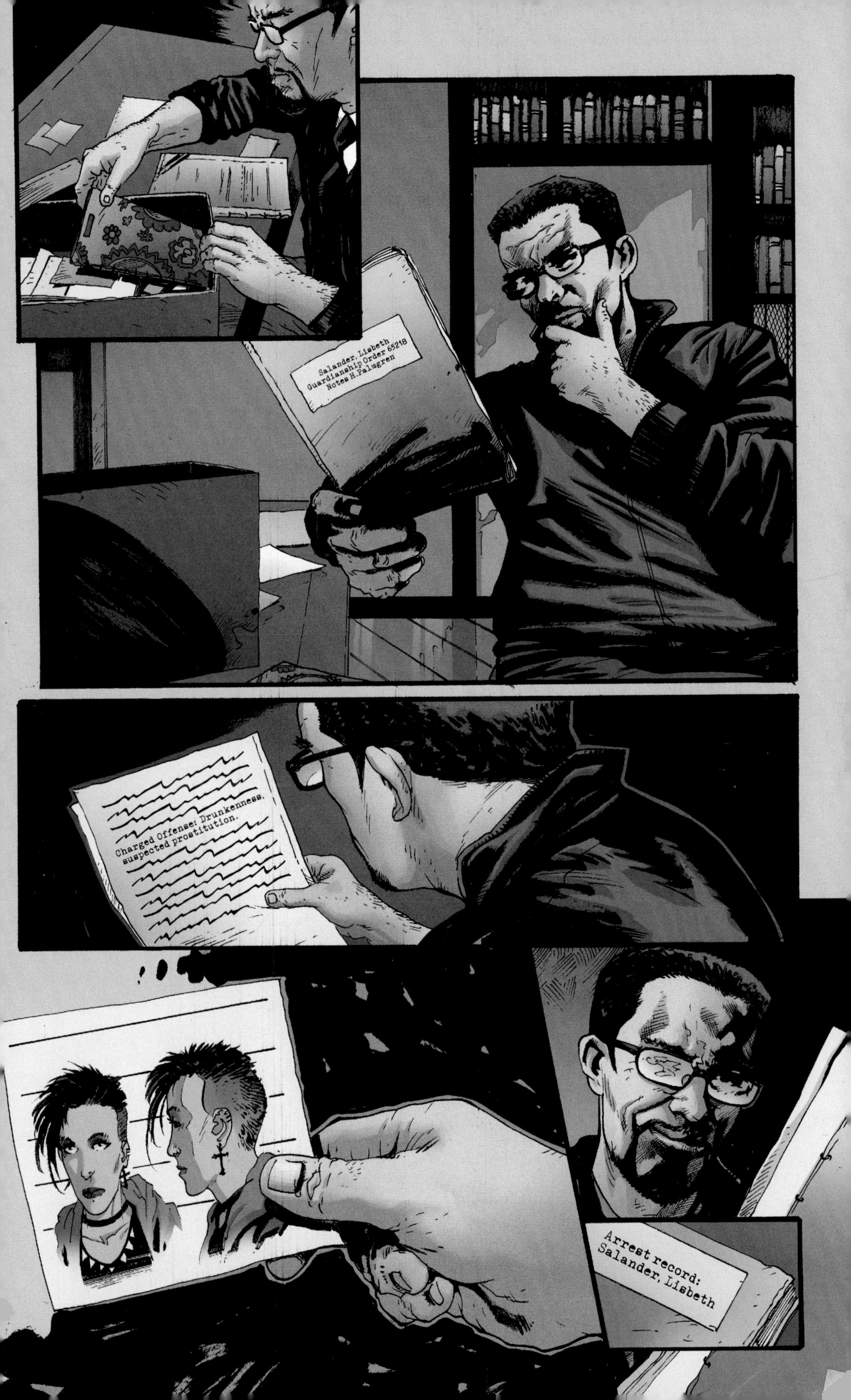
Salander, Lisbeth
Guardianship Order 65218
Notes H.Palmgren
Charged Offense: Drunkenness,
suspected prostitution.
Arrest record:
Salander, Lisbeth

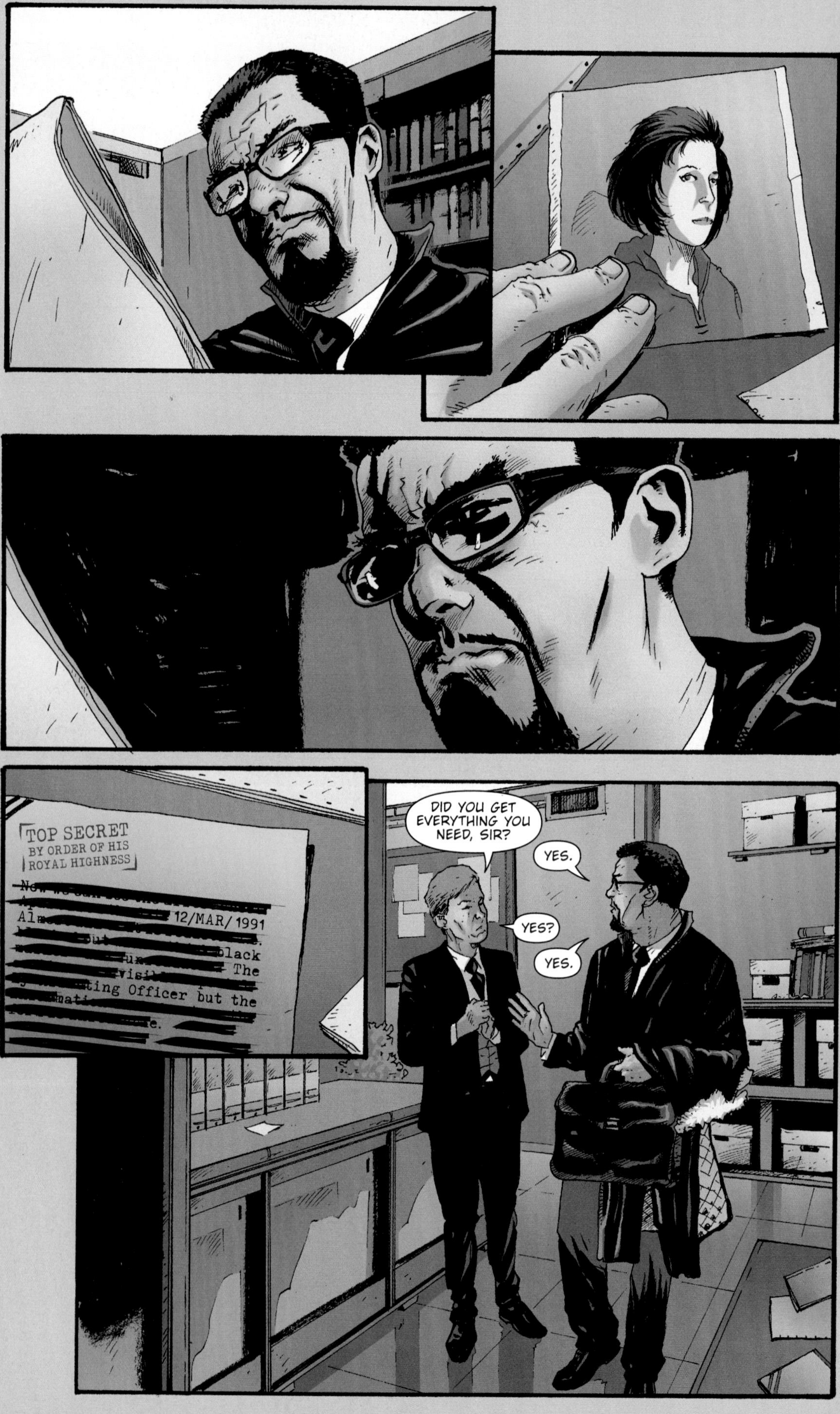
TOP SECRET
BY ORDER OF HIS
ROYAL HIGHNESS
[redacted] 12/MAR/1991
[redacted] black
[redacted] The
[redacted] Officer but the
[redacted] e.
[redacted]
DID YOU GET EVERYTHING YOU NEED, SIR?
YES.
YES?
YES.

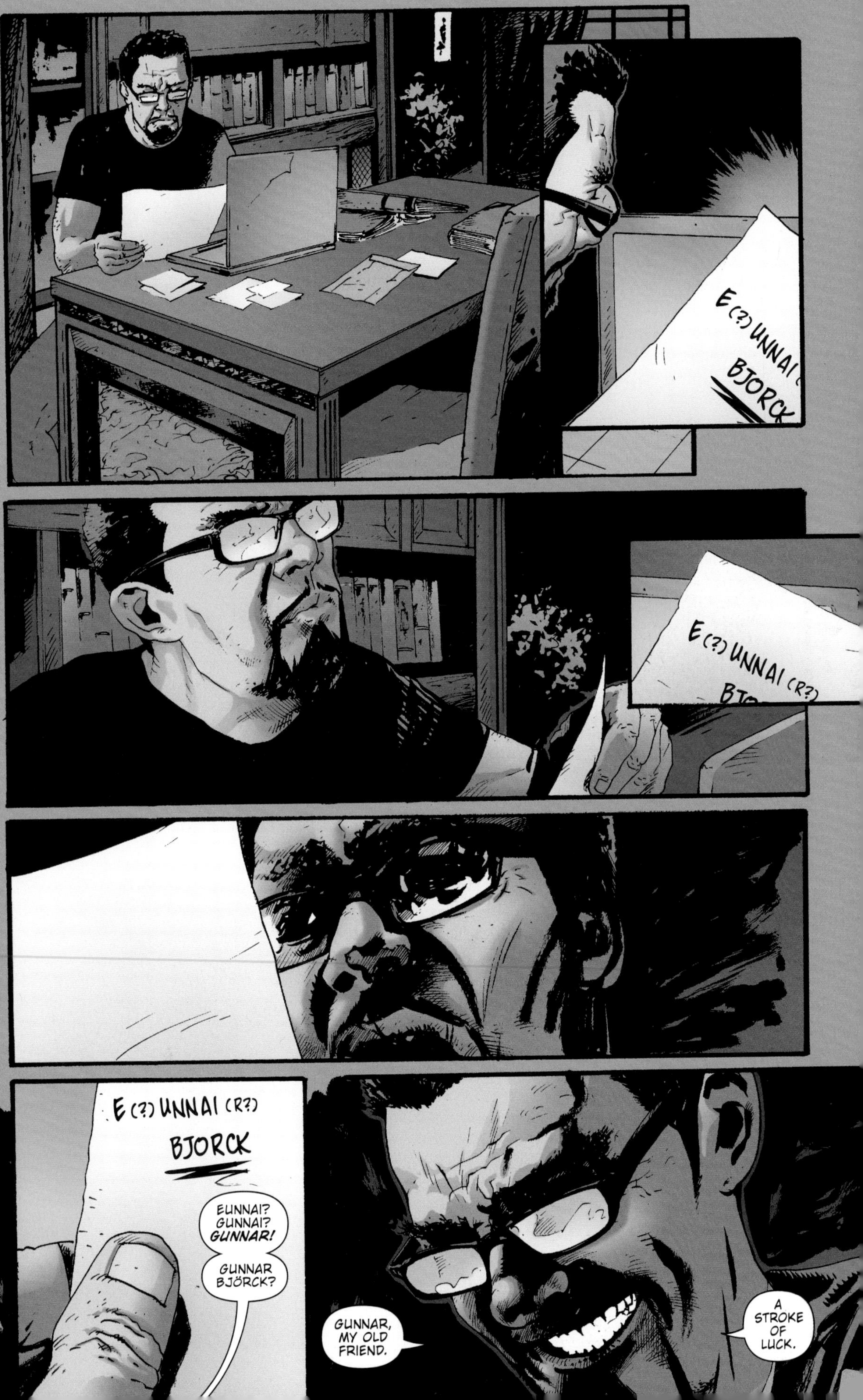
E (?) UNNAI (R?)
BJORCK
E (?) UNNAI (R?)
BJ
E (?) UNNAI (R?)
BJORCK
EUNNAI? GUNNAI? GUNNAR!
GUNNAR BJÖRCK?
GUNNAR, MY OLD FRIEND.
A STROKE OF LUCK.

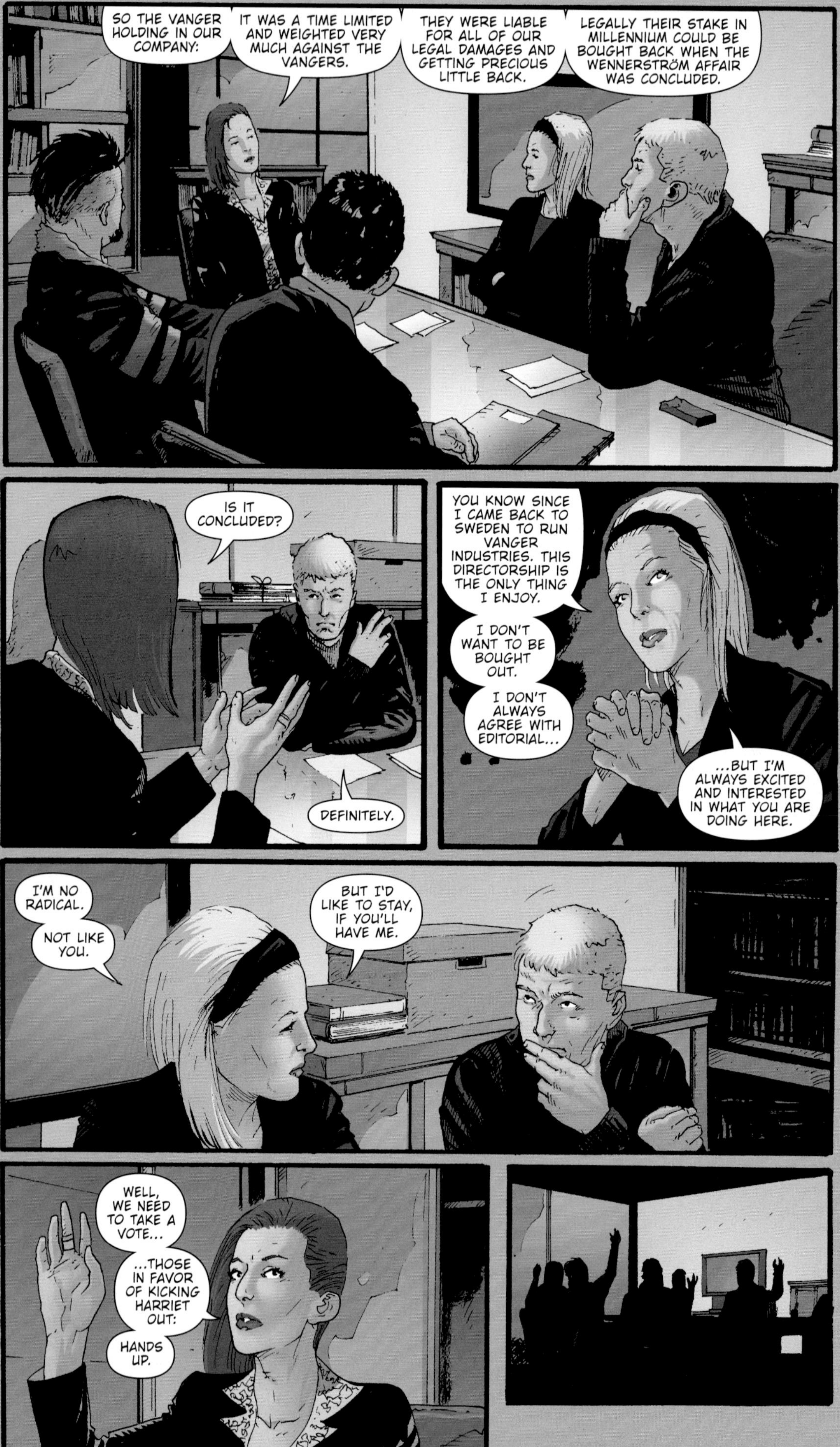
SO THE VANGER HOLDING IN OUR COMPANY:
IT WAS A TIME LIMITED AND WEIGHTED VERY MUCH AGAINST THE VANGERS.
THEY WERE LIABLE FOR ALL OF OUR LEGAL DAMAGES AND GETTING PRECIOUS LITTLE BACK.
LEGALLY THEIR STAKE IN MILLENNIUM COULD BE BOUGHT BACK WHEN THE WENNERSTRÖM AFFAIR WAS CONCLUDED.
IS IT CONCLUDED?
DEFINITELY.
YOU KNOW SINCE I CAME BACK TO SWEDEN TO RUN VANGER INDUSTRIES. THIS DIRECTORSHIP IS THE ONLY THING I ENJOY.
I DON'T WANT TO BE BOUGHT OUT.
I DON'T ALWAYS AGREE WITH EDITORIAL...
...BUT I'M ALWAYS EXCITED AND INTERESTED IN WHAT YOU ARE DOING HERE.
I'M NO RADICAL.
NOT LIKE YOU.
BUT I'D LIKE TO STAY, IF YOU'LL HAVE ME.
WELL, WE NEED TO TAKE A VOTE...
...THOSE IN FAVOR OF KICKING HARRIET OUT:
HANDS UP.

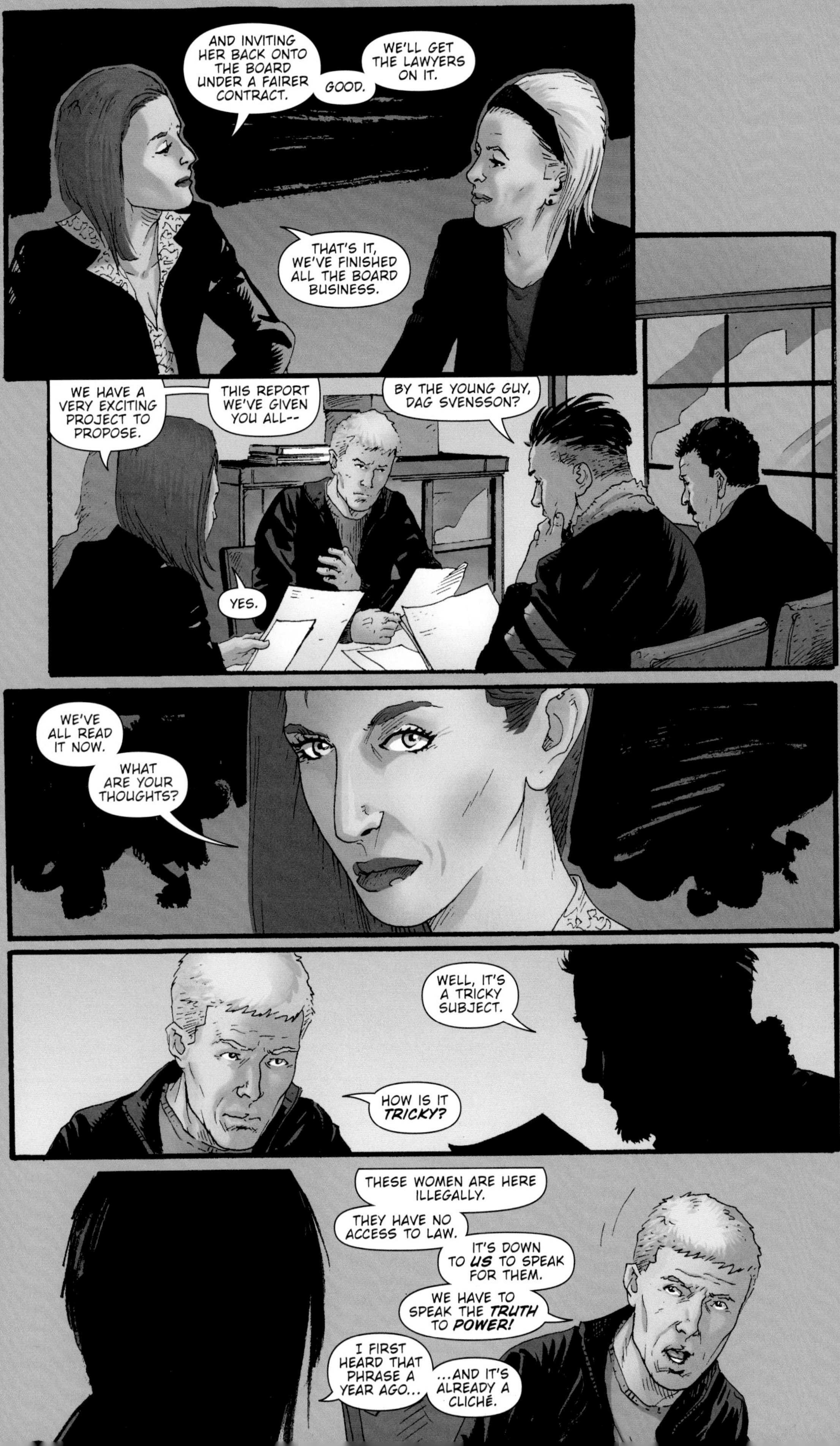
AND INVITING HER BACK ONTO THE BOARD UNDER A FAIRER CONTRACT.
GOOD.
WE'LL GET THE LAWYERS ON IT.
THAT'S IT, WE'VE FINISHED ALL THE BOARD BUSINESS.
WE HAVE A VERY EXCITING PROJECT TO PROPOSE.
THIS REPORT WE'VE GIVEN YOU ALL--
BY THE YOUNG GUY, DAG SVENSSON?
YES.
WE'VE ALL READ IT NOW.
WHAT ARE YOUR THOUGHTS?
WELL, IT'S A TRICKY SUBJECT.
HOW IS IT *TRICKY?*
THESE WOMEN ARE HERE ILLEGALLY.
THEY HAVE NO ACCESS TO LAW.
IT'S DOWN TO **US** TO SPEAK FOR THEM.
WE HAVE TO SPEAK THE **TRUTH** TO **POWER!**
I FIRST HEARD THAT PHRASE A YEAR AGO...
...AND IT'S ALREADY A CLICHÉ.

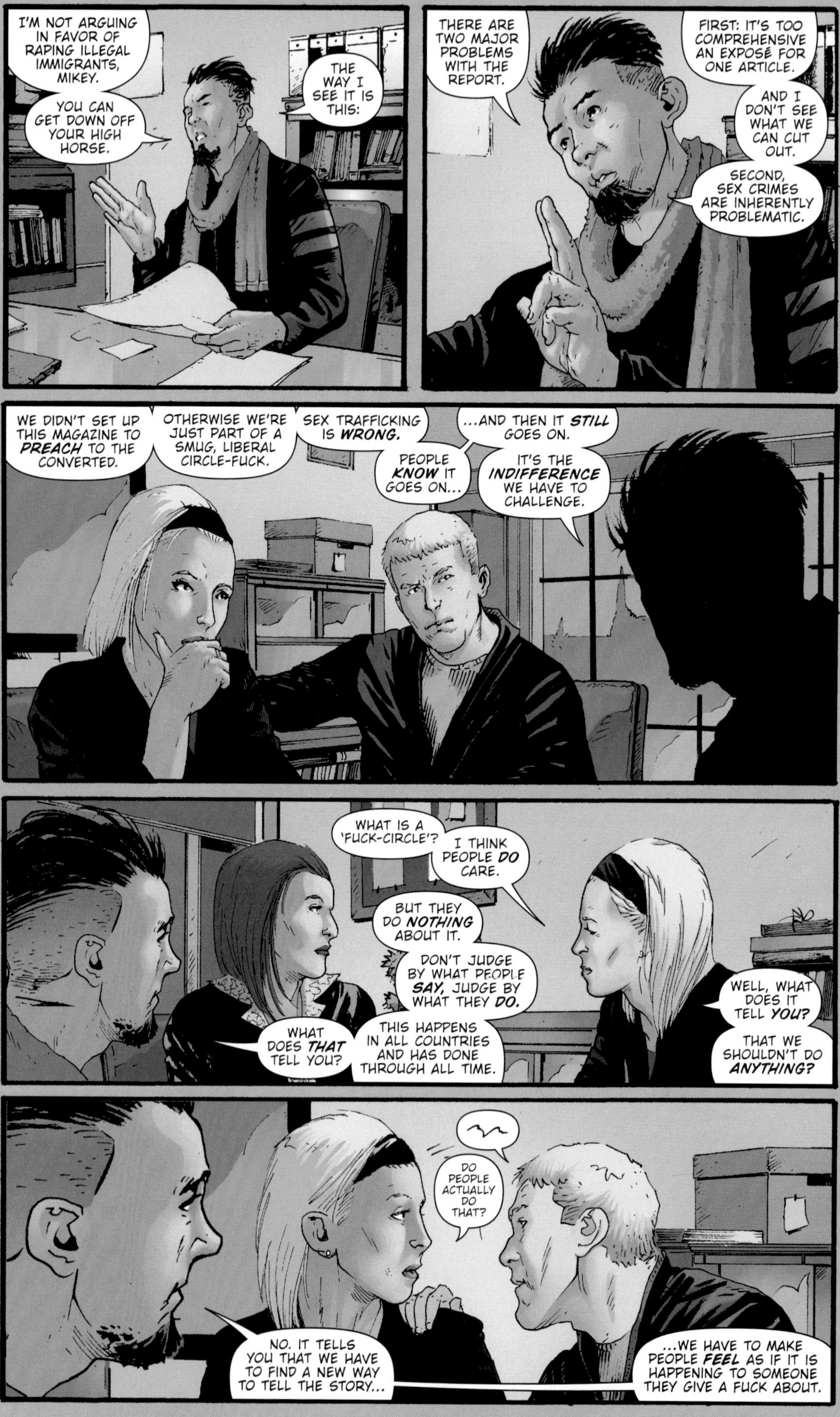
I'M NOT ARGUING IN FAVOR OF RAPING ILLEGAL IMMIGRANTS, MIKEY.
YOU CAN GET DOWN OFF YOUR HIGH HORSE.
THE WAY I SEE IT IS THIS:
THERE ARE TWO MAJOR PROBLEMS WITH THE REPORT.
FIRST: IT'S TOO COMPREHENSIVE AN EXPOSÉ FOR ONE ARTICLE.
AND I DON'T SEE WHAT WE CAN CUT OUT.
SECOND, SEX CRIMES ARE INHERENTLY PROBLEMATIC.
WE DIDN'T SET UP THIS MAGAZINE TO **PREACH** TO THE CONVERTED.
OTHERWISE WE'RE JUST PART OF A SMUG, LIBERAL CIRCLE-FUCK.
SEX TRAFFICKING IS **WRONG.**
PEOPLE **KNOW** IT GOES ON...
...AND THEN IT **STILL** GOES ON.
IT'S THE **INDIFFERENCE** WE HAVE TO CHALLENGE.
WHAT IS A 'FUCK-CIRCLE'?
I THINK PEOPLE **DO** CARE.
BUT THEY DO **NOTHING** ABOUT IT.
DON'T JUDGE BY WHAT PEOPLE **SAY,** JUDGE BY WHAT THEY **DO.**
THIS HAPPENS IN ALL COUNTRIES AND HAS DONE THROUGH ALL TIME.
WHAT DOES **THAT** TELL YOU?
WELL, WHAT DOES IT TELL **YOU?**
THAT WE SHOULDN'T DO **ANYTHING?**
DO PEOPLE ACTUALLY DO THAT?
NO. IT TELLS YOU THAT WE HAVE TO FIND A NEW WAY TO TELL THE STORY...
...WE HAVE TO MAKE PEOPLE **FEEL** AS IF IT IS HAPPENING TO SOMEONE THEY GIVE A FUCK ABOUT.

GOOD! IDENTIFY THE PROBLEMS WITH THE STORY.

THEN WE'LL SEE IF WE CAN FIX THEM.

I SUPPOSE ANYONE WHO USES ANY PART OF THE SEX INDUSTRY FEELS IMPLICATED.

OFTEN A DIFFERENT SKIN COLOR OR RACE.

YEAH, AND VICTIMS ARE HARD TO IDENTIFY WITH:

FOREIGN, POOR, SOMEONE ELSE'S DAUGHTER OR SON.

POWERLESS AND FROM ANOTHER COUNTRY.

WAIT, WAIT, I FEEL AS IF WE'RE HEADING TO A FIRST-PERSON ACCOUNT OF SEXUAL EXPLOITATION.

I DON'T WANT THAT.

I *SWEAR* PEOPLE READ THEM FOR TITILLATION.

AND THESE PEOPLE ARE EPIC HEROES:

WE REDUCE THEM TO A SLACK-JAWED VICTIM.

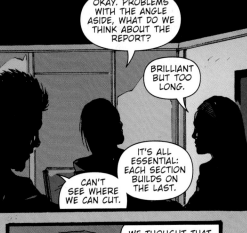

OKAY. PROBLEMS WITH THE ANGLE ASIDE, WHAT DO WE THINK ABOUT THE REPORT?

BRILLIANT BUT TOO LONG.

IT'S ALL ESSENTIAL: EACH SECTION BUILDS ON THE LAST.

CAN'T SEE WHERE WE CAN CUT.

WE THOUGHT THAT, DIDN'T WE?

MIKAEL HAD A SUGGESTION.

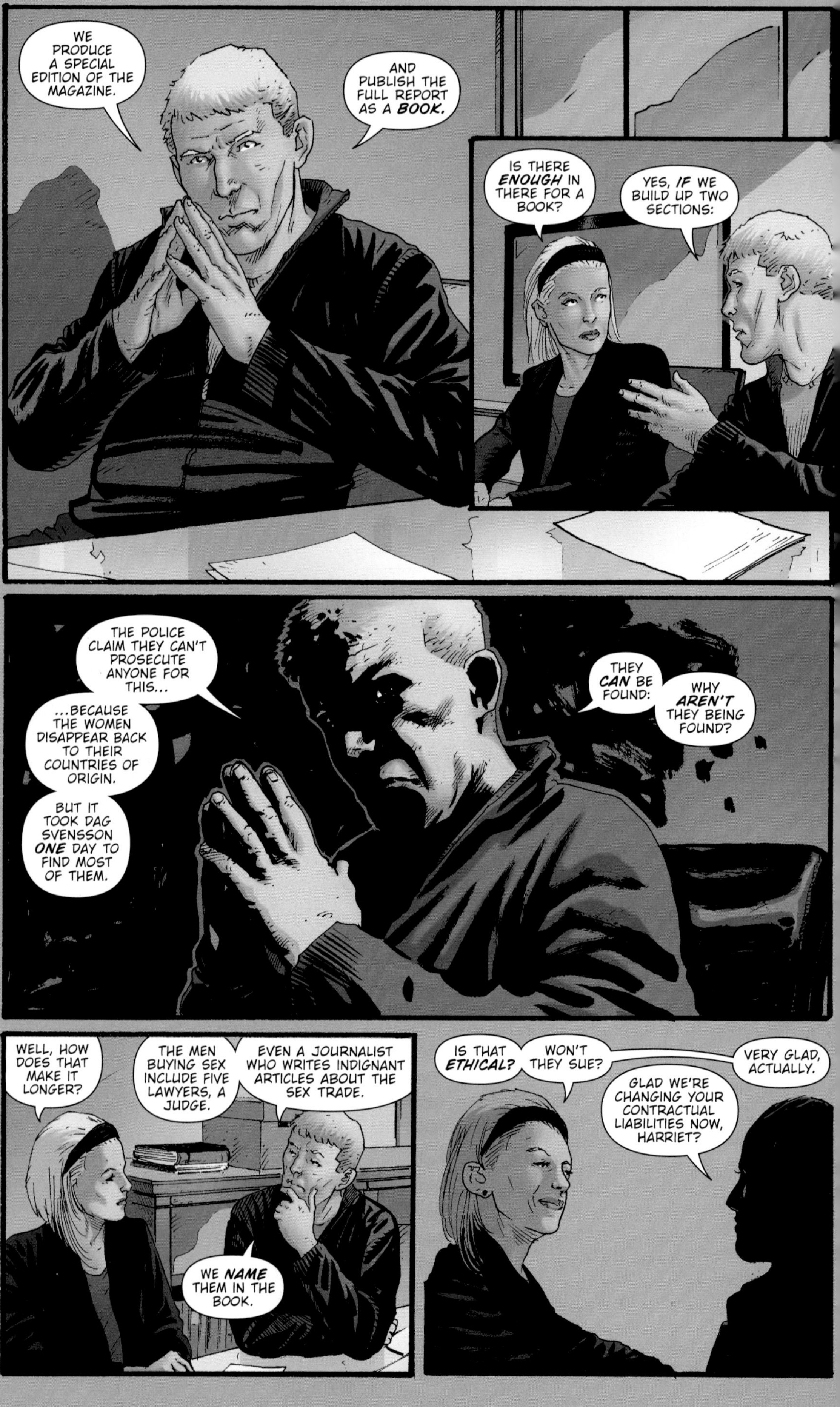
WE PRODUCE A SPECIAL EDITION OF THE MAGAZINE.
AND PUBLISH THE FULL REPORT AS A BOOK.
IS THERE ENOUGH IN THERE FOR A BOOK?
YES, IF WE BUILD UP TWO SECTIONS:
THE POLICE CLAIM THEY CAN'T PROSECUTE ANYONE FOR THIS...
...BECAUSE THE WOMEN DISAPPEAR BACK TO THEIR COUNTRIES OF ORIGIN.
BUT IT TOOK DAG SVENSSON ONE DAY TO FIND MOST OF THEM.
THEY CAN BE FOUND:
WHY AREN'T THEY BEING FOUND?
WELL, HOW DOES THAT MAKE IT LONGER?
THE MEN BUYING SEX INCLUDE FIVE LAWYERS, A JUDGE.
EVEN A JOURNALIST WHO WRITES INDIGNANT ARTICLES ABOUT THE SEX TRADE.
WE NAME THEM IN THE BOOK.
IS THAT ETHICAL?
WON'T THEY SUE?
VERY GLAD, ACTUALLY.
GLAD WE'RE CHANGING YOUR CONTRACTUAL LIABILITIES NOW, HARRIET?

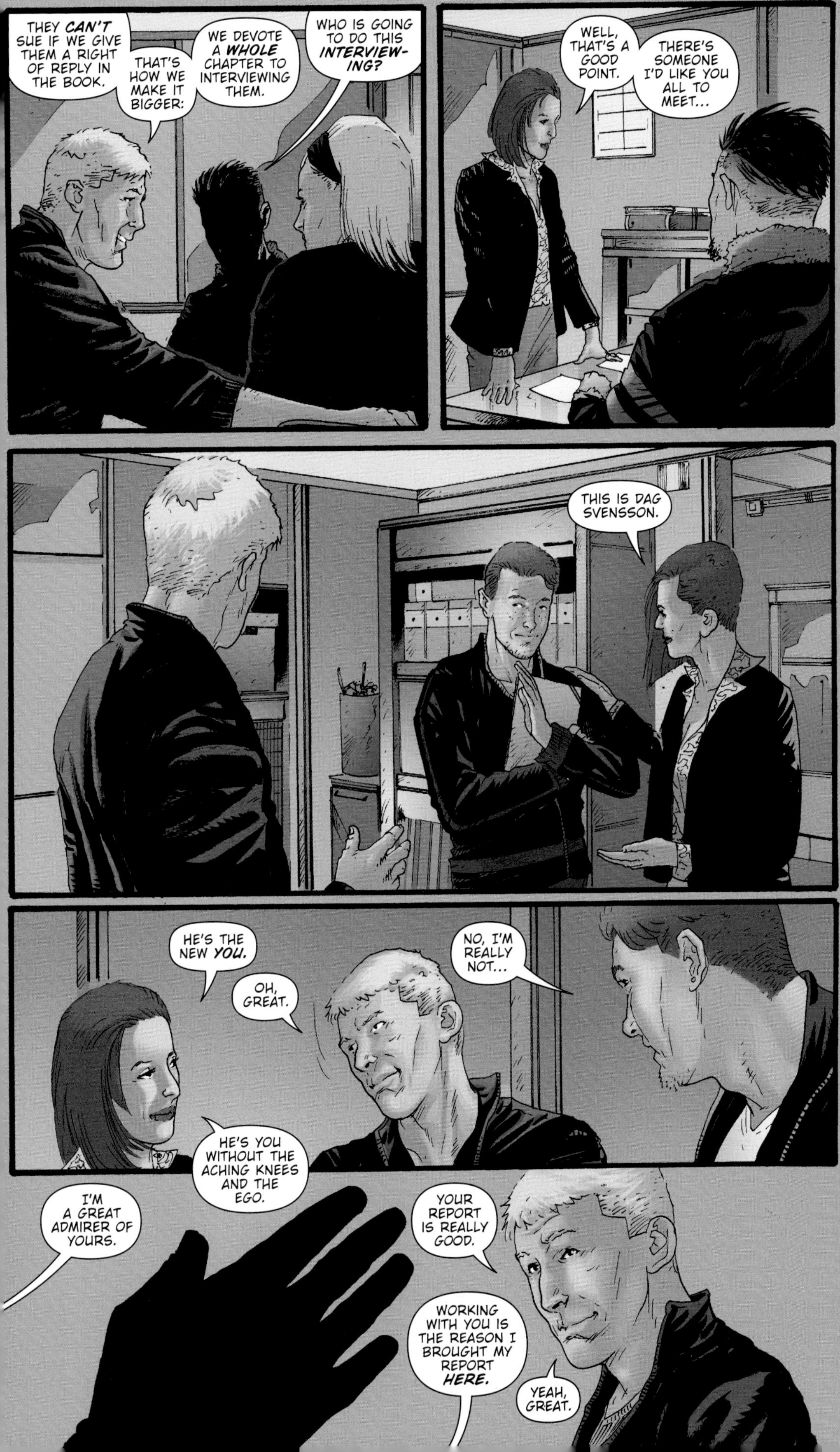
THEY CAN'T SUE IF WE GIVE THEM A RIGHT OF REPLY IN THE BOOK.
THAT'S HOW WE MAKE IT BIGGER:
WE DEVOTE A WHOLE CHAPTER TO INTERVIEWING THEM.
WHO IS GOING TO DO THIS INTERVIEWING?
WELL, THAT'S A GOOD POINT.
THERE'S SOMEONE I'D LIKE YOU ALL TO MEET...
THIS IS DAG SVENSSON.
HE'S THE NEW YOU.
OH, GREAT.
NO, I'M REALLY NOT...
HE'S YOU WITHOUT THE ACHING KNEES AND THE EGO.
I'M A GREAT ADMIRER OF YOURS.
YOUR REPORT IS REALLY GOOD.
WORKING WITH YOU IS THE REASON I BROUGHT MY REPORT HERE.
YEAH, GREAT.

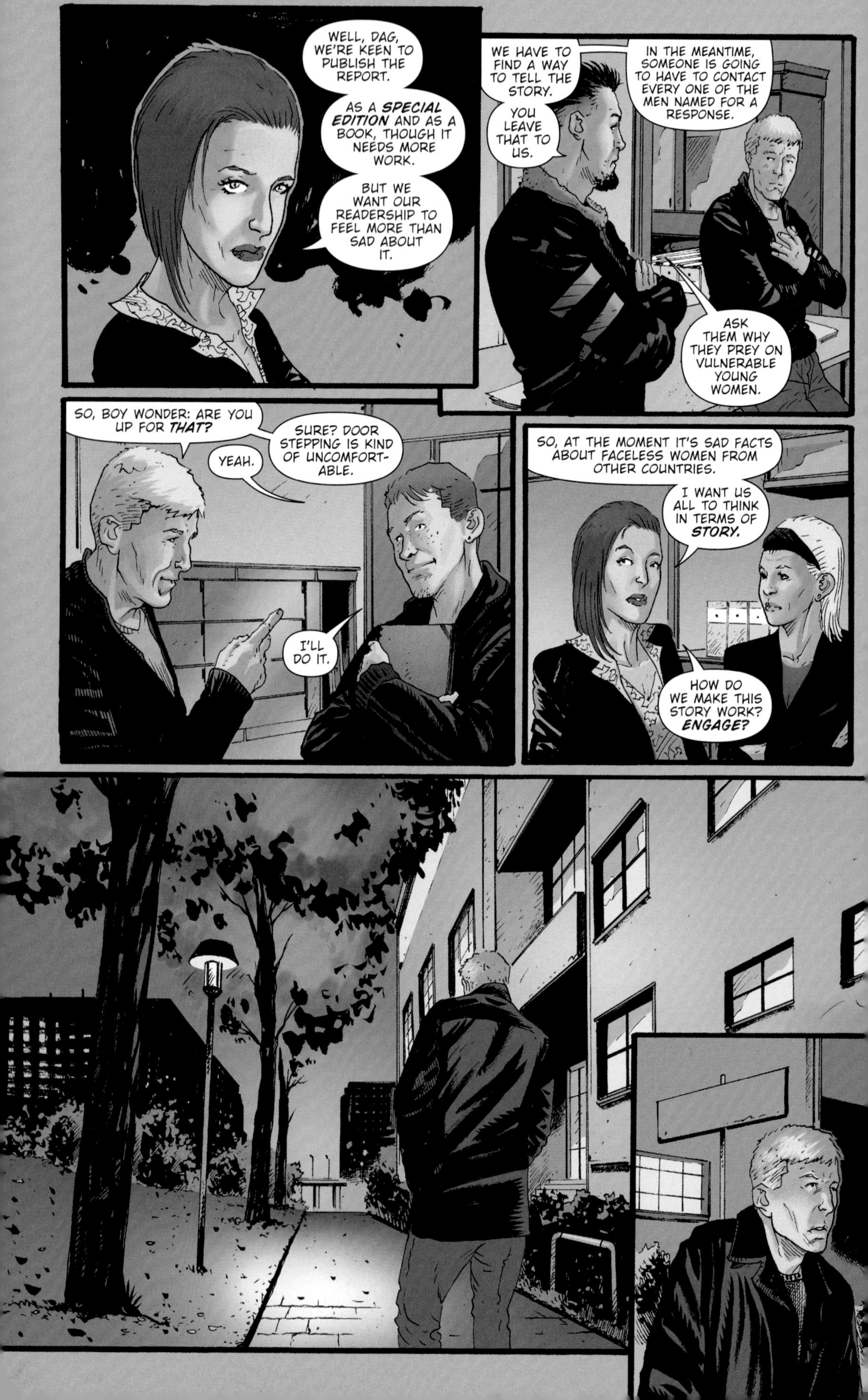

WELL, DAG, WE'RE KEEN TO PUBLISH THE REPORT.
AS A **SPECIAL EDITION** AND AS A BOOK, THOUGH IT NEEDS MORE WORK.
BUT WE WANT OUR READERSHIP TO FEEL MORE THAN SAD ABOUT IT.
WE HAVE TO FIND A WAY TO TELL THE STORY.
YOU LEAVE THAT TO US.
IN THE MEANTIME, SOMEONE IS GOING TO HAVE TO CONTACT EVERY ONE OF THE MEN NAMED FOR A RESPONSE.
ASK THEM WHY THEY PREY ON VULNERABLE YOUNG WOMEN.
SO, BOY WONDER: ARE YOU UP FOR ***THAT?***
YEAH.
SURE? DOOR STEPPING IS KIND OF UNCOMFORTABLE.
I'LL DO IT.
SO, AT THE MOMENT IT'S SAD FACTS ABOUT FACELESS WOMEN FROM OTHER COUNTRIES.
I WANT US ALL TO THINK IN TERMS OF ***STORY.***
HOW DO WE MAKE THIS STORY WORK? ***ENGAGE?***

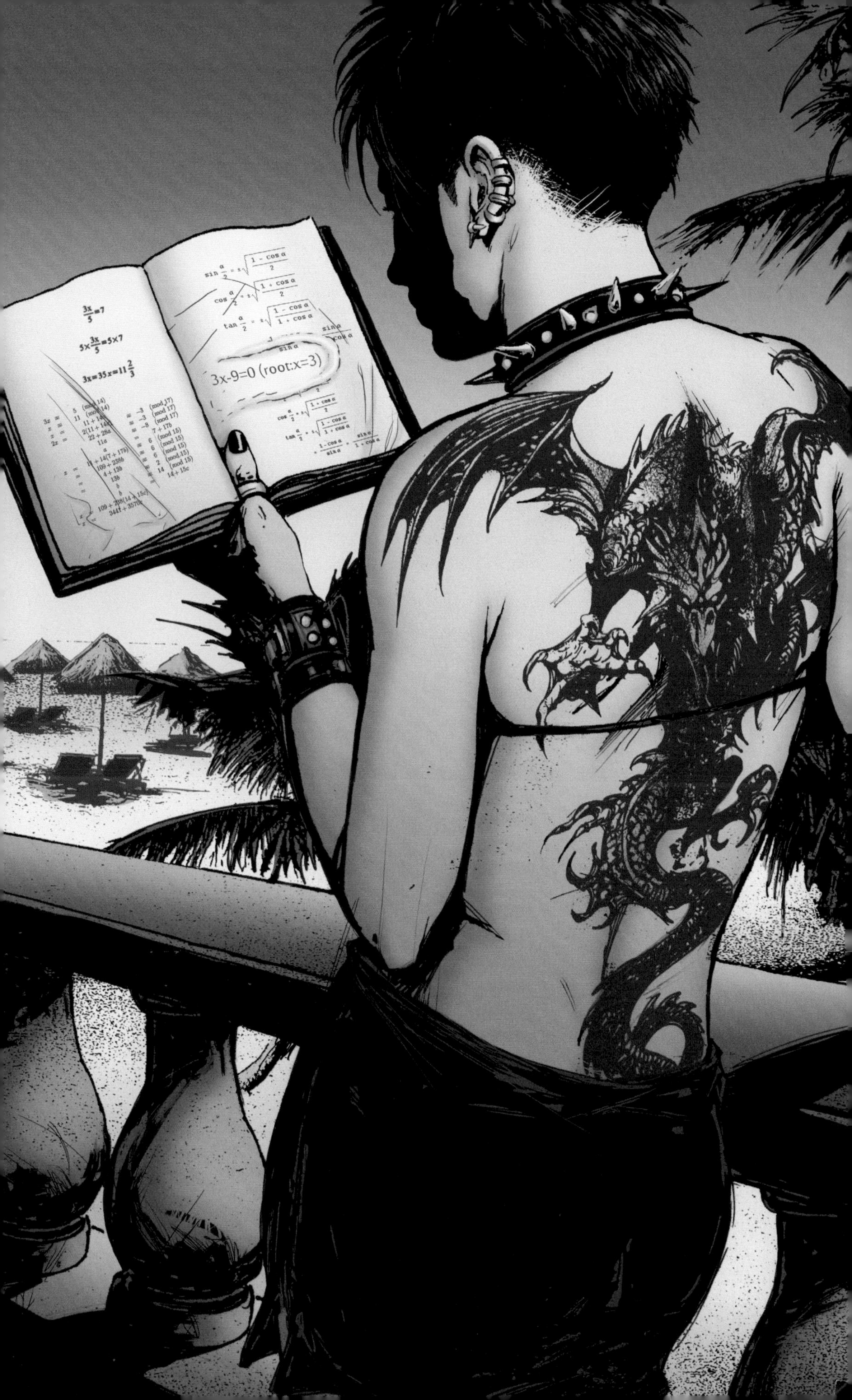

3x/5=7
5×3x/5=5×7
3x=35x=11 2/3
3x-9=0 (root:x=3)

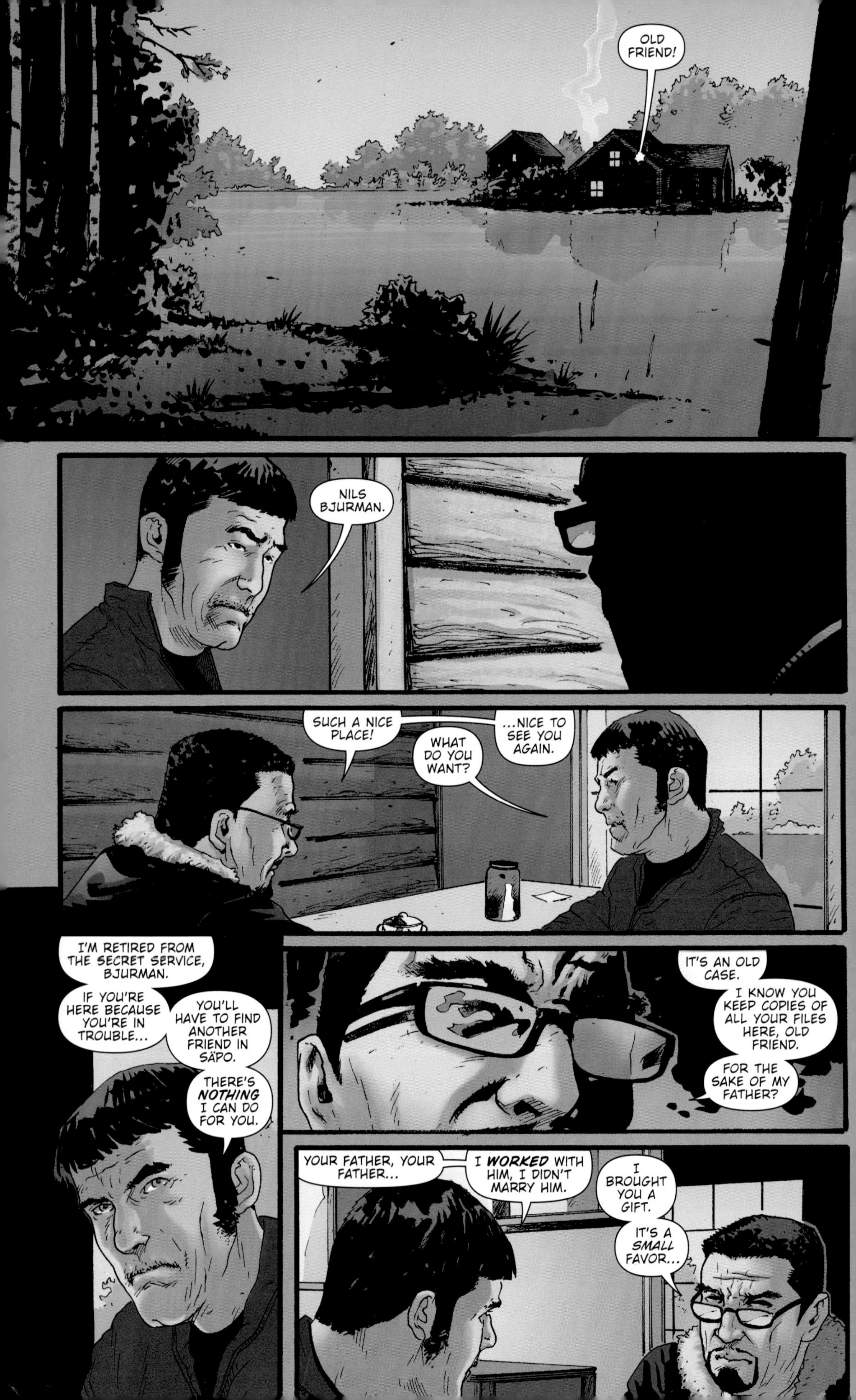
OLD FRIEND!
NILS BJURMAN.
SUCH A NICE PLACE!
...NICE TO SEE YOU AGAIN.
WHAT DO YOU WANT?
I'M RETIRED FROM THE SECRET SERVICE, BJURMAN.
IF YOU'RE HERE BECAUSE YOU'RE IN TROUBLE...
YOU'LL HAVE TO FIND ANOTHER FRIEND IN SÄPO.
THERE'S **NOTHING** I CAN DO FOR YOU.
IT'S AN OLD CASE.
I KNOW YOU KEEP COPIES OF ALL YOUR FILES HERE, OLD FRIEND.
FOR THE SAKE OF MY FATHER?
YOUR FATHER, YOUR FATHER...
I **WORKED** WITH HIM, I DIDN'T MARRY HIM.
I BROUGHT YOU A GIFT.
IT'S A *SMALL* FAVOR...

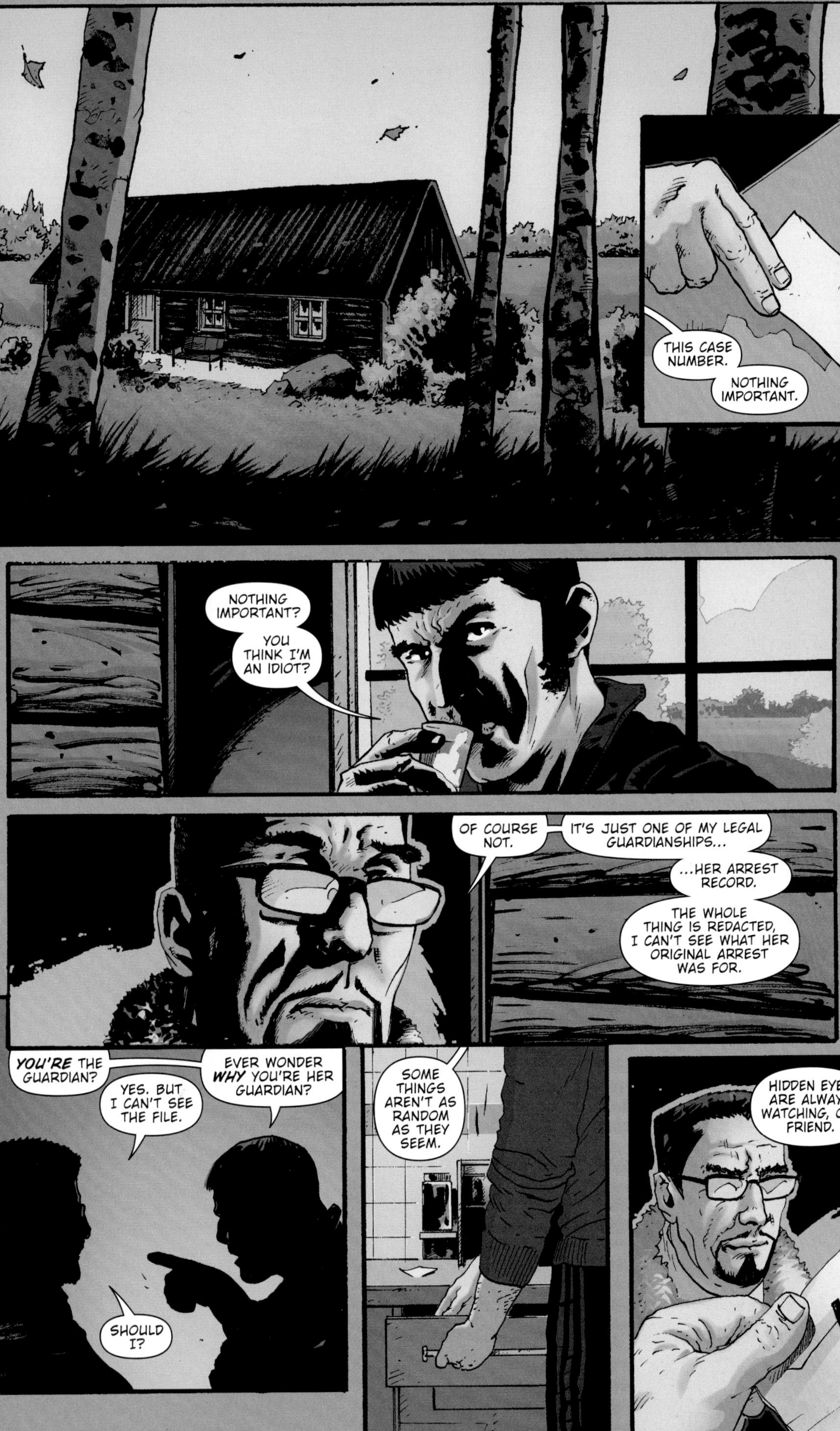
THIS CASE NUMBER.
NOTHING IMPORTANT.
NOTHING IMPORTANT?
YOU THINK I'M AN IDIOT?
OF COURSE NOT.
IT'S JUST ONE OF MY LEGAL GUARDIANSHIPS...
...HER ARREST RECORD.
THE WHOLE THING IS REDACTED, I CAN'T SEE WHAT HER ORIGINAL ARREST WAS FOR.
YOU'RE THE GUARDIAN?
YES. BUT I CAN'T SEE THE FILE.
EVER WONDER WHY YOU'RE HER GUARDIAN?
SHOULD I?
SOME THINGS AREN'T AS RANDOM AS THEY SEEM.
HIDDEN EYES ARE ALWAYS WATCHING, OLD FRIEND.

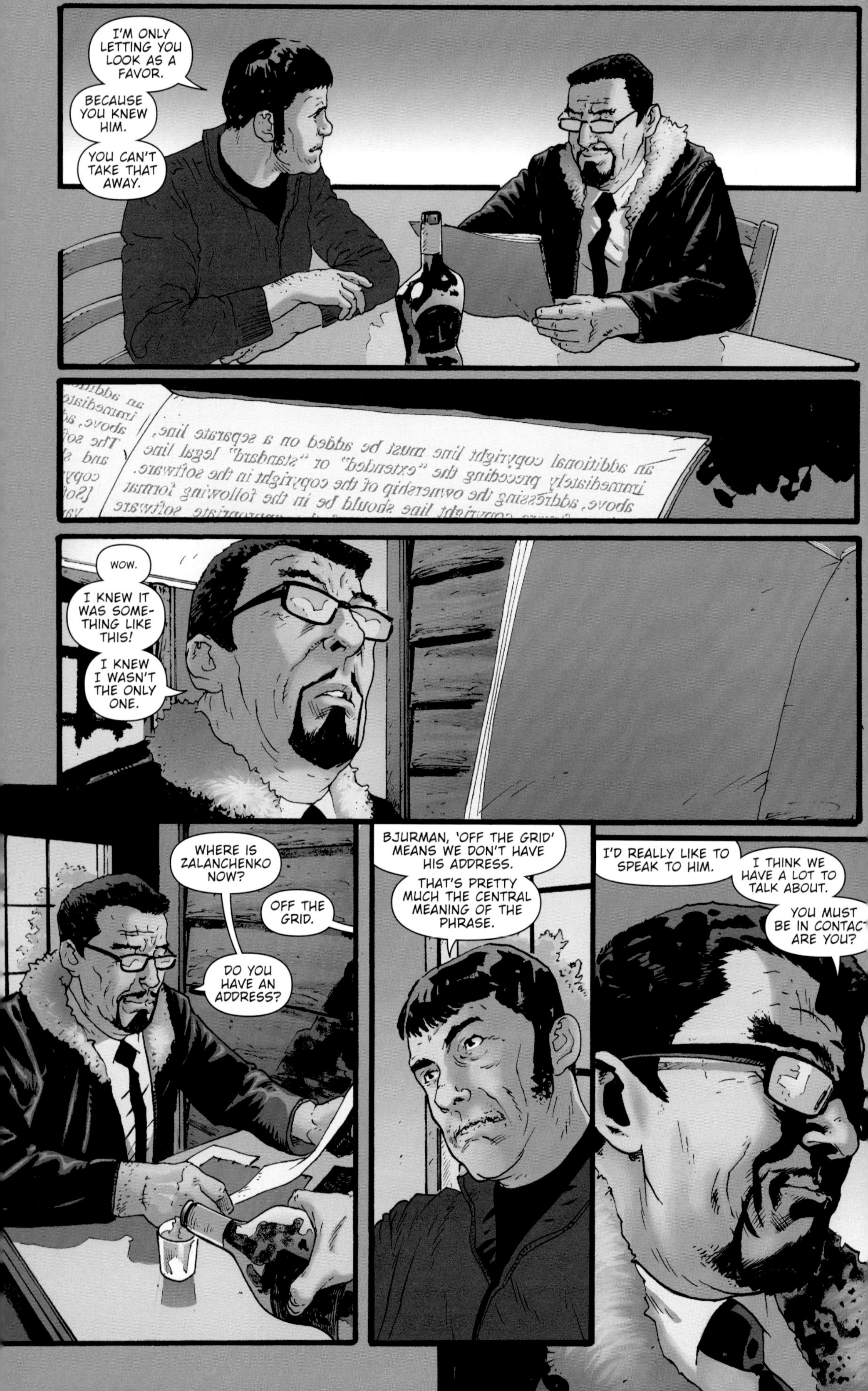
I'M ONLY LETTING YOU LOOK AS A FAVOR.
BECAUSE YOU KNEW HIM.
YOU CAN'T TAKE THAT AWAY.
WOW.
I KNEW IT WAS SOMETHING LIKE THIS!
I KNEW I WASN'T THE ONLY ONE.
WHERE IS ZALANCHENKO NOW?
OFF THE GRID.
DO YOU HAVE AN ADDRESS?
BJURMAN, 'OFF THE GRID' MEANS WE DON'T HAVE HIS ADDRESS.
THAT'S PRETTY MUCH THE CENTRAL MEANING OF THE PHRASE.
I'D REALLY LIKE TO SPEAK TO HIM.
I THINK WE HAVE A LOT TO TALK ABOUT.
YOU MUST BE IN CONTAC ARE YOU?

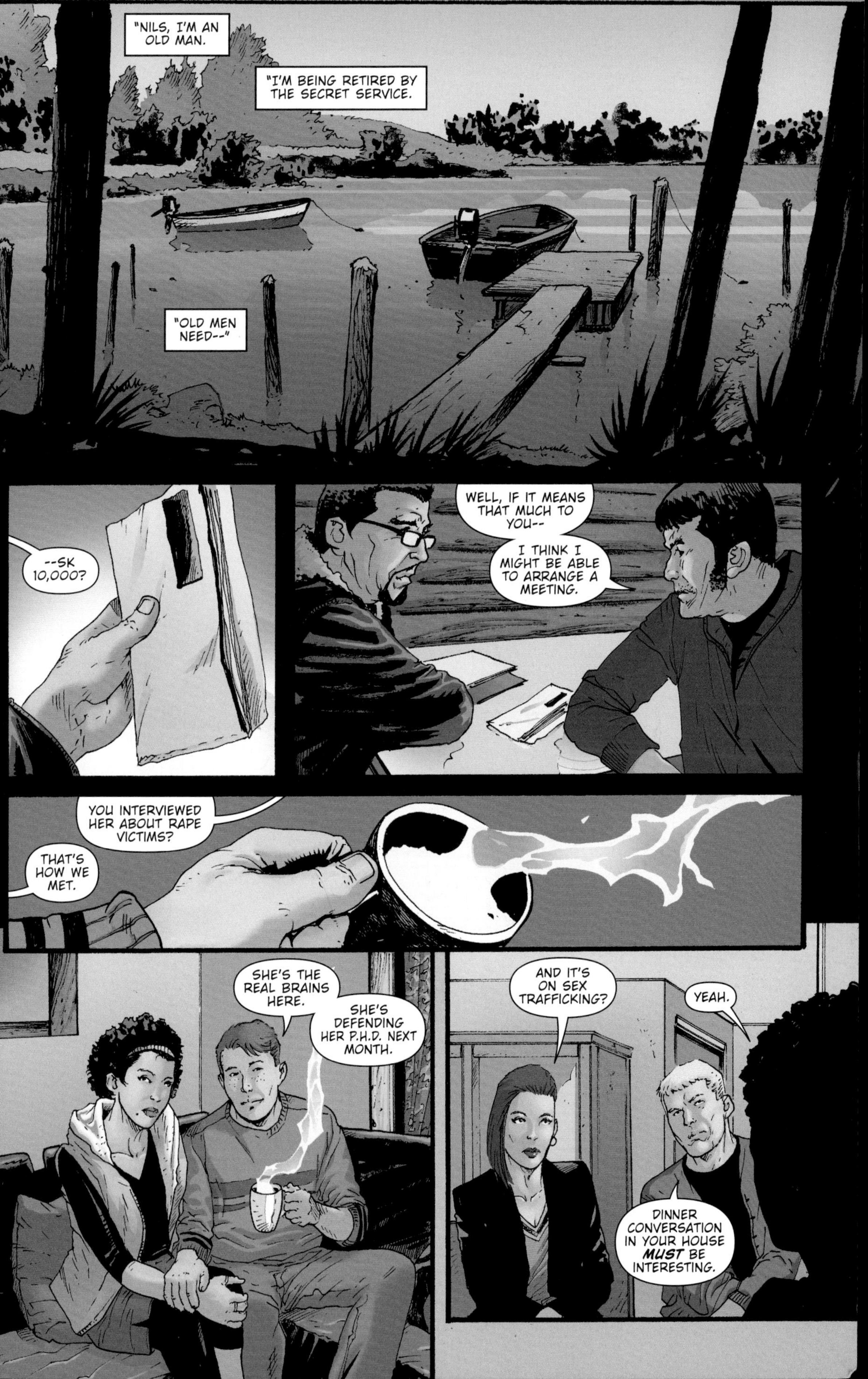
"NILS, I'M AN OLD MAN.
"I'M BEING RETIRED BY THE SECRET SERVICE.
"OLD MEN NEED--"
--SK 10,000?
WELL, IF IT MEANS THAT MUCH TO YOU--
I THINK I MIGHT BE ABLE TO ARRANGE A MEETING.
YOU INTERVIEWED HER ABOUT RAPE VICTIMS?
THAT'S HOW WE MET.
SHE'S THE REAL BRAINS HERE.
SHE'S DEFENDING HER P.H.D. NEXT MONTH.
AND IT'S ON SEX TRAFFICKING?
YEAH.
DINNER CONVERSATION IN YOUR HOUSE MUST BE INTERESTING.

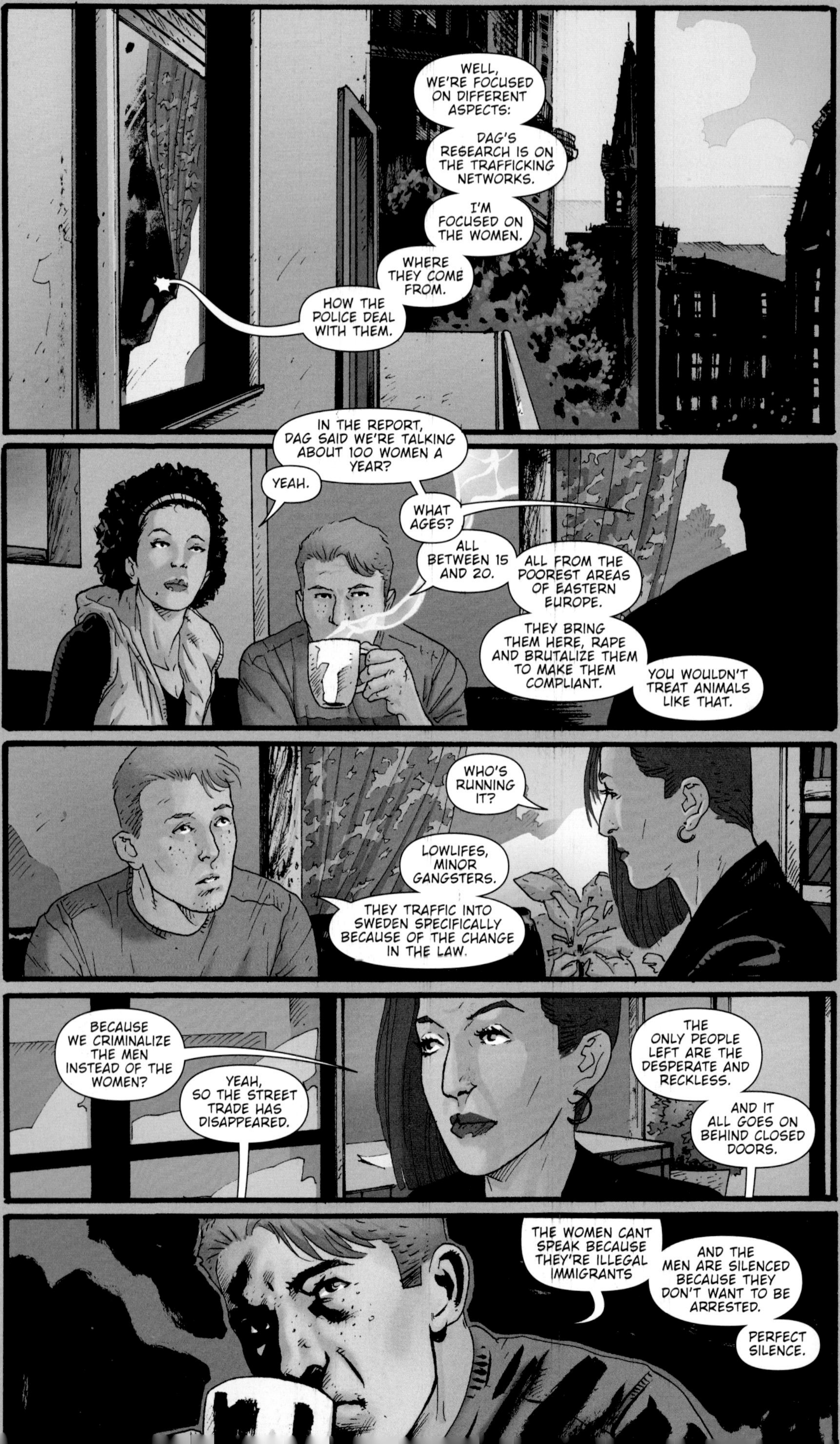
WELL, WE'RE FOCUSED ON DIFFERENT ASPECTS:
DAG'S RESEARCH IS ON THE TRAFFICKING NETWORKS.
I'M FOCUSED ON THE WOMEN.
WHERE THEY COME FROM.
HOW THE POLICE DEAL WITH THEM.
IN THE REPORT, DAG SAID WE'RE TALKING ABOUT 100 WOMEN A YEAR?
YEAH.
WHAT AGES?
ALL BETWEEN 15 AND 20.
ALL FROM THE POOREST AREAS OF EASTERN EUROPE.
THEY BRING THEM HERE, RAPE AND BRUTALIZE THEM TO MAKE THEM COMPLIANT.
YOU WOULDN'T TREAT ANIMALS LIKE THAT.
WHO'S RUNNING IT?
LOWLIFES, MINOR GANGSTERS.
THEY TRAFFIC INTO SWEDEN SPECIFICALLY BECAUSE OF THE CHANGE IN THE LAW.
BECAUSE WE CRIMINALIZE THE MEN INSTEAD OF THE WOMEN?
YEAH, SO THE STREET TRADE HAS DISAPPEARED.
THE ONLY PEOPLE LEFT ARE THE DESPERATE AND RECKLESS.
AND IT ALL GOES ON BEHIND CLOSED DOORS.
THE WOMEN CANT SPEAK BECAUSE THEY'RE ILLEGAL IMMIGRANTS
AND THE MEN ARE SILENCED BECAUSE THEY DON'T WANT TO BE ARRESTED.
PERFECT SILENCE.

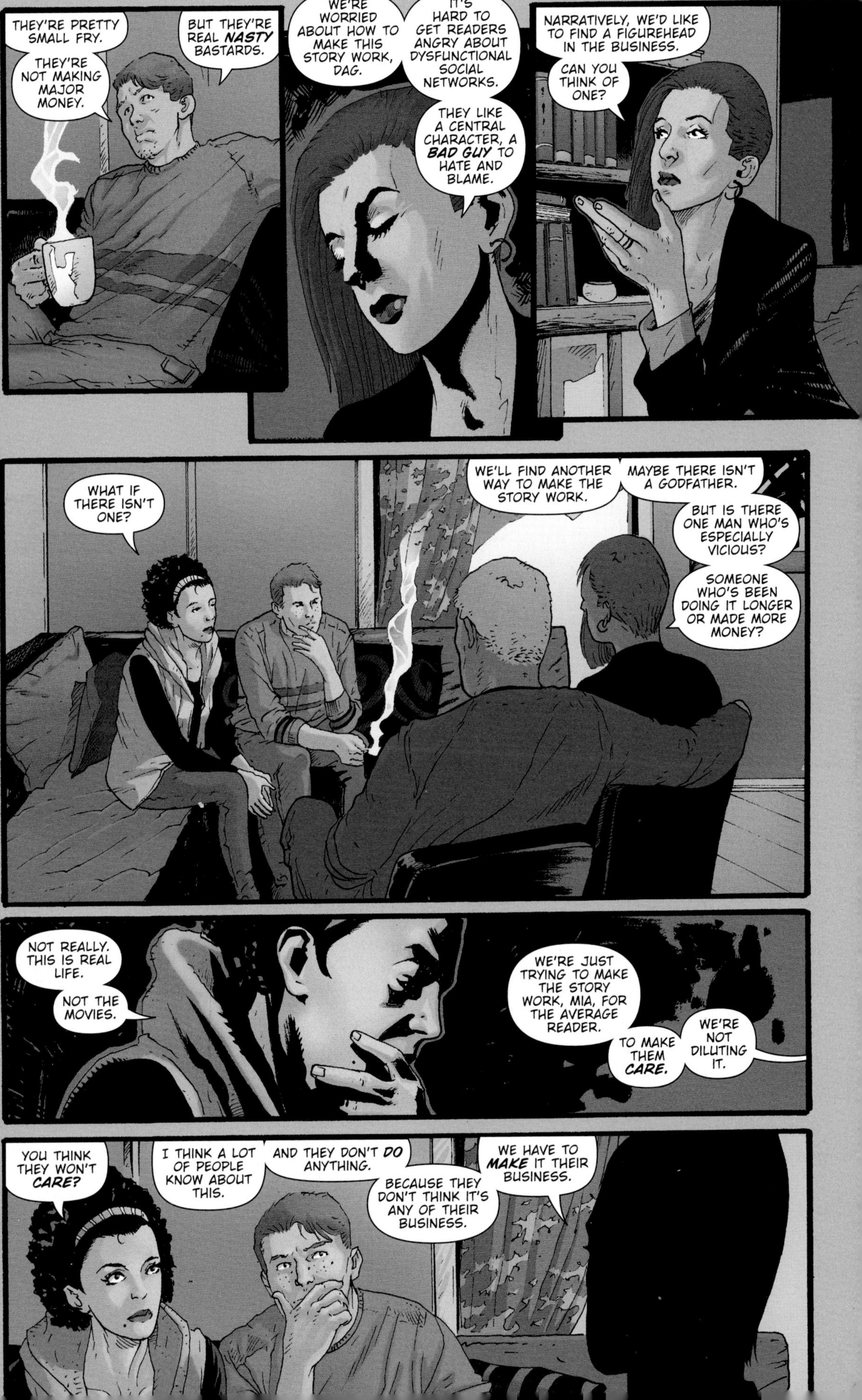
THEY'RE PRETTY SMALL FRY.
THEY'RE NOT MAKING MAJOR MONEY.
BUT THEY'RE REAL NASTY BASTARDS.
WE'RE WORRIED ABOUT HOW TO MAKE THIS STORY WORK, DAG.
IT'S HARD TO GET READERS ANGRY ABOUT DYSFUNCTIONAL SOCIAL NETWORKS.
THEY LIKE A CENTRAL CHARACTER, A BAD GUY TO HATE AND BLAME.
NARRATIVELY, WE'D LIKE TO FIND A FIGUREHEAD IN THE BUSINESS.
CAN YOU THINK OF ONE?
WHAT IF THERE ISN'T ONE?
WE'LL FIND ANOTHER WAY TO MAKE THE STORY WORK.
MAYBE THERE ISN'T A GODFATHER.
BUT IS THERE ONE MAN WHO'S ESPECIALLY VICIOUS?
SOMEONE WHO'S BEEN DOING IT LONGER OR MADE MORE MONEY?
NOT REALLY. THIS IS REAL LIFE.
NOT THE MOVIES.
WE'RE JUST TRYING TO MAKE THE STORY WORK, MIA, FOR THE AVERAGE READER.
TO MAKE THEM CARE.
WE'RE NOT DILUTING IT.
YOU THINK THEY WON'T CARE?
I THINK A LOT OF PEOPLE KNOW ABOUT THIS.
AND THEY DON'T DO ANYTHING.
BECAUSE THEY DON'T THINK IT'S ANY OF THEIR BUSINESS.
WE HAVE TO MAKE IT THEIR BUSINESS.

IS THERE ANOTHER WAY TO DO THAT?

WELL, CONTRAST IS ALSO GOOD:

IS THERE A REVEREND INVOLVED?

I FEEL SO CHEAP.

WERE WE EV THAT EARNES

WE ARE JUST CHEAP HACKS TO THEM.

I THINK WE WER INSUFFE ABLE.

I NEED A REAL COFFEE.

COME ON...

WE'RE TWO BLOCKS FROM THE OFFICE, MIKEY!

BLOOD SUGAR CRASHING, CAFFEINE ESSENTIAL.

HAPPY NOW?

GOD YEAH, I NEED THIS.

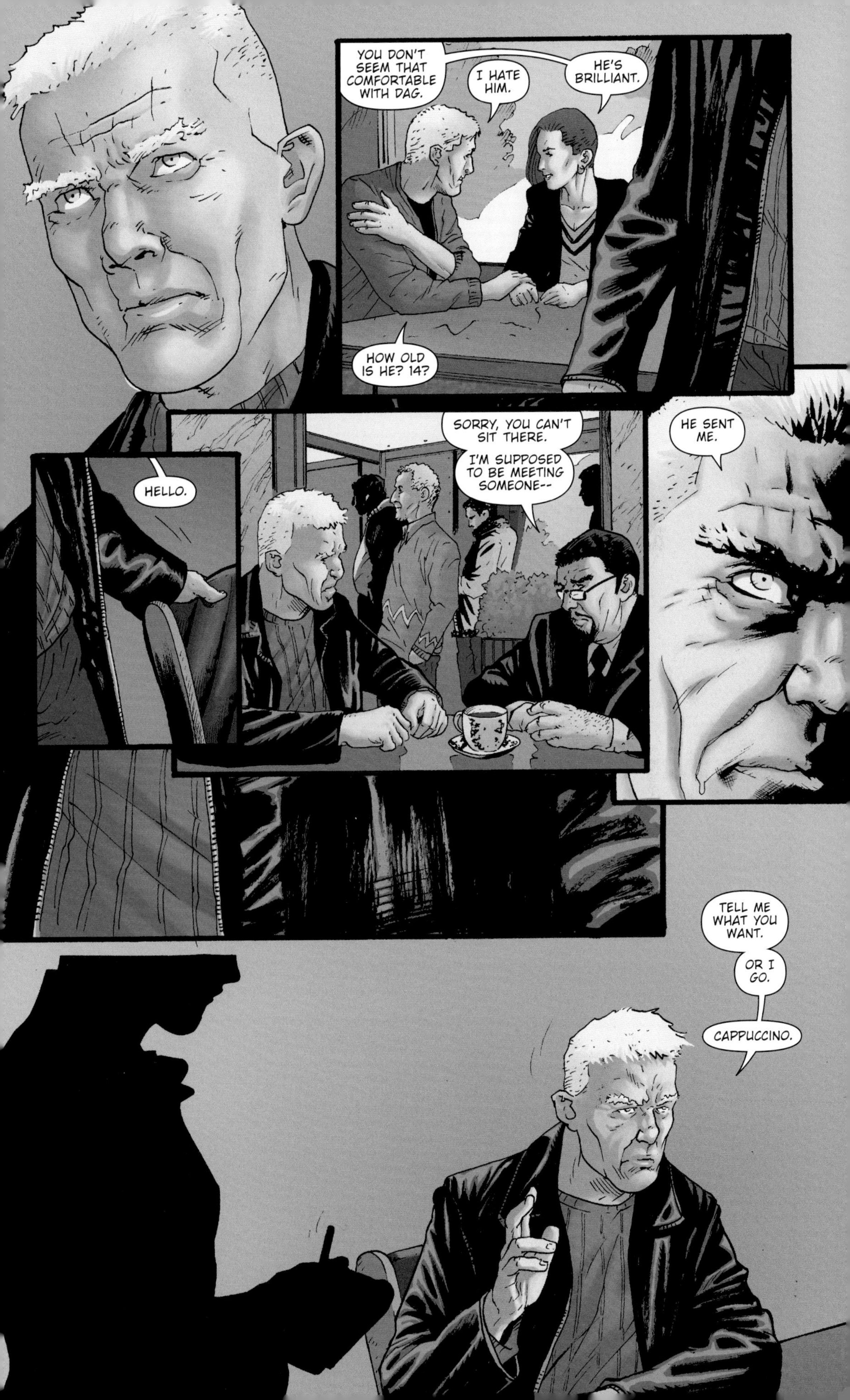
YOU DON'T SEEM THAT COMFORTABLE WITH DAG.
I HATE HIM.
HE'S BRILLIANT.
HOW OLD IS HE? 14?
HELLO.
SORRY, YOU CAN'T SIT THERE.
I'M SUPPOSED TO BE MEETING SOMEONE--
HE SENT ME.
TELL ME WHAT YOU WANT.
OR I GO.
CAPPUCCINO.

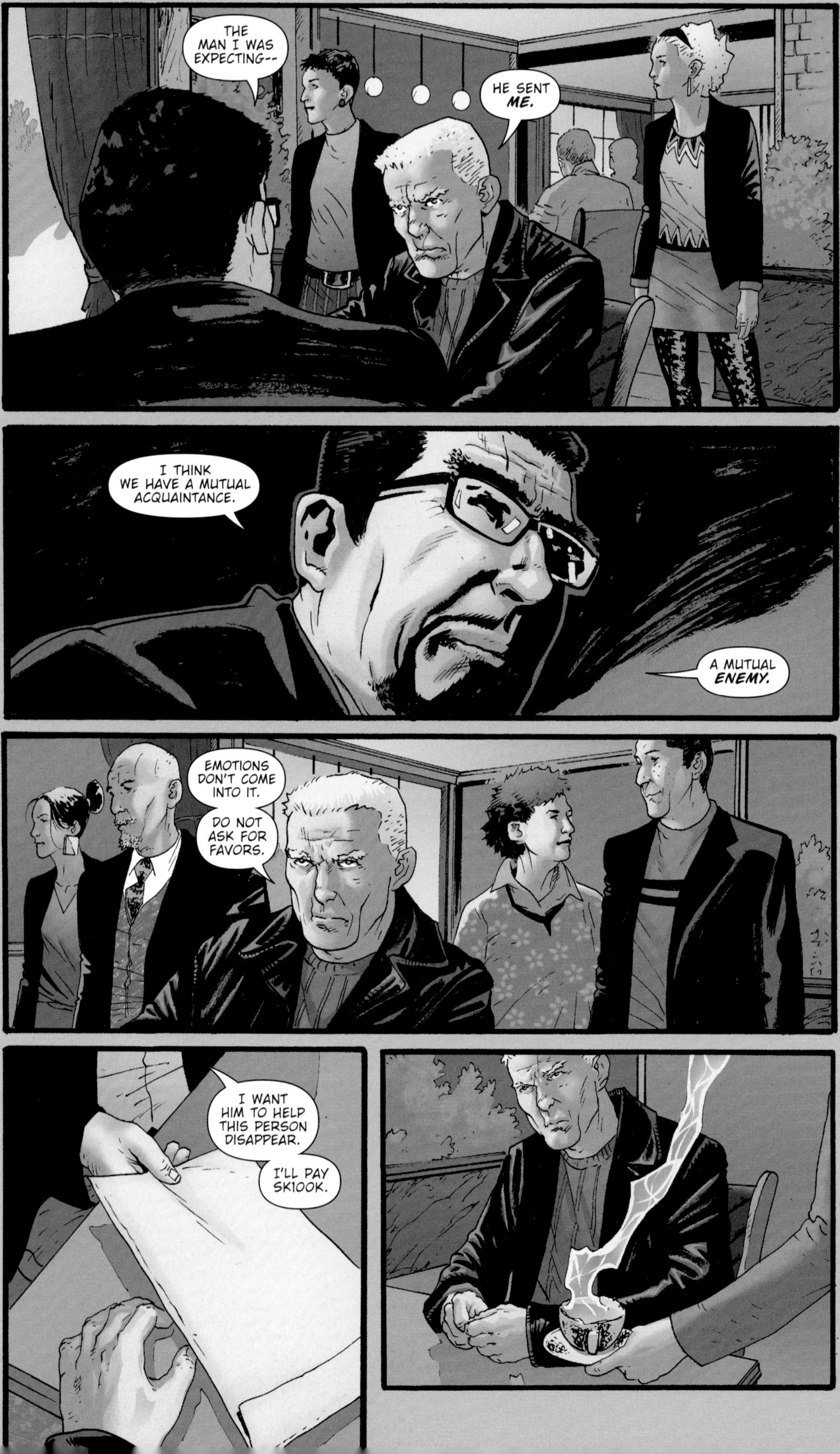
THE MAN I WAS EXPECTING--
HE SENT ME.
I THINK WE HAVE A MUTUAL ACQUAINTANCE.
A MUTUAL ENEMY.
EMOTIONS DON'T COME INTO IT.
DO NOT ASK FOR FAVORS.
I WANT HIM TO HELP THIS PERSON DISAPPEAR.
I'LL PAY $100K.

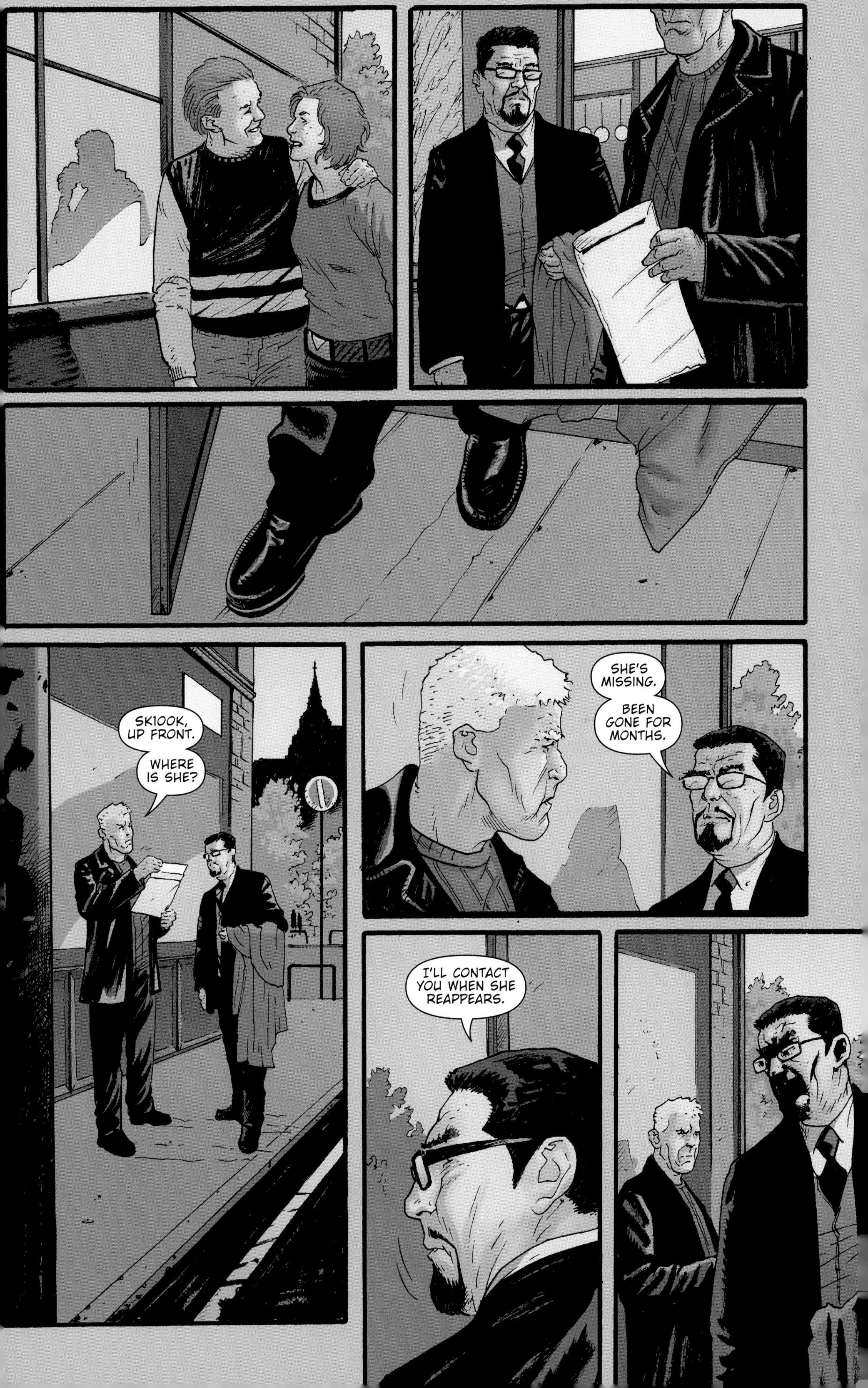
SK100K, UP FRONT.
WHERE IS SHE?
SHE'S MISSING.
BEEN GONE FOR MONTHS.
I'LL CONTACT YOU WHEN SHE REAPPEARS.

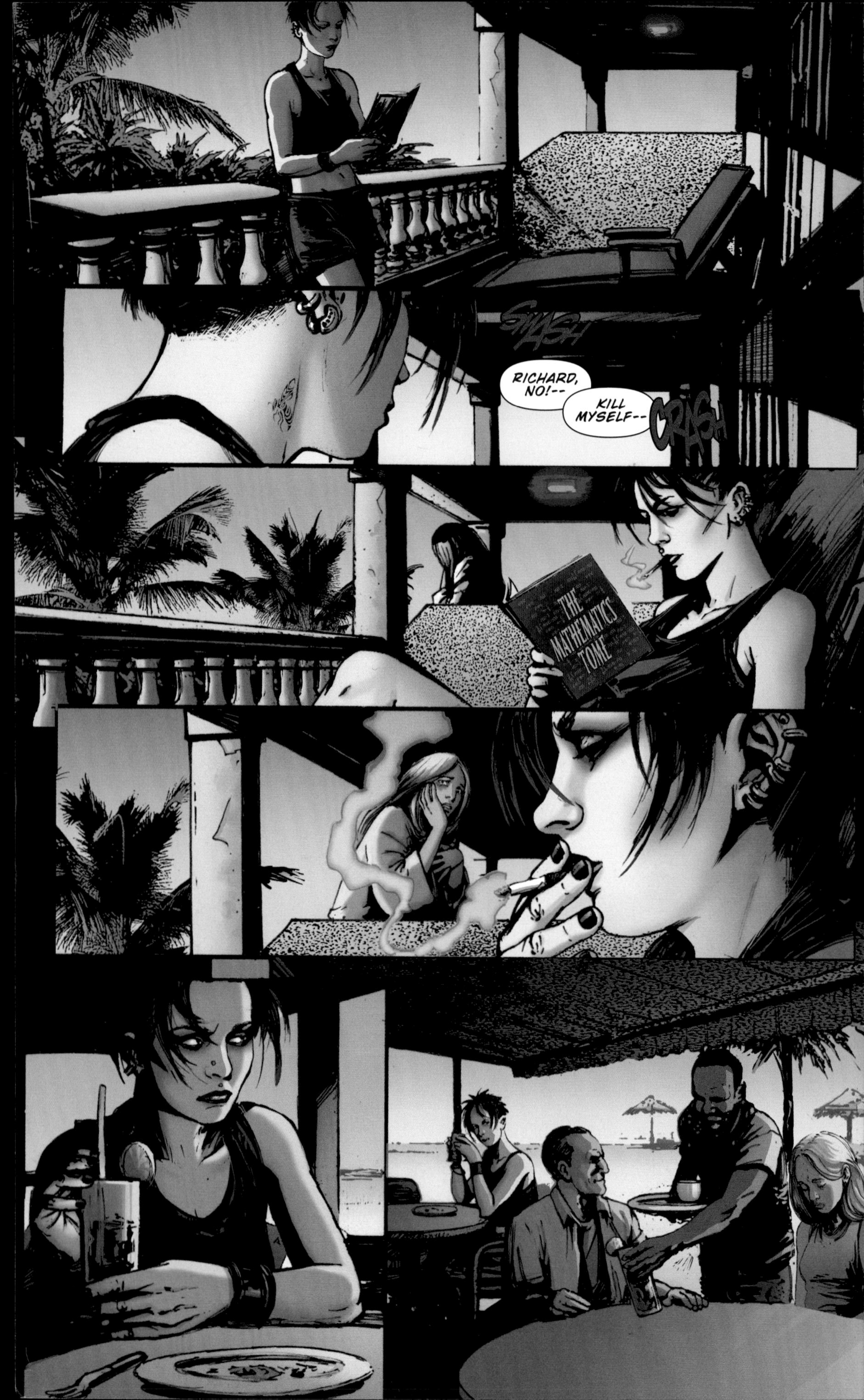
SMASH
RICHARD, NO!--
KILL MYSELF--
CRASH
THE MATHEMATICS TOME

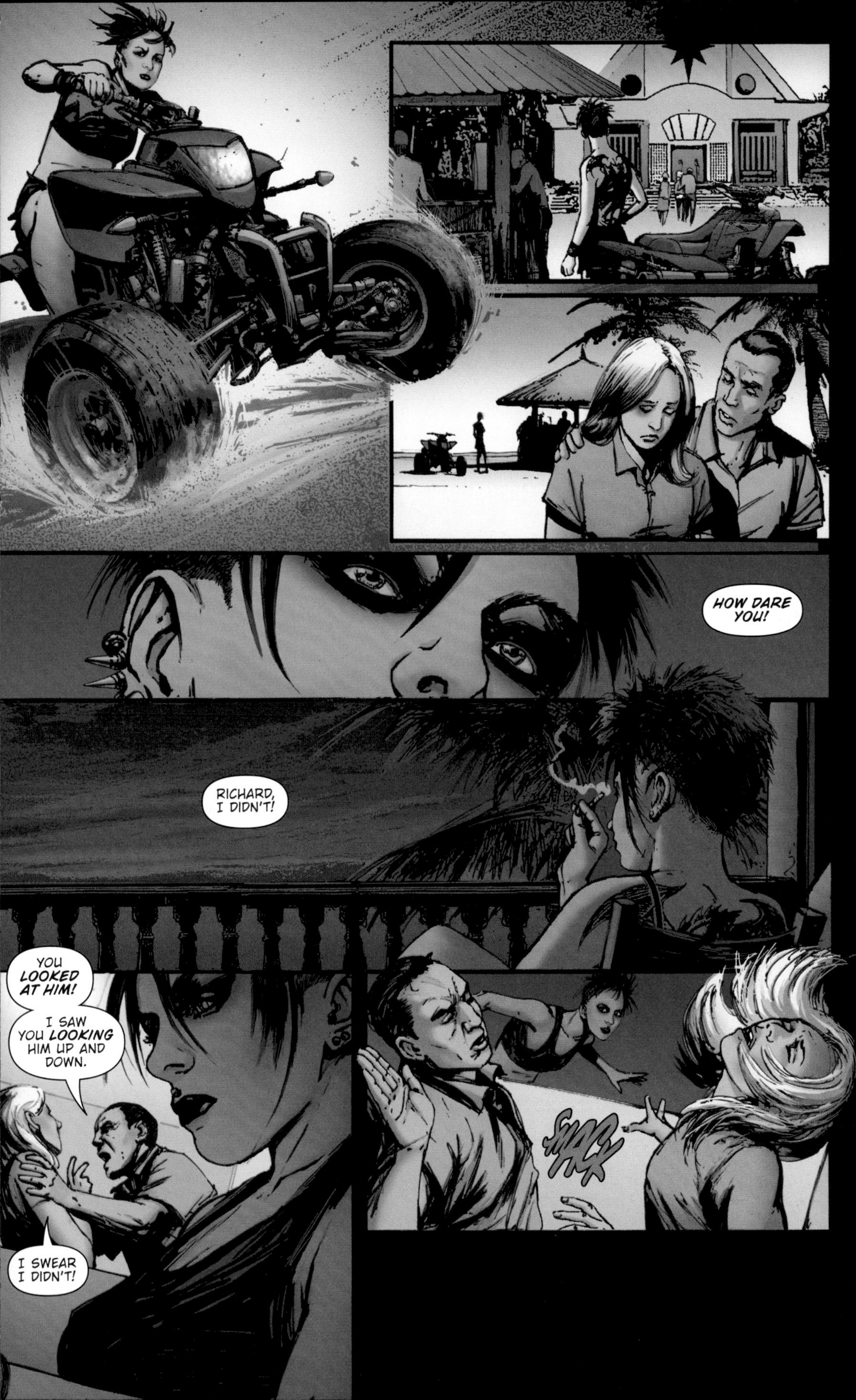
HOW DARE YOU!
RICHARD, I DIDN'T!
YOU LOOKED AT HIM!
I SAW YOU LOOKING HIM UP AND DOWN.
I SWEAR I DIDN'T!
SMACK

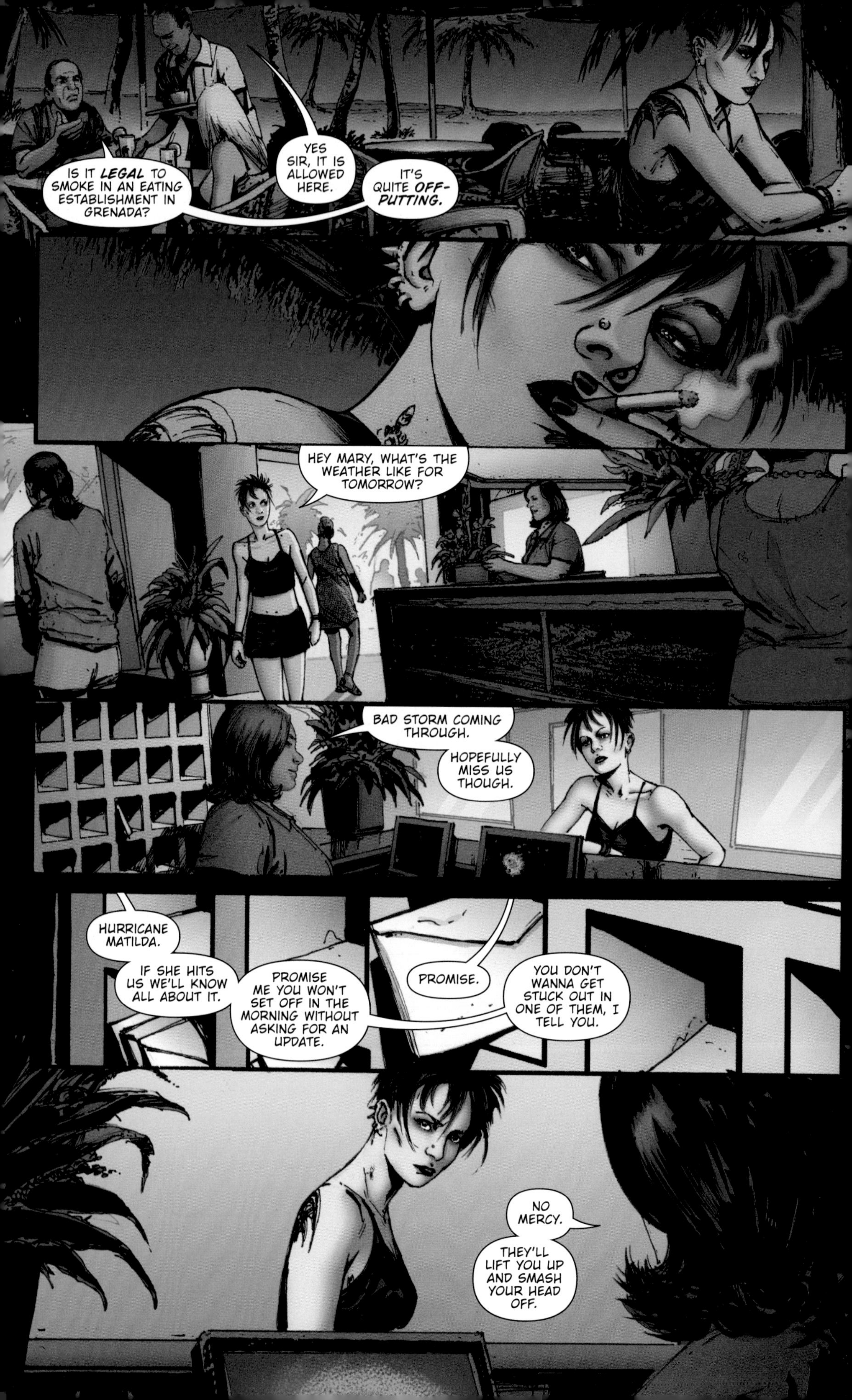
IS IT LEGAL TO SMOKE IN AN EATING ESTABLISHMENT IN GRENADA?
YES SIR, IT IS ALLOWED HERE.
IT'S QUITE OFF-PUTTING.
HEY MARY, WHAT'S THE WEATHER LIKE FOR TOMORROW?
BAD STORM COMING THROUGH.
HOPEFULLY MISS US THOUGH.
HURRICANE MATILDA.
IF SHE HITS US WE'LL KNOW ALL ABOUT IT.
PROMISE ME YOU WON'T SET OFF IN THE MORNING WITHOUT ASKING FOR AN UPDATE.
PROMISE.
YOU DON'T WANNA GET STUCK OUT IN ONE OF THEM, I TELL YOU.
NO MERCY.
THEY'LL LIFT YOU UP AND SMASH YOUR HEAD OFF.

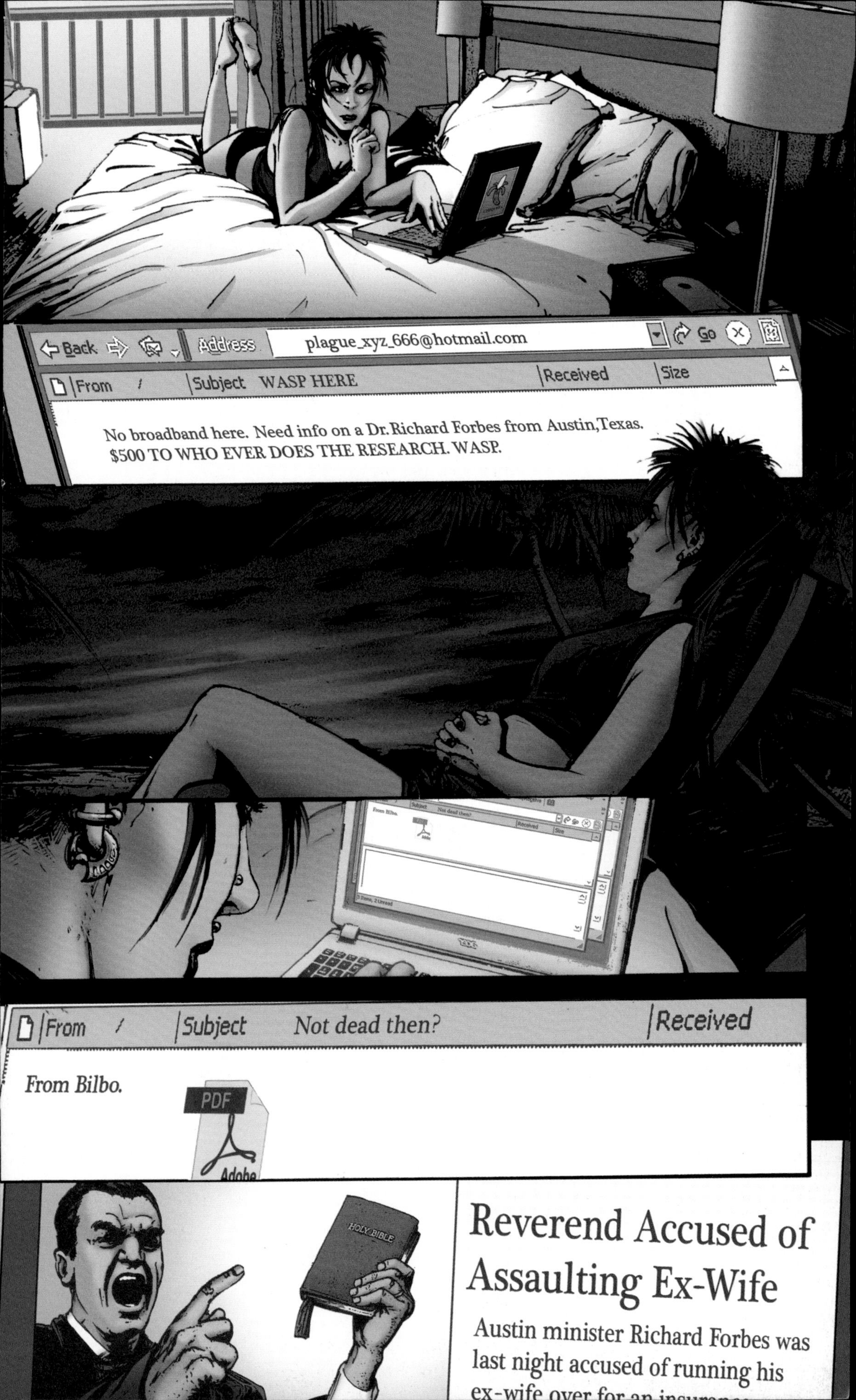

Back
Address
plague_xyz_666@hotmail.com
Go
From
Subject WASP HERE
Received
Size
No broadband here. Need info on a Dr.Richard Forbes from Austin,Texas.
$500 TO WHO EVER DOES THE RESEARCH. WASP.
From
Subject Not dead then?
Received
From Bilbo.
PDF
Adobe
HOLY BIBLE
Reverend Accused of Assaulting Ex-Wife
Austin minister Richard Forbes was last night accused of running his

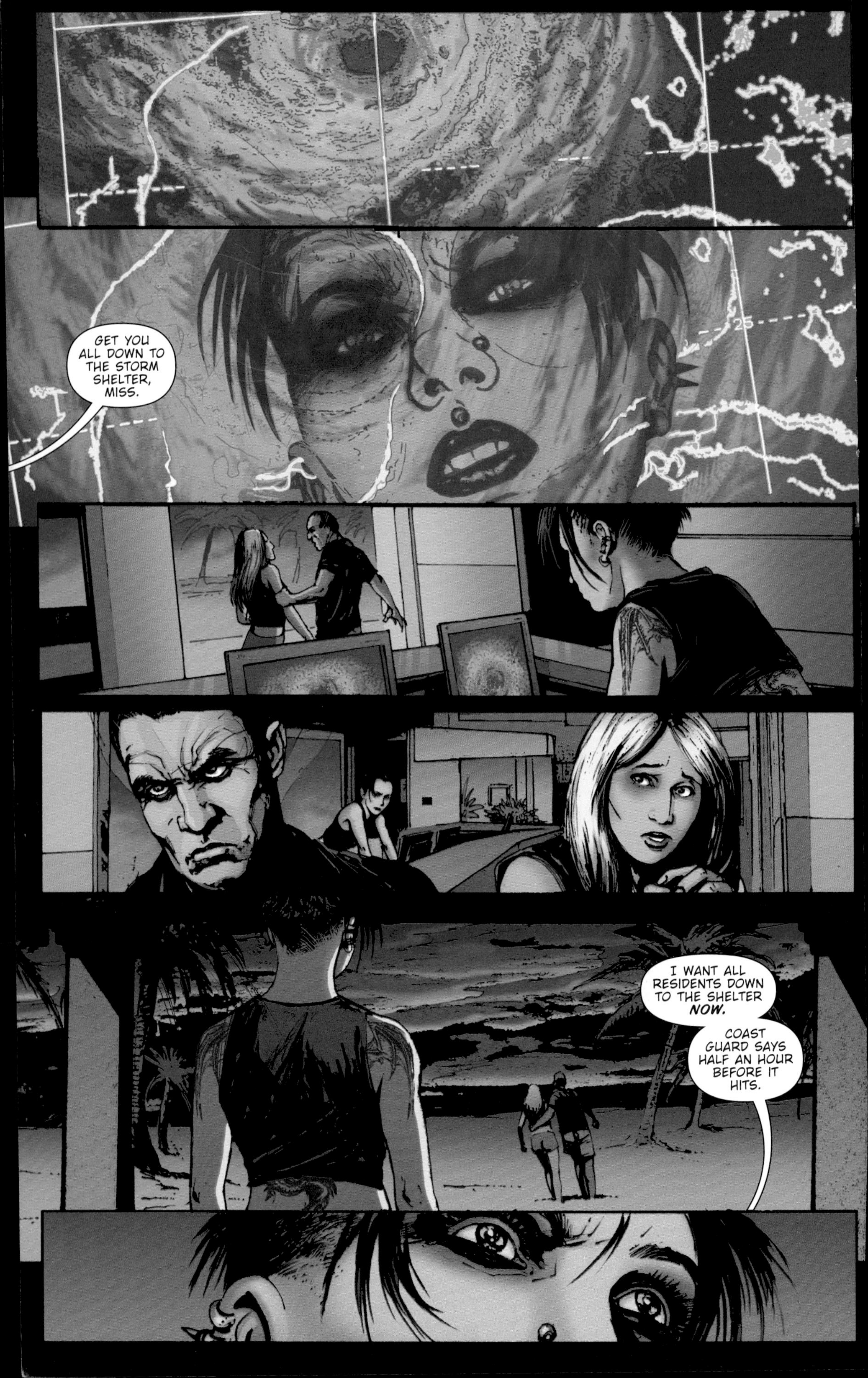
GET YOU ALL DOWN TO THE STORM SHELTER, MISS.
I WANT ALL RESIDENTS DOWN TO THE SHELTER ***NOW.***
COAST GUARD SAYS HALF AN HOUR BEFORE IT HITS.

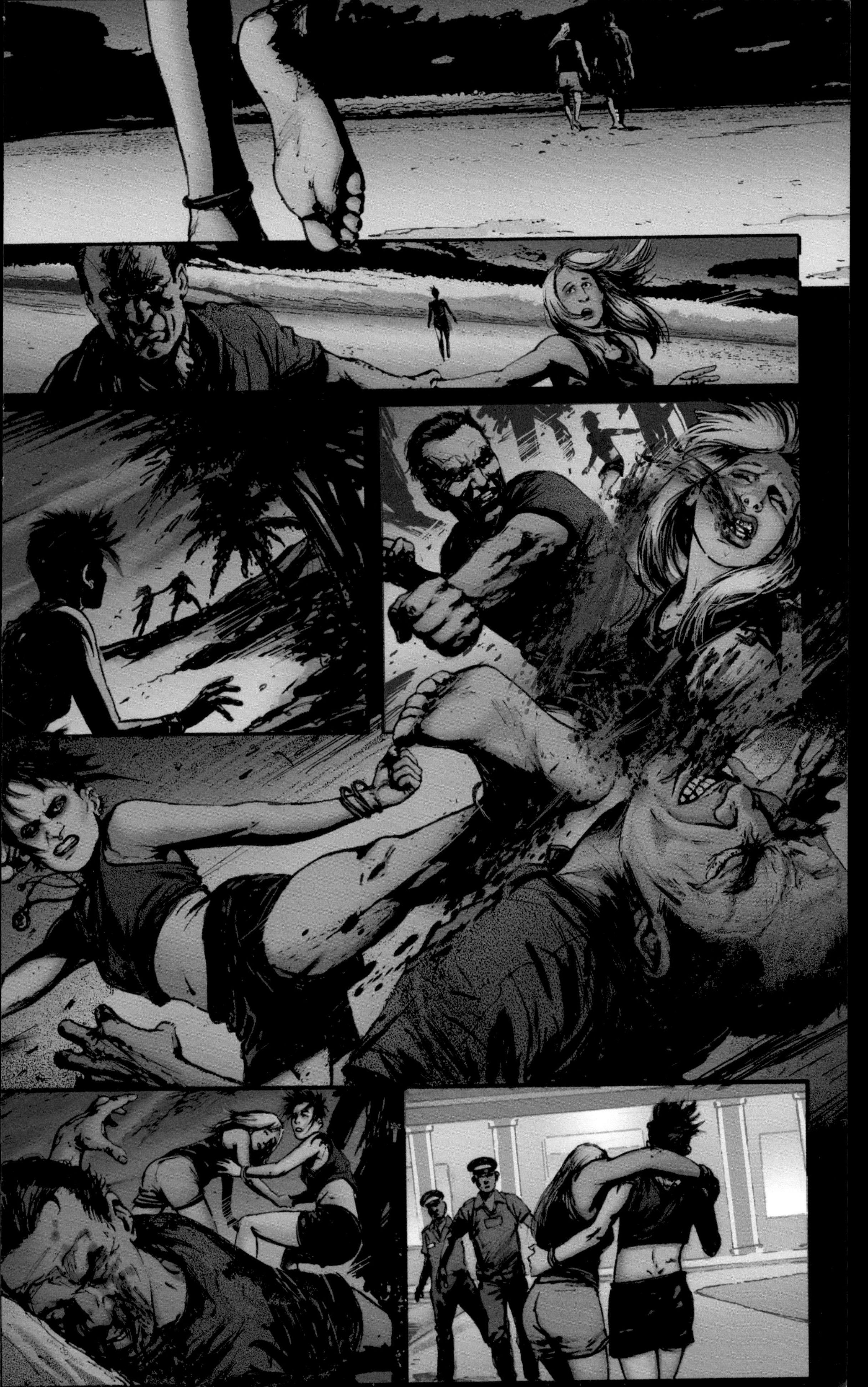

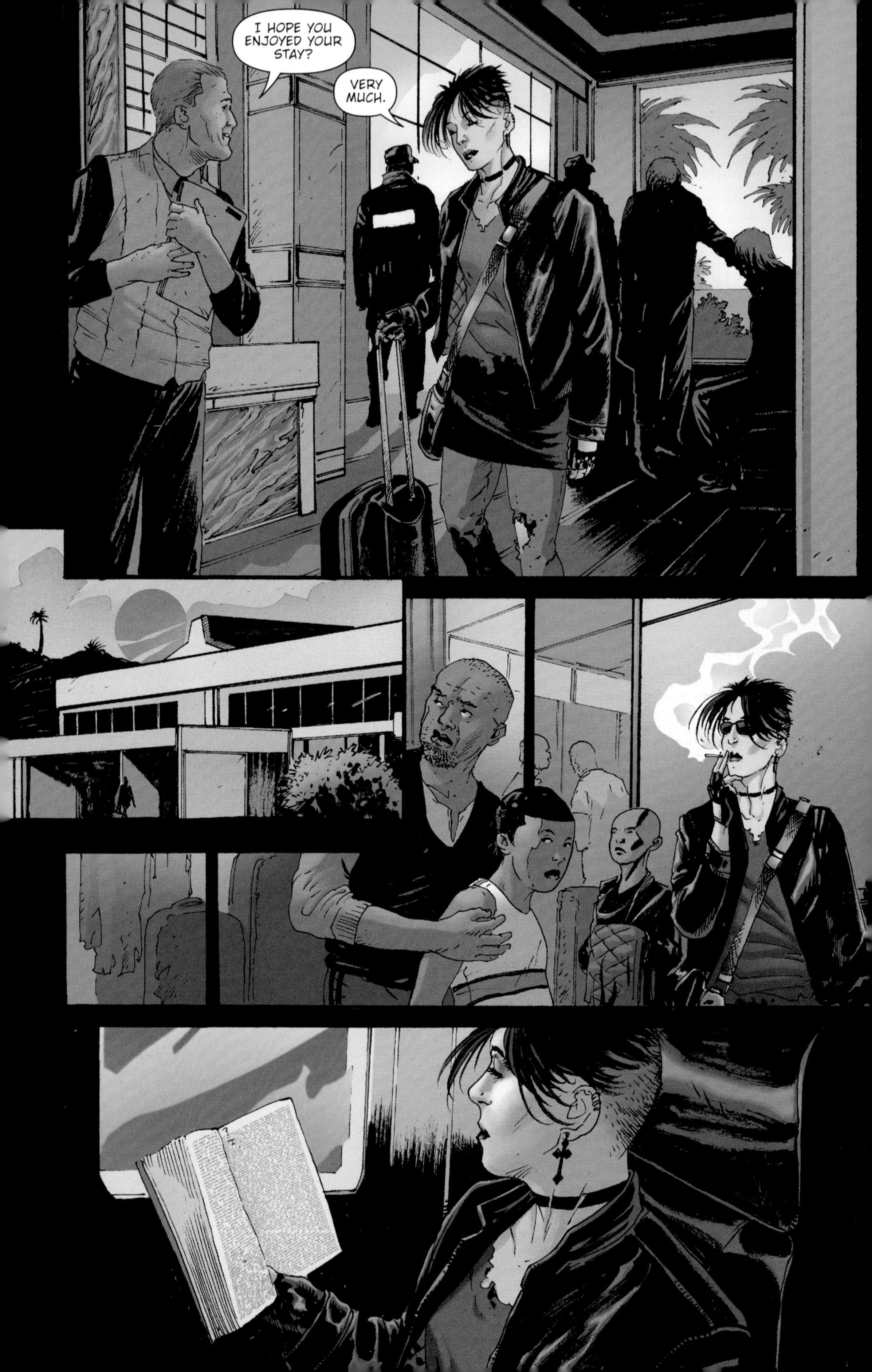
I HOPE YOU ENJOYED YOUR STAY?
VERY MUCH.

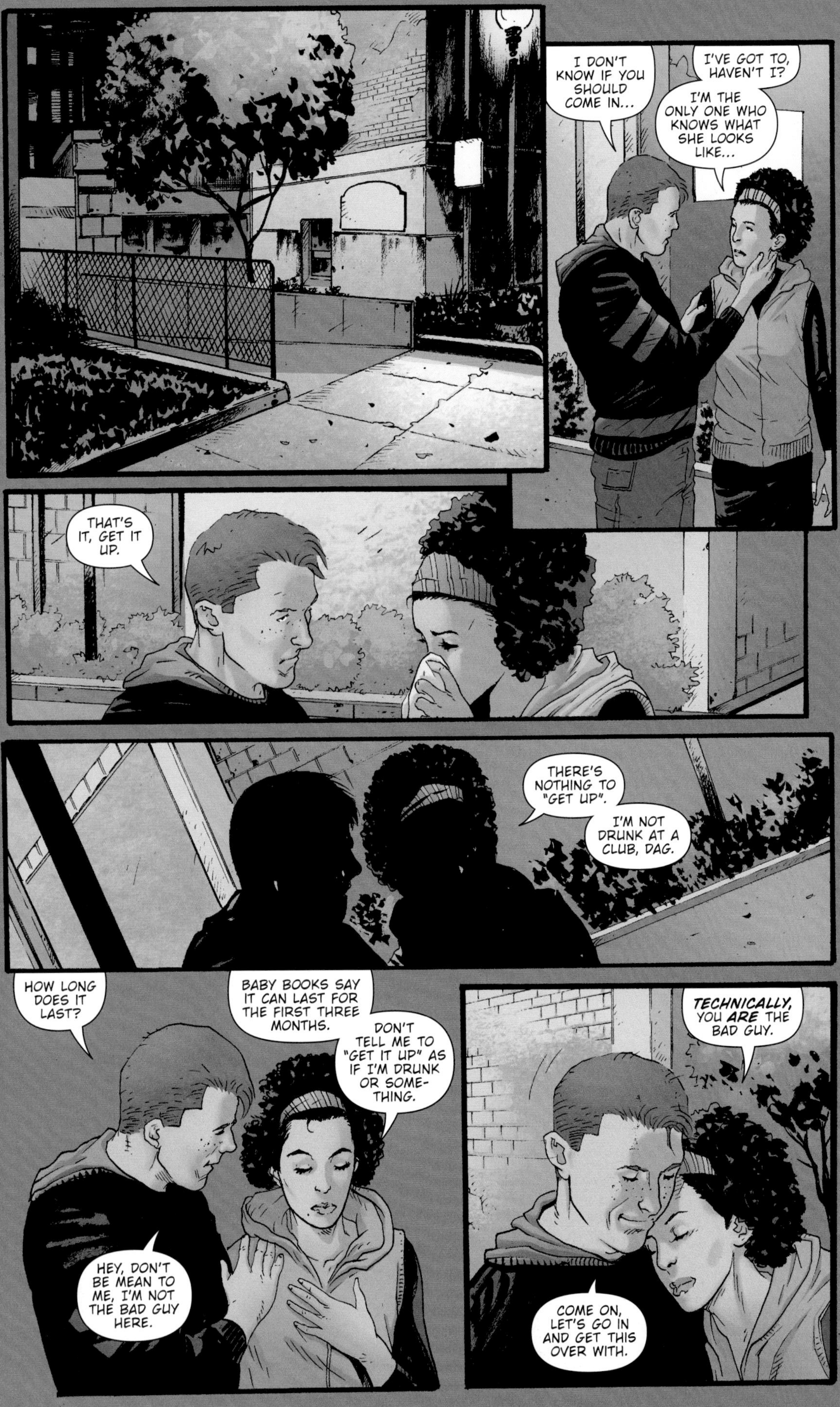
I DON'T KNOW IF YOU SHOULD COME IN...
I'VE GOT TO, HAVEN'T I?
I'M THE ONLY ONE WHO KNOWS WHAT SHE LOOKS LIKE...
THAT'S IT, GET IT UP.
THERE'S NOTHING TO "GET UP".
I'M NOT DRUNK AT A CLUB, DAG.
HOW LONG DOES IT LAST?
BABY BOOKS SAY IT CAN LAST FOR THE FIRST THREE MONTHS.
DON'T TELL ME TO "GET IT UP" AS IF I'M DRUNK OR SOME-THING.
HEY, DON'T BE MEAN TO ME, I'M NOT THE BAD GUY HERE.
TECHNICALLY, YOU ARE THE BAD GUY.
COME ON, LET'S GO IN AND GET THIS OVER WITH.

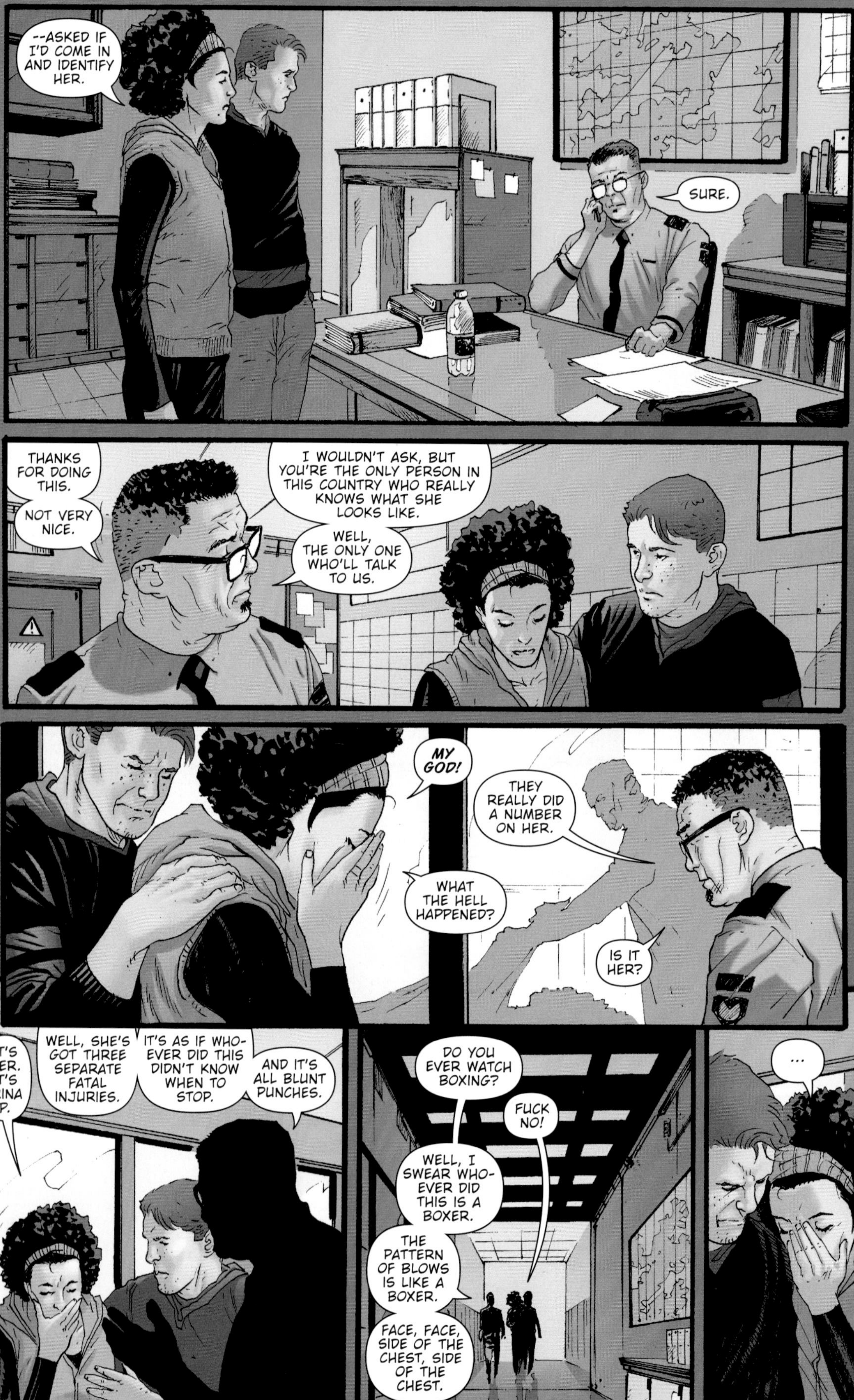
--ASKED IF I'D COME IN AND IDENTIFY HER.
SURE.
THANKS FOR DOING THIS.
NOT VERY NICE.
I WOULDN'T ASK, BUT YOU'RE THE ONLY PERSON IN THIS COUNTRY WHO REALLY KNOWS WHAT SHE LOOKS LIKE.
WELL, THE ONLY ONE WHO'LL TALK TO US.
MY GOD!
WHAT THE HELL HAPPENED?
THEY REALLY DID A NUMBER ON HER.
IS IT HER?
IT'S HER. IT'S IRINA P.
WELL, SHE'S GOT THREE SEPARATE FATAL INJURIES.
IT'S AS IF WHO-EVER DID THIS DIDN'T KNOW WHEN TO STOP.
AND IT'S ALL BLUNT PUNCHES.
DO YOU EVER WATCH BOXING?
FUCK NO!
WELL, I SWEAR WHO-EVER DID THIS IS A BOXER.
THE PATTERN OF BLOWS IS LIKE A BOXER.
FACE, FACE, SIDE OF THE CHEST, SIDE OF THE CHEST.
...

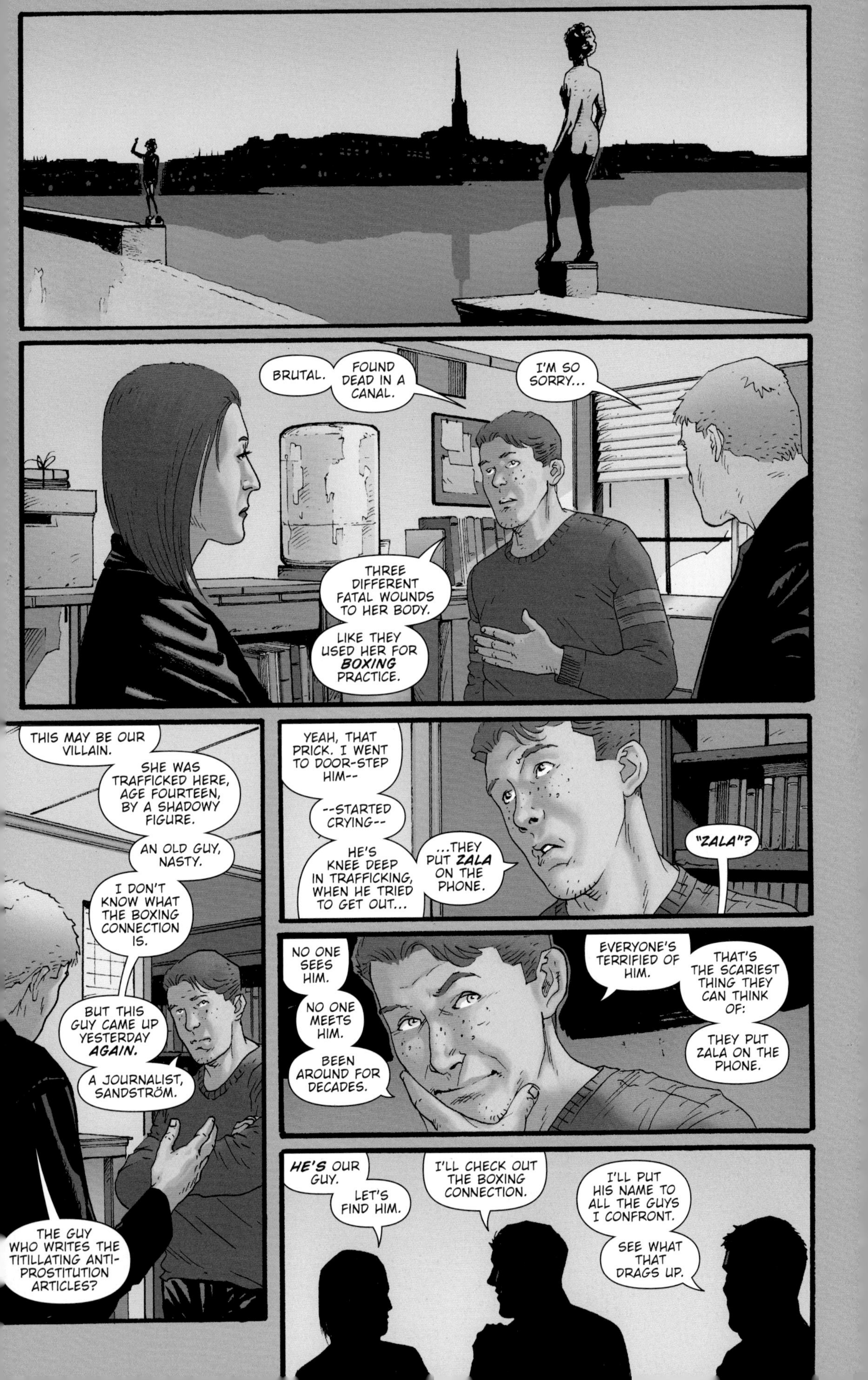
BRUTAL.
FOUND DEAD IN A CANAL.
I'M SO SORRY...
THREE DIFFERENT FATAL WOUNDS TO HER BODY.
LIKE THEY USED HER FOR **BOXING** PRACTICE.
THIS MAY BE OUR VILLAIN.
SHE WAS TRAFFICKED HERE, AGE FOURTEEN, BY A SHADOWY FIGURE.
AN OLD GUY, NASTY.
I DON'T KNOW WHAT THE BOXING CONNECTION IS.
BUT THIS GUY CAME UP YESTERDAY **AGAIN.**
A JOURNALIST, SANDSTRÖM.
THE GUY WHO WRITES THE TITILLATING ANTI-PROSTITUTION ARTICLES?
YEAH, THAT PRICK. I WENT TO DOOR-STEP HIM--
--STARTED CRYING--
HE'S KNEE DEEP IN TRAFFICKING, WHEN HE TRIED TO GET OUT...
...THEY PUT **ZALA** ON THE PHONE.
"ZALA"?
NO ONE SEES HIM.
NO ONE MEETS HIM.
BEEN AROUND FOR DECADES.
EVERYONE'S TERRIFIED OF HIM.
THAT'S THE SCARIEST THING THEY CAN THINK OF:
THEY PUT ZALA ON THE PHONE.
HE'S OUR GUY.
LET'S FIND HIM.
I'LL CHECK OUT THE BOXING CONNECTION.
I'LL PUT HIS NAME TO ALL THE GUYS I CONFRONT.
SEE WHAT THAT DRAGS UP.

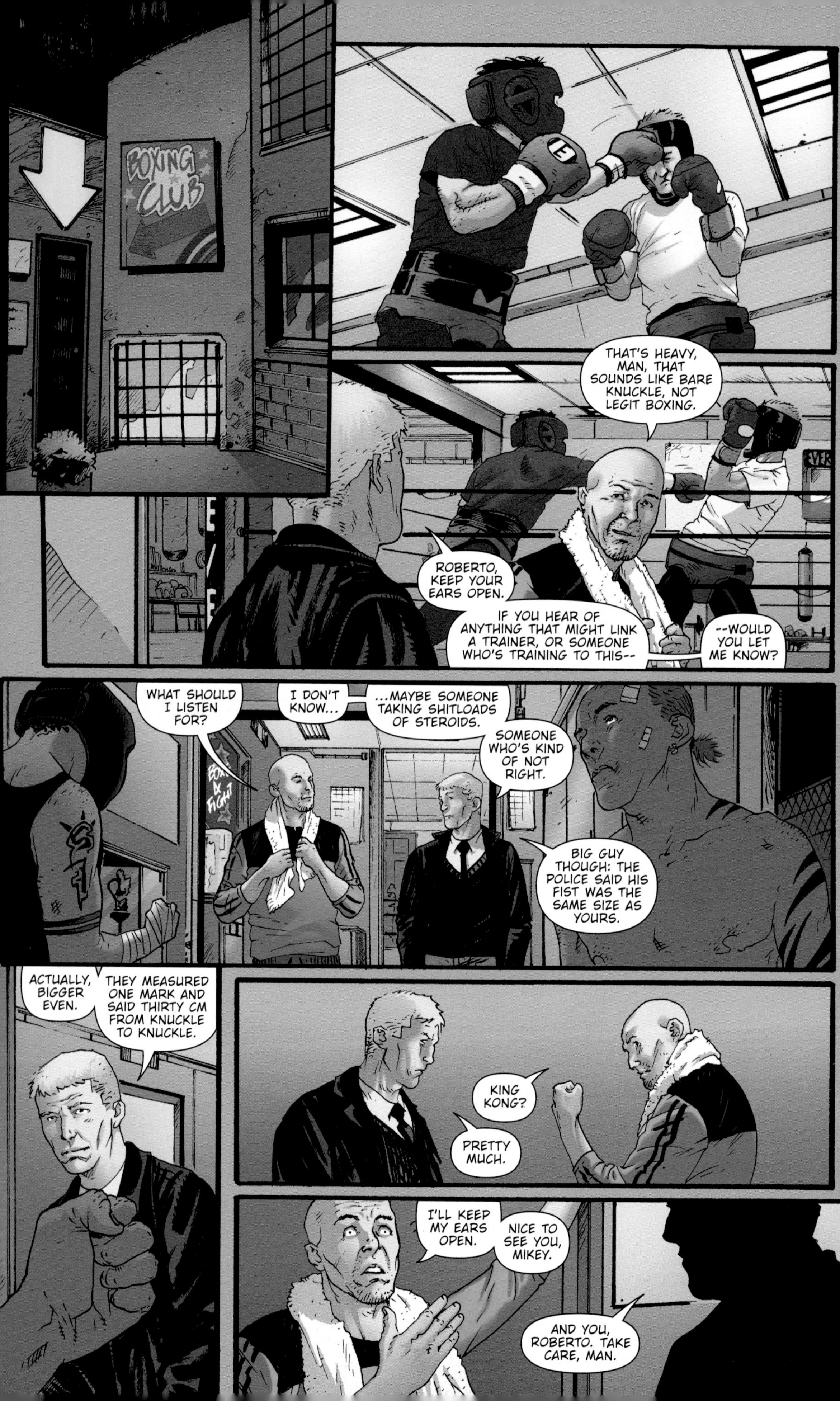
BOXING CLUB
THAT'S HEAVY, MAN, THAT SOUNDS LIKE BARE KNUCKLE, NOT LEGIT BOXING.
ROBERTO, KEEP YOUR EARS OPEN.
IF YOU HEAR OF ANYTHING THAT MIGHT LINK A TRAINER, OR SOMEONE WHO'S TRAINING TO THIS--
--WOULD YOU LET ME KNOW?
WHAT SHOULD I LISTEN FOR?
I DON'T KNOW...
...MAYBE SOMEONE TAKING SHITLOADS OF STEROIDS.
SOMEONE WHO'S KIND OF NOT RIGHT.
BIG GUY THOUGH: THE POLICE SAID HIS FIST WAS THE SAME SIZE AS YOURS.
ACTUALLY, BIGGER EVEN.
THEY MEASURED ONE MARK AND SAID THIRTY CM FROM KNUCKLE TO KNUCKLE.
KING KONG?
PRETTY MUCH.
I'LL KEEP MY EARS OPEN.
NICE TO SEE YOU, MIKEY.
AND YOU, ROBERTO. TAKE CARE, MAN.

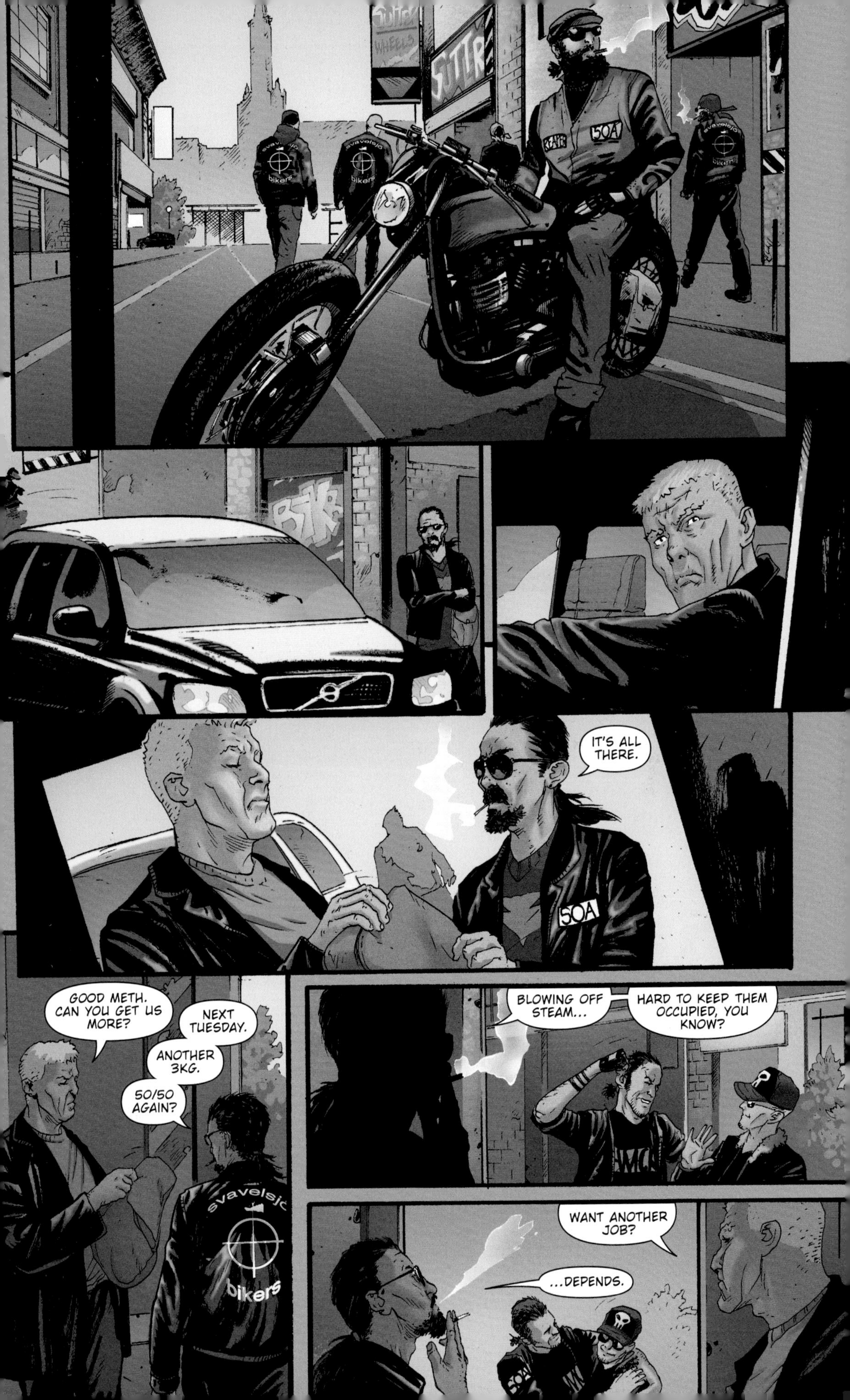
IT'S ALL THERE.
GOOD METH. CAN YOU GET US MORE?
NEXT TUESDAY.
ANOTHER 3KG.
50/50 AGAIN?
BLOWING OFF STEAM...
HARD TO KEEP THEM OCCUPIED, YOU KNOW?
WANT ANOTHER JOB?
...DEPENDS.

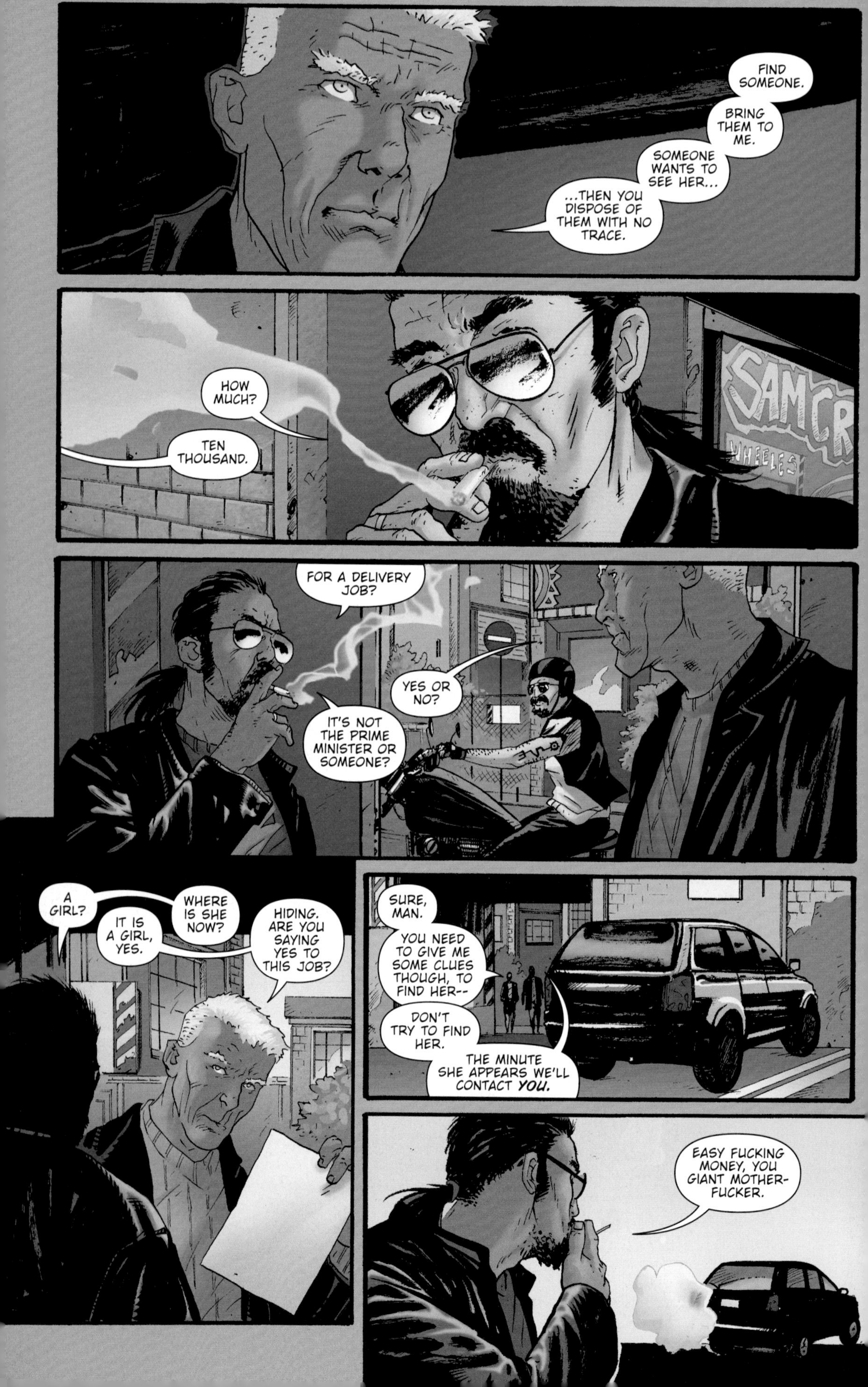
FIND SOMEONE.
BRING THEM TO ME.
SOMEONE WANTS TO SEE HER...
...THEN YOU DISPOSE OF THEM WITH NO TRACE.
SAMCR
WHEELES
HOW MUCH?
TEN THOUSAND.
FOR A DELIVERY JOB?
IT'S NOT THE PRIME MINISTER OR SOMEONE?
YES OR NO?
A GIRL?
IT IS A GIRL, YES.
WHERE IS SHE NOW?
HIDING. ARE YOU SAYING YES TO THIS JOB?
SURE, MAN.
YOU NEED TO GIVE ME SOME CLUES THOUGH, TO FIND HER--
DON'T TRY TO FIND HER.
THE MINUTE SHE APPEARS WE'LL CONTACT *YOU.*
EASY FUCKING MONEY, YOU GIANT MOTHER-FUCKER.

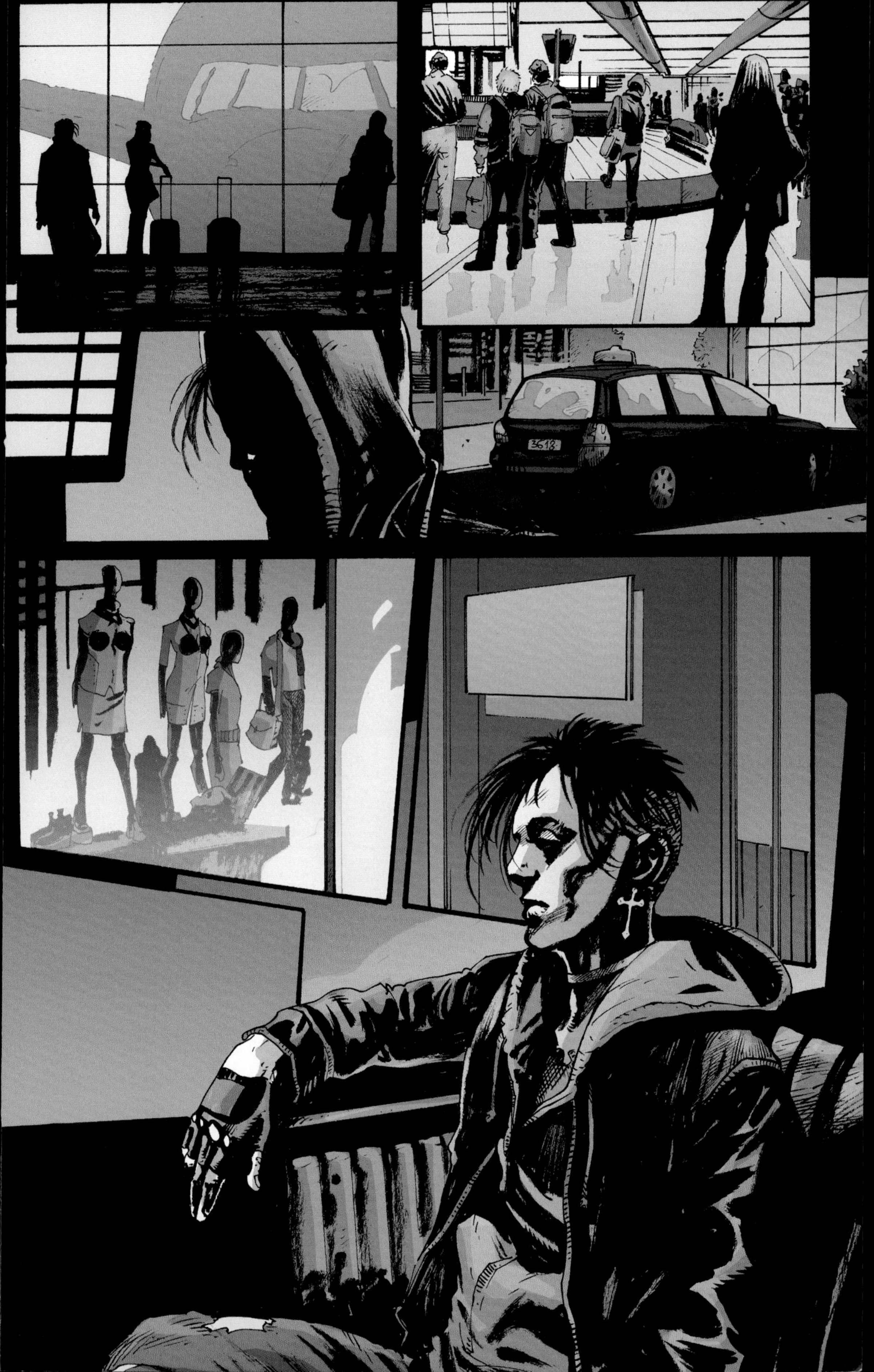
3618

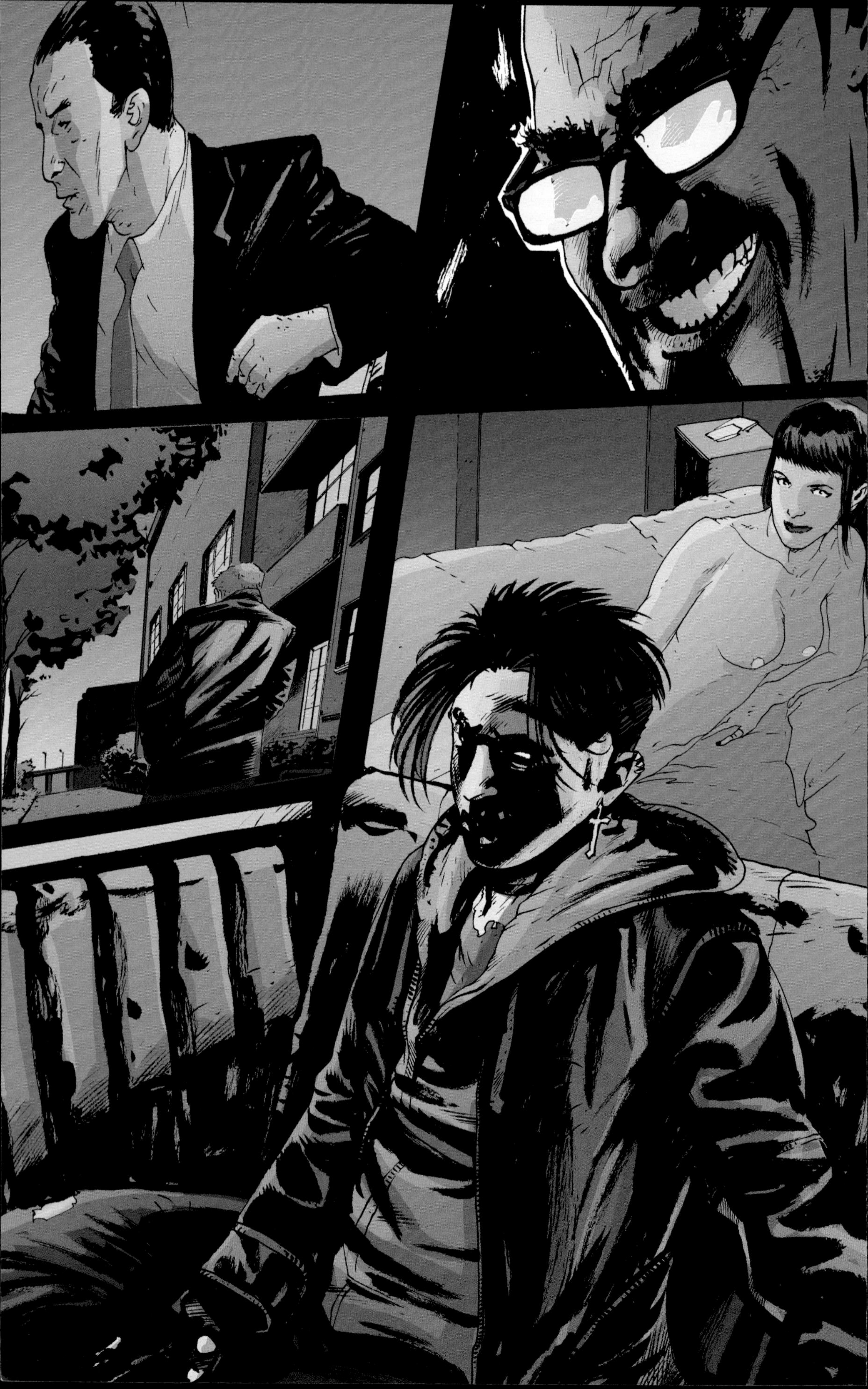

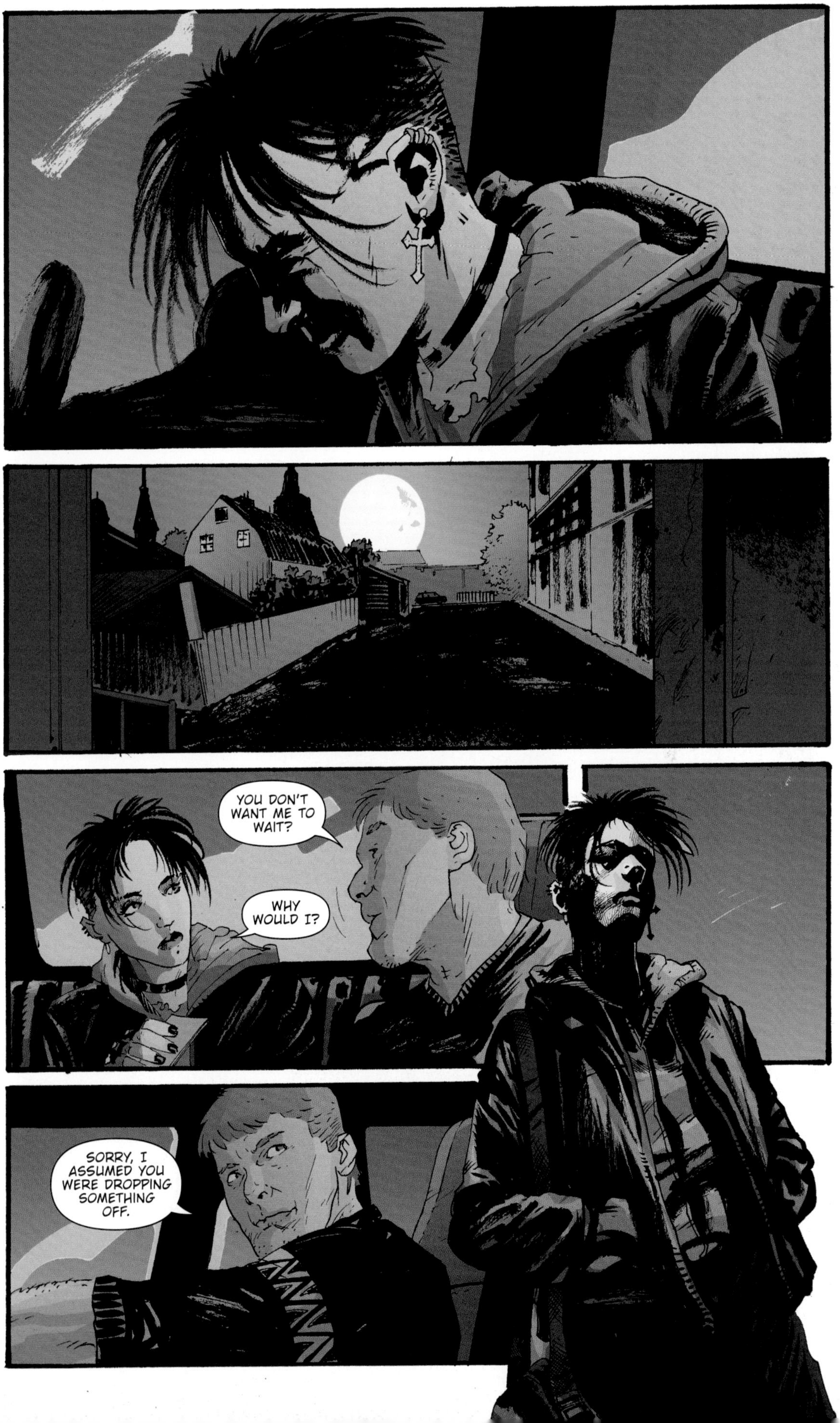
YOU DON'T WANT ME TO WAIT?
WHY WOULD I?
SORRY, I ASSUMED YOU WERE DROPPING SOMETHING OFF.

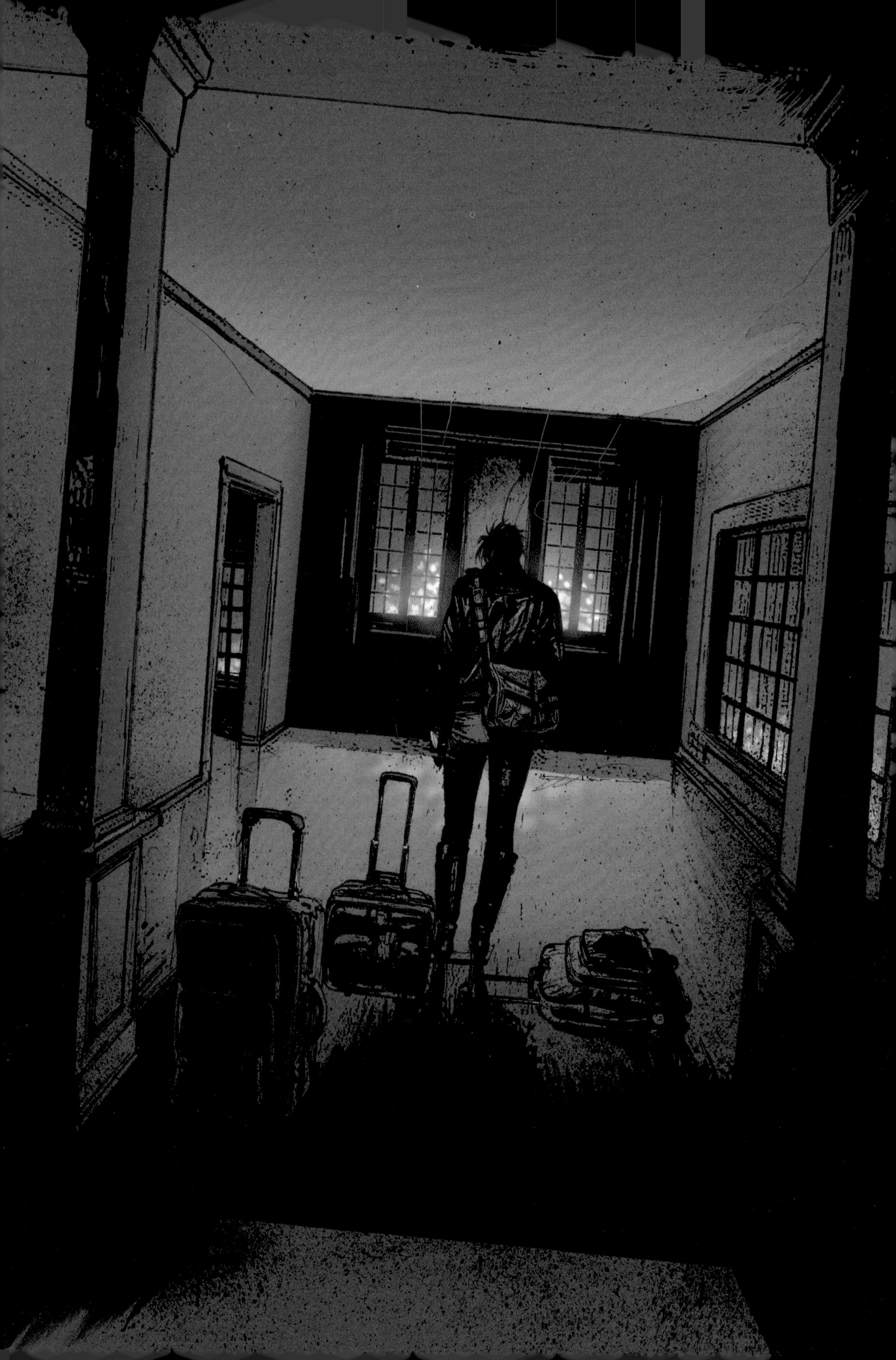

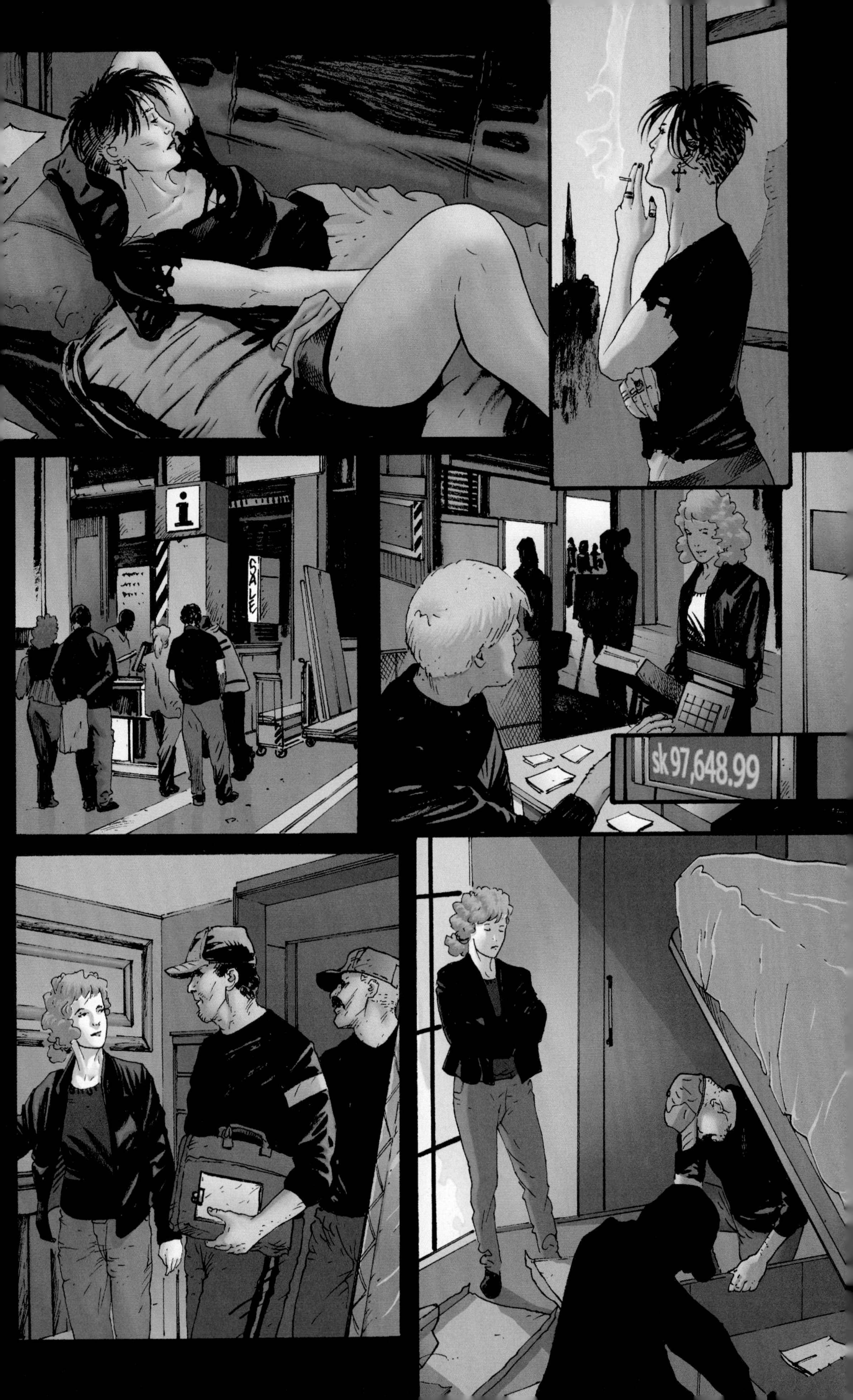
i
SALE
sk 97,648.99

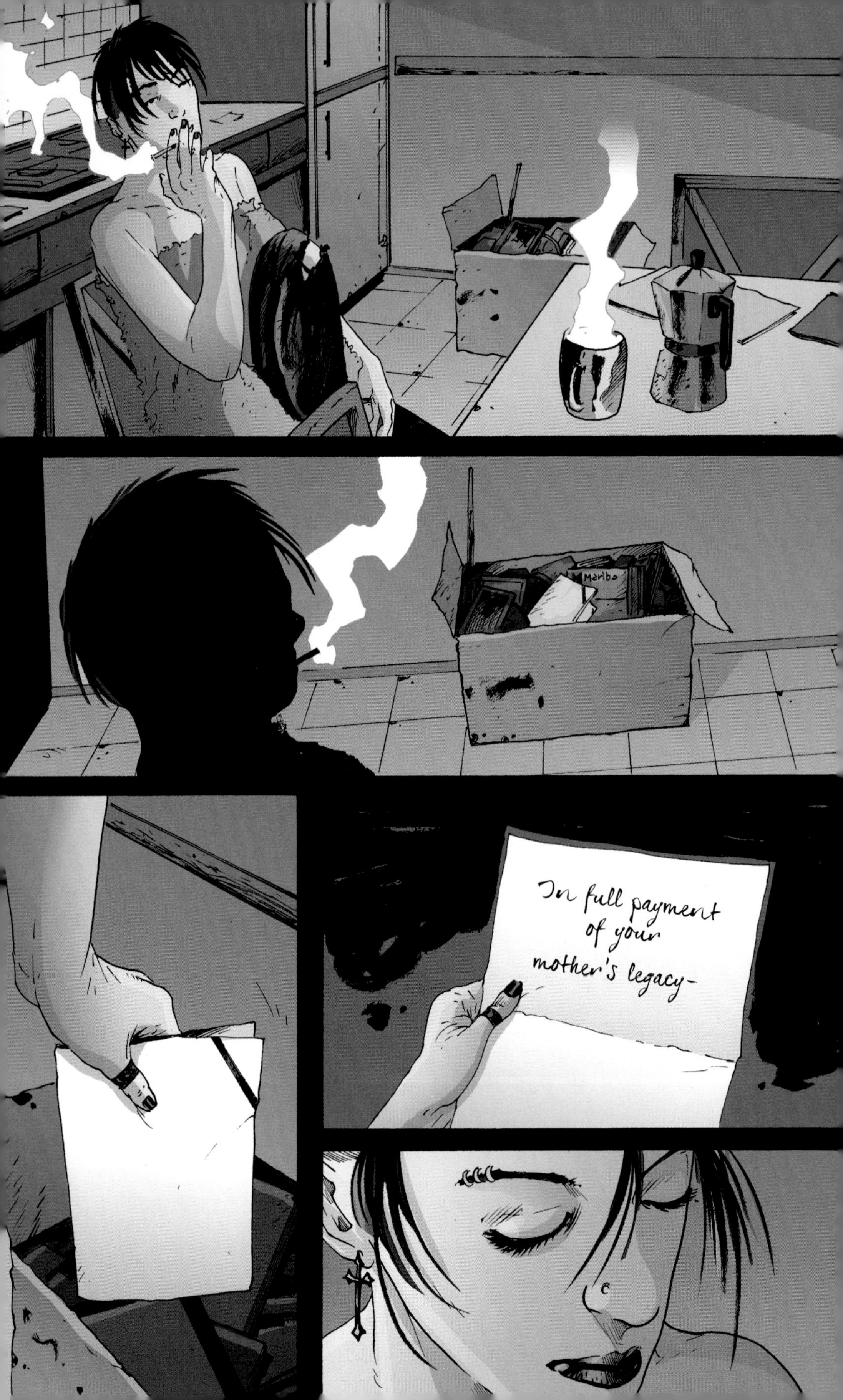
Marlbo
In full payment of your mother's legacy-

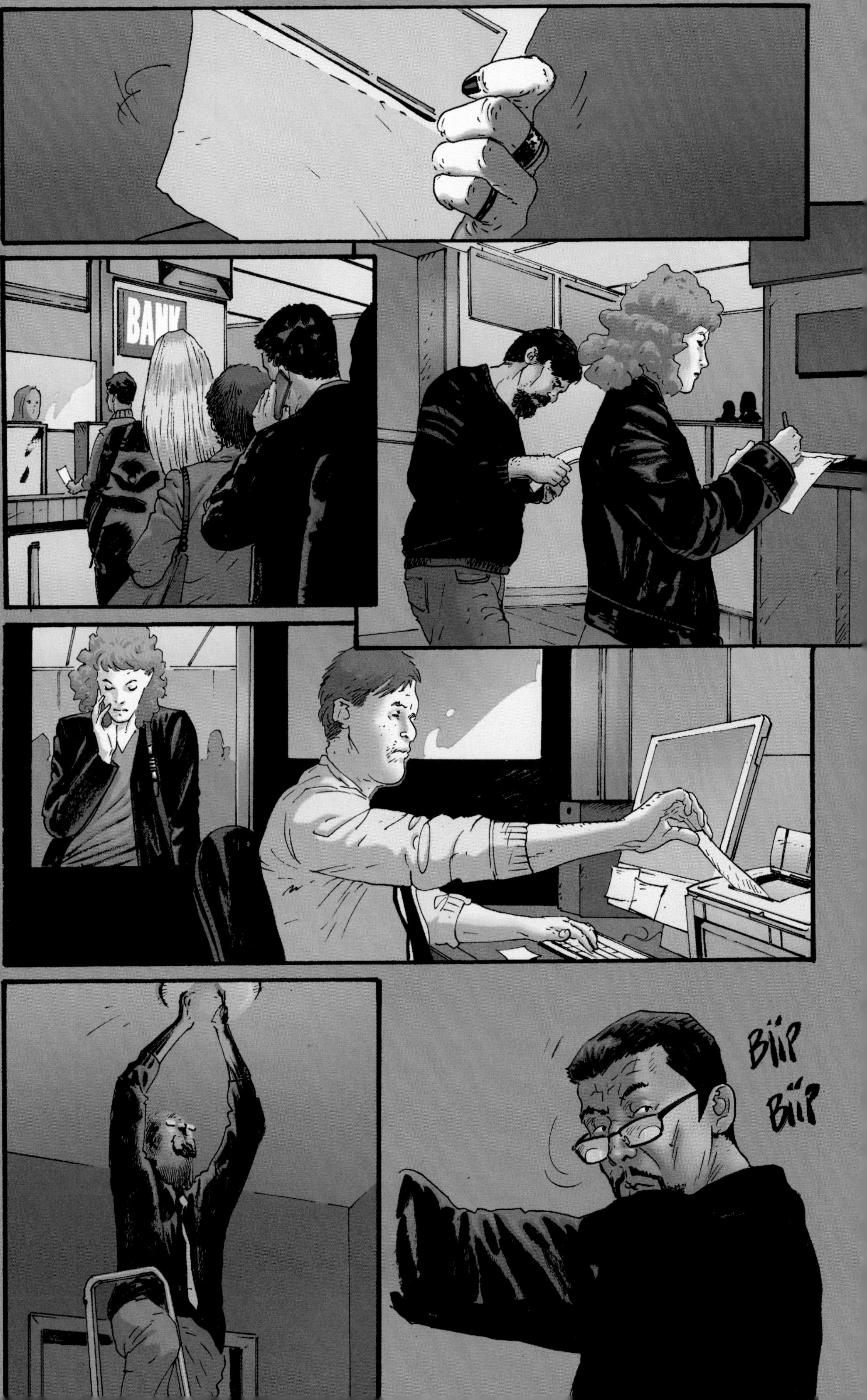
BANK
BIIP
BIIP

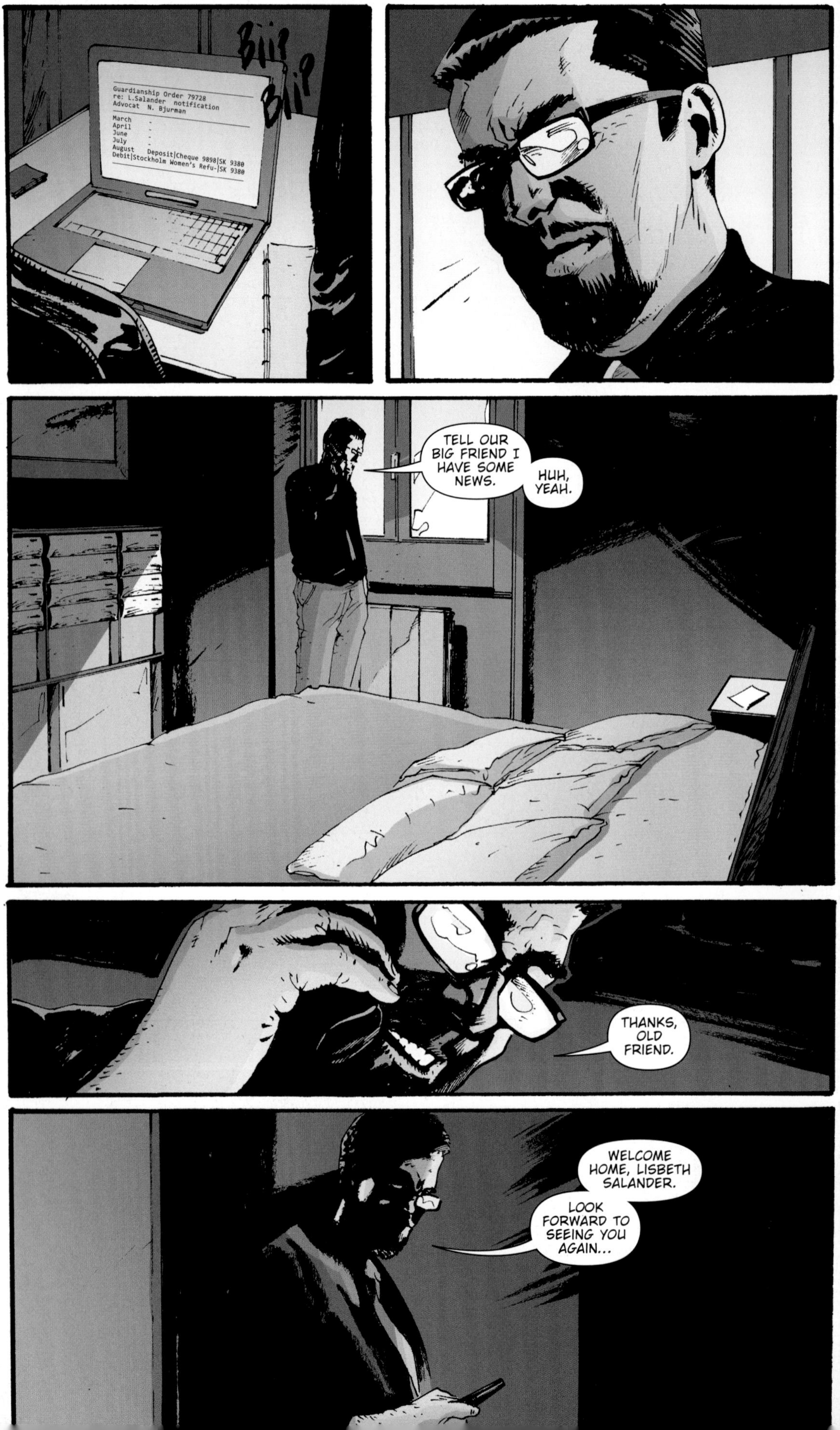
Guardianship Order 79728
re: L.Salander notification
Advocat N. Bjurman
March -
April -
June -
July -
August Deposit|Cheque 9898|SK 9380
Debit|Stockholm Women's Refu-|SK 9380
BIIP
BIIP
TELL OUR BIG FRIEND I HAVE SOME NEWS.
HUH, YEAH.
THANKS, OLD FRIEND.
WELCOME HOME, LISBETH SALANDER.
LOOK FORWARD TO SEEING YOU AGAIN...

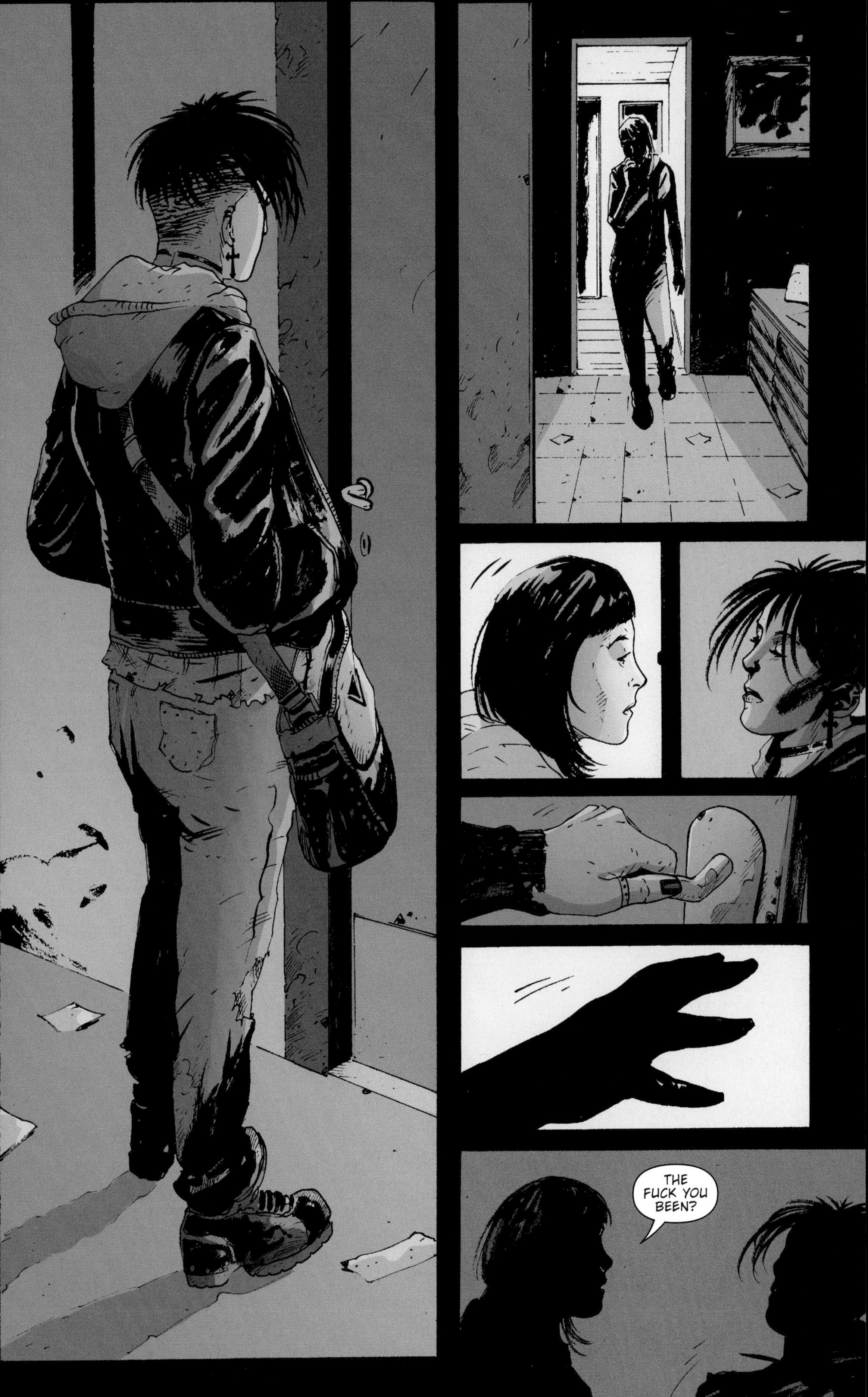
THE FUCK YOU BEEN?

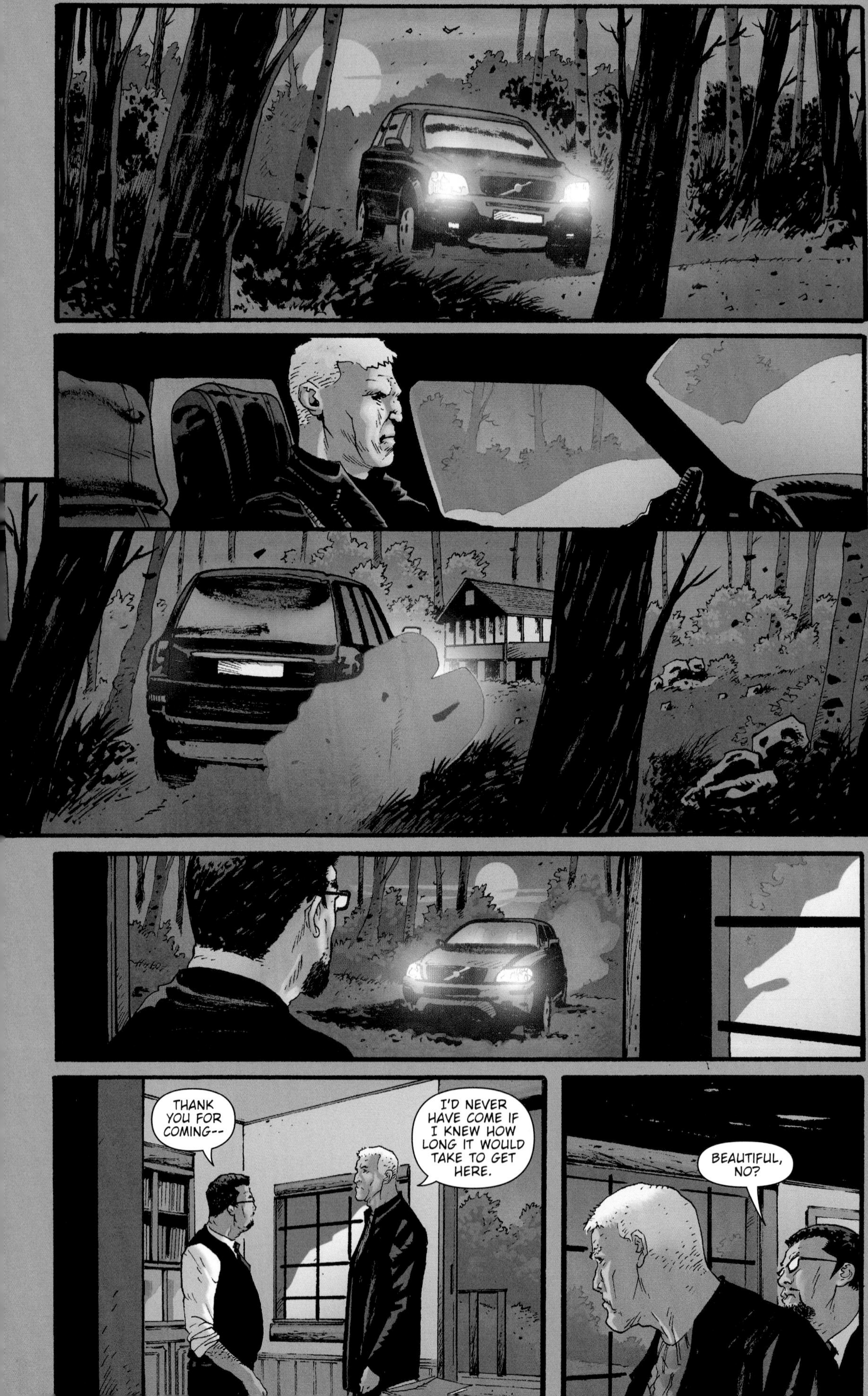
THANK YOU FOR COMING--
I'D NEVER HAVE COME IF I KNEW HOW LONG IT WOULD TAKE TO GET HERE.
BEAUTIFUL, NO?

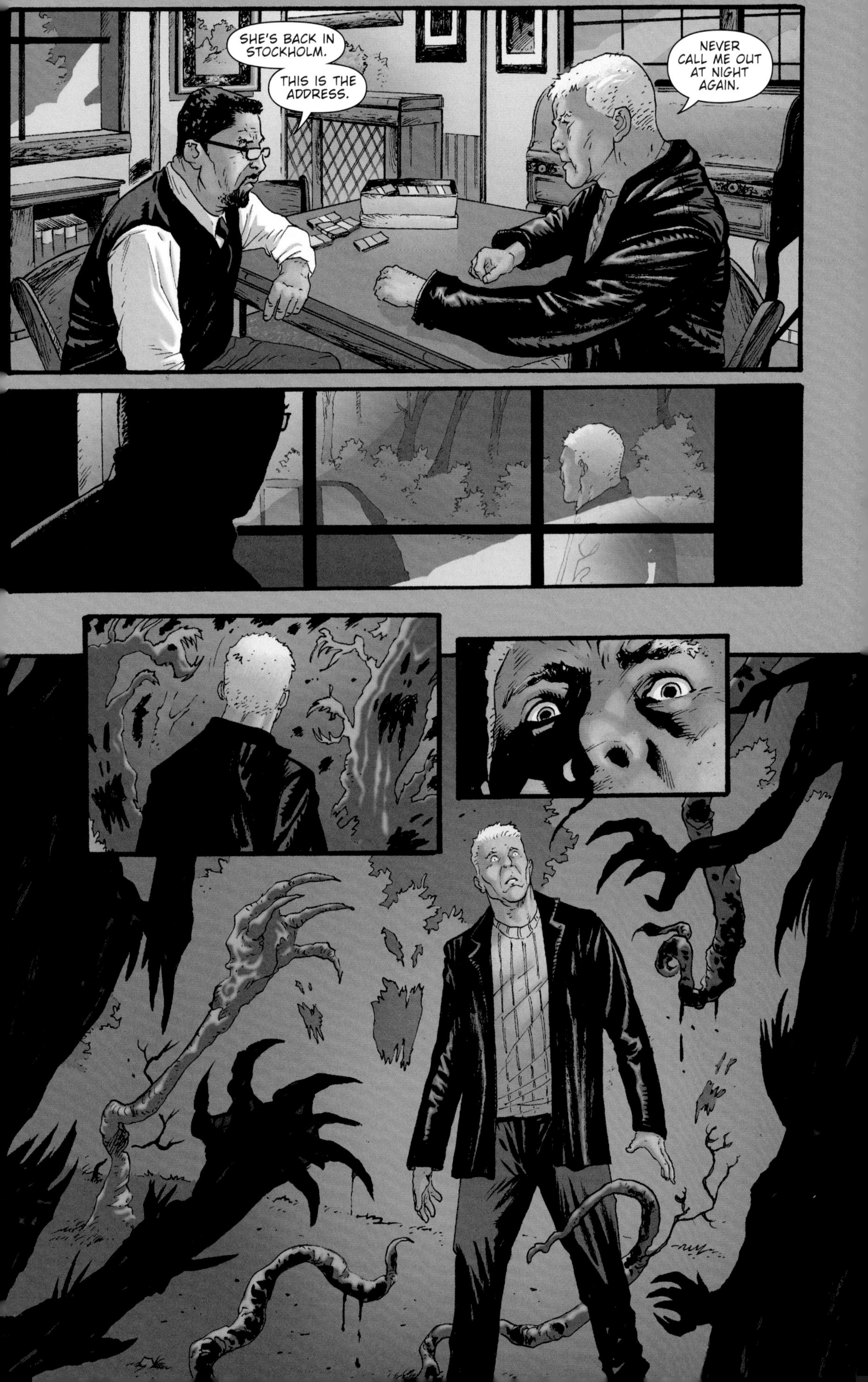
SHE'S BACK IN STOCKHOLM.
THIS IS THE ADDRESS.
NEVER CALL ME OUT AT NIGHT AGAIN.

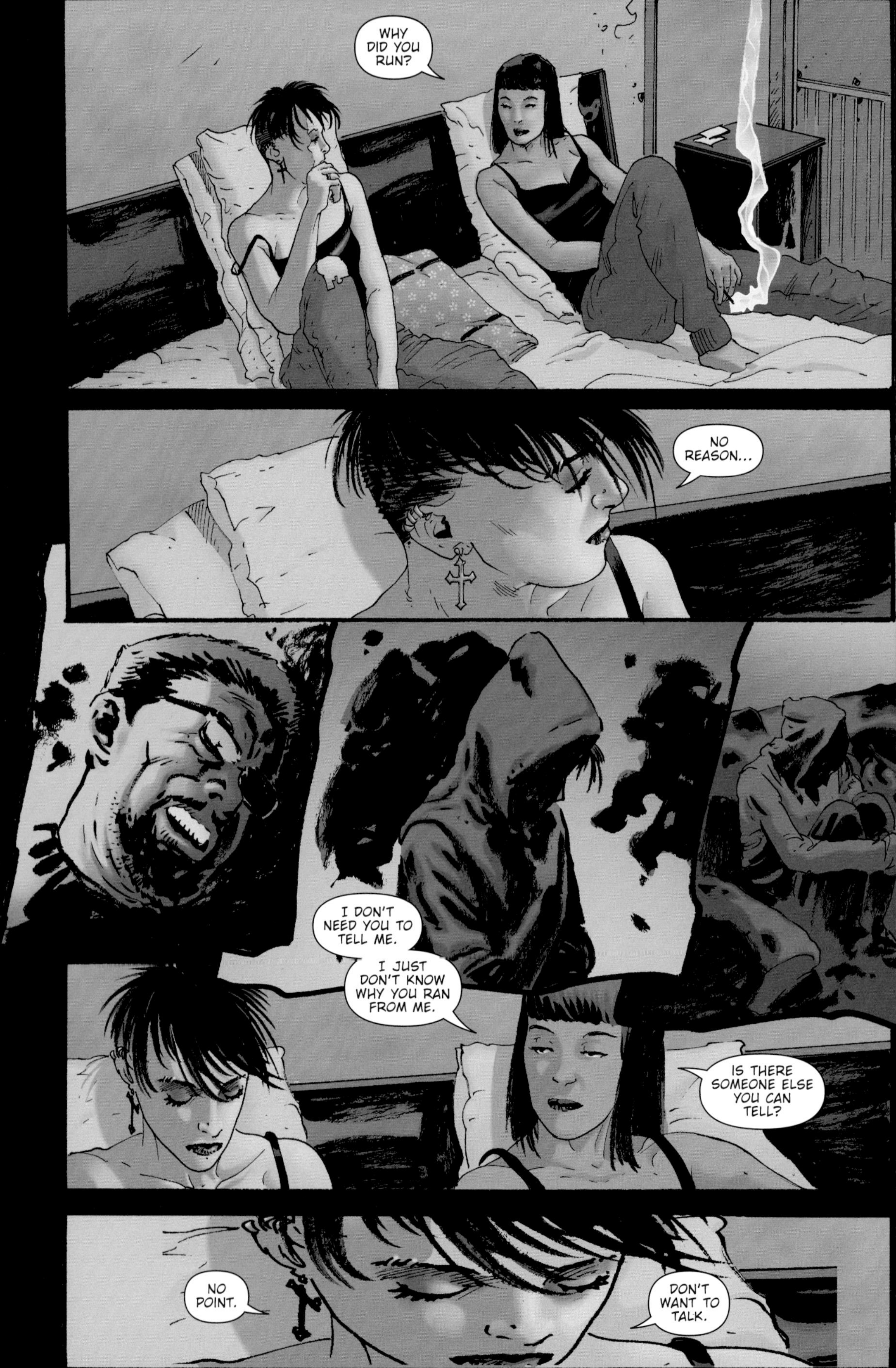
WHY DID YOU RUN?
NO REASON...
I DON'T NEED YOU TO TELL ME.
I JUST DON'T KNOW WHY YOU RAN FROM ME.
IS THERE SOMEONE ELSE YOU CAN TELL?
NO POINT.
DON'T WANT TO TALK.

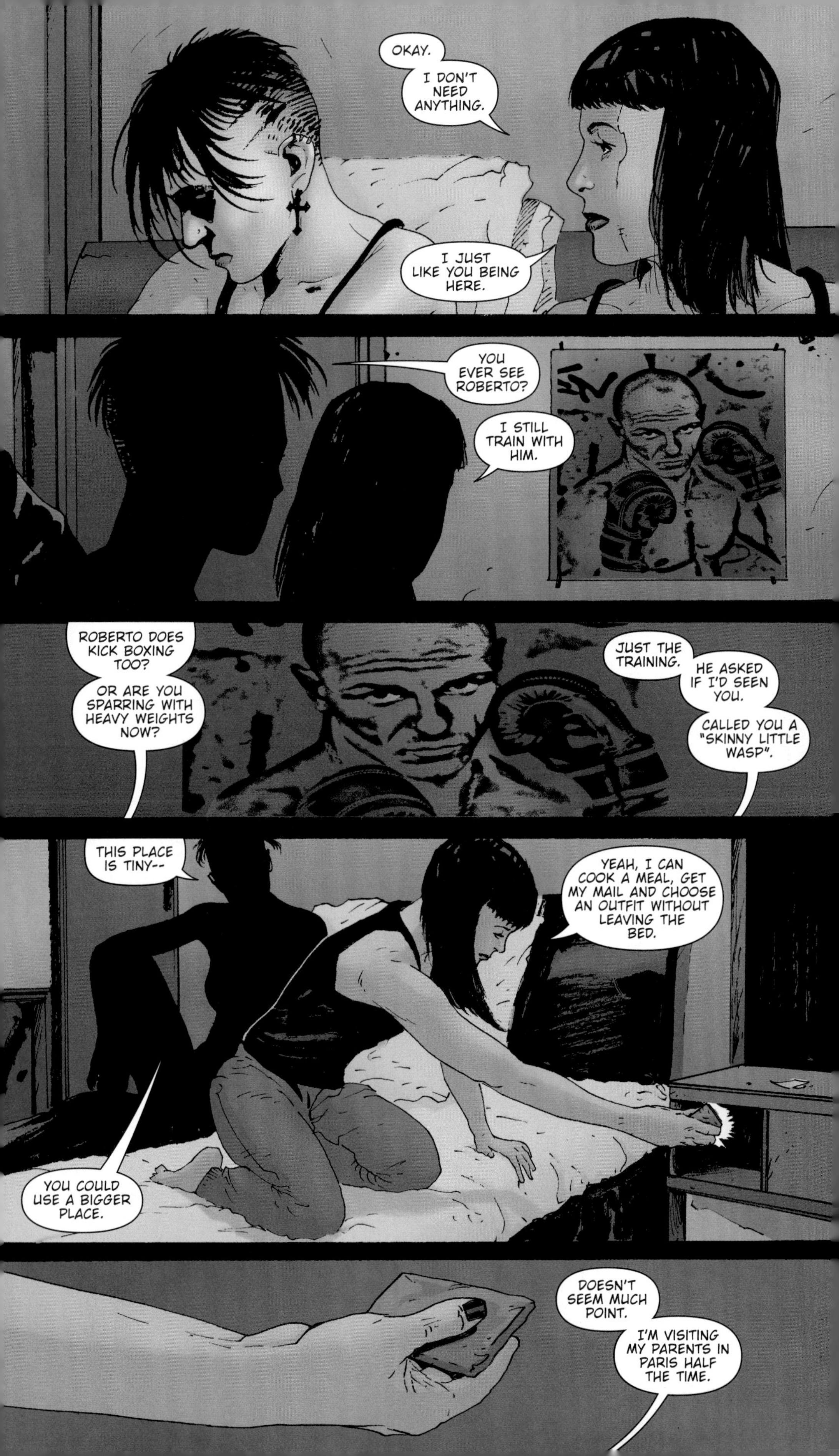
OKAY.
I DON'T NEED ANYTHING.
I JUST LIKE YOU BEING HERE.
YOU EVER SEE ROBERTO?
I STILL TRAIN WITH HIM.
ROBERTO DOES KICK BOXING TOO?
OR ARE YOU SPARRING WITH HEAVY WEIGHTS NOW?
JUST THE TRAINING.
HE ASKED IF I'D SEEN YOU.
CALLED YOU A "SKINNY LITTLE WASP".
THIS PLACE IS TINY--
YEAH, I CAN COOK A MEAL, GET MY MAIL AND CHOOSE AN OUTFIT WITHOUT LEAVING THE BED.
YOU COULD USE A BIGGER PLACE.
DOESN'T SEEM MUCH POINT.
I'M VISITING MY PARENTS IN PARIS HALF THE TIME.

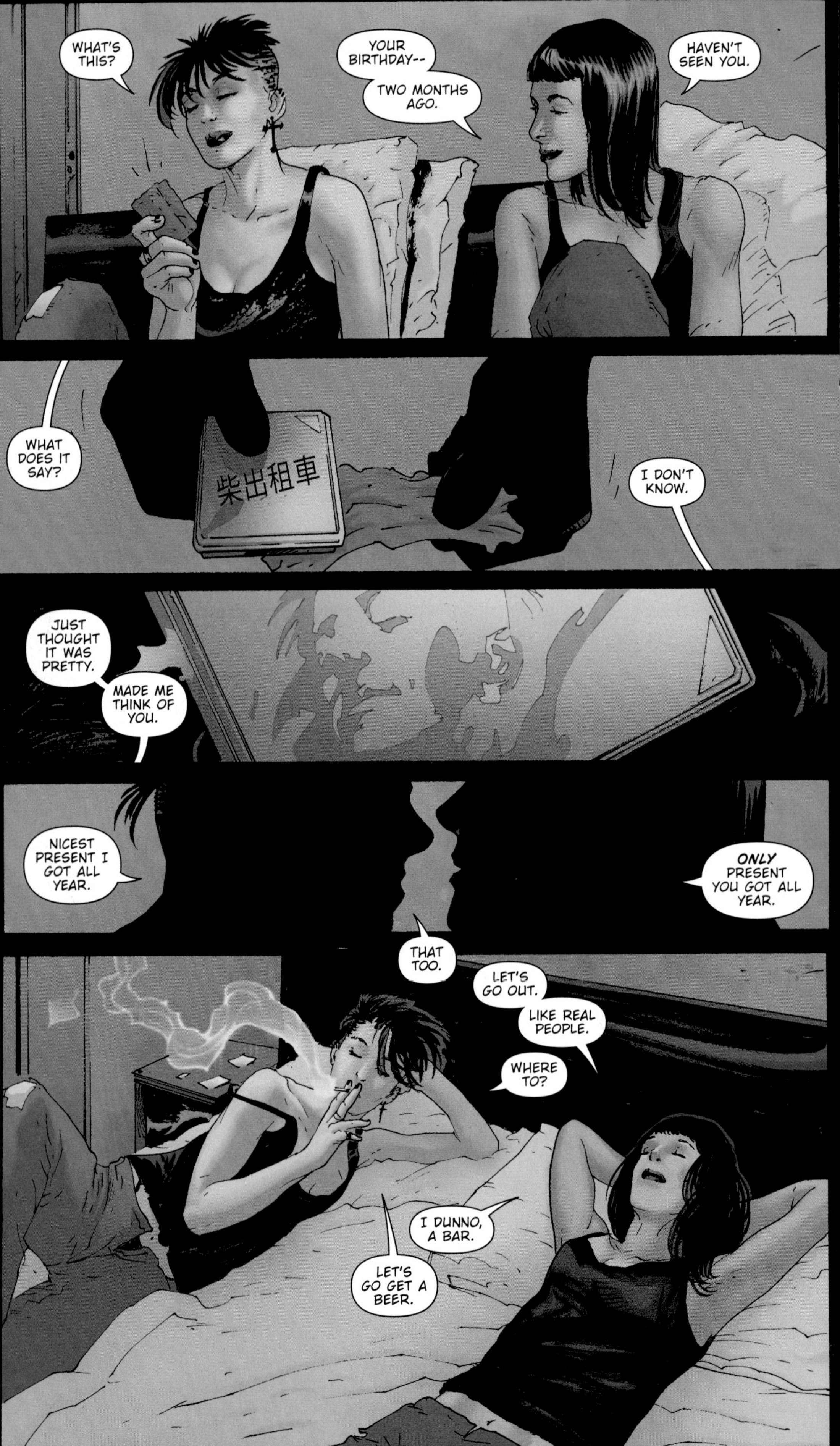
WHAT'S THIS?
YOUR BIRTHDAY--
TWO MONTHS AGO.
HAVEN'T SEEN YOU.
WHAT DOES IT SAY?
柴出租車
I DON'T KNOW.
JUST THOUGHT IT WAS PRETTY.
MADE ME THINK OF YOU.
NICEST PRESENT I GOT ALL YEAR.
ONLY PRESENT YOU GOT ALL YEAR.
THAT TOO.
LET'S GO OUT.
LIKE REAL PEOPLE.
WHERE TO?
I DUNNO, A BAR.
LET'S GO GET A BEER.

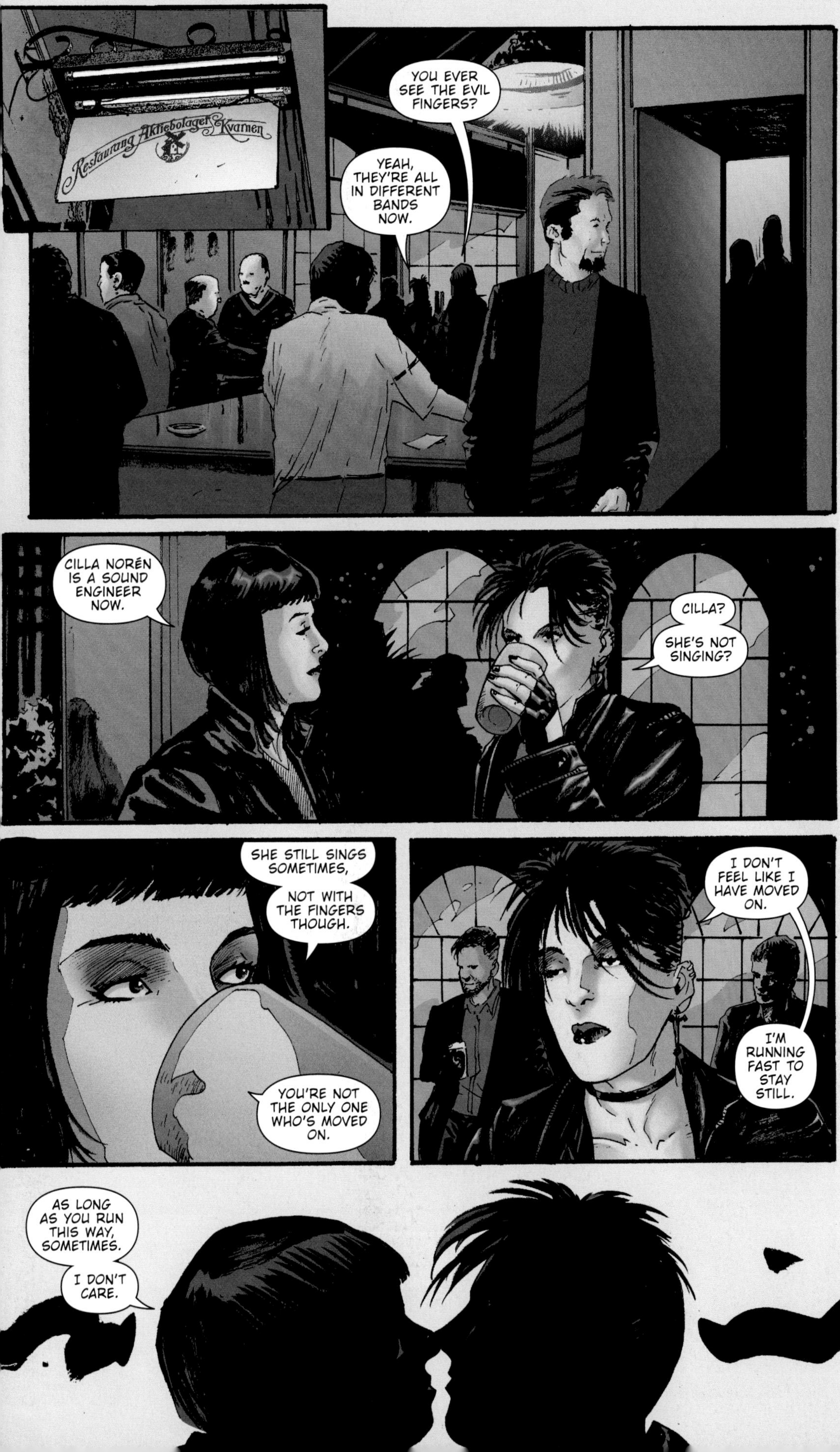
Restaurang Aktiebolaget Kvarnen
YOU EVER SEE THE EVIL FINGERS?
YEAH, THEY'RE ALL IN DIFFERENT BANDS NOW.
CILLA NORÉN IS A SOUND ENGINEER NOW.
CILLA?
SHE'S NOT SINGING?
SHE STILL SINGS SOMETIMES,
NOT WITH THE FINGERS THOUGH.
YOU'RE NOT THE ONLY ONE WHO'S MOVED ON.
I DON'T FEEL LIKE I HAVE MOVED ON.
I'M RUNNING FAST TO STAY STILL.
AS LONG AS YOU RUN THIS WAY, SOMETIMES.
I DON'T CARE.

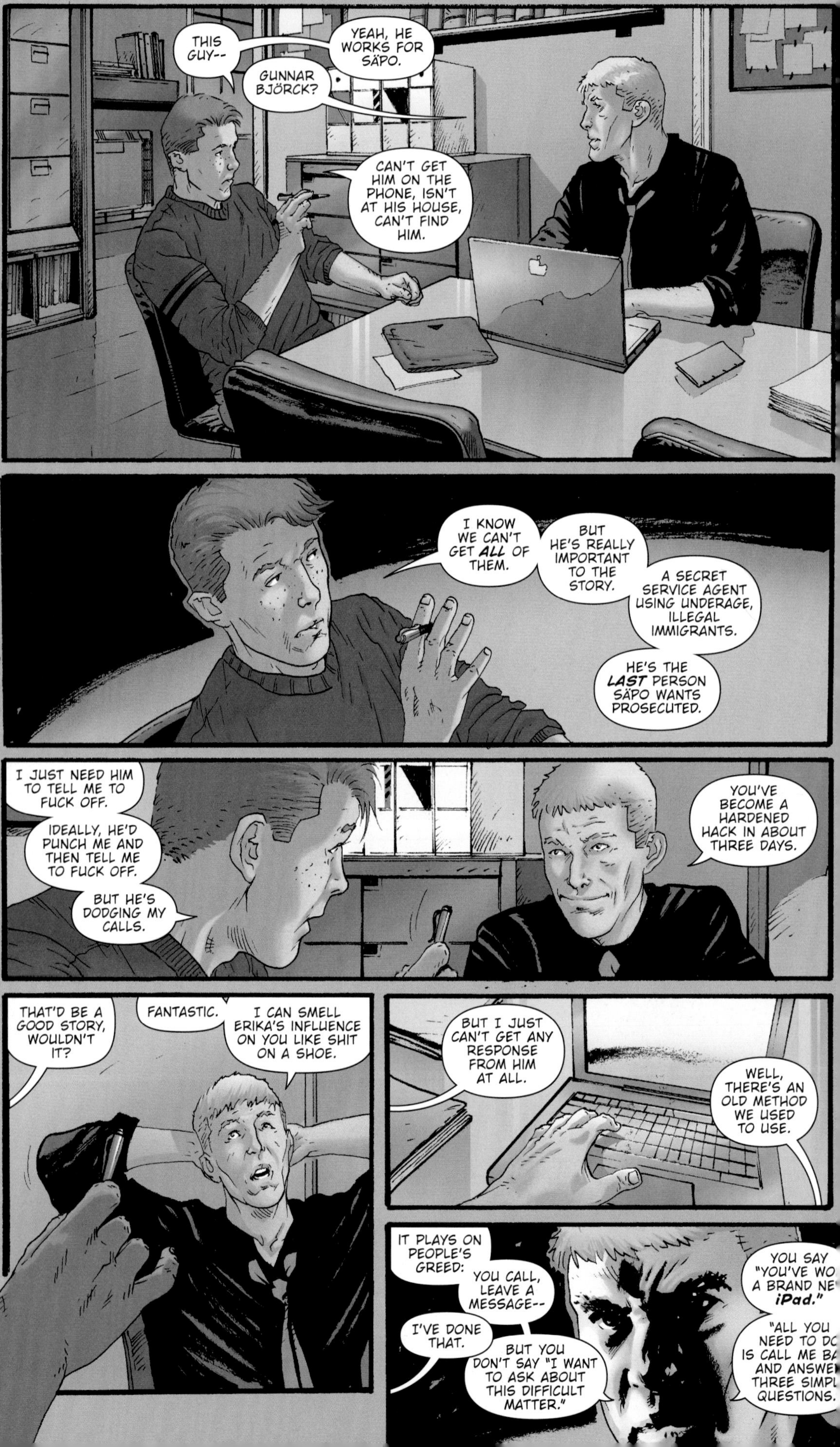
THIS GUY--
YEAH, HE WORKS FOR SÄPO.
GUNNAR BJÖRCK?
CAN'T GET HIM ON THE PHONE, ISN'T AT HIS HOUSE, CAN'T FIND HIM.
I KNOW WE CAN'T GET *ALL* OF THEM.
BUT HE'S REALLY IMPORTANT TO THE STORY.
A SECRET SERVICE AGENT USING UNDERAGE, ILLEGAL IMMIGRANTS.
HE'S THE *LAST* PERSON SÄPO WANTS PROSECUTED.
I JUST NEED HIM TO TELL ME TO FUCK OFF.
IDEALLY, HE'D PUNCH ME AND THEN TELL ME TO FUCK OFF.
BUT HE'S DODGING MY CALLS.
YOU'VE BECOME A HARDENED HACK IN ABOUT THREE DAYS.
THAT'D BE A GOOD STORY, WOULDN'T IT?
FANTASTIC.
I CAN SMELL ERIKA'S INFLUENCE ON YOU LIKE SHIT ON A SHOE.
BUT I JUST CAN'T GET ANY RESPONSE FROM HIM AT ALL.
WELL, THERE'S AN OLD METHOD WE USED TO USE.
IT PLAYS ON PEOPLE'S GREED:
YOU CALL, LEAVE A MESSAGE--
I'VE DONE THAT.
BUT YOU DON'T SAY "I WANT TO ASK ABOUT THIS DIFFICULT MATTER."
YOU SAY "YOU'VE WO A BRAND NE ***iPad.***"
"ALL YOU NEED TO DO IS CALL ME BA AND ANSWE THREE SIMPL QUESTIONS.

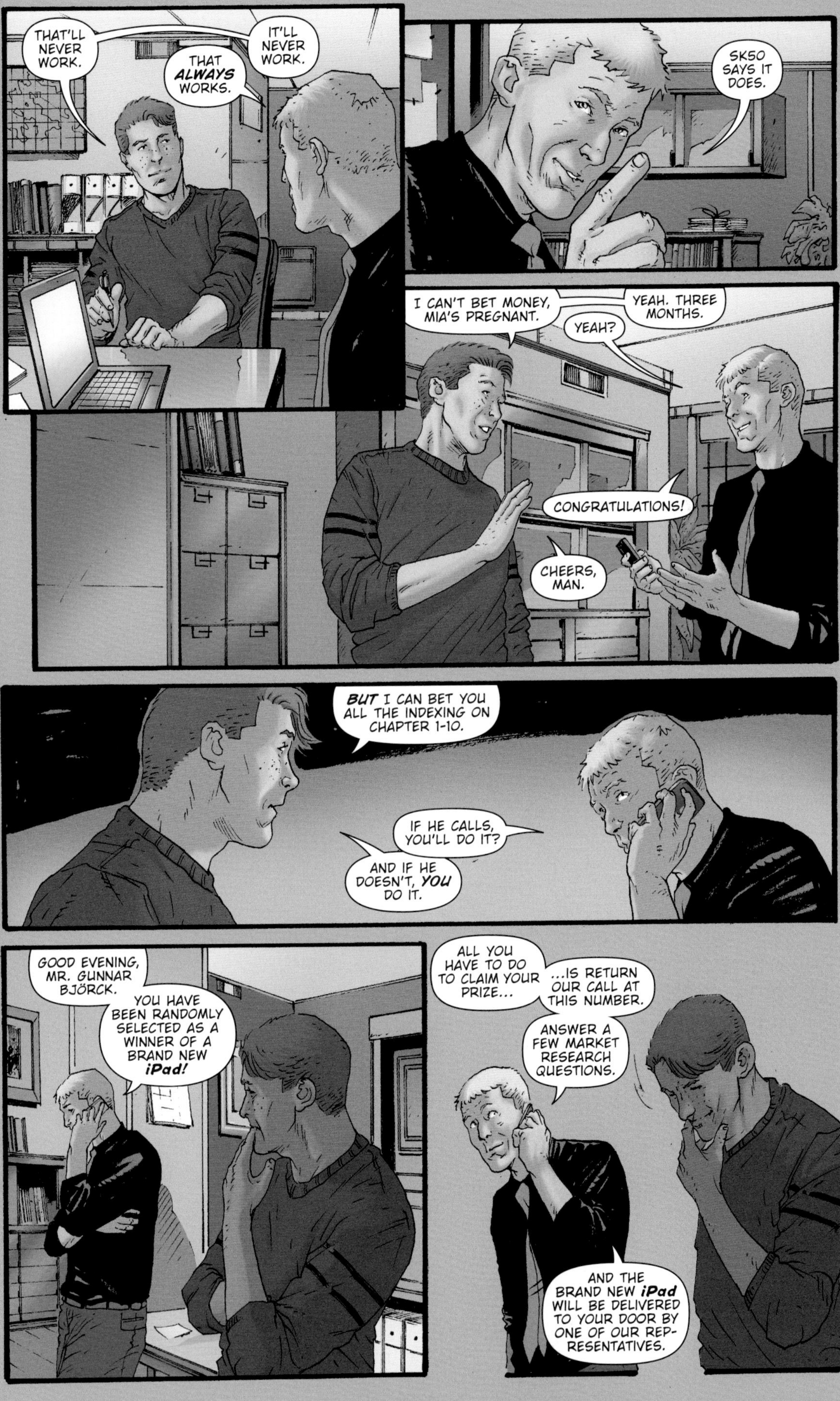
THAT'LL NEVER WORK.
THAT ALWAYS WORKS.
IT'LL NEVER WORK.
SK50 SAYS IT DOES.
I CAN'T BET MONEY, MIA'S PREGNANT.
YEAH?
YEAH. THREE MONTHS.
CONGRATULATIONS!
CHEERS, MAN.
BUT I CAN BET YOU ALL THE INDEXING ON CHAPTER 1-10.
IF HE CALLS, YOU'LL DO IT?
AND IF HE DOESN'T, YOU DO IT.
GOOD EVENING, MR. GUNNAR BJÖRCK.
YOU HAVE BEEN RANDOMLY SELECTED AS A WINNER OF A BRAND NEW iPad!
ALL YOU HAVE TO DO TO CLAIM YOUR PRIZE...
...IS RETURN OUR CALL AT THIS NUMBER.
ANSWER A FEW MARKET RESEARCH QUESTIONS.
AND THE BRAND NEW iPad WILL BE DELIVERED TO YOUR DOOR BY ONE OF OUR REP-RESENTATIVES.

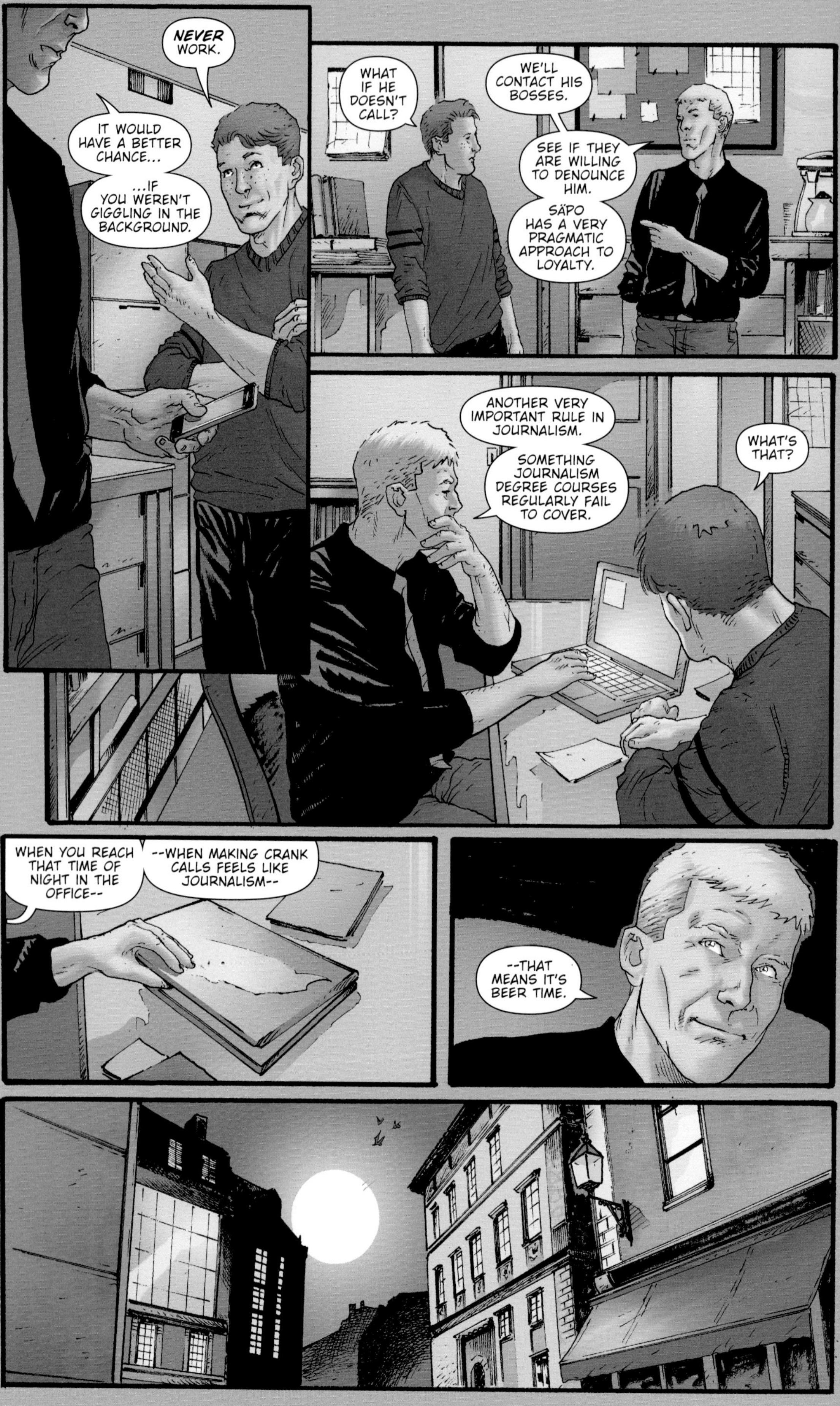
NEVER WORK.
IT WOULD HAVE A BETTER CHANCE...
...IF YOU WEREN'T GIGGLING IN THE BACKGROUND.
WHAT IF HE DOESN'T CALL?
WE'LL CONTACT HIS BOSSES.
SEE IF THEY ARE WILLING TO DENOUNCE HIM.
SÄPO HAS A VERY PRAGMATIC APPROACH TO LOYALTY.
ANOTHER VERY IMPORTANT RULE IN JOURNALISM.
SOMETHING JOURNALISM DEGREE COURSES REGULARLY FAIL TO COVER.
WHAT'S THAT?
WHEN YOU REACH THAT TIME OF NIGHT IN THE OFFICE--
--WHEN MAKING CRANK CALLS FEELS LIKE JOURNALISM--
--THAT MEANS IT'S BEER TIME.

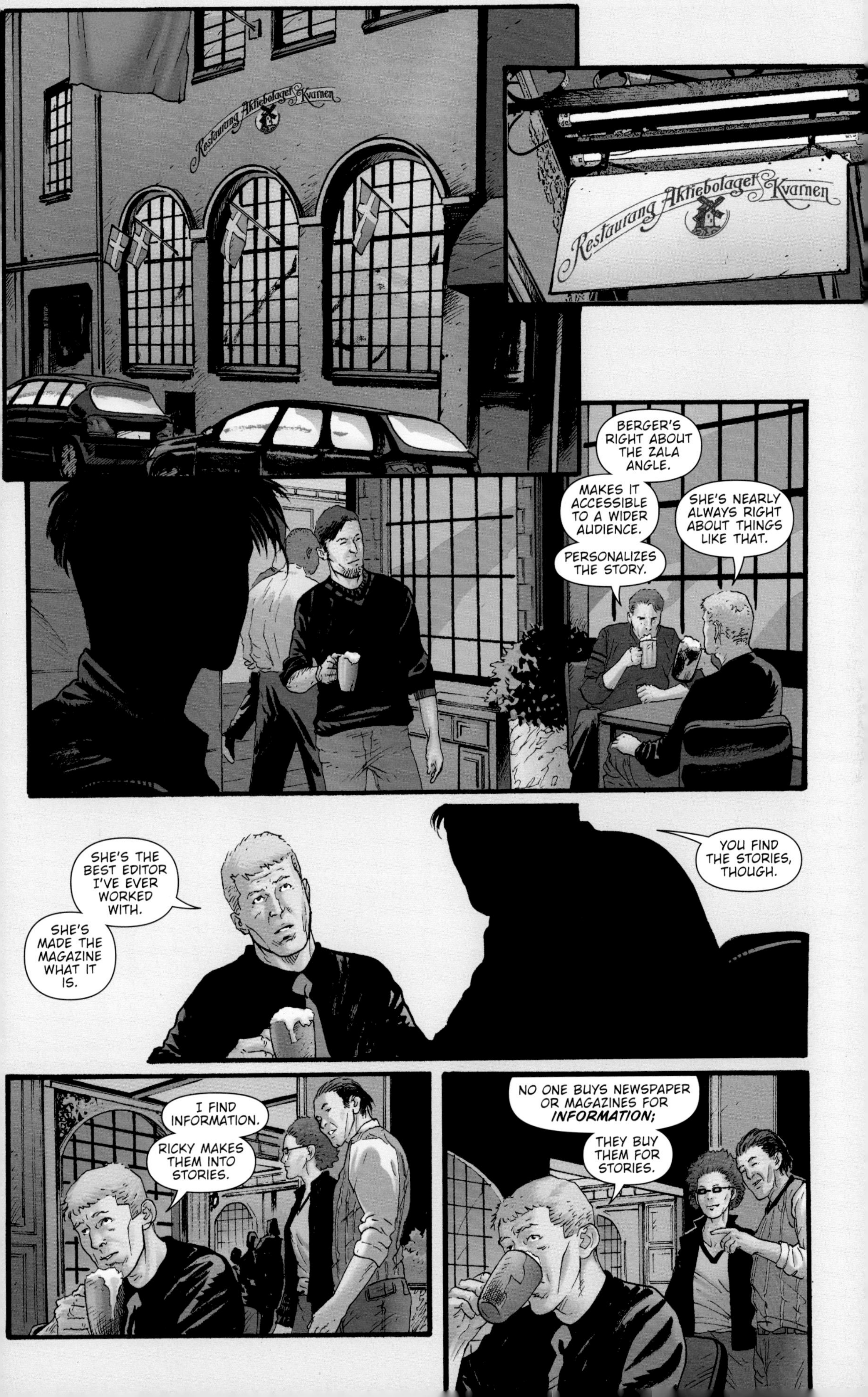
Restaurang Aktiebolaget Kvarnen
Restaurang Aktiebolaget Kvarnen
BERGER'S RIGHT ABOUT THE ZALA ANGLE.
MAKES IT ACCESSIBLE TO A WIDER AUDIENCE.
PERSONALIZES THE STORY.
SHE'S NEARLY ALWAYS RIGHT ABOUT THINGS LIKE THAT.
SHE'S THE BEST EDITOR I'VE EVER WORKED WITH.
SHE'S MADE THE MAGAZINE WHAT IT IS.
YOU FIND THE STORIES, THOUGH.
I FIND INFORMATION.
RICKY MAKES THEM INTO STORIES.
NO ONE BUYS NEWSPAPER OR MAGAZINES FOR ***INFORMATION;***
THEY BUY THEM FOR STORIES.

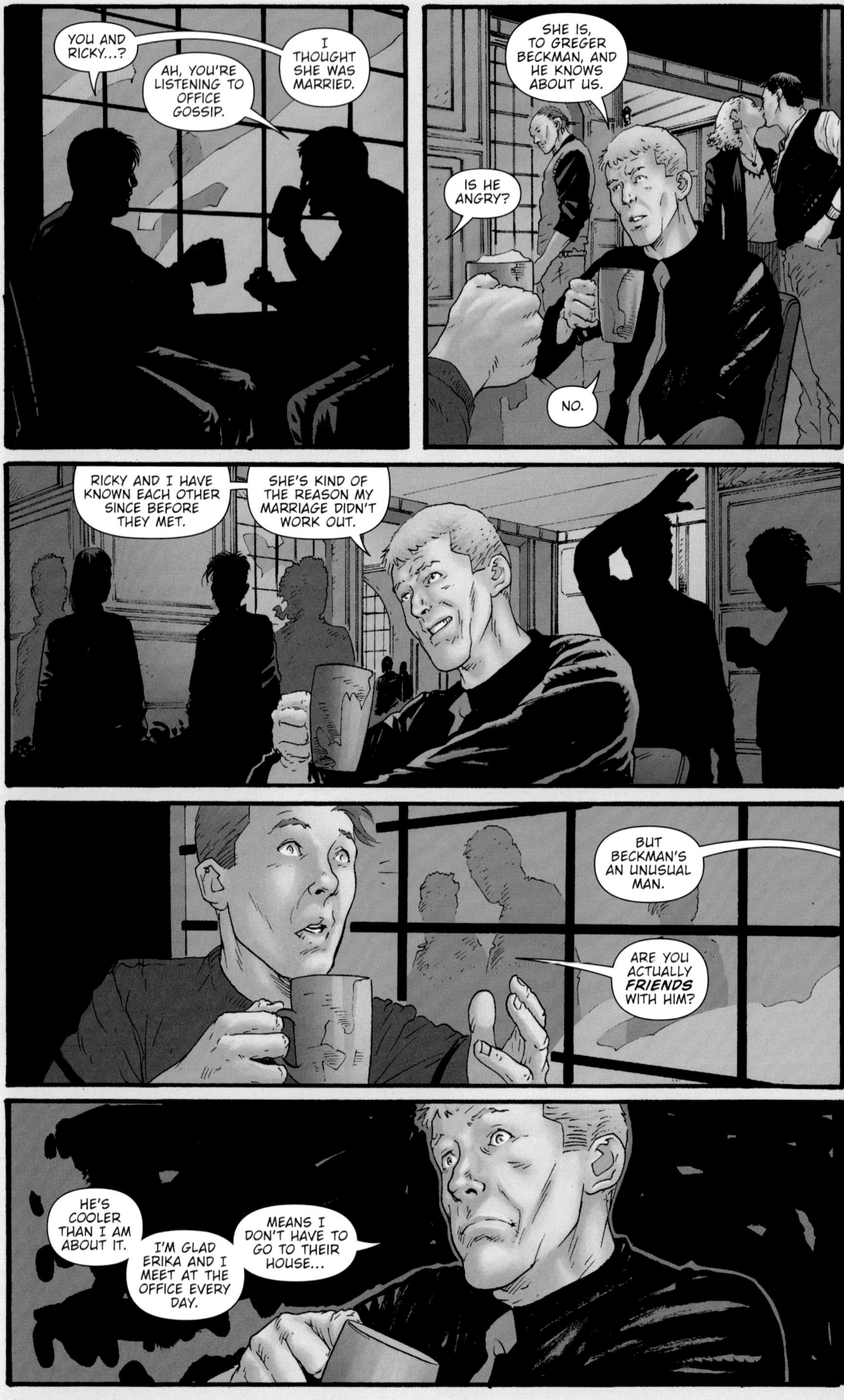
YOU AND RICKY...?
I THOUGHT SHE WAS MARRIED.
AH, YOU'RE LISTENING TO OFFICE GOSSIP.
SHE IS, TO GREGER BECKMAN, AND HE KNOWS ABOUT US.
IS HE ANGRY?
NO.
RICKY AND I HAVE KNOWN EACH OTHER SINCE BEFORE THEY MET.
SHE'S KIND OF THE REASON MY MARRIAGE DIDN'T WORK OUT.
BUT BECKMAN'S AN UNUSUAL MAN.
ARE YOU ACTUALLY **FRIENDS** WITH HIM?
HE'S COOLER THAN I AM ABOUT IT.
I'M GLAD ERIKA AND I MEET AT THE OFFICE EVERY DAY.
MEANS I DON'T HAVE TO GO TO THEIR HOUSE...

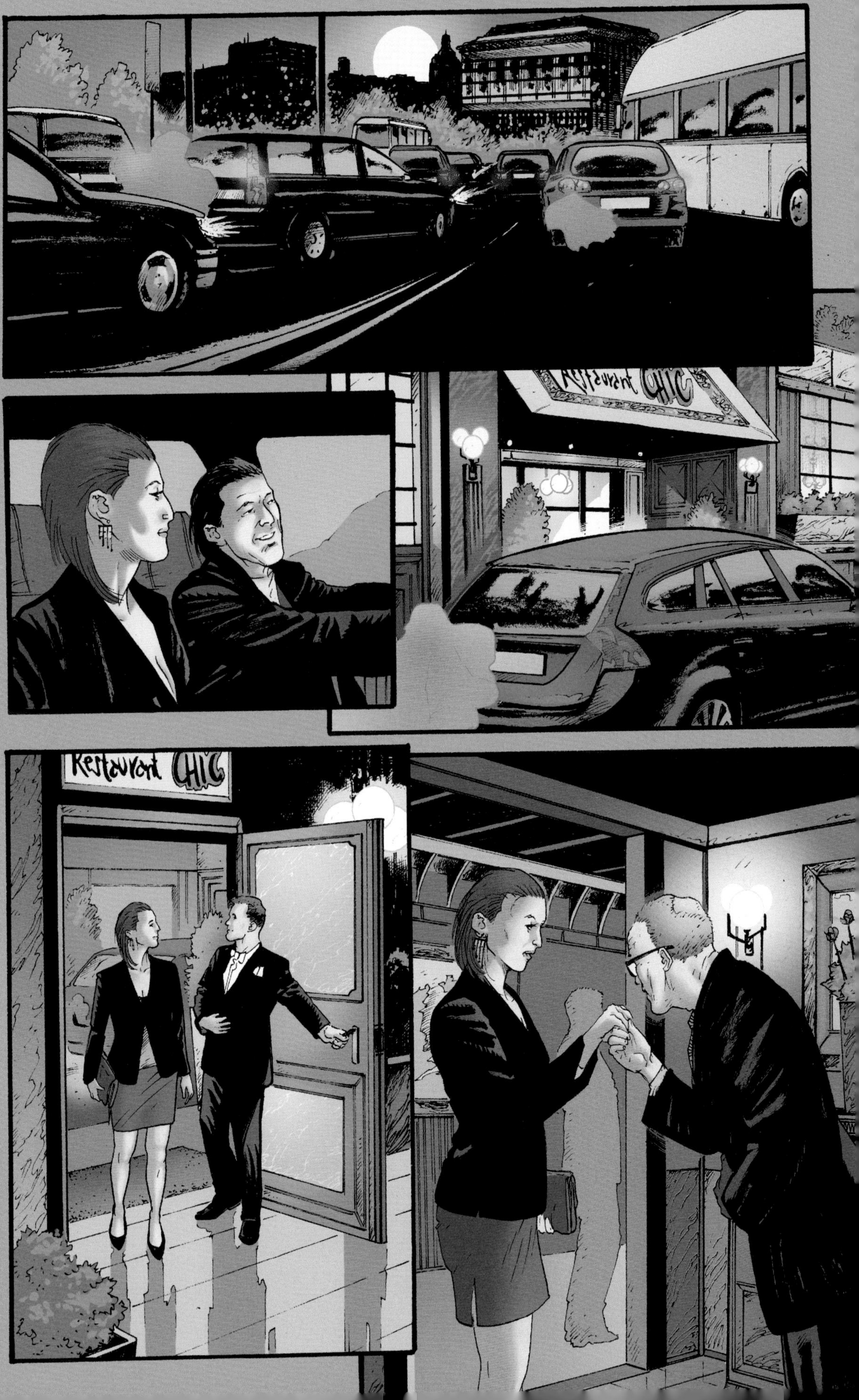
Restaurant CHIC
Restaurant CHIC

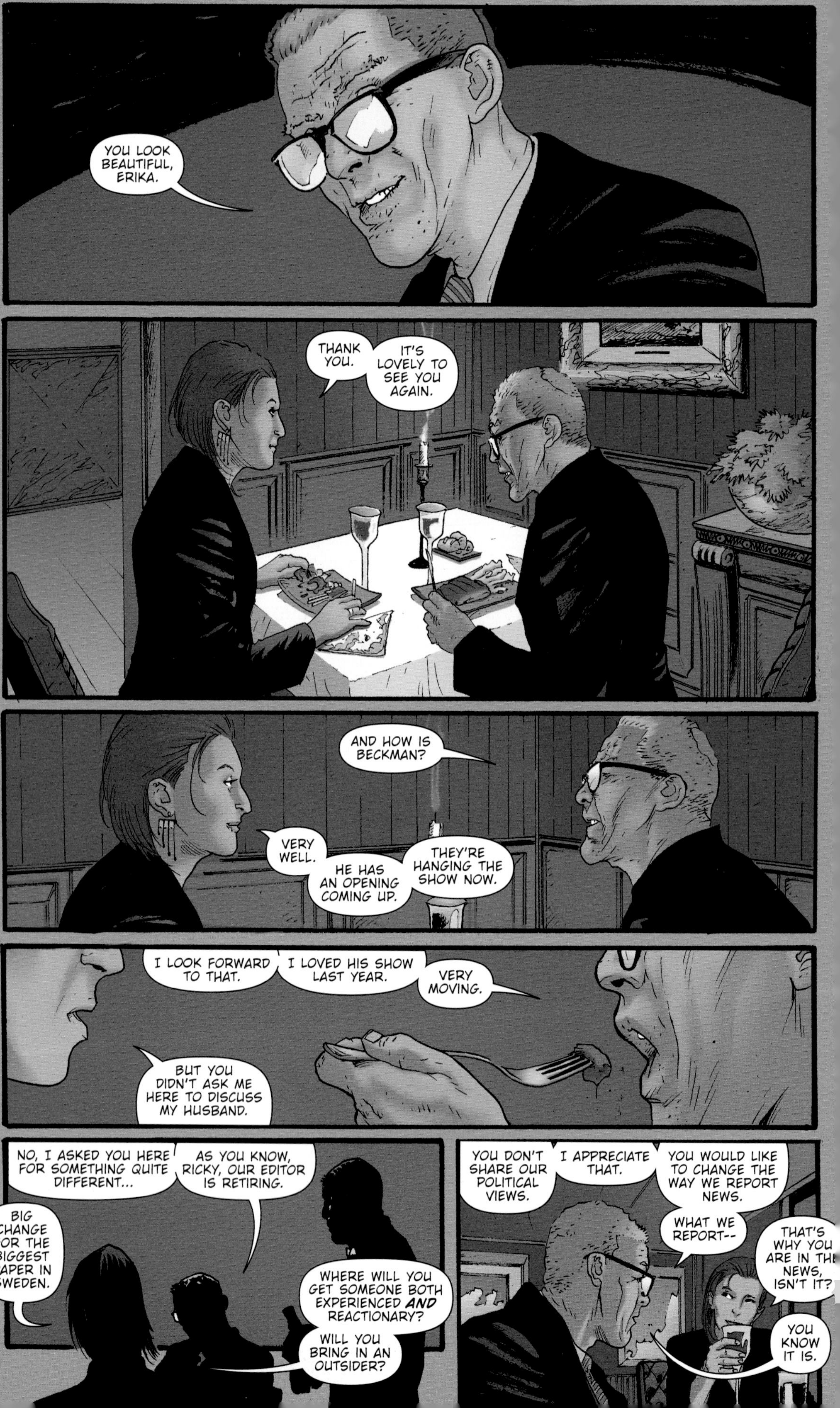
YOU LOOK BEAUTIFUL, ERIKA.
THANK YOU.
IT'S LOVELY TO SEE YOU AGAIN.
AND HOW IS BECKMAN?
VERY WELL.
HE HAS AN OPENING COMING UP.
THEY'RE HANGING THE SHOW NOW.
I LOOK FORWARD TO THAT.
I LOVED HIS SHOW LAST YEAR.
VERY MOVING.
BUT YOU DIDN'T ASK ME HERE TO DISCUSS MY HUSBAND.
NO, I ASKED YOU HERE FOR SOMETHING QUITE DIFFERENT...
AS YOU KNOW, RICKY, OUR EDITOR IS RETIRING.
BIG CHANGE FOR THE BIGGEST PAPER IN SWEDEN.
WHERE WILL YOU GET SOMEONE BOTH EXPERIENCED *AND* REACTIONARY?
WILL YOU BRING IN AN OUTSIDER?
YOU DON'T SHARE OUR POLITICAL VIEWS.
I APPRECIATE THAT.
YOU WOULD LIKE TO CHANGE THE WAY WE REPORT NEWS.
WHAT WE REPORT--
THAT'S WHY YOU ARE IN THE NEWS, ISN'T IT?
YOU KNOW IT IS.

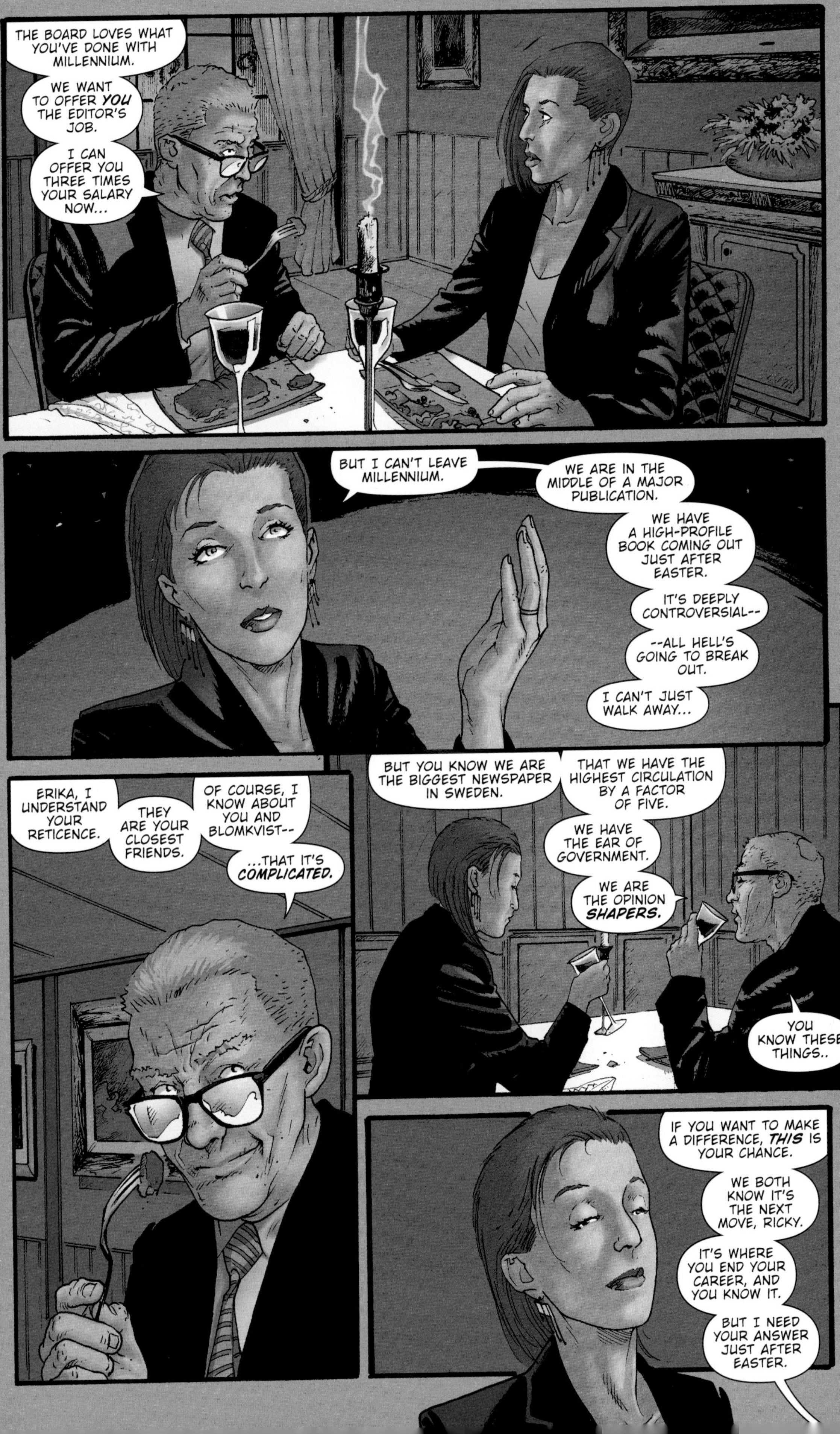
THE BOARD LOVES WHAT YOU'VE DONE WITH MILLENNIUM.
WE WANT TO OFFER **YOU** THE EDITOR'S JOB.
I CAN OFFER YOU THREE TIMES YOUR SALARY NOW...
BUT I CAN'T LEAVE MILLENNIUM.
WE ARE IN THE MIDDLE OF A MAJOR PUBLICATION.
WE HAVE A HIGH-PROFILE BOOK COMING OUT JUST AFTER EASTER.
IT'S DEEPLY CONTROVERSIAL--
--ALL HELL'S GOING TO BREAK OUT.
I CAN'T JUST WALK AWAY...
ERIKA, I UNDERSTAND YOUR RETICENCE.
THEY ARE YOUR CLOSEST FRIENDS.
OF COURSE, I KNOW ABOUT YOU AND BLOMKVIST--
...THAT IT'S **COMPLICATED.**
BUT YOU KNOW WE ARE THE BIGGEST NEWSPAPER IN SWEDEN.
THAT WE HAVE THE HIGHEST CIRCULATION BY A FACTOR OF FIVE.
WE HAVE THE EAR OF GOVERNMENT.
WE ARE THE OPINION **SHAPERS.**
YOU KNOW THESE THINGS..
IF YOU WANT TO MAKE A DIFFERENCE, **THIS** IS YOUR CHANCE.
WE BOTH KNOW IT'S THE NEXT MOVE, RICKY.
IT'S WHERE YOU END YOUR CAREER, AND YOU KNOW IT.
BUT I NEED YOUR ANSWER JUST AFTER EASTER.

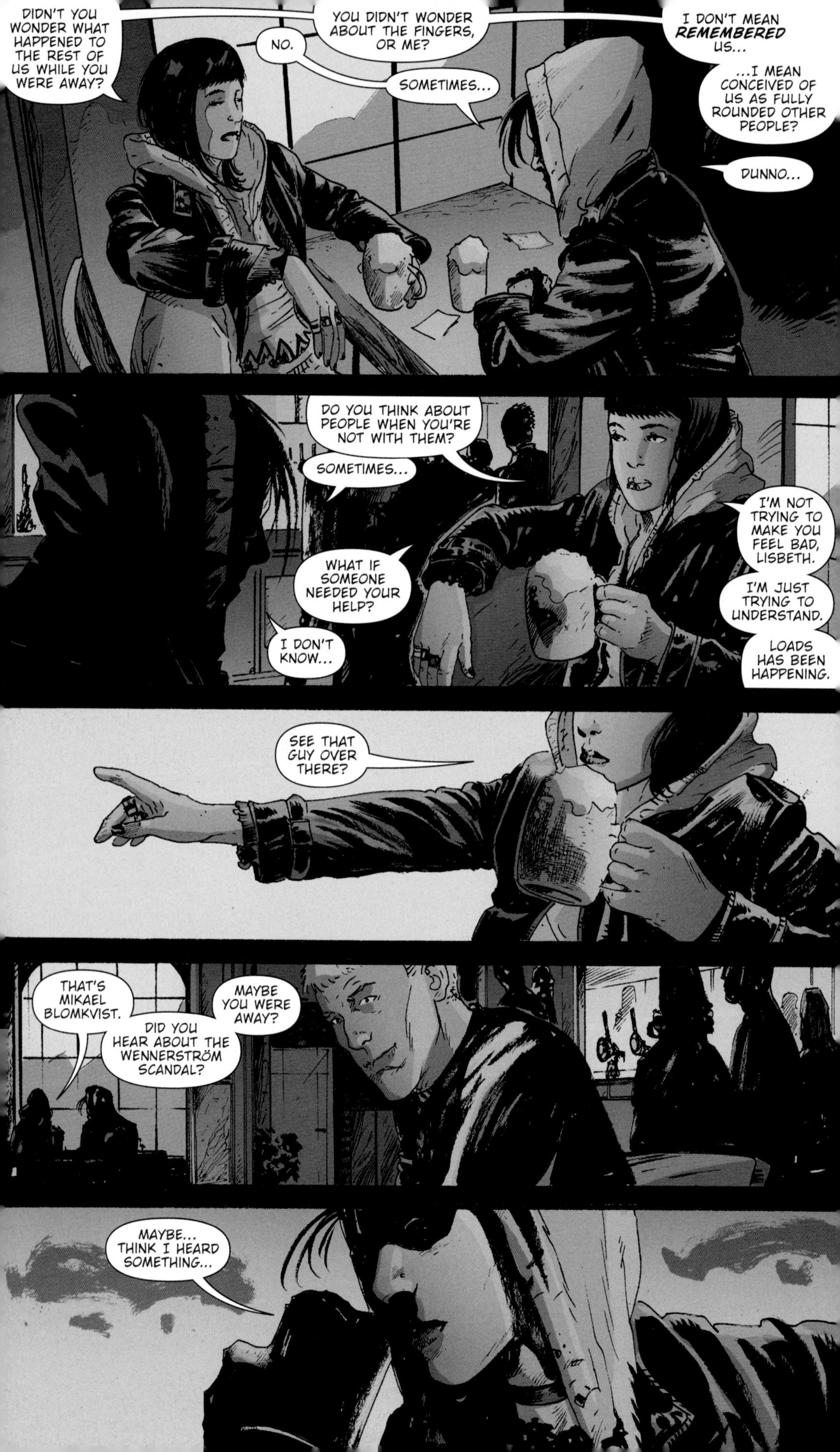
DIDN'T YOU WONDER WHAT HAPPENED TO THE REST OF US WHILE YOU WERE AWAY?
NO.
YOU DIDN'T WONDER ABOUT THE FINGERS, OR ME?
SOMETIMES...
I DON'T MEAN REMEMBERED US...
...I MEAN CONCEIVED OF US AS FULLY ROUNDED OTHER PEOPLE?
DUNNO...
DO YOU THINK ABOUT PEOPLE WHEN YOU'RE NOT WITH THEM?
SOMETIMES...
I'M NOT TRYING TO MAKE YOU FEEL BAD, LISBETH.
I'M JUST TRYING TO UNDERSTAND.
WHAT IF SOMEONE NEEDED YOUR HELP?
I DON'T KNOW...
LOADS HAS BEEN HAPPENING.
SEE THAT GUY OVER THERE?
THAT'S MIKAEL BLOMKVIST.
DID YOU HEAR ABOUT THE WENNERSTRÖM SCANDAL?
MAYBE YOU WERE AWAY?
MAYBE... THINK I HEARD SOMETHING...

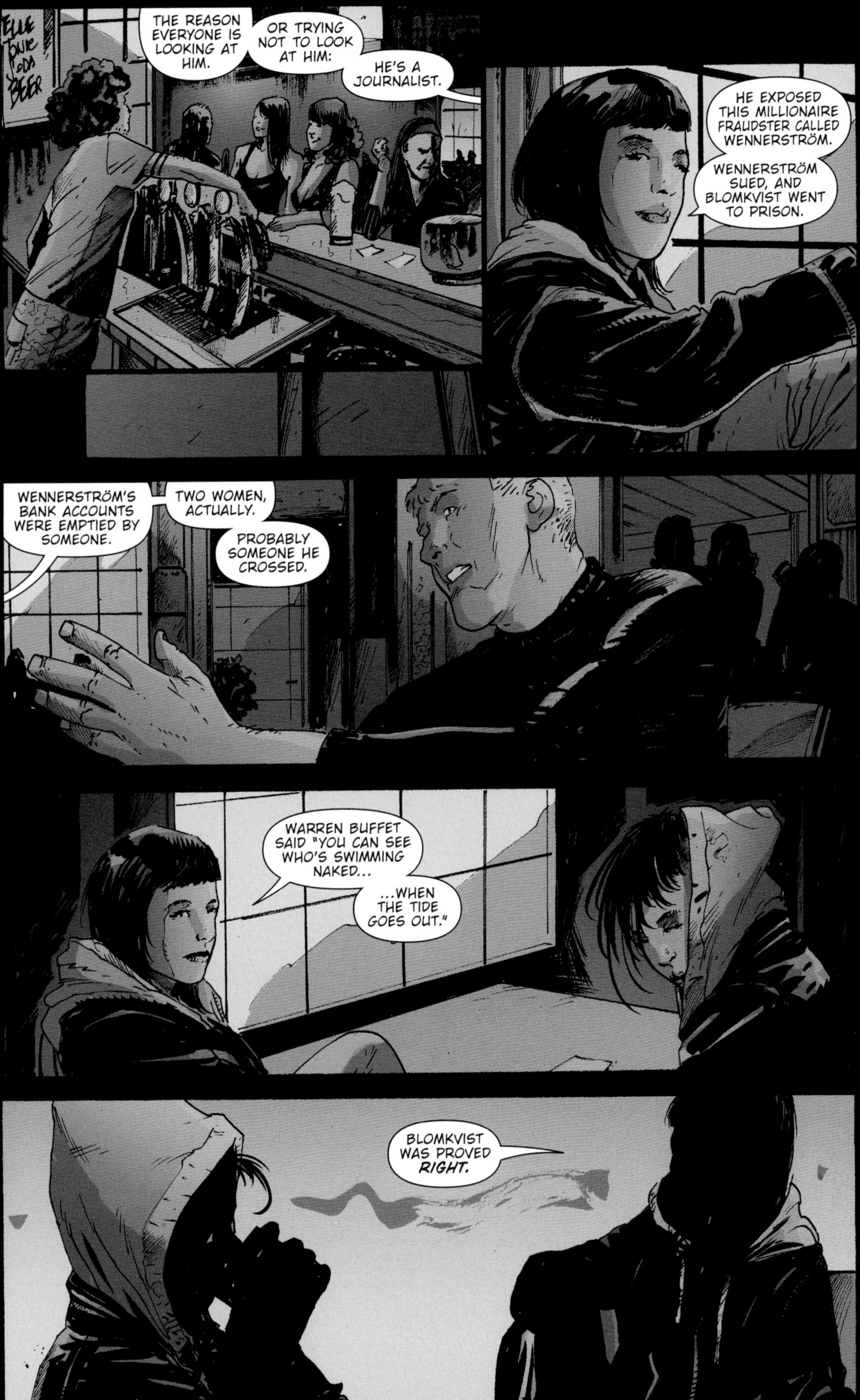
THE REASON EVERYONE IS LOOKING AT HIM.
OR TRYING NOT TO LOOK AT HIM:
HE'S A JOURNALIST.
HE EXPOSED THIS MILLIONAIRE FRAUDSTER CALLED WENNERSTRÖM.
WENNERSTRÖM SUED, AND BLOMKVIST WENT TO PRISON.
WENNERSTRÖM'S BANK ACCOUNTS WERE EMPTIED BY SOMEONE.
TWO WOMEN, ACTUALLY.
PROBABLY SOMEONE HE CROSSED.
WARREN BUFFET SAID "YOU CAN SEE WHO'S SWIMMING NAKED...
...WHEN THE TIDE GOES OUT."
BLOMKVIST WAS PROVED *RIGHT.*

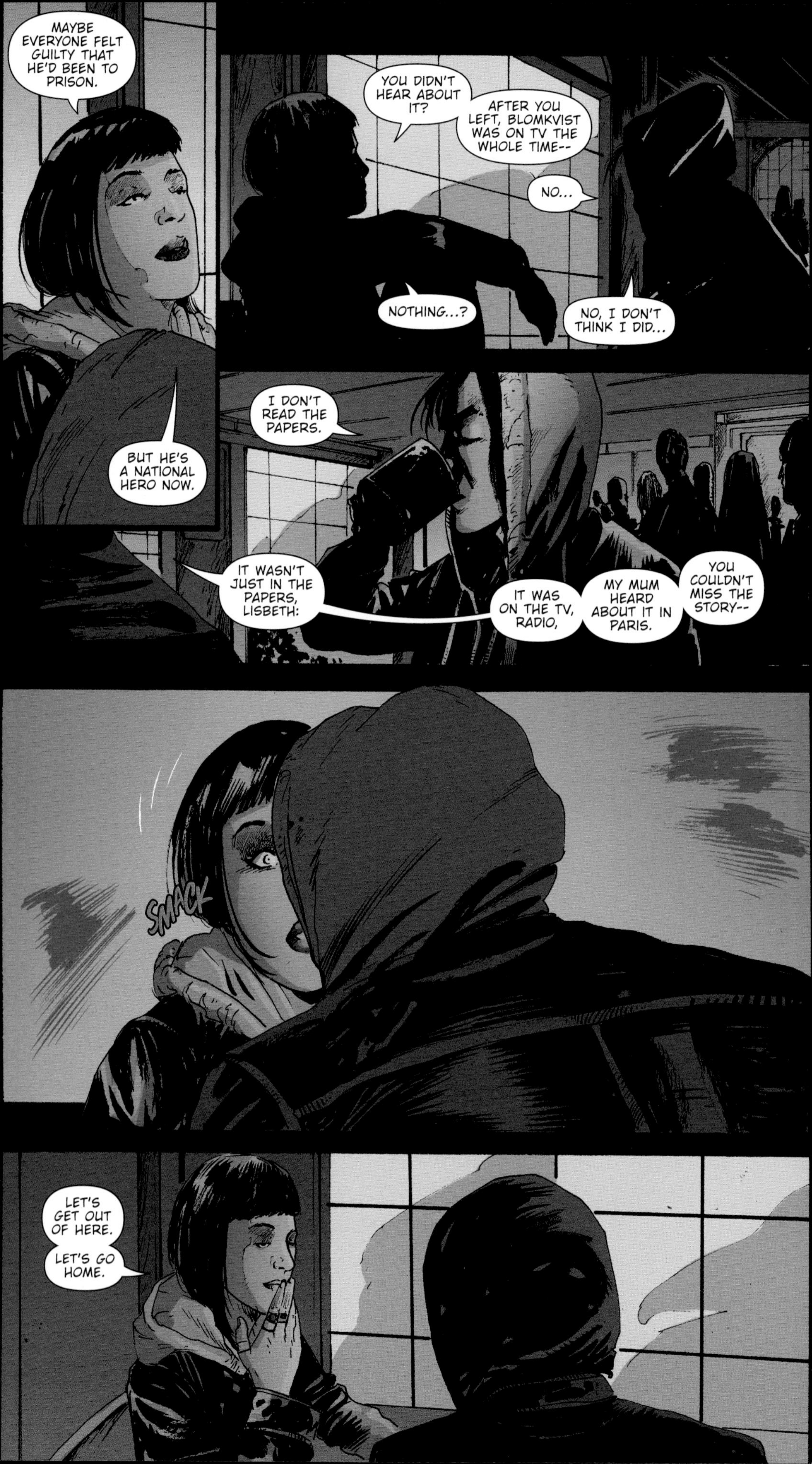
MAYBE EVERYONE FELT GUILTY THAT HE'D BEEN TO PRISON.
YOU DIDN'T HEAR ABOUT IT?
AFTER YOU LEFT, BLOMKVIST WAS ON TV THE WHOLE TIME--
NO...
NOTHING...?
NO, I DON'T THINK I DID...
BUT HE'S A NATIONAL HERO NOW.
I DON'T READ THE PAPERS.
IT WASN'T JUST IN THE PAPERS, LISBETH:
IT WAS ON THE TV, RADIO,
MY MUM HEARD ABOUT IT IN PARIS.
YOU COULDN'T MISS THE STORY--
SMACK
LET'S GET OUT OF HERE.
LET'S GO HOME.

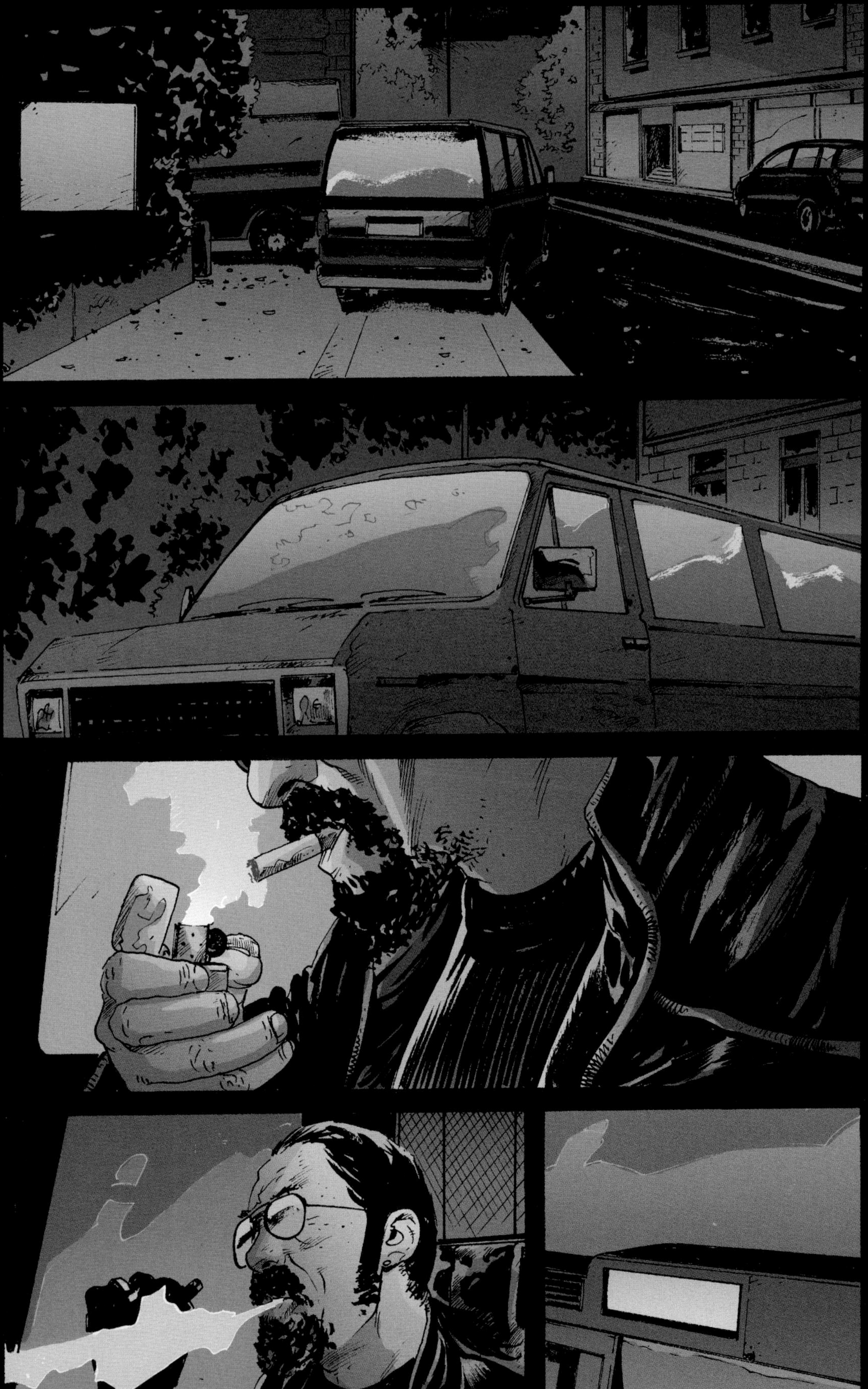

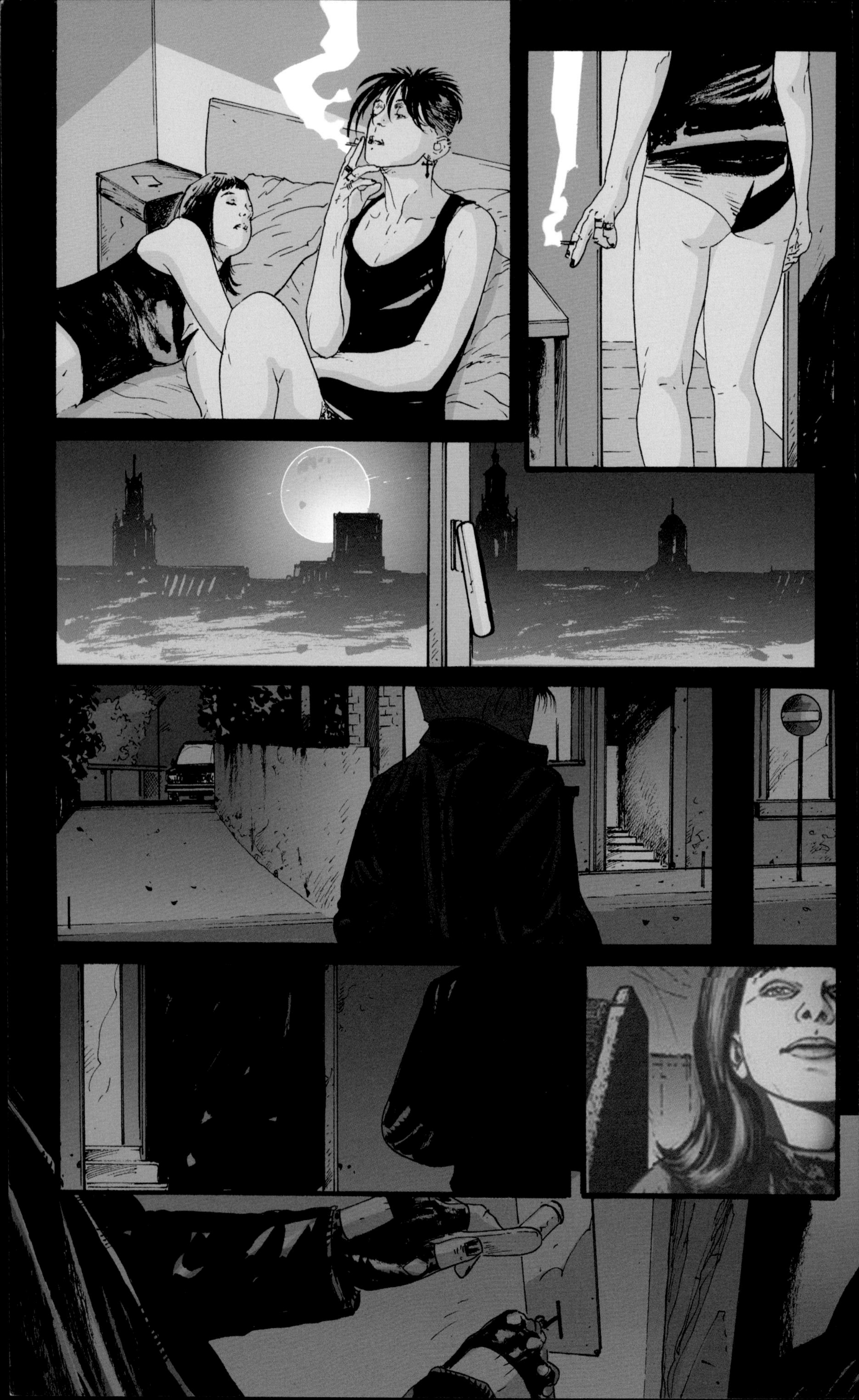

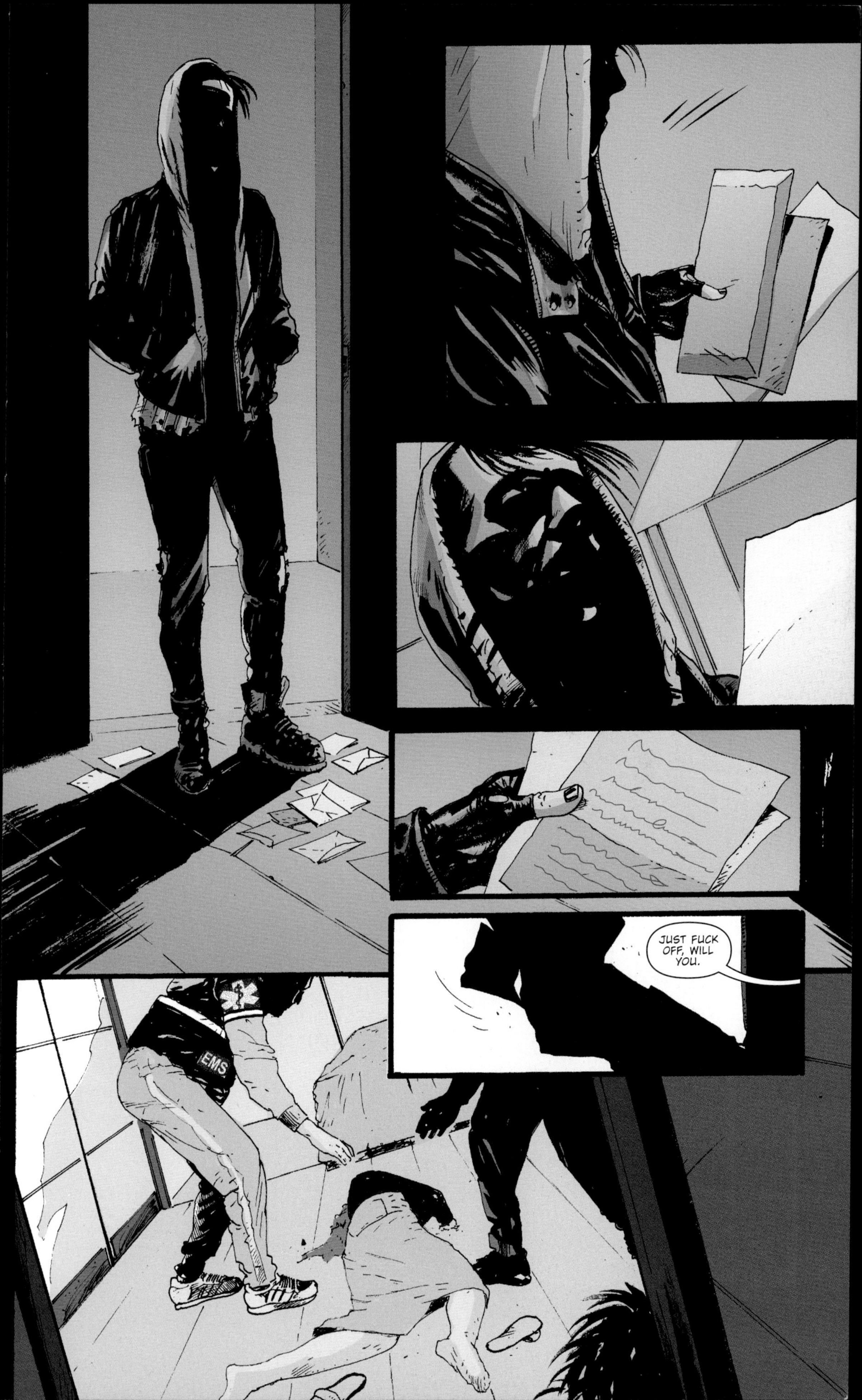
JUST FUCK OFF, WILL YOU.
EMS

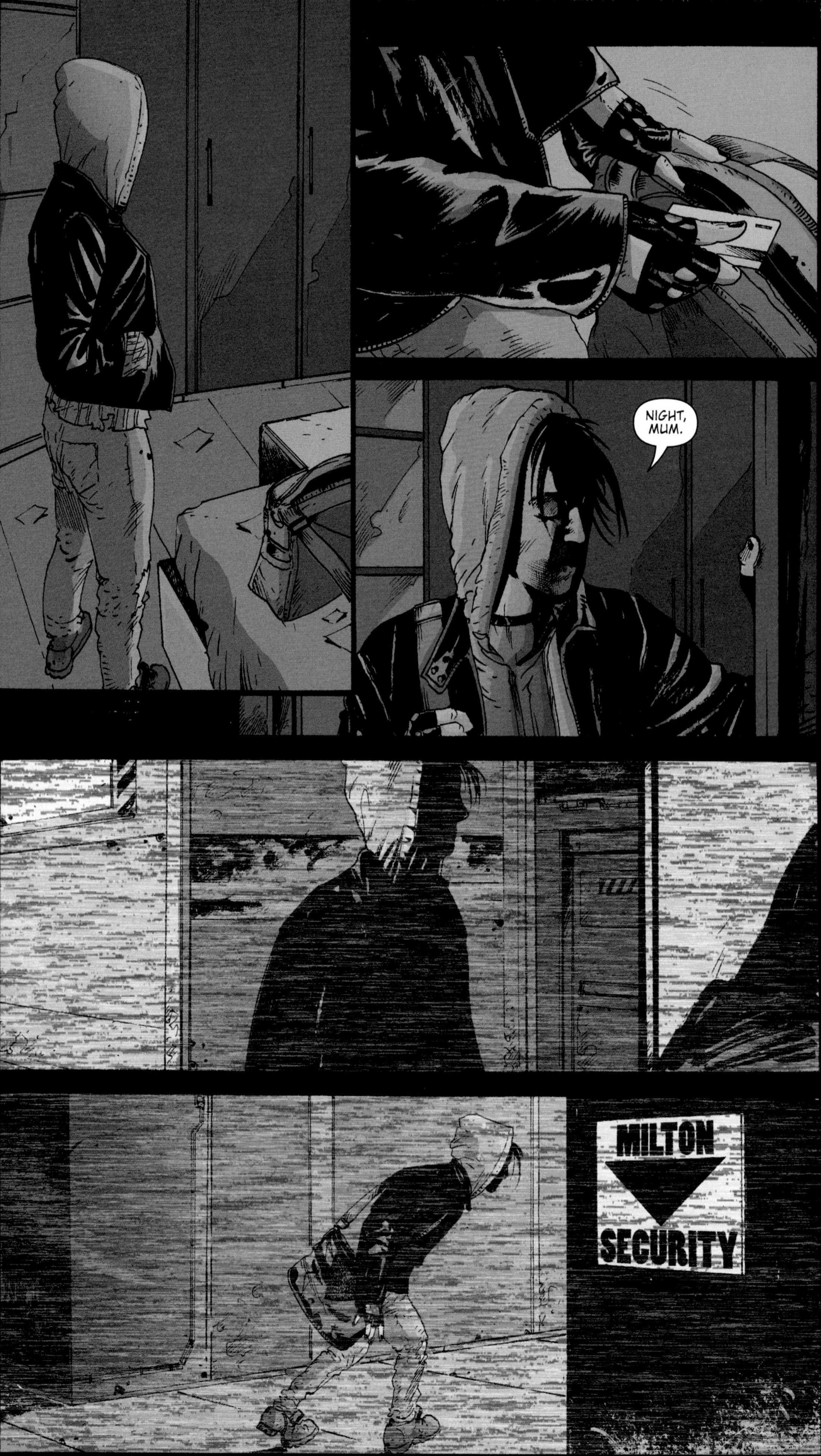
NIGHT, MUM.
MILTON
SECURITY

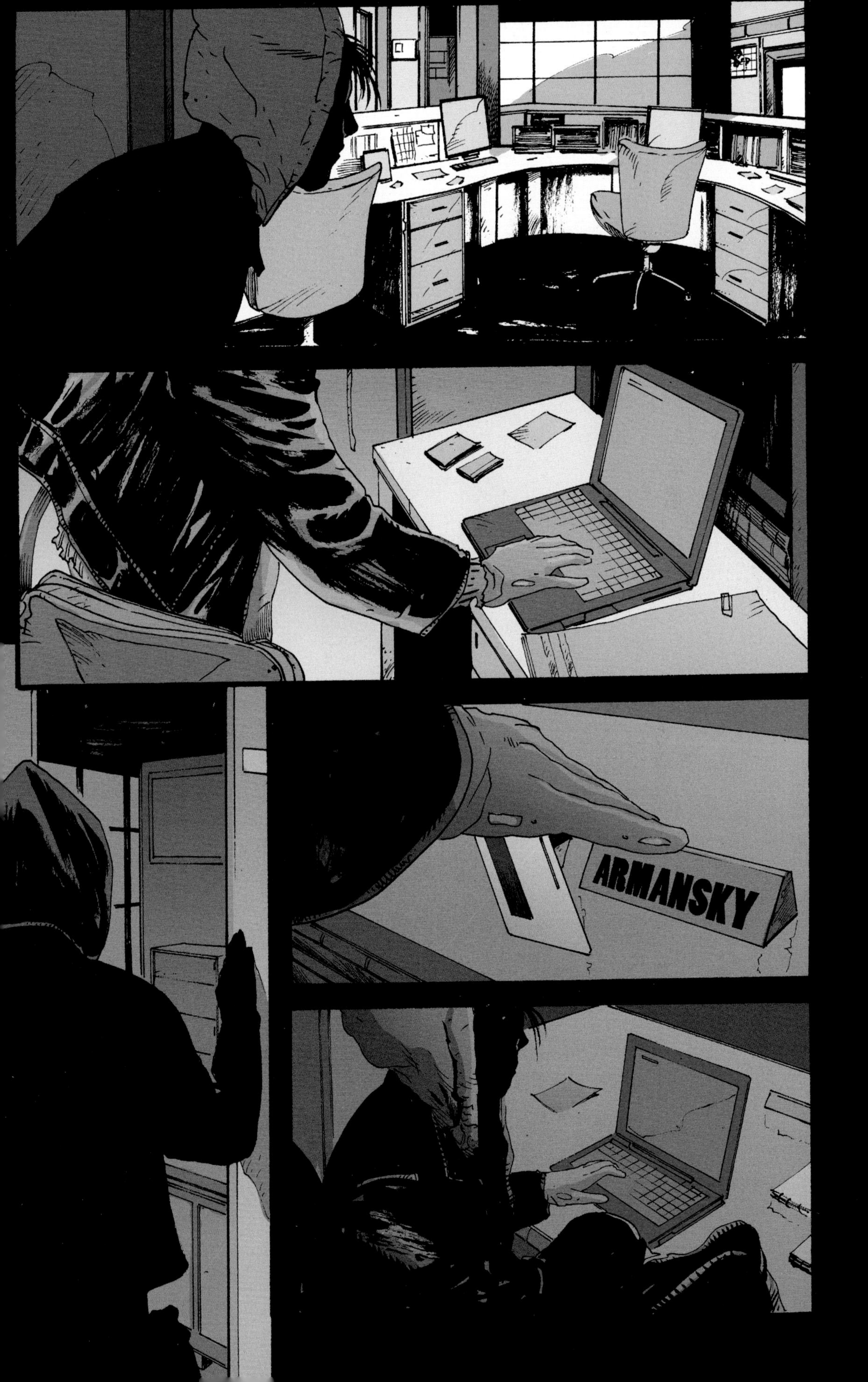
ARMANSKY

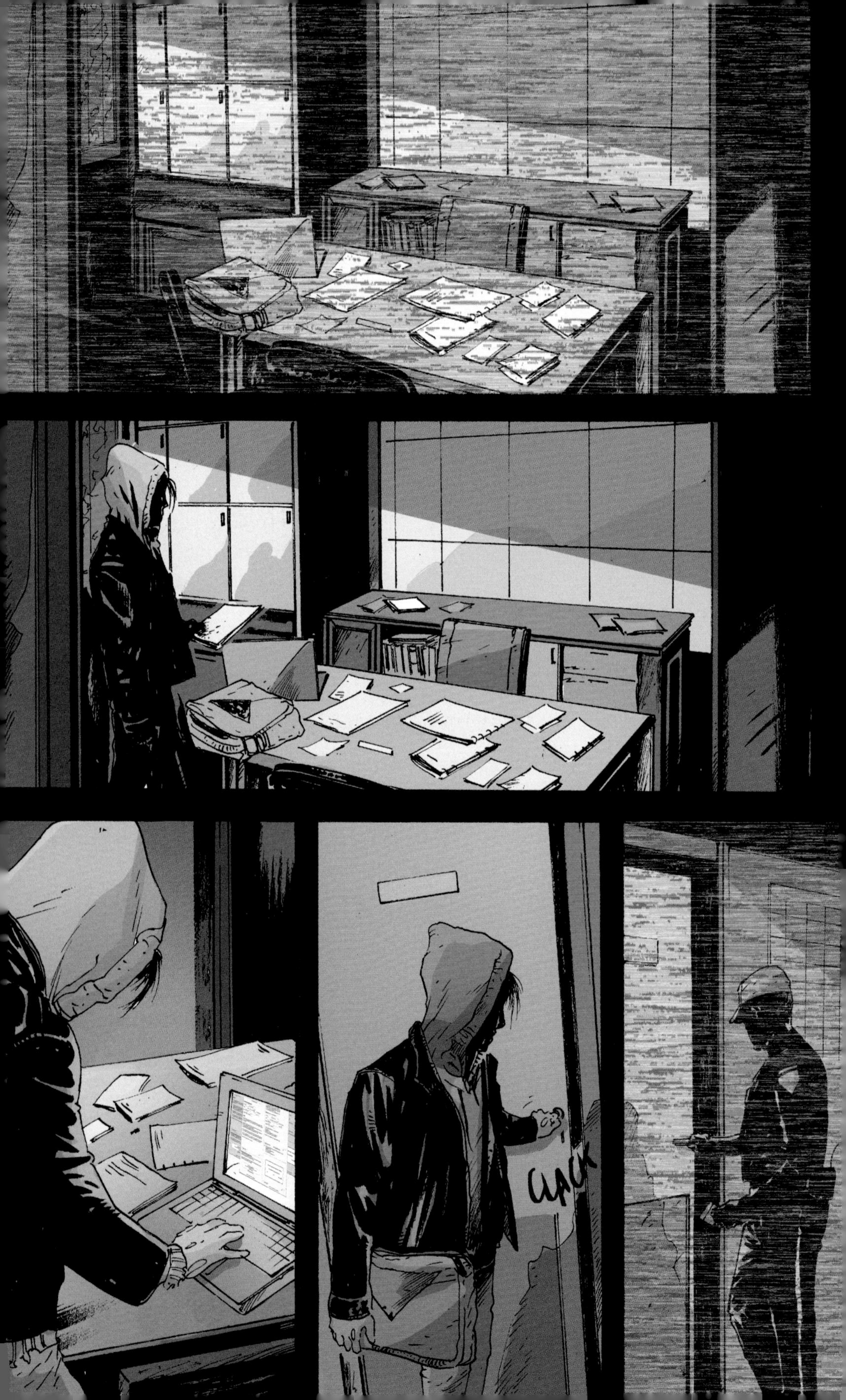
CLACK

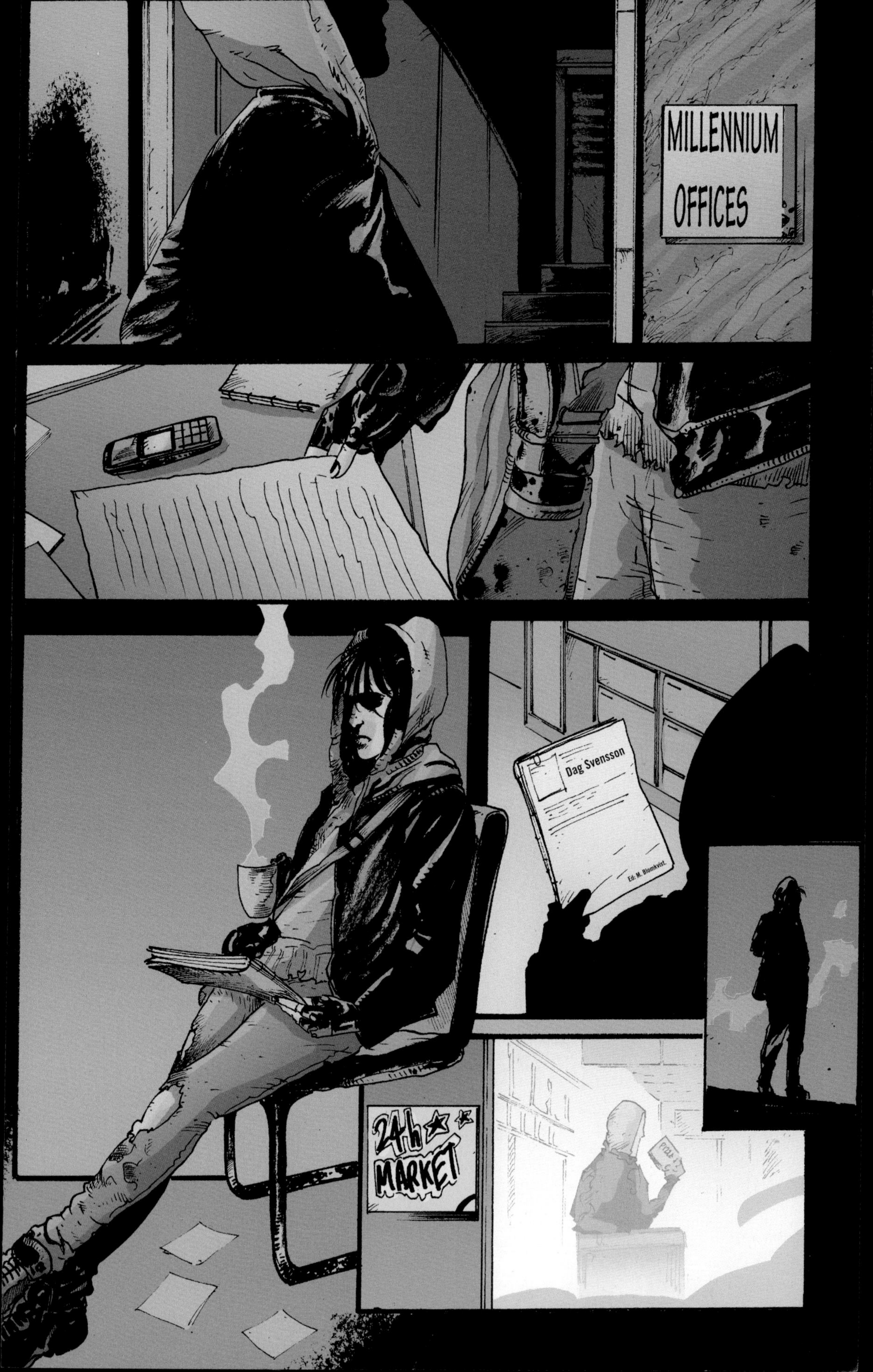
MILLENNIUM
OFFICES
Dag Svensson
Ed: M. Blomkvist.
24h
MARKET

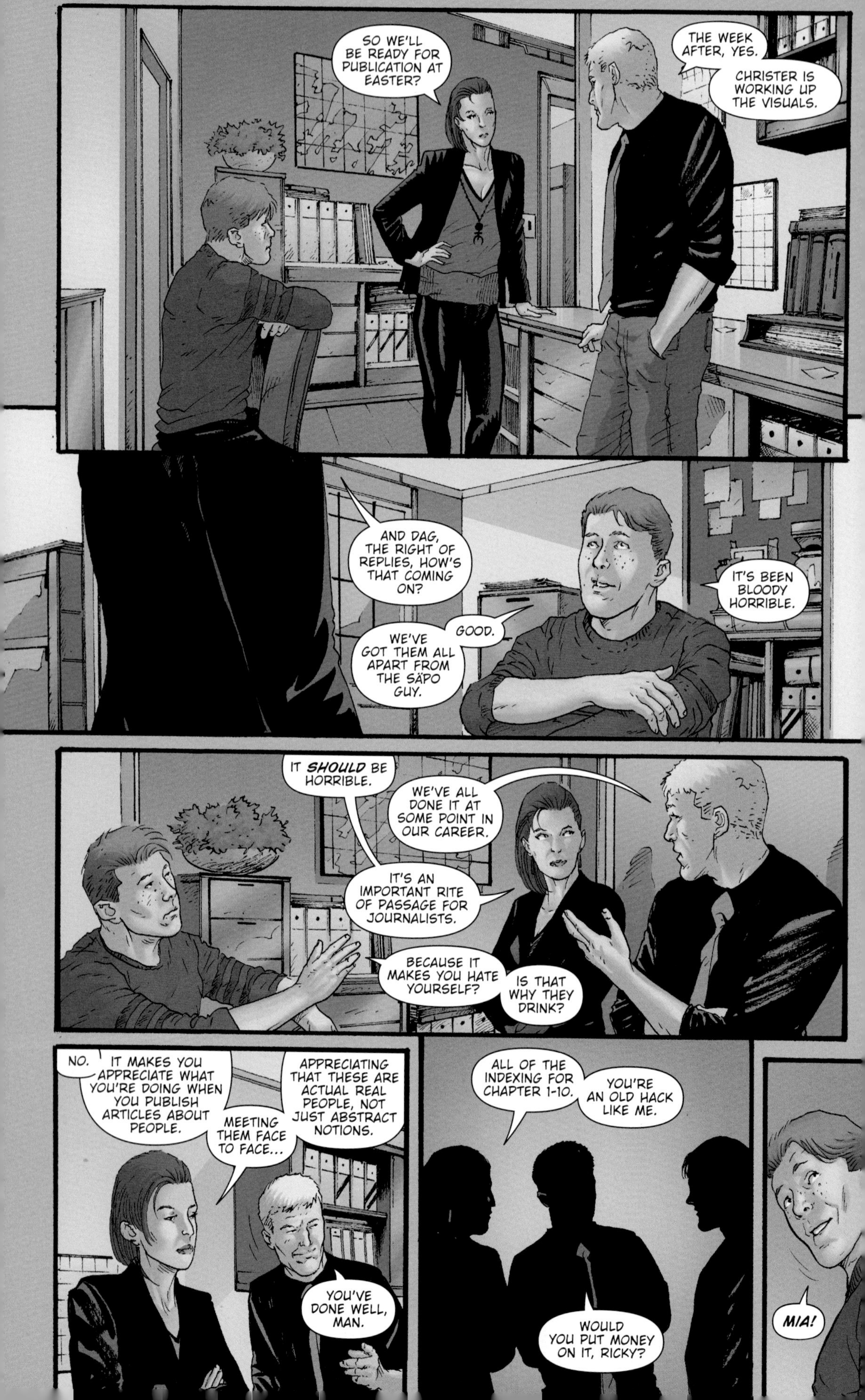
SO WE'LL BE READY FOR PUBLICATION AT EASTER?
THE WEEK AFTER, YES.
CHRISTER IS WORKING UP THE VISUALS.
AND DAG, THE RIGHT OF REPLIES, HOW'S THAT COMING ON?
GOOD.
WE'VE GOT THEM ALL APART FROM THE SÄPO GUY.
IT'S BEEN BLOODY HORRIBLE.
IT *SHOULD* BE HORRIBLE.
WE'VE ALL DONE IT AT SOME POINT IN OUR CAREER.
IT'S AN IMPORTANT RITE OF PASSAGE FOR JOURNALISTS.
BECAUSE IT MAKES YOU HATE YOURSELF?
IS THAT WHY THEY DRINK?
NO.
IT MAKES YOU APPRECIATE WHAT YOU'RE DOING WHEN YOU PUBLISH ARTICLES ABOUT PEOPLE.
MEETING THEM FACE TO FACE...
APPRECIATING THAT THESE ARE ACTUAL REAL PEOPLE, NOT JUST ABSTRACT NOTIONS.
YOU'VE DONE WELL, MAN.
ALL OF THE INDEXING FOR CHAPTER 1-10.
YOU'RE AN OLD HACK LIKE ME.
WOULD YOU PUT MONEY ON IT, RICKY?
MIA!

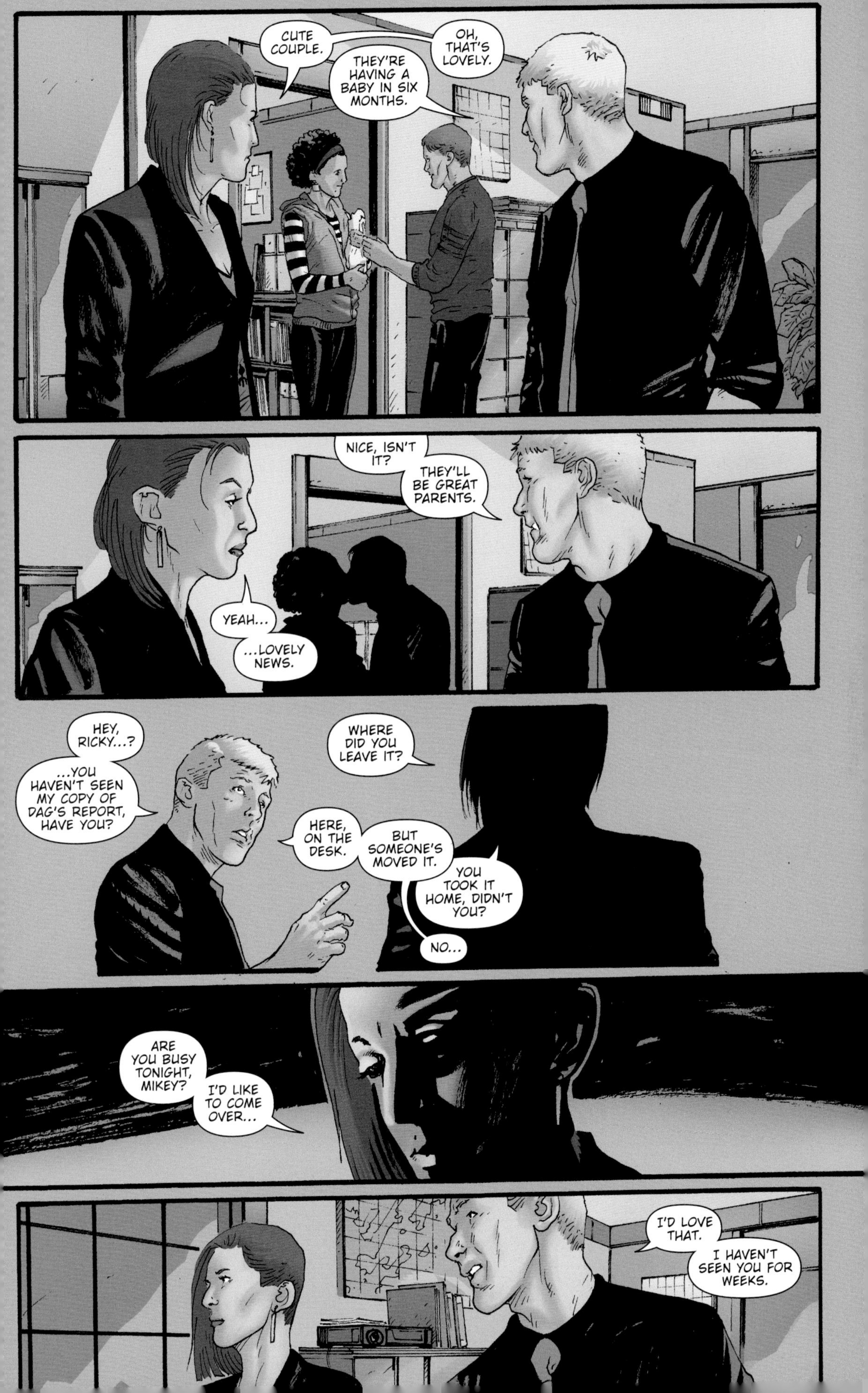
CUTE COUPLE.
OH, THAT'S LOVELY.
THEY'RE HAVING A BABY IN SIX MONTHS.
NICE, ISN'T IT?
THEY'LL BE GREAT PARENTS.
YEAH...
...LOVELY NEWS.
HEY, RICKY...?
...YOU HAVEN'T SEEN MY COPY OF DAG'S REPORT, HAVE YOU?
WHERE DID YOU LEAVE IT?
HERE, ON THE DESK.
BUT SOMEONE'S MOVED IT.
YOU TOOK IT HOME, DIDN'T YOU?
NO...
ARE YOU BUSY TONIGHT, MIKEY?
I'D LIKE TO COME OVER...
I'D LOVE THAT.
I HAVEN'T SEEN YOU FOR WEEKS.

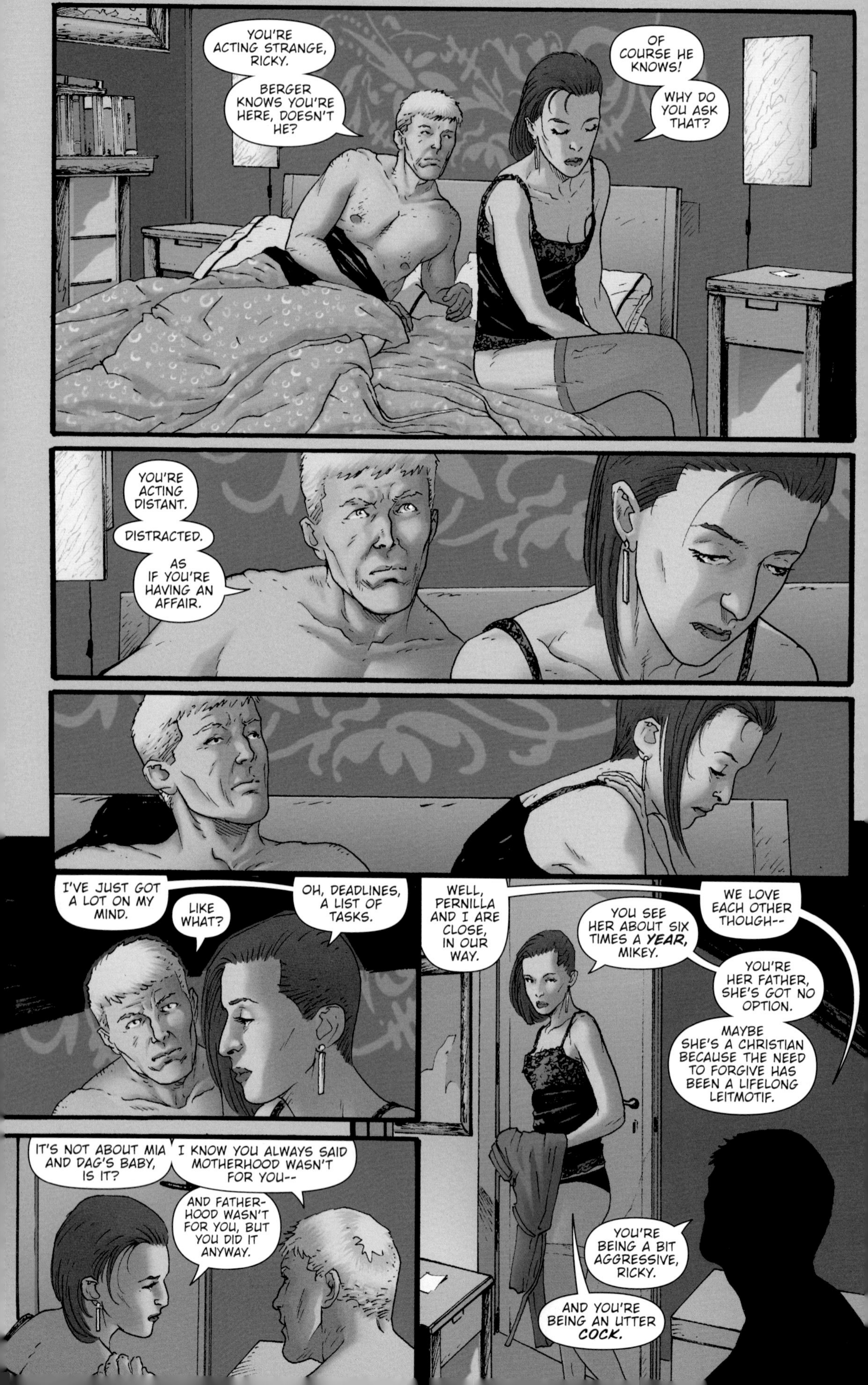

YOU'RE ACTING STRANGE, RICKY.
BERGER KNOWS YOU'RE HERE, DOESN'T HE?
OF COURSE HE KNOWS!
WHY DO YOU ASK THAT?
YOU'RE ACTING DISTANT.
DISTRACTED.
AS IF YOU'RE HAVING AN AFFAIR.
I'VE JUST GOT A LOT ON MY MIND.
LIKE WHAT?
OH, DEADLINES, A LIST OF TASKS.
IT'S NOT ABOUT MIA AND DAG'S BABY, IS IT?
I KNOW YOU ALWAYS SAID MOTHERHOOD WASN'T FOR YOU--
AND FATHER-HOOD WASN'T FOR YOU, BUT YOU DID IT ANYWAY.
WELL, PERNILLA AND I ARE CLOSE, IN OUR WAY.
YOU SEE HER ABOUT SIX TIMES A ***YEAR,*** MIKEY.
WE LOVE EACH OTHER THOUGH--
YOU'RE HER FATHER, SHE'S GOT NO OPTION.
MAYBE SHE'S A CHRISTIAN BECAUSE THE NEED TO FORGIVE HAS BEEN A LIFELONG LEITMOTIF.
YOU'RE BEING A BIT AGGRESSIVE, RICKY.
AND YOU'RE BEING AN UTTER ***COCK.***

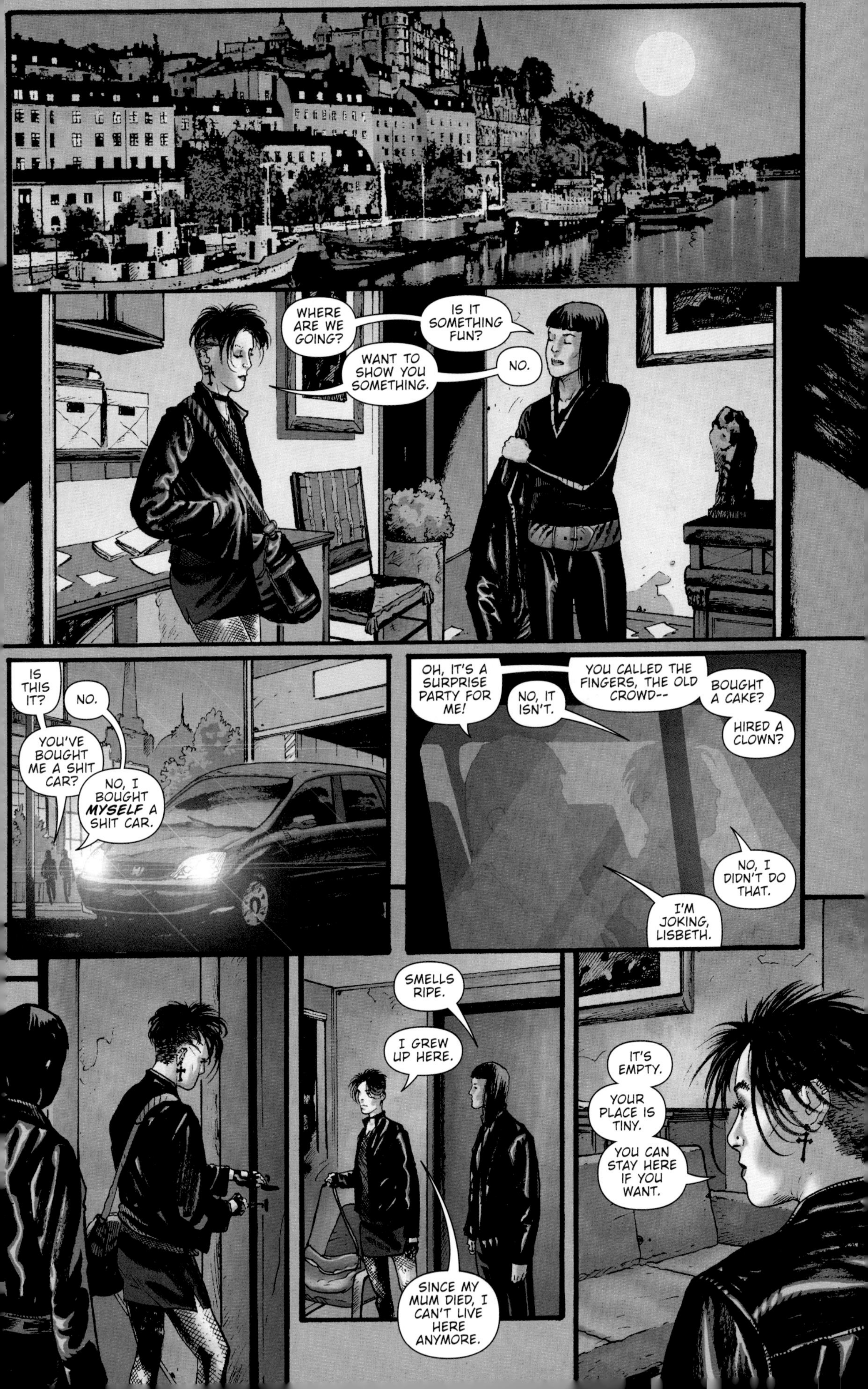

WHERE ARE WE GOING?
IS IT SOMETHING FUN?
WANT TO SHOW YOU SOMETHING.
NO.
IS THIS IT?
NO.
YOU'VE BOUGHT ME A SHIT CAR?
NO, I BOUGHT *MYSELF* A SHIT CAR.
OH, IT'S A SURPRISE PARTY FOR ME!
NO, IT ISN'T.
YOU CALLED THE FINGERS, THE OLD CROWD--
BOUGHT A CAKE?
HIRED A CLOWN?
NO, I DIDN'T DO THAT.
I'M JOKING, LISBETH.
SMELLS RIPE.
I GREW UP HERE.
SINCE MY MUM DIED, I CAN'T LIVE HERE ANYMORE.
IT'S EMPTY.
YOUR PLACE IS TINY.
YOU CAN STAY HERE IF YOU WANT.

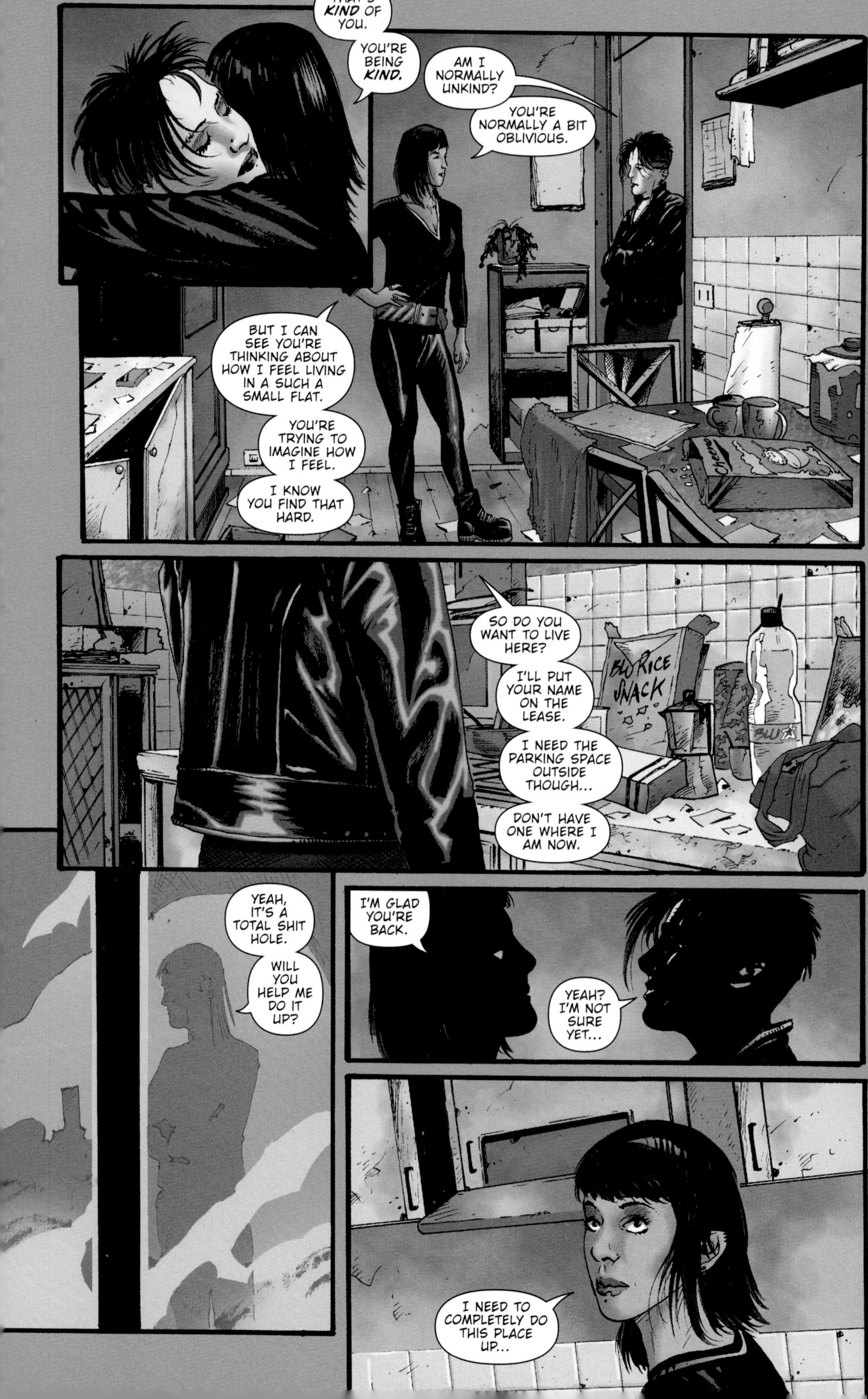
THAT'S *KIND* OF YOU.
YOU'RE BEING *KIND.*
AM I NORMALLY UNKIND?
YOU'RE NORMALLY A BIT OBLIVIOUS.
BUT I CAN SEE YOU'RE THINKING ABOUT HOW I FEEL LIVING IN A SUCH A SMALL FLAT.
YOU'RE TRYING TO IMAGINE HOW I FEEL.
I KNOW YOU FIND THAT HARD.
SO DO YOU WANT TO LIVE HERE?
I'LL PUT YOUR NAME ON THE LEASE.
I NEED THE PARKING SPACE OUTSIDE THOUGH...
DON'T HAVE ONE WHERE I AM NOW.
BLU RICE SNACK
YEAH, IT'S A TOTAL SHIT HOLE.
WILL YOU HELP ME DO IT UP?
I'M GLAD YOU'RE BACK.
YEAH? I'M NOT SURE YET...
I NEED TO COMPLETELY DO THIS PLACE UP...

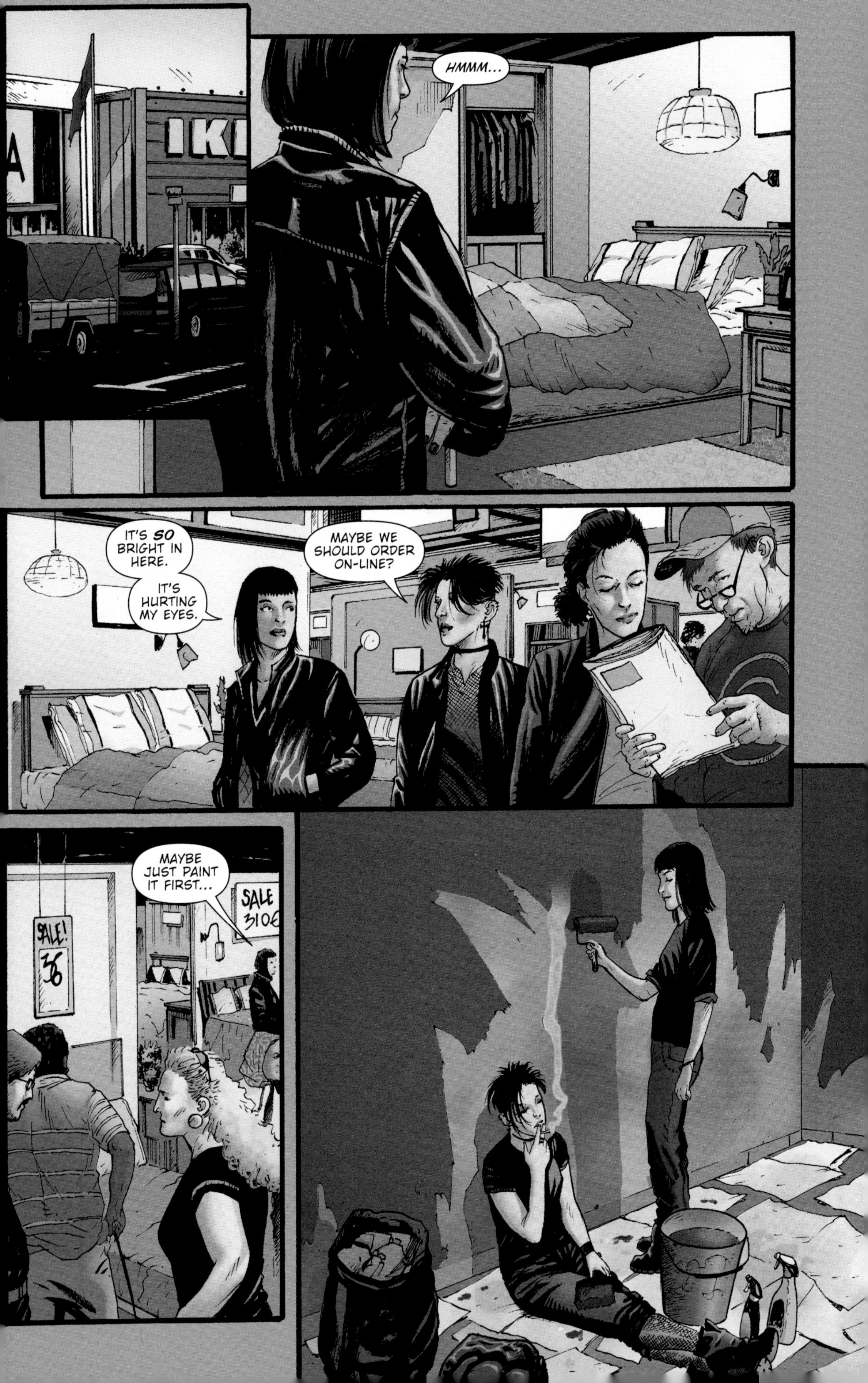
IKI
HMMM...
IT'S *SO* BRIGHT IN HERE.
IT'S HURTING MY EYES.
MAYBE WE SHOULD ORDER ON-LINE?
MAYBE JUST PAINT IT FIRST...
SALE! 36
SALE 310

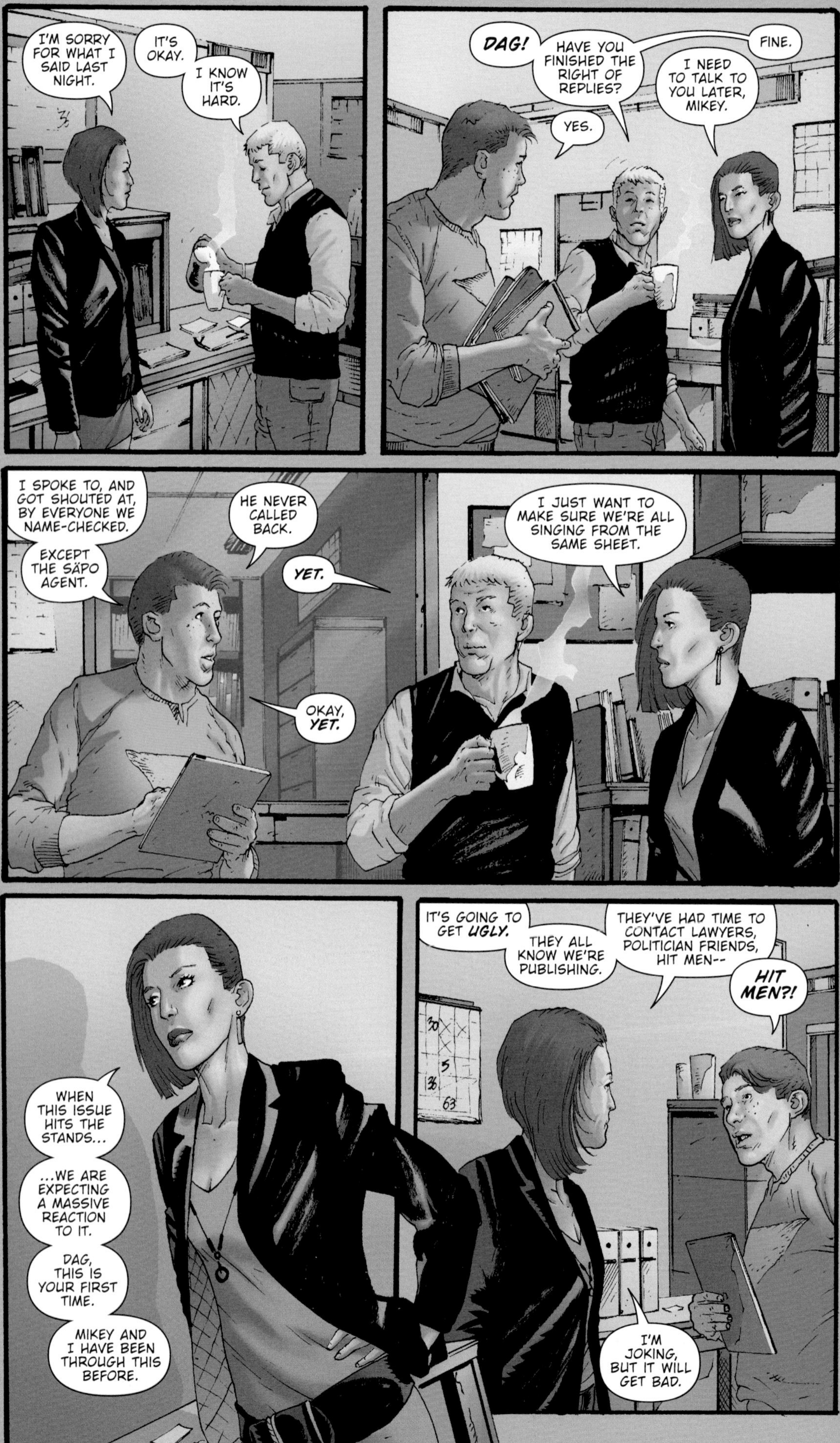
I'M SORRY FOR WHAT I SAID LAST NIGHT.
IT'S OKAY.
I KNOW IT'S HARD.
DAG!
HAVE YOU FINISHED THE RIGHT OF REPLIES?
FINE.
I NEED TO TALK TO YOU LATER, MIKEY.
YES.
I SPOKE TO, AND GOT SHOUTED AT, BY EVERYONE WE NAME-CHECKED.
EXCEPT THE SÄPO AGENT.
HE NEVER CALLED BACK.
YET.
OKAY, YET.
I JUST WANT TO MAKE SURE WE'RE ALL SINGING FROM THE SAME SHEET.
WHEN THIS ISSUE HITS THE STANDS...
...WE ARE EXPECTING A MASSIVE REACTION TO IT.
DAG, THIS IS YOUR FIRST TIME.
MIKEY AND I HAVE BEEN THROUGH THIS BEFORE.
IT'S GOING TO GET UGLY.
THEY ALL KNOW WE'RE PUBLISHING.
THEY'VE HAD TIME TO CONTACT LAWYERS, POLITICIAN FRIENDS, HIT MEN--
HIT MEN?!
I'M JOKING, BUT IT WILL GET BAD.

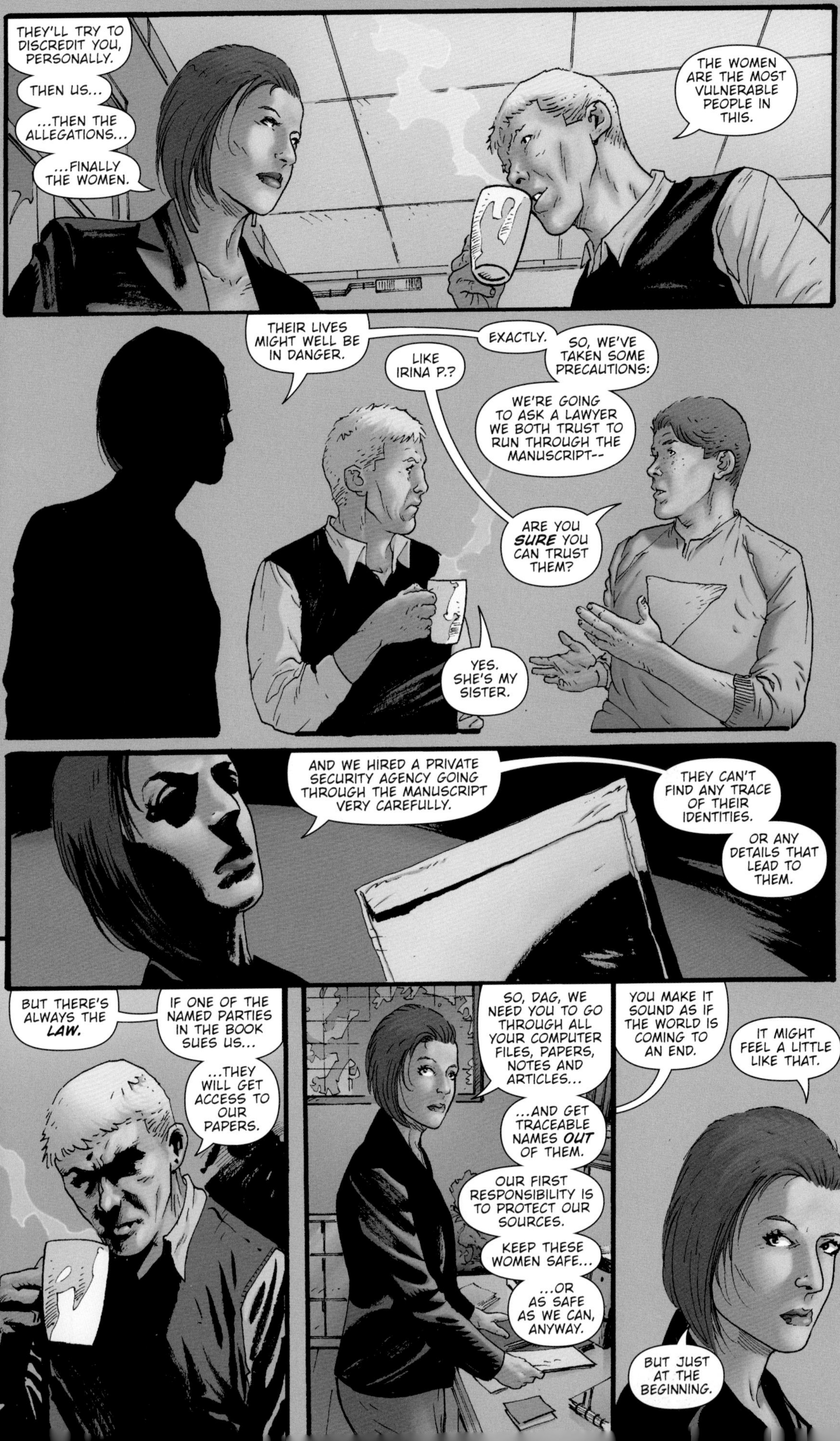

THEY'LL TRY TO DISCREDIT YOU, PERSONALLY.
THEN US...
...THEN THE ALLEGATIONS...
...FINALLY THE WOMEN.
THE WOMEN ARE THE MOST VULNERABLE PEOPLE IN THIS.
THEIR LIVES MIGHT WELL BE IN DANGER.
EXACTLY.
SO, WE'VE TAKEN SOME PRECAUTIONS:
LIKE IRINA P.?
WE'RE GOING TO ASK A LAWYER WE BOTH TRUST TO RUN THROUGH THE MANUSCRIPT--
ARE YOU **SURE** YOU CAN TRUST THEM?
YES. SHE'S MY SISTER.
AND WE HIRED A PRIVATE SECURITY AGENCY GOING THROUGH THE MANUSCRIPT VERY CAREFULLY.
THEY CAN'T FIND ANY TRACE OF THEIR IDENTITIES.
OR ANY DETAILS THAT LEAD TO THEM.
BUT THERE'S ALWAYS THE **LAW.**
IF ONE OF THE NAMED PARTIES IN THE BOOK SUES US...
...THEY WILL GET ACCESS TO OUR PAPERS.
SO, DAG, WE NEED YOU TO GO THROUGH ALL YOUR COMPUTER FILES, PAPERS, NOTES AND ARTICLES...
...AND GET TRACEABLE NAMES **OUT** OF THEM.
OUR FIRST RESPONSIBILITY IS TO PROTECT OUR SOURCES.
KEEP THESE WOMEN SAFE...
...OR AS SAFE AS WE CAN, ANYWAY.
YOU MAKE IT SOUND AS IF THE WORLD IS COMING TO AN END.
IT MIGHT FEEL A LITTLE LIKE THAT.
BUT JUST AT THE BEGINNING.

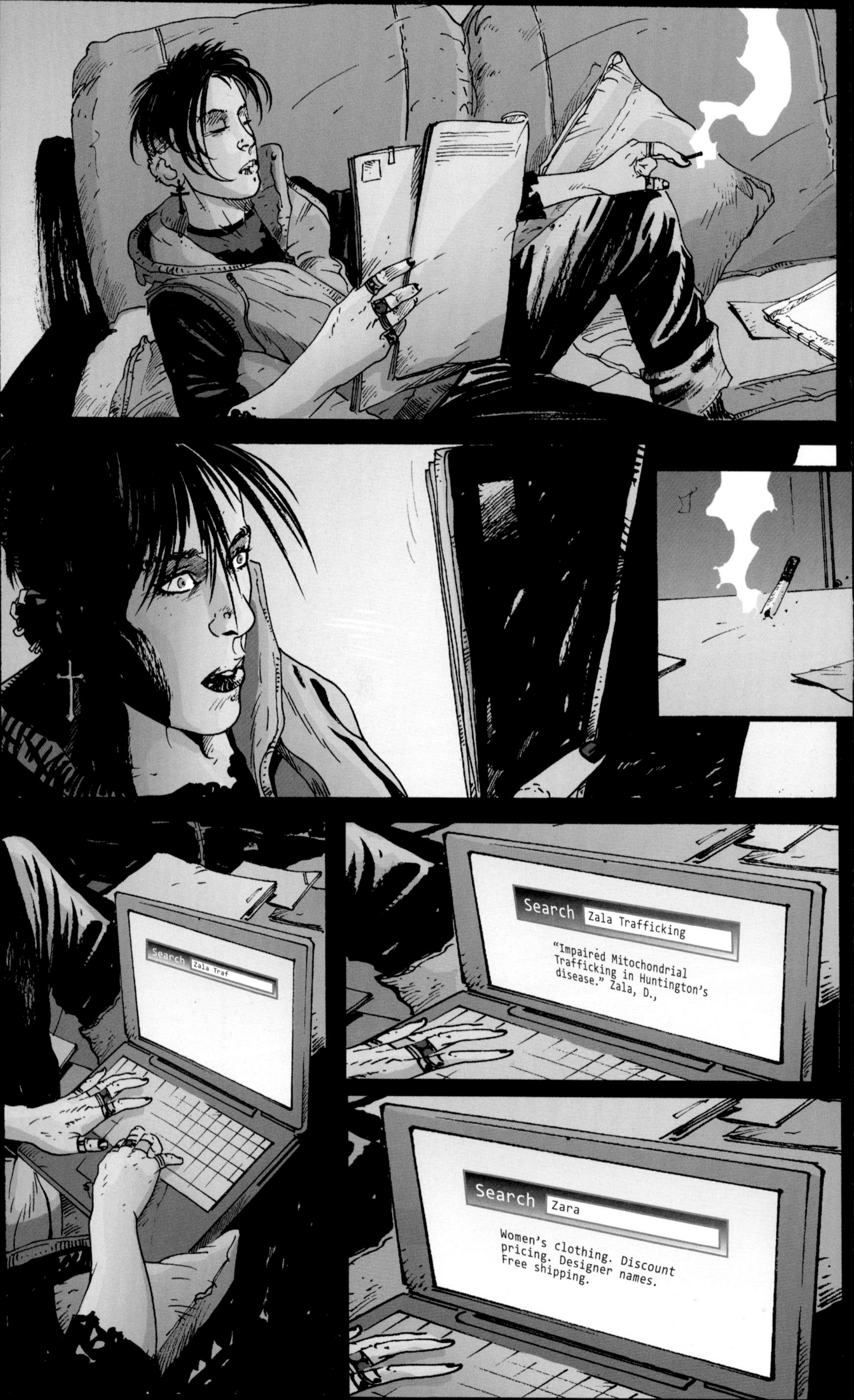
Search Zala Traf
Search Zala Trafficking
"Impaired Mitochondrial Trafficking in Huntington's disease." Zala, D.,
Search Zara
Women's clothing. Discount pricing. Designer names. Free shipping.

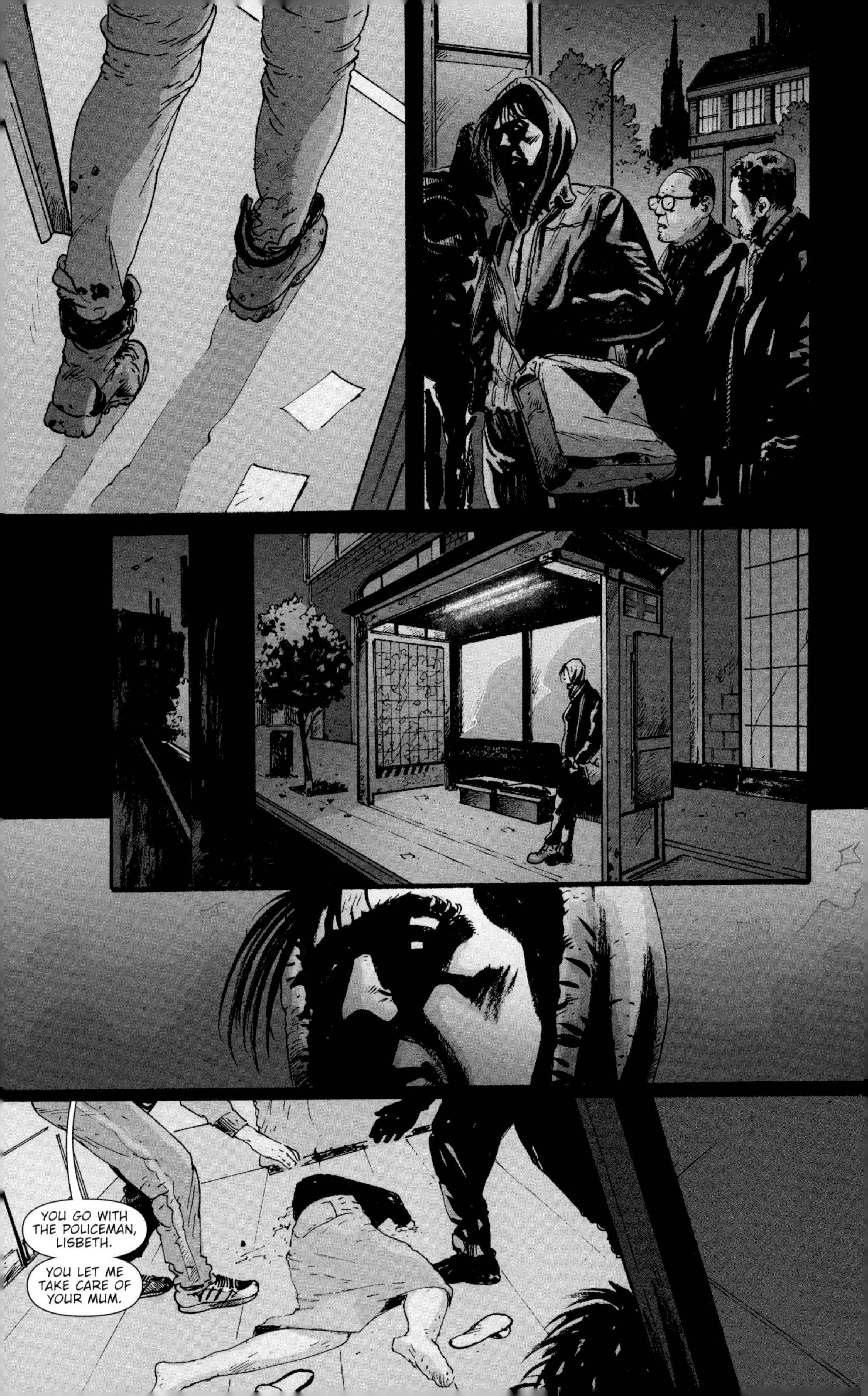
YOU GO WITH THE POLICEMAN, LISBETH.
YOU LET ME TAKE CARE OF YOUR MUM.

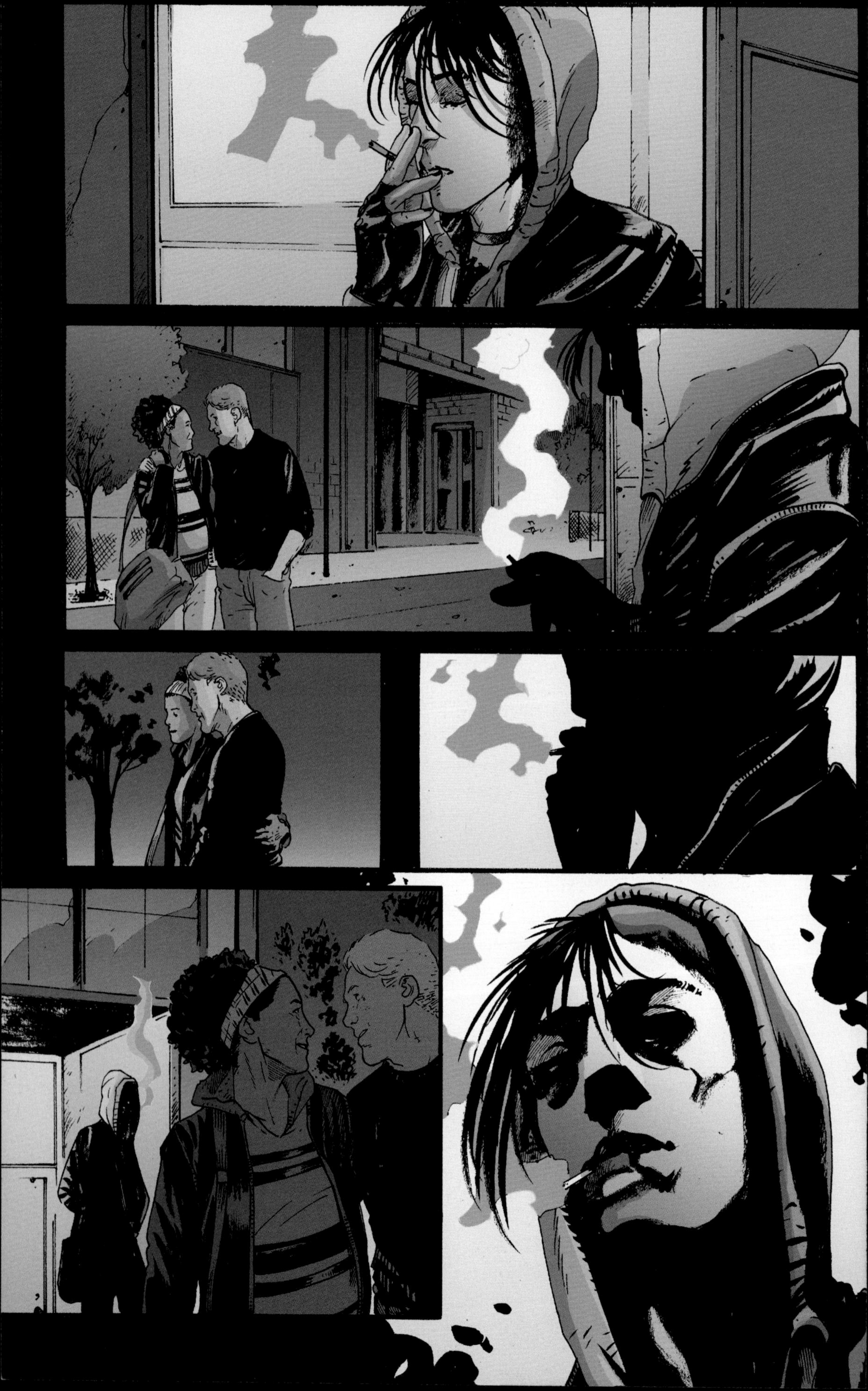

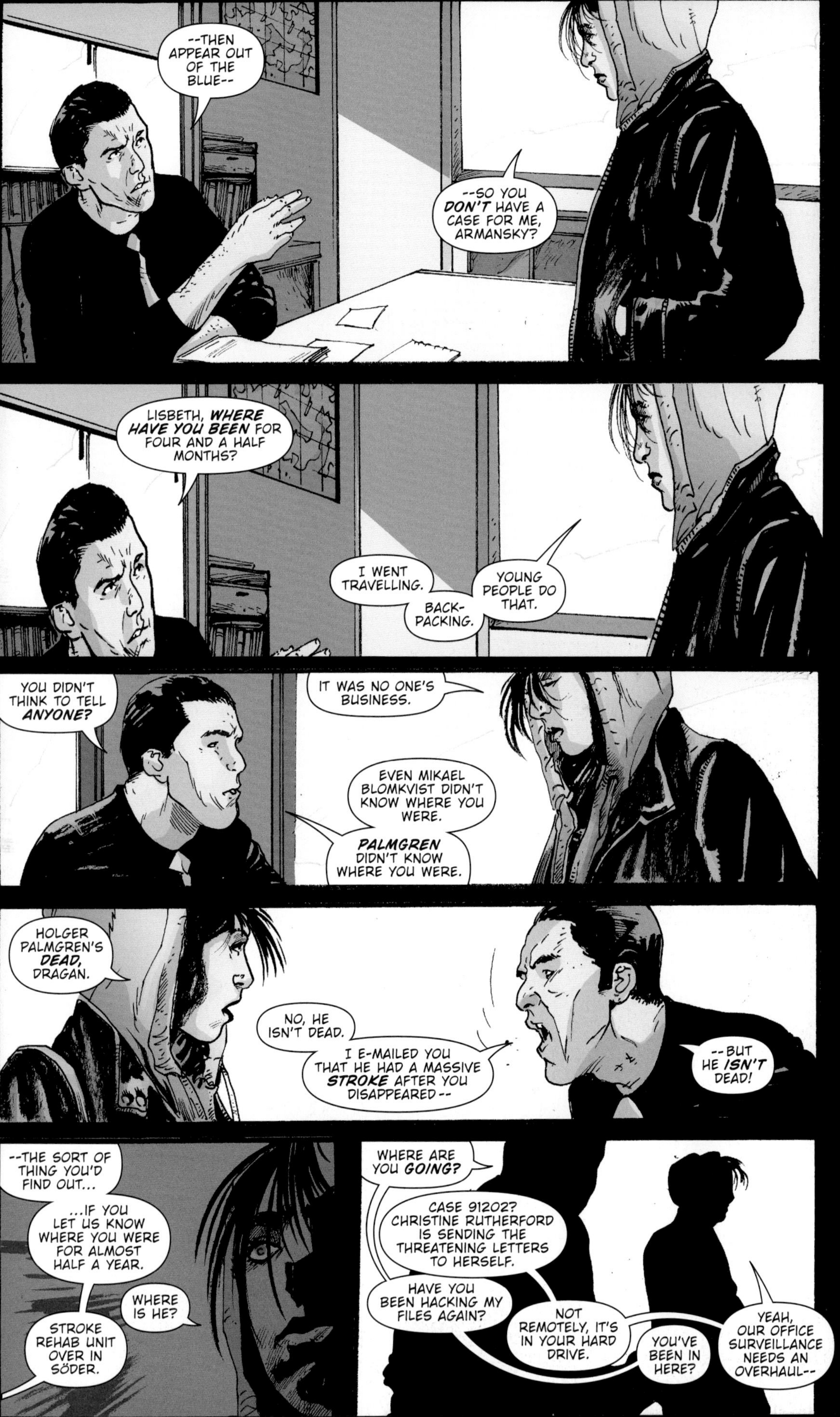
--THEN APPEAR OUT OF THE BLUE--
--SO YOU DON'T HAVE A CASE FOR ME, ARMANSKY?
LISBETH, WHERE HAVE YOU BEEN FOR FOUR AND A HALF MONTHS?
I WENT TRAVELLING.
BACK-PACKING.
YOUNG PEOPLE DO THAT.
YOU DIDN'T THINK TO TELL ANYONE?
IT WAS NO ONE'S BUSINESS.
EVEN MIKAEL BLOMKVIST DIDN'T KNOW WHERE YOU WERE.
PALMGREN DIDN'T KNOW WHERE YOU WERE.
HOLGER PALMGREN'S DEAD, DRAGAN.
NO, HE ISN'T DEAD.
I E-MAILED YOU THAT HE HAD A MASSIVE STROKE AFTER YOU DISAPPEARED--
--BUT HE ISN'T DEAD!
--THE SORT OF THING YOU'D FIND OUT...
...IF YOU LET US KNOW WHERE YOU WERE FOR ALMOST HALF A YEAR.
WHERE IS HE?
STROKE REHAB UNIT OVER IN SÖDER.
WHERE ARE YOU GOING?
CASE 91202? CHRISTINE RUTHERFORD IS SENDING THE THREATENING LETTERS TO HERSELF.
HAVE YOU BEEN HACKING MY FILES AGAIN?
NOT REMOTELY, IT'S IN YOUR HARD DRIVE.
YOU'VE BEEN IN HERE?
YEAH, OUR OFFICE SURVEILLANCE NEEDS AN OVERHAUL--

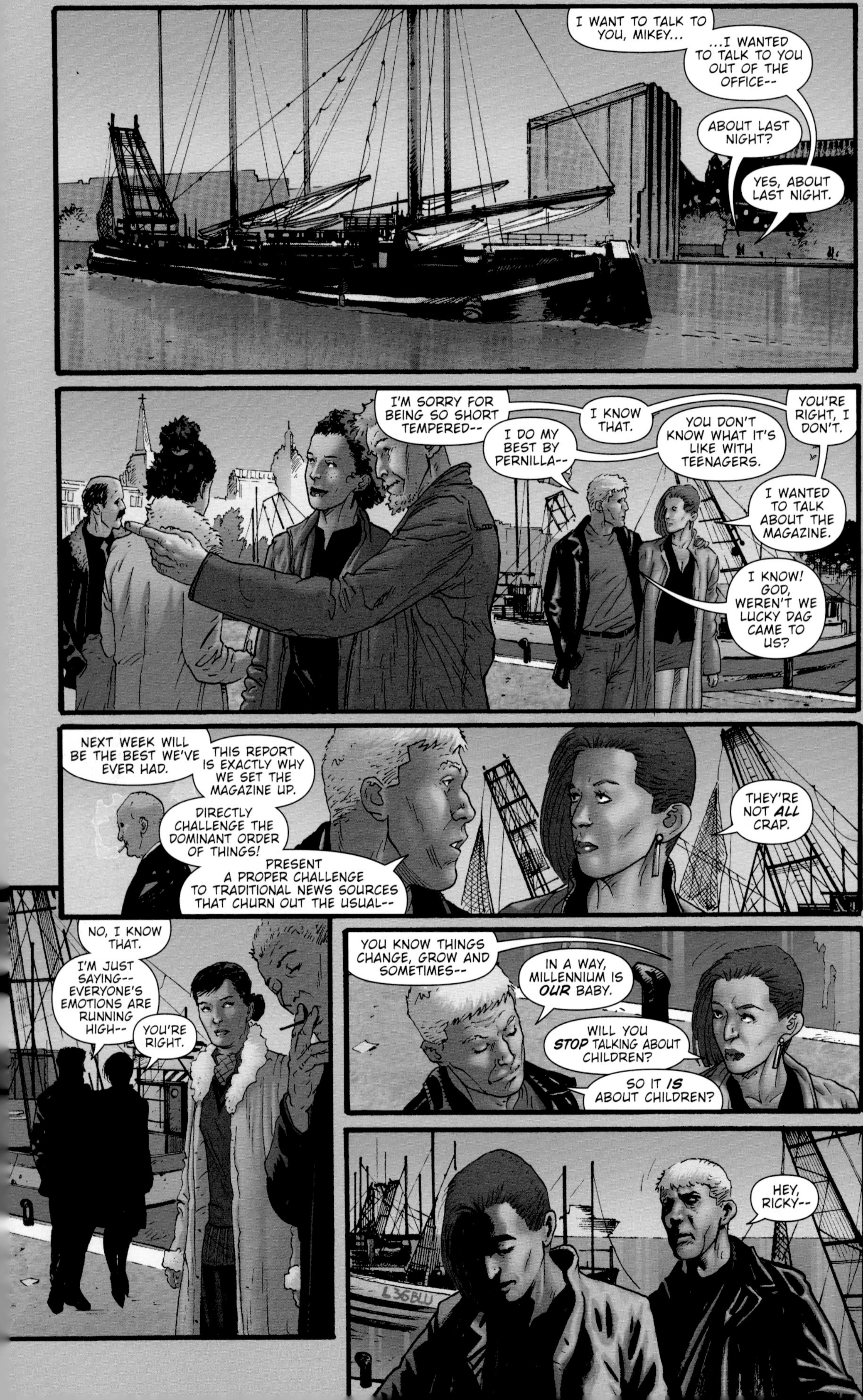
I WANT TO TALK TO YOU, MIKEY...
...I WANTED TO TALK TO YOU OUT OF THE OFFICE--
ABOUT LAST NIGHT?
YES, ABOUT LAST NIGHT.
I'M SORRY FOR BEING SO SHORT TEMPERED--
I DO MY BEST BY PERNILLA--
I KNOW THAT.
YOU DON'T KNOW WHAT IT'S LIKE WITH TEENAGERS.
YOU'RE RIGHT, I DON'T.
I WANTED TO TALK ABOUT THE MAGAZINE.
I KNOW! GOD, WEREN'T WE LUCKY DAG CAME TO US?
NEXT WEEK WILL BE THE BEST WE'VE EVER HAD.
THIS REPORT IS EXACTLY WHY WE SET THE MAGAZINE UP.
DIRECTLY CHALLENGE THE DOMINANT ORDER OF THINGS!
PRESENT A PROPER CHALLENGE TO TRADITIONAL NEWS SOURCES THAT CHURN OUT THE USUAL--
THEY'RE NOT ALL CRAP.
NO, I KNOW THAT.
I'M JUST SAYING-- EVERYONE'S EMOTIONS ARE RUNNING HIGH--
YOU'RE RIGHT.
YOU KNOW THINGS CHANGE, GROW AND SOMETIMES--
IN A WAY, MILLENNIUM IS OUR BABY.
WILL YOU STOP TALKING ABOUT CHILDREN?
SO IT IS ABOUT CHILDREN?
HEY, RICKY--

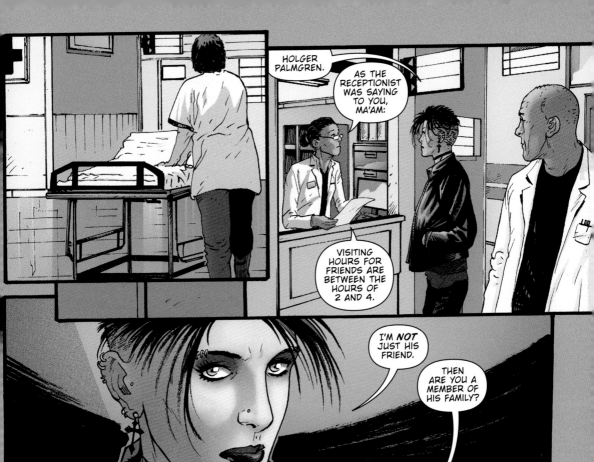

HOLGER PALMGREN.

AS THE RECEPTIONIST WAS SAYING TO YOU, MA'AM:

VISITING HOURS FOR FRIENDS ARE BETWEEN THE HOURS OF 2 AND 4.

I'M *NOT* JUST HIS FRIEND.

THEN ARE YOU A MEMBER OF HIS FAMILY?

MR. PALMGREN? YOU HAVE A VISITOR.

YOUR FOSTER DAUGHTER IS HERE, TO VISIT YOU.

SHE *IS* YOUR FOSTER DAUGHTER, ISN'T SHE?

YESH. YESH, SHE *IS*.

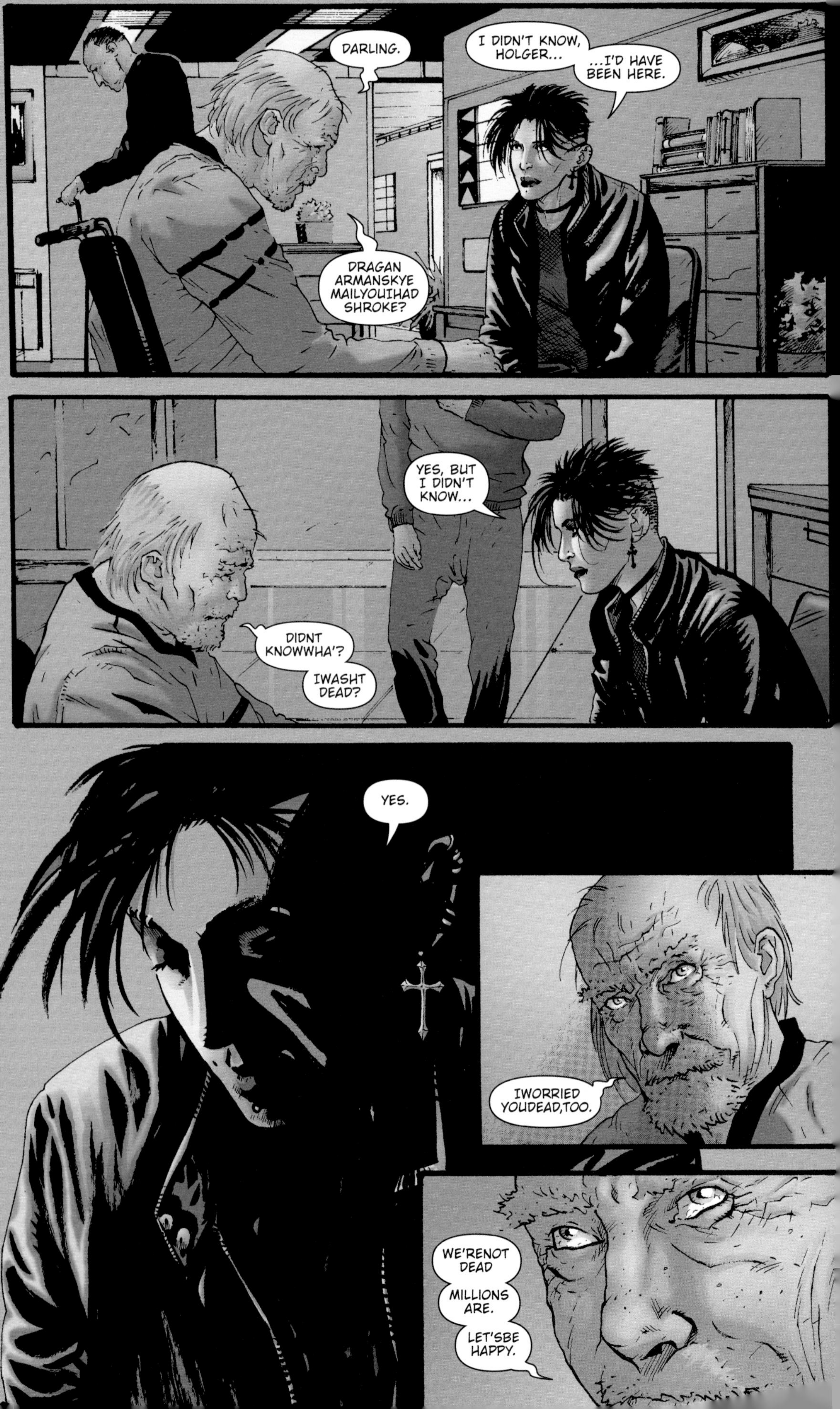
DARLING.
I DIDN'T KNOW, HOLGER...
...I'D HAVE BEEN HERE.
DRAGAN ARMANSKYE MAILYOUIHAD SHROKE?
YES, BUT I DIDN'T KNOW...
DIDNT KNOWWHA'?
IWASHT DEAD?
YES.
IWORRIED YOUDEAD,TOO.
WE'RENOT DEAD
MILLIONS ARE.
LET'SBE HAPPY.

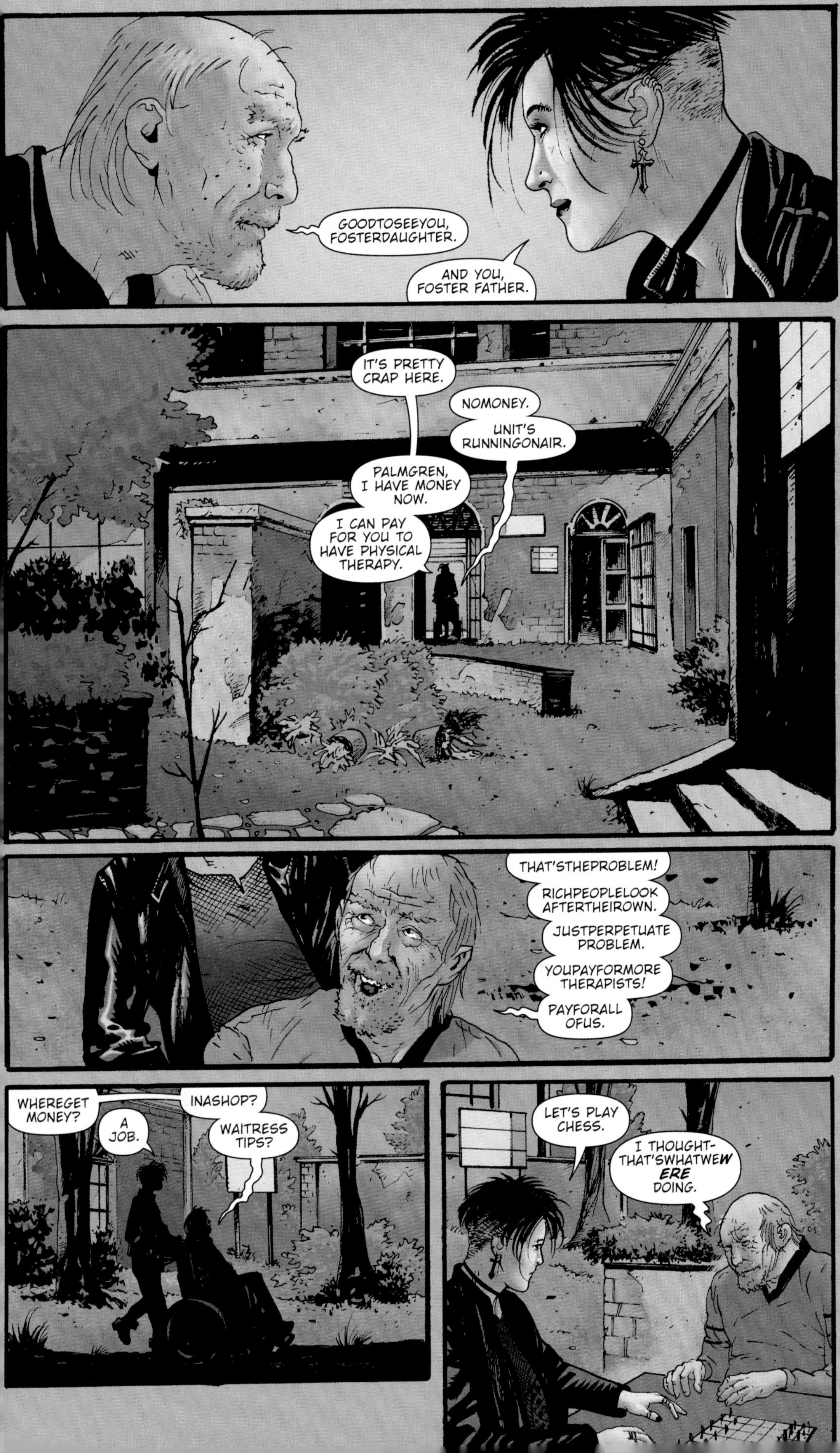
GOODTOSEEYOU, FOSTERDAUGHTER.
AND YOU, FOSTER FATHER.
IT'S PRETTY CRAP HERE.
NOMONEY.
UNIT'S RUNNINGONAIR.
PALMGREN, I HAVE MONEY NOW.
I CAN PAY FOR YOU TO HAVE PHYSICAL THERAPY.
THAT'STHEPROBLEM!
RICHPEOPLELOOK AFTERTHEIROWN.
JUSTPERPETUATE PROBLEM.
YOUPAYFORMORE THERAPISTS!
PAYFORALL OFUS.
WHEREGET MONEY?
A JOB.
INASHOP?
WAITRESS TIPS?
LET'S PLAY CHESS.
I THOUGHT-THAT'SWHATWEW*ERE* DOING.

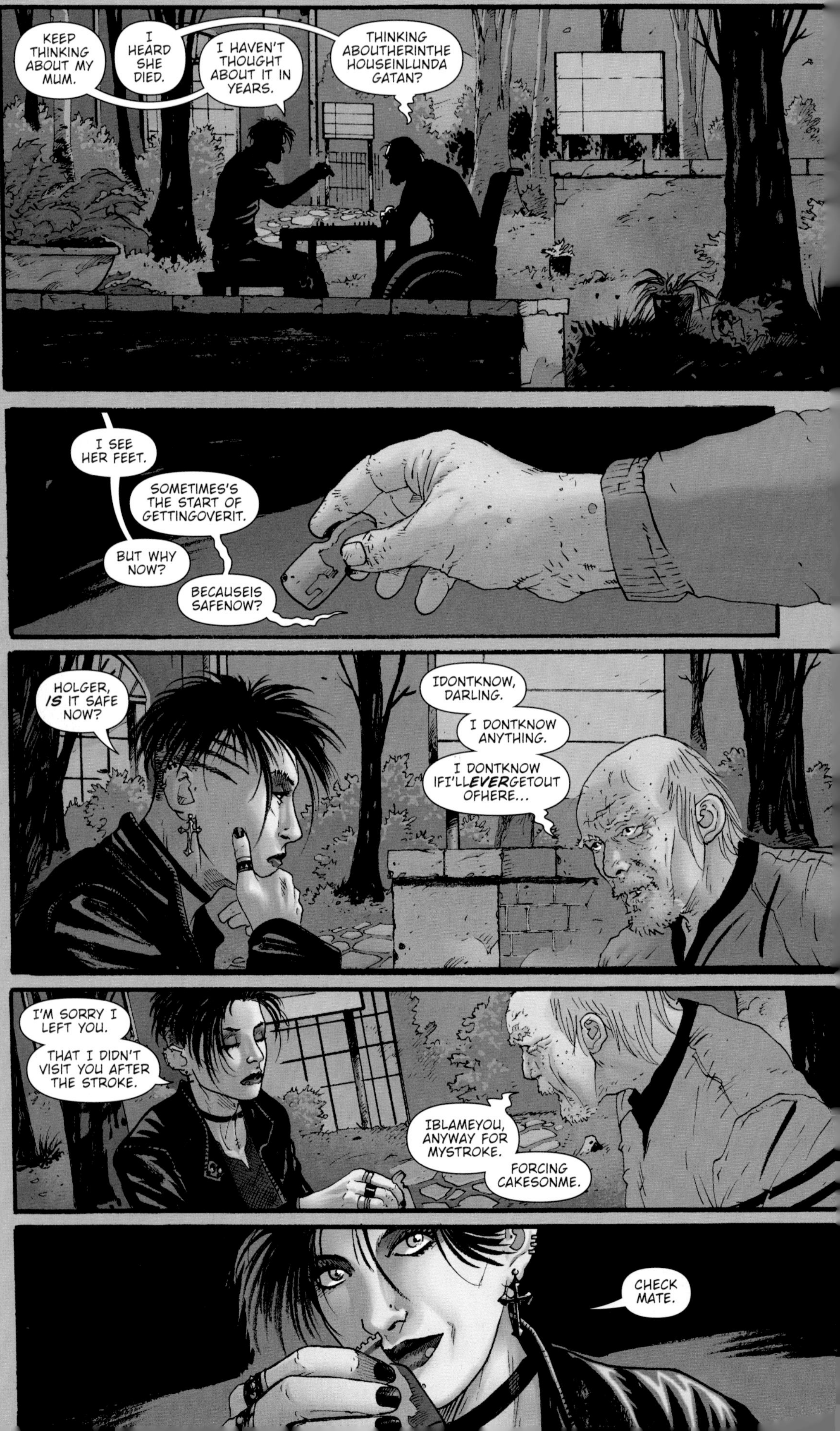
KEEP THINKING ABOUT MY MUM.
I HEARD SHE DIED.
I HAVEN'T THOUGHT ABOUT IT IN YEARS.
THINKING ABOUTHERINTHE HOUSEINLUNDA GATAN?
I SEE HER FEET.
SOMETIMES'S THE START OF GETTINGOVERIT.
BUT WHY NOW?
BECAUSEIS SAFENOW?
HOLGER, *IS* IT SAFE NOW?
IDONTKNOW, DARLING.
I DONTKNOW ANYTHING.
I DONTKNOW IFI'LL*EVER*GETOUT OFHERE...
I'M SORRY I LEFT YOU.
THAT I DIDN'T VISIT YOU AFTER THE STROKE.
IBLAMEYOU, ANYWAY FOR MYSTROKE.
FORCING CAKESONME.
CHECK MATE.

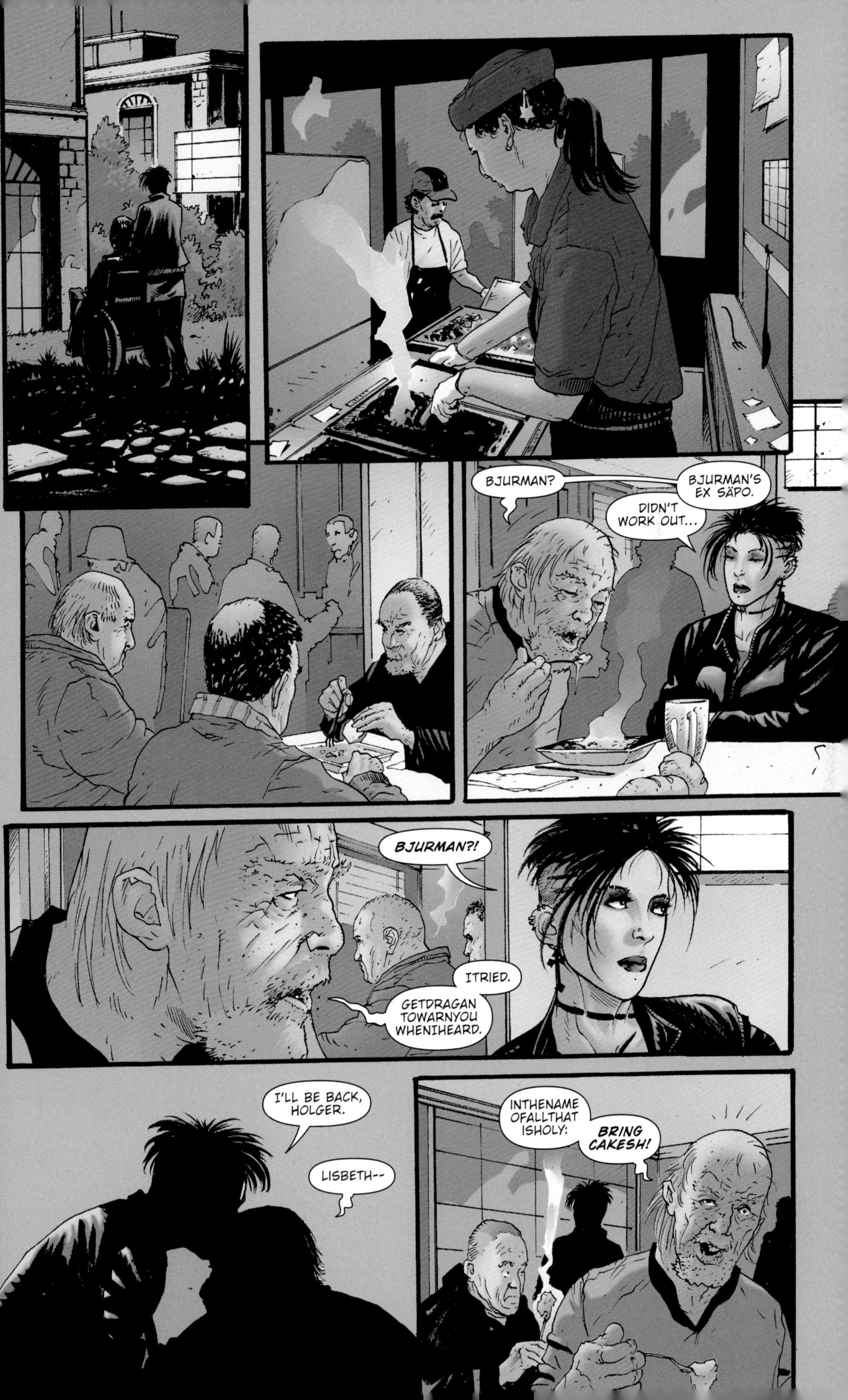
BJURMAN?
BJURMAN'S EX SÄPO.
DIDN'T WORK OUT...
BJURMAN?!
ITRIED.
GETDRAGAN TOWARNYOU WHENIHEARD.
I'LL BE BACK, HOLGER.
LISBETH--
INTHENAME OFALLTHAT ISHOLY:
BRING CAKESH!

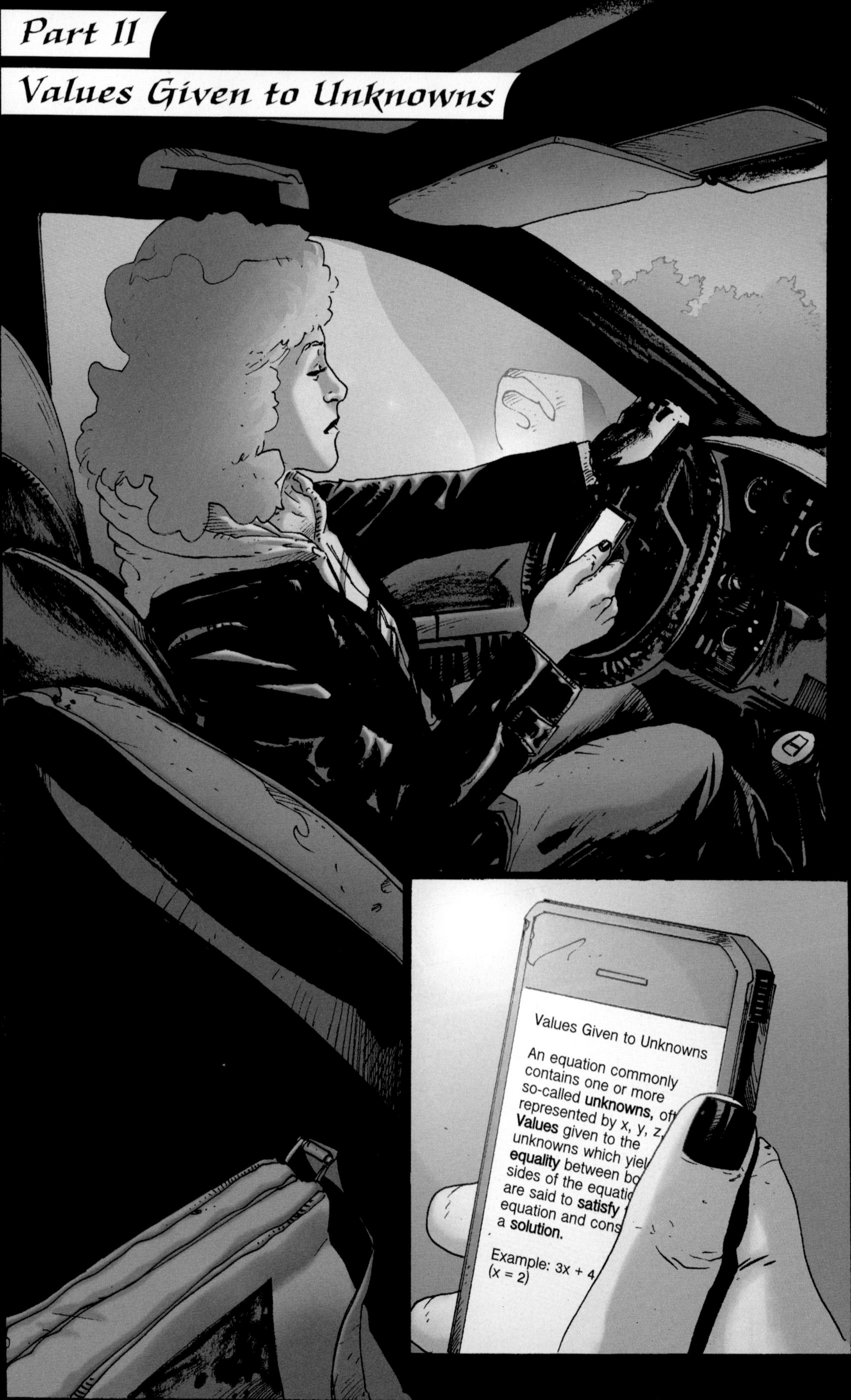

Part II
Values Given to Unknowns
Values Given to Unknowns
An equation commonly
contains one or more
so-called unknowns, oft
represented by x, y, z,
Values given to the
unknowns which yiel
equality between bo
sides of the equatio
are said to satisfy
equation and cons
a solution.
Example: 3x + 4
(x = 2)

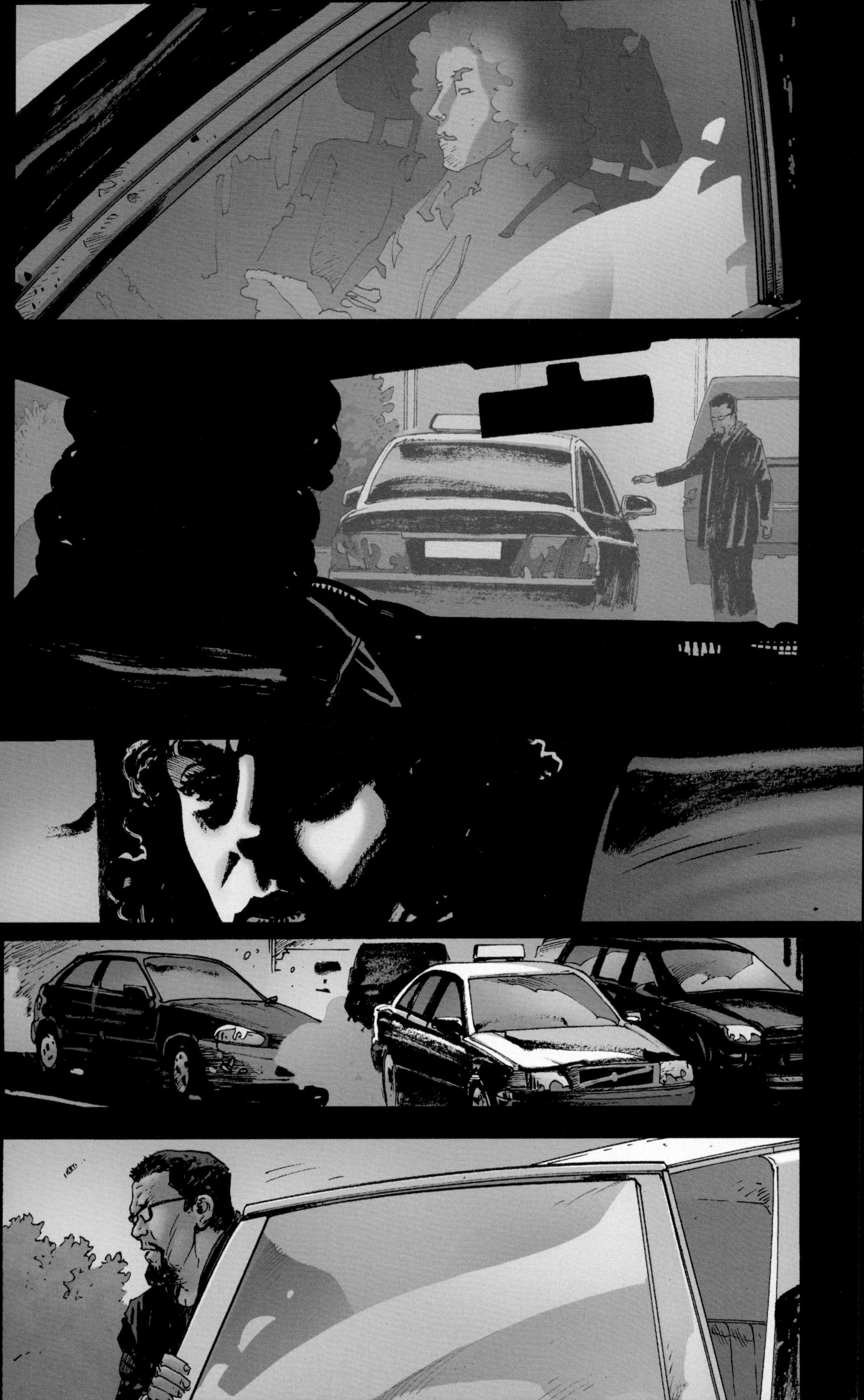

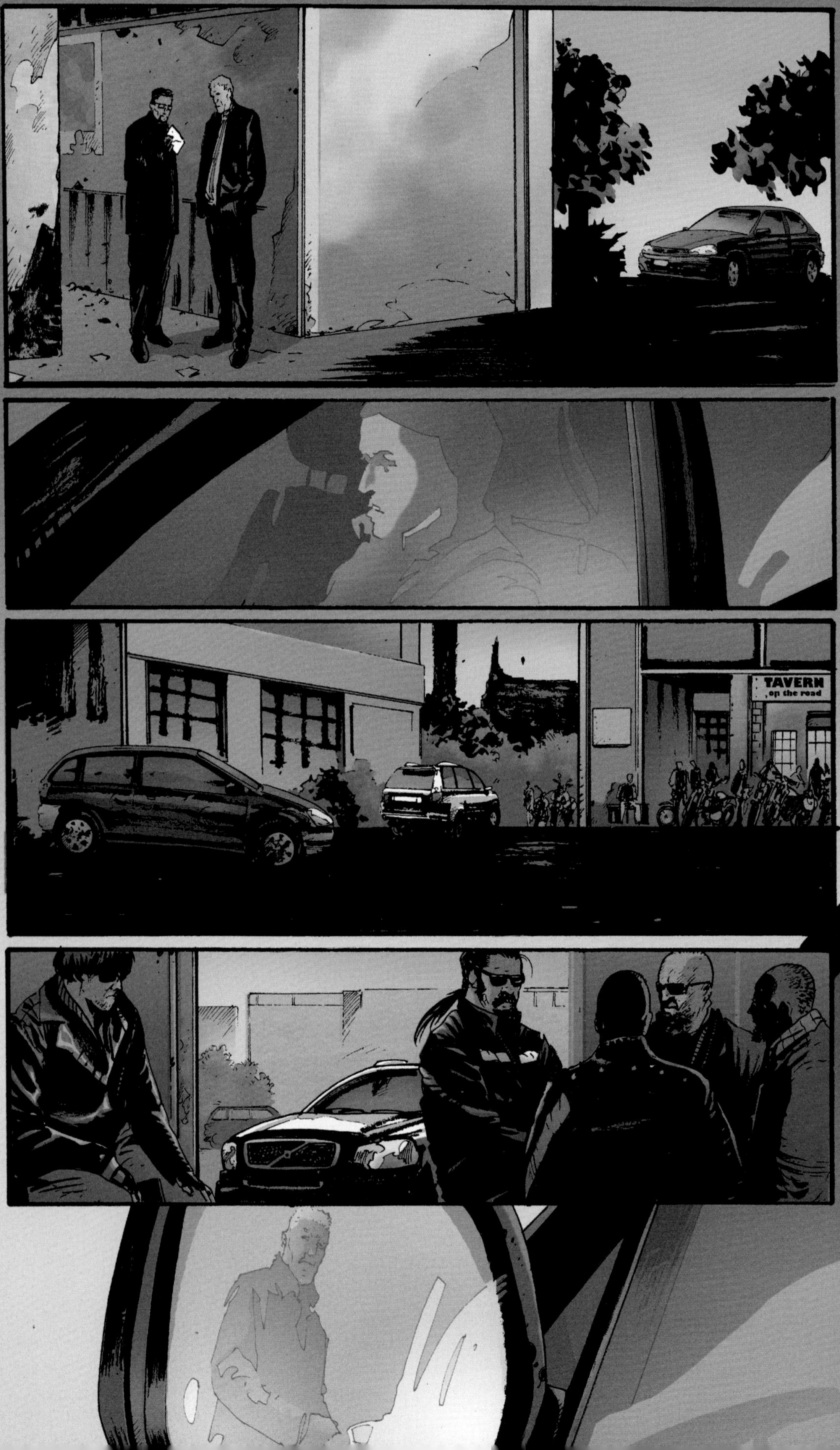
TAVERN
on the road

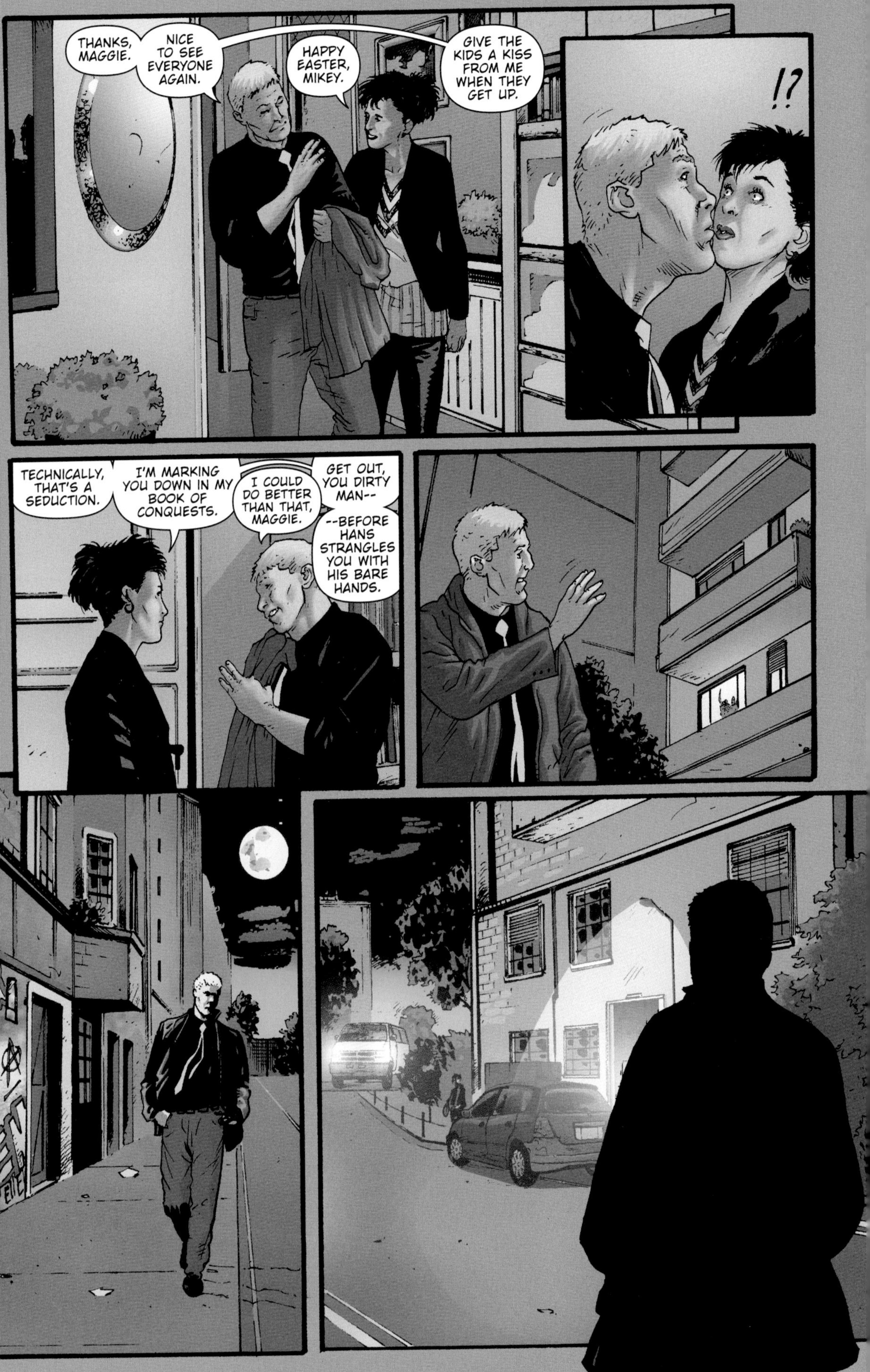
THANKS, MAGGIE.
NICE TO SEE EVERYONE AGAIN.
HAPPY EASTER, MIKEY.
GIVE THE KIDS A KISS FROM ME WHEN THEY GET UP.
!?
TECHNICALLY, THAT'S A SEDUCTION.
I'M MARKING YOU DOWN IN MY BOOK OF CONQUESTS.
I COULD DO BETTER THAN THAT, MAGGIE.
GET OUT, YOU DIRTY MAN--
--BEFORE HANS STRANGLES YOU WITH HIS BARE HANDS.

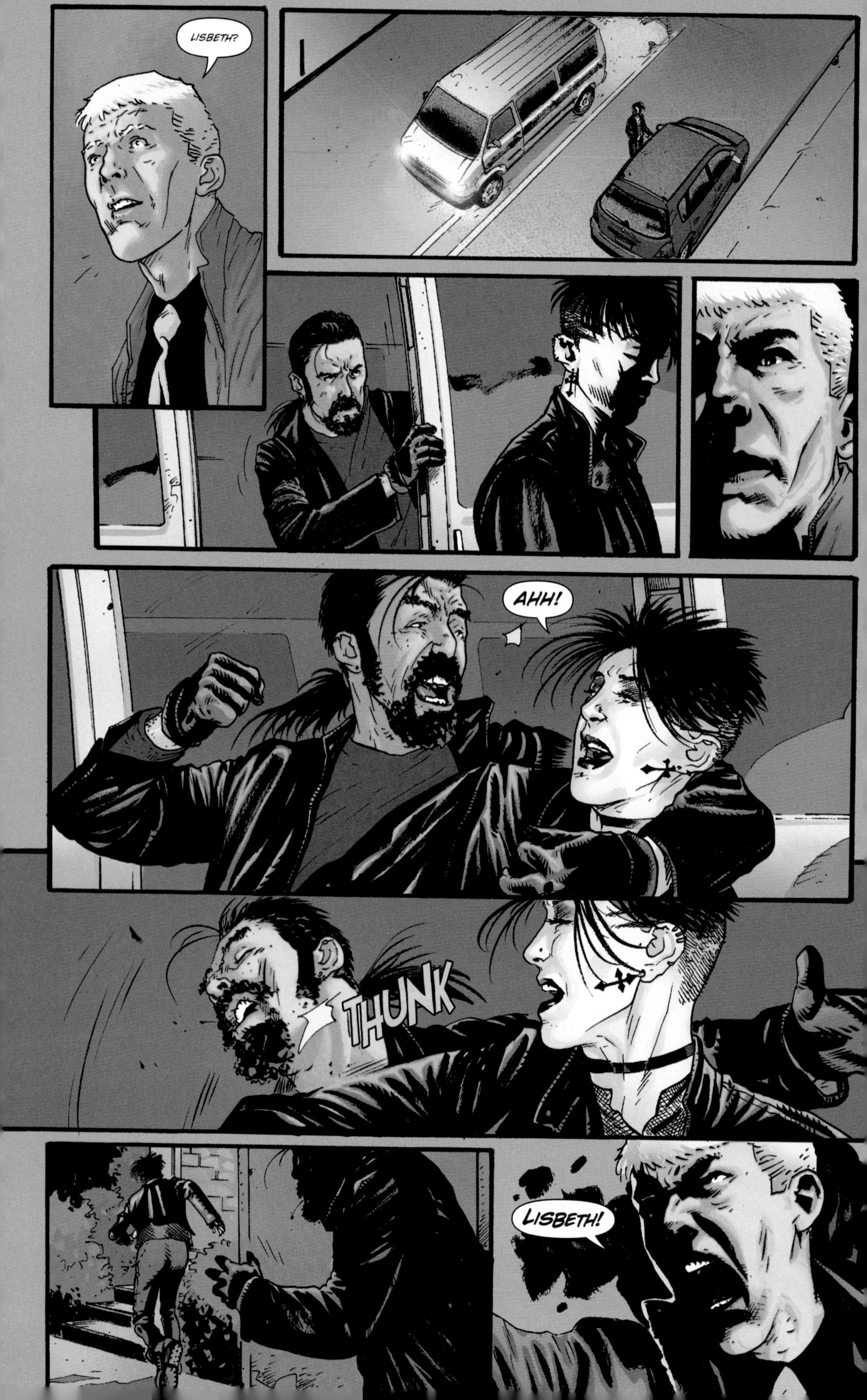
LISBETH?
AHH!
THUNK
LISBETH!

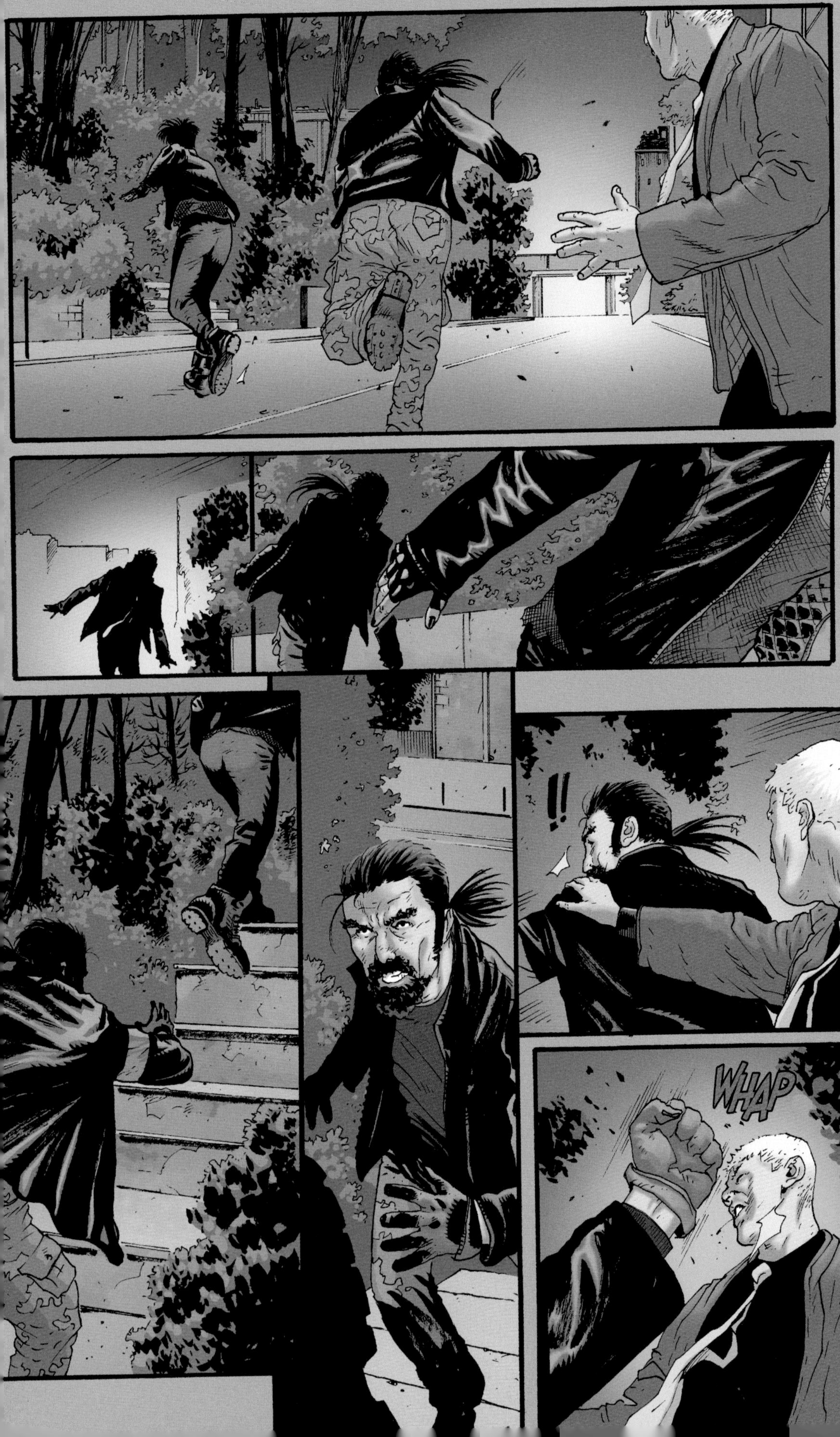
!!
WHAP

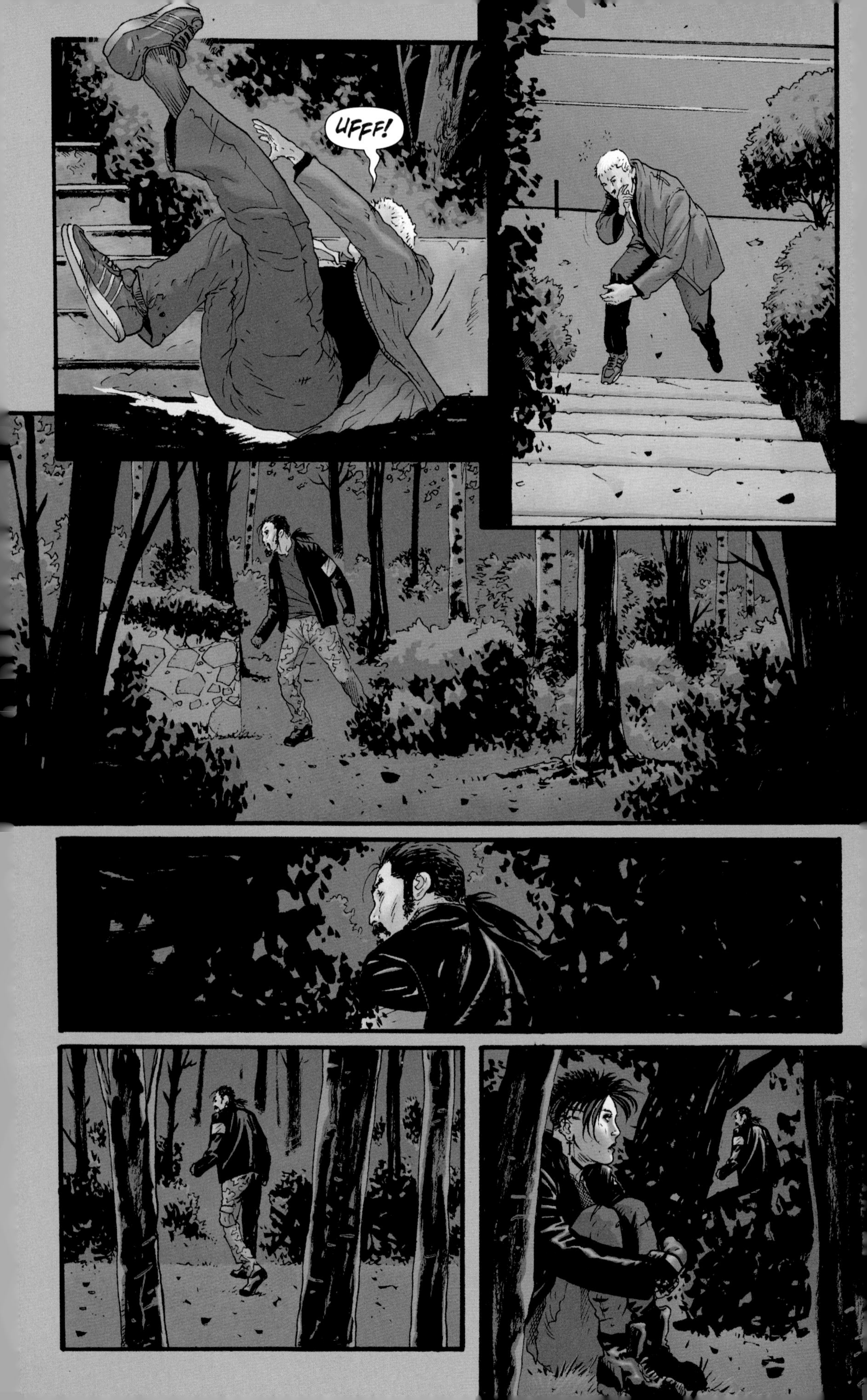
UFFF!

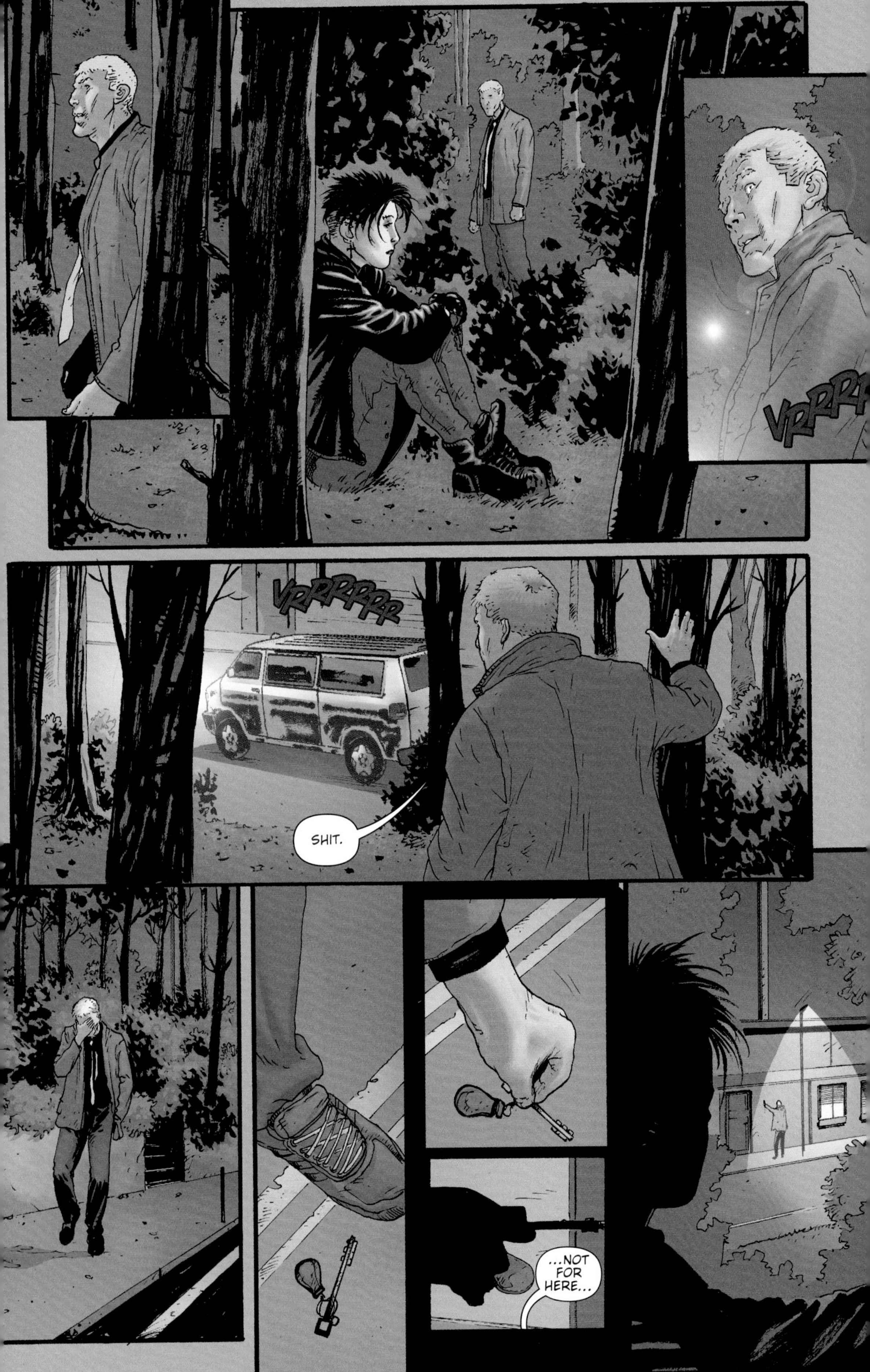
VRRRR
VRRRRRRR
SHIT.
...NOT FOR HERE...

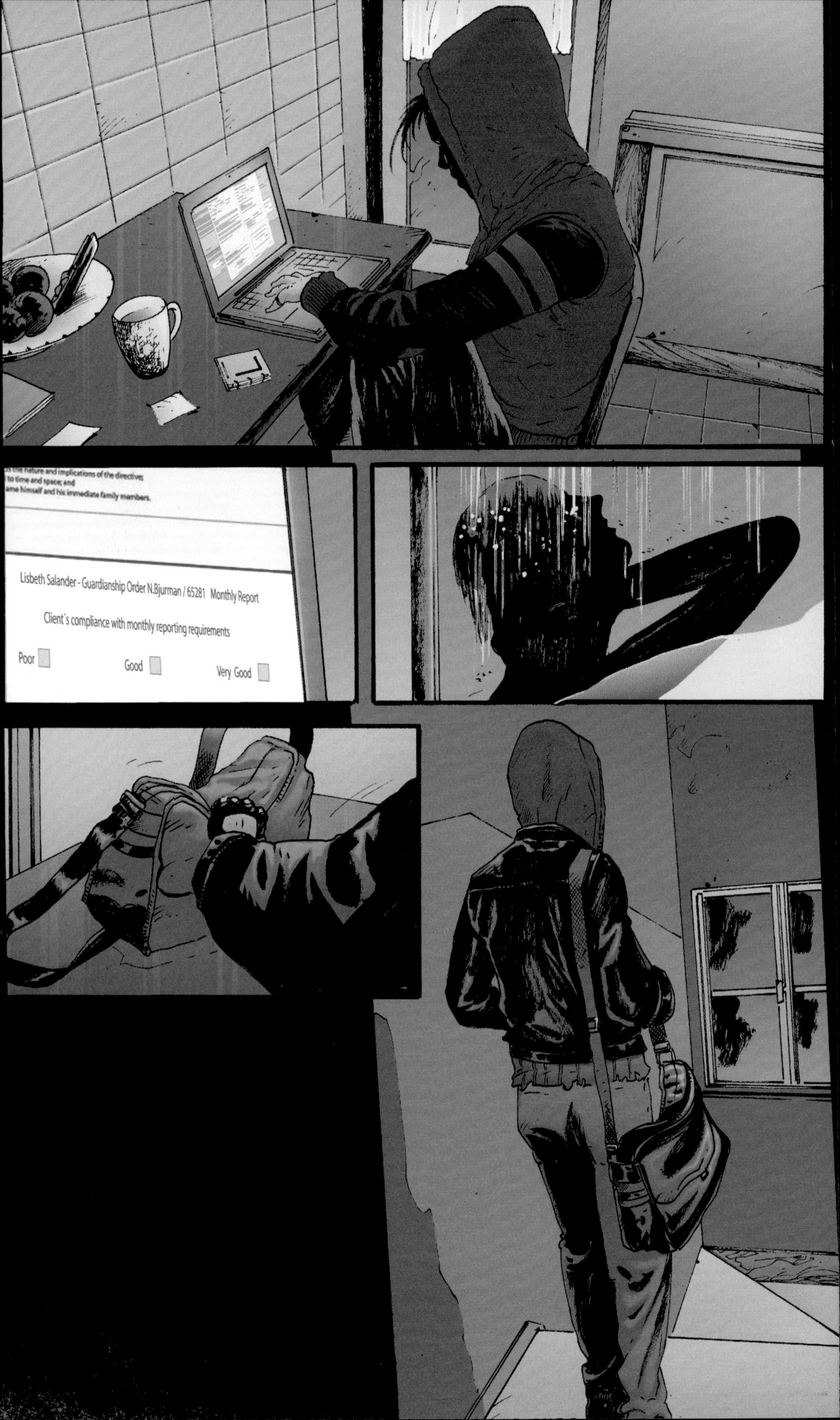

the nature and implications of the directive;
to time and space; and
himself and his immediate family members.
Lisbeth Salander - Guardianship Order N.Bjurman / 65281 Monthly Report
Client´s compliance with monthly reporting requirements
Poor
Good
Very Good

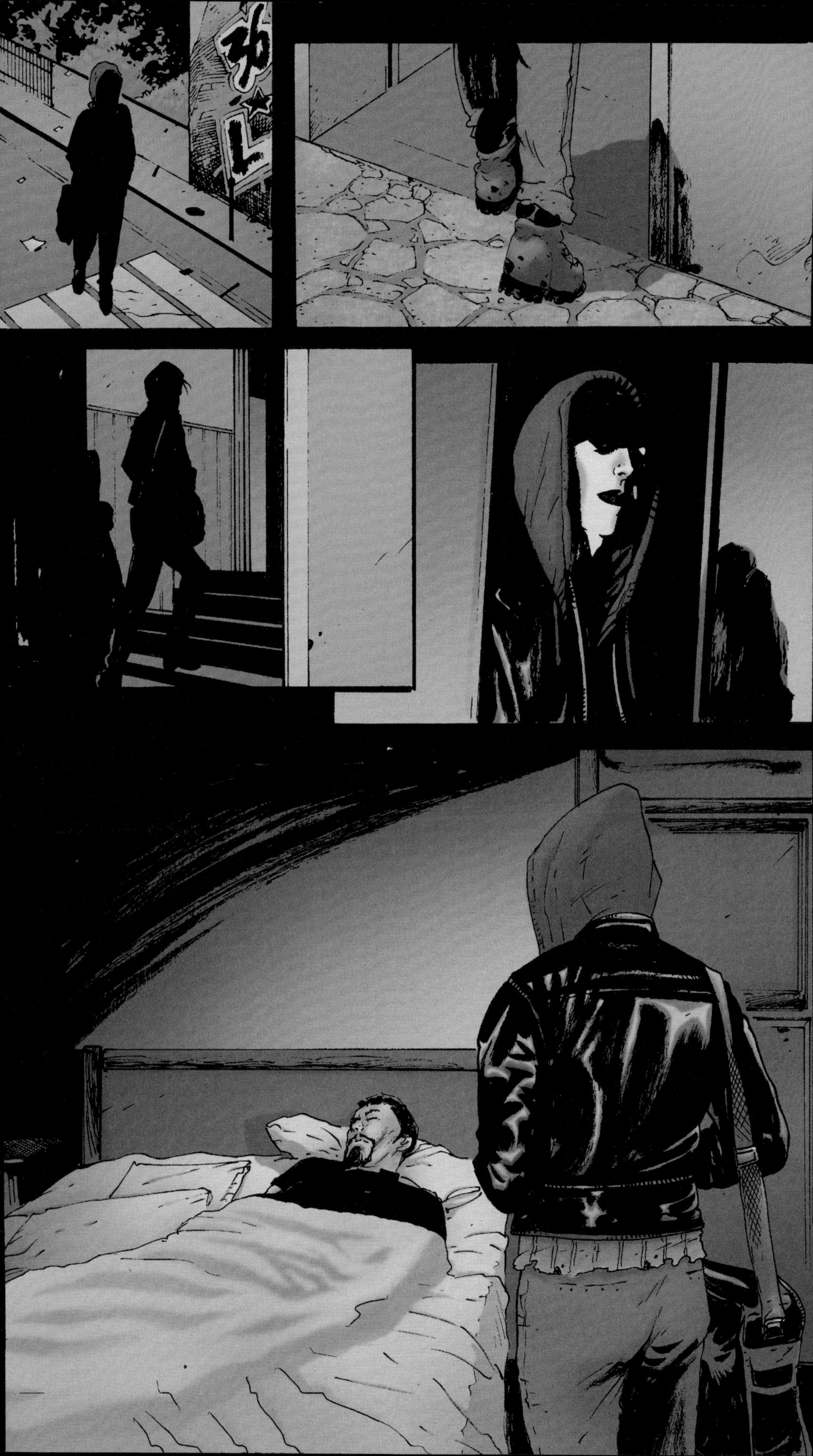

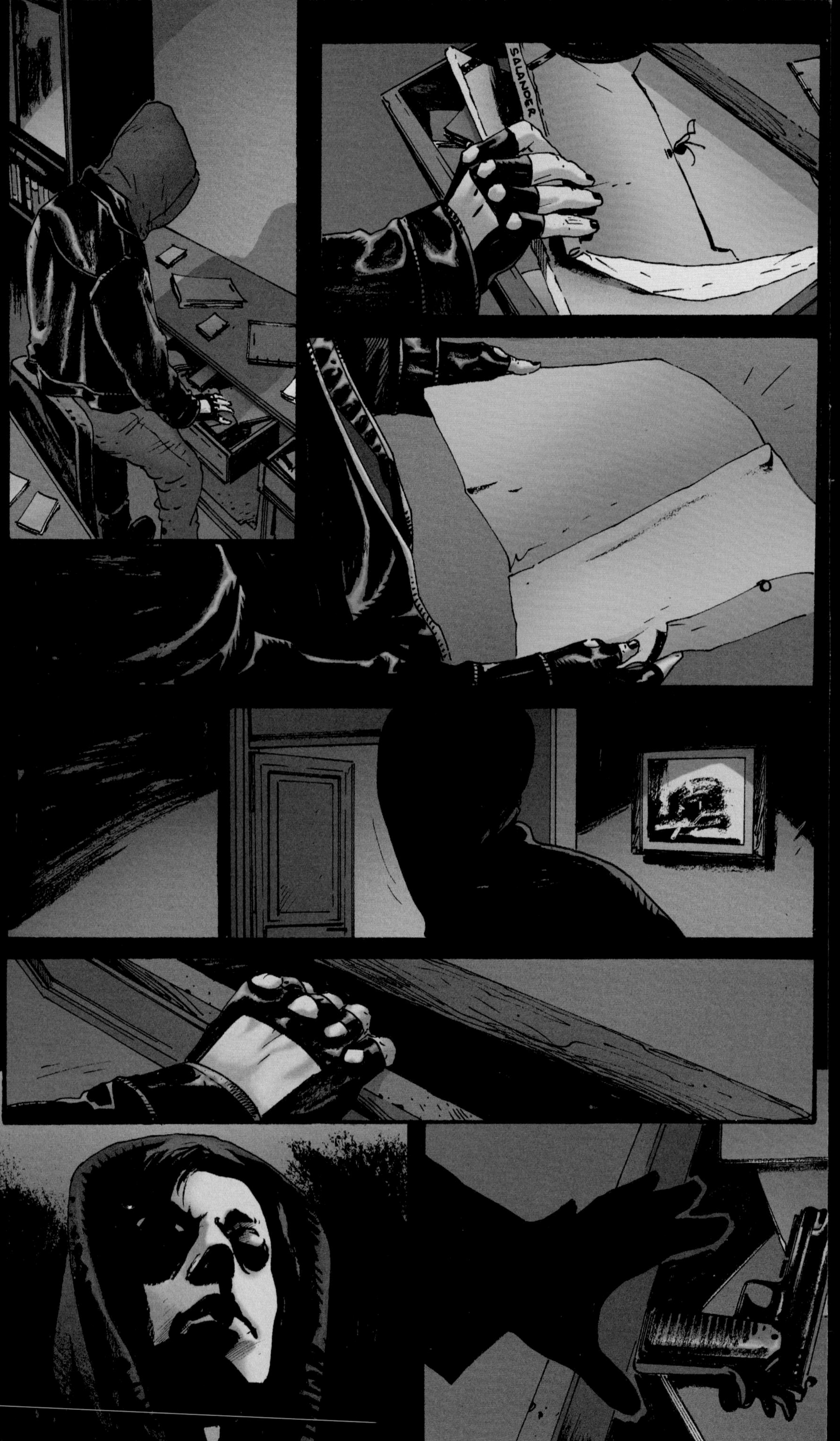
SALANDER

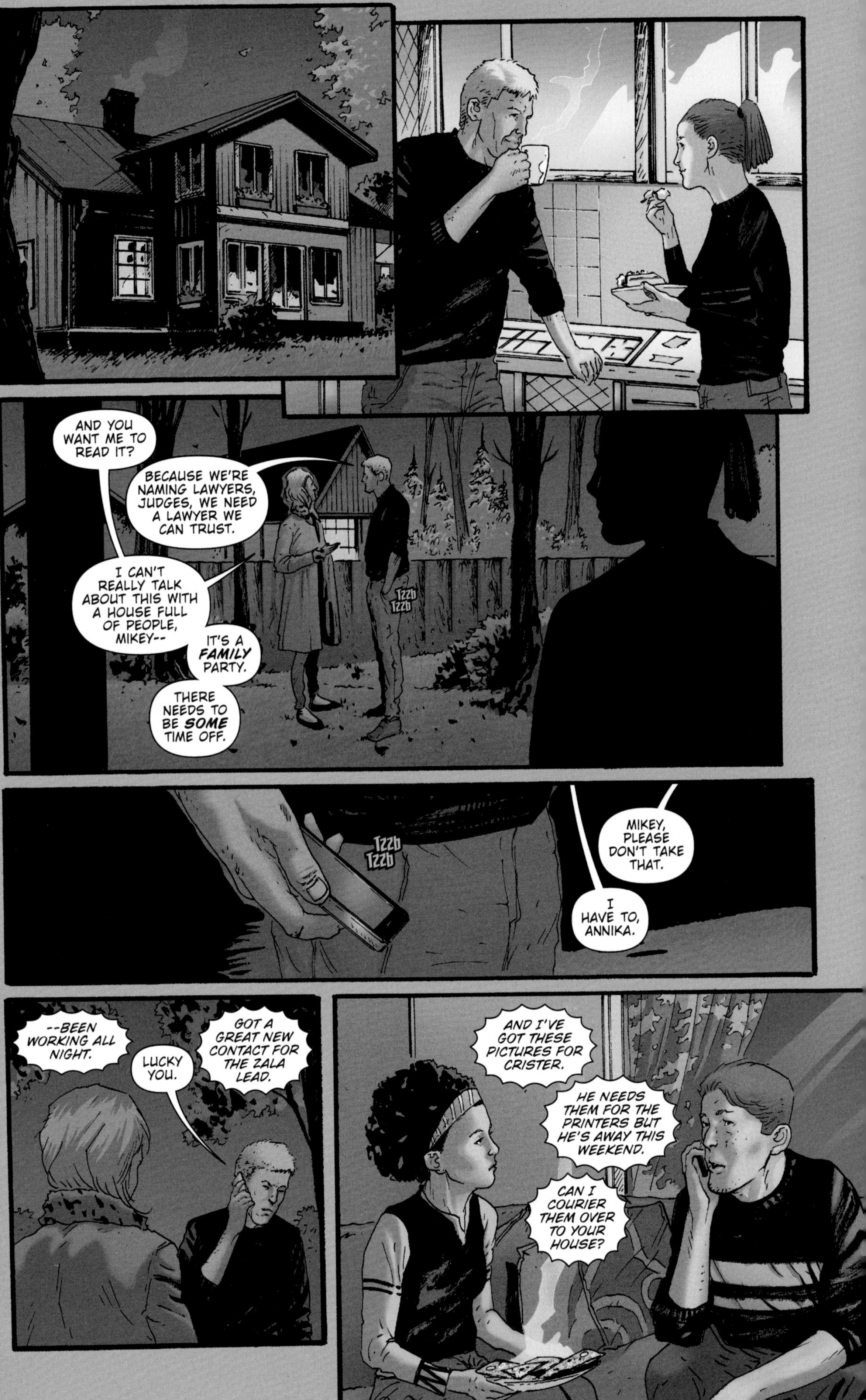
AND YOU WANT ME TO READ IT?
BECAUSE WE'RE NAMING LAWYERS, JUDGES, WE NEED A LAWYER WE CAN TRUST.
I CAN'T REALLY TALK ABOUT THIS WITH A HOUSE FULL OF PEOPLE, MIKEY--
TZZB TZZB
IT'S A FAMILY PARTY.
THERE NEEDS TO BE SOME TIME OFF.
TZZB TZZB
MIKEY, PLEASE DON'T TAKE THAT.
I HAVE TO, ANNIKA.
--BEEN WORKING ALL NIGHT.
LUCKY YOU.
GOT A GREAT NEW CONTACT FOR THE ZALA LEAD.
AND I'VE GOT THESE PICTURES FOR CRISTER.
HE NEEDS THEM FOR THE PRINTERS BUT HE'S AWAY THIS WEEKEND.
CAN I COURIER THEM OVER TO YOUR HOUSE?

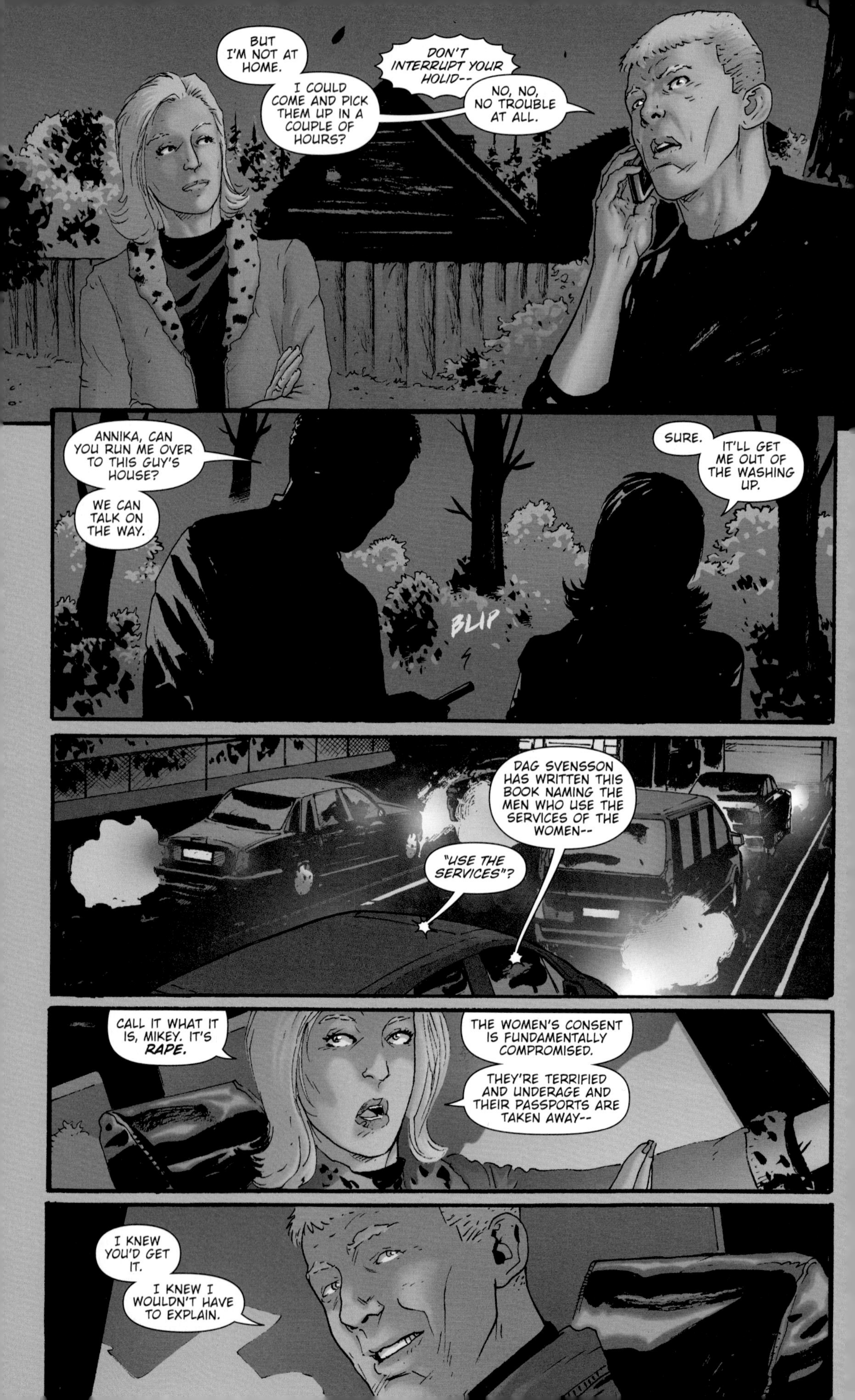
BUT I'M NOT AT HOME.
I COULD COME AND PICK THEM UP IN A COUPLE OF HOURS?
DON'T INTERRUPT YOUR HOLID--
NO, NO, NO TROUBLE AT ALL.
ANNIKA, CAN YOU RUN ME OVER TO THIS GUY'S HOUSE?
WE CAN TALK ON THE WAY.
SURE.
IT'LL GET ME OUT OF THE WASHING UP.
BLIP
DAG SVENSSON HAS WRITTEN THIS BOOK NAMING THE MEN WHO USE THE SERVICES OF THE WOMEN--
"USE THE SERVICES"?
CALL IT WHAT IT IS, MIKEY. IT'S *RAPE.*
THE WOMEN'S CONSENT IS FUNDAMENTALLY COMPROMISED.
THEY'RE TERRIFIED AND UNDERAGE AND THEIR PASSPORTS ARE TAKEN AWAY--
I KNEW YOU'D GET IT.
I KNEW I WOULDN'T HAVE TO EXPLAIN.

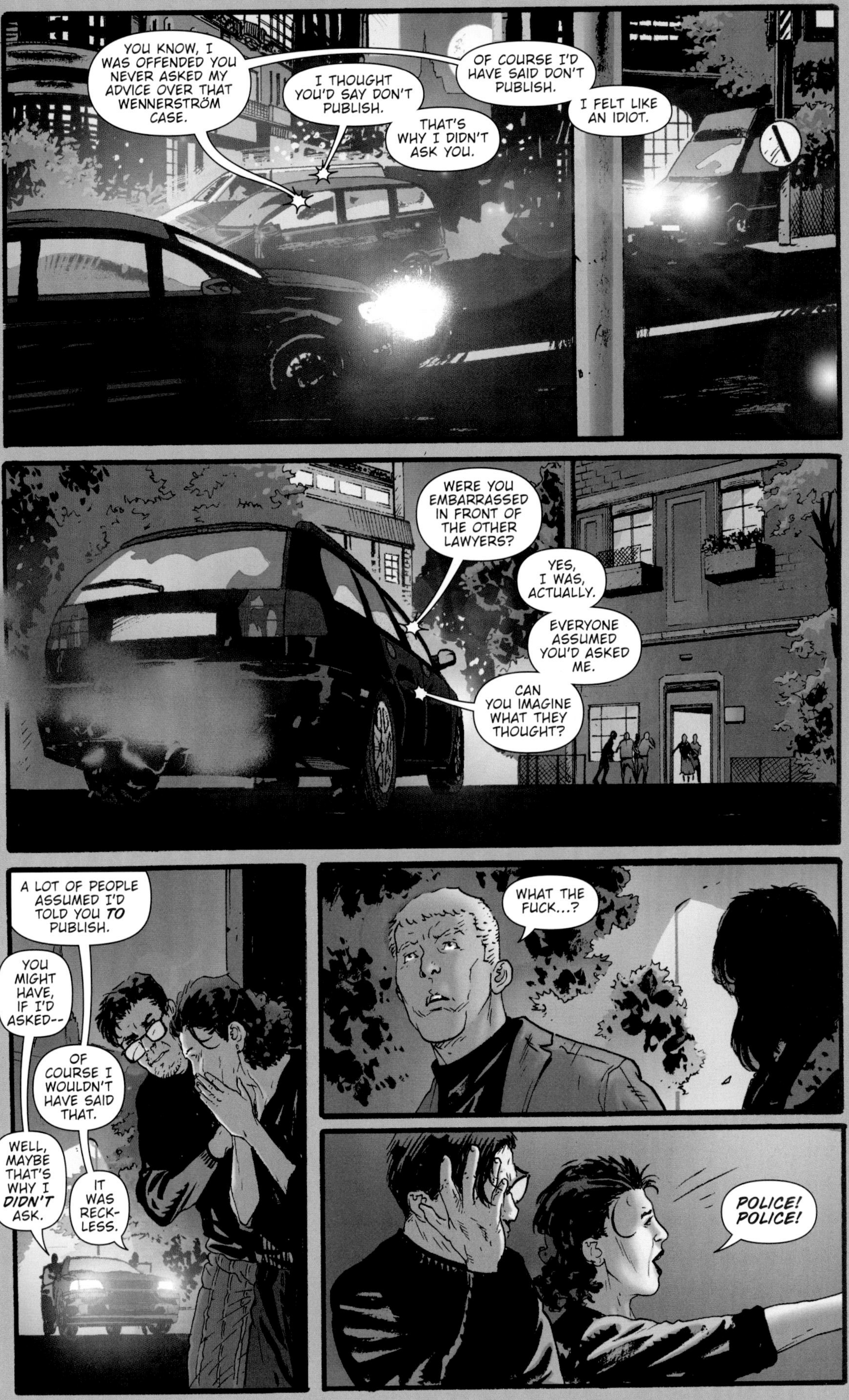
YOU KNOW, I WAS OFFENDED YOU NEVER ASKED MY ADVICE OVER THAT WENNERSTRÖM CASE.
I THOUGHT YOU'D SAY DON'T PUBLISH.
THAT'S WHY I DIDN'T ASK YOU.
OF COURSE I'D HAVE SAID DON'T PUBLISH.
I FELT LIKE AN IDIOT.
WERE YOU EMBARRASSED IN FRONT OF THE OTHER LAWYERS?
YES, I WAS, ACTUALLY.
EVERYONE ASSUMED YOU'D ASKED ME.
CAN YOU IMAGINE WHAT THEY THOUGHT?
A LOT OF PEOPLE ASSUMED I'D TOLD YOU ***TO*** PUBLISH.
YOU MIGHT HAVE, IF I'D ASKED--
OF COURSE I WOULDN'T HAVE SAID THAT.
WELL, MAYBE THAT'S WHY I ***DIDN'T*** ASK.
IT WAS RECK-LESS.
WHAT THE FUCK...?
POLICE! POLICE!

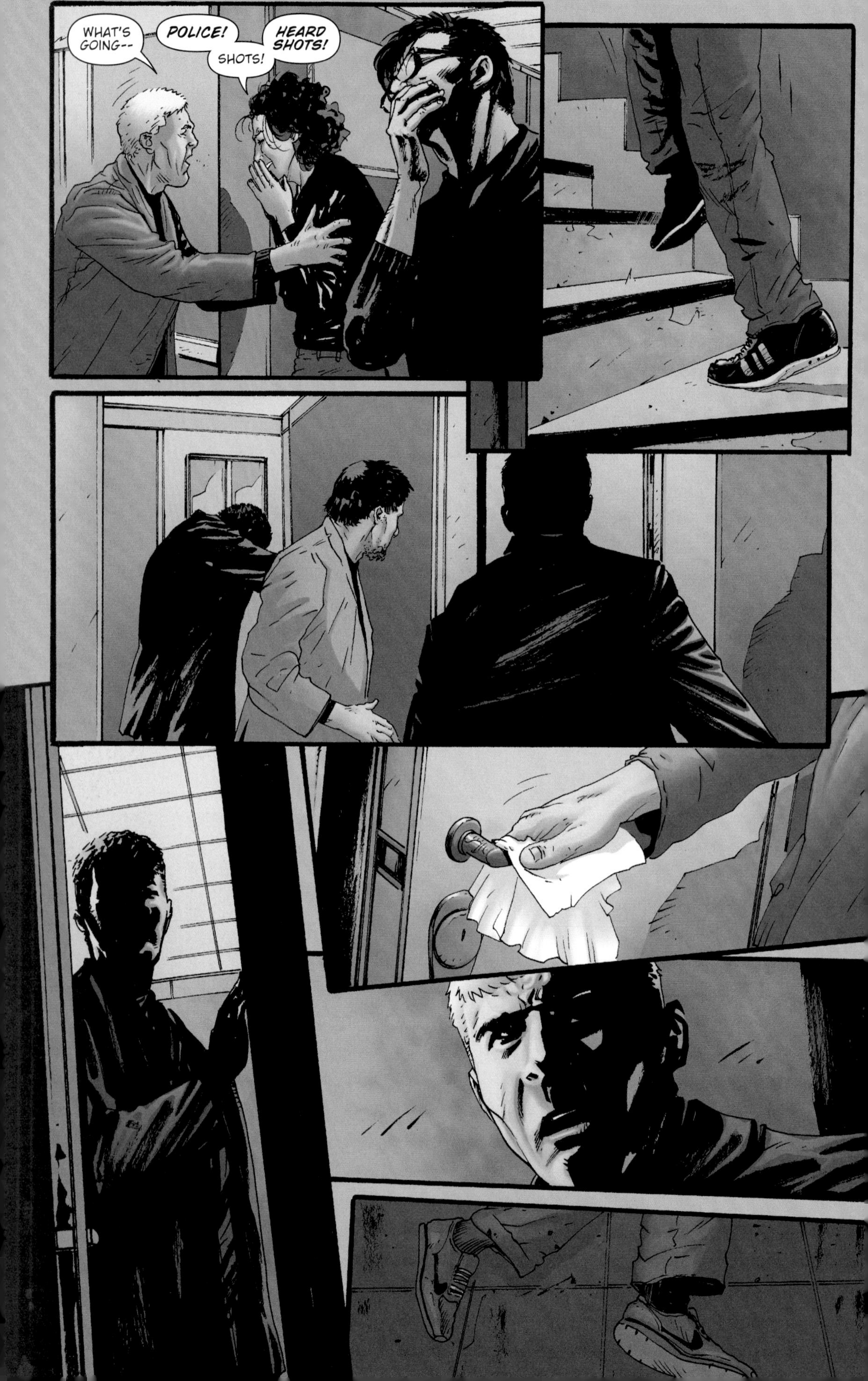
WHAT'S GOING--
POLICE!
SHOTS!
HEARD SHOTS!

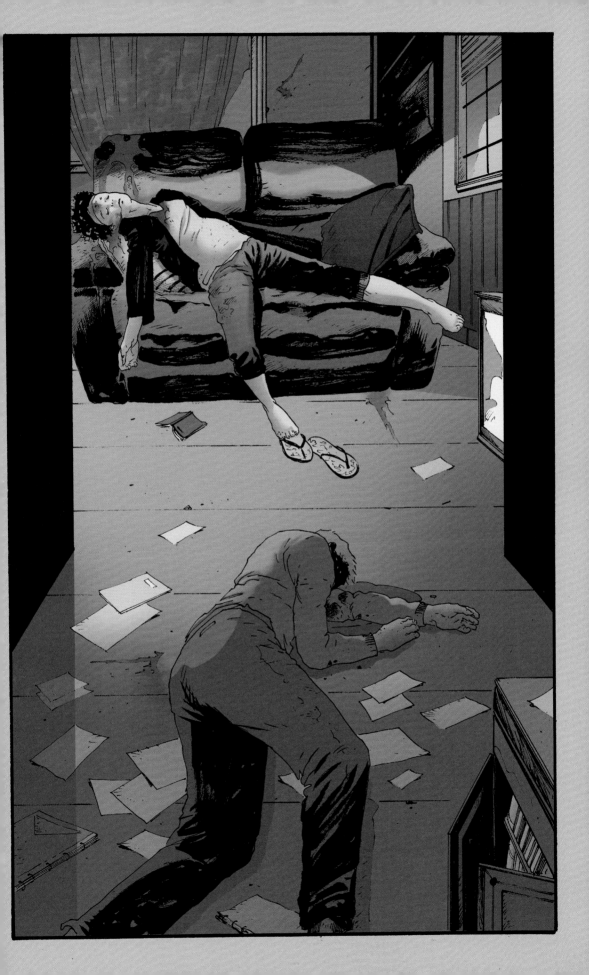

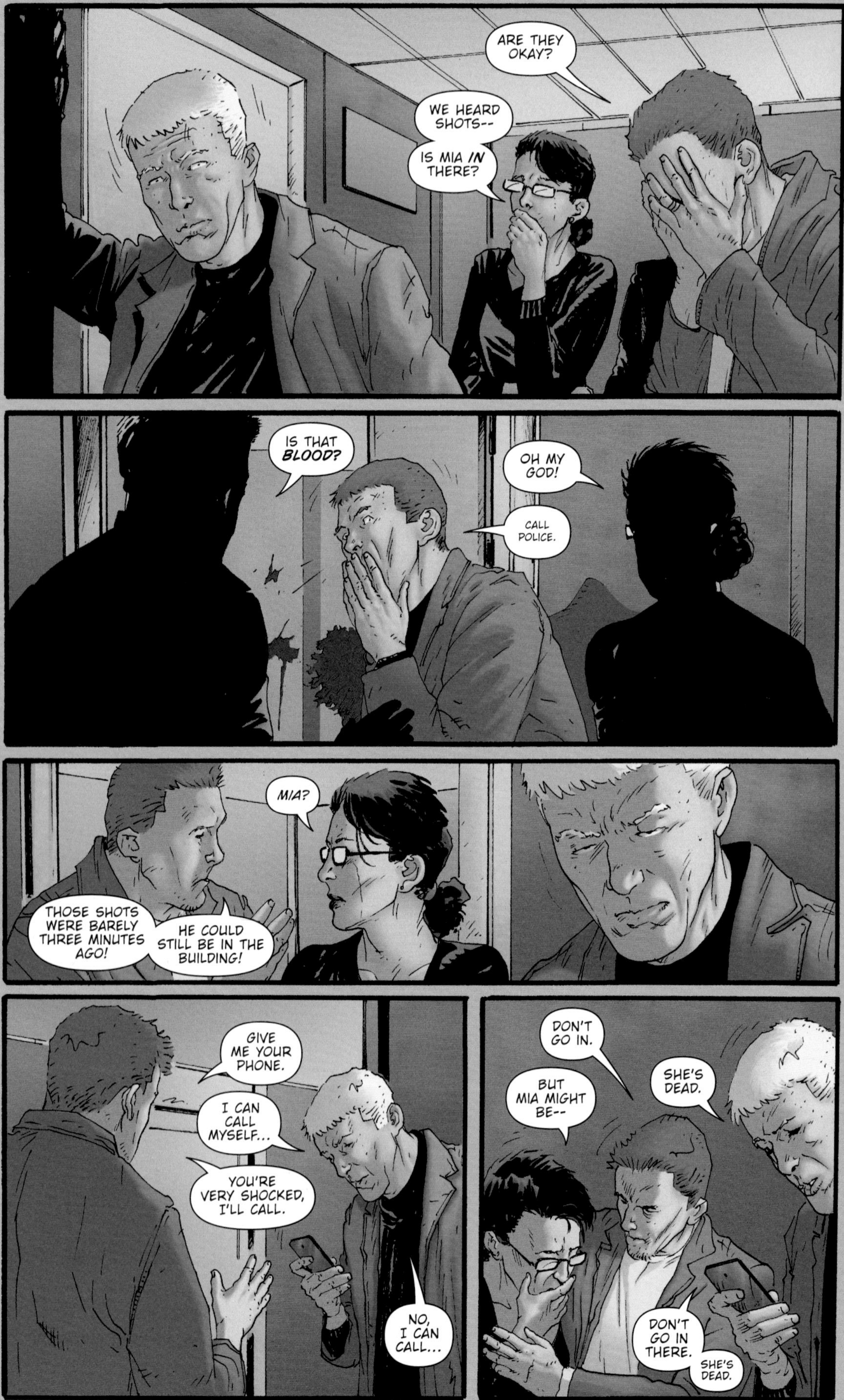
ARE THEY OKAY?
WE HEARD SHOTS--
IS MIA *IN* THERE?
IS THAT *BLOOD?*
OH MY GOD!
CALL POLICE.
MIA?
THOSE SHOTS WERE BARELY THREE MINUTES AGO!
HE COULD STILL BE IN THE BUILDING!
GIVE ME YOUR PHONE.
I CAN CALL MYSELF...
YOU'RE VERY SHOCKED, I'LL CALL.
NO, I CAN CALL...
DON'T GO IN.
BUT MIA MIGHT BE--
SHE'S DEAD.
DON'T GO IN THERE.
SHE'S DEAD.

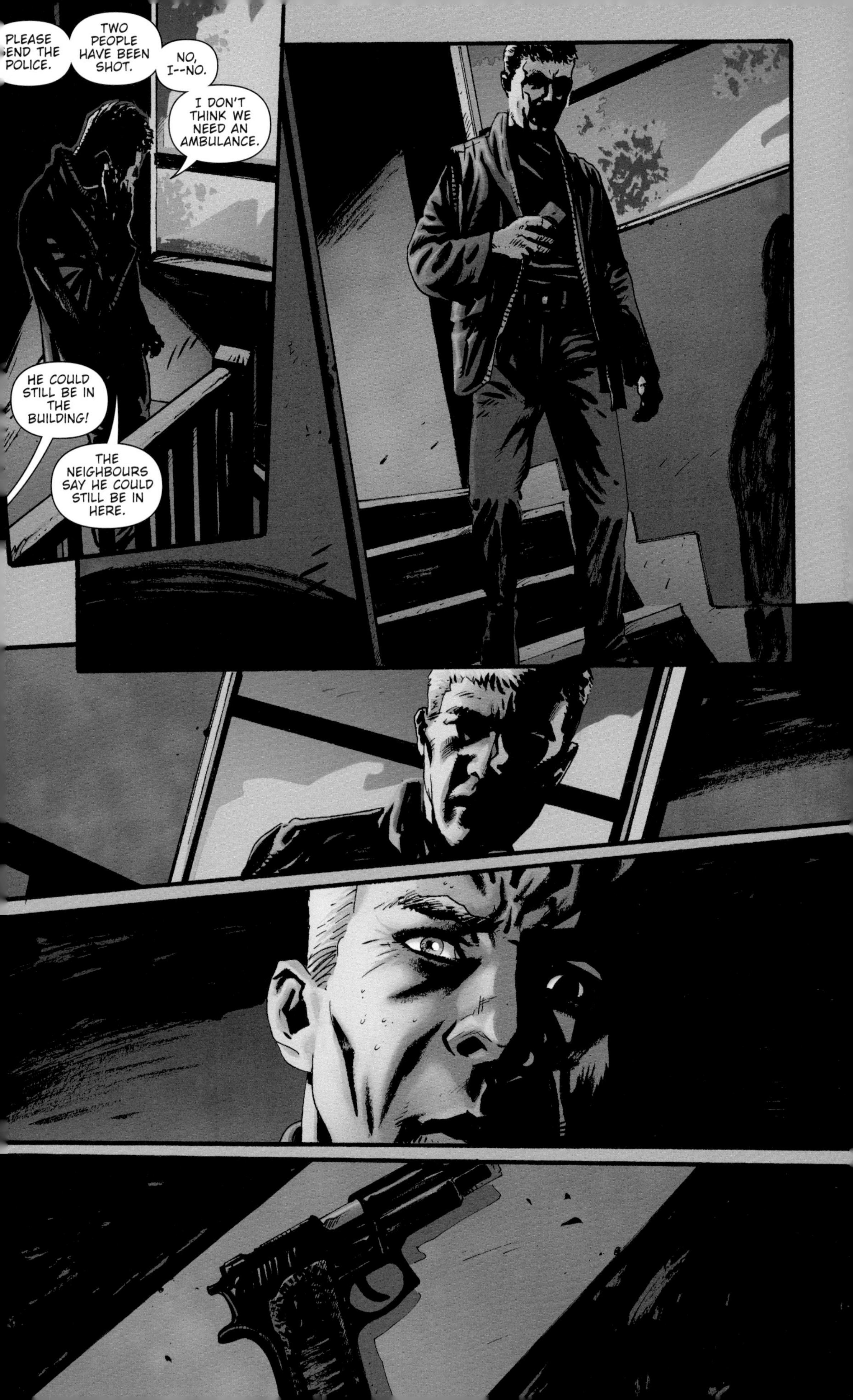
PLEASE SEND THE POLICE.
TWO PEOPLE HAVE BEEN SHOT.
NO, I--NO.
I DON'T THINK WE NEED AN AMBULANCE.
HE COULD STILL BE IN THE BUILDING!
THE NEIGHBOURS SAY HE COULD STILL BE IN HERE.

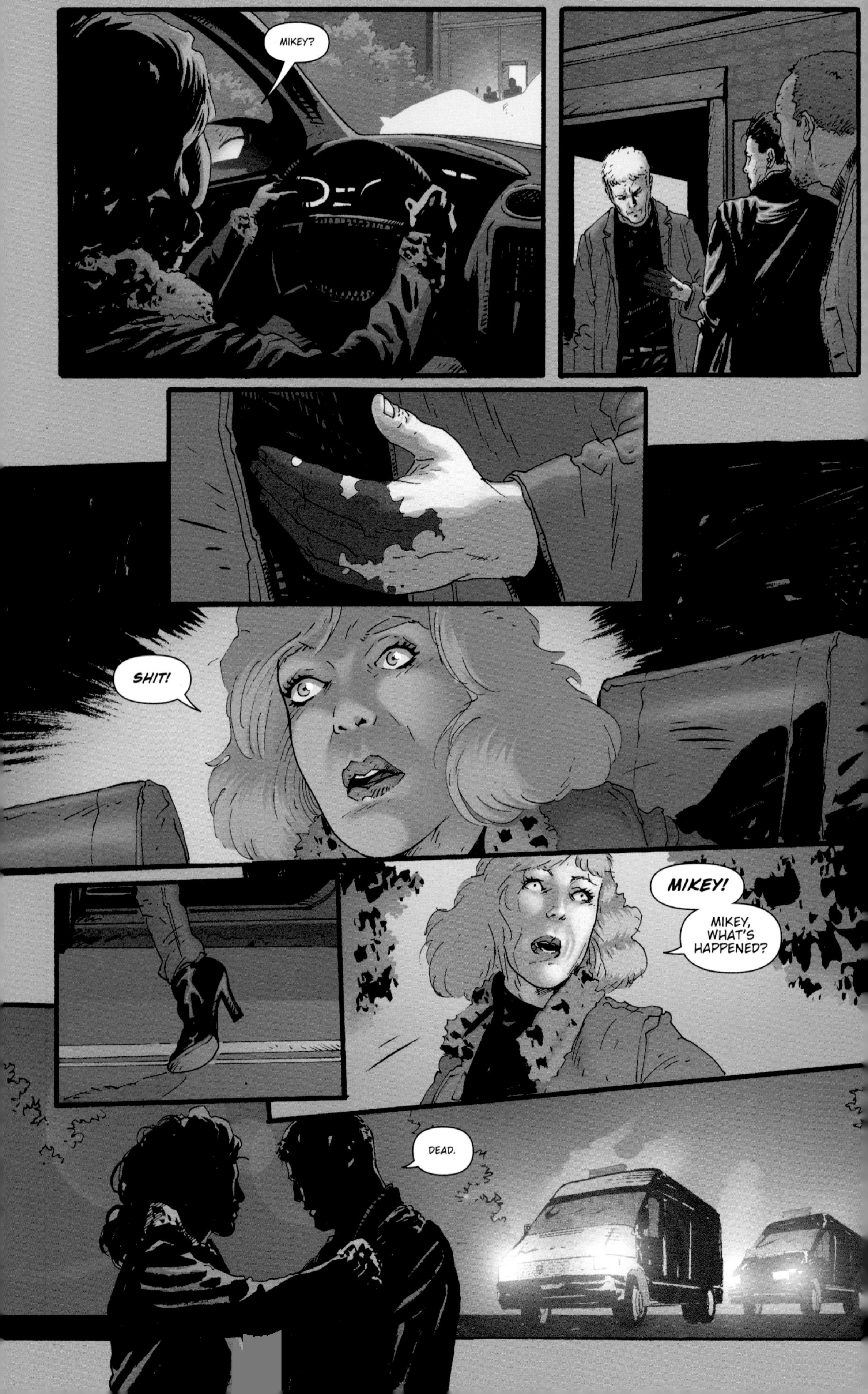
MIKEY?
SHIT!
MIKEY!
MIKEY, WHAT'S HAPPENED?
DEAD.

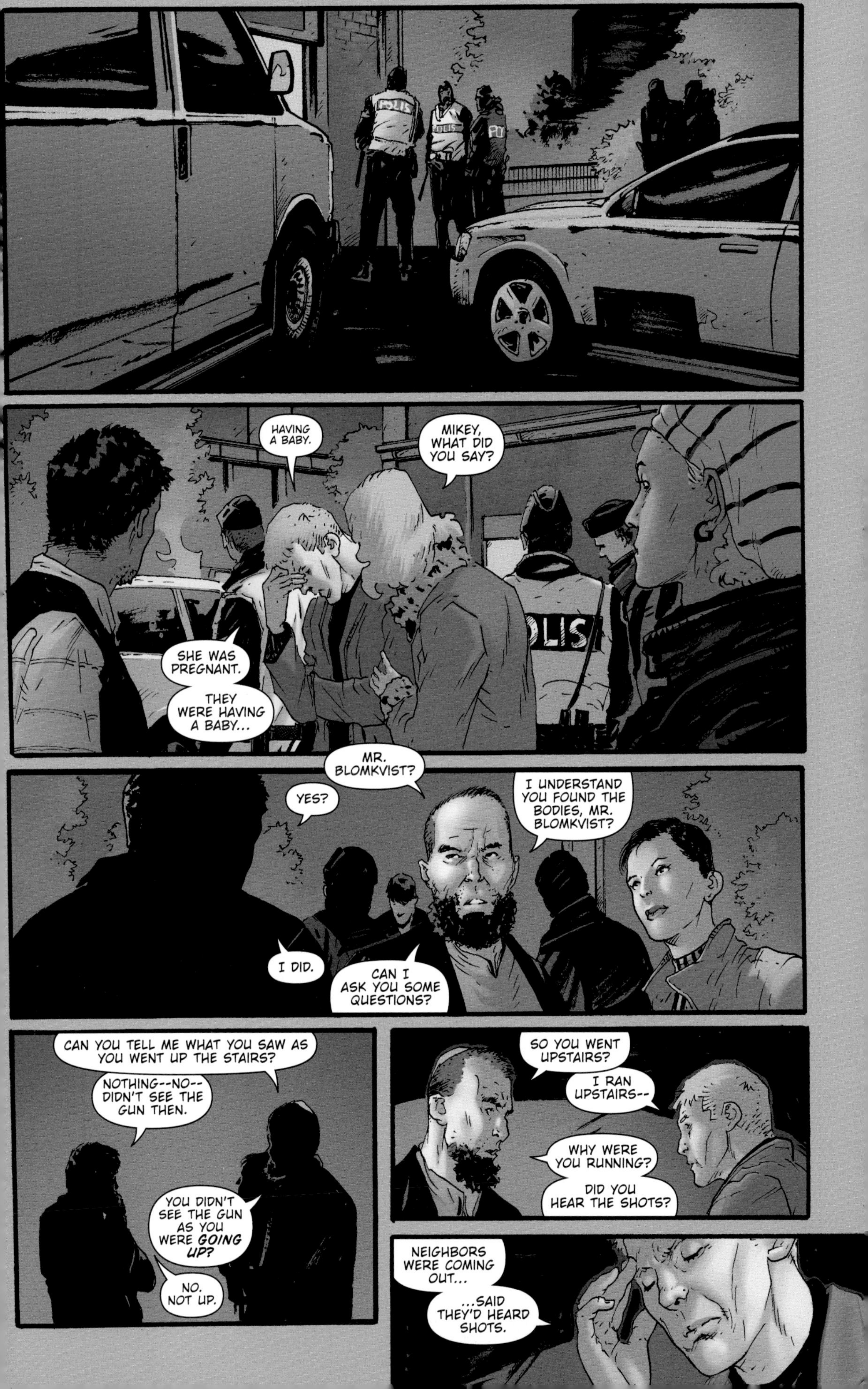
POLIS
POLIS
HAVING A BABY.
MIKEY, WHAT DID YOU SAY?
SHE WAS PREGNANT.
THEY WERE HAVING A BABY...
POLIS
MR. BLOMKVIST?
YES?
I UNDERSTAND YOU FOUND THE BODIES, MR. BLOMKVIST?
I DID.
CAN I ASK YOU SOME QUESTIONS?
CAN YOU TELL ME WHAT YOU SAW AS YOU WENT UP THE STAIRS?
NOTHING--NO--DIDN'T SEE THE GUN THEN.
YOU DIDN'T SEE THE GUN AS YOU WERE *GOING UP?*
NO. NOT UP.
SO YOU WENT UPSTAIRS?
I RAN UPSTAIRS--
WHY WERE YOU RUNNING?
DID YOU HEAR THE SHOTS?
NEIGHBORS WERE COMING OUT...
...SAID THEY'D HEARD SHOTS.

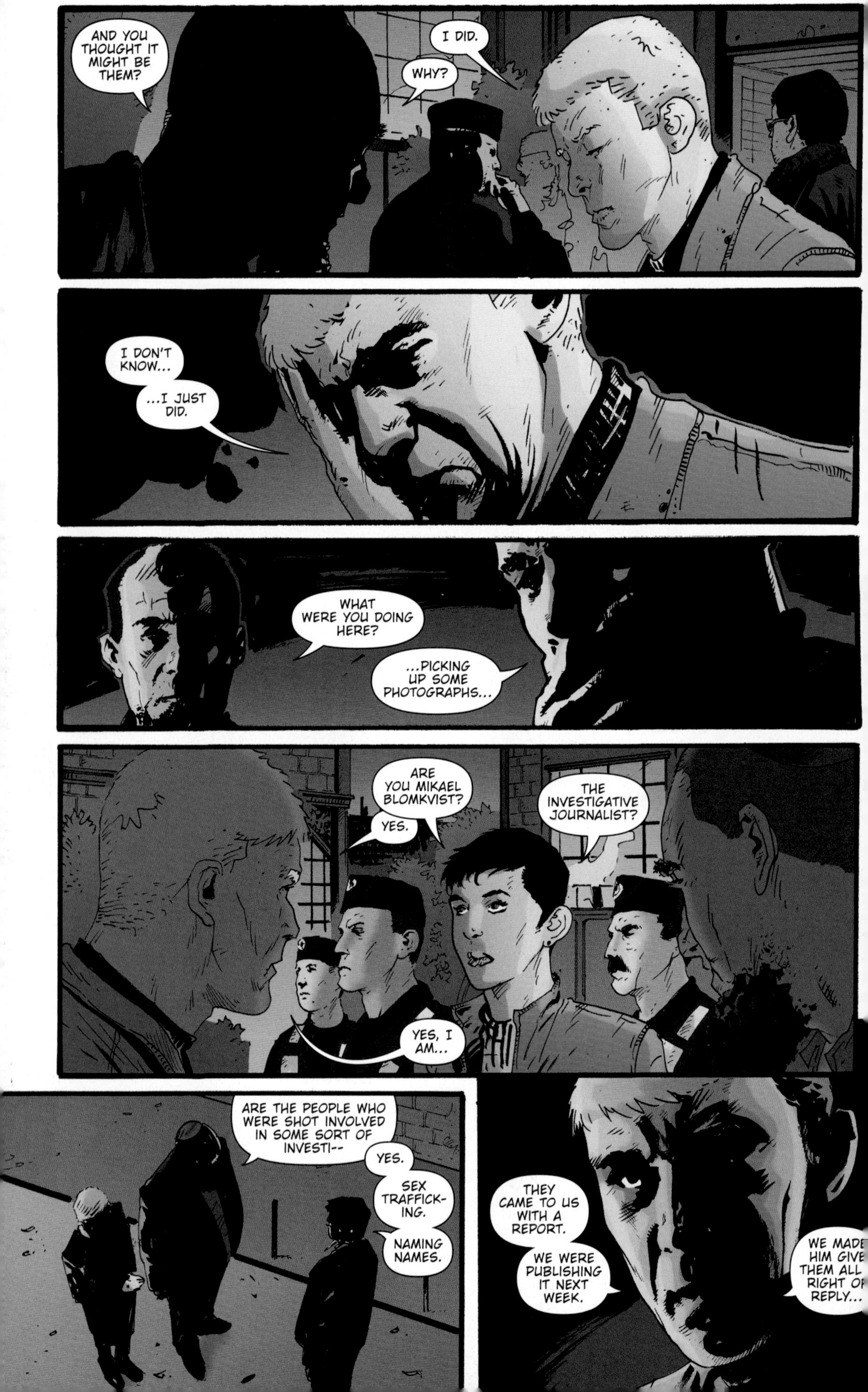
AND YOU THOUGHT IT MIGHT BE THEM?
I DID.
WHY?
I DON'T KNOW...
...I JUST DID.
WHAT WERE YOU DOING HERE?
...PICKING UP SOME PHOTOGRAPHS...
ARE YOU MIKAEL BLOMKVIST?
YES.
THE INVESTIGATIVE JOURNALIST?
YES, I AM...
ARE THE PEOPLE WHO WERE SHOT INVOLVED IN SOME SORT OF INVESTI--
YES.
SEX TRAFFICK-ING.
NAMING NAMES.
THEY CAME TO US WITH A REPORT.
WE WERE PUBLISHING IT NEXT WEEK.
WE MADE HIM GIVE THEM ALL RIGHT OF REPLY...

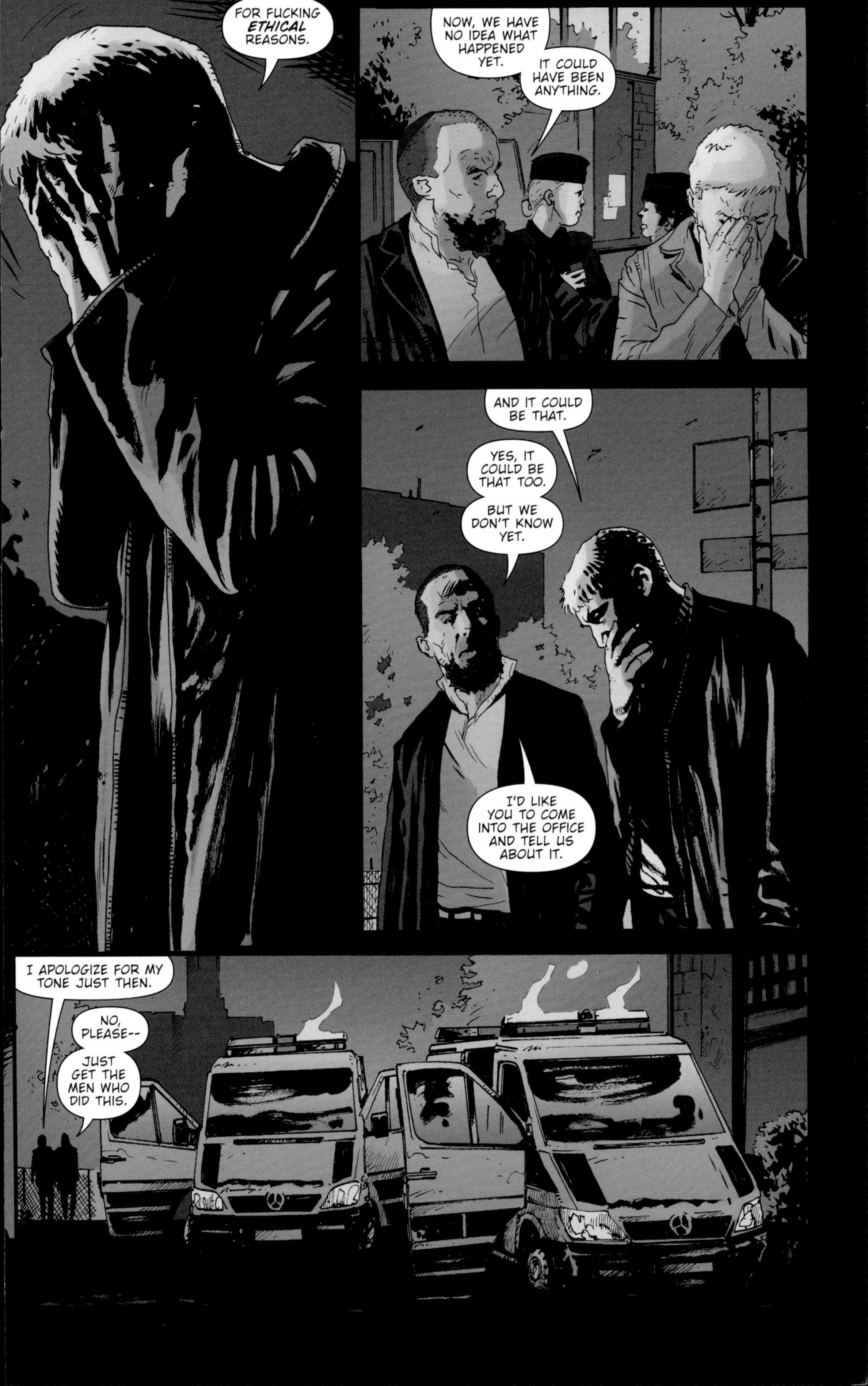
FOR FUCKING ETHICAL REASONS.
NOW, WE HAVE NO IDEA WHAT HAPPENED YET.
IT COULD HAVE BEEN ANYTHING.
AND IT COULD BE THAT.
YES, IT COULD BE THAT TOO.
BUT WE DON'T KNOW YET.
I'D LIKE YOU TO COME INTO THE OFFICE AND TELL US ABOUT IT.
I APOLOGIZE FOR MY TONE JUST THEN.
NO, PLEASE--
JUST GET THE MEN WHO DID THIS.

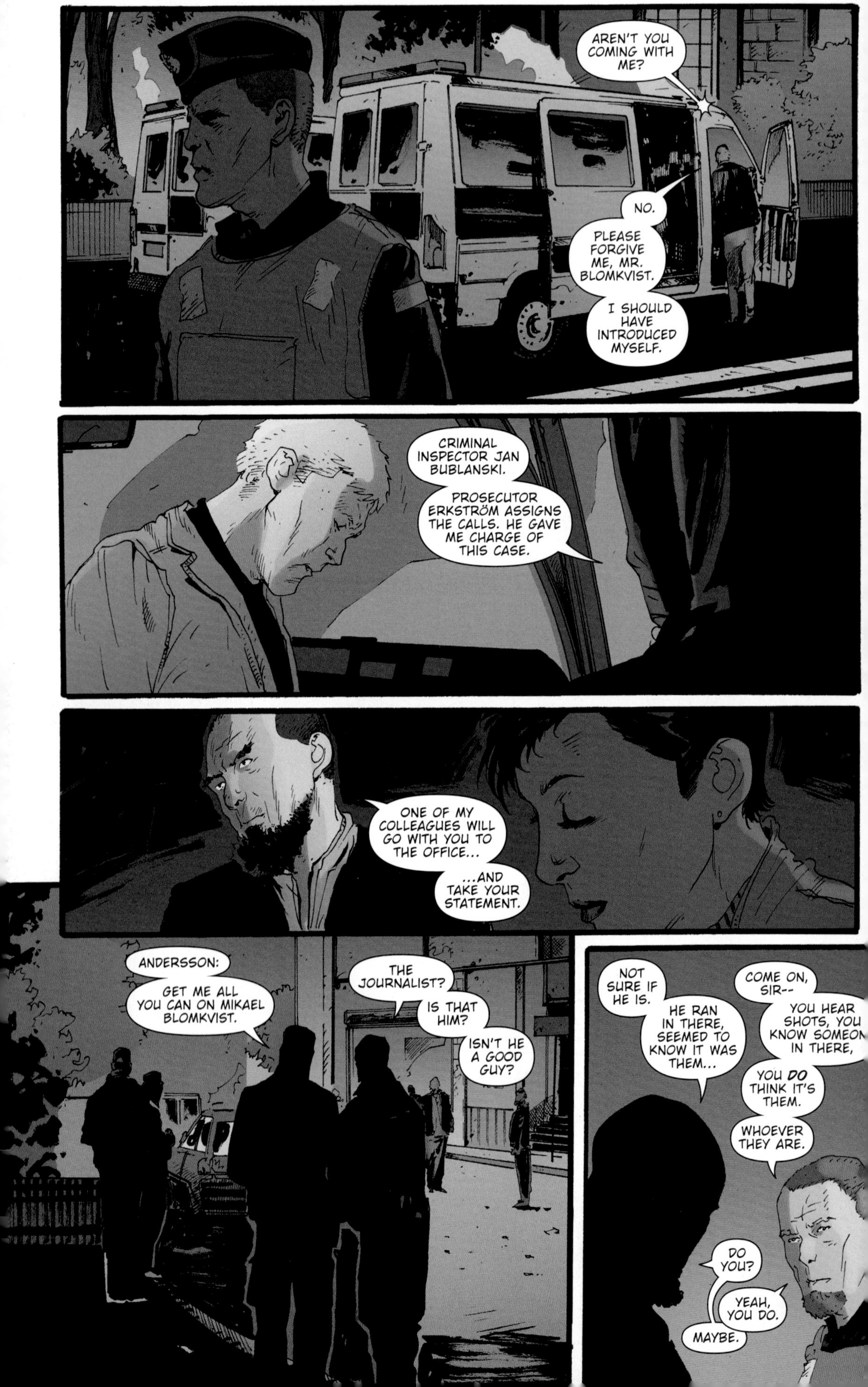
AREN'T YOU COMING WITH ME?
NO.
PLEASE FORGIVE ME, MR. BLOMKVIST.
I SHOULD HAVE INTRODUCED MYSELF.
CRIMINAL INSPECTOR JAN BUBLANSKI.
PROSECUTOR ERKSTRÖM ASSIGNS THE CALLS. HE GAVE ME CHARGE OF THIS CASE.
ONE OF MY COLLEAGUES WILL GO WITH YOU TO THE OFFICE...
...AND TAKE YOUR STATEMENT.
ANDERSSON:
GET ME ALL YOU CAN ON MIKAEL BLOMKVIST.
THE JOURNALIST?
IS THAT HIM?
ISN'T HE A GOOD GUY?
NOT SURE IF HE IS.
HE RAN IN THERE, SEEMED TO KNOW IT WAS THEM...
COME ON, SIR--
YOU HEAR SHOTS, YOU KNOW SOMEON IN THERE,
YOU DO THINK IT'S THEM.
WHOEVER THEY ARE.
DO YOU?
YEAH, YOU DO.
MAYBE.

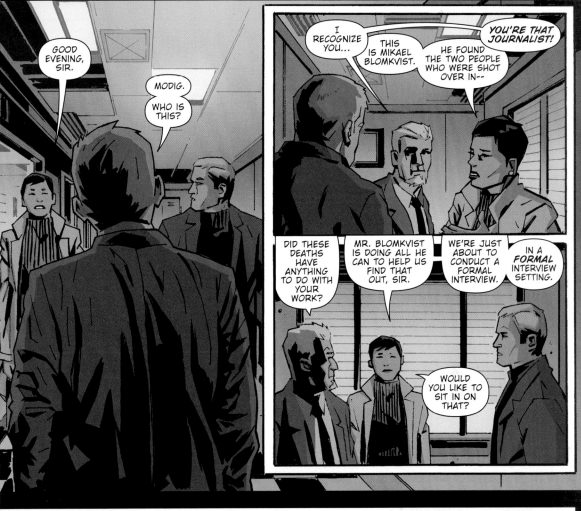

GOOD EVENING, SIR.

MODIG. WHO IS THIS?

I RECOGNIZE YOU...

THIS IS MIKAEL BLOMKVIST.

HE FOUND THE TWO PEOPLE WHO WERE SHOT OVER IN--

YOU'RE THAT JOURNALIST!

DID THESE DEATHS HAVE ANYTHING TO DO WITH YOUR WORK?

MR. BLOMKVIST IS DOING ALL HE CAN TO HELP US FIND THAT OUT, SIR.

WE'RE JUST ABOUT TO CONDUCT A FORMAL INTERVIEW.

IN A FORMAL INTERVIEW SETTING.

WOULD YOU LIKE TO SIT IN ON THAT?

NO, I HAVE TOO MUCH TO DO.

I'LL GET THE TRANSCRIPTS ANYWAY.

MR. BLOMKVIST, I AM PROSECUTOR RICHARD EKSTRÖM.

I AM IN OVERALL CHARGE OF THIS CASE.

IF I CAN BE OF ANY ASSISTANCE...

...OR YOU HAVE ANY INFORMATION TO SHARE WITH US LATER.

PLEASE FEEL FREE TO CONTACT ME DIRECTLY.

I HAVE THE GREATEST RESPECT FOR THE PRESS.

HE'S AMBITIOUS, ISN'T HE?

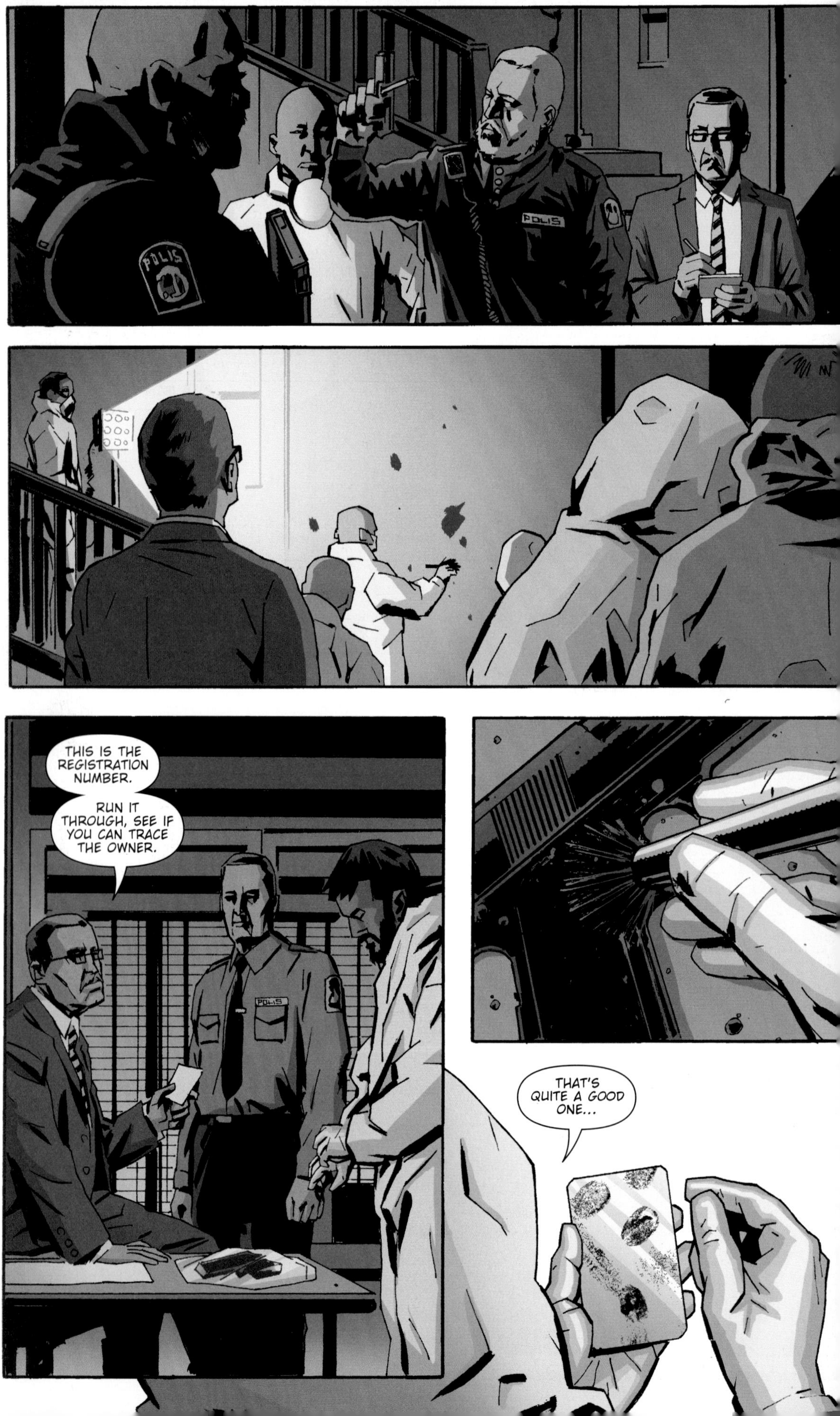

POLIS
POLIS
THIS IS THE REGISTRATION NUMBER.
RUN IT THROUGH, SEE IF YOU CAN TRACE THE OWNER.
POLIS
THAT'S QUITE A GOOD ONE...

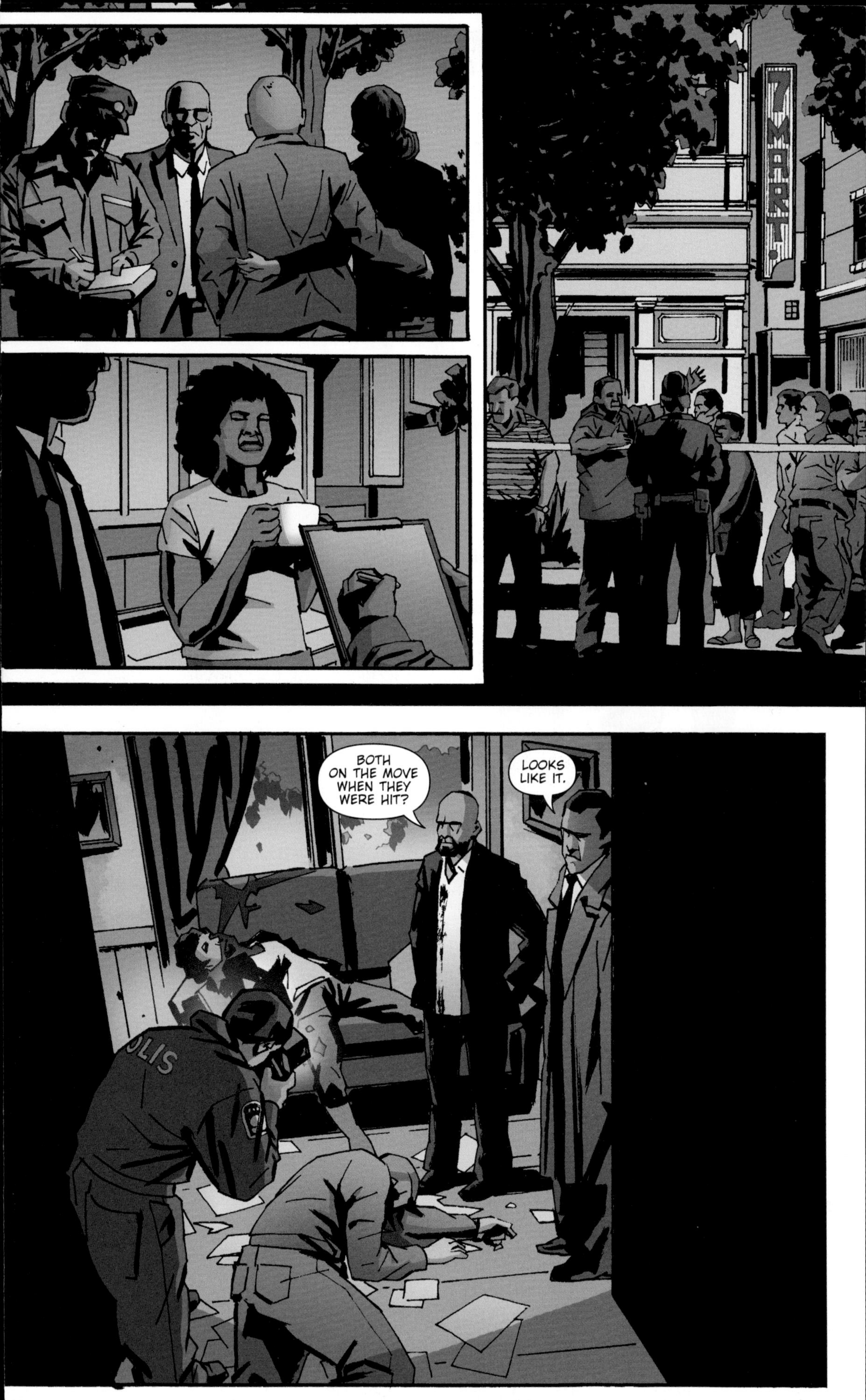
7 MART
BOTH ON THE MOVE WHEN THEY WERE HIT?
LOOKS LIKE IT.
POLIS

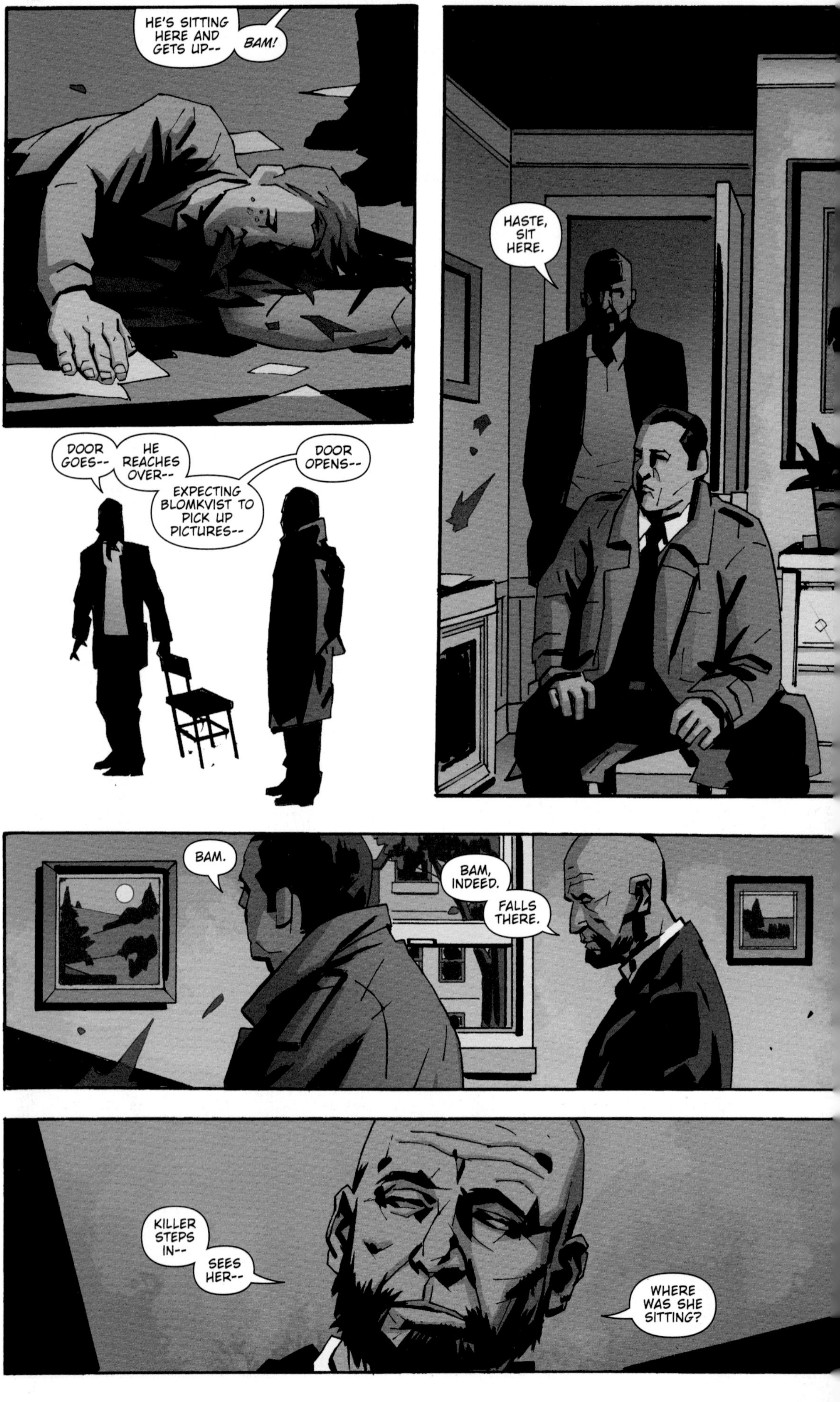

HE'S SITTING HERE AND GETS UP--
BAM!
DOOR GOES--
HE REACHES OVER--
EXPECTING BLOMKVIST TO PICK UP PICTURES--
DOOR OPENS--
HASTE, SIT HERE.
BAM.
BAM, INDEED.
FALLS THERE.
KILLER STEPS IN--
SEES HER--
WHERE WAS SHE SITTING?

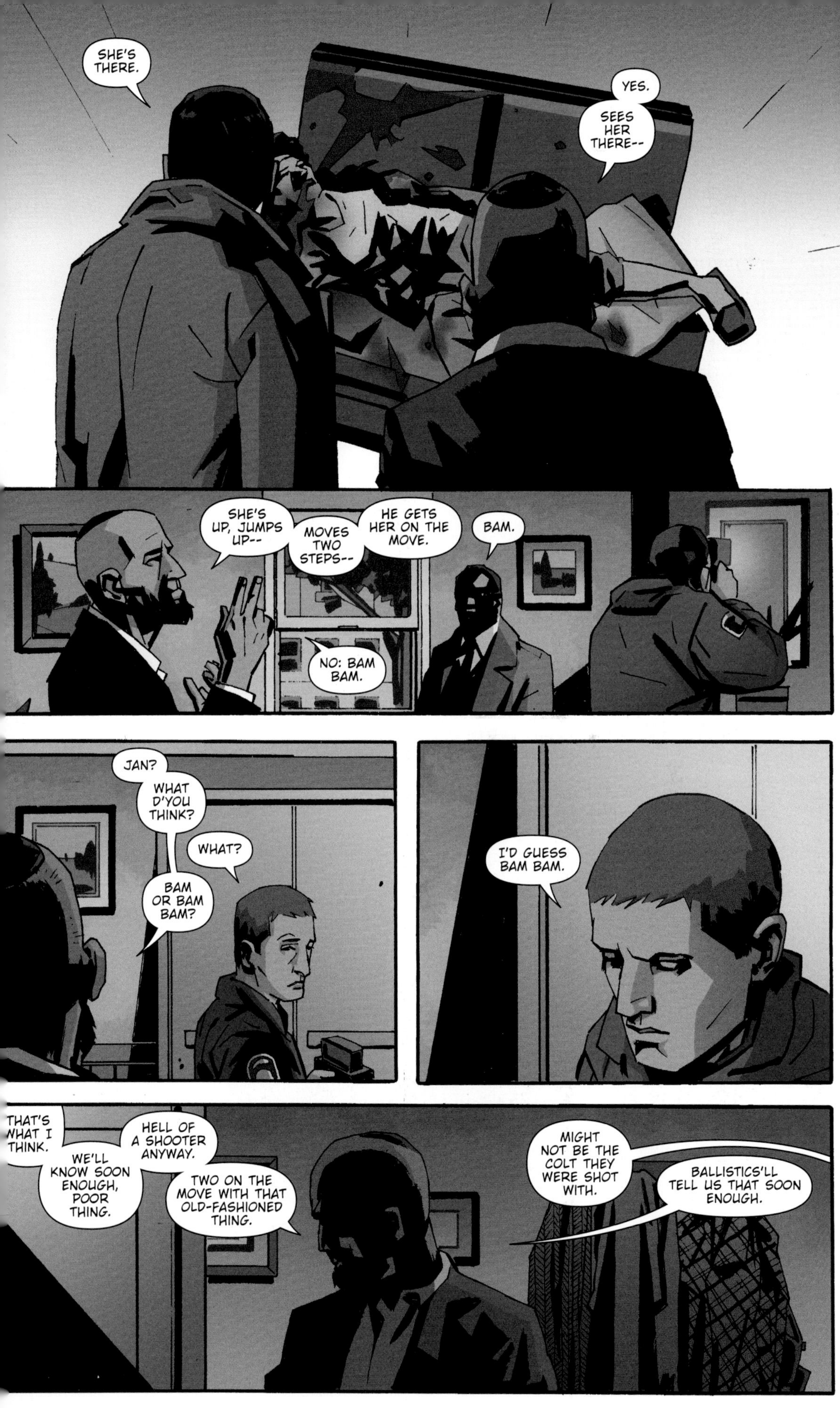
SHE'S THERE.
YES.
SEES HER THERE--
SHE'S UP, JUMPS UP--
MOVES TWO STEPS--
HE GETS HER ON THE MOVE.
BAM.
NO: BAM BAM.
JAN?
WHAT D'YOU THINK?
WHAT?
BAM OR BAM BAM?
I'D GUESS BAM BAM.
THAT'S WHAT I THINK.
HELL OF A SHOOTER ANYWAY.
WE'LL KNOW SOON ENOUGH, POOR THING.
TWO ON THE MOVE WITH THAT OLD-FASHIONED THING.
MIGHT NOT BE THE COLT THEY WERE SHOT WITH.
BALLISTICS'LL TELL US THAT SOON ENOUGH.

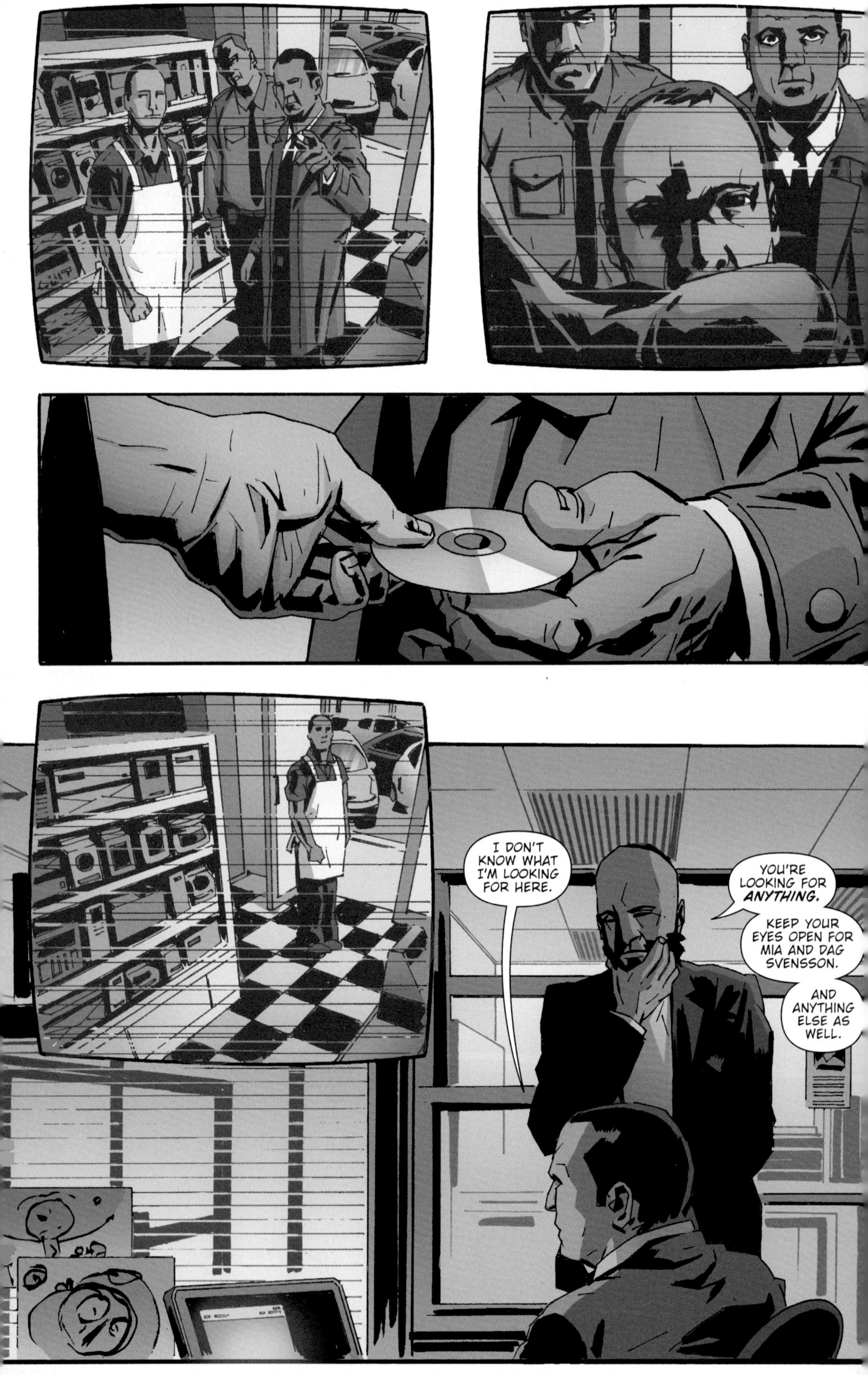

I DON'T KNOW WHAT I'M LOOKING FOR HERE.
YOU'RE LOOKING FOR *ANYTHING.*
KEEP YOUR EYES OPEN FOR MIA AND DAG SVENSSON.
AND ANYTHING ELSE AS WELL.

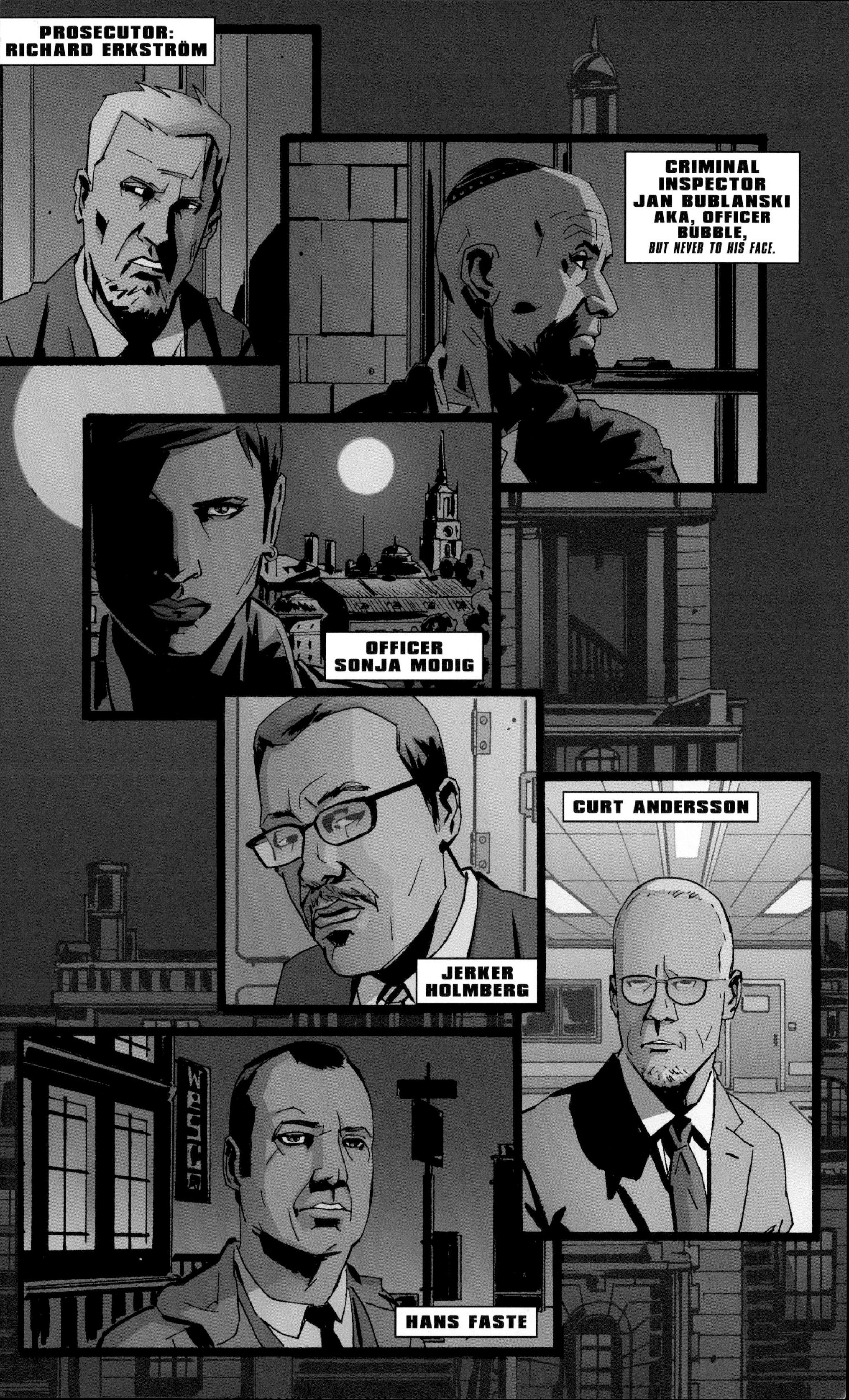
PROSECUTOR: RICHARD ERKSTRÖM
CRIMINAL INSPECTOR JAN BUBLANSKI AKA, OFFICER BUBBLE, BUT NEVER TO HIS FACE.
OFFICER SONJA MODIG
JERKER HOLMBERG
CURT ANDERSSON
HANS FASTE

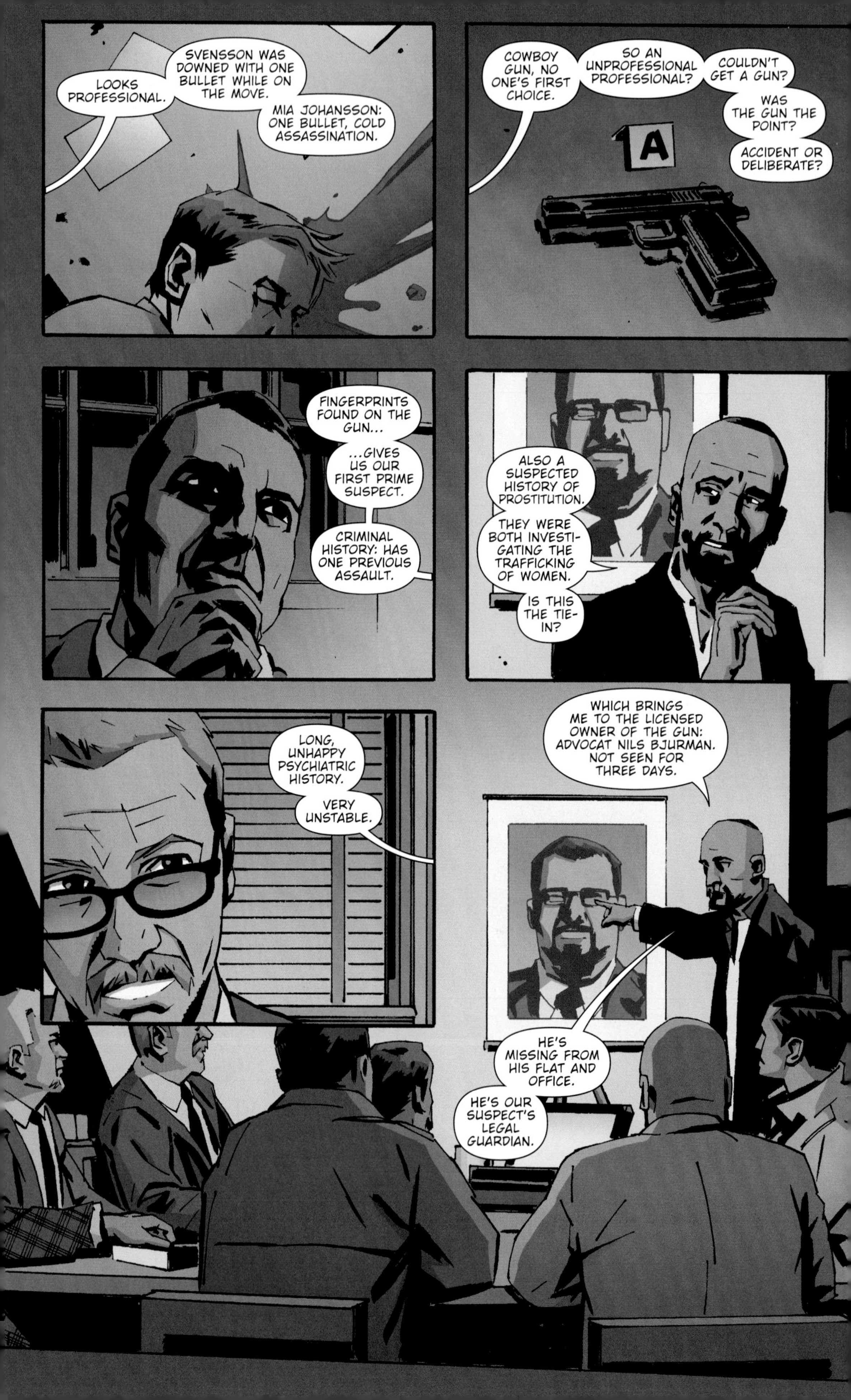
LOOKS PROFESSIONAL.
SVENSSON WAS DOWNED WITH ONE BULLET WHILE ON THE MOVE.
MIA JOHANSSON: ONE BULLET, COLD ASSASSINATION.
COWBOY GUN, NO ONE'S FIRST CHOICE.
SO AN UNPROFESSIONAL PROFESSIONAL?
COULDN'T GET A GUN?
WAS THE GUN THE POINT?
ACCIDENT OR DELIBERATE?
A
FINGERPRINTS FOUND ON THE GUN...
...GIVES US OUR FIRST PRIME SUSPECT.
CRIMINAL HISTORY: HAS ONE PREVIOUS ASSAULT.
ALSO A SUSPECTED HISTORY OF PROSTITUTION.
THEY WERE BOTH INVESTI-GATING THE TRAFFICKING OF WOMEN.
IS THIS THE TIE-IN?
LONG, UNHAPPY PSYCHIATRIC HISTORY.
VERY UNSTABLE.
WHICH BRINGS ME TO THE LICENSED OWNER OF THE GUN: ADVOCAT NILS BJURMAN. NOT SEEN FOR THREE DAYS.
HE'S MISSING FROM HIS FLAT AND OFFICE.
HE'S OUR SUSPECT'S LEGAL GUARDIAN.

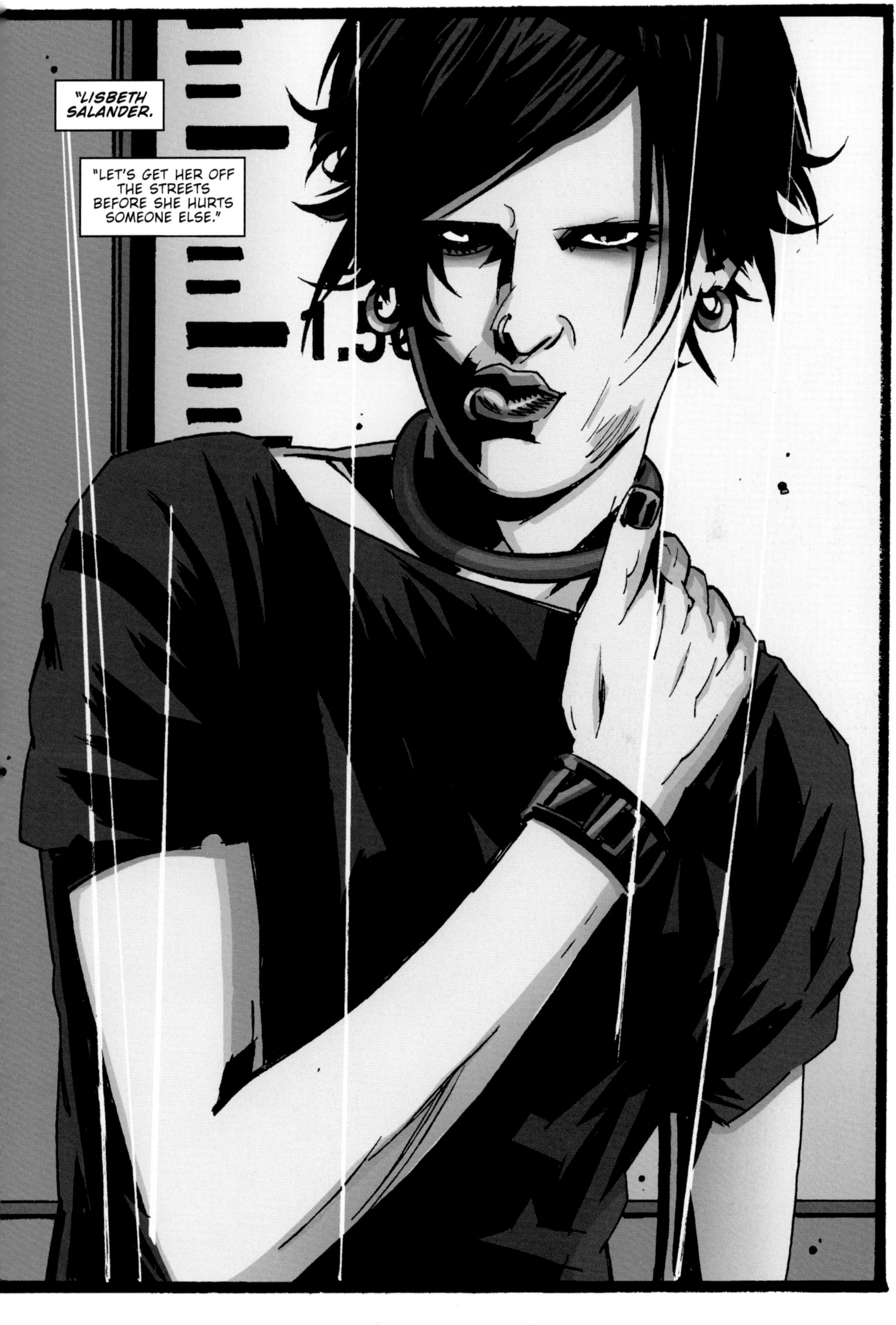
"LISBETH SALANDER.
"LET'S GET HER OFF THE STREETS BEFORE SHE HURTS SOMEONE ELSE."

–SALANDER L.–

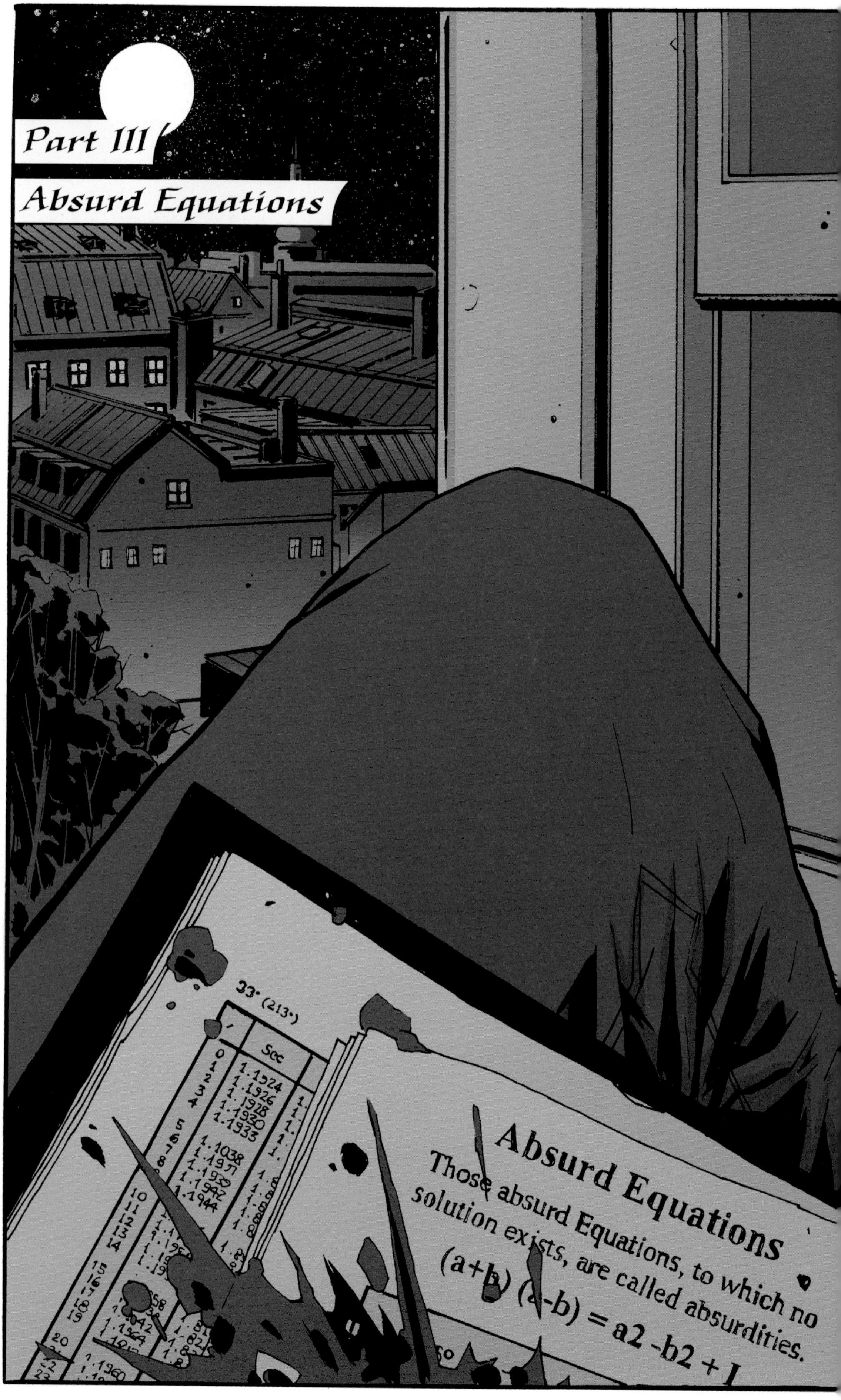
Part III
Absurd Equations
33° (213°)
Sec
Absurd Equations
Those absurd Equations, to which no solution exists, are called absurdities.
(a+b) (a-b) = a2 -b2 + 1

...FUCK...
...STUPID...
Abs
Those absurd
solution exists
(a+b) (a-
36°(216')
Sec
Auto-Expert car hire,
Eskilstuna office_
33°(213')
Sec
0 1.924 1.803
1 1.926

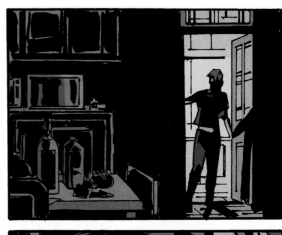

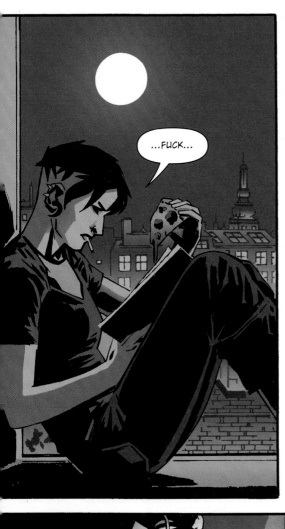

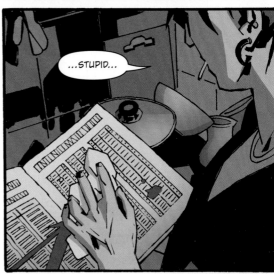

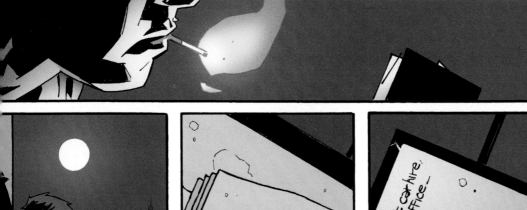

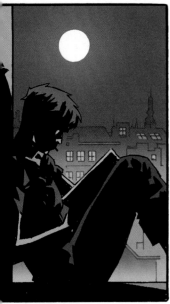

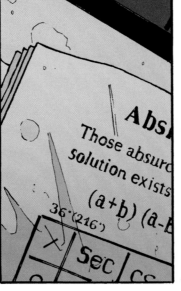

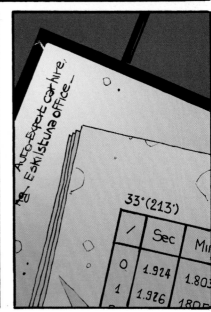

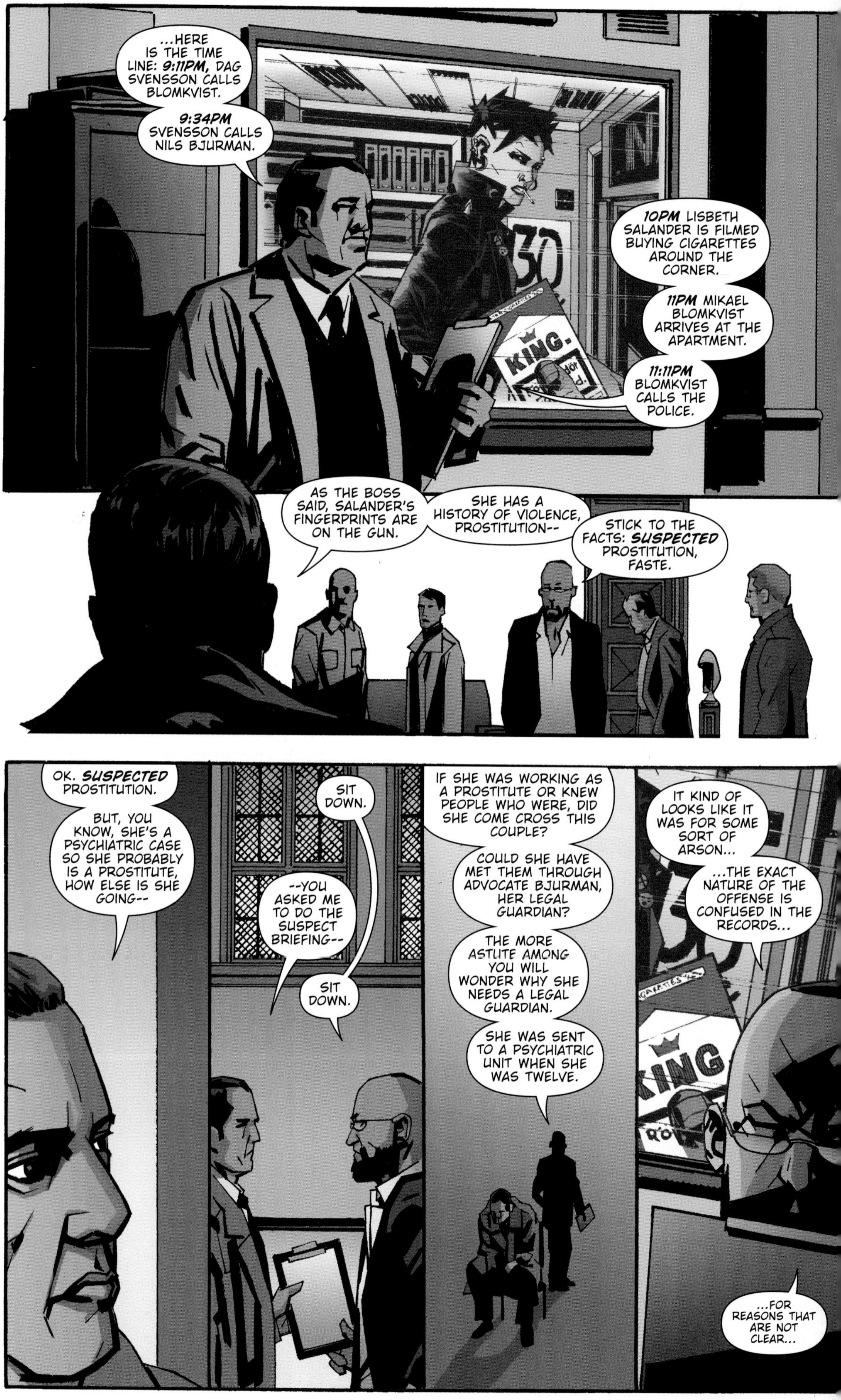
...HERE IS THE TIME LINE: 9:11PM, DAG SVENSSON CALLS BLOMKVIST.
9:34PM SVENSSON CALLS NILS BJURMAN.
10PM LISBETH SALANDER IS FILMED BUYING CIGARETTES AROUND THE CORNER.
11PM MIKAEL BLOMKVIST ARRIVES AT THE APARTMENT.
11:11PM BLOMKVIST CALLS THE POLICE.
KING.
30
AS THE BOSS SAID, SALANDER'S FINGERPRINTS ARE ON THE GUN.
SHE HAS A HISTORY OF VIOLENCE, PROSTITUTION--
STICK TO THE FACTS: SUSPECTED PROSTITUTION, FASTE.
OK. SUSPECTED PROSTITUTION.
BUT, YOU KNOW, SHE'S A PSYCHIATRIC CASE SO SHE PROBABLY IS A PROSTITUTE, HOW ELSE IS SHE GOING--
SIT DOWN.
--YOU ASKED ME TO DO THE SUSPECT BRIEFING--
SIT DOWN.
IF SHE WAS WORKING AS A PROSTITUTE OR KNEW PEOPLE WHO WERE, DID SHE COME CROSS THIS COUPLE?
COULD SHE HAVE MET THEM THROUGH ADVOCATE BJURMAN, HER LEGAL GUARDIAN?
THE MORE ASTUTE AMONG YOU WILL WONDER WHY SHE NEEDS A LEGAL GUARDIAN.
SHE WAS SENT TO A PSYCHIATRIC UNIT WHEN SHE WAS TWELVE.
IT KIND OF LOOKS LIKE IT WAS FOR SOME SORT OF ARSON...
...THE EXACT NATURE OF THE OFFENSE IS CONFUSED IN THE RECORDS...
KING
...FOR REASONS THAT ARE NOT CLEAR...

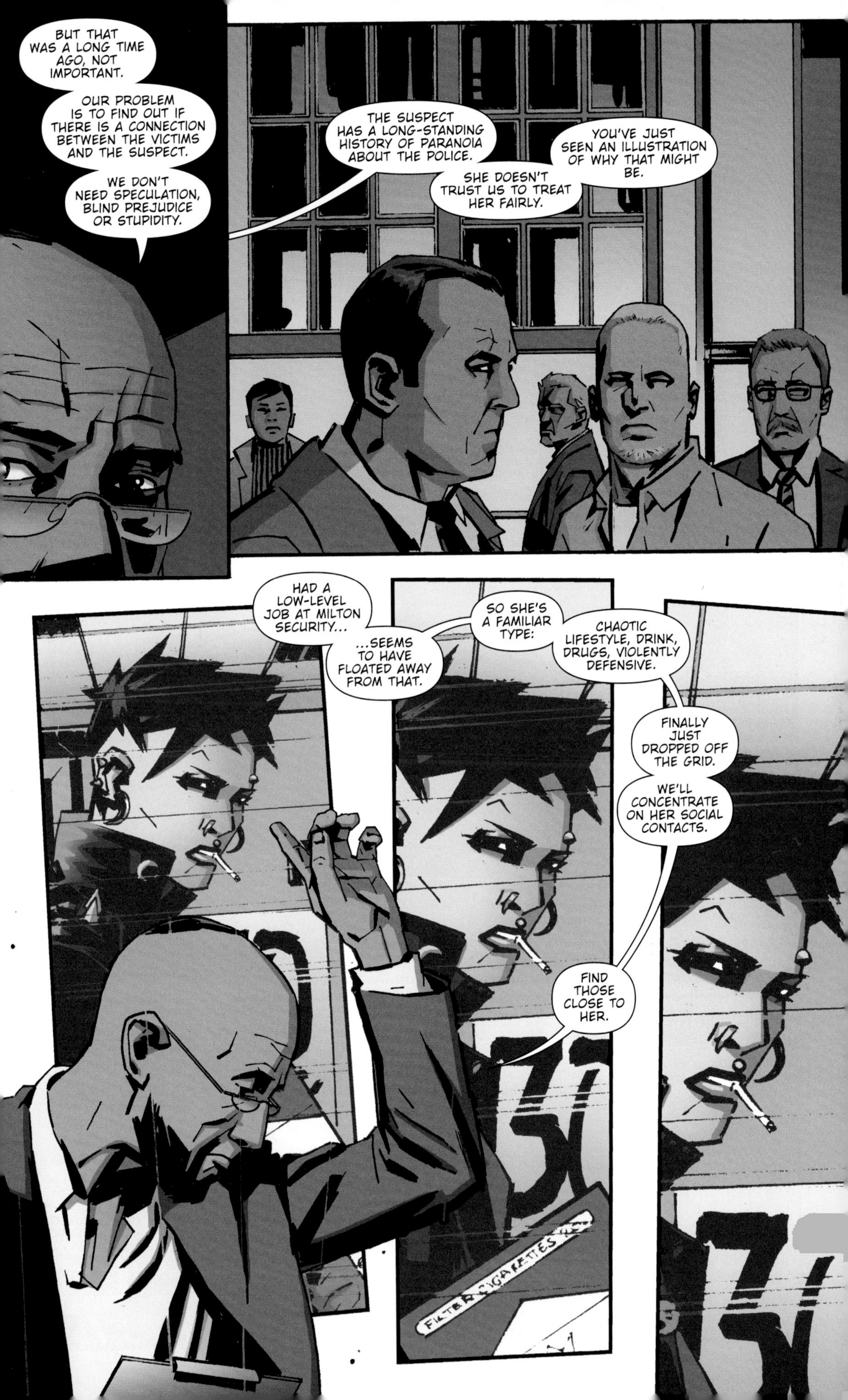
BUT THAT WAS A LONG TIME AGO, NOT IMPORTANT.
OUR PROBLEM IS TO FIND OUT IF THERE IS A CONNECTION BETWEEN THE VICTIMS AND THE SUSPECT.
WE DON'T NEED SPECULATION, BLIND PREJUDICE OR STUPIDITY.
THE SUSPECT HAS A LONG-STANDING HISTORY OF PARANOIA ABOUT THE POLICE.
SHE DOESN'T TRUST US TO TREAT HER FAIRLY.
YOU'VE JUST SEEN AN ILLUSTRATION OF WHY THAT MIGHT BE.
HAD A LOW-LEVEL JOB AT MILTON SECURITY...
...SEEMS TO HAVE FLOATED AWAY FROM THAT.
SO SHE'S A FAMILIAR TYPE:
CHAOTIC LIFESTYLE, DRINK, DRUGS, VIOLENTLY DEFENSIVE.
FINALLY JUST DROPPED OFF THE GRID.
WE'LL CONCENTRATE ON HER SOCIAL CONTACTS.
FIND THOSE CLOSE TO HER.

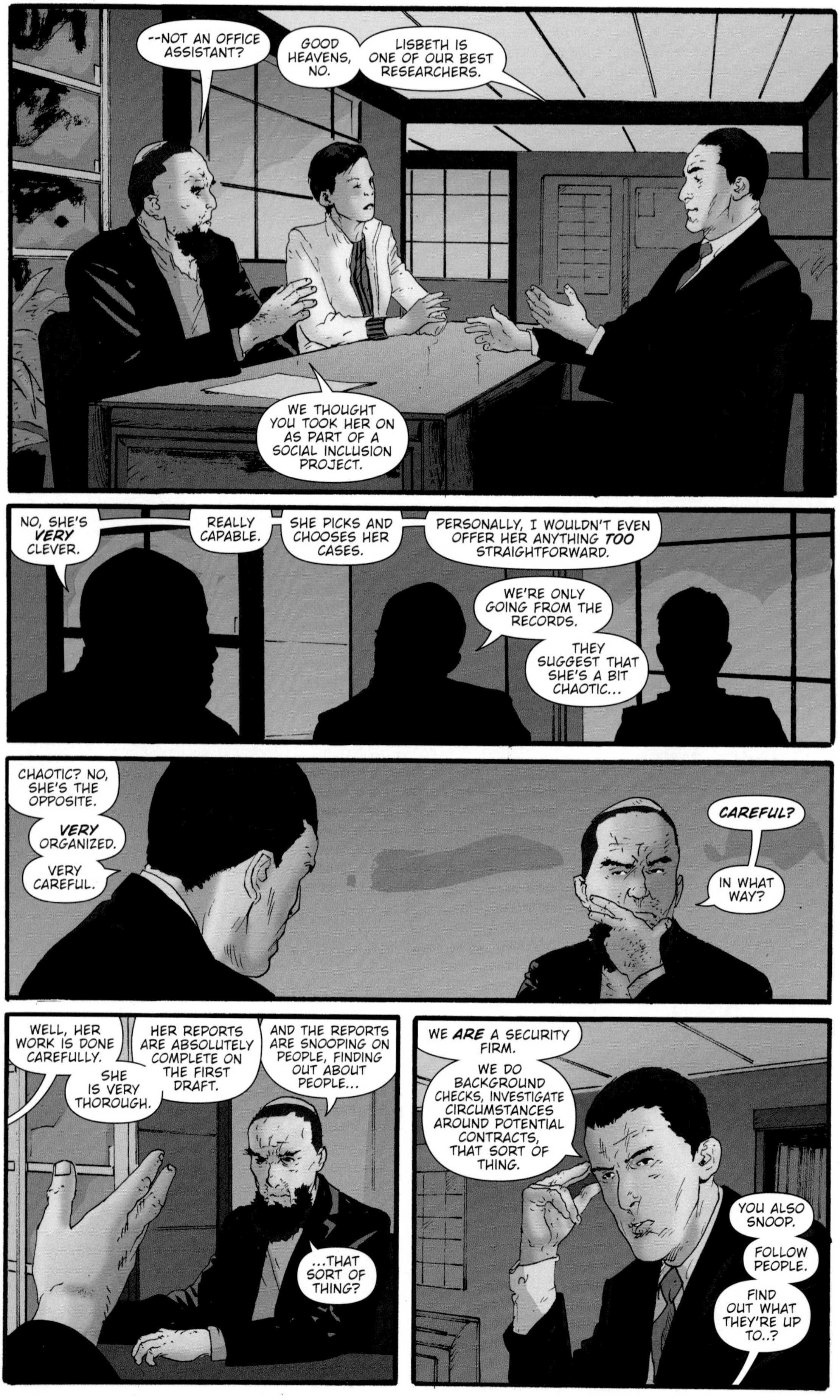
--NOT AN OFFICE ASSISTANT?
GOOD HEAVENS, NO.
LISBETH IS ONE OF OUR BEST RESEARCHERS.
WE THOUGHT YOU TOOK HER ON AS PART OF A SOCIAL INCLUSION PROJECT.
NO, SHE'S *VERY* CLEVER.
REALLY CAPABLE.
SHE PICKS AND CHOOSES HER CASES.
PERSONALLY, I WOULDN'T EVEN OFFER HER ANYTHING *TOO* STRAIGHTFORWARD.
WE'RE ONLY GOING FROM THE RECORDS.
THEY SUGGEST THAT SHE'S A BIT CHAOTIC...
CHAOTIC? NO, SHE'S THE OPPOSITE.
VERY ORGANIZED.
VERY CAREFUL.
CAREFUL?
IN WHAT WAY?
WELL, HER WORK IS DONE CAREFULLY.
SHE IS VERY THOROUGH.
HER REPORTS ARE ABSOLUTELY COMPLETE ON THE FIRST DRAFT.
AND THE REPORTS ARE SNOOPING ON PEOPLE, FINDING OUT ABOUT PEOPLE...
...THAT SORT OF THING?
WE *ARE* A SECURITY FIRM.
WE DO BACKGROUND CHECKS, INVESTIGATE CIRCUMSTANCES AROUND POTENTIAL CONTRACTS, THAT SORT OF THING.
YOU ALSO SNOOP.
FOLLOW PEOPLE.
FIND OUT WHAT THEY'RE UP TO..?

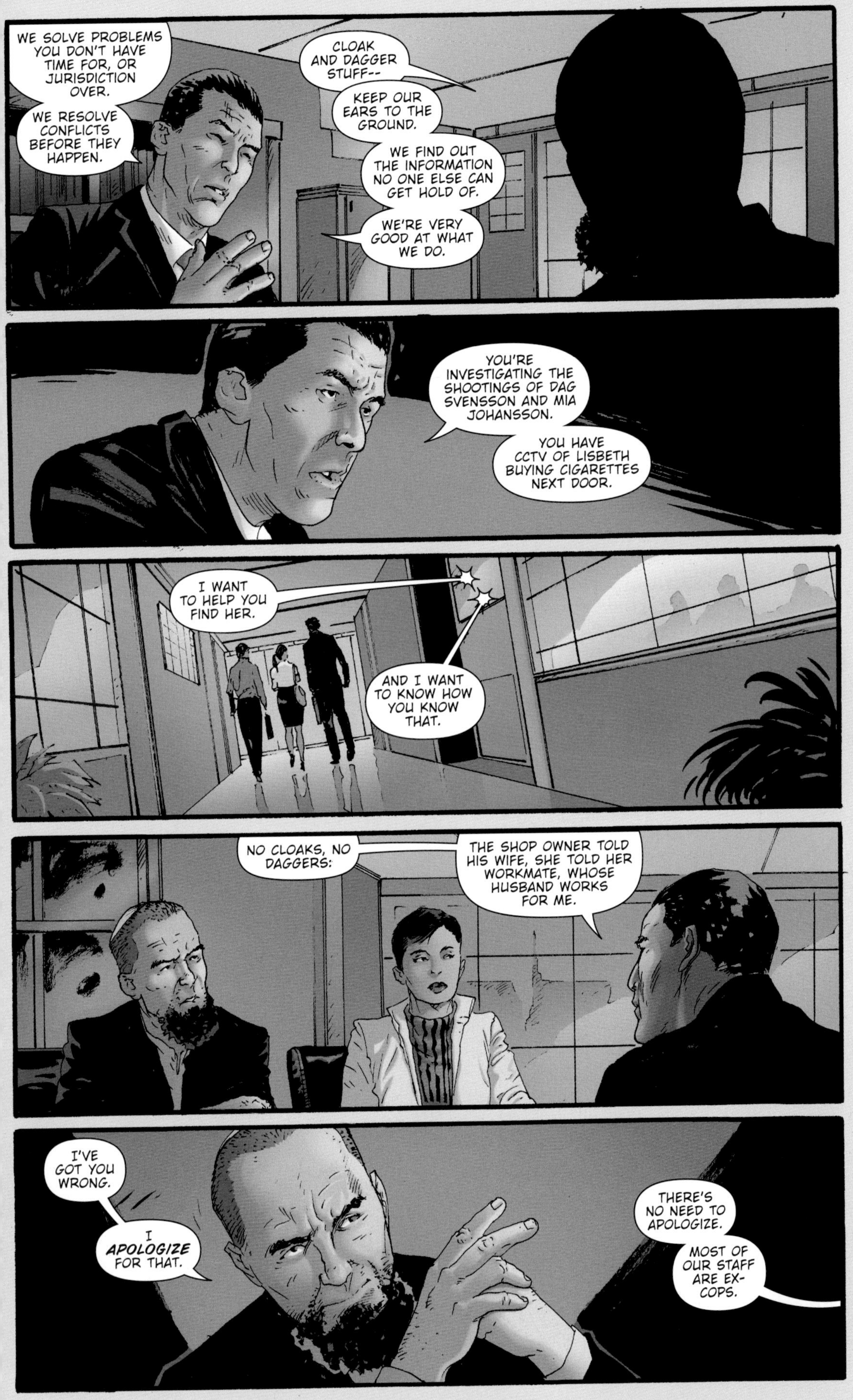
WE SOLVE PROBLEMS YOU DON'T HAVE TIME FOR, OR JURISDICTION OVER.
WE RESOLVE CONFLICTS BEFORE THEY HAPPEN.
CLOAK AND DAGGER STUFF--
KEEP OUR EARS TO THE GROUND.
WE FIND OUT THE INFORMATION NO ONE ELSE CAN GET HOLD OF.
WE'RE VERY GOOD AT WHAT WE DO.
YOU'RE INVESTIGATING THE SHOOTINGS OF DAG SVENSSON AND MIA JOHANSSON.
YOU HAVE CCTV OF LISBETH BUYING CIGARETTES NEXT DOOR.
I WANT TO HELP YOU FIND HER.
AND I WANT TO KNOW HOW YOU KNOW THAT.
NO CLOAKS, NO DAGGERS:
THE SHOP OWNER TOLD HIS WIFE, SHE TOLD HER WORKMATE, WHOSE HUSBAND WORKS FOR ME.
I'VE GOT YOU WRONG.
I *APOLOGIZE* FOR THAT.
THERE'S NO NEED TO APOLOGIZE.
MOST OF OUR STAFF ARE EX-COPS.

THE GUN BELONGED TO HER NEW LEGAL GUARDIAN, NILS BJURMAN.

SHE TALK ABOUT HIM?

NO.

BUT IF I WAS INVESTIGATING THIS I'D BE ASKING MYSELF WHY A LAWYER WOULD NEED A GUN.

DO YOU THINK SALANDER IS CAPABLE OF THIS?

I THINK *ANYONE* IS CAPABLE OF ANYTHING, BUT I'D BE SURPRISED:

SHE DOESN'T USE GUNS.

SHE'S MORE LIKELY TO CLOSE YOUR BANK ACCOUNTS.

SHE'S *SMART.*

FRIENDS? FAMILY?

I KNOW SHE GREW UP IN A GROUP HOME.

NO FOSTER PLACEMENTS OR ANYTHING.

SHE DOES HAVE A FAMILY.

SHE'S CREATED ONE FOR HERSELF:

HOLGER PALMGREN, HER EX-LEGAL GUARDIAN, HE'S LIKE HER *FATHER.*

HOW DID HE COME TO BE "EX"?

DID SHE ATTACK HIM?

PALMGREN HAD A STROKE. HAD TO RETIRE.

LISBETH PRETTY MUCH HAD A BREAKDOWN THEN, A GRIEF REACTION.

I'M HER ANNOYING, SENSIBLE OLDER BROTHER.

I GIVE HER SOUND ADVICE AND SHE IGNORES IT.

BUT SHE ALWAYS COMES BACK.

IT'S A VERY COMMON BEHAVIORAL TRAIT IN PEOPLE FROM CHAOTIC AN TRAUMATIZED BACKGROUNDS:

FIERCE LOYALTY, EVEN IN THE FACE OF EVIDENCE THAT IT'S UNDESERVED.

LISBETH *ALWAYS* COMES BACK.

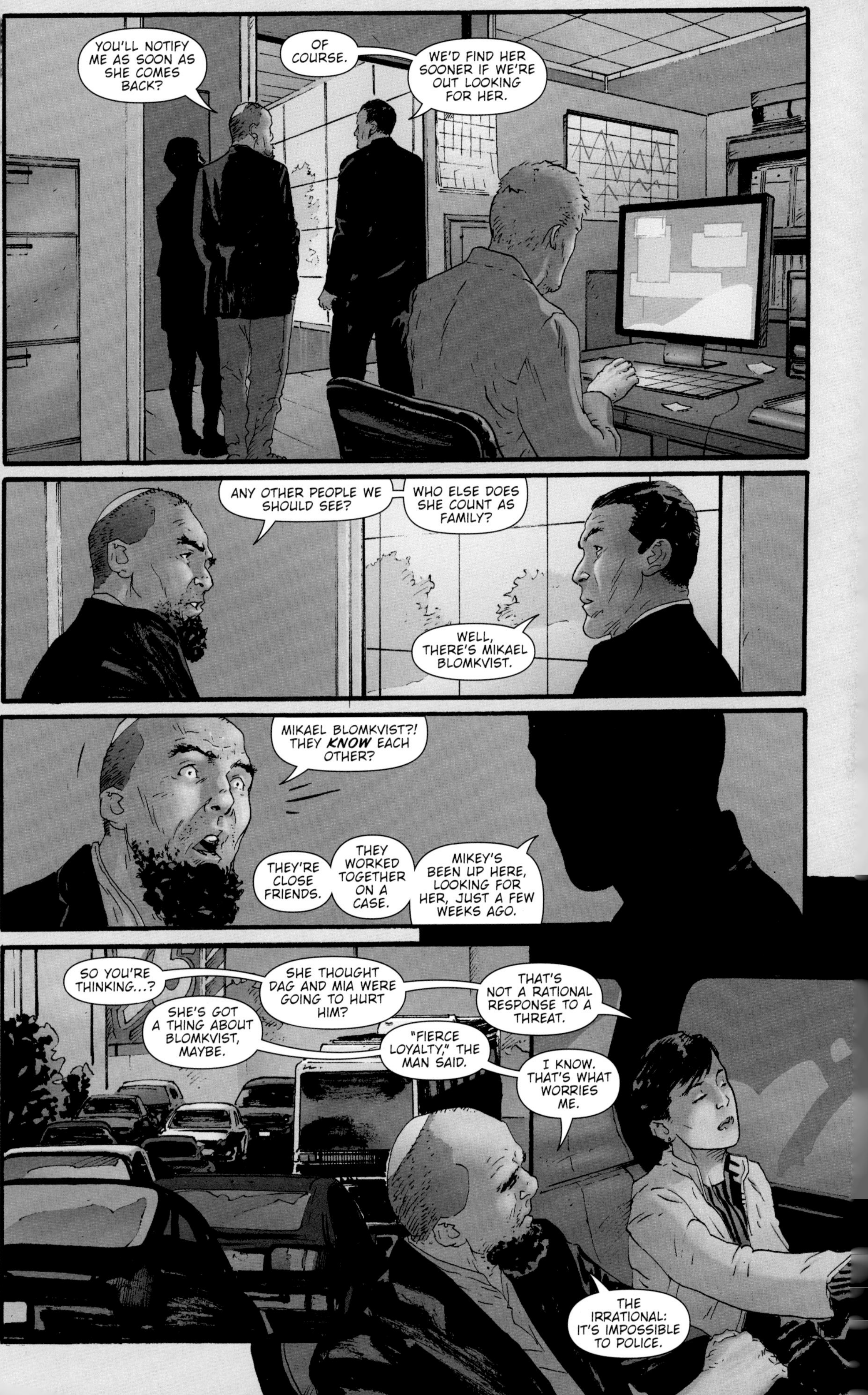
YOU'LL NOTIFY ME AS SOON AS SHE COMES BACK?
OF COURSE.
WE'D FIND HER SOONER IF WE'RE OUT LOOKING FOR HER.
ANY OTHER PEOPLE WE SHOULD SEE?
WHO ELSE DOES SHE COUNT AS FAMILY?
WELL, THERE'S MIKAEL BLOMKVIST.
MIKAEL BLOMKVIST?! THEY KNOW EACH OTHER?
THEY'RE CLOSE FRIENDS.
THEY WORKED TOGETHER ON A CASE.
MIKEY'S BEEN UP HERE, LOOKING FOR HER, JUST A FEW WEEKS AGO.
SO YOU'RE THINKING...?
SHE THOUGHT DAG AND MIA WERE GOING TO HURT HIM?
THAT'S NOT A RATIONAL RESPONSE TO A THREAT.
SHE'S GOT A THING ABOUT BLOMKVIST, MAYBE.
"FIERCE LOYALTY," THE MAN SAID.
I KNOW. THAT'S WHAT WORRIES ME.
THE IRRATIONAL: IT'S IMPOSSIBLE TO POLICE.

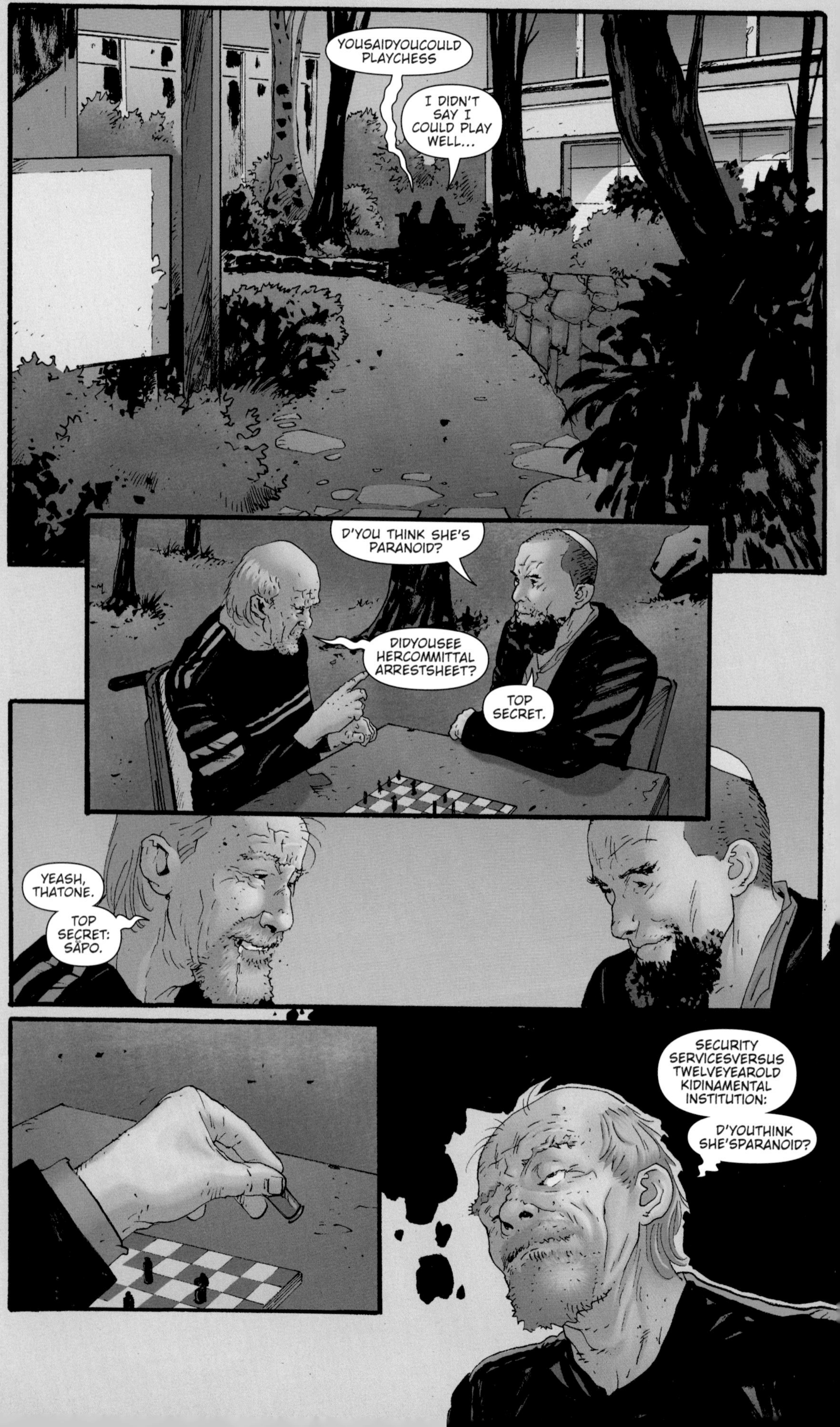
YOUSAIDYOUCOULD PLAYCHESS
I DIDN'T SAY I COULD PLAY WELL...
D'YOU THINK SHE'S PARANOID?
DIDYOUSEE HERCOMMITTAL ARRESTSHEET?
TOP SECRET.
YEASH, THATONE.
TOP SECRET: SÄPO.
SECURITY SERVICESVERSUS TWELVEYEAROLD KIDINAMENTAL INSTITUTION:
D'YOUTHINK SHE'SPARANOID?

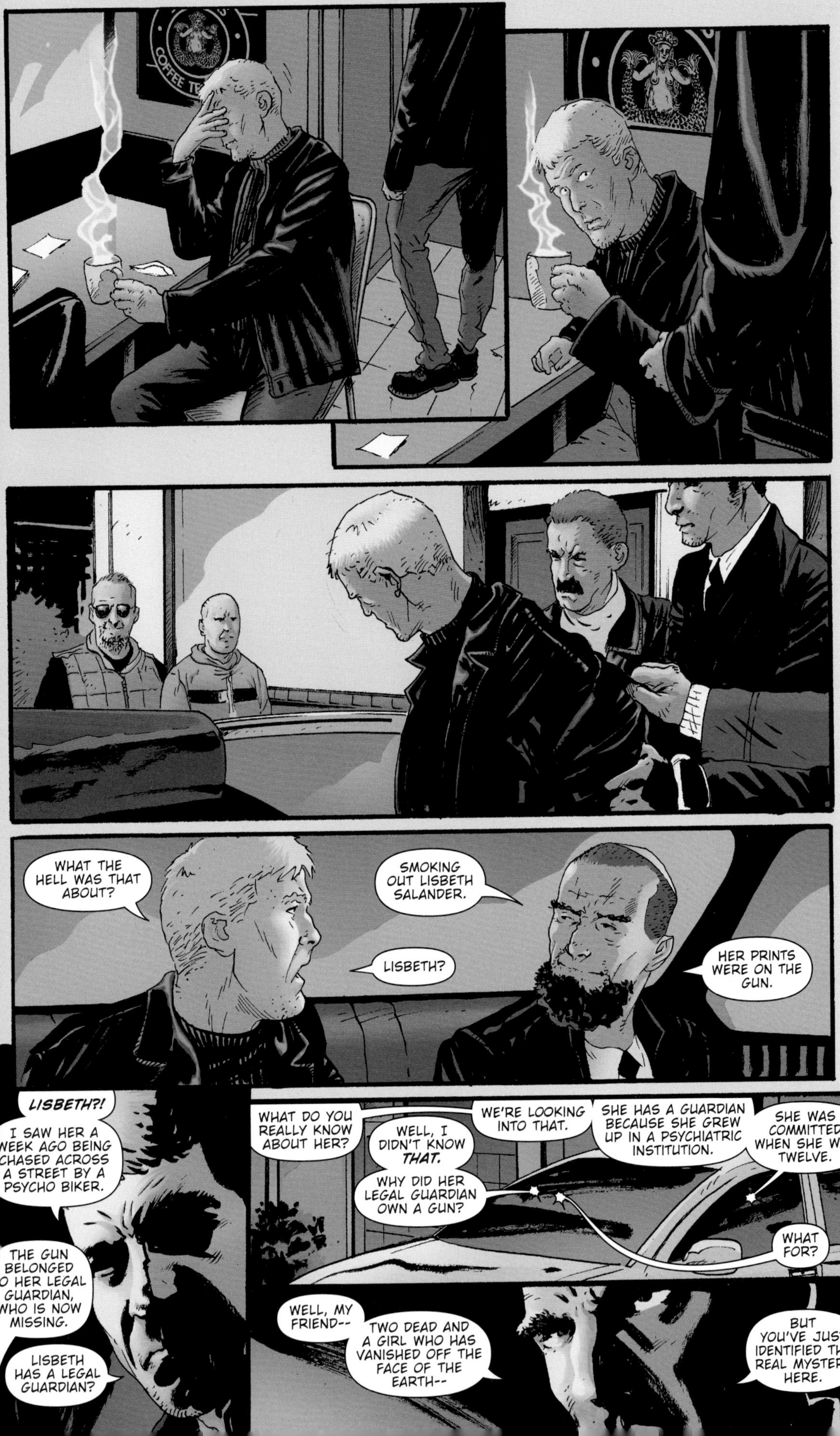

WHAT THE HELL WAS THAT ABOUT?
SMOKING OUT LISBETH SALANDER.
LISBETH?
HER PRINTS WERE ON THE GUN.
LISBETH?!
I SAW HER A WEEK AGO BEING CHASED ACROSS A STREET BY A PSYCHO BIKER.
THE GUN BELONGED O HER LEGAL GUARDIAN, WHO IS NOW MISSING.
LISBETH HAS A LEGAL GUARDIAN?
SHE HAS A GUARDIAN BECAUSE SHE GREW UP IN A PSYCHIATRIC INSTITUTION.
SHE WAS COMMITTED WHEN SHE WAS TWELVE.
WHAT FOR?
WELL, I DIDN'T KNOW THAT.
WHY DID HER LEGAL GUARDIAN OWN A GUN?
WE'RE LOOKING INTO THAT.
WHAT DO YOU REALLY KNOW ABOUT HER?
WELL, MY FRIEND--
TWO DEAD AND A GIRL WHO HAS VANISHED OFF THE FACE OF THE EARTH--
BUT YOU'VE JUST IDENTIFIED THE REAL MYSTERY HERE.

STILL NO SIGN?

NO, MA'AM.

STILL NO SIGN OF ADVOKAT BJURMAN?

I'M AFRAID NOT.

YOU MUST THINK WE'RE BAD NEIGHBORS.

BUT HE WENT AWAY MOST WEEKENDS.

WENT AWAY FOR MONTHS IN THE SUMMER TOO.

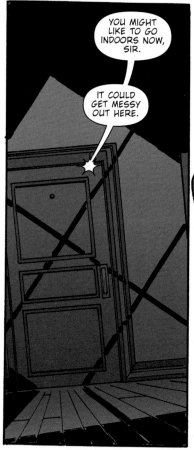

YOU MIGHT LIKE TO GO INDOORS NOW, SIR.

IT COULD GET MESSY OUT HERE.

CRRPCK

AH, AN END TO WAITING.

I ALWAYS ENJOY THIS.

GIVE IT ANOTHER ONE, BOYS.

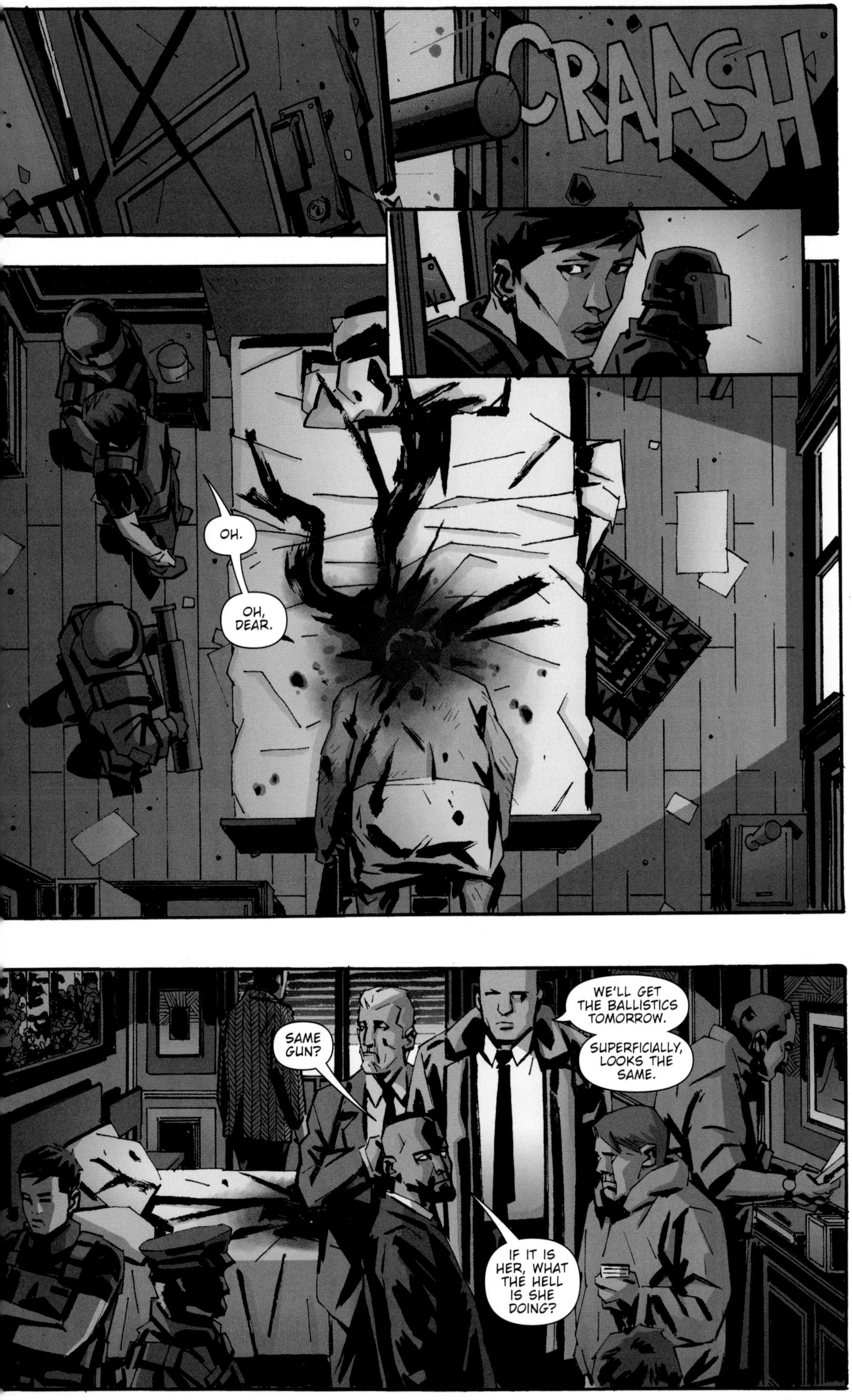
CRAASH
OH.
OH, DEAR.
SAME GUN?
WE'LL GET THE BALLISTICS TOMORROW.
SUPERFICIALLY, LOOKS THE SAME.
IF IT IS HER, WHAT THE HELL IS SHE DOING?

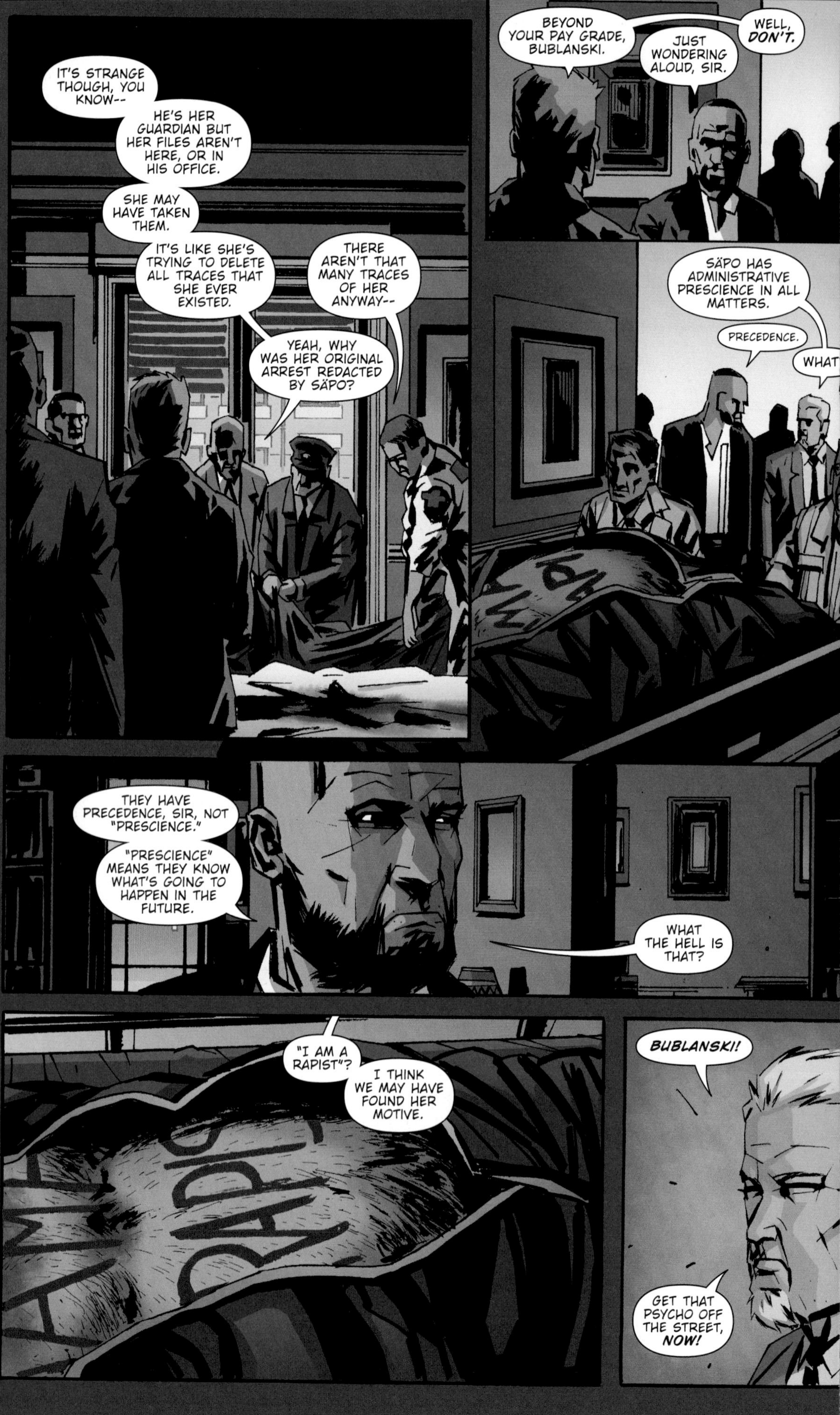
IT'S STRANGE THOUGH, YOU KNOW--
HE'S HER GUARDIAN BUT HER FILES AREN'T HERE, OR IN HIS OFFICE.
SHE MAY HAVE TAKEN THEM.
IT'S LIKE SHE'S TRYING TO DELETE ALL TRACES THAT SHE EVER EXISTED.
THERE AREN'T THAT MANY TRACES OF HER ANYWAY--
YEAH, WHY WAS HER ORIGINAL ARREST REDACTED BY SÄPO?
BEYOND YOUR PAY GRADE, BUBLANSKI.
JUST WONDERING ALOUD, SIR.
WELL, DON'T.
SÄPO HAS ADMINISTRATIVE PRESCIENCE IN ALL MATTERS.
PRECEDENCE.
WHAT
THEY HAVE PRECEDENCE, SIR, NOT "PRESCIENCE."
"PRESCIENCE" MEANS THEY KNOW WHAT'S GOING TO HAPPEN IN THE FUTURE.
WHAT THE HELL IS THAT?
"I AM A RAPIST"?
I THINK WE MAY HAVE FOUND HER MOTIVE.
BUBLANSKI!
GET THAT PSYCHO OFF THE STREET, NOW!

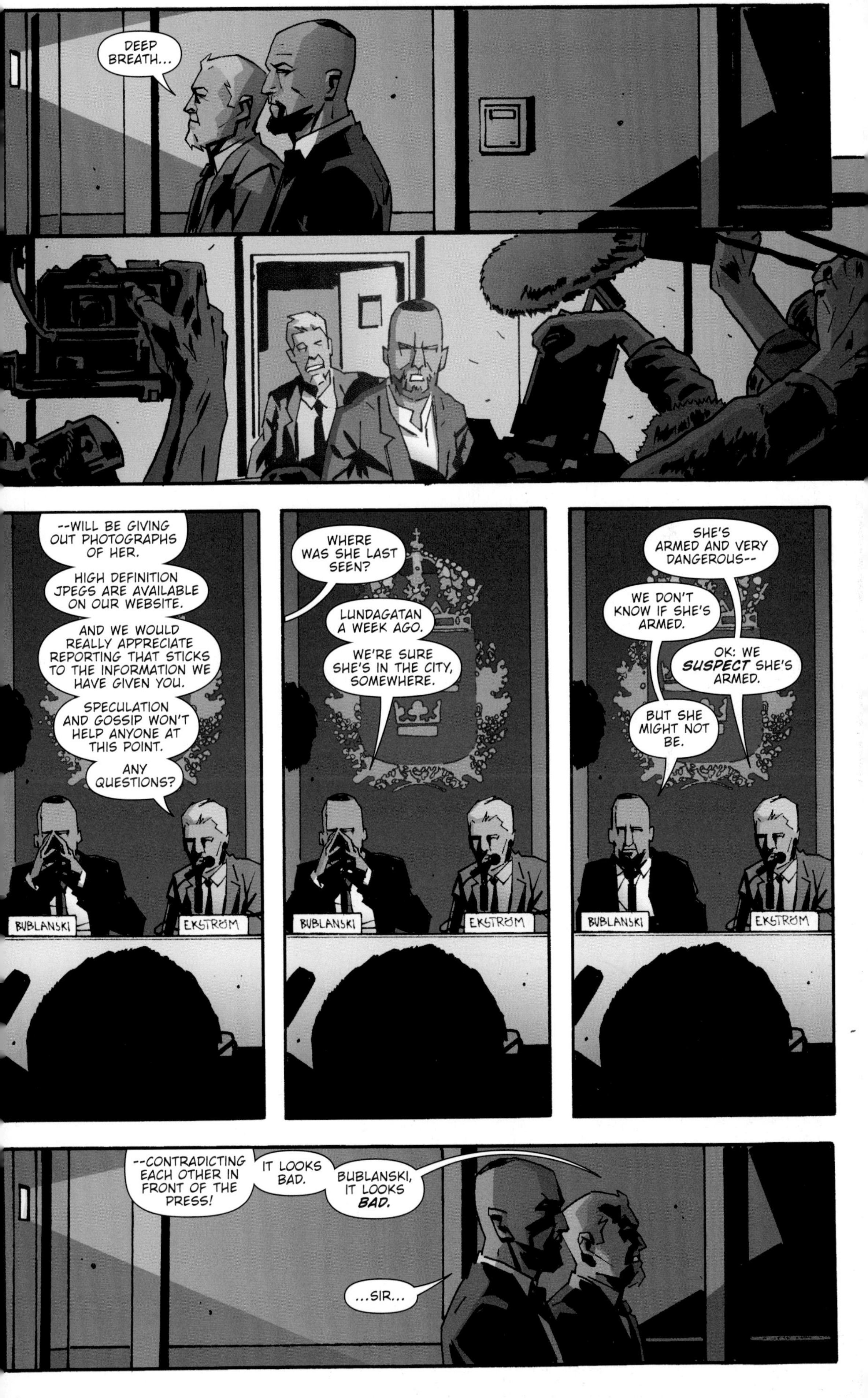
DEEP BREATH...
--WILL BE GIVING OUT PHOTOGRAPHS OF HER.
HIGH DEFINITION JPEGS ARE AVAILABLE ON OUR WEBSITE.
AND WE WOULD REALLY APPRECIATE REPORTING THAT STICKS TO THE INFORMATION WE HAVE GIVEN YOU.
SPECULATION AND GOSSIP WON'T HELP ANYONE AT THIS POINT.
ANY QUESTIONS?
BUBLANSKI
EKSTRÖM
WHERE WAS SHE LAST SEEN?
LUNDAGATAN A WEEK AGO.
WE'RE SURE SHE'S IN THE CITY, SOMEWHERE.
BUBLANSKI
EKSTRÖM
SHE'S ARMED AND VERY DANGEROUS--
WE DON'T KNOW IF SHE'S ARMED.
OK: WE ***SUSPECT*** SHE'S ARMED.
BUT SHE MIGHT NOT BE.
BUBLANSKI
EKSTRÖM
--CONTRADICTING EACH OTHER IN FRONT OF THE PRESS!
IT LOOKS BAD.
BUBLANSKI, IT LOOKS ***BAD.***
...SIR...

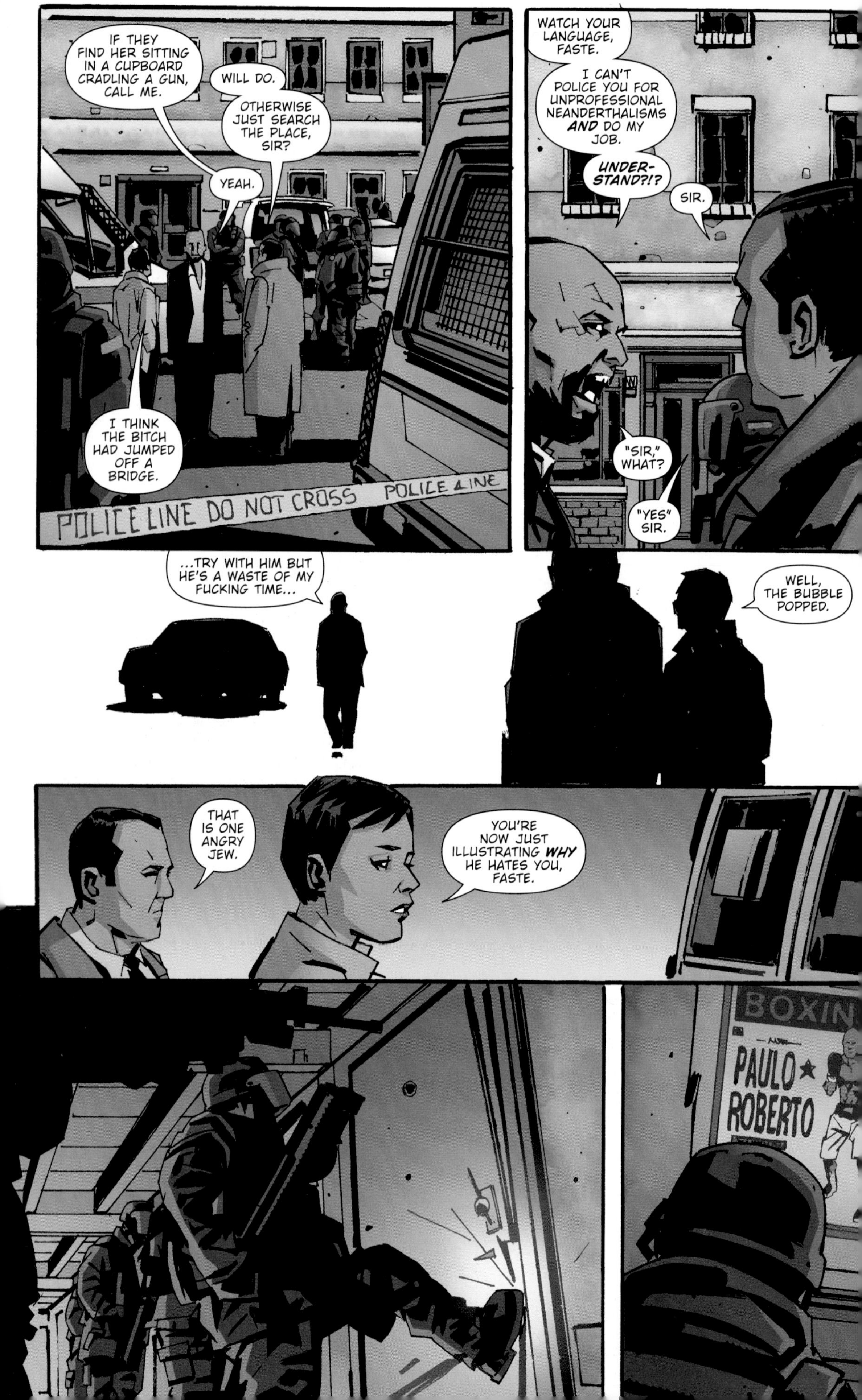
IF THEY FIND HER SITTING IN A CUPBOARD CRADLING A GUN, CALL ME.
WILL DO.
OTHERWISE JUST SEARCH THE PLACE, SIR?
YEAH.
I THINK THE BITCH HAD JUMPED OFF A BRIDGE.
POLICE LINE DO NOT CROSS POLICE LINE
WATCH YOUR LANGUAGE, FASTE.
I CAN'T POLICE YOU FOR UNPROFESSIONAL NEANDERTHALISMS AND DO MY JOB.
UNDER-STAND?!?
SIR.
"SIR," WHAT?
"YES" SIR.
...TRY WITH HIM BUT HE'S A WASTE OF MY FUCKING TIME...
WELL, THE BUBBLE POPPED.
THAT IS ONE ANGRY JEW.
YOU'RE NOW JUST ILLUSTRATING WHY HE HATES YOU, FASTE.
BOXIN
PAULO ROBERTO

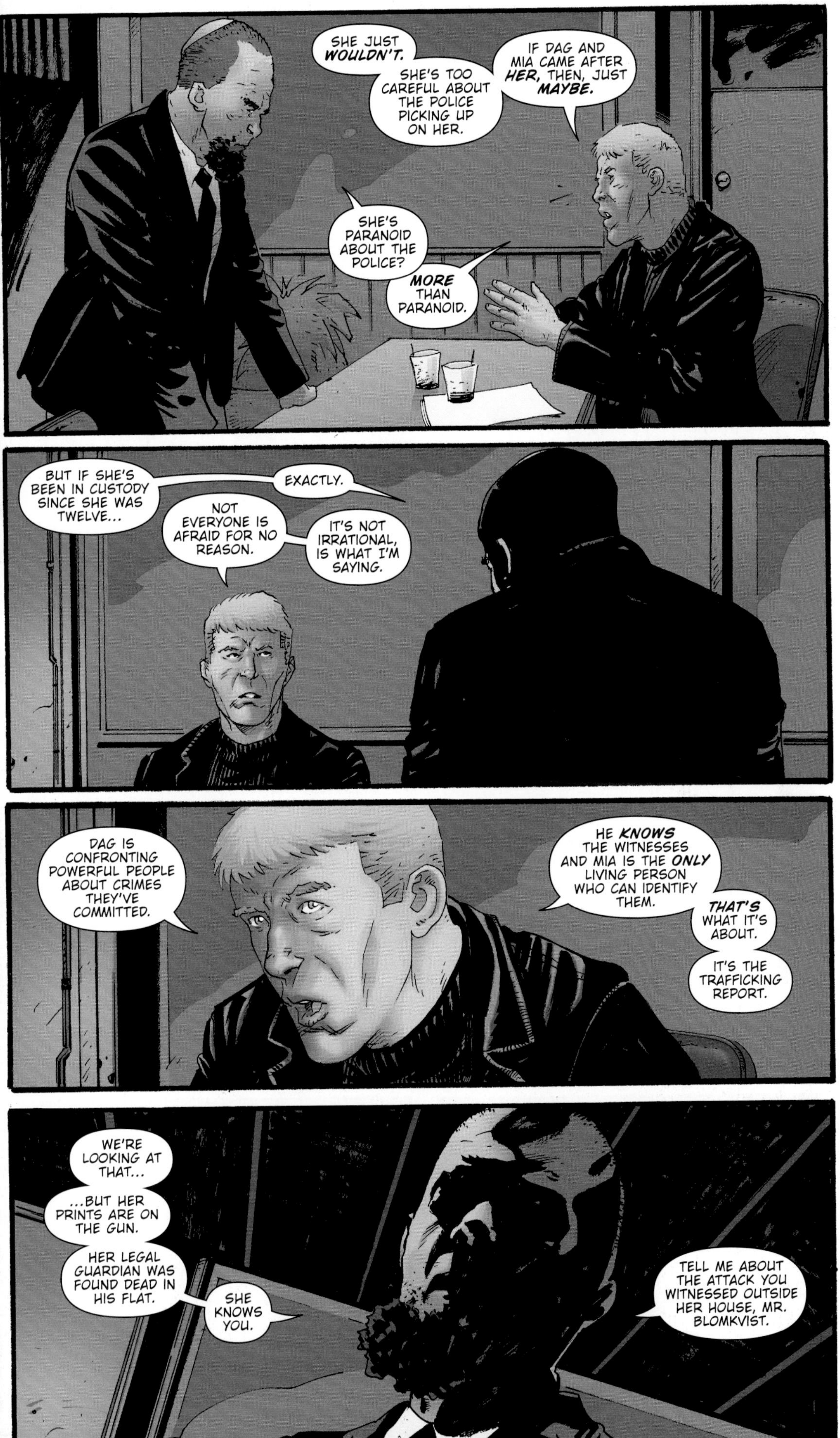
SHE JUST WOULDN'T.
SHE'S TOO CAREFUL ABOUT THE POLICE PICKING UP ON HER.
IF DAG AND MIA CAME AFTER HER, THEN, JUST MAYBE.
SHE'S PARANOID ABOUT THE POLICE?
MORE THAN PARANOID.
BUT IF SHE'S BEEN IN CUSTODY SINCE SHE WAS TWELVE...
EXACTLY.
NOT EVERYONE IS AFRAID FOR NO REASON.
IT'S NOT IRRATIONAL, IS WHAT I'M SAYING.
DAG IS CONFRONTING POWERFUL PEOPLE ABOUT CRIMES THEY'VE COMMITTED.
HE KNOWS THE WITNESSES AND MIA IS THE ONLY LIVING PERSON WHO CAN IDENTIFY THEM.
THAT'S WHAT IT'S ABOUT.
IT'S THE TRAFFICKING REPORT.
WE'RE LOOKING AT THAT...
...BUT HER PRINTS ARE ON THE GUN.
HER LEGAL GUARDIAN WAS FOUND DEAD IN HIS FLAT.
SHE KNOWS YOU.
TELL ME ABOUT THE ATTACK YOU WITNESSED OUTSIDE HER HOUSE, MR. BLOMKVIST.

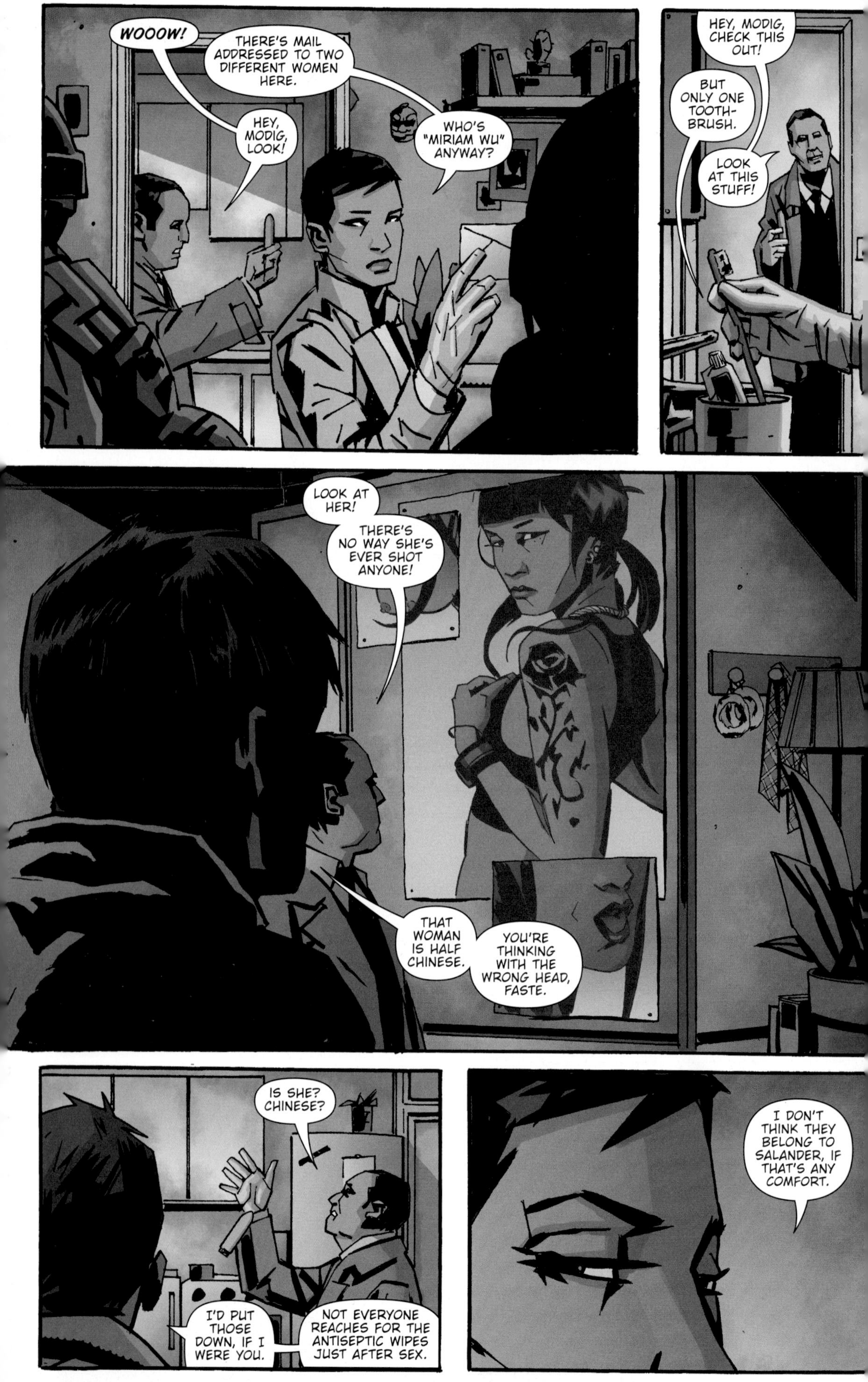
WOOOW!
THERE'S MAIL ADDRESSED TO TWO DIFFERENT WOMEN HERE.
HEY, MODIG, LOOK!
WHO'S "MIRIAM WU" ANYWAY?
HEY, MODIG, CHECK THIS OUT!
BUT ONLY ONE TOOTH-BRUSH.
LOOK AT THIS STUFF!
LOOK AT HER!
THERE'S NO WAY SHE'S EVER SHOT ANYONE!
THAT WOMAN IS HALF CHINESE.
YOU'RE THINKING WITH THE WRONG HEAD, FASTE.
IS SHE? CHINESE?
I'D PUT THOSE DOWN, IF I WERE YOU.
NOT EVERYONE REACHES FOR THE ANTISEPTIC WIPES JUST AFTER SEX.
I DON'T THINK THEY BELONG TO SALANDER, IF THAT'S ANY COMFORT.

SHARE DROP 4.6% OF VALUE WITHIN TWO HOURS OF MARKET

OF VALUE WITHIN TWO HOURS OF MARKET

VALUE WITHIN TWO HOURS OF MARKET

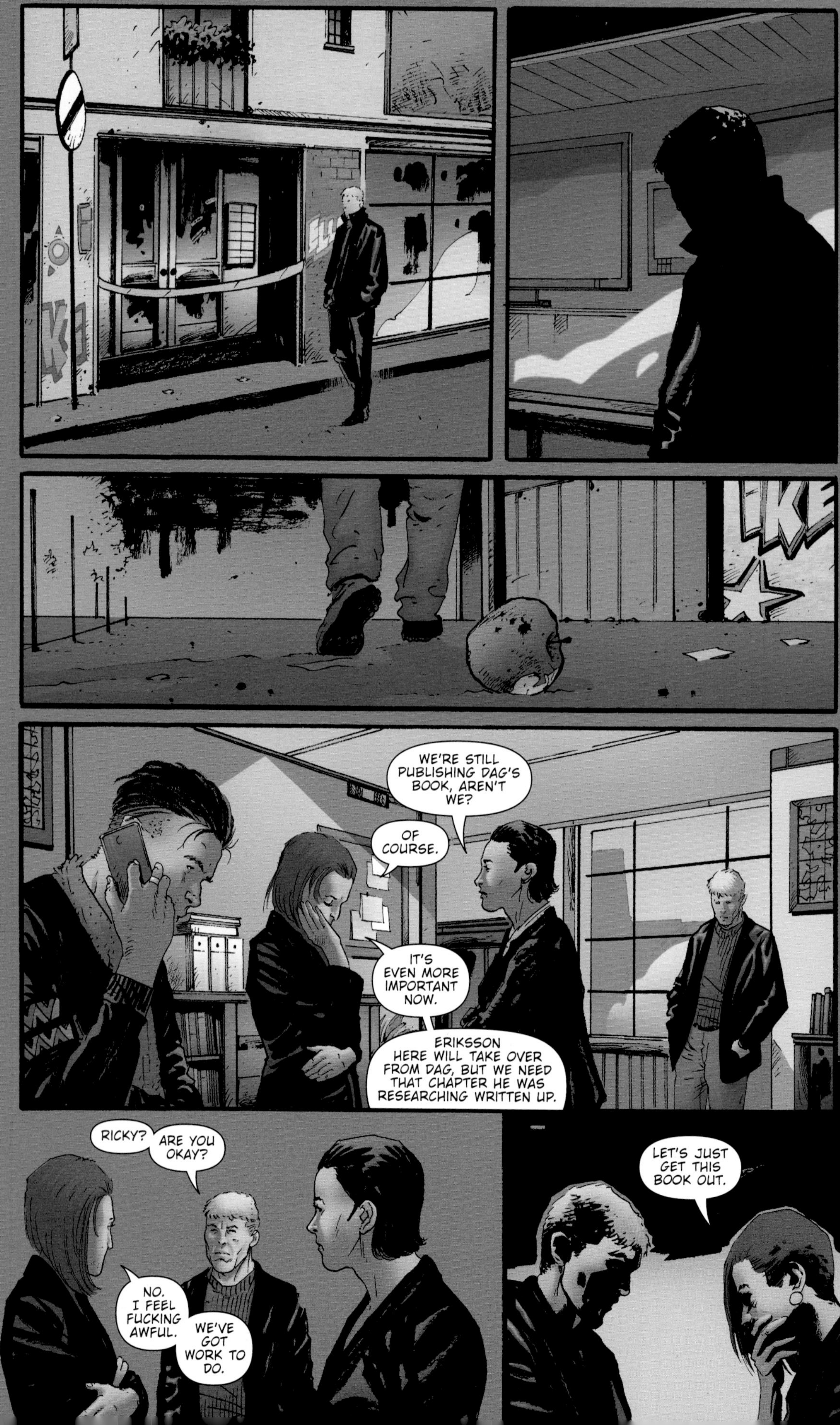
WE'RE STILL PUBLISHING DAG'S BOOK, AREN'T WE?
OF COURSE.
IT'S EVEN MORE IMPORTANT NOW.
ERIKSSON HERE WILL TAKE OVER FROM DAG, BUT WE NEED THAT CHAPTER HE WAS RESEARCHING WRITTEN UP.
RICKY?
ARE YOU OKAY?
NO. I FEEL FUCKING AWFUL.
WE'VE GOT WORK TO DO.
LET'S JUST GET THIS BOOK OUT.

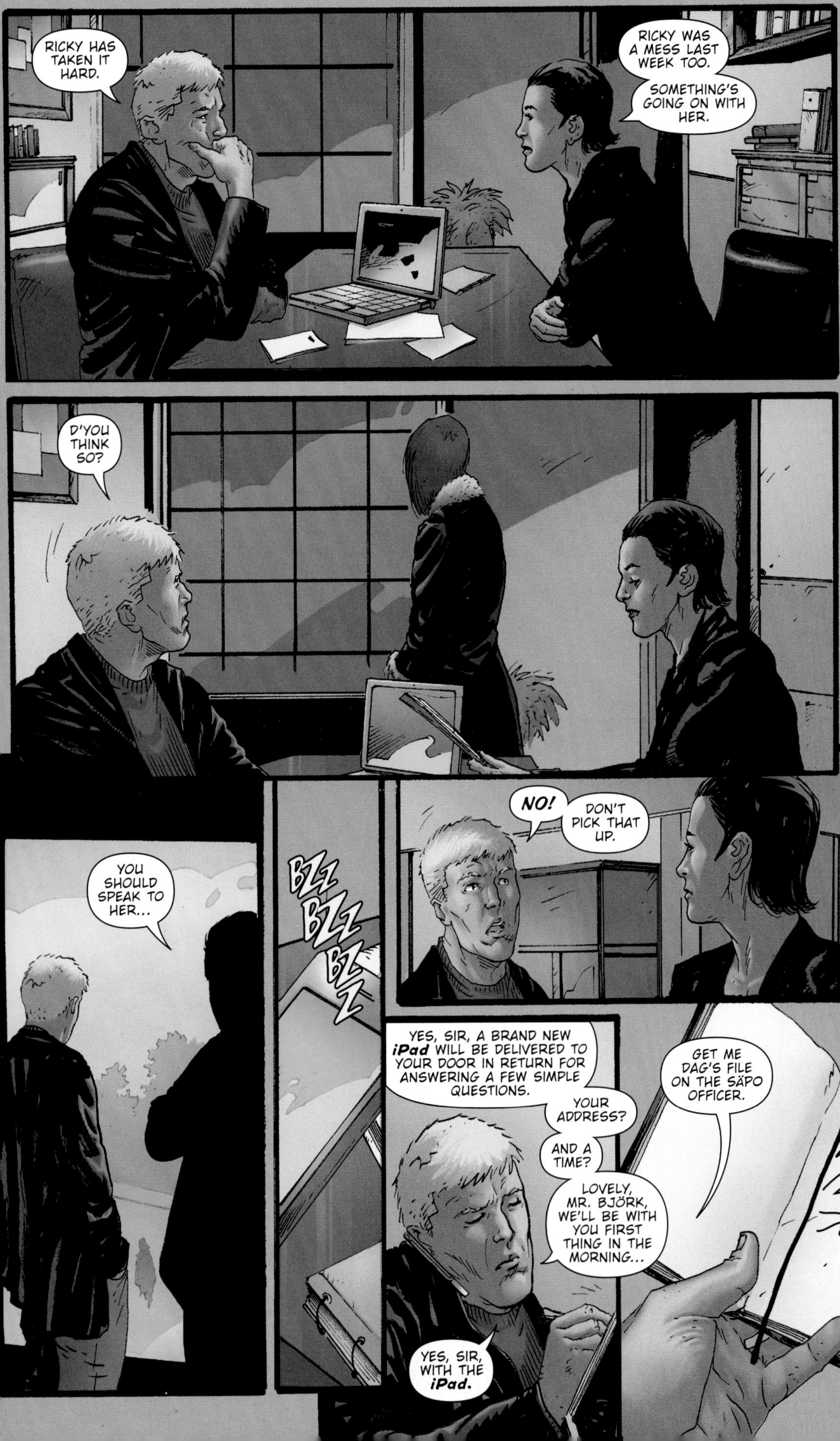
RICKY HAS TAKEN IT HARD.
RICKY WAS A MESS LAST WEEK TOO.
SOMETHING'S GOING ON WITH HER.
D'YOU THINK SO?
YOU SHOULD SPEAK TO HER...
BZZ BZZ BZZ
NO!
DON'T PICK THAT UP.
YES, SIR, A BRAND NEW iPad WILL BE DELIVERED TO YOUR DOOR IN RETURN FOR ANSWERING A FEW SIMPLE QUESTIONS.
YOUR ADDRESS?
AND A TIME?
LOVELY, MR. BJÖRK, WE'LL BE WITH YOU FIRST THING IN THE MORNING...
YES, SIR, WITH THE iPad.
GET ME DAG'S FILE ON THE SÄPO OFFICER.

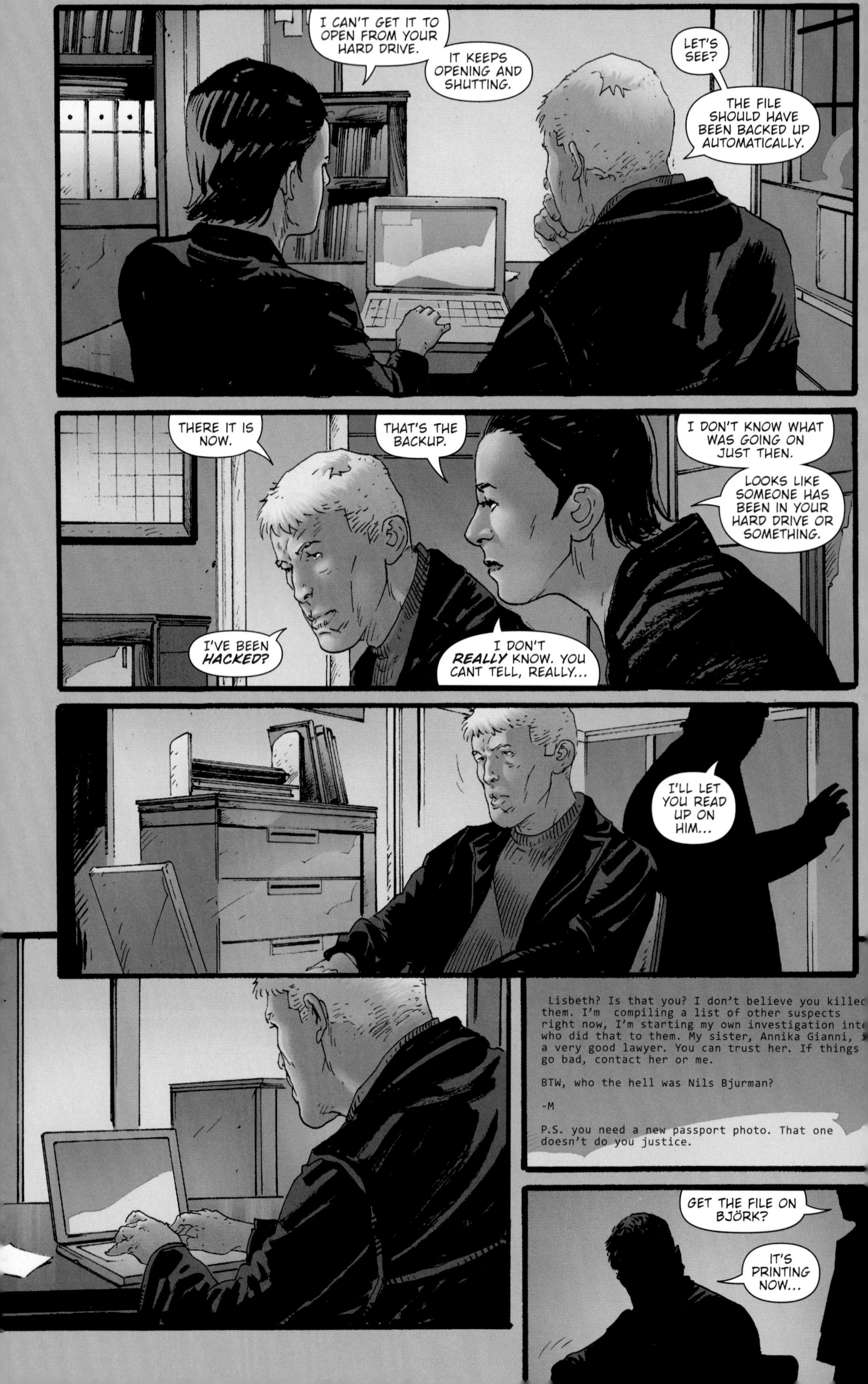

I CAN'T GET IT TO OPEN FROM YOUR HARD DRIVE.
IT KEEPS OPENING AND SHUTTING.
LET'S SEE?
THE FILE SHOULD HAVE BEEN BACKED UP AUTOMATICALLY.
THERE IT IS NOW.
THAT'S THE BACKUP.
I DON'T KNOW WHAT WAS GOING ON JUST THEN.
LOOKS LIKE SOMEONE HAS BEEN IN YOUR HARD DRIVE OR SOMETHING.
I'VE BEEN **HACKED?**
I DON'T **REALLY** KNOW. YOU CANT TELL, REALLY...
I'LL LET YOU READ UP ON HIM...
Lisbeth? Is that you? I don't believe you kille
them. I'm compiling a list of other suspects
right now, I'm starting my own investigation int
who did that to them. My sister, Annika Gianni,
a very good lawyer. You can trust her. If things
go bad, contact her or me.
BTW, who the hell was Nils Bjurman?
-M
P.S. you need a new passport photo. That one
doesn't do you justice.
GET THE FILE ON BJÖRK?
IT'S PRINTING NOW...

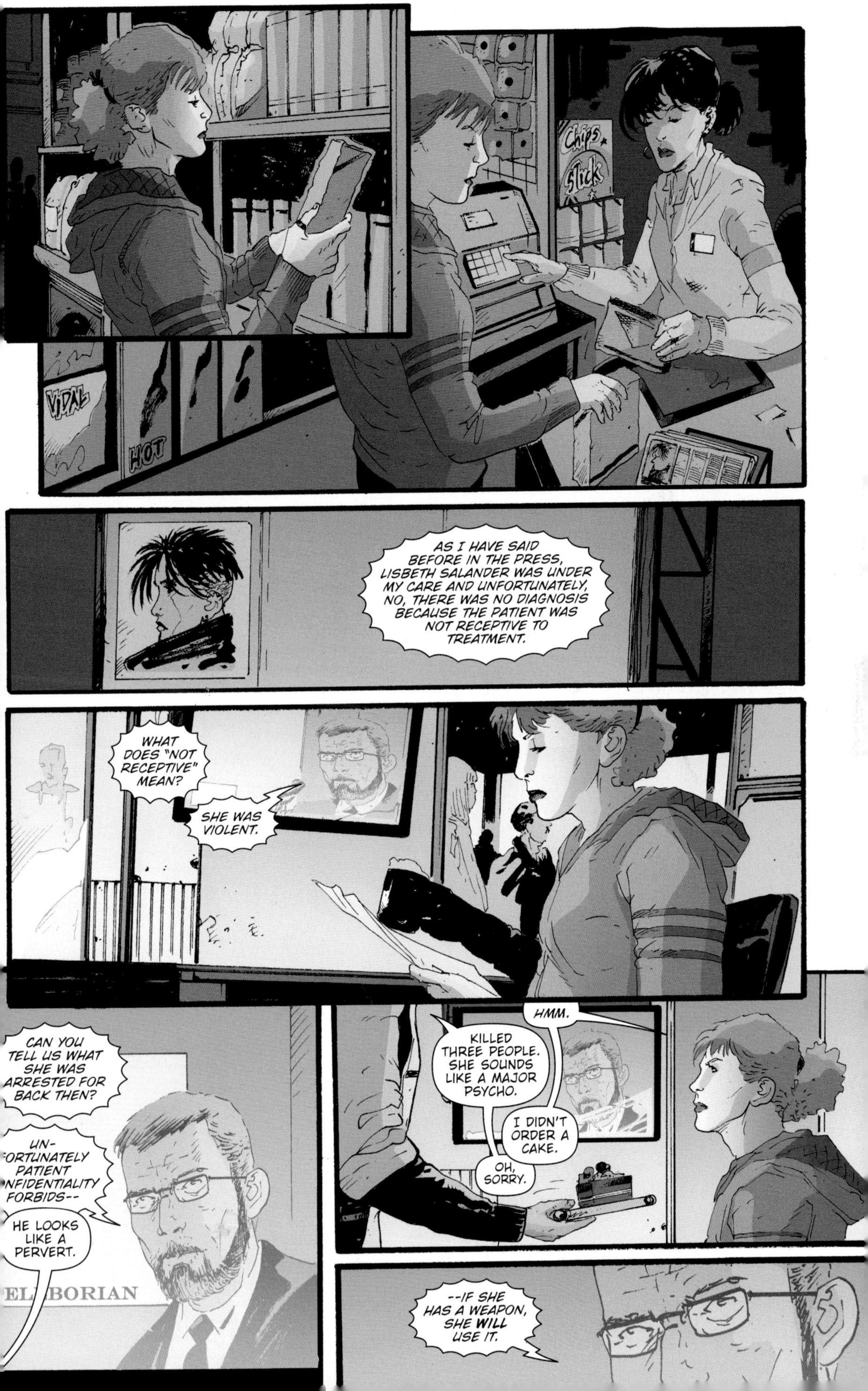
VIDAL
HOT
Chips Stick
AS I HAVE SAID BEFORE IN THE PRESS, LISBETH SALANDER WAS UNDER MY CARE AND UNFORTUNATELY, NO, THERE WAS NO DIAGNOSIS BECAUSE THE PATIENT WAS NOT RECEPTIVE TO TREATMENT.
WHAT DOES "NOT RECEPTIVE" MEAN?
SHE WAS VIOLENT.
CAN YOU TELL US WHAT SHE WAS ARRESTED FOR BACK THEN?
UN-FORTUNATELY PATIENT NFIDENTIALITY FORBIDS--
HE LOOKS LIKE A PERVERT.
EL BORIAN
HMM.
KILLED THREE PEOPLE. SHE SOUNDS LIKE A MAJOR PSYCHO.
I DIDN'T ORDER A CAKE.
OH, SORRY.
--IF SHE HAS A WEAPON, SHE **WILL** USE IT.

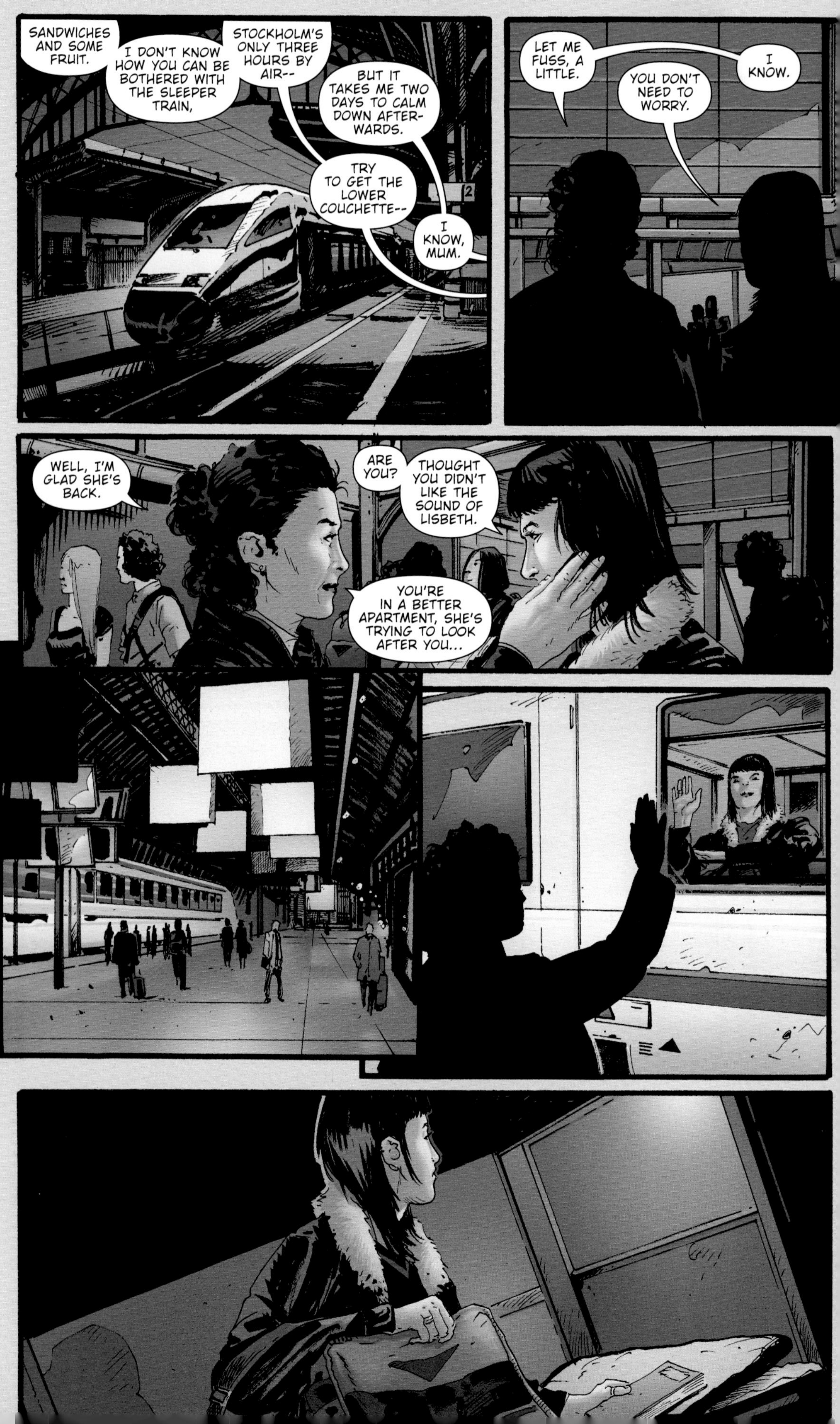
SANDWICHES AND SOME FRUIT.
I DON'T KNOW HOW YOU CAN BE BOTHERED WITH THE SLEEPER TRAIN,
STOCKHOLM'S ONLY THREE HOURS BY AIR--
BUT IT TAKES ME TWO DAYS TO CALM DOWN AFTER-WARDS.
TRY TO GET THE LOWER COUCHETTE--
I KNOW, MUM.
LET ME FUSS, A LITTLE.
YOU DON'T NEED TO WORRY.
I KNOW.
WELL, I'M GLAD SHE'S BACK.
ARE YOU?
THOUGHT YOU DIDN'T LIKE THE SOUND OF LISBETH.
YOU'RE IN A BETTER APARTMENT, SHE'S TRYING TO LOOK AFTER YOU...

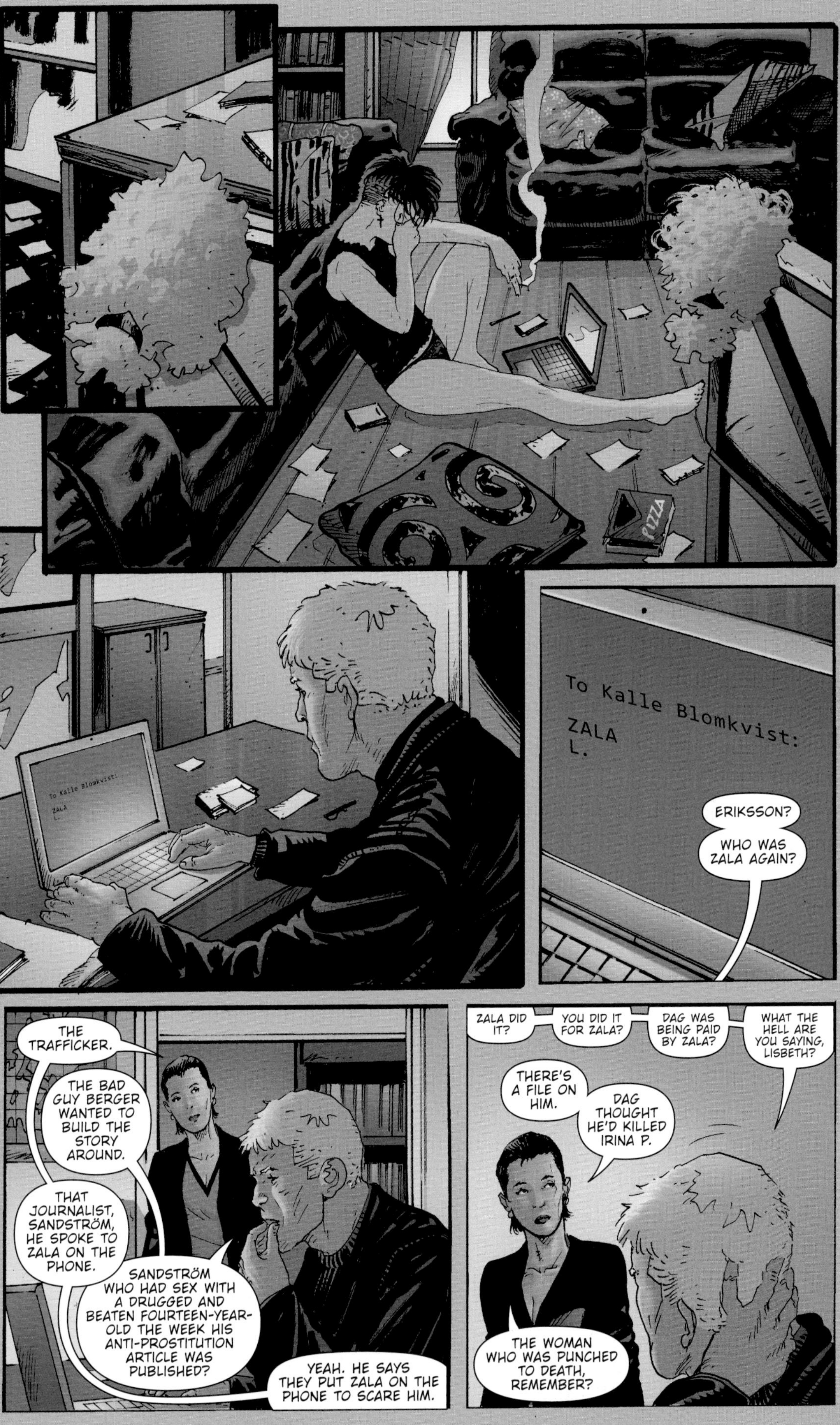
To Kalle Blomkvist:
ZALA
L.
To Kalle Blomkvist:
ZALA
L.
ERIKSSON?
WHO WAS ZALA AGAIN?
THE TRAFFICKER.
THE BAD GUY BERGER WANTED TO BUILD THE STORY AROUND.
THAT JOURNALIST, SANDSTRÖM, HE SPOKE TO ZALA ON THE PHONE.
SANDSTRÖM WHO HAD SEX WITH A DRUGGED AND BEATEN FOURTEEN-YEAR-OLD THE WEEK HIS ANTI-PROSTITUTION ARTICLE WAS PUBLISHED?
YEAH. HE SAYS THEY PUT ZALA ON THE PHONE TO SCARE HIM.
ZALA DID IT?
YOU DID IT FOR ZALA?
DAG WAS BEING PAID BY ZALA?
WHAT THE HELL ARE YOU SAYING, LISBETH?
THERE'S A FILE ON HIM.
DAG THOUGHT HE'D KILLED IRINA P.
THE WOMAN WHO WAS PUNCHED TO DEATH, REMEMBER?

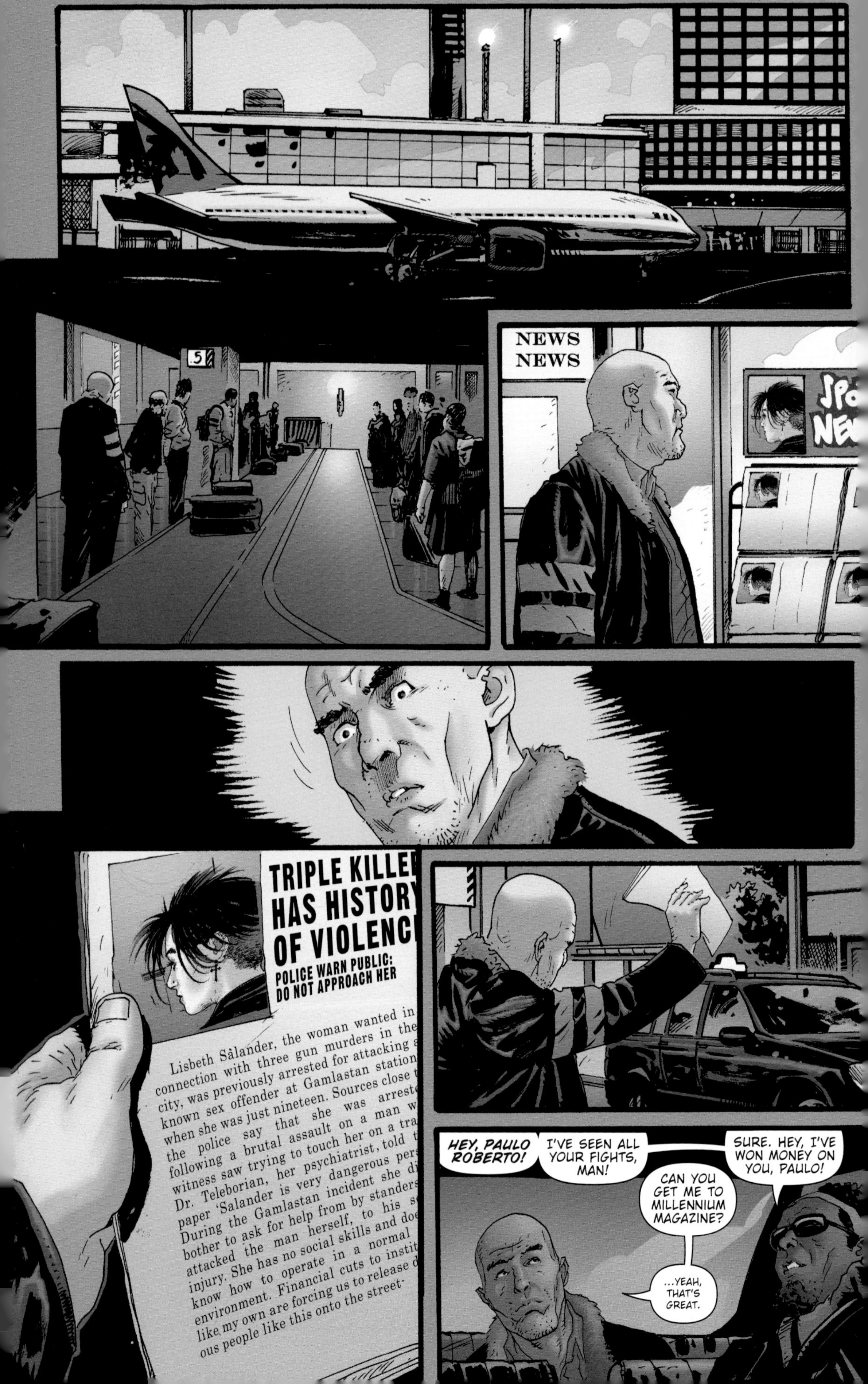

NEWS
NEWS
TRIPLE KILLE
HAS HISTORY
OF VIOLENC
POLICE WARN PUBLIC:
DO NOT APPROACH HER
Lisbeth Salander, the woman wanted in
connection with three gun murders in the
city, was previously arrested for attacking a
known sex offender at Gamlastan station
when she was just nineteen. Sources close t
the police say that she was arreste
following a brutal assault on a man w
witness saw trying to touch her on a tra
Dr. Teleborian, her psychiatrist, told t
paper 'Salander is very dangerous pers
During the Gamlastan incident she di
bother to ask for help from by standers
attacked the man herself, to his s
injury. She has no social skills and doe
know how to operate in a normal
environment. Financial cuts to instit
like my own are forcing us to release d
ous people like this onto the street-
HEY, PAULO ROBERTO!
I'VE SEEN ALL YOUR FIGHTS, MAN!
SURE. HEY, I'VE WON MONEY ON YOU, PAULO!
CAN YOU GET ME TO MILLENNIUM MAGAZINE?
...YEAH, THAT'S GREAT.

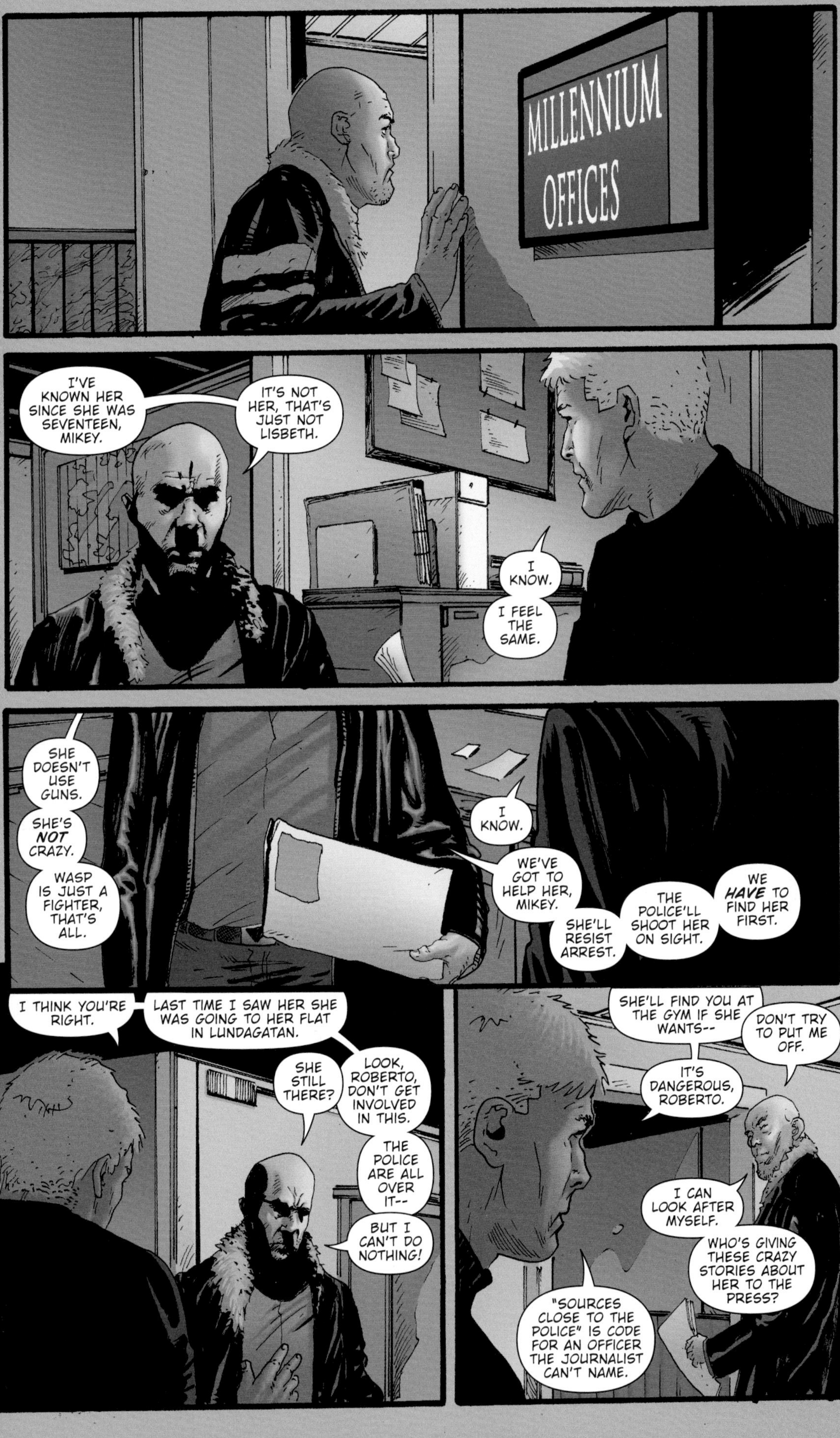
MILLENNIUM OFFICES
I'VE KNOWN HER SINCE SHE WAS SEVENTEEN, MIKEY.
IT'S NOT HER, THAT'S JUST NOT LISBETH.
I KNOW.
I FEEL THE SAME.
SHE DOESN'T USE GUNS.
SHE'S ***NOT*** CRAZY.
WASP IS JUST A FIGHTER, THAT'S ALL.
I KNOW.
WE'VE GOT TO HELP HER, MIKEY.
SHE'LL RESIST ARREST.
THE POLICE'LL SHOOT HER ON SIGHT.
WE ***HAVE*** TO FIND HER FIRST.
I THINK YOU'RE RIGHT.
LAST TIME I SAW HER SHE WAS GOING TO HER FLAT IN LUNDAGATAN.
SHE STILL THERE?
LOOK, ROBERTO, DON'T GET INVOLVED IN THIS.
THE POLICE ARE ALL OVER IT--
BUT I CAN'T DO NOTHING!
SHE'LL FIND YOU AT THE GYM IF SHE WANTS--
DON'T TRY TO PUT ME OFF.
IT'S DANGEROUS, ROBERTO.
I CAN LOOK AFTER MYSELF.
WHO'S GIVING THESE CRAZY STORIES ABOUT HER TO THE PRESS?
"SOURCES CLOSE TO THE POLICE" IS CODE FOR AN OFFICER THE JOURNALIST CAN'T NAME.

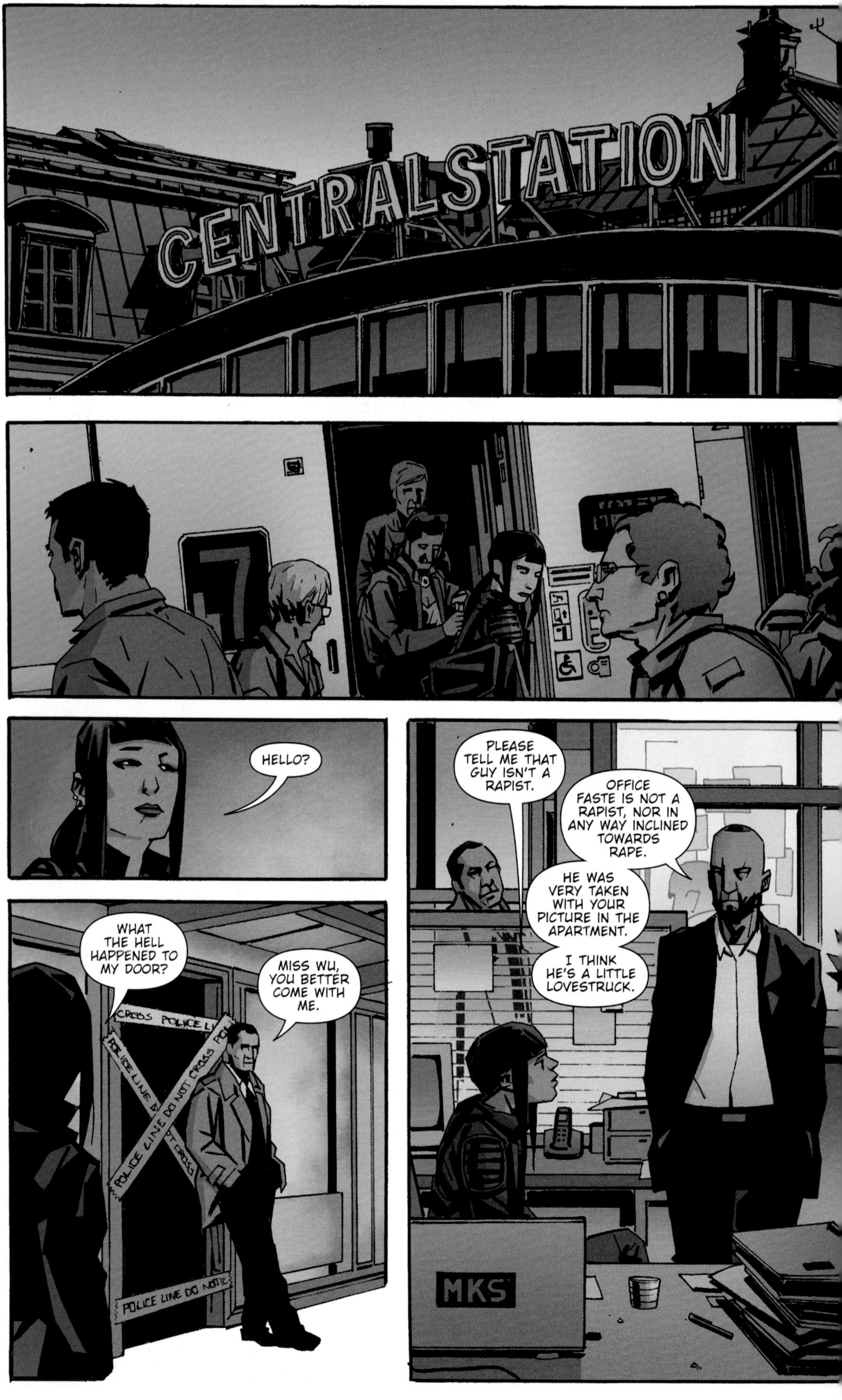
CENTRALSTATION
HELLO?
WHAT THE HELL HAPPENED TO MY DOOR?
MISS WU, YOU BETTER COME WITH ME.
POLICE LINE DO NOT CROSS
PLEASE TELL ME THAT GUY ISN'T A RAPIST.
OFFICE FASTE IS NOT A RAPIST, NOR IN ANY WAY INCLINED TOWARDS RAPE.
HE WAS VERY TAKEN WITH YOUR PICTURE IN THE APARTMENT.
I THINK HE'S A LITTLE LOVESTRUCK.
MKS

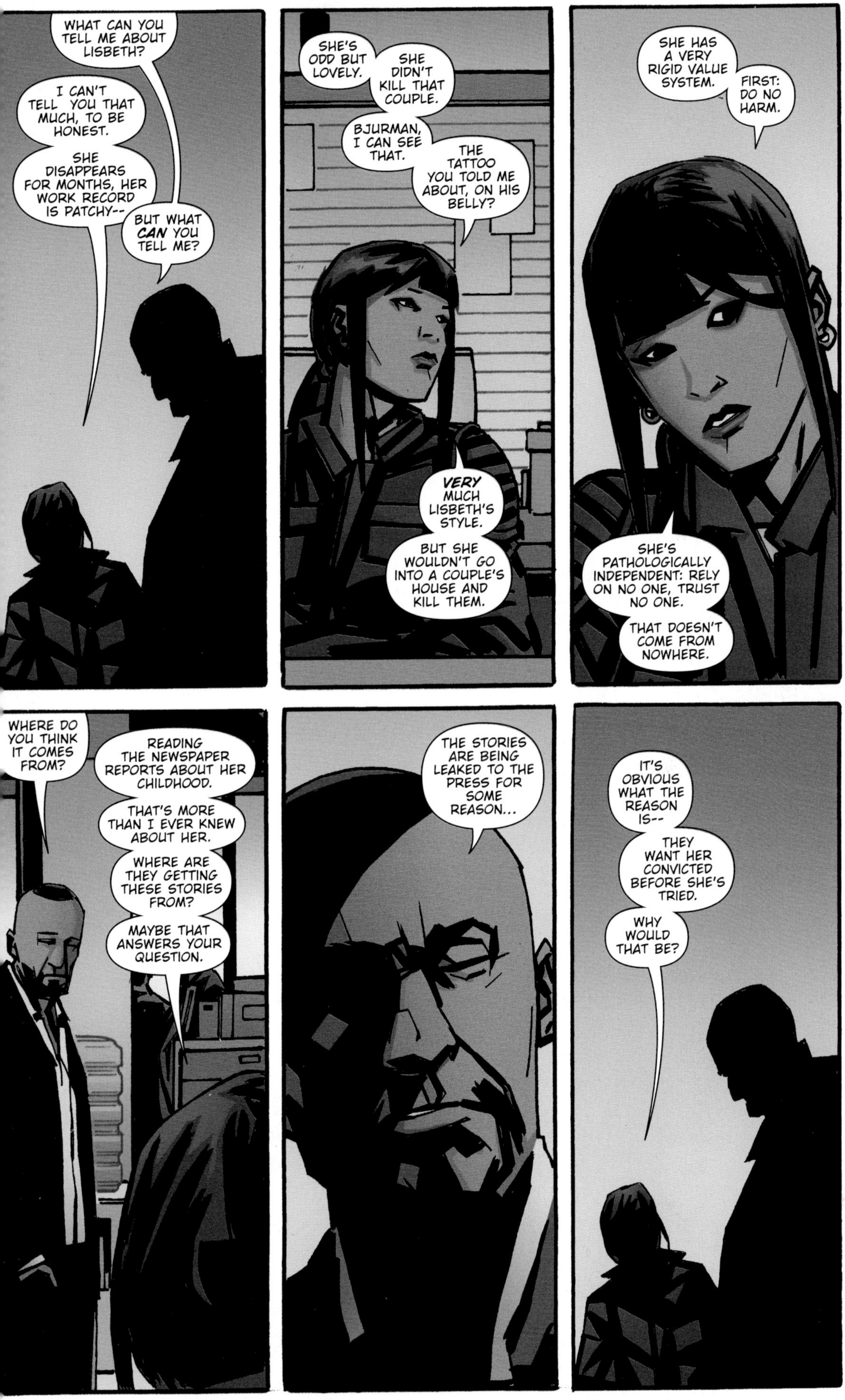
WHAT CAN YOU TELL ME ABOUT LISBETH?
I CAN'T TELL YOU THAT MUCH, TO BE HONEST.
SHE DISAPPEARS FOR MONTHS, HER WORK RECORD IS PATCHY--
BUT WHAT CAN YOU TELL ME?
SHE'S ODD BUT LOVELY.
SHE DIDN'T KILL THAT COUPLE.
BJURMAN, I CAN SEE THAT.
THE TATTOO YOU TOLD ME ABOUT, ON HIS BELLY?
VERY MUCH LISBETH'S STYLE.
BUT SHE WOULDN'T GO INTO A COUPLE'S HOUSE AND KILL THEM.
SHE HAS A VERY RIGID VALUE SYSTEM.
FIRST: DO NO HARM.
SHE'S PATHOLOGICALLY INDEPENDENT: RELY ON NO ONE, TRUST NO ONE.
THAT DOESN'T COME FROM NOWHERE.
WHERE DO YOU THINK IT COMES FROM?
READING THE NEWSPAPER REPORTS ABOUT HER CHILDHOOD.
THAT'S MORE THAN I EVER KNEW ABOUT HER.
WHERE ARE THEY GETTING THESE STORIES FROM?
MAYBE THAT ANSWERS YOUR QUESTION.
THE STORIES ARE BEING LEAKED TO THE PRESS FOR SOME REASON...
IT'S OBVIOUS WHAT THE REASON IS--
THEY WANT HER CONVICTED BEFORE SHE'S TRIED.
WHY WOULD THAT BE?

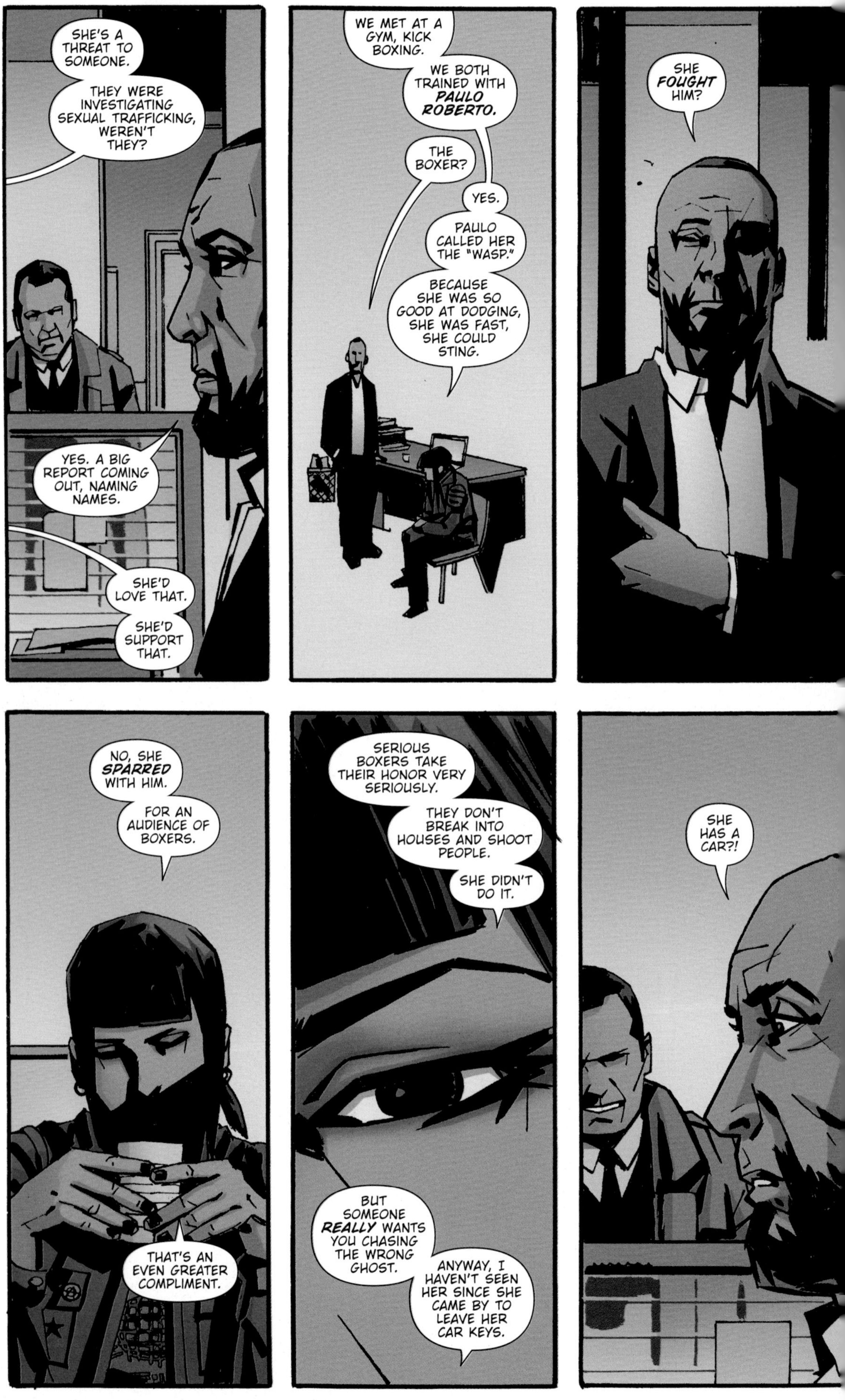
SHE'S A THREAT TO SOMEONE.
THEY WERE INVESTIGATING SEXUAL TRAFFICKING, WEREN'T THEY?
YES. A BIG REPORT COMING OUT, NAMING NAMES.
SHE'D LOVE THAT.
SHE'D SUPPORT THAT.
WE MET AT A GYM, KICK BOXING.
WE BOTH TRAINED WITH PAULO ROBERTO.
THE BOXER?
YES.
PAULO CALLED HER THE "WASP."
BECAUSE SHE WAS SO GOOD AT DODGING, SHE WAS FAST, SHE COULD STING.
SHE FOUGHT HIM?
NO, SHE SPARRED WITH HIM.
FOR AN AUDIENCE OF BOXERS.
THAT'S AN EVEN GREATER COMPLIMENT.
SERIOUS BOXERS TAKE THEIR HONOR VERY SERIOUSLY.
THEY DON'T BREAK INTO HOUSES AND SHOOT PEOPLE.
SHE DIDN'T DO IT.
BUT SOMEONE REALLY WANTS YOU CHASING THE WRONG GHOST.
ANYWAY, I HAVEN'T SEEN HER SINCE SHE CAME BY TO LEAVE HER CAR KEYS.
SHE HAS A CAR?!

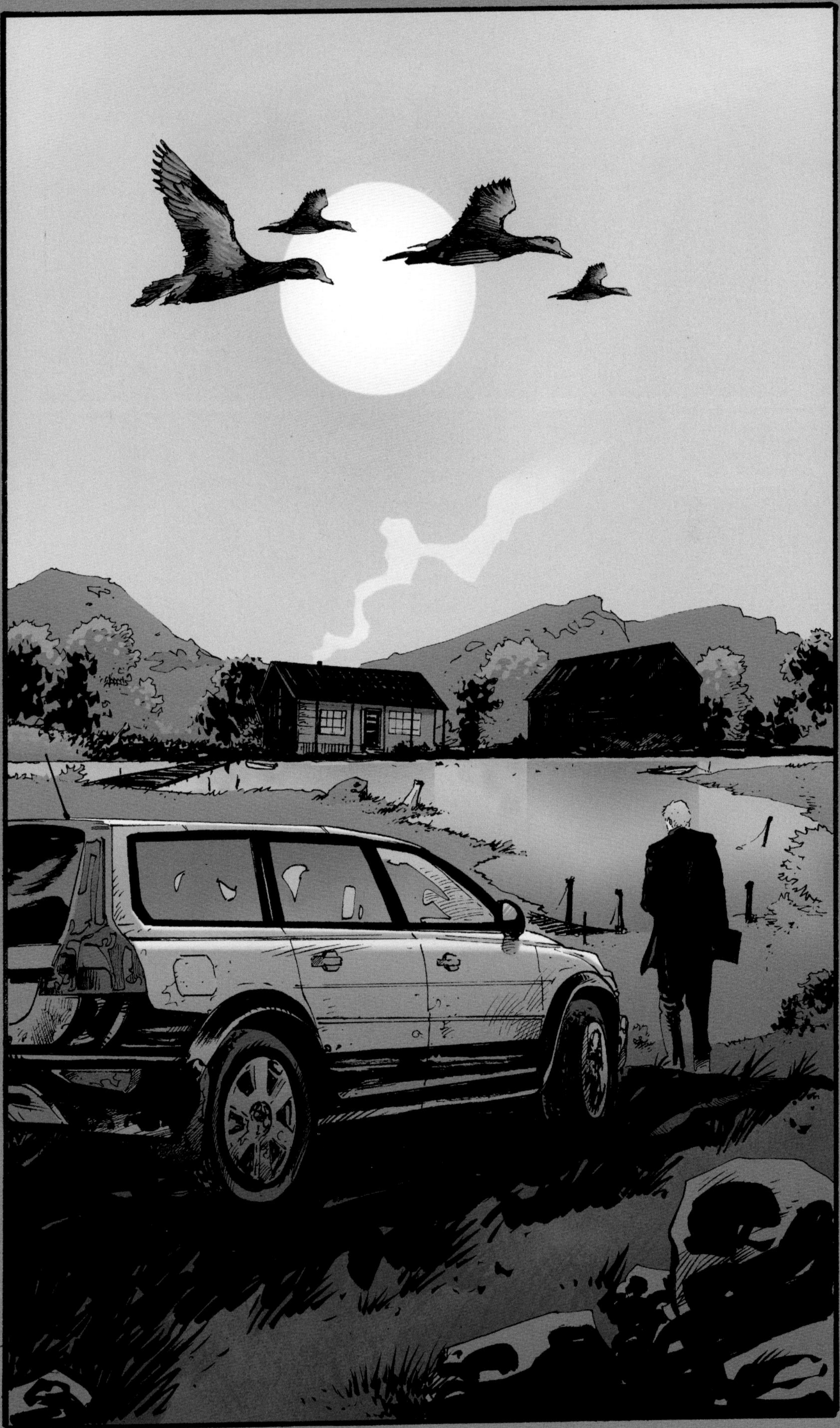

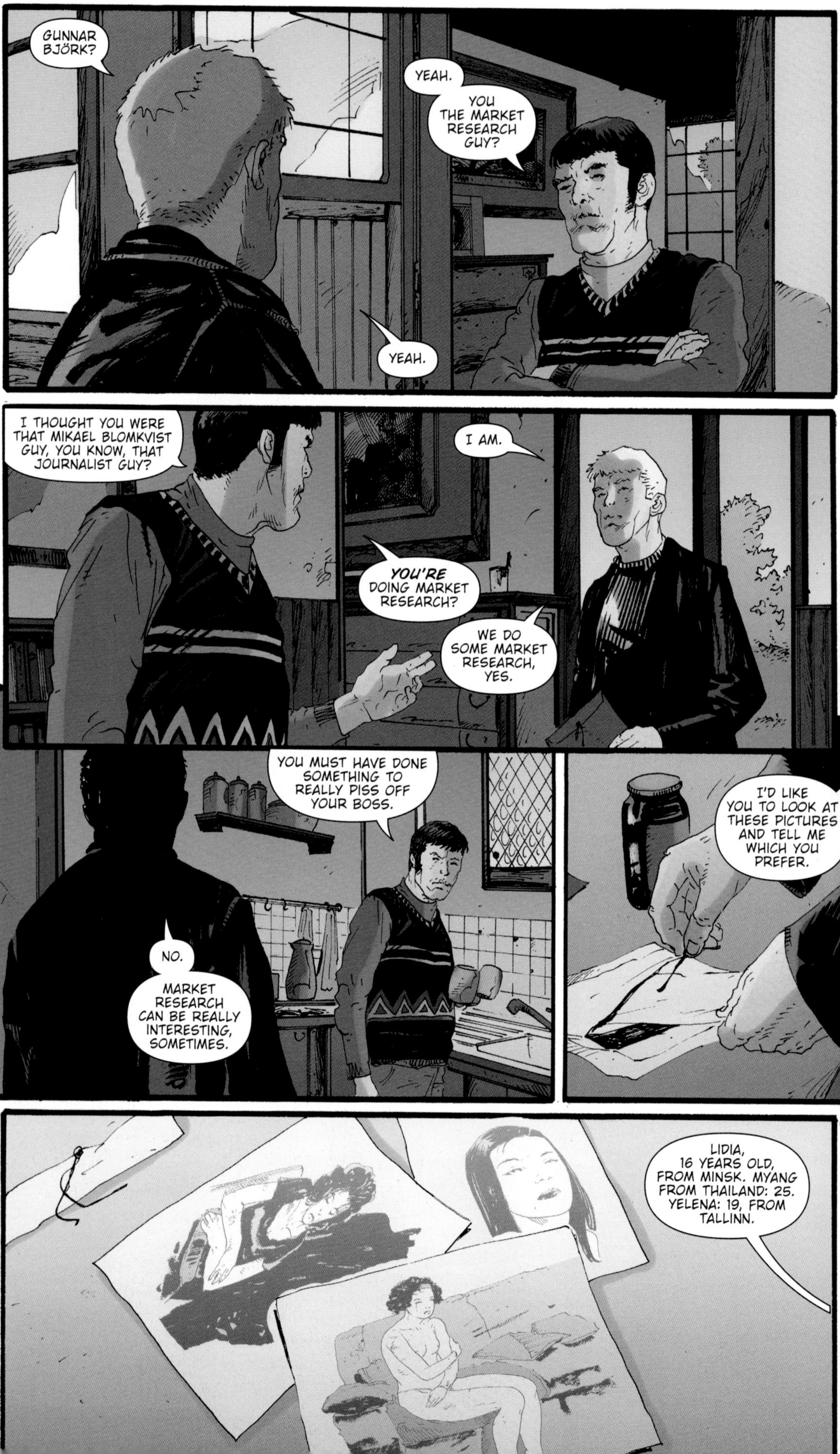

GUNNAR BJÖRK?
YEAH.
YOU THE MARKET RESEARCH GUY?
YEAH.
I THOUGHT YOU WERE THAT MIKAEL BLOMKVIST GUY, YOU KNOW, THAT JOURNALIST GUY?
I AM.
YOU'RE DOING MARKET RESEARCH?
WE DO SOME MARKET RESEARCH, YES.
YOU MUST HAVE DONE SOMETHING TO REALLY PISS OFF YOUR BOSS.
NO.
MARKET RESEARCH CAN BE REALLY INTERESTING, SOMETIMES.
I'D LIKE YOU TO LOOK AT THESE PICTURES AND TELL ME WHICH YOU PREFER.
LIDIA, 16 YEARS OLD, FROM MINSK. MYANG FROM THAILAND: 25. YELENA: 19, FROM TALLINN.

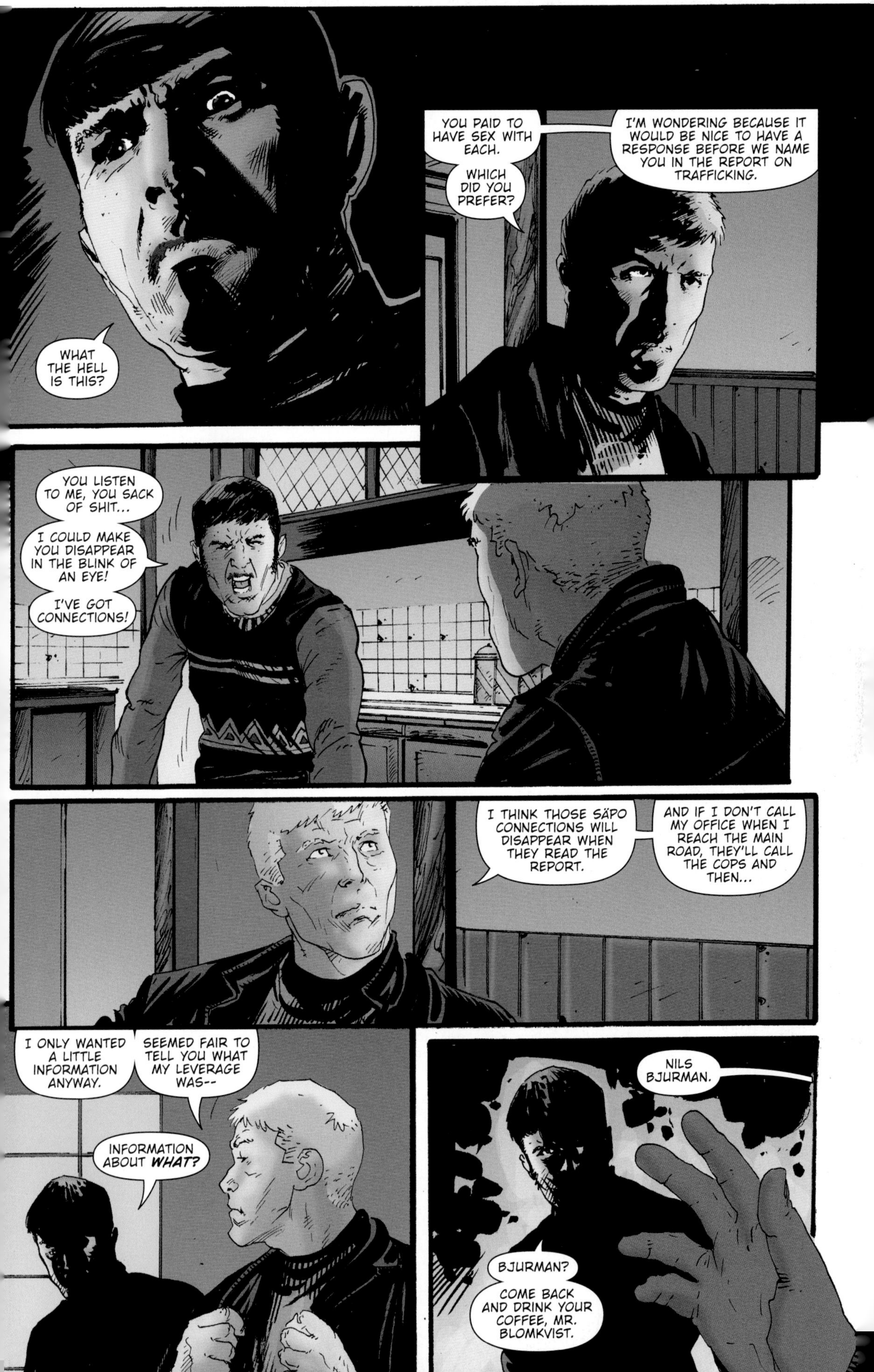
WHAT THE HELL IS THIS?
YOU PAID TO HAVE SEX WITH EACH.
WHICH DID YOU PREFER?
I'M WONDERING BECAUSE IT WOULD BE NICE TO HAVE A RESPONSE BEFORE WE NAME YOU IN THE REPORT ON TRAFFICKING.
YOU LISTEN TO ME, YOU SACK OF SHIT...
I COULD MAKE YOU DISAPPEAR IN THE BLINK OF AN EYE!
I'VE GOT CONNECTIONS!
I THINK THOSE SÄPO CONNECTIONS WILL DISAPPEAR WHEN THEY READ THE REPORT.
AND IF I DON'T CALL MY OFFICE WHEN I REACH THE MAIN ROAD, THEY'LL CALL THE COPS AND THEN...
I ONLY WANTED A LITTLE INFORMATION ANYWAY.
SEEMED FAIR TO TELL YOU WHAT MY LEVERAGE WAS--
INFORMATION ABOUT ***WHAT?***
NILS BJURMAN.
BJURMAN?
COME BACK AND DRINK YOUR COFFEE, MR. BLOMKVIST.

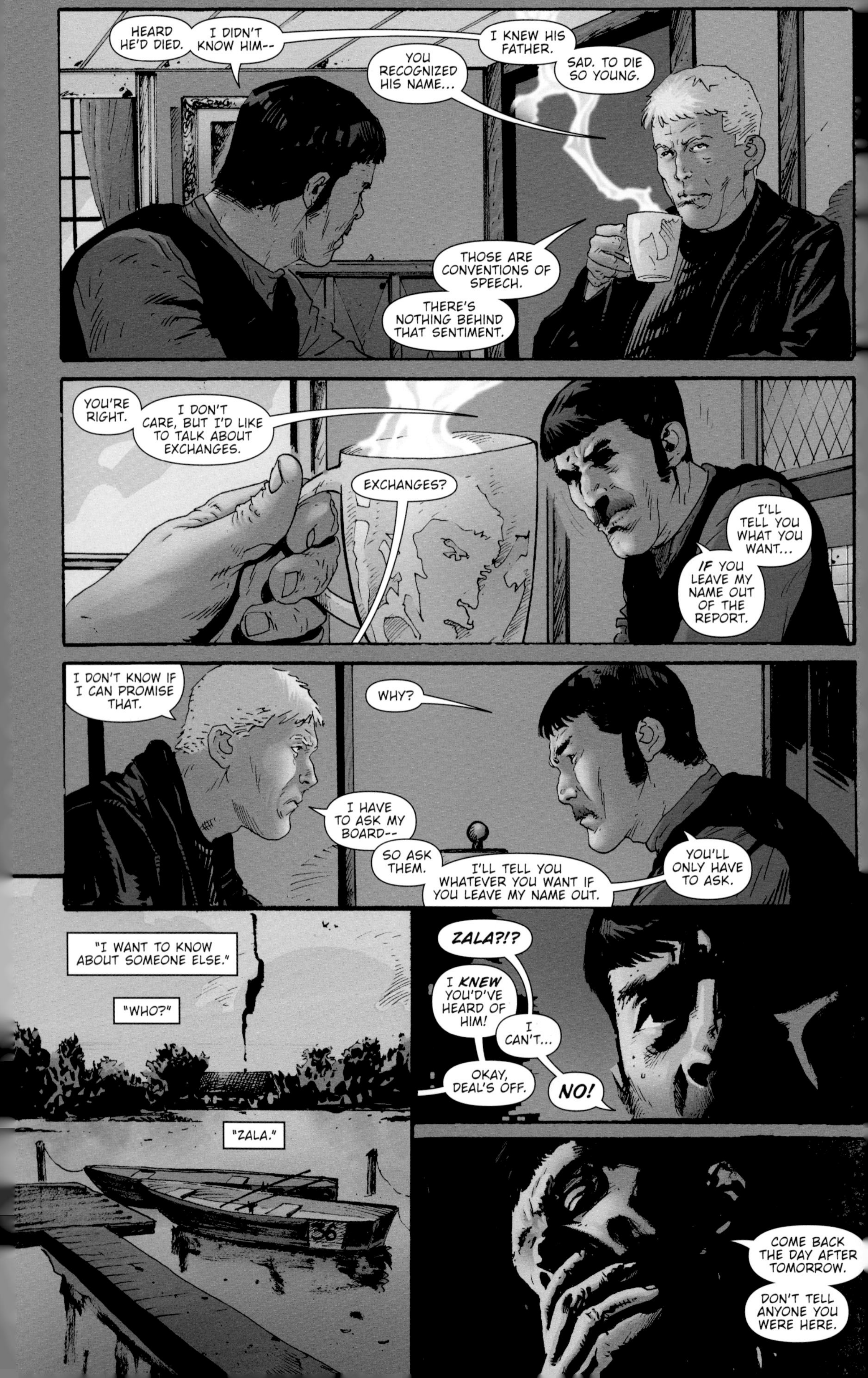
HEARD HE'D DIED.
I DIDN'T KNOW HIM--
I KNEW HIS FATHER.
YOU RECOGNIZED HIS NAME...
SAD. TO DIE SO YOUNG.
THOSE ARE CONVENTIONS OF SPEECH.
THERE'S NOTHING BEHIND THAT SENTIMENT.
YOU'RE RIGHT.
I DON'T CARE, BUT I'D LIKE TO TALK ABOUT EXCHANGES.
EXCHANGES?
I'LL TELL YOU WHAT YOU WANT...
IF YOU LEAVE MY NAME OUT OF THE REPORT.
I DON'T KNOW IF I CAN PROMISE THAT.
WHY?
I HAVE TO ASK MY BOARD--
SO ASK THEM.
I'LL TELL YOU WHATEVER YOU WANT IF YOU LEAVE MY NAME OUT.
YOU'LL ONLY HAVE TO ASK.
"I WANT TO KNOW ABOUT SOMEONE ELSE."
"WHO?"
"ZALA."
ZALA?!?
I KNEW YOU'D'VE HEARD OF HIM!
I CAN'T...
OKAY, DEAL'S OFF.
NO!
COME BACK THE DAY AFTER TOMORROW.
DON'T TELL ANYONE YOU WERE HERE.

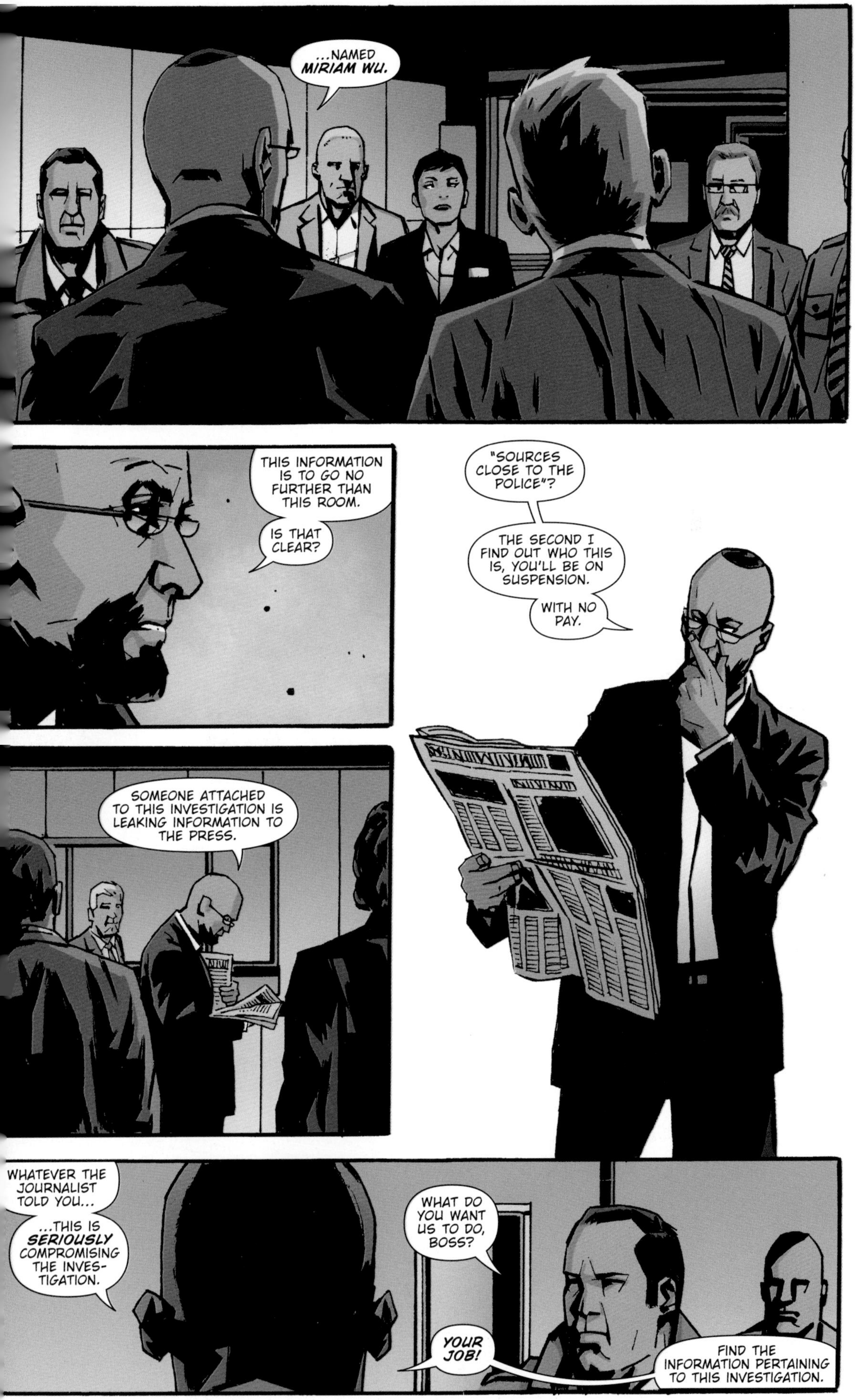
...NAMED MIRIAM WU.
THIS INFORMATION IS TO GO NO FURTHER THAN THIS ROOM.
IS THAT CLEAR?
SOMEONE ATTACHED TO THIS INVESTIGATION IS LEAKING INFORMATION TO THE PRESS.
"SOURCES CLOSE TO THE POLICE"?
THE SECOND I FIND OUT WHO THIS IS, YOU'LL BE ON SUSPENSION.
WITH NO PAY.
WHATEVER THE JOURNALIST TOLD YOU...
...THIS IS SERIOUSLY COMPROMISING THE INVES-TIGATION.
WHAT DO YOU WANT US TO DO, BOSS?
YOUR JOB!
FIND THE INFORMATION PERTAINING TO THIS INVESTIGATION.

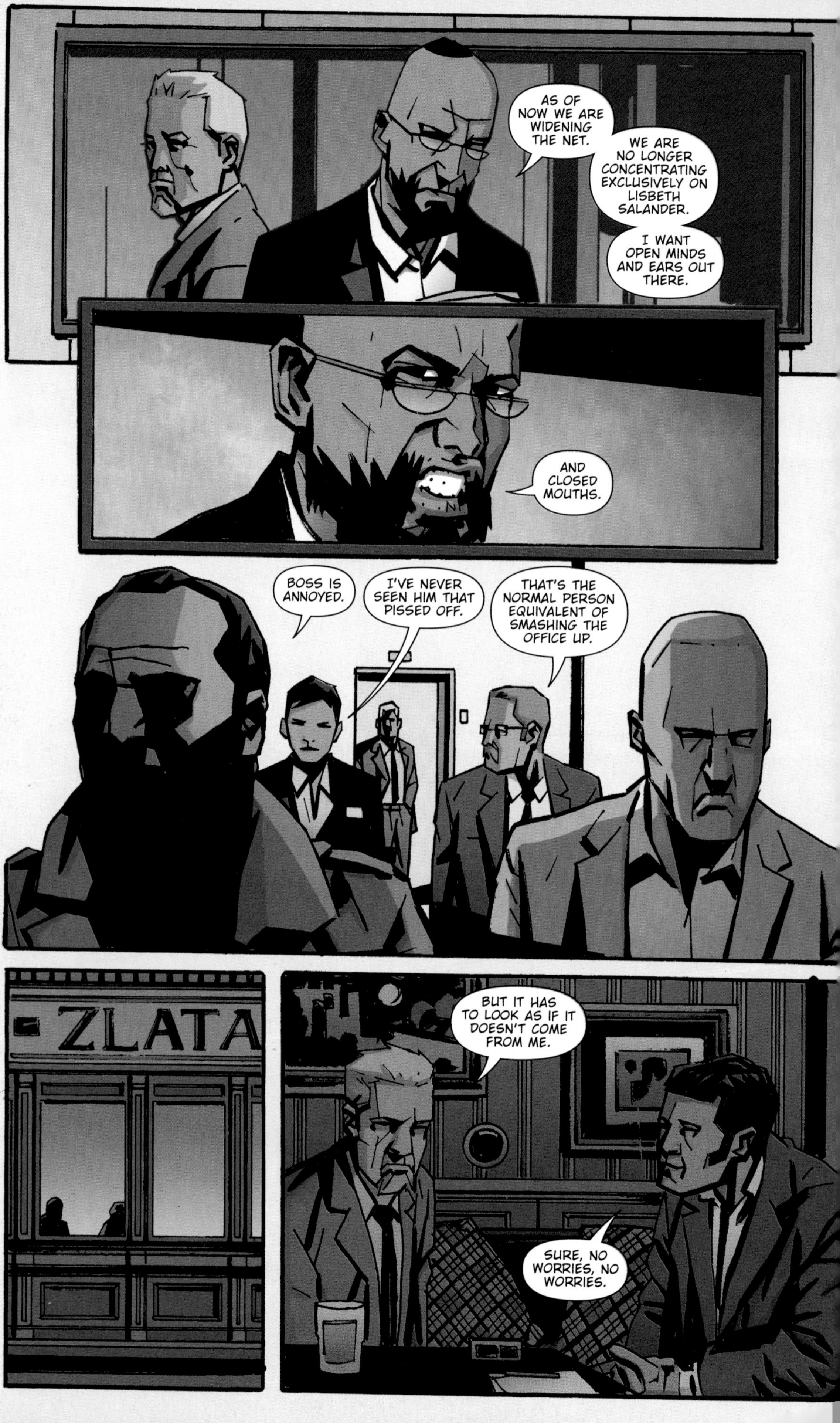
AS OF NOW WE ARE WIDENING THE NET.
WE ARE NO LONGER CONCENTRATING EXCLUSIVELY ON LISBETH SALANDER.
I WANT OPEN MINDS AND EARS OUT THERE.
AND CLOSED MOUTHS.
BOSS IS ANNOYED.
I'VE NEVER SEEN HIM THAT PISSED OFF.
THAT'S THE NORMAL PERSON EQUIVALENT OF SMASHING THE OFFICE UP.
ZLATA
BUT IT HAS TO LOOK AS IF IT DOESN'T COME FROM ME.
SURE, NO WORRIES, NO WORRIES.

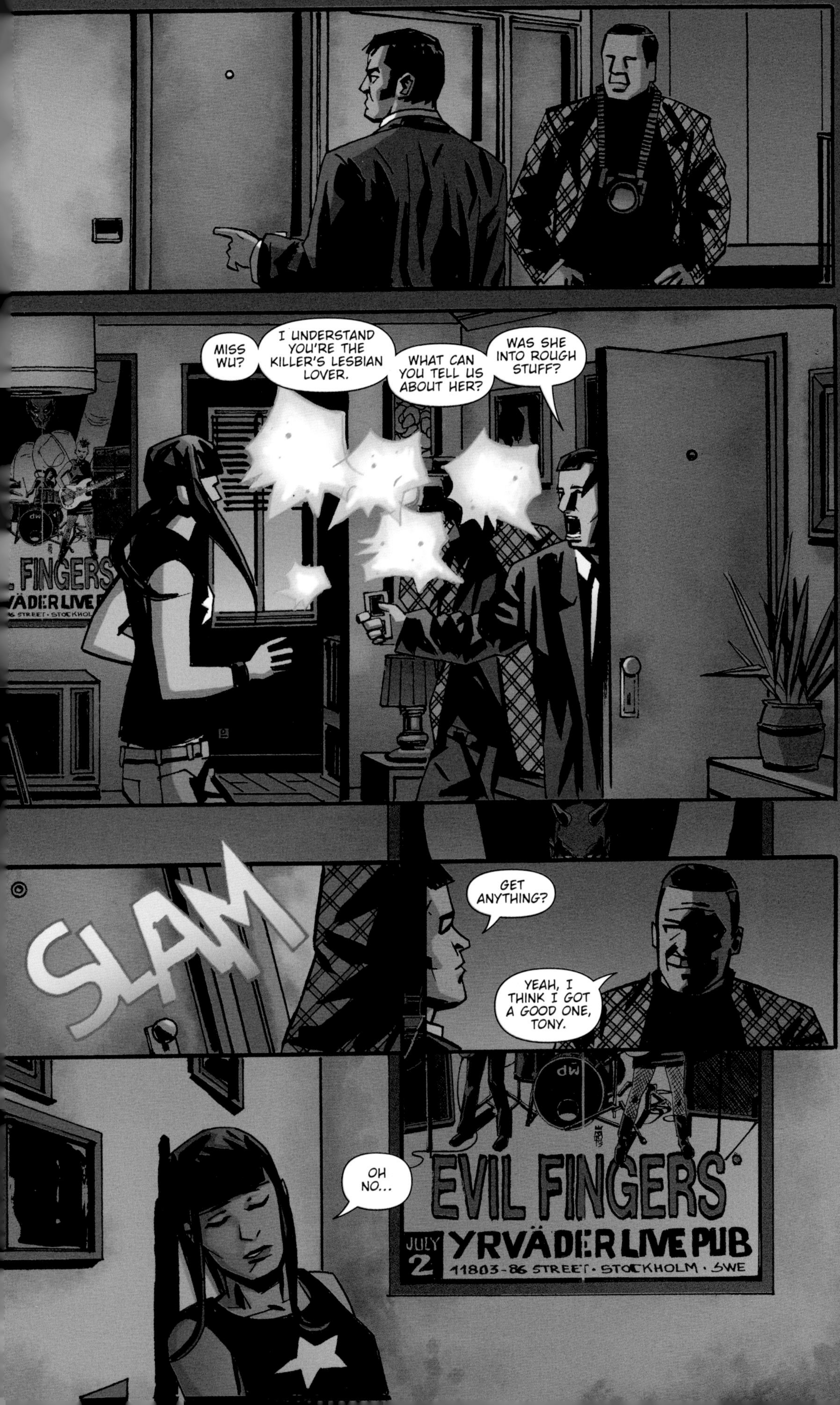
MISS WU?
I UNDERSTAND YOU'RE THE KILLER'S LESBIAN LOVER.
WHAT CAN YOU TELL US ABOUT HER?
WAS SHE INTO ROUGH STUFF?
FINGERS
VÄDER LIVE
SLAM
GET ANYTHING?
YEAH, I THINK I GOT A GOOD ONE, TONY.
OH NO...
EVIL FINGERS
JULY 2
YRVÄDER LIVE PUB
11803-86 STREET · STOCKHOLM · SWE

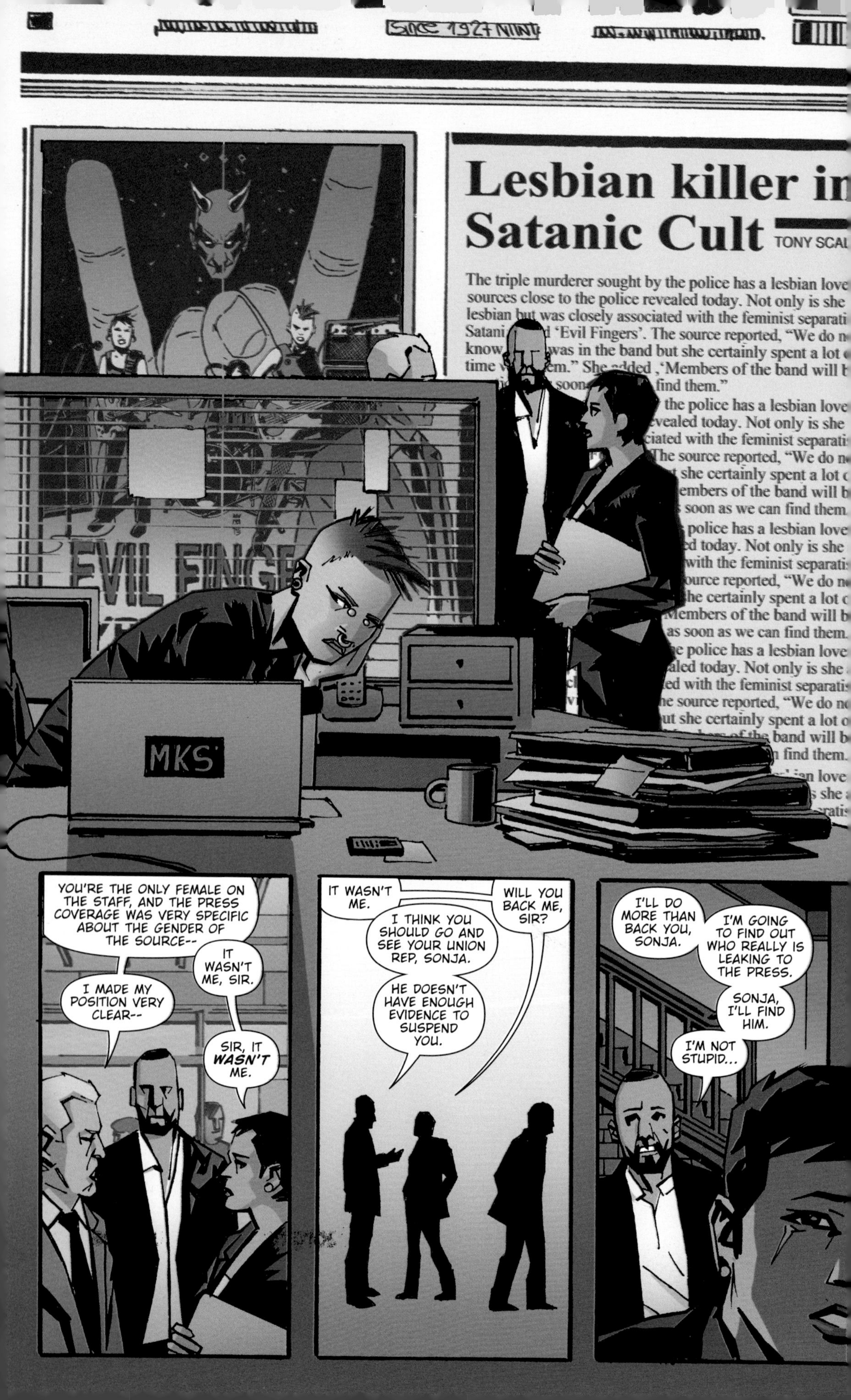
Since 1927
Lesbian killer in Satanic Cult
TONY SCAL
The triple murderer sought by the police has a lesbian love sources close to the police revealed today. Not only is she lesbian but was closely associated with the feminist separati Satani 'Evil Fingers'. The source reported, "We do n know was in the band but she certainly spent a lot time em." She added ,'Members of the band will b soon find them."
EVIL FINGE
MKS
YOU'RE THE ONLY FEMALE ON THE STAFF, AND THE PRESS COVERAGE WAS VERY SPECIFIC ABOUT THE GENDER OF THE SOURCE--
IT WASN'T ME, SIR.
I MADE MY POSITION VERY CLEAR--
SIR, IT *WASN'T* ME.
IT WASN'T ME.
WILL YOU BACK ME, SIR?
I THINK YOU SHOULD GO AND SEE YOUR UNION REP, SONJA.
HE DOESN'T HAVE ENOUGH EVIDENCE TO SUSPEND YOU.
I'LL DO MORE THAN BACK YOU, SONJA.
I'M GOING TO FIND OUT WHO REALLY IS LEAKING TO THE PRESS.
SONJA, I'LL FIND HIM.
I'M NOT STUPID...

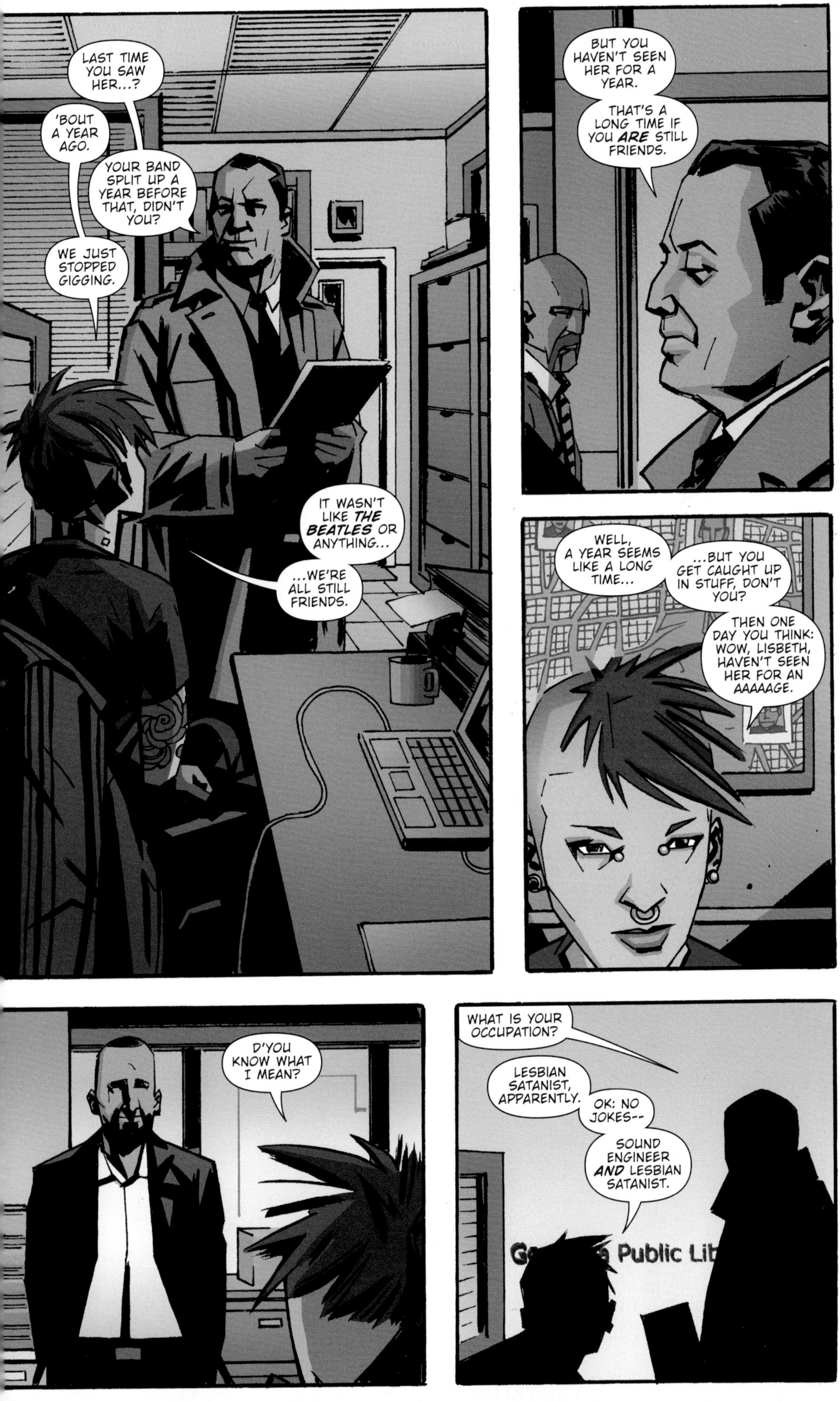
LAST TIME YOU SAW HER...?
'BOUT A YEAR AGO.
YOUR BAND SPLIT UP A YEAR BEFORE THAT, DIDN'T YOU?
WE JUST STOPPED GIGGING.
IT WASN'T LIKE ***THE BEATLES*** OR ANYTHING...
...WE'RE ALL STILL FRIENDS.
BUT YOU HAVEN'T SEEN HER FOR A YEAR.
THAT'S A LONG TIME IF YOU ***ARE*** STILL FRIENDS.
WELL, A YEAR SEEMS LIKE A LONG TIME...
...BUT YOU GET CAUGHT UP IN STUFF, DON'T YOU?
THEN ONE DAY YOU THINK: WOW, LISBETH, HAVEN'T SEEN HER FOR AN AAAAAGE.
D'YOU KNOW WHAT I MEAN?
WHAT IS YOUR OCCUPATION?
LESBIAN SATANIST, APPARENTLY.
OK: NO JOKES--
SOUND ENGINEER ***AND*** LESBIAN SATANIST.
Public Lib

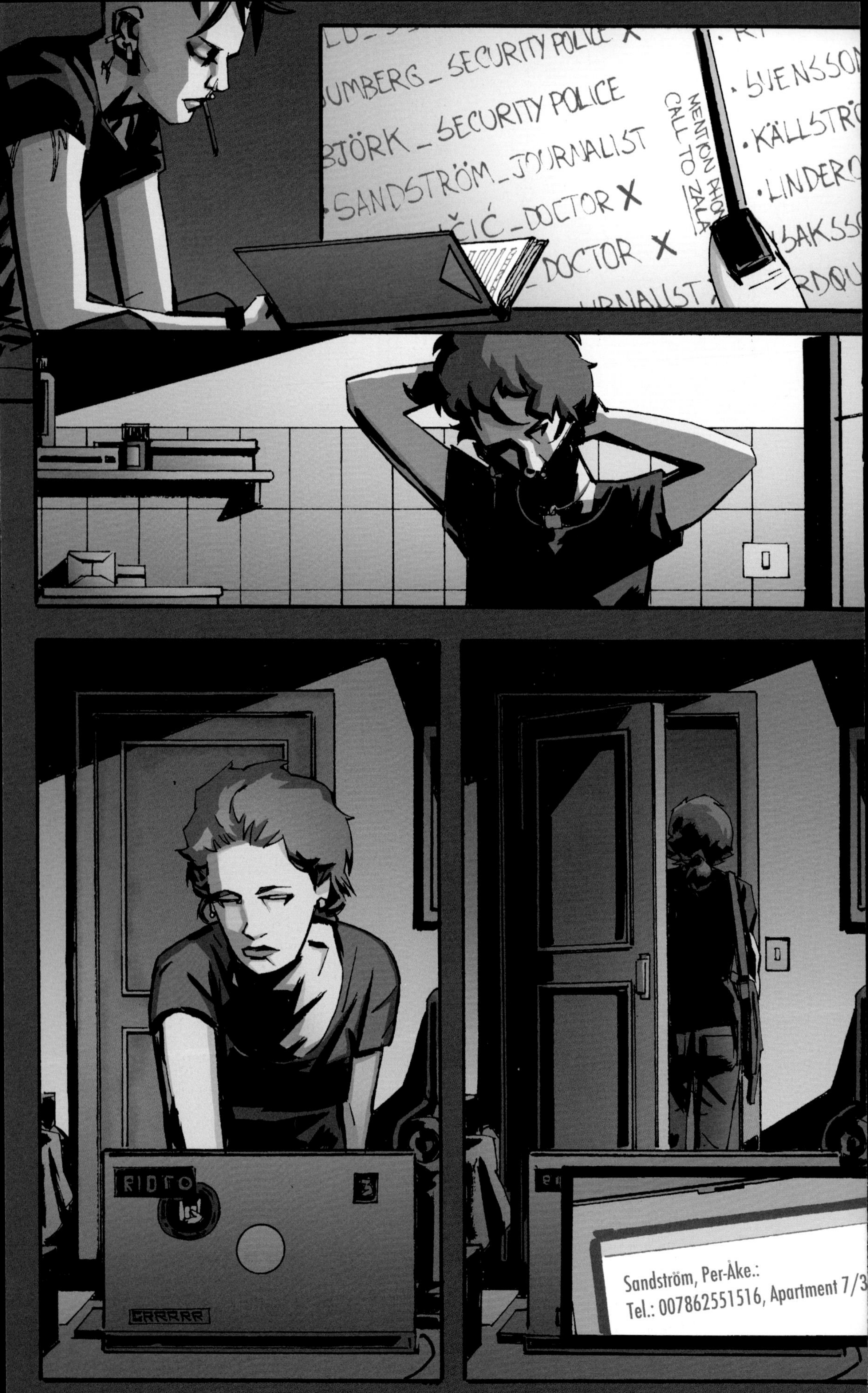

UMBERG_SECURITY POLICE X
BJÖRK_SECURITY POLICE
SANDSTRÖM_JOURNALIST
ČIĆ_DOCTOR X
_DOCTOR X
CALL TO ZALA
SVENSSO
KÄLLSTR
LINDER
Sandström, Per-Åke.:
Tel.: 007862551516, Apartment 7/3

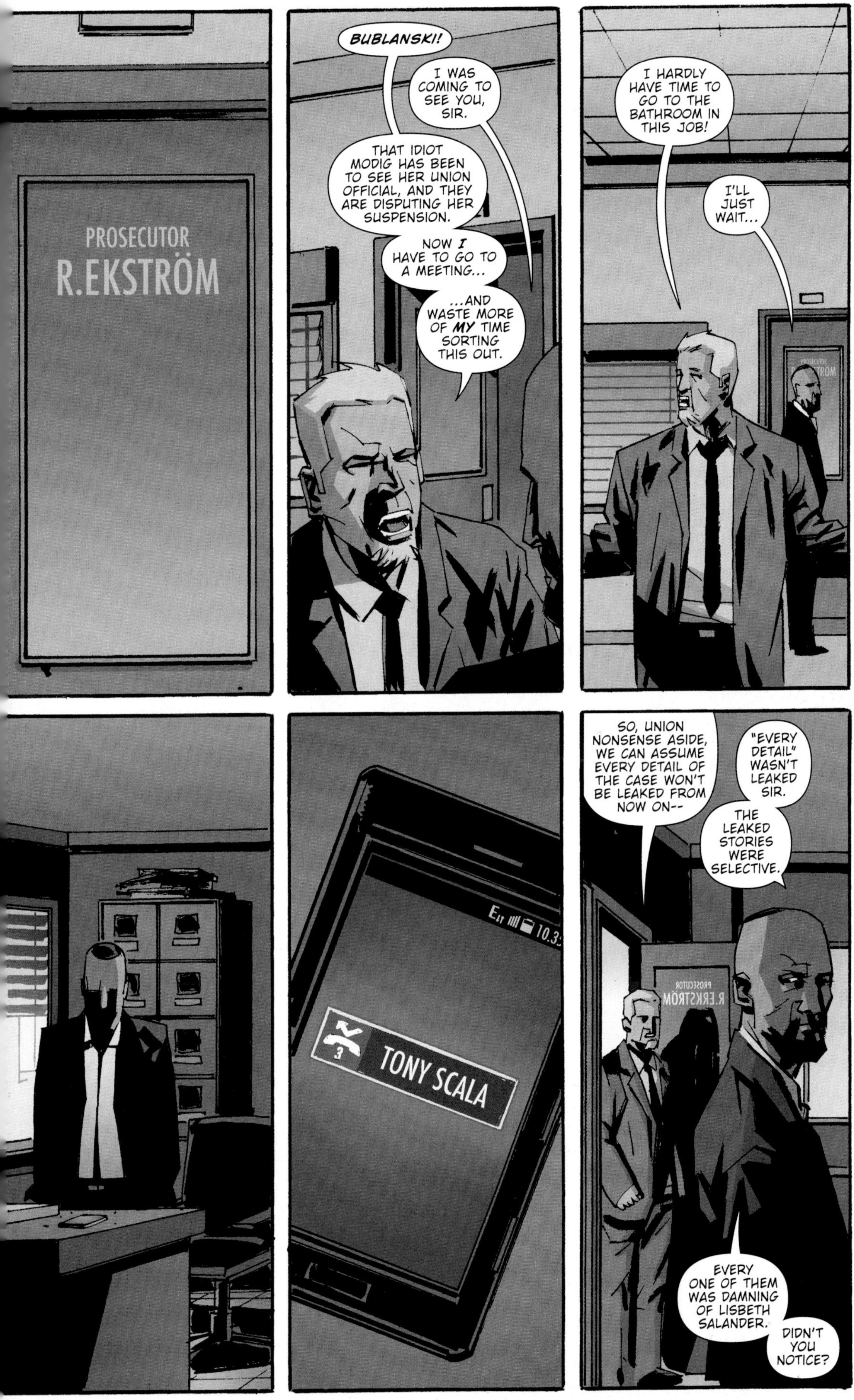
PROSECUTOR
R.EKSTRÖM
BUBLANSKI!
I WAS COMING TO SEE YOU, SIR.
THAT IDIOT MODIG HAS BEEN TO SEE HER UNION OFFICIAL, AND THEY ARE DISPUTING HER SUSPENSION.
NOW I HAVE TO GO TO A MEETING...
...AND WASTE MORE OF MY TIME SORTING THIS OUT.
I HARDLY HAVE TIME TO GO TO THE BATHROOM IN THIS JOB!
I'LL JUST WAIT...
TONY SCALA
SO, UNION NONSENSE ASIDE, WE CAN ASSUME EVERY DETAIL OF THE CASE WON'T BE LEAKED FROM NOW ON--
"EVERY DETAIL" WASN'T LEAKED SIR.
THE LEAKED STORIES WERE SELECTIVE.
EVERY ONE OF THEM WAS DAMNING OF LISBETH SALANDER.
DIDN'T YOU NOTICE?

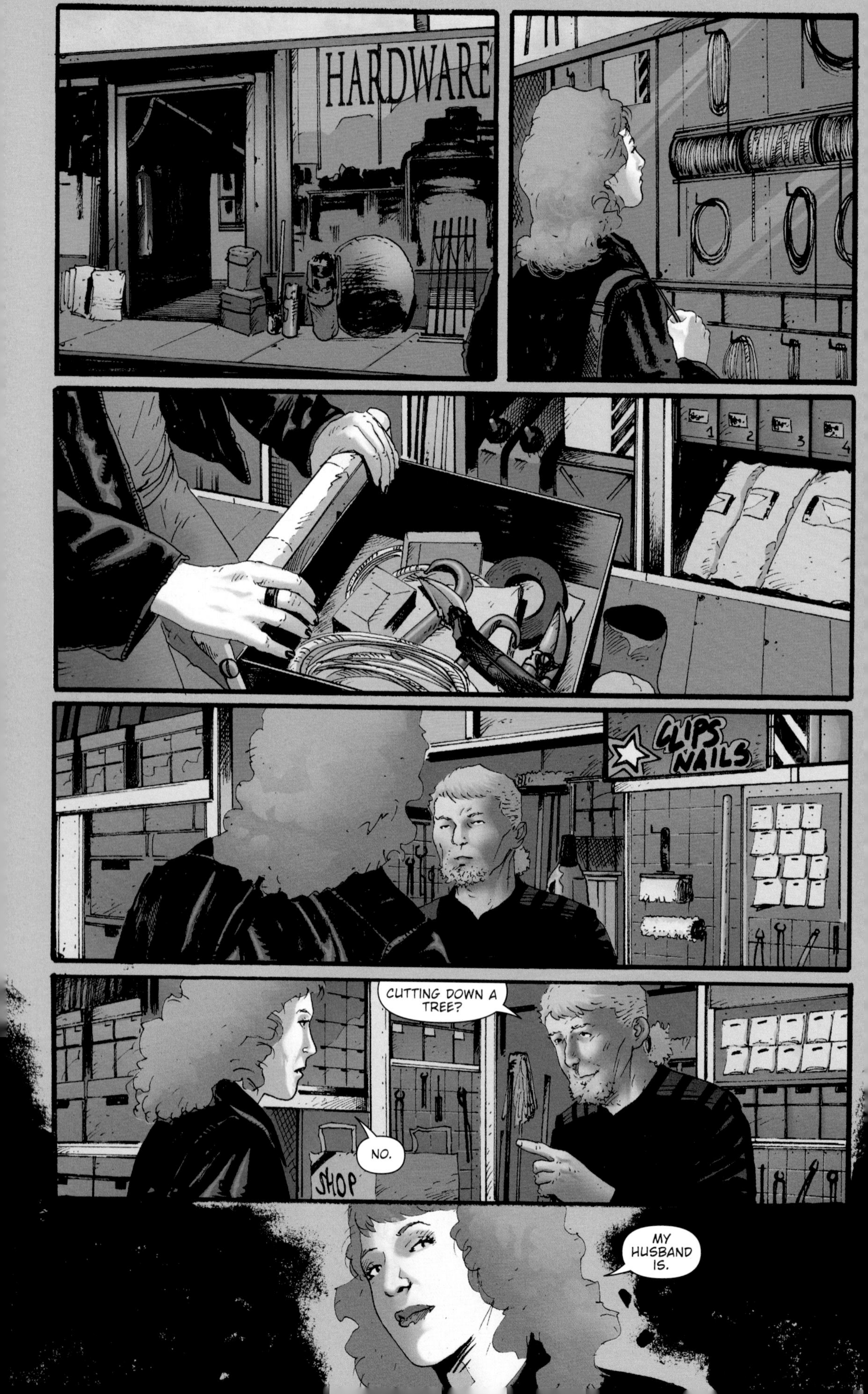
HARDWARE
1
2
3
4
CLIPS
NAILS
CUTTING DOWN A TREE?
NO.
SHOP
MY HUSBAND IS.

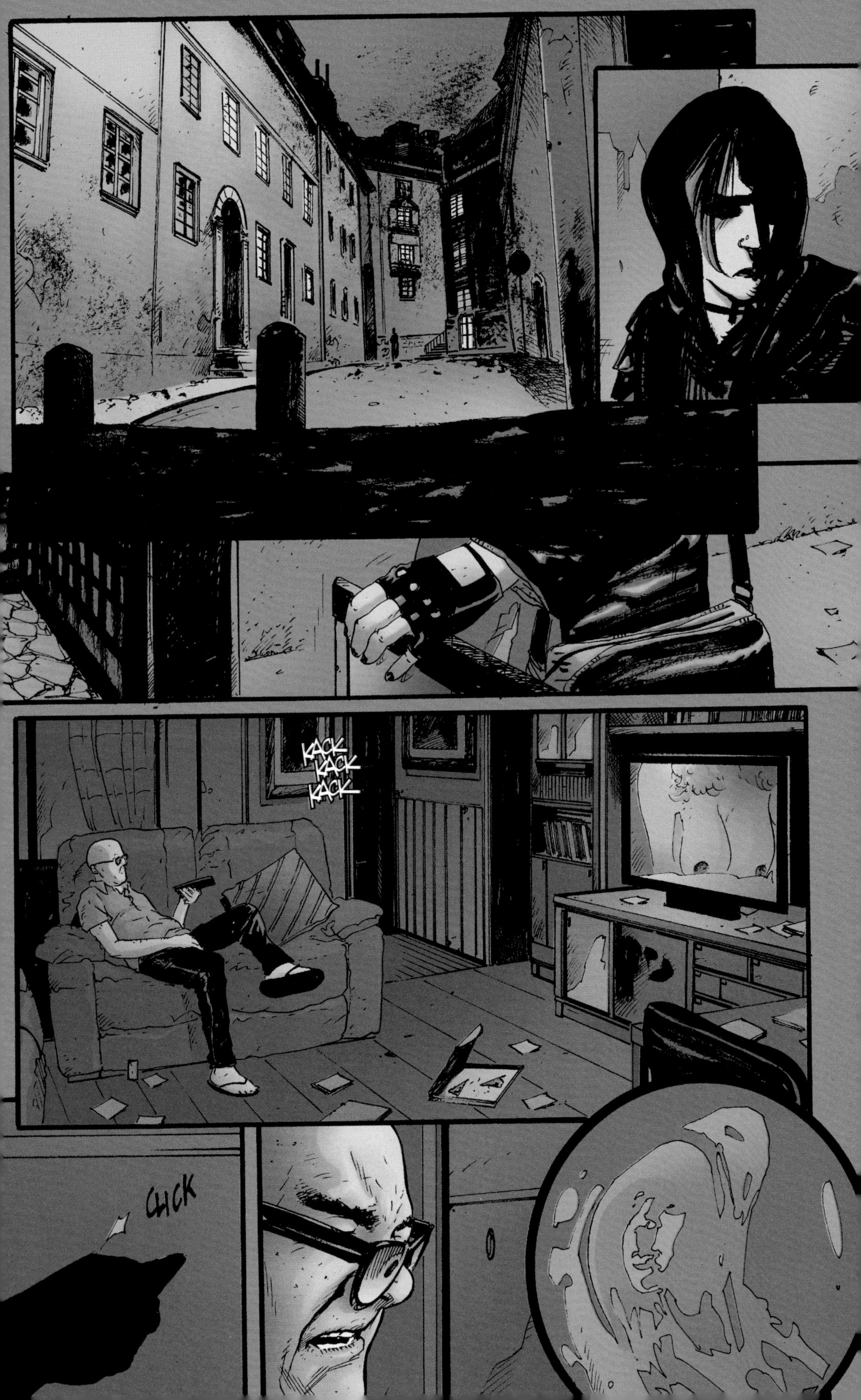
KACK
KACK
KACK
CLICK

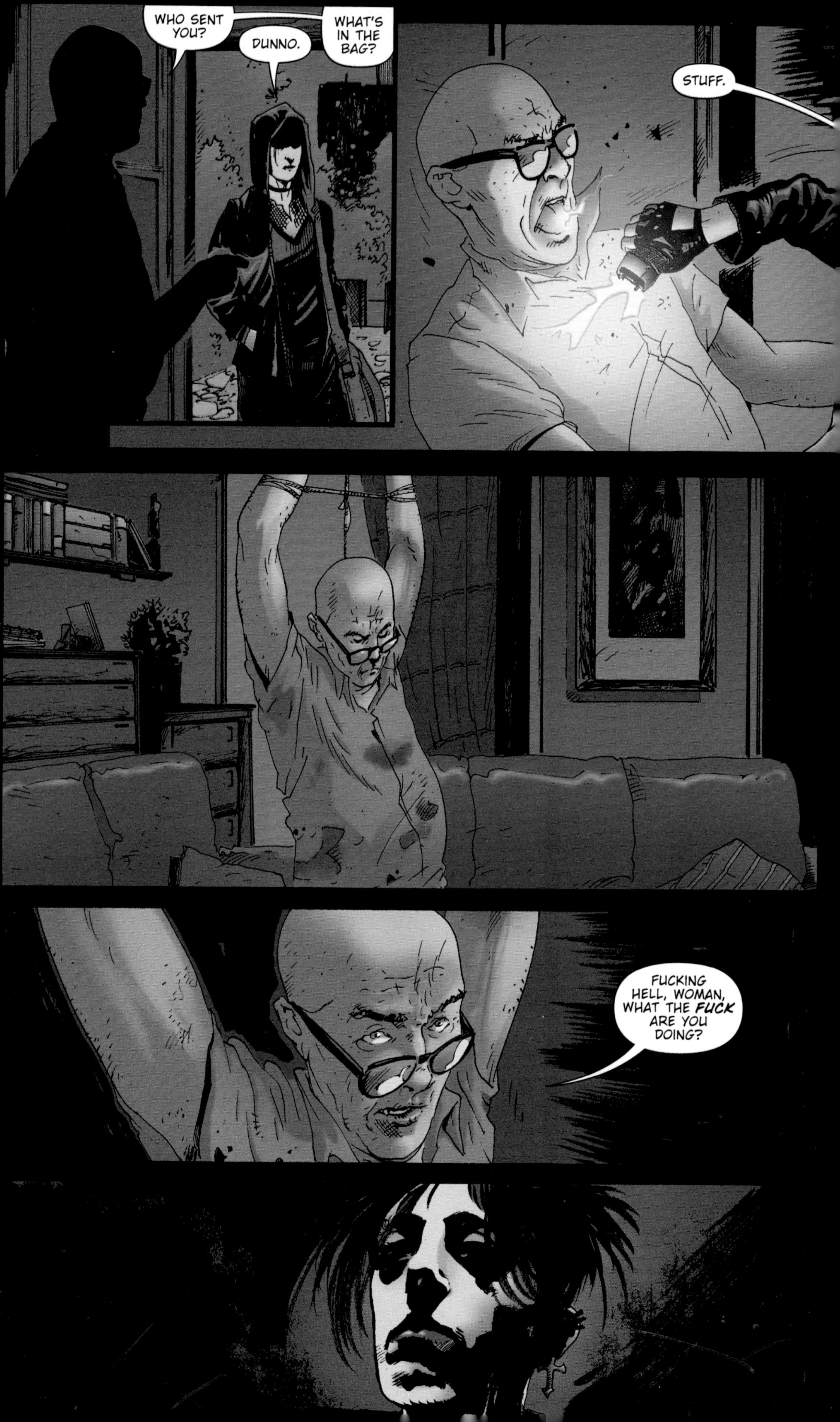
WHO SENT YOU?
DUNNO.
WHAT'S IN THE BAG?
STUFF.
FUCKING HELL, WOMAN, WHAT THE FUCK ARE YOU DOING?

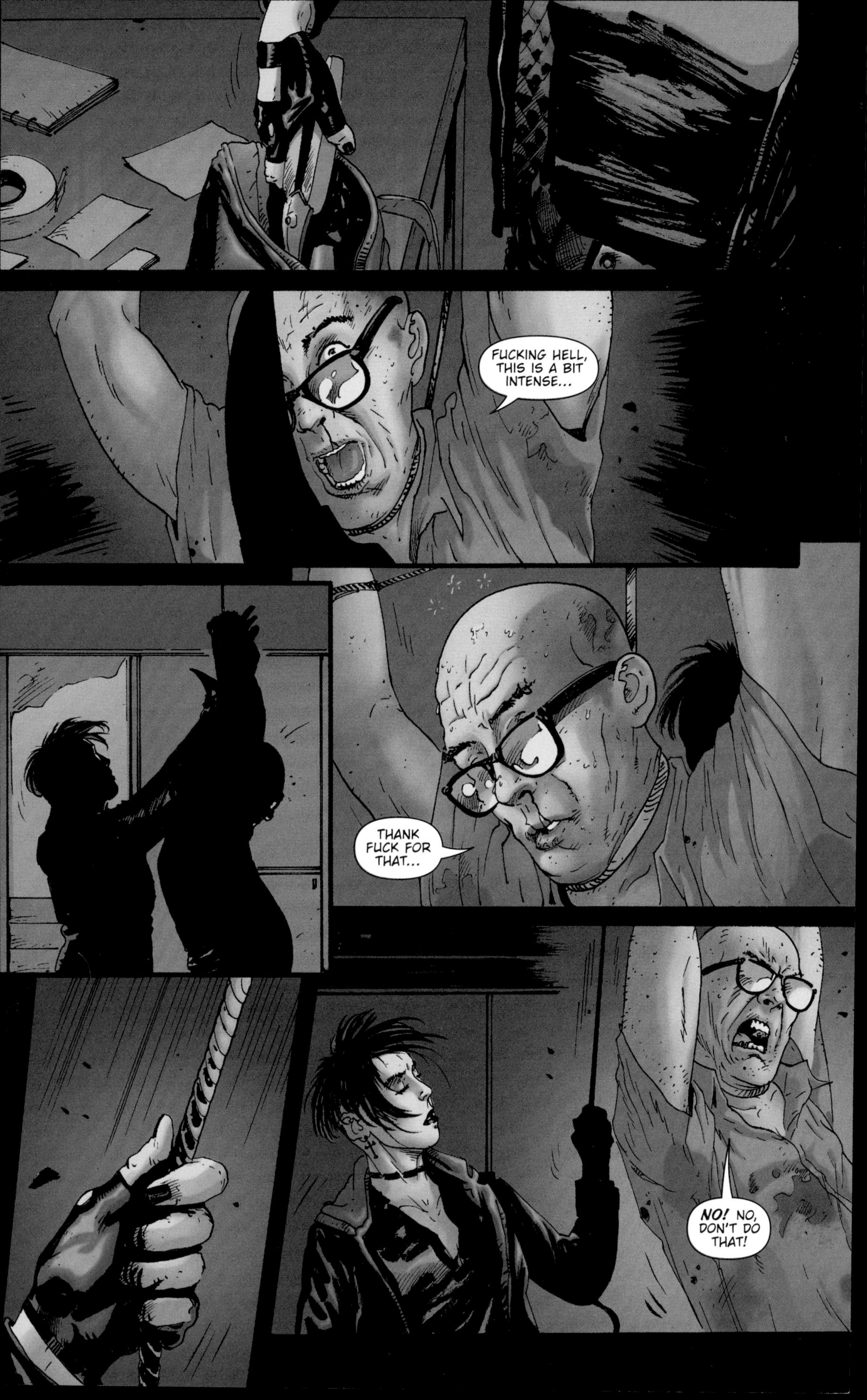
FUCKING HELL, THIS IS A BIT INTENSE...
THANK FUCK FOR THAT...
NO! NO, DON'T DO THAT!

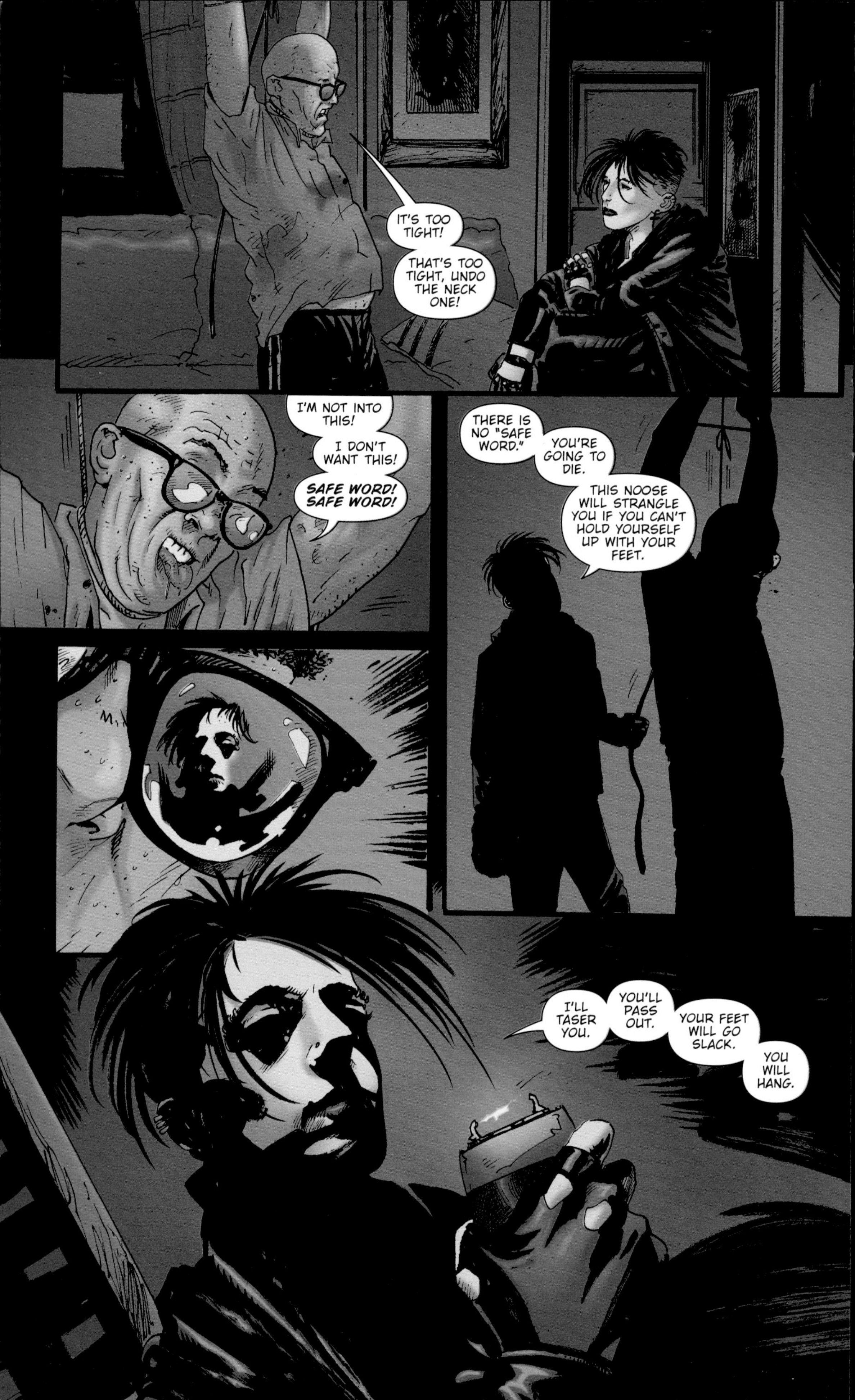

IT'S TOO TIGHT!
THAT'S TOO TIGHT, UNDO THE NECK ONE!
I'M NOT INTO THIS!
I DON'T WANT THIS!
SAFE WORD! SAFE WORD!
THERE IS NO "SAFE WORD."
YOU'RE GOING TO DIE.
THIS NOOSE WILL STRANGLE YOU IF YOU CAN'T HOLD YOURSELF UP WITH YOUR FEET.
I'LL TASER YOU.
YOU'LL PASS OUT.
YOUR FEET WILL GO SLACK.
YOU WILL HANG.

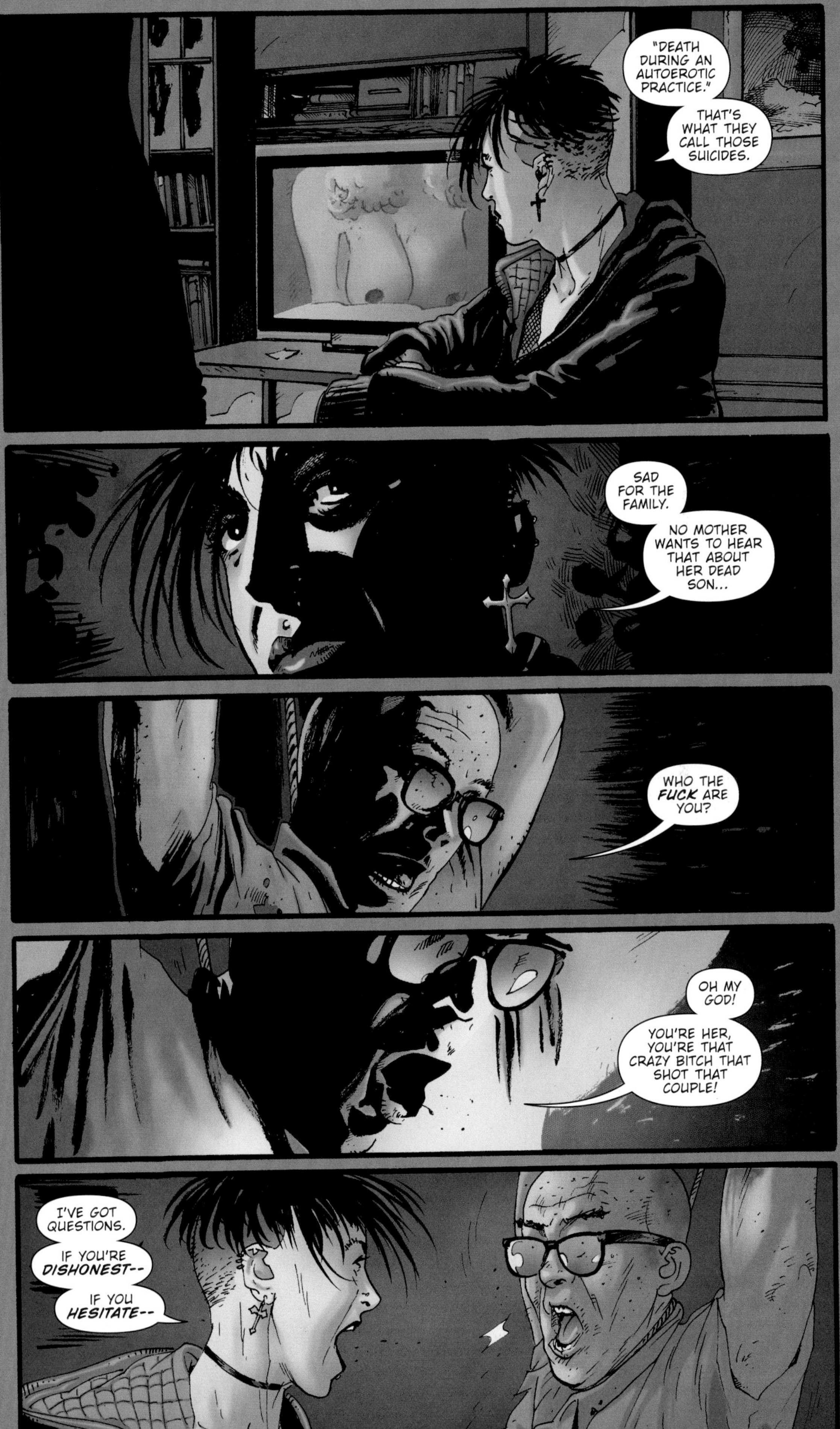
"DEATH DURING AN AUTOEROTIC PRACTICE."
THAT'S WHAT THEY CALL THOSE SUICIDES.
SAD FOR THE FAMILY.
NO MOTHER WANTS TO HEAR THAT ABOUT HER DEAD SON...
WHO THE *FUCK* ARE YOU?
OH MY GOD!
YOU'RE HER, YOU'RE THAT CRAZY BITCH THAT SHOT THAT COUPLE!
I'VE GOT QUESTIONS.
IF YOU'RE *DISHONEST--*
IF YOU *HESITATE--*

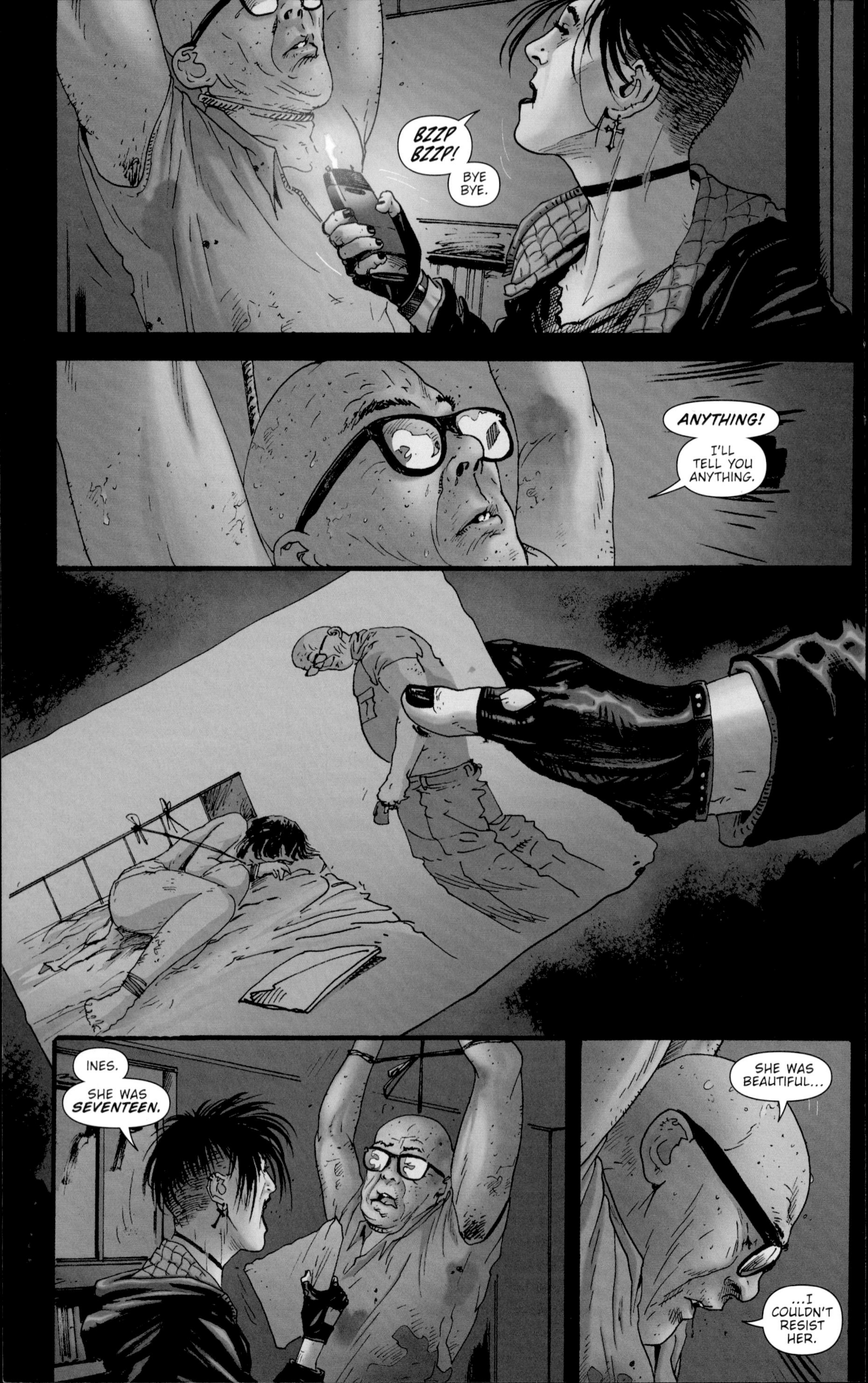
BZZP BZZP!
BYE BYE.
ANYTHING!
I'LL TELL YOU ANYTHING.
INES.
SHE WAS SEVENTEEN.
SHE WAS BEAUTIFUL...
...I COULDN'T RESIST HER.

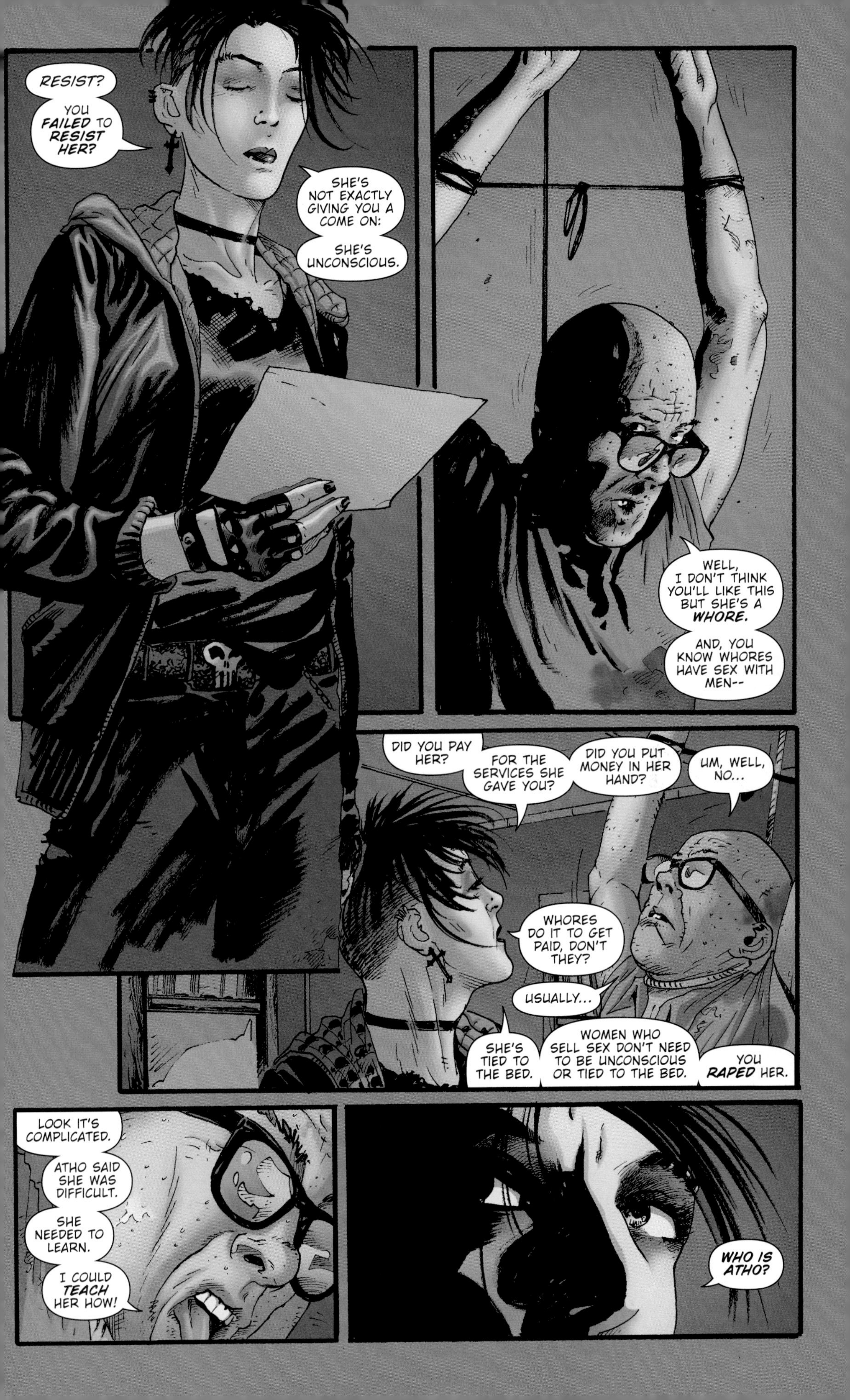

RESIST?
YOU *FAILED* TO *RESIST HER?*
SHE'S NOT EXACTLY GIVING YOU A COME ON:
SHE'S UNCONSCIOUS.
WELL, I DON'T THINK YOU'LL LIKE THIS BUT SHE'S A *WHORE.*
AND, YOU KNOW WHORES HAVE SEX WITH MEN--
DID YOU PAY HER?
FOR THE SERVICES SHE GAVE YOU?
DID YOU PUT MONEY IN HER HAND?
UM, WELL, NO...
WHORES DO IT TO GET PAID, DON'T THEY?
USUALLY...
SHE'S TIED TO THE BED.
WOMEN WHO SELL SEX DON'T NEED TO BE UNCONSCIOUS OR TIED TO THE BED.
YOU *RAPED* HER.
LOOK IT'S COMPLICATED.
ATHO SAID SHE WAS DIFFICULT.
SHE NEEDED TO LEARN.
I COULD *TEACH* HER HOW!
WHO IS ATHO?

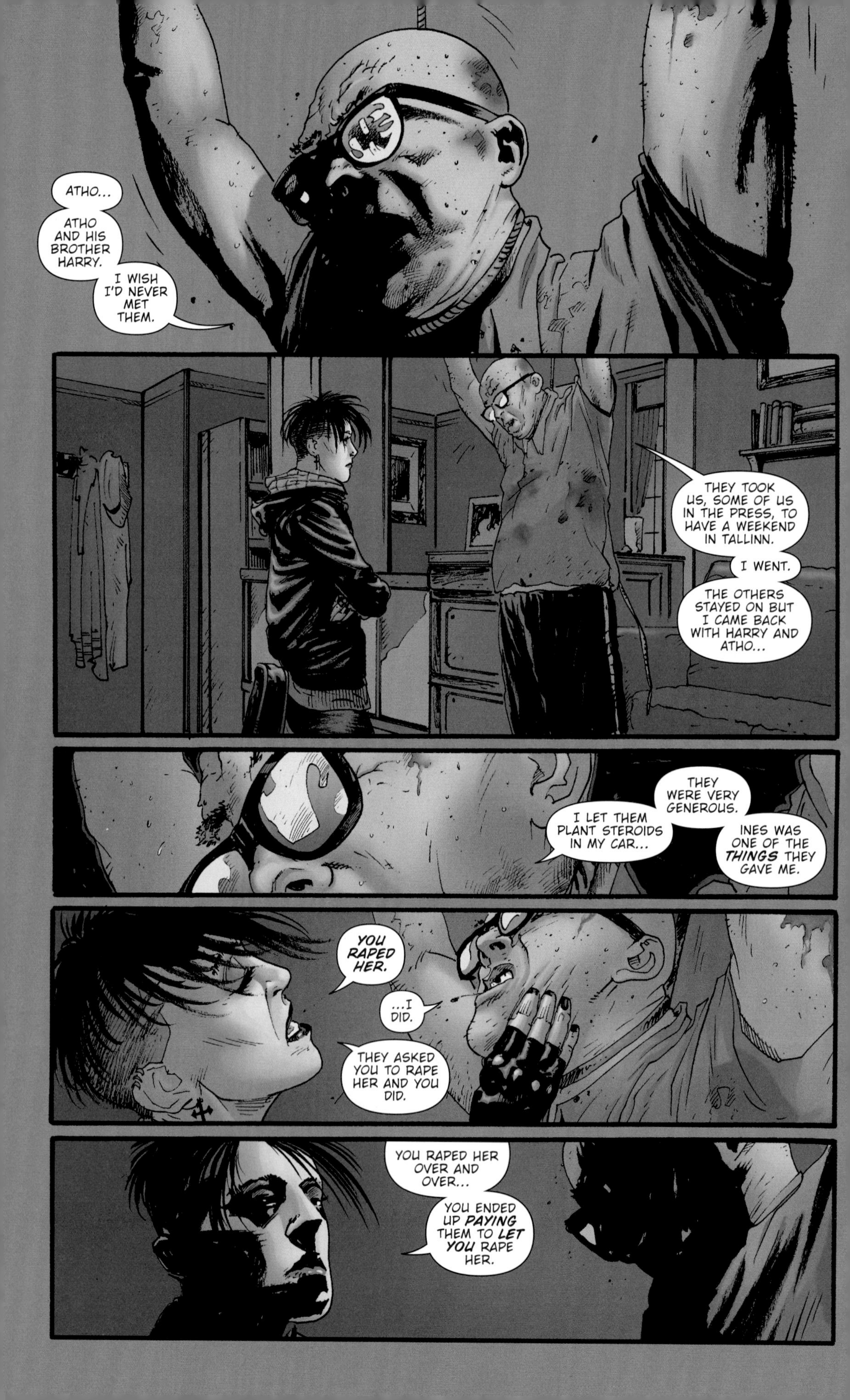
ATHO...
ATHO AND HIS BROTHER HARRY.
I WISH I'D NEVER MET THEM.
THEY TOOK US, SOME OF US IN THE PRESS, TO HAVE A WEEKEND IN TALLINN.
I WENT.
THE OTHERS STAYED ON BUT I CAME BACK WITH HARRY AND ATHO...
I LET THEM PLANT STEROIDS IN MY CAR...
THEY WERE VERY GENEROUS.
INES WAS ONE OF THE *THINGS* THEY GAVE ME.
YOU RAPED HER.
...I DID.
THEY ASKED YOU TO RAPE HER AND YOU DID.
YOU RAPED HER OVER AND OVER...
YOU ENDED UP *PAYING* THEM TO *LET YOU* RAPE HER.

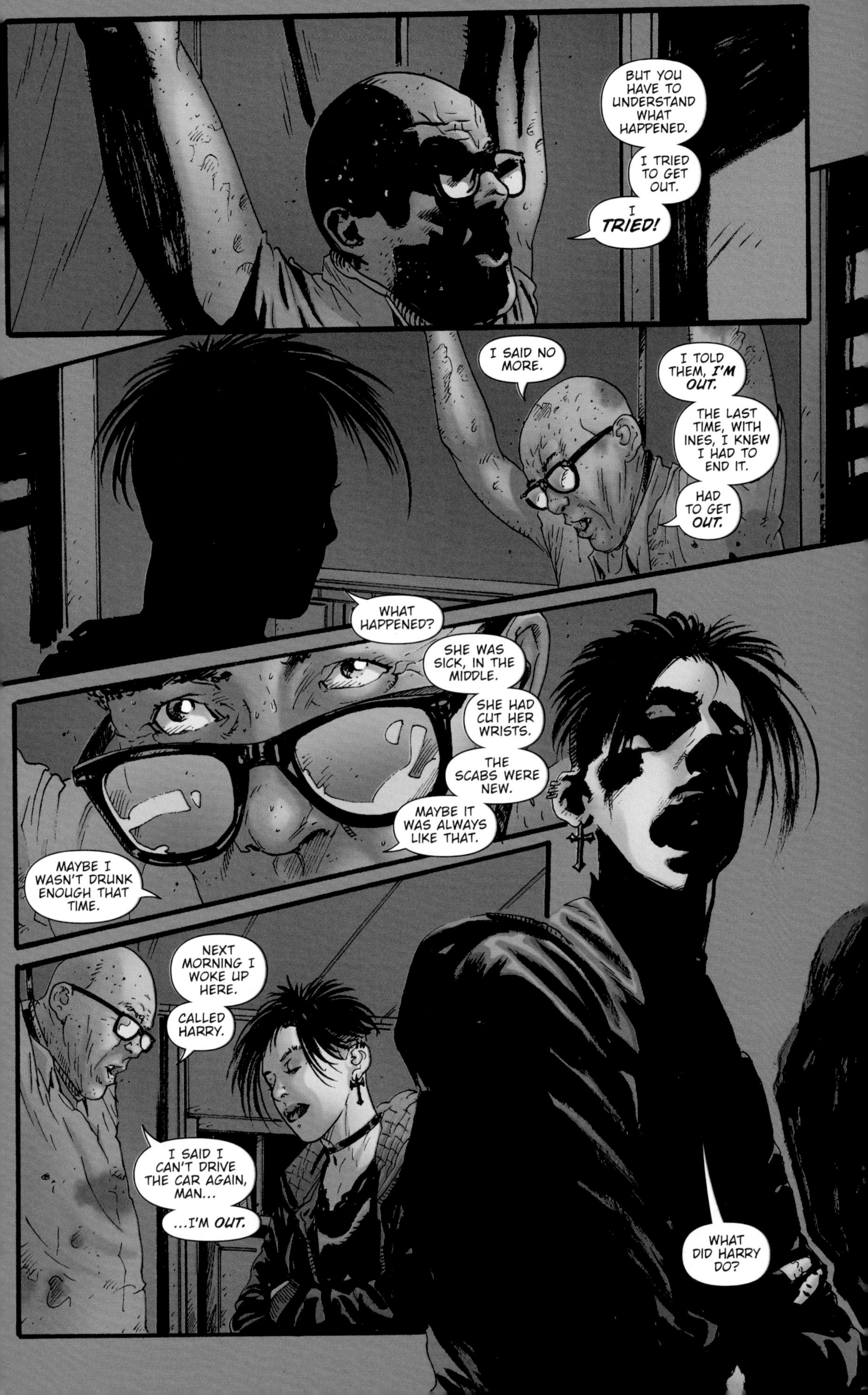
BUT YOU HAVE TO UNDERSTAND WHAT HAPPENED.
I TRIED TO GET OUT.
I *TRIED!*
I SAID NO MORE.
I TOLD THEM, *I'M OUT.*
THE LAST TIME, WITH INES, I KNEW I HAD TO END IT.
HAD TO GET *OUT.*
WHAT HAPPENED?
SHE WAS SICK, IN THE MIDDLE.
SHE HAD CUT HER WRISTS.
THE SCABS WERE NEW.
MAYBE IT WAS ALWAYS LIKE THAT.
MAYBE I WASN'T DRUNK ENOUGH THAT TIME.
NEXT MORNING I WOKE UP HERE.
CALLED HARRY.
I SAID I CAN'T DRIVE THE CAR AGAIN, MAN...
...I'M *OUT.*
WHAT DID HARRY DO?

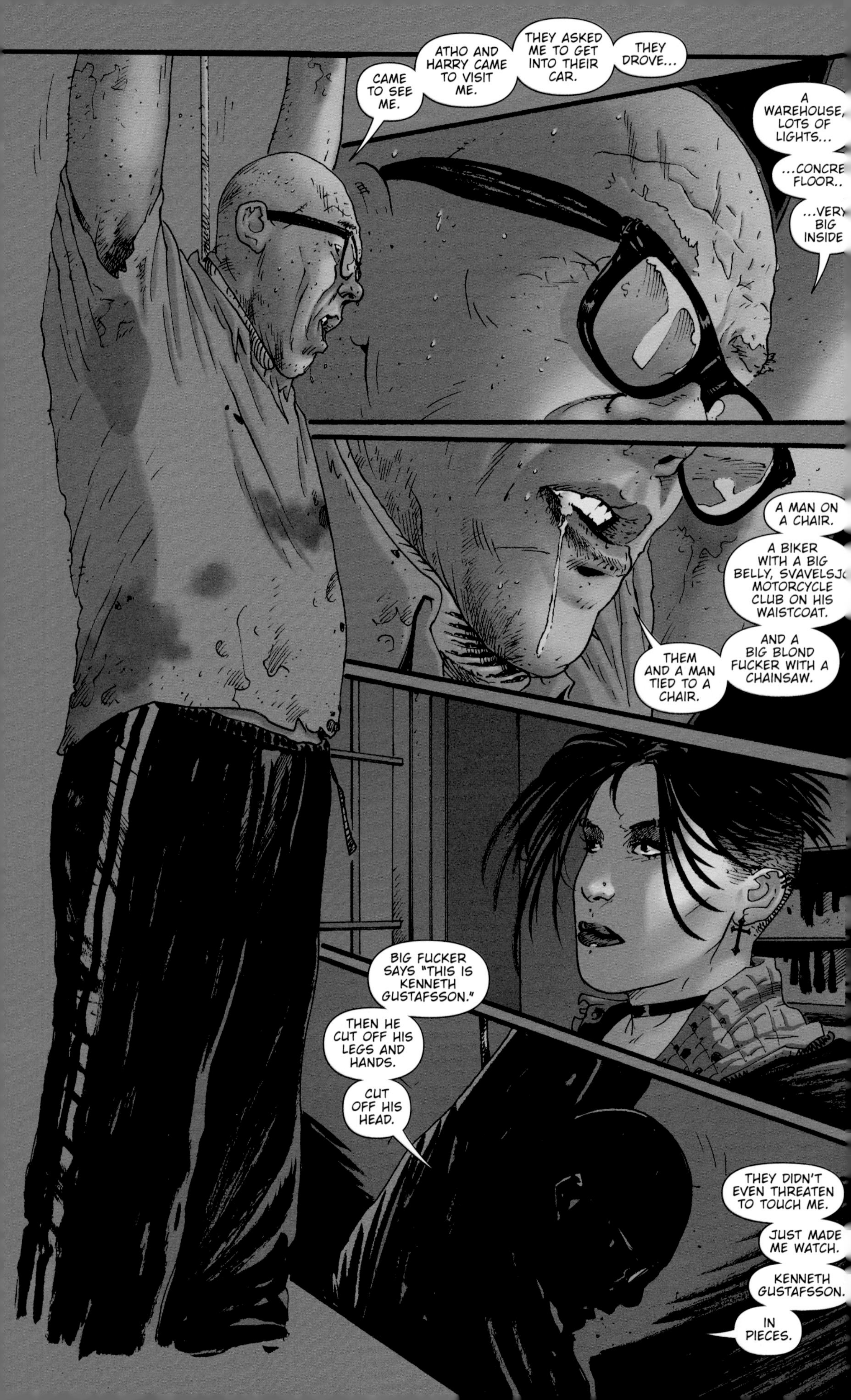

CAME TO SEE ME.
ATHO AND HARRY CAME TO VISIT ME.
THEY ASKED ME TO GET INTO THEIR CAR.
THEY DROVE...
A WAREHOUSE, LOTS OF LIGHTS...
...CONCRE FLOOR..
...VERY BIG INSIDE
A MAN ON A CHAIR.
A BIKER WITH A BIG BELLY, SVAVELSJ MOTORCYCLE CLUB ON HIS WAISTCOAT.
THEM AND A MAN TIED TO A CHAIR.
AND A BIG BLOND FUCKER WITH A CHAINSAW.
BIG FUCKER SAYS "THIS IS KENNETH GUSTAFSSON."
THEN HE CUT OFF HIS LEGS AND HANDS.
CUT OFF HIS HEAD.
THEY DIDN'T EVEN THREATEN TO TOUCH ME.
JUST MADE ME WATCH.
KENNETH GUSTAFSSON.
IN PIECES.

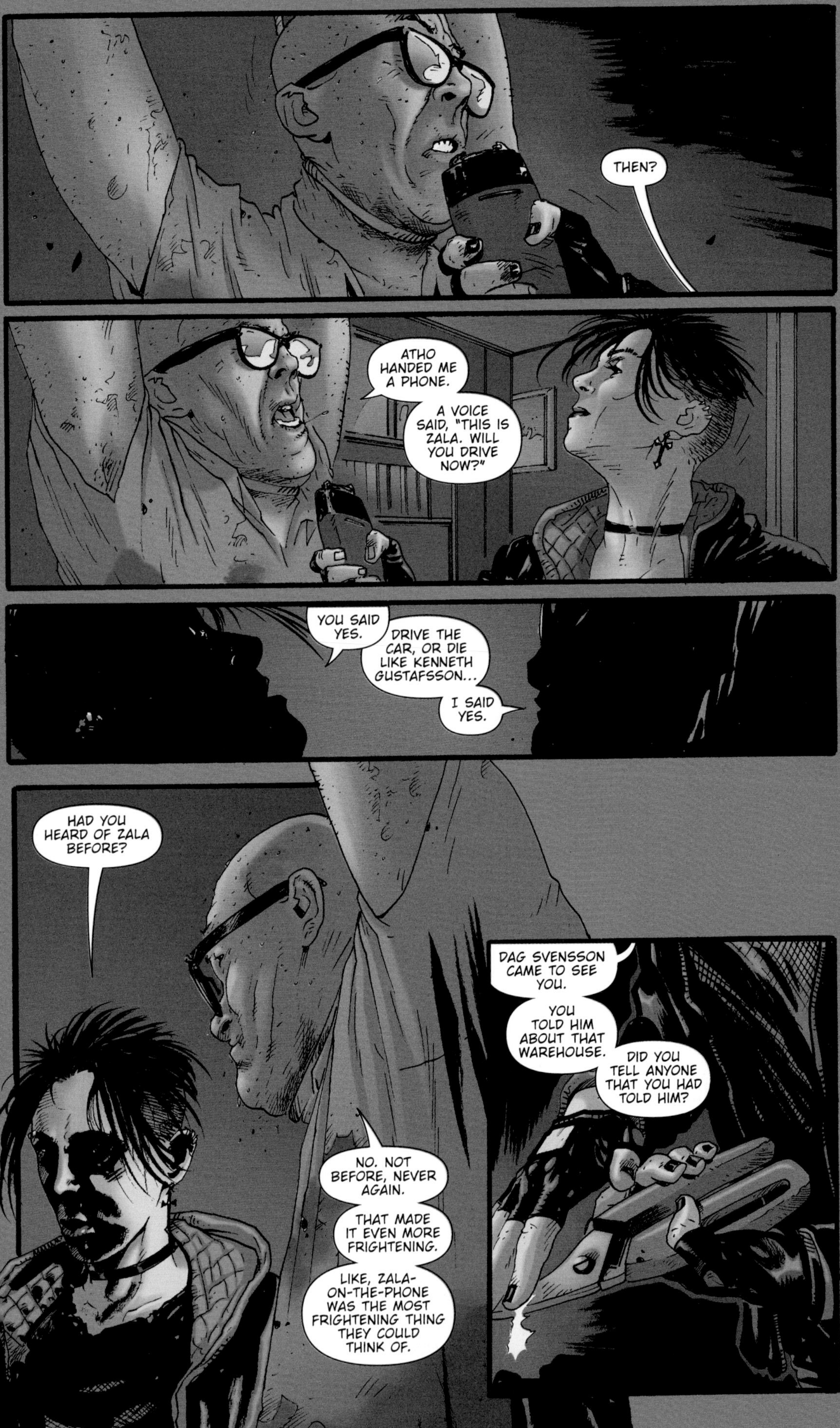
THEN?
ATHO HANDED ME A PHONE.
A VOICE SAID, "THIS IS ZALA. WILL YOU DRIVE NOW?"
YOU SAID YES.
DRIVE THE CAR, OR DIE LIKE KENNETH GUSTAFSSON...
I SAID YES.
HAD YOU HEARD OF ZALA BEFORE?
NO. NOT BEFORE, NEVER AGAIN.
THAT MADE IT EVEN MORE FRIGHTENING.
LIKE, ZALA-ON-THE-PHONE WAS THE MOST FRIGHTENING THING THEY COULD THINK OF.
DAG SVENSSON CAME TO SEE YOU.
YOU TOLD HIM ABOUT THAT WAREHOUSE.
DID YOU TELL ANYONE THAT YOU HAD TOLD HIM?

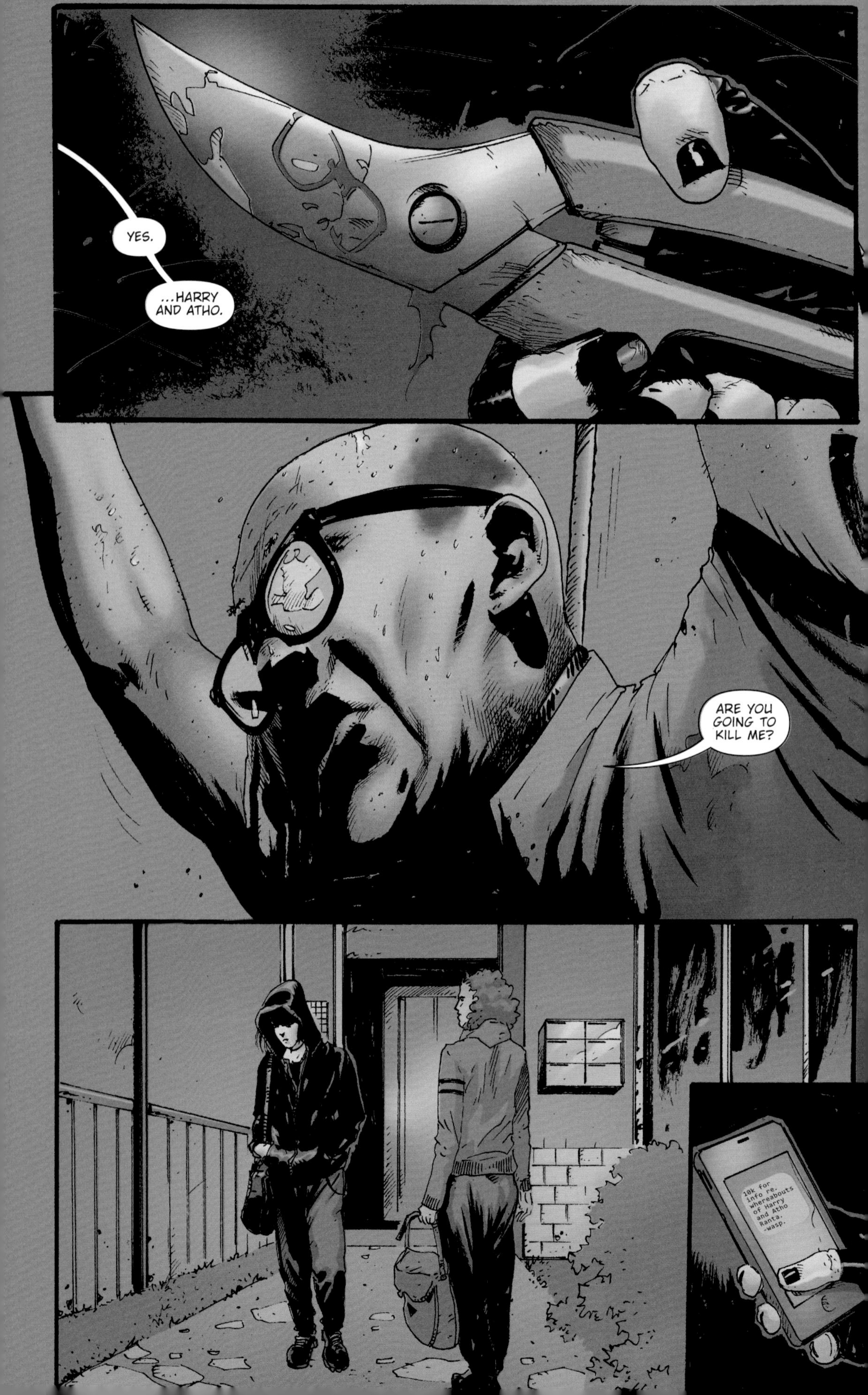
YES.
...HARRY AND ATHO.
ARE YOU GOING TO KILL ME?
10k for info re. whereabouts of Harry and Atho Ranta.
-wasp.

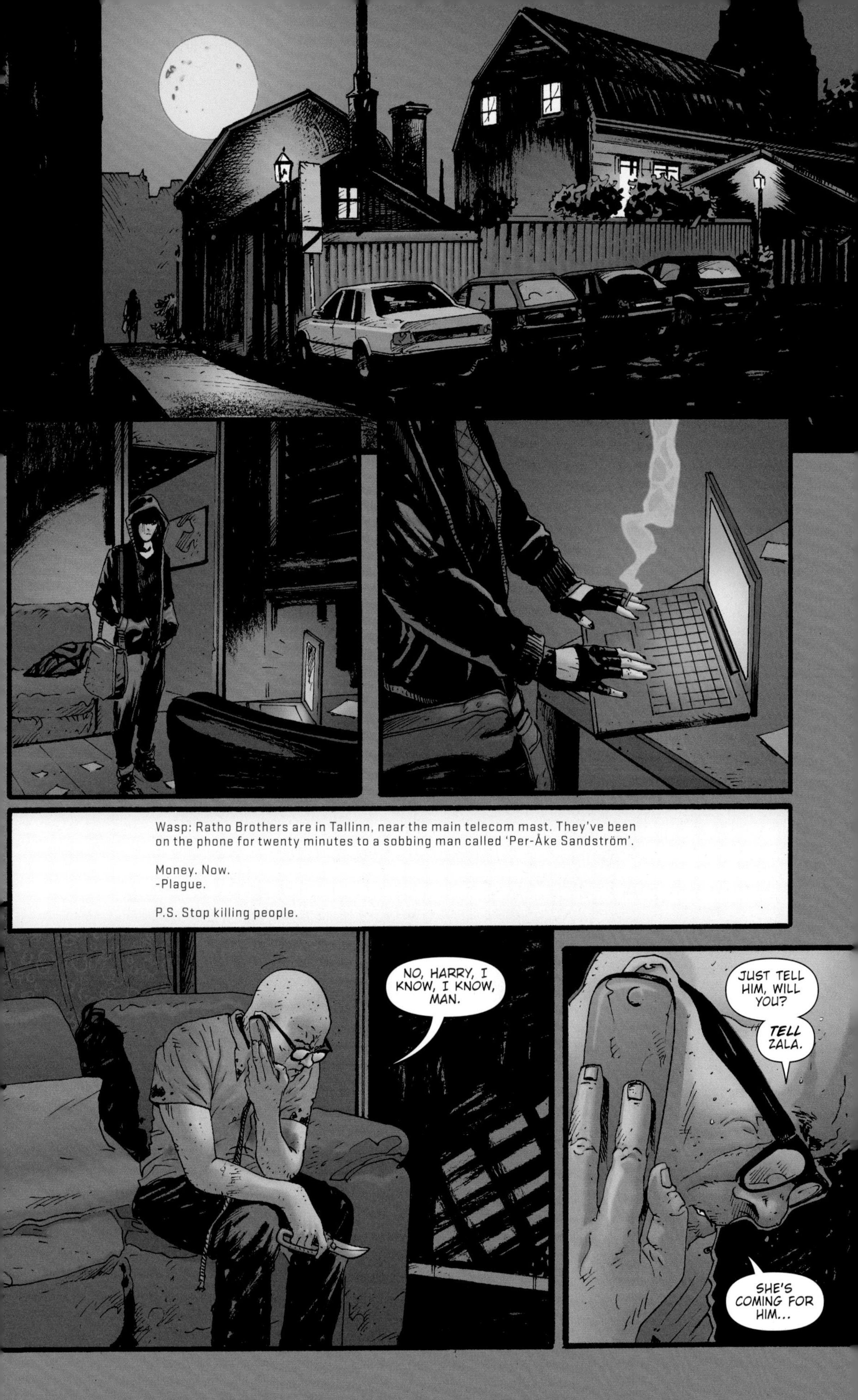
Wasp: Ratho Brothers are in Tallinn, near the main telecom mast. They've been on the phone for twenty minutes to a sobbing man called 'Per-Åke Sandström'.
Money. Now.
-Plague.
P.S. Stop killing people.
NO, HARRY, I KNOW, I KNOW, MAN.
JUST TELL HIM, WILL YOU?
TELL ZALA.
SHE'S COMING FOR HIM...

IT IS DONE. MY ONLY RESERVATION IS GUNNAR BJÖRK.

THE SÄPO OFFICER?

YES.

HE SAYS HE CAN GIVE ME INFORMATION ABOUT THIS ZALA CHARACTER.

BUT ONLY ON THE CONDITION THAT WE LEAVE HIS NAME OUT OF DAG'S BOOK.

IF WE LEAVE HIS NAME OUT, THE BOOK SUFFERS.

BUT IF WE GET THE INFORMATION FROM HIM.

IT COULD GIVE US A SERIOUS CHANCE OF DEFENDING LISBETH SALANDER WHEN SHE REAPPEARS.

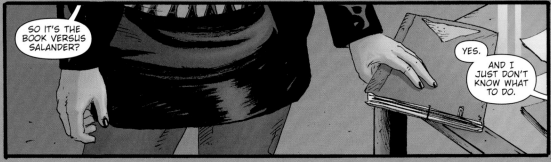

SO IT'S THE BOOK VERSUS SALANDER?

YES.

AND I JUST DON'T KNOW WHAT TO DO.

HAVE YOU CONSIDERED THE POSSIBILITY THAT SHE KILLED THEM, MIKEY, SERIOUSLY?

I DON'T THINK SHE DID.

BUT SHE MIGHT HAVE.

I DON'T THINK SHE DID.

BUT I DON'T HAVE ANY EVIDENCE FOR THAT...

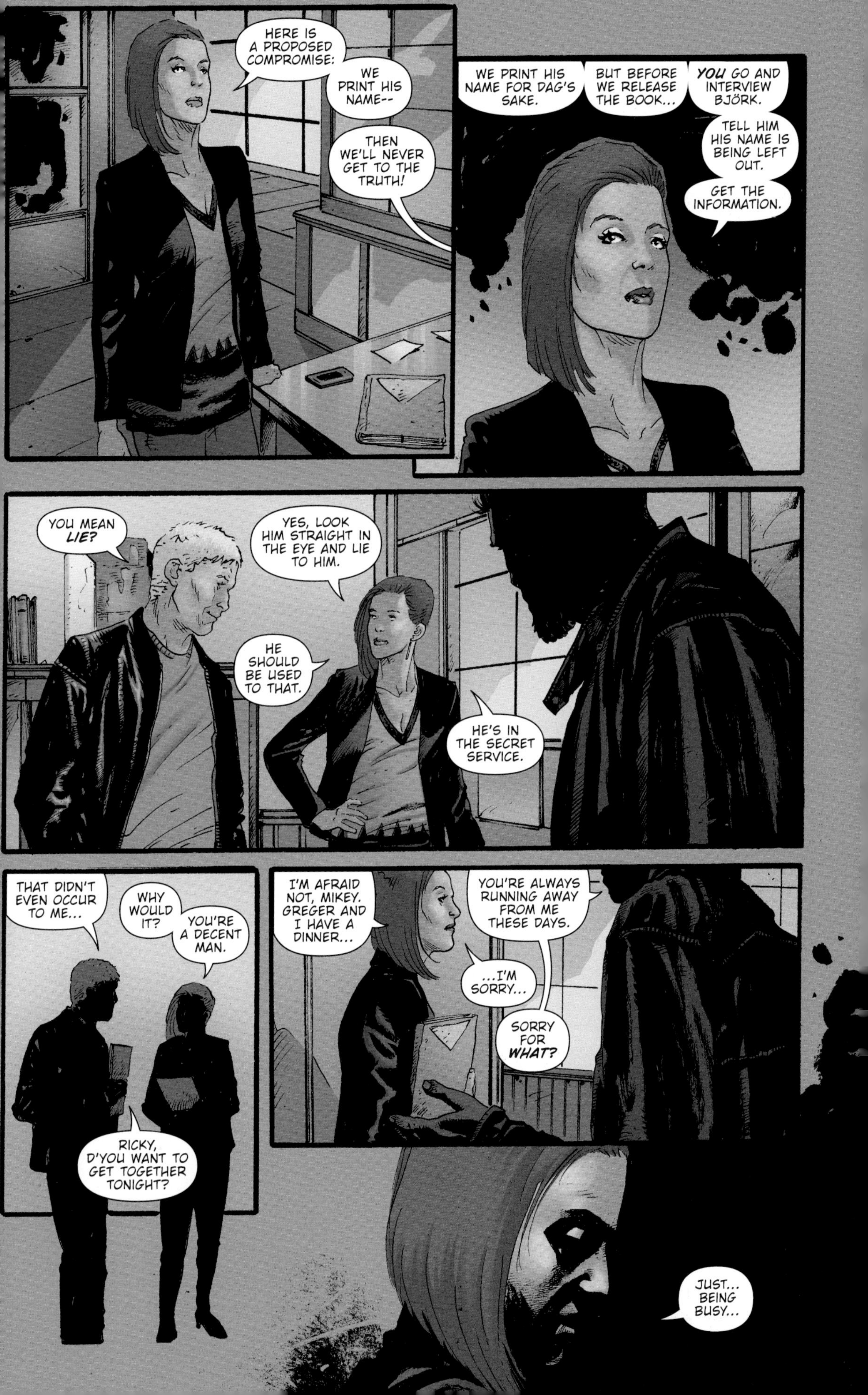
HERE IS A PROPOSED COMPROMISE:
WE PRINT HIS NAME--
THEN WE'LL NEVER GET TO THE TRUTH!
WE PRINT HIS NAME FOR DAG'S SAKE.
BUT BEFORE WE RELEASE THE BOOK...
YOU GO AND INTERVIEW BJÖRK.
TELL HIM HIS NAME IS BEING LEFT OUT.
GET THE INFORMATION.
YOU MEAN LIE?
YES, LOOK HIM STRAIGHT IN THE EYE AND LIE TO HIM.
HE SHOULD BE USED TO THAT.
HE'S IN THE SECRET SERVICE.
THAT DIDN'T EVEN OCCUR TO ME...
WHY WOULD IT?
YOU'RE A DECENT MAN.
RICKY, D'YOU WANT TO GET TOGETHER TONIGHT?
I'M AFRAID NOT, MIKEY. GREGER AND I HAVE A DINNER...
YOU'RE ALWAYS RUNNING AWAY FROM ME THESE DAYS.
...I'M SORRY...
SORRY FOR WHAT?
JUST... BEING BUSY...

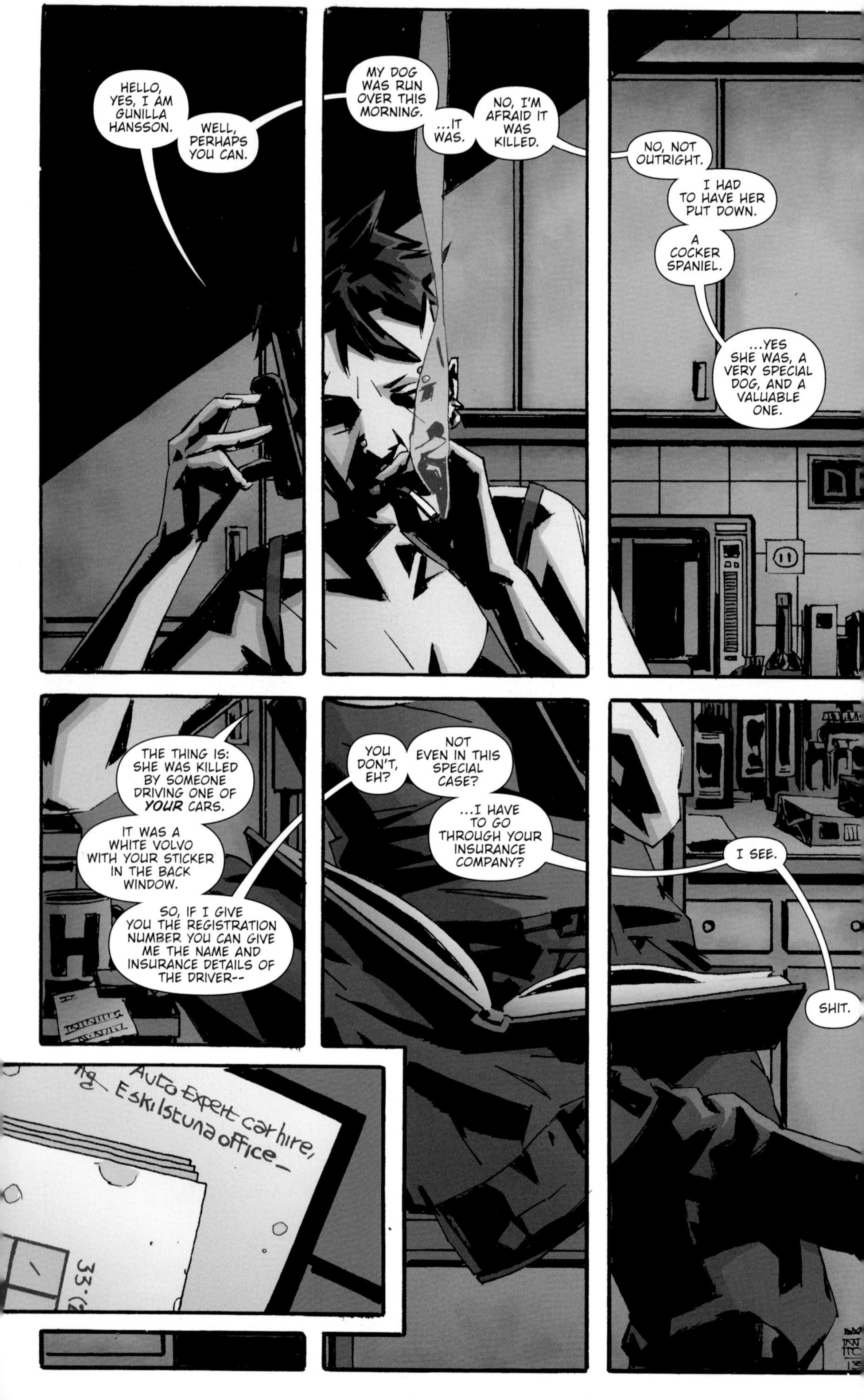
HELLO, YES, I AM GUNILLA HANSSON.
WELL, PERHAPS YOU CAN.
MY DOG WAS RUN OVER THIS MORNING.
...IT WAS.
NO, I'M AFRAID IT WAS KILLED.
NO, NOT OUTRIGHT.
I HAD TO HAVE HER PUT DOWN.
A COCKER SPANIEL.
...YES SHE WAS, A VERY SPECIAL DOG, AND A VALUABLE ONE.
THE THING IS: SHE WAS KILLED BY SOMEONE DRIVING ONE OF YOUR CARS.
IT WAS A WHITE VOLVO WITH YOUR STICKER IN THE BACK WINDOW.
SO, IF I GIVE YOU THE REGISTRATION NUMBER YOU CAN GIVE ME THE NAME AND INSURANCE DETAILS OF THE DRIVER--
YOU DON'T, EH?
NOT EVEN IN THIS SPECIAL CASE?
...I HAVE TO GO THROUGH YOUR INSURANCE COMPANY?
I SEE.
SHIT.
Auto Expert car hire,
Eskilstuna office-

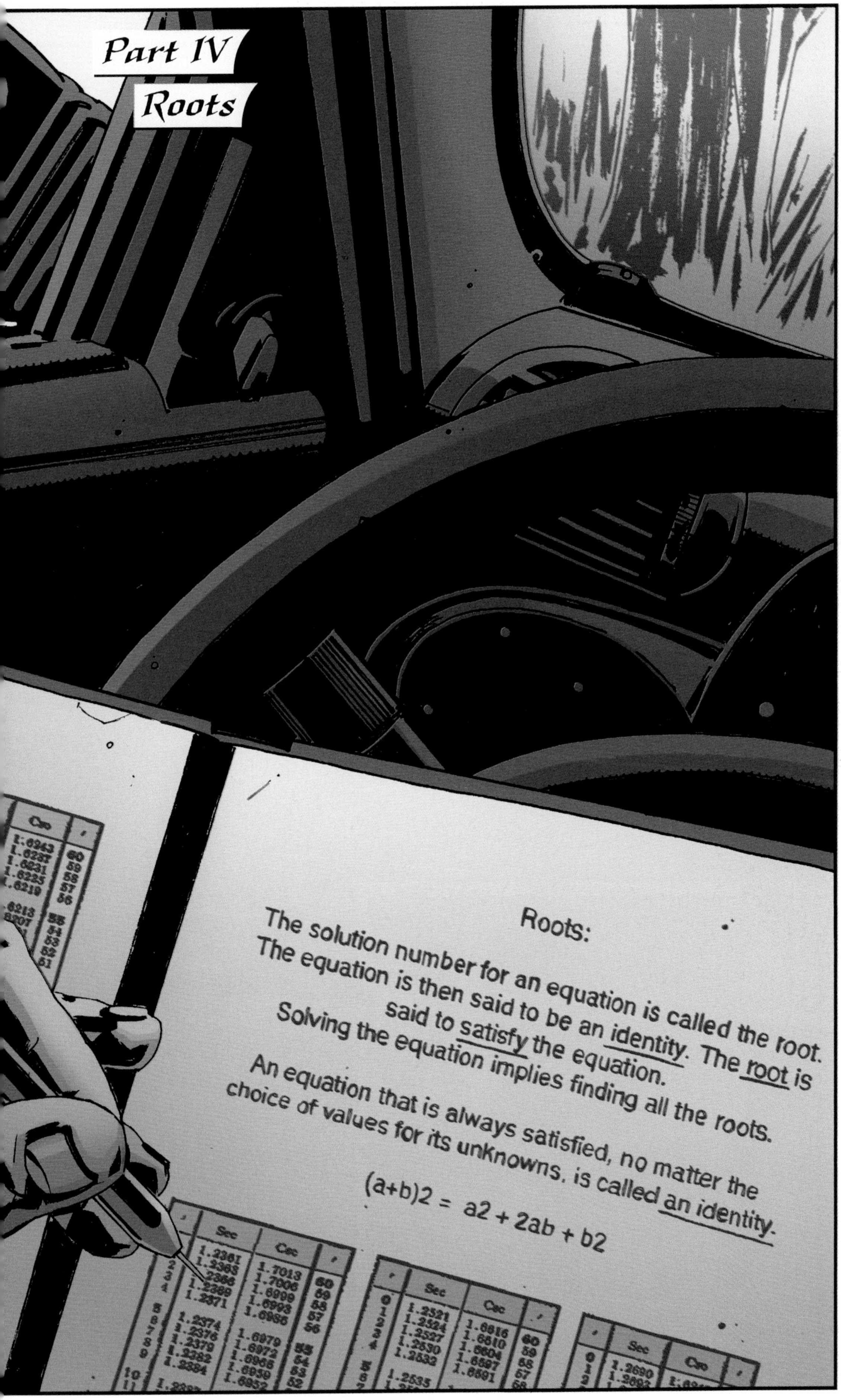
Part IV
Roots
Roots:
The solution number for an equation is called the root.
The equation is then said to be an identity. The root is
said to satisfy the equation.
Solving the equation implies finding all the roots.
An equation that is always satisfied, no matter the
choice of values for its unknowns, is called an identity.
(a+b)2 = a2 + 2ab + b2

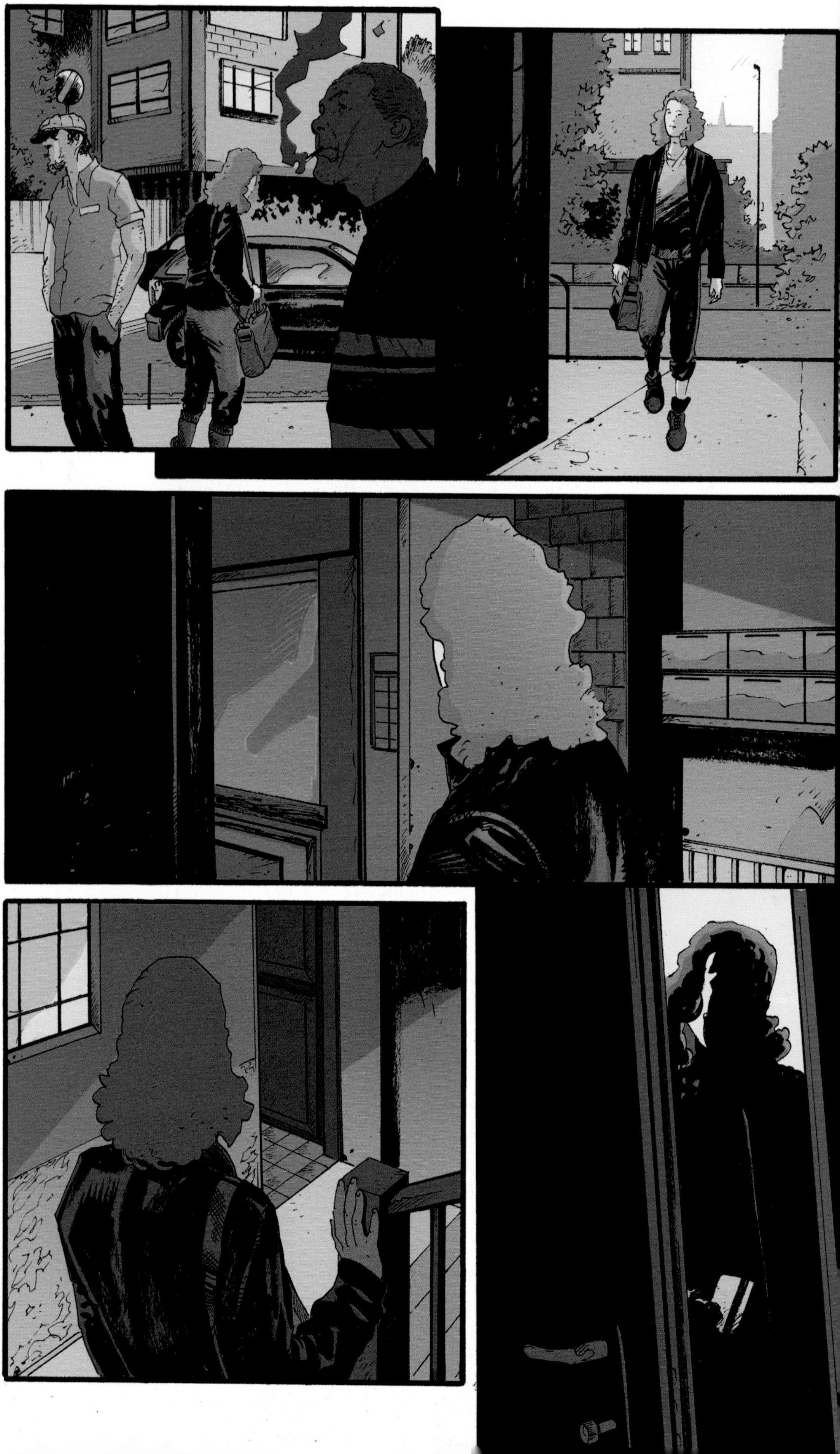

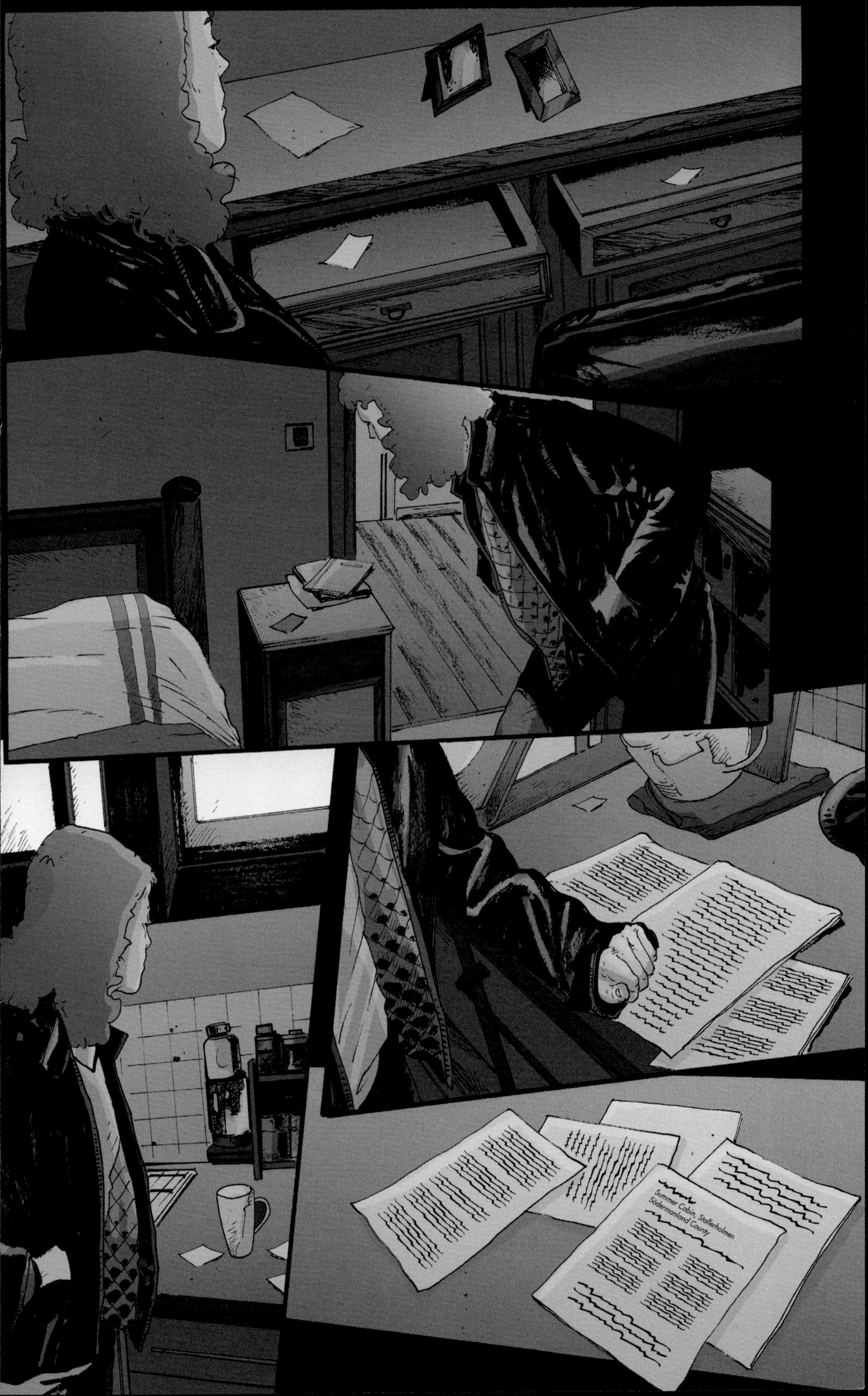
Summer Cabin, Stallerholmen
Södermanland County

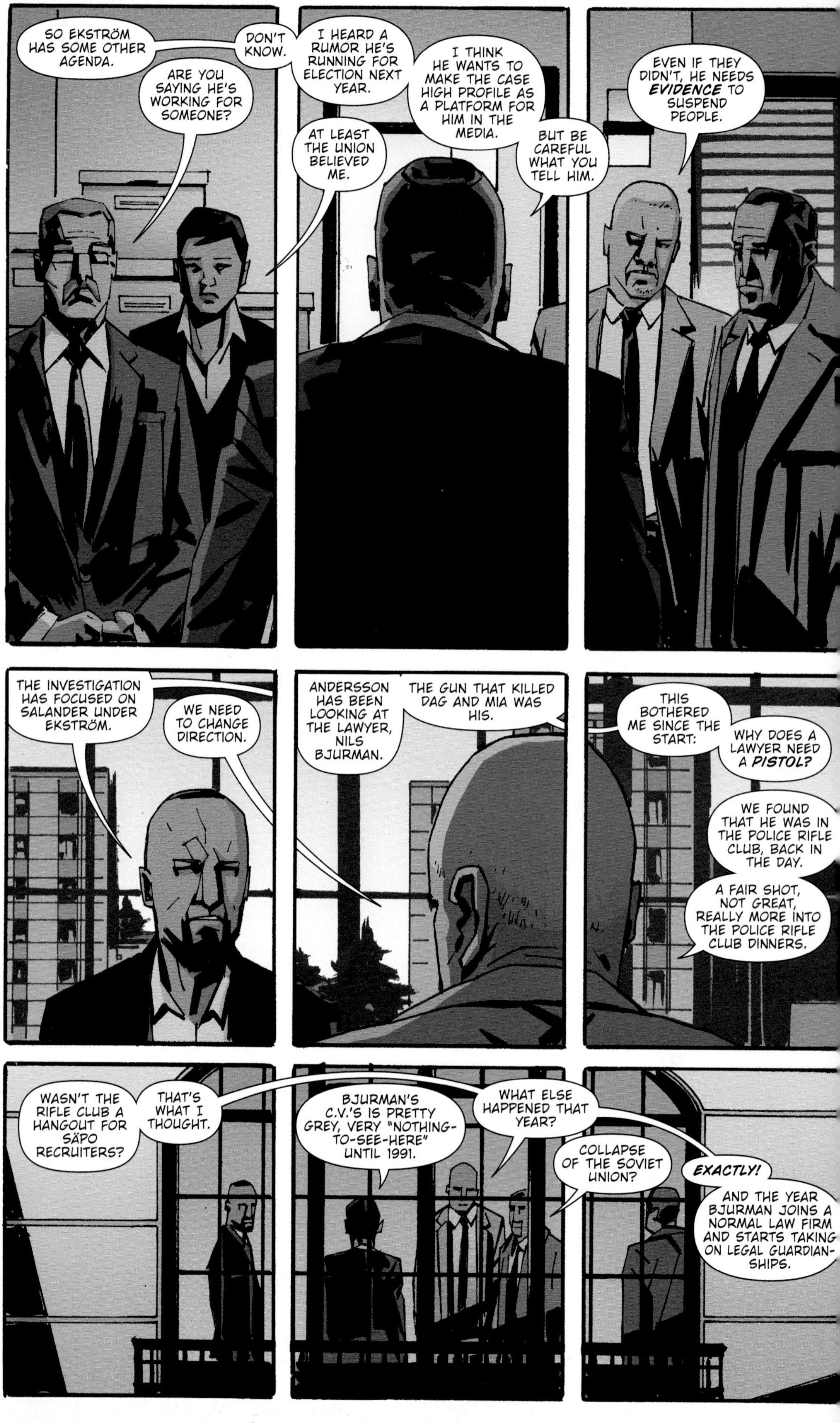
SO EKSTRÖM HAS SOME OTHER AGENDA.
ARE YOU SAYING HE'S WORKING FOR SOMEONE?
DON'T KNOW.
I HEARD A RUMOR HE'S RUNNING FOR ELECTION NEXT YEAR.
AT LEAST THE UNION BELIEVED ME.
I THINK HE WANTS TO MAKE THE CASE HIGH PROFILE AS A PLATFORM FOR HIM IN THE MEDIA.
BUT BE CAREFUL WHAT YOU TELL HIM.
EVEN IF THEY DIDN'T, HE NEEDS EVIDENCE TO SUSPEND PEOPLE.
THE INVESTIGATION HAS FOCUSED ON SALANDER UNDER EKSTRÖM.
WE NEED TO CHANGE DIRECTION.
ANDERSSON HAS BEEN LOOKING AT THE LAWYER, NILS BJURMAN.
THE GUN THAT KILLED DAG AND MIA WAS HIS.
THIS BOTHERED ME SINCE THE START:
WHY DOES A LAWYER NEED A PISTOL?
WE FOUND THAT HE WAS IN THE POLICE RIFLE CLUB, BACK IN THE DAY.
A FAIR SHOT, NOT GREAT, REALLY MORE INTO THE POLICE RIFLE CLUB DINNERS.
WASN'T THE RIFLE CLUB A HANGOUT FOR SÄPO RECRUITERS?
THAT'S WHAT I THOUGHT.
BJURMAN'S C.V.'S IS PRETTY GREY, VERY "NOTHING-TO-SEE-HERE" UNTIL 1991.
WHAT ELSE HAPPENED THAT YEAR?
COLLAPSE OF THE SOVIET UNION?
EXACTLY!
AND THE YEAR BJURMAN JOINS A NORMAL LAW FIRM AND STARTS TAKING ON LEGAL GUARDIAN-SHIPS.

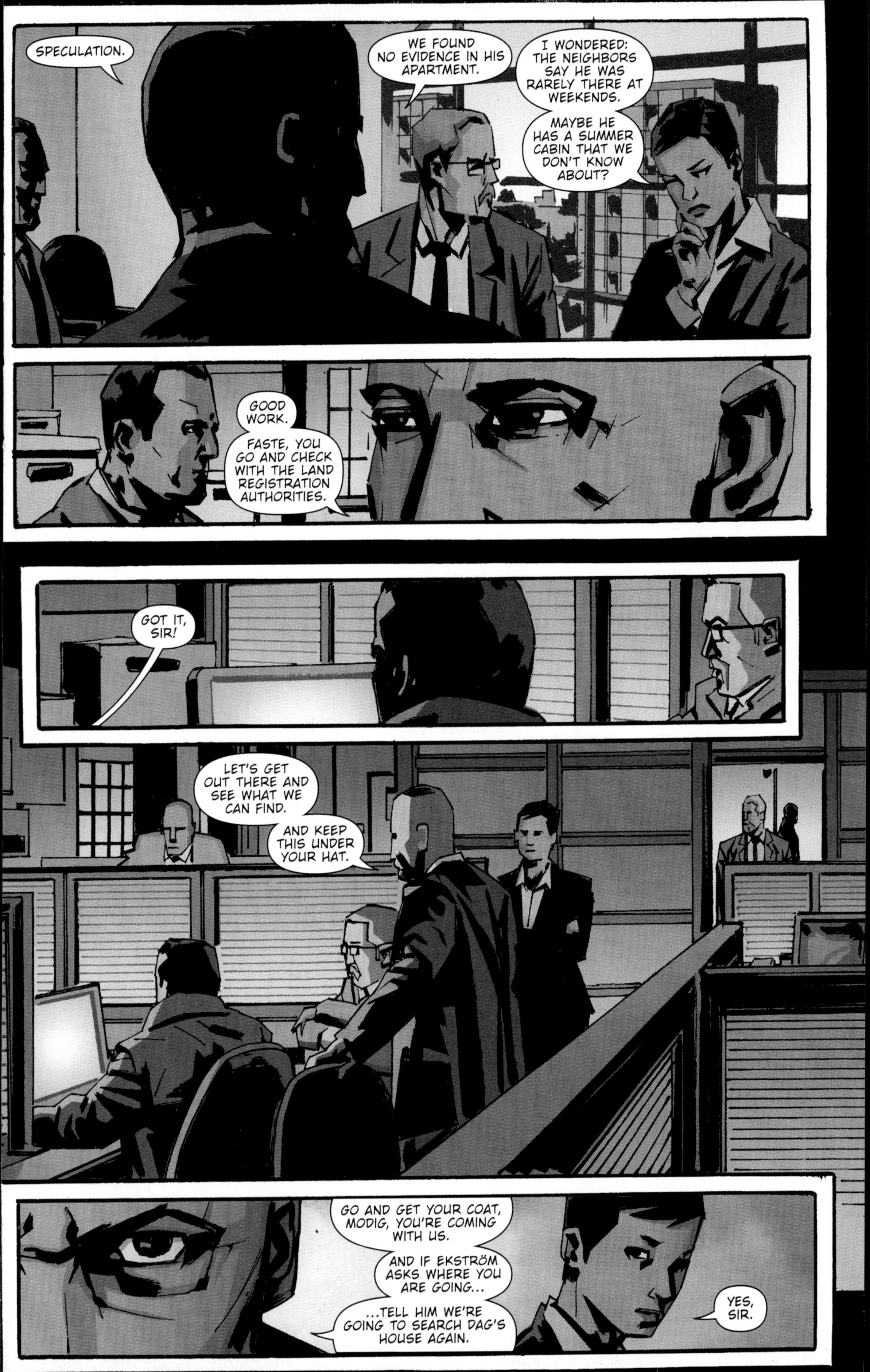
SPECULATION.
WE FOUND NO EVIDENCE IN HIS APARTMENT.
I WONDERED: THE NEIGHBORS SAY HE WAS RARELY THERE AT WEEKENDS.
MAYBE HE HAS A SUMMER CABIN THAT WE DON'T KNOW ABOUT?
GOOD WORK.
FASTE, YOU GO AND CHECK WITH THE LAND REGISTRATION AUTHORITIES.
GOT IT, SIR!
LET'S GET OUT THERE AND SEE WHAT WE CAN FIND.
AND KEEP THIS UNDER YOUR HAT.
GO AND GET YOUR COAT, MODIG, YOU'RE COMING WITH US.
AND IF EKSTRÖM ASKS WHERE YOU ARE GOING...
...TELL HIM WE'RE GOING TO SEARCH DAG'S HOUSE AGAIN.
YES, SIR.

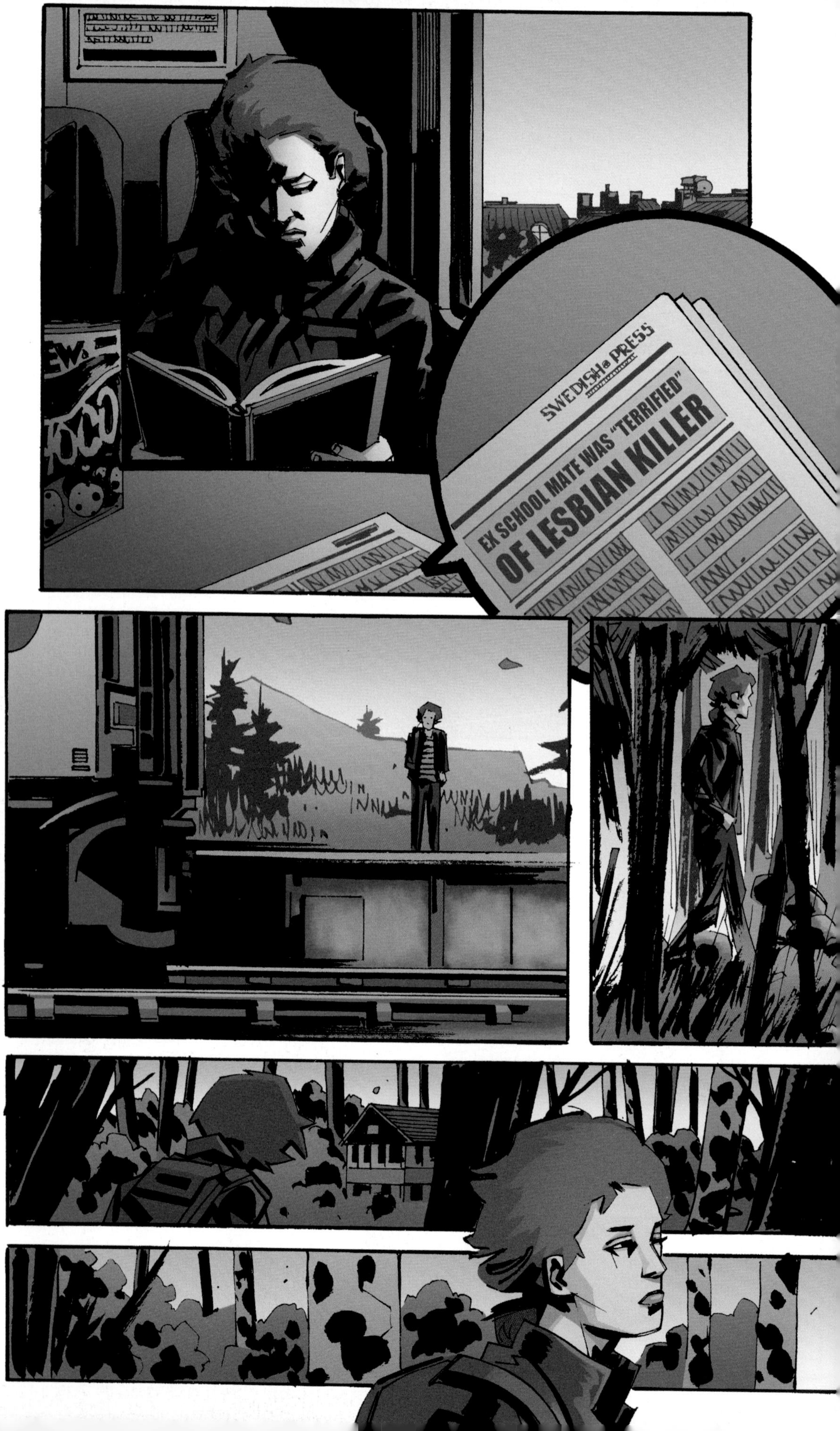
SWEDISH PRESS
EX SCHOOL MATE WAS "TERRIFIED" OF LESBIAN KILLER

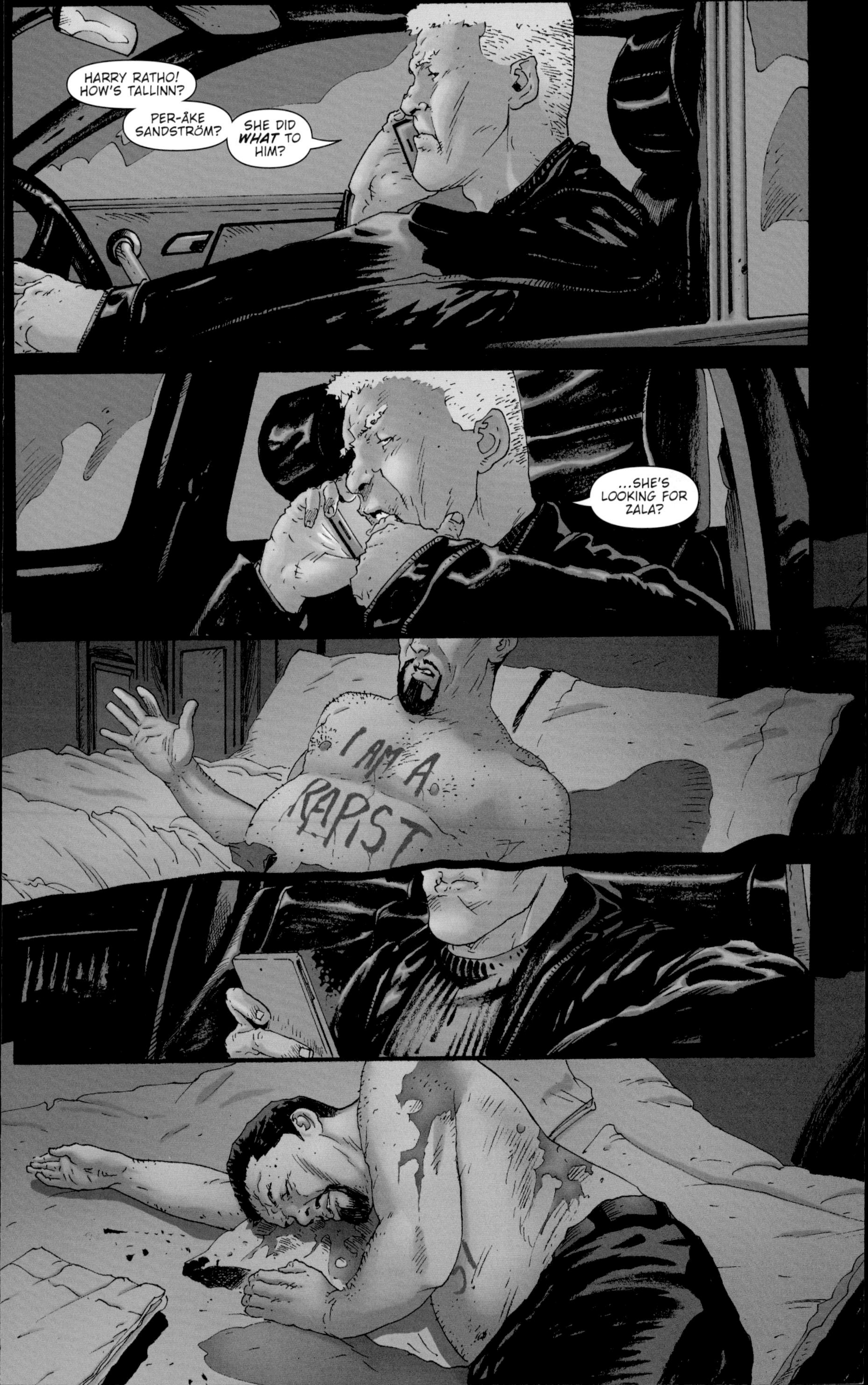
HARRY RATHO! HOW'S TALLINN?
PER-ÅKE SANDSTRÖM?
SHE DID **WHAT** TO HIM?
...SHE'S LOOKING FOR ZALA?
I AM A RAPIST

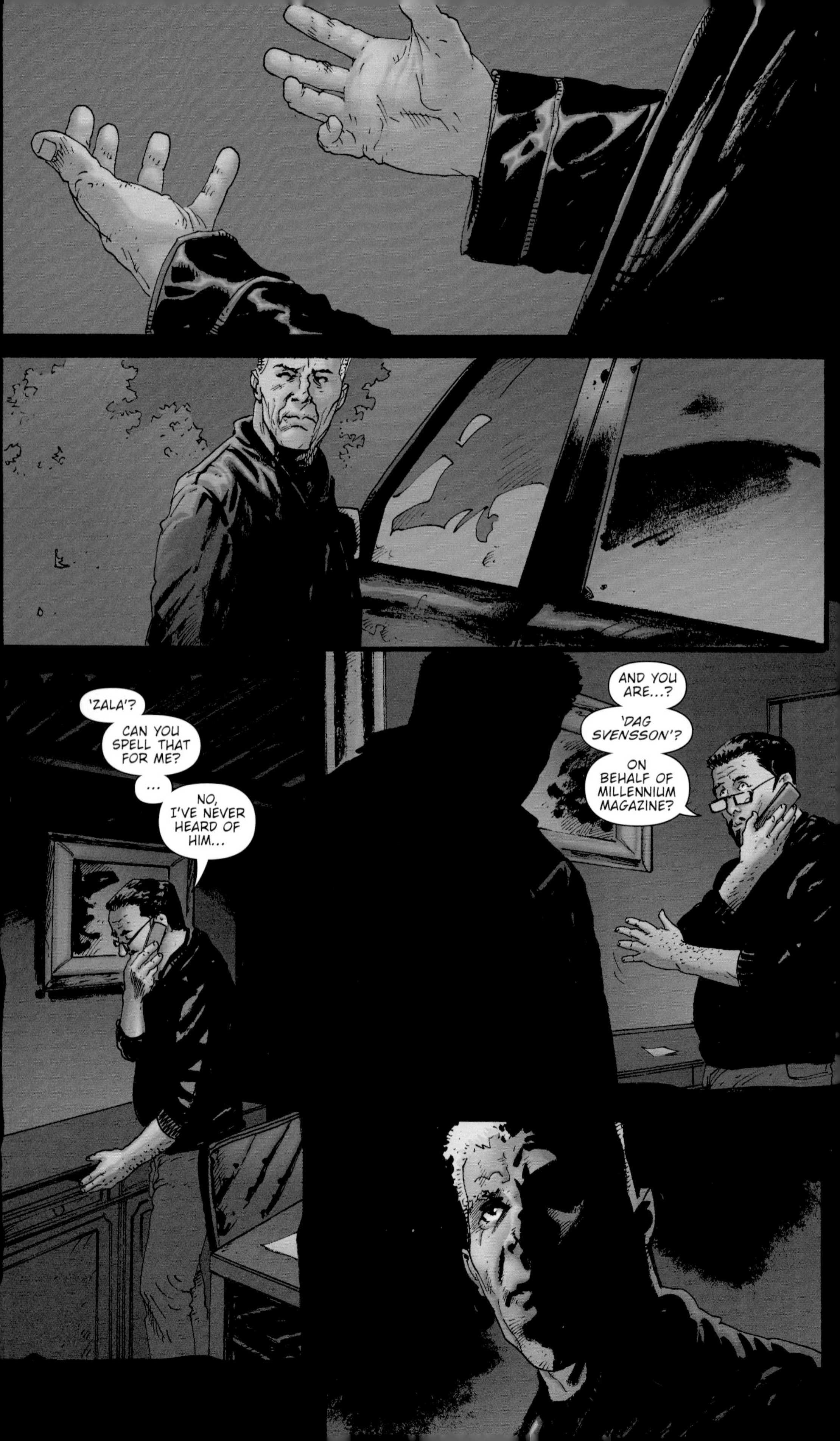
'ZALA'?
CAN YOU SPELL THAT FOR ME?
...
NO, I'VE NEVER HEARD OF HIM...
AND YOU ARE...?
'DAG SVENSSON'?
ON BEHALF OF MILLENNIUM MAGAZINE?

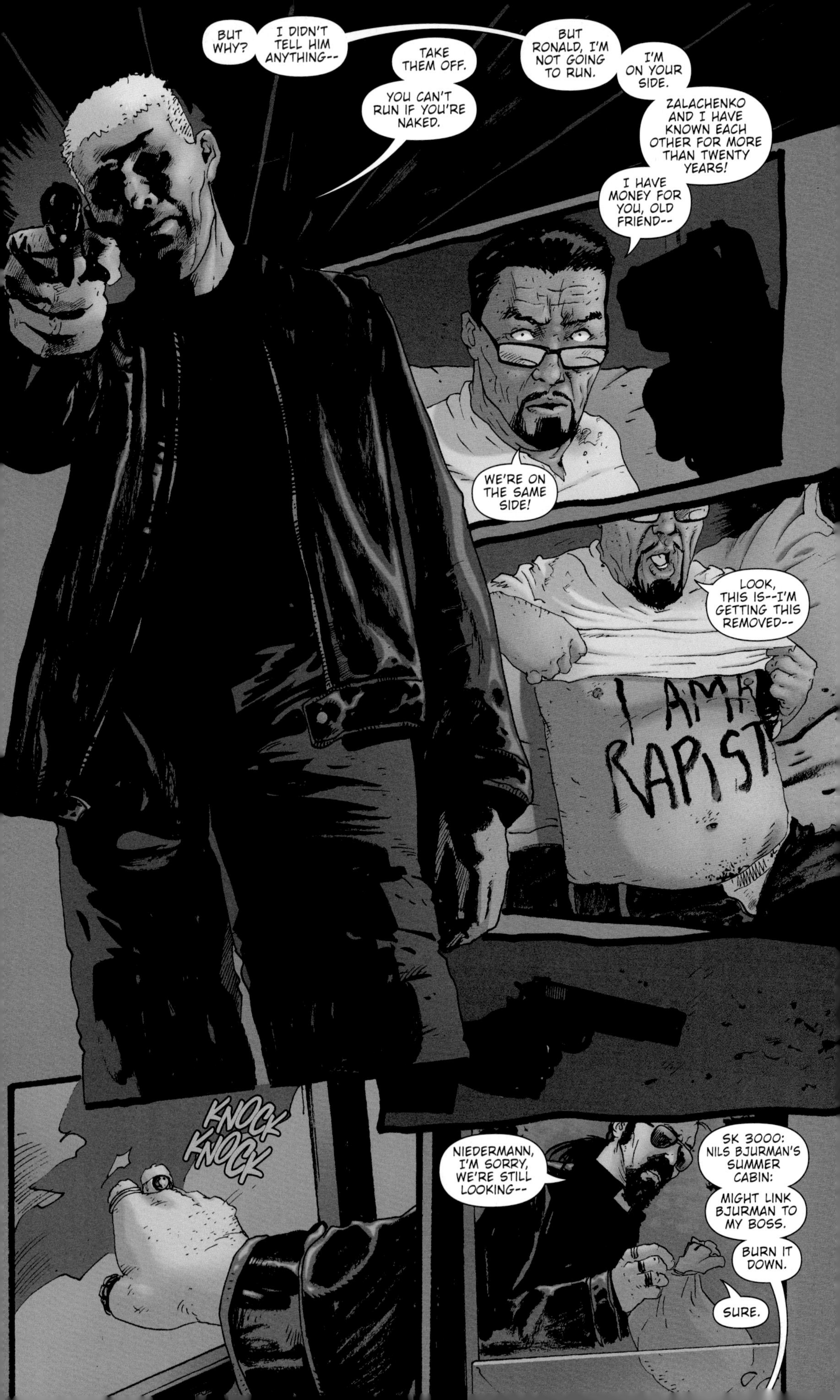
BUT WHY?
I DIDN'T TELL HIM ANYTHING--
TAKE THEM OFF.
YOU CAN'T RUN IF YOU'RE NAKED.
BUT RONALD, I'M NOT GOING TO RUN.
I'M ON YOUR SIDE.
ZALACHENKO AND I HAVE KNOWN EACH OTHER FOR MORE THAN TWENTY YEARS!
I HAVE MONEY FOR YOU, OLD FRIEND--
WE'RE ON THE SAME SIDE!
LOOK, THIS IS--I'M GETTING THIS REMOVED--
I AM A RAPIST
KNOCK KNOCK
NIEDERMANN, I'M SORRY, WE'RE STILL LOOKING--
SK 3000: NILS BJURMAN'S SUMMER CABIN:
MIGHT LINK BJURMAN TO MY BOSS.
BURN IT DOWN.
SURE.

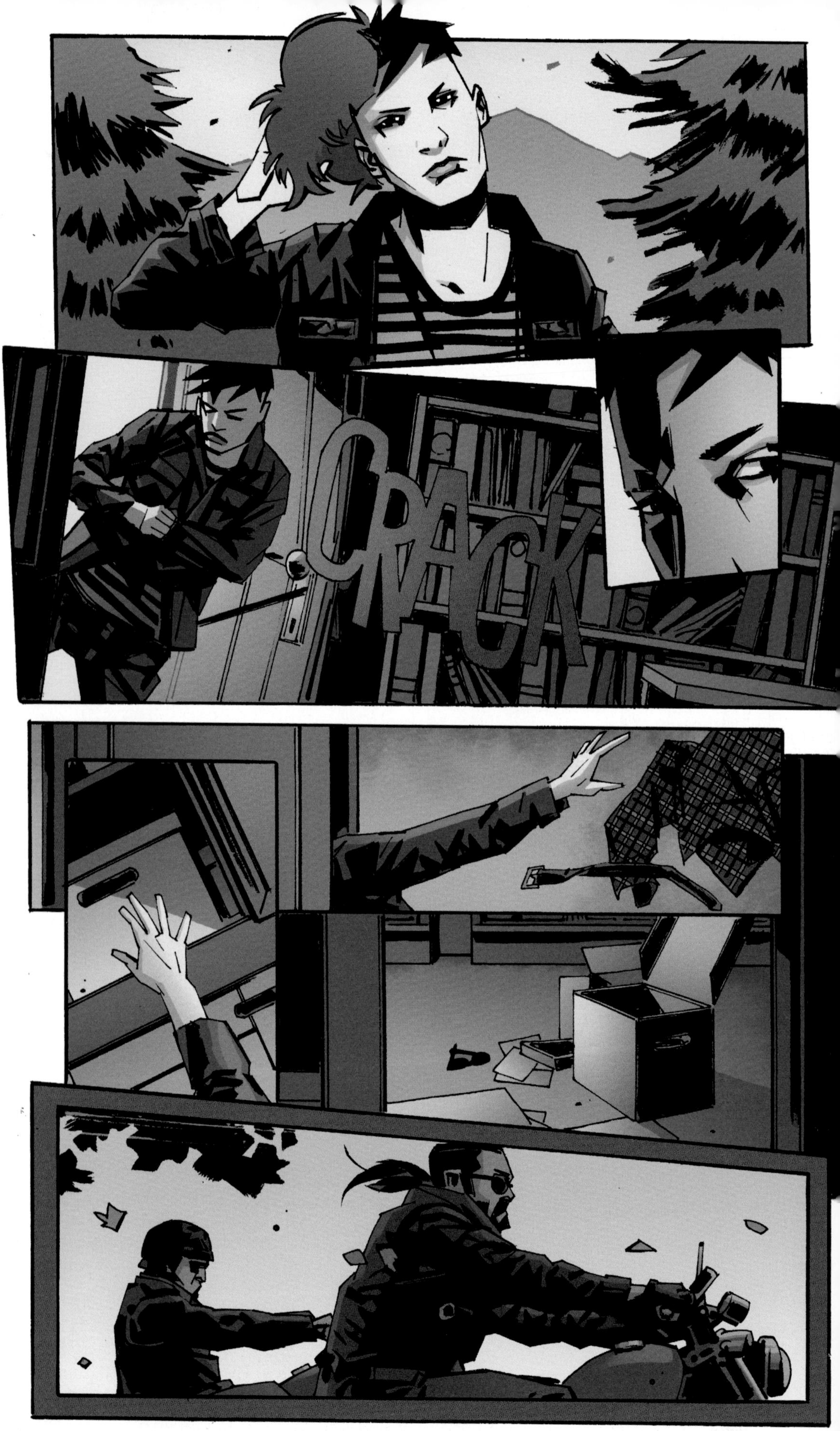
CRACK

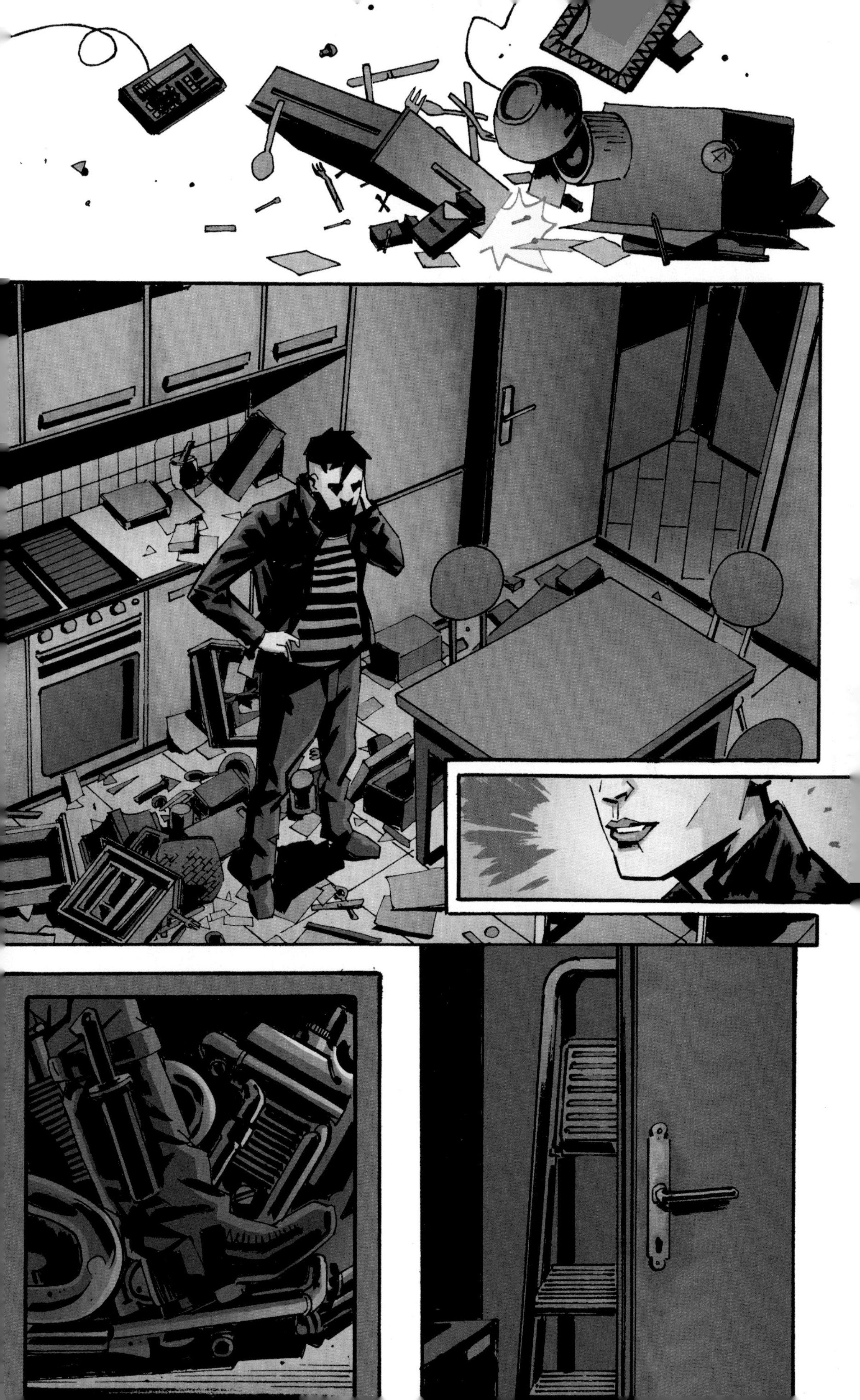

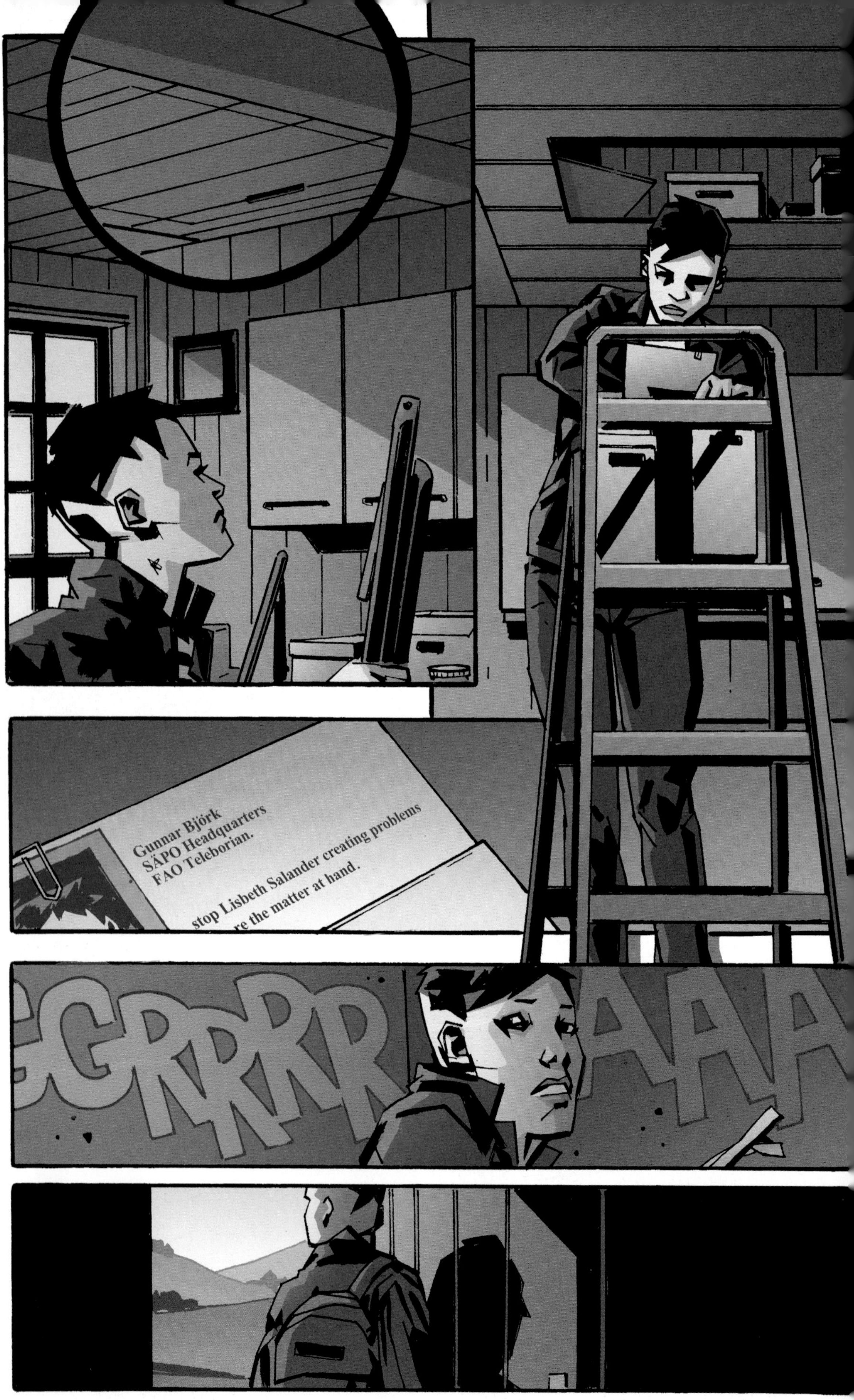
Gunnar Björk
SÄPO Headquarters
FAO Teleborian.
stop Lisbeth Salander creating problems
re the matter at hand.
GRRRRAAAA

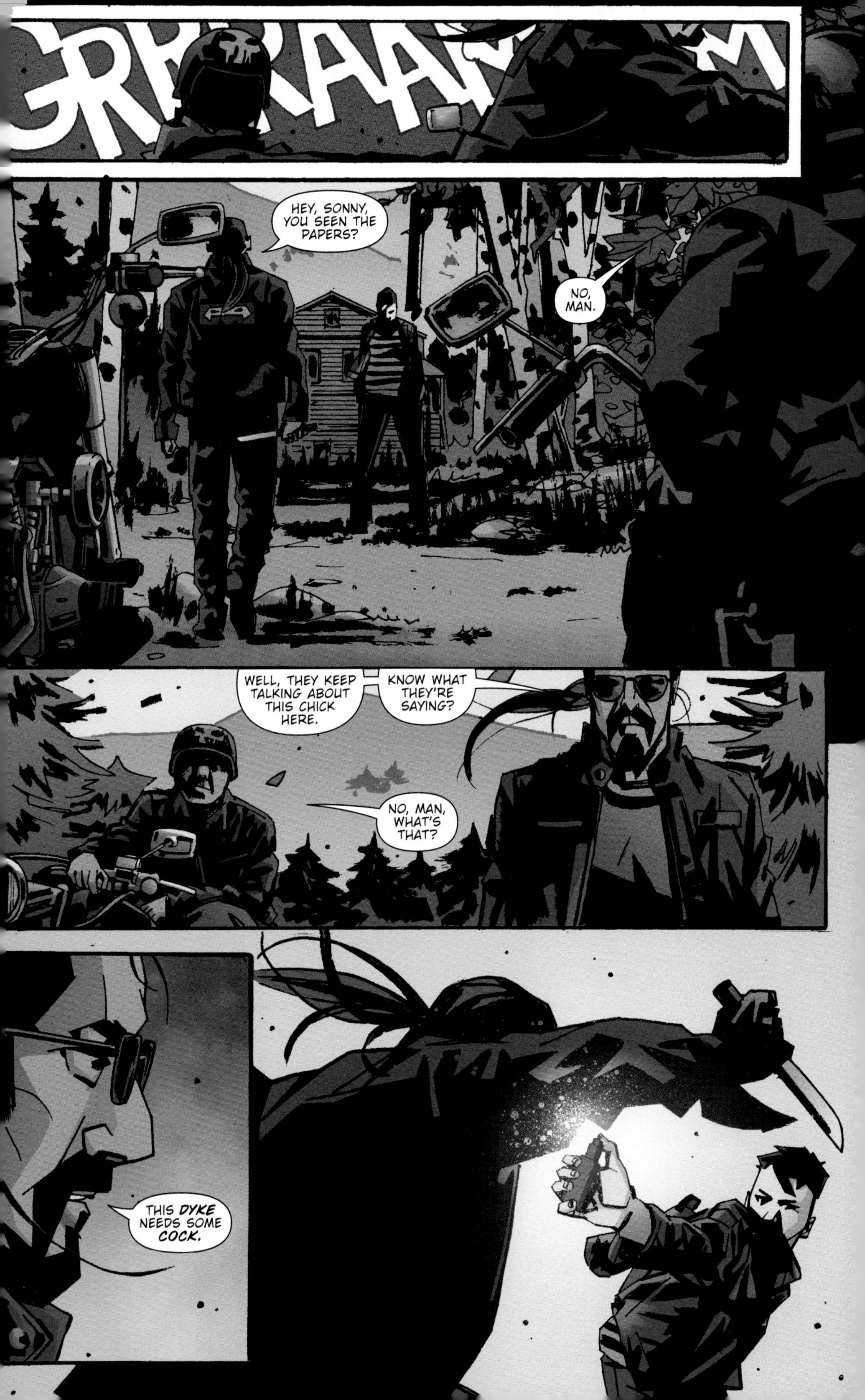
GRRAAAM
HEY, SONNY, YOU SEEN THE PAPERS?
NO, MAN.
WELL, THEY KEEP TALKING ABOUT THIS CHICK HERE.
KNOW WHAT THEY'RE SAYING?
NO, MAN, WHAT'S THAT?
THIS *DYKE* NEEDS SOME *COCK.*

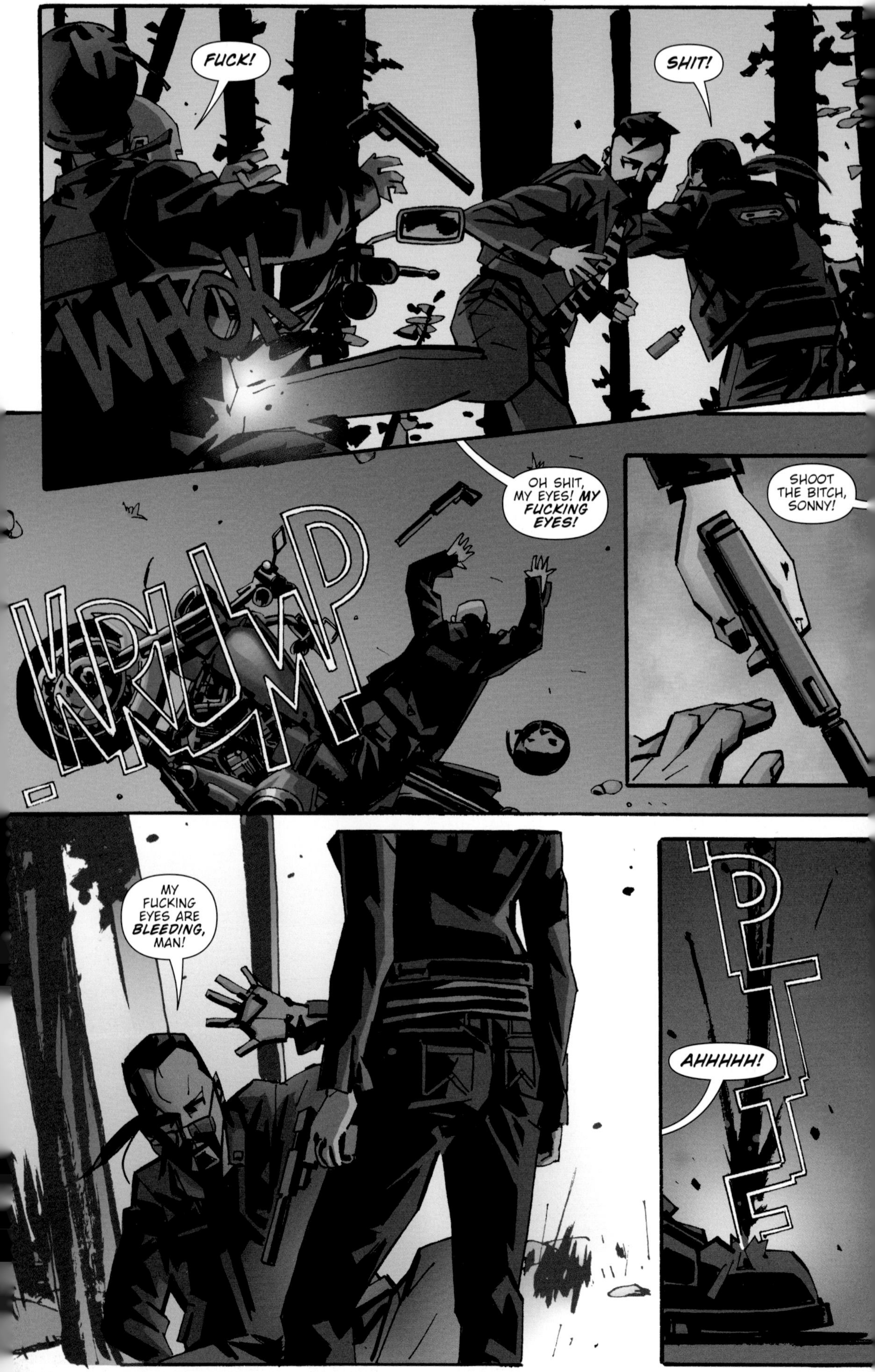
FUCK!
SHIT!
WHOK
OH SHIT, MY EYES! MY FUCKING EYES!
SHOOT THE BITCH, SONNY!
KRUMP
MY FUCKING EYES ARE BLEEDING, MAN!
AHHHHH!

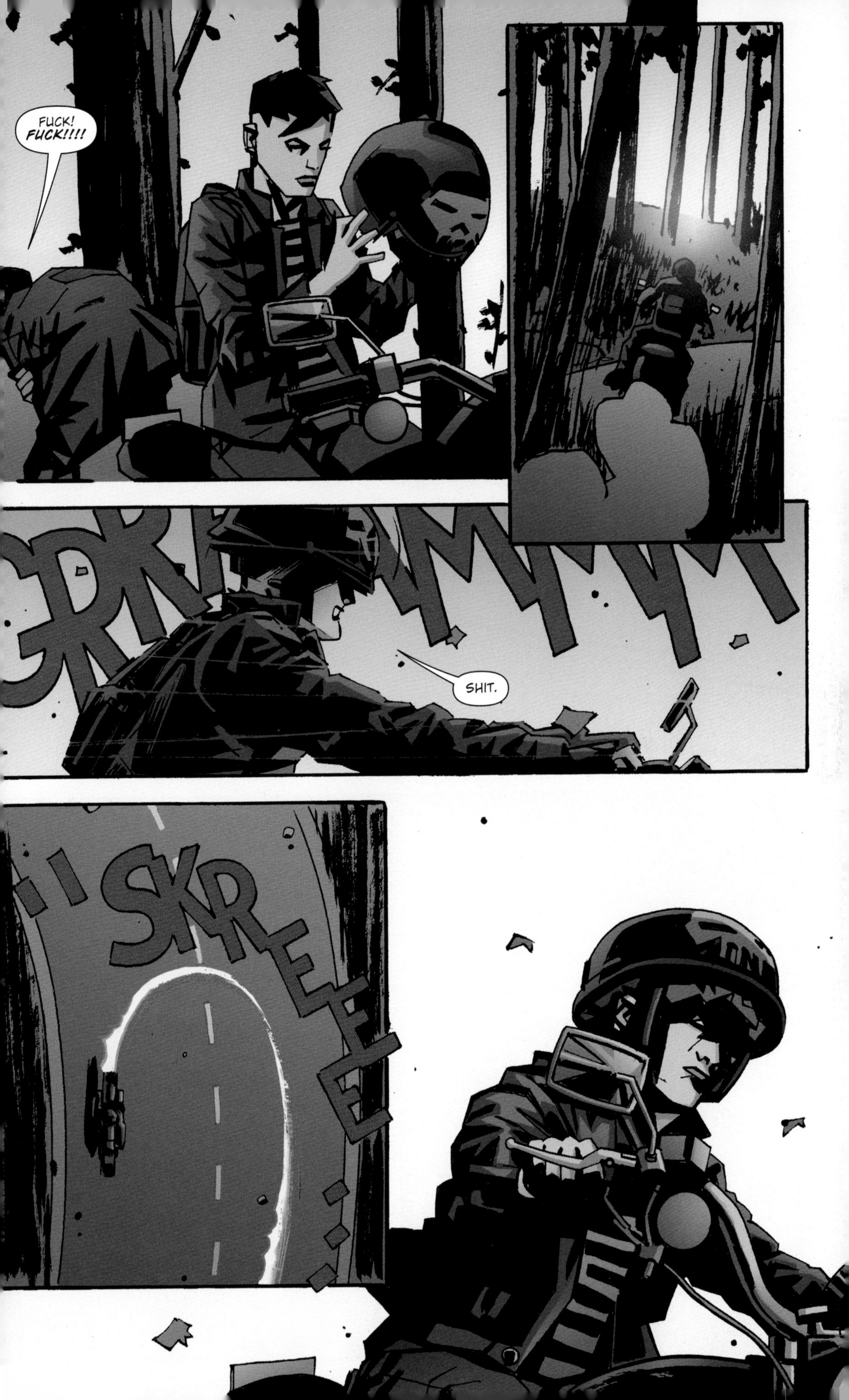
FUCK!
FUCK!!!!
GRRAAMMMM
SHIT.
SKREEEEE

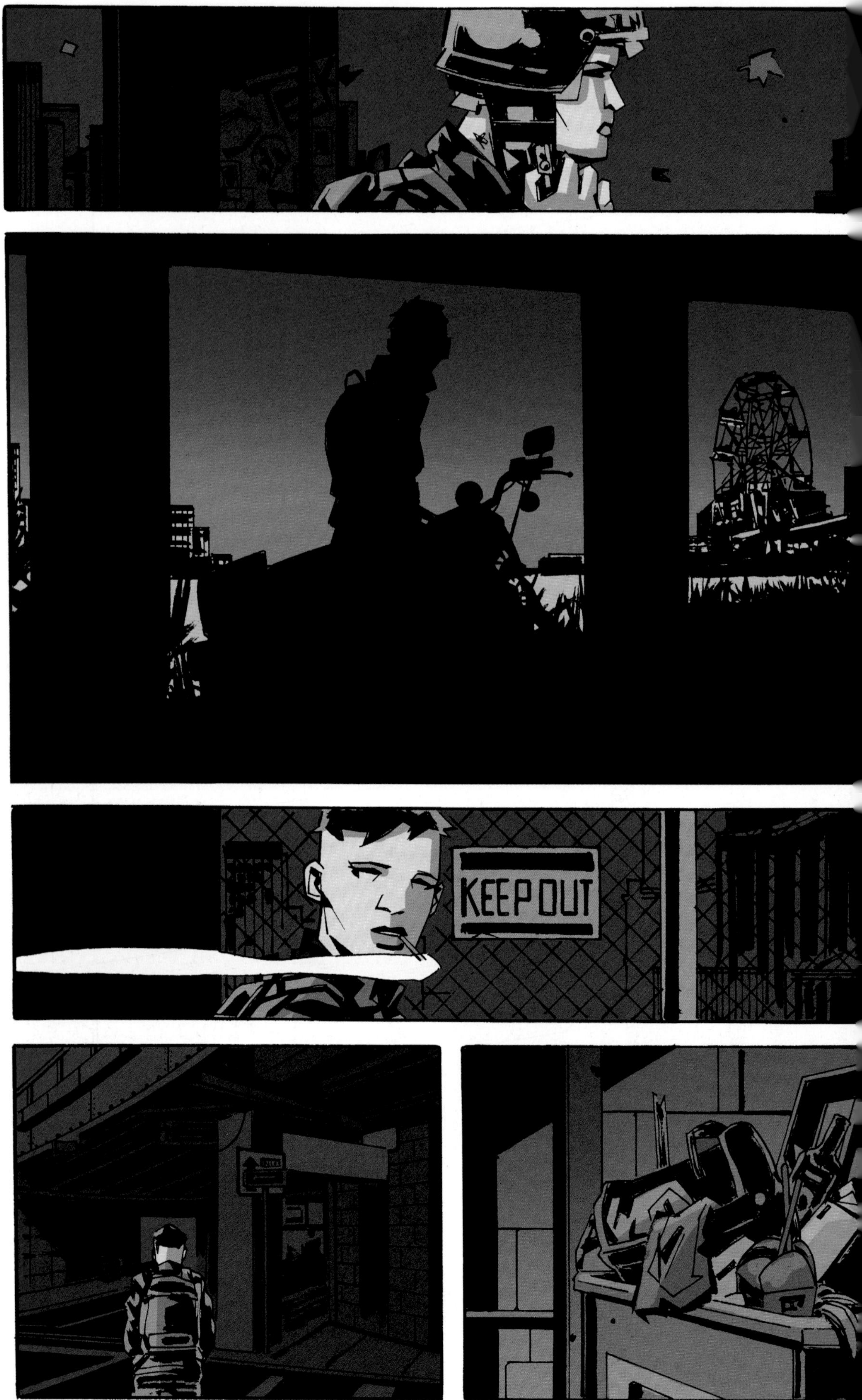
KEEP OUT

THAT WAS VERY IRRESPONSIBLE DRIVING.

FUCK OFF, PIG.

OH, NOW YOU'RE BEING QUITE RUDE.

QUITE RUDE **AND** A LITTLE BIT IRRESPONSIBLE.

I DON'T KNOW HOW YOU CAN SLEEP.

SONNY!

YOU PRICK!

YOU TOOK MY **FUCKING** BIKE AND LEFT ME, YOU **ASSHOLE!**

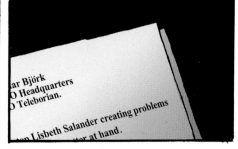

...ar Björk
...O Headquarters
...O Teleborian.

...en Lisbeth Salander creating problems
...ter at hand.

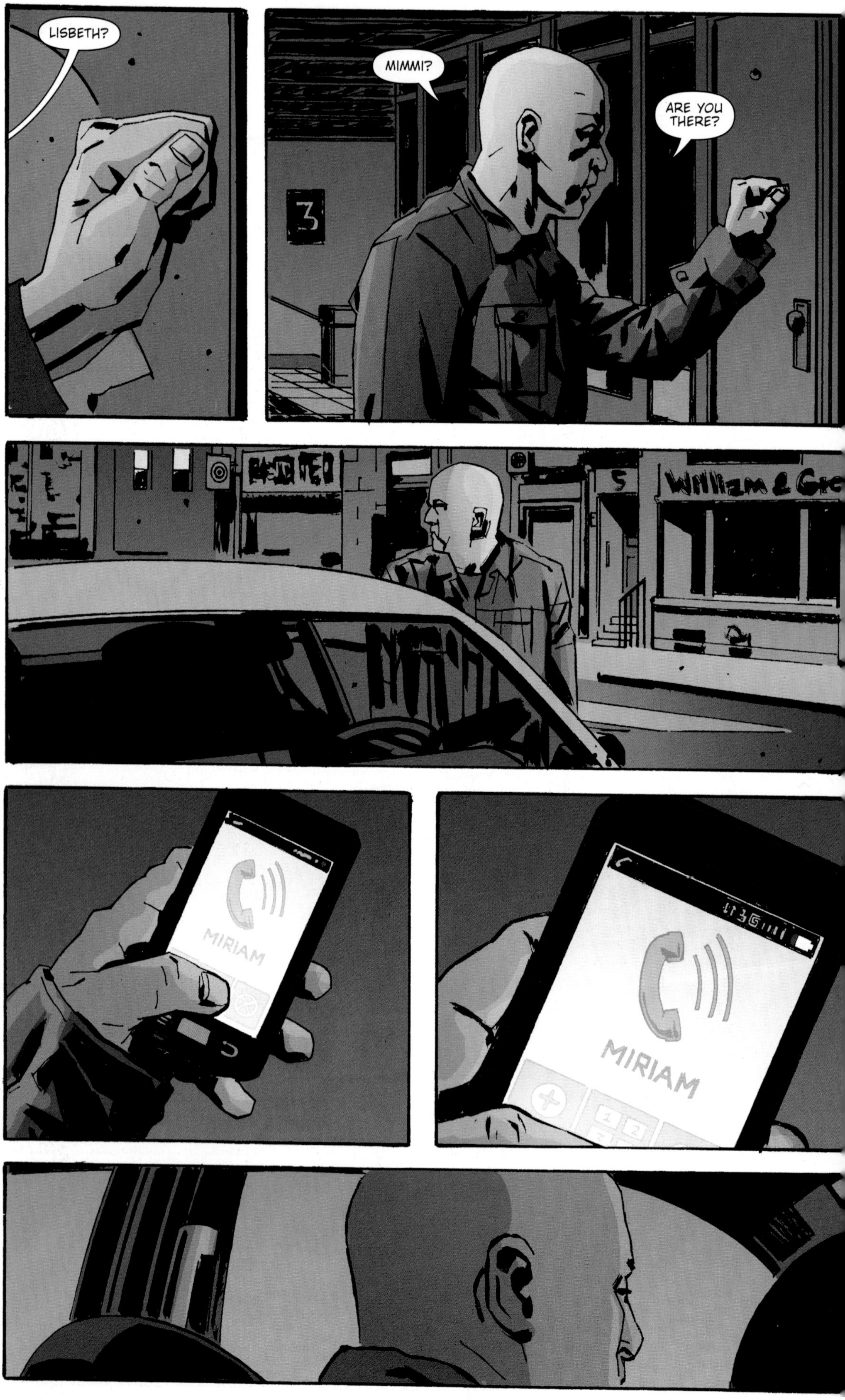
LISBETH?
MIMMI?
ARE YOU THERE?
William & Gr
MIRIAM
MIRIAM

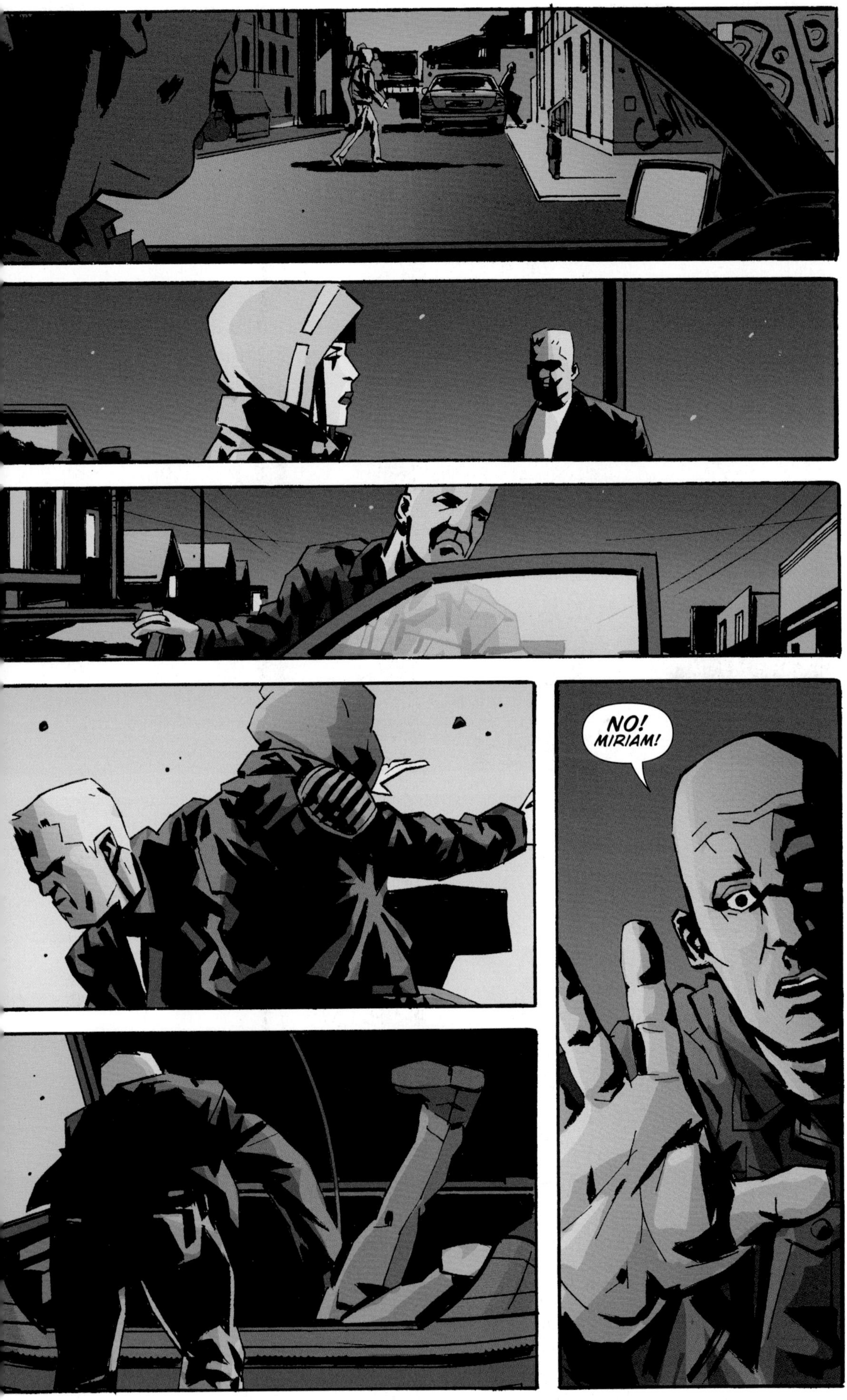
NO! MIRIAM!

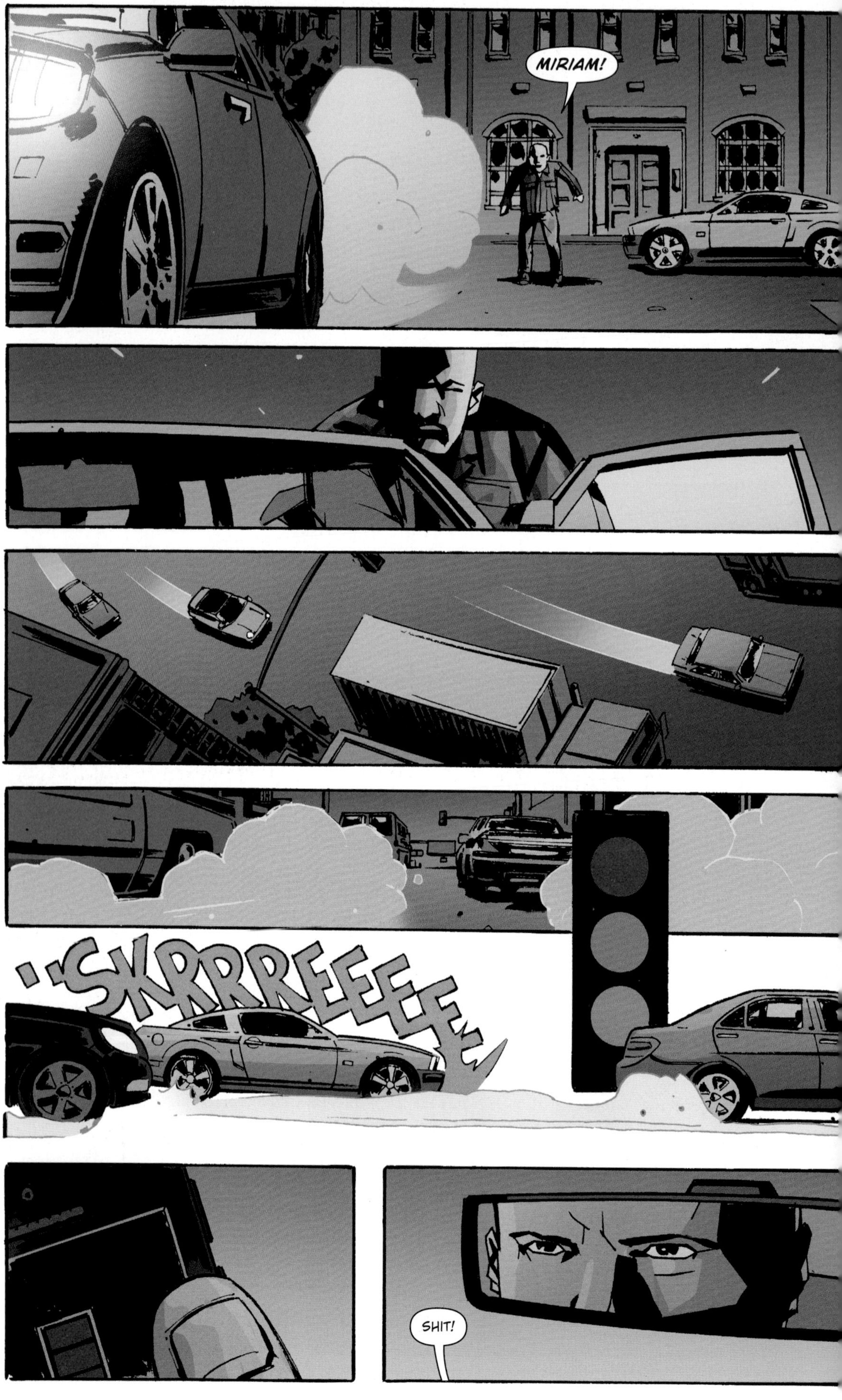
MIRIAM!
SKRRREEEEE
SHIT!

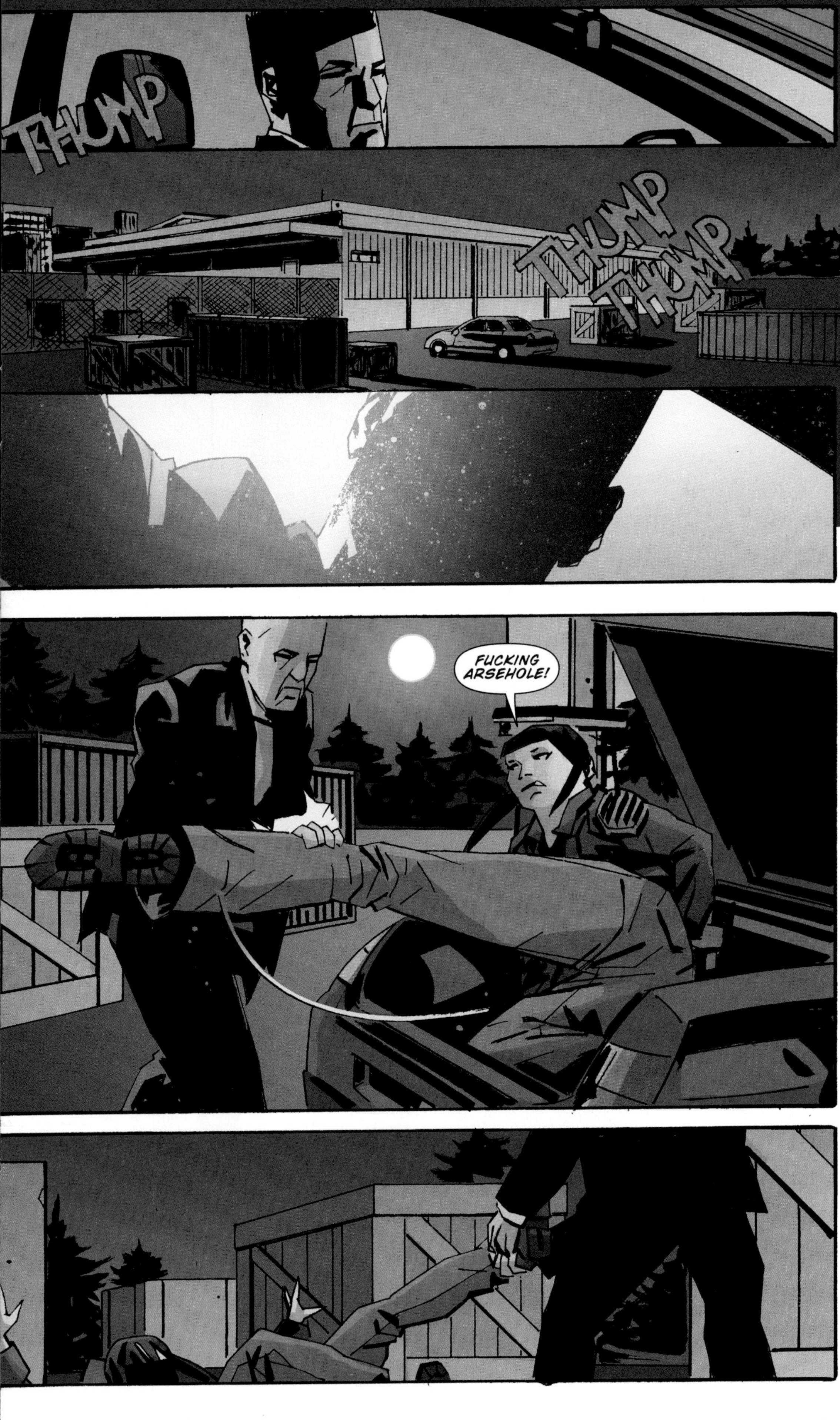
THUMP
THUMP
THUMP
FUCKING ARSEHOLE!

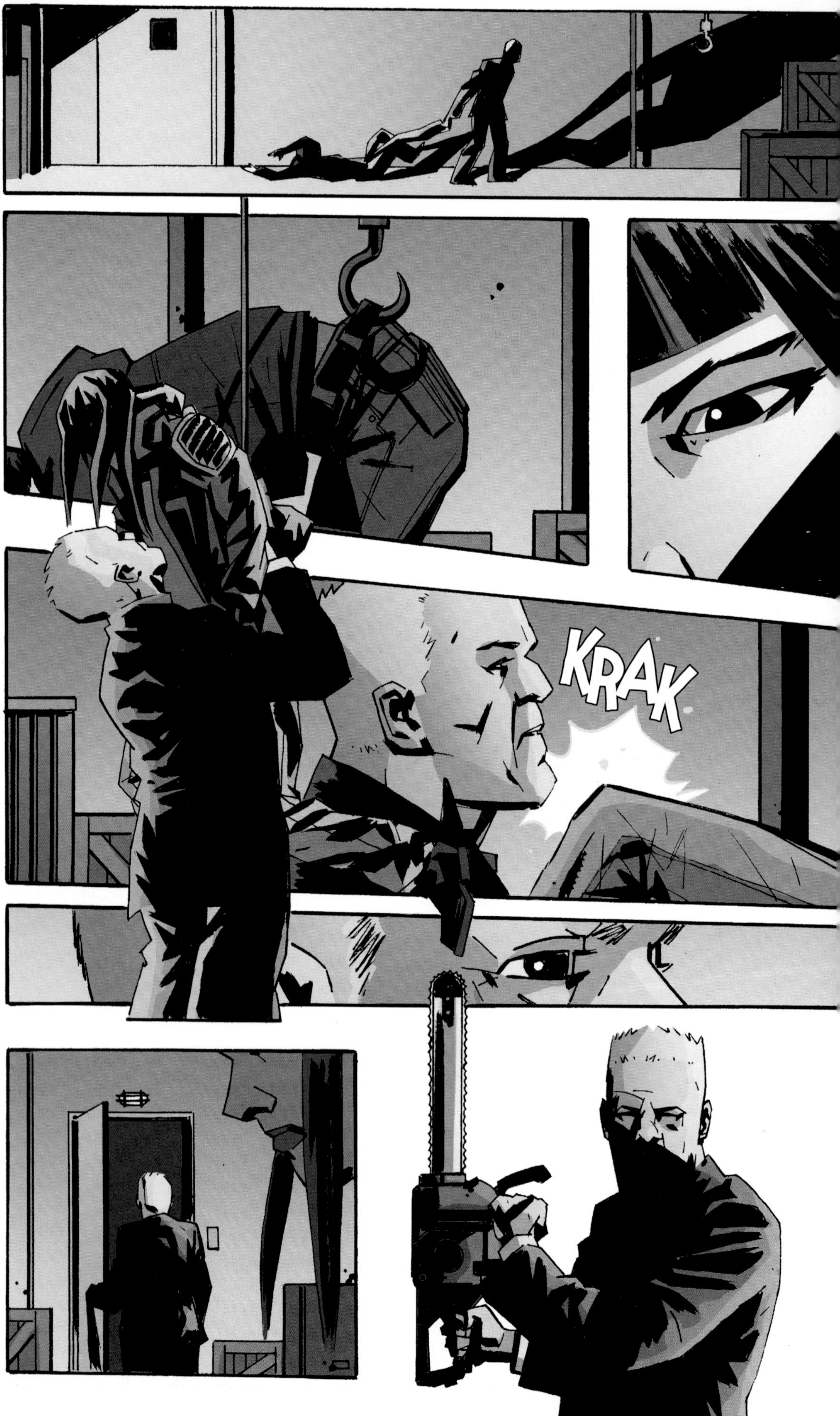
KRAK

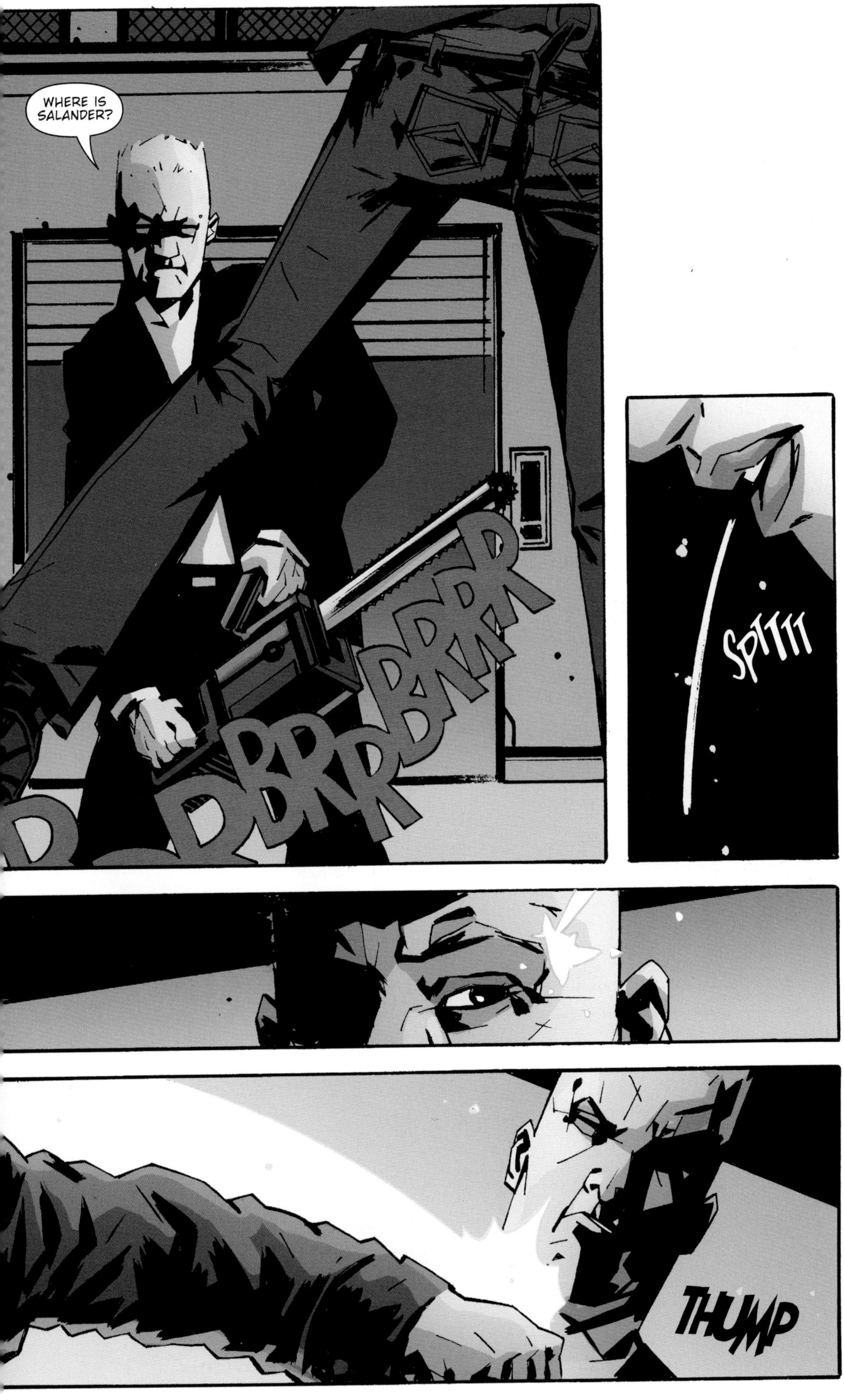
WHERE IS SALANDER?
BRRBRRBRRRR
SPTTTT
THUMP

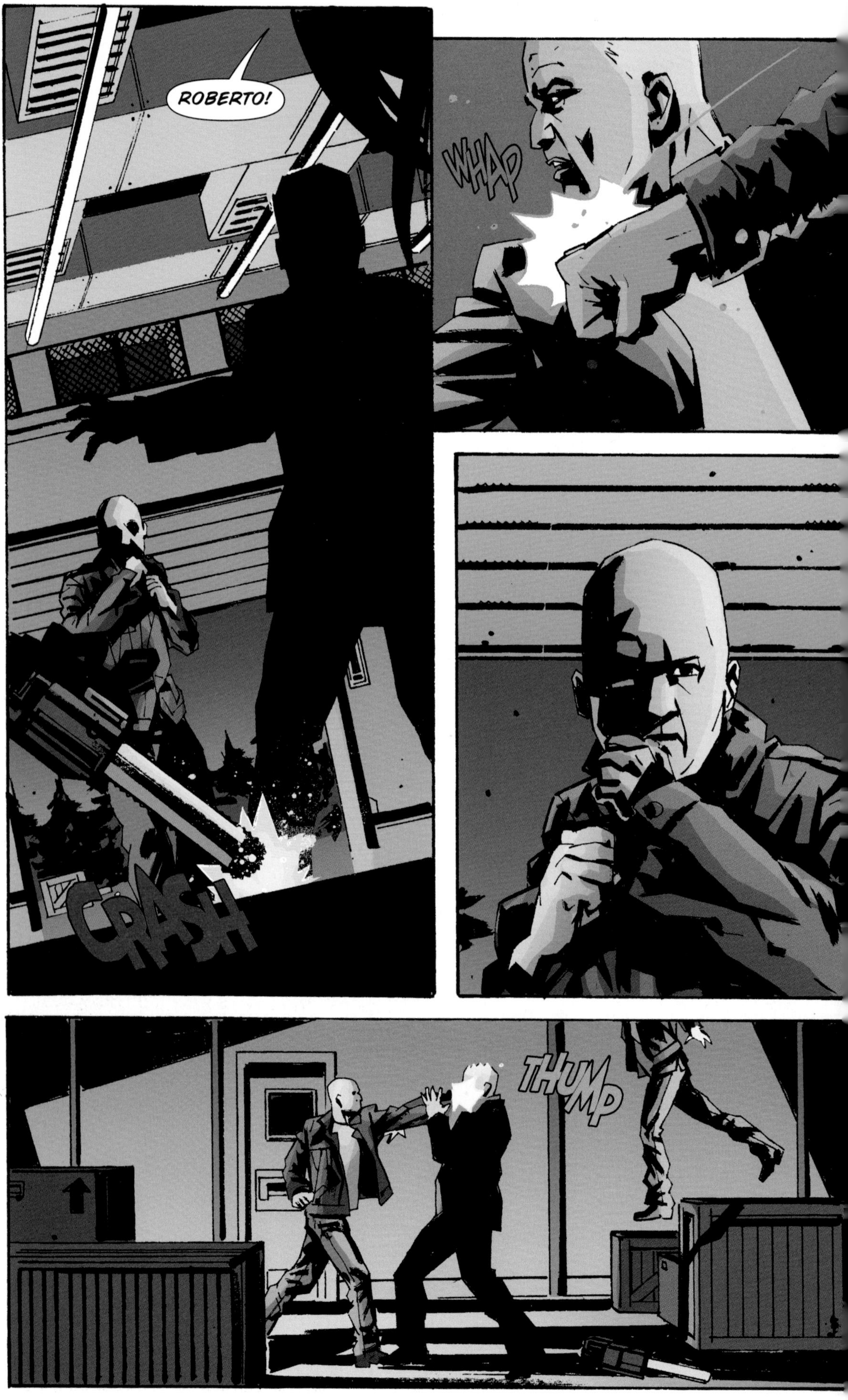
ROBERTO!
CRASH
WHAP
THUMP

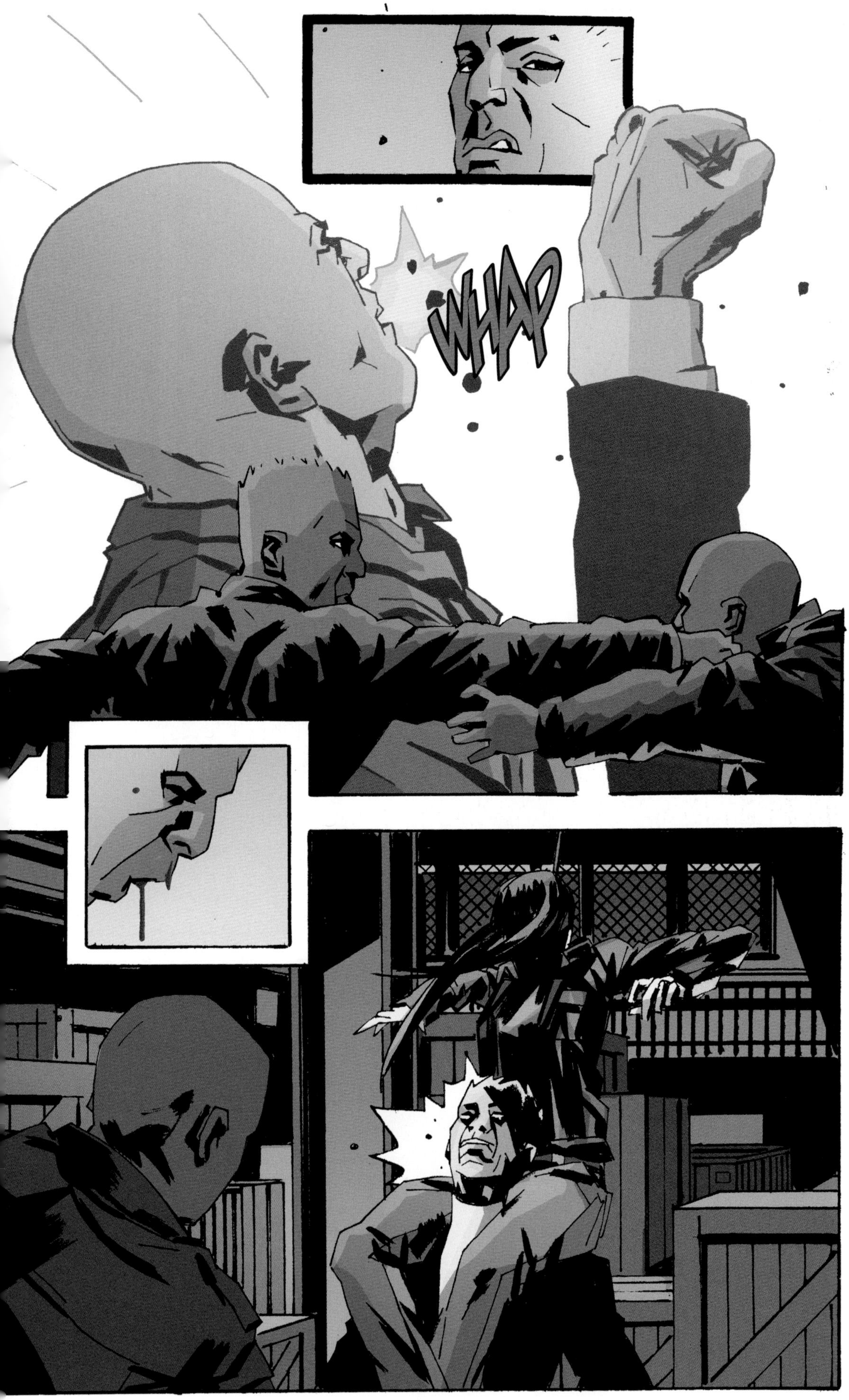
WHAP

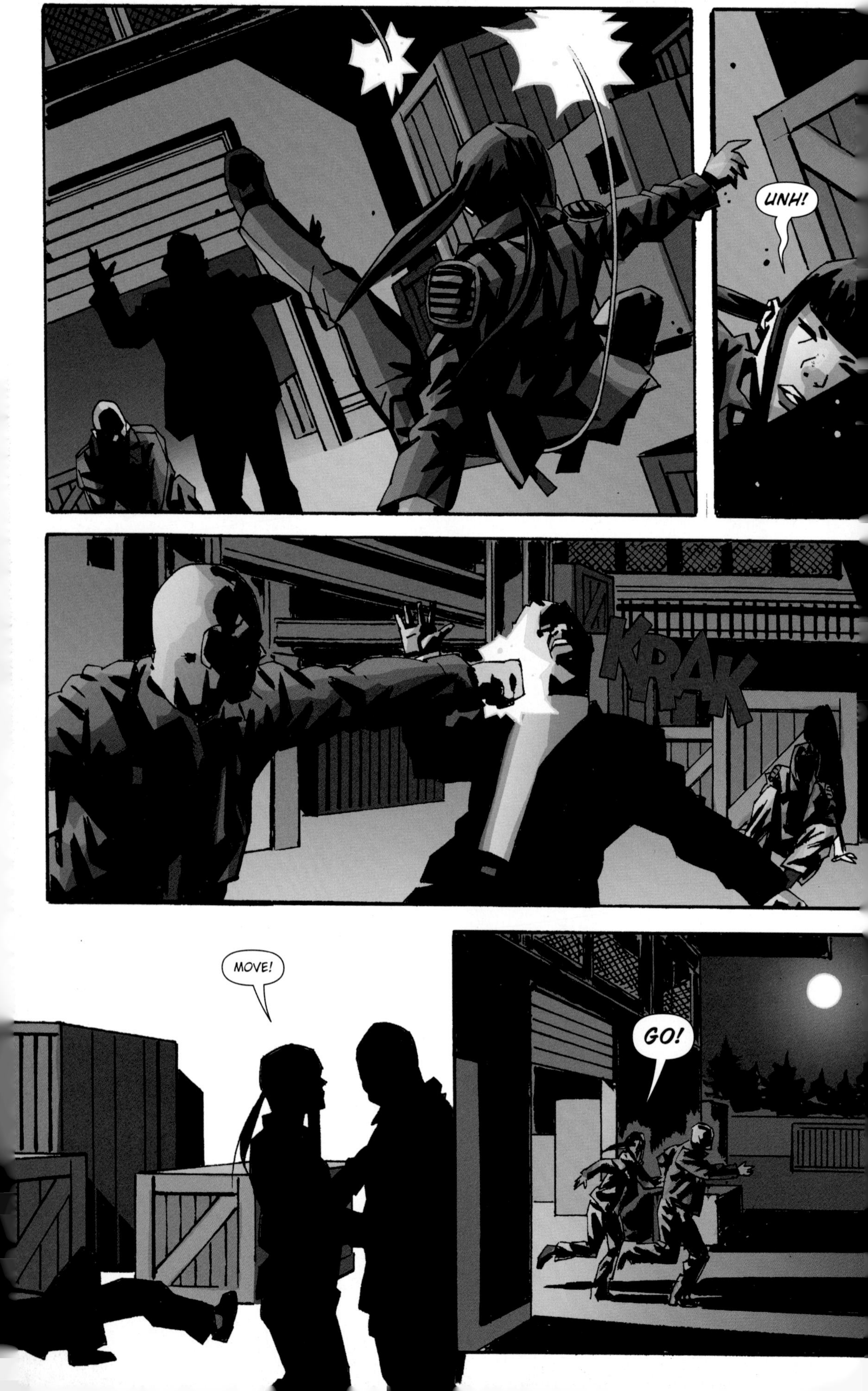
UNH!
KRAK
MOVE!
GO!

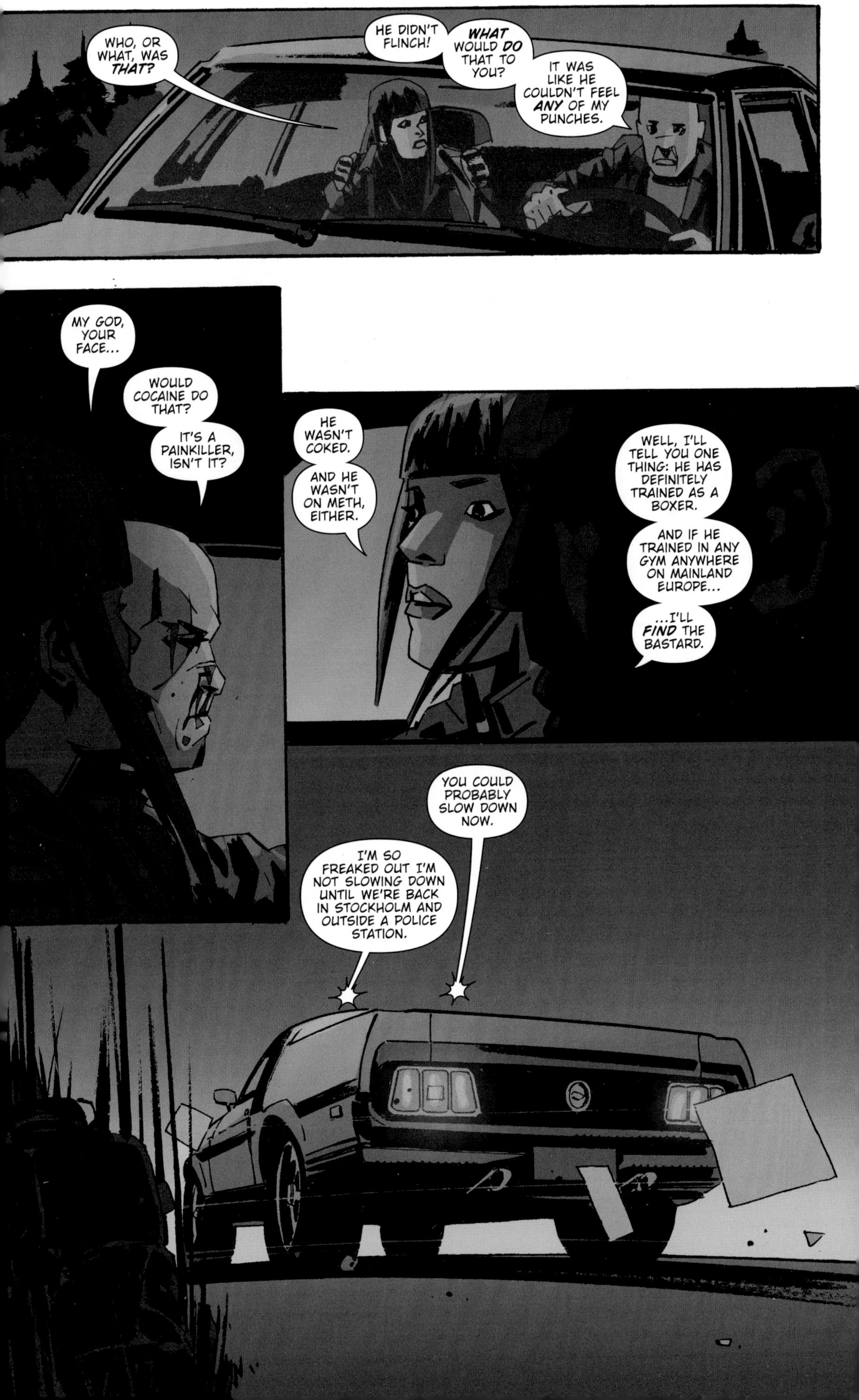
WHO, OR WHAT, WAS *THAT?*
HE DIDN'T FLINCH!
WHAT WOULD *DO* THAT TO YOU?
IT WAS LIKE HE COULDN'T FEEL *ANY* OF MY PUNCHES.
MY GOD, YOUR FACE...
WOULD COCAINE DO THAT?
IT'S A PAINKILLER, ISN'T IT?
HE WASN'T COKED.
AND HE WASN'T ON METH, EITHER.
WELL, I'LL TELL YOU ONE THING: HE HAS DEFINITELY TRAINED AS A BOXER.
AND IF HE TRAINED IN ANY GYM ANYWHERE ON MAINLAND EUROPE...
...I'LL *FIND* THE BASTARD.
YOU COULD PROBABLY SLOW DOWN NOW.
I'M SO FREAKED OUT I'M NOT SLOWING DOWN UNTIL WE'RE BACK IN STOCKHOLM AND OUTSIDE A POLICE STATION.

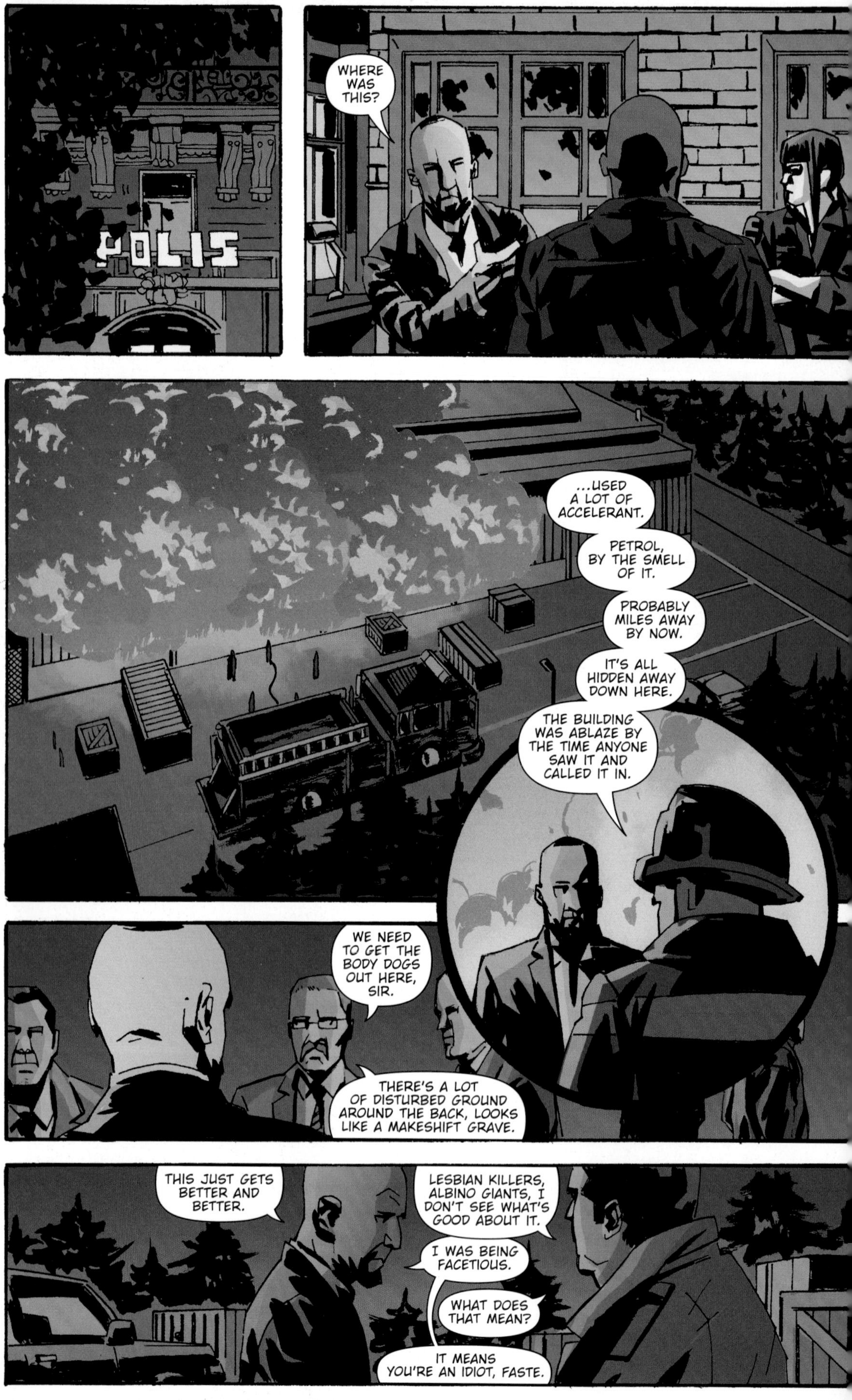
POLIS
WHERE WAS THIS?
...USED A LOT OF ACCELERANT.
PETROL, BY THE SMELL OF IT.
PROBABLY MILES AWAY BY NOW.
IT'S ALL HIDDEN AWAY DOWN HERE.
THE BUILDING WAS ABLAZE BY THE TIME ANYONE SAW IT AND CALLED IT IN.
WE NEED TO GET THE BODY DOGS OUT HERE, SIR.
THERE'S A LOT OF DISTURBED GROUND AROUND THE BACK, LOOKS LIKE A MAKESHIFT GRAVE.
THIS JUST GETS BETTER AND BETTER.
LESBIAN KILLERS, ALBINO GIANTS, I DON'T SEE WHAT'S GOOD ABOUT IT.
I WAS BEING FACETIOUS.
WHAT DOES THAT MEAN?
IT MEANS YOU'RE AN IDIOT, FASTE.

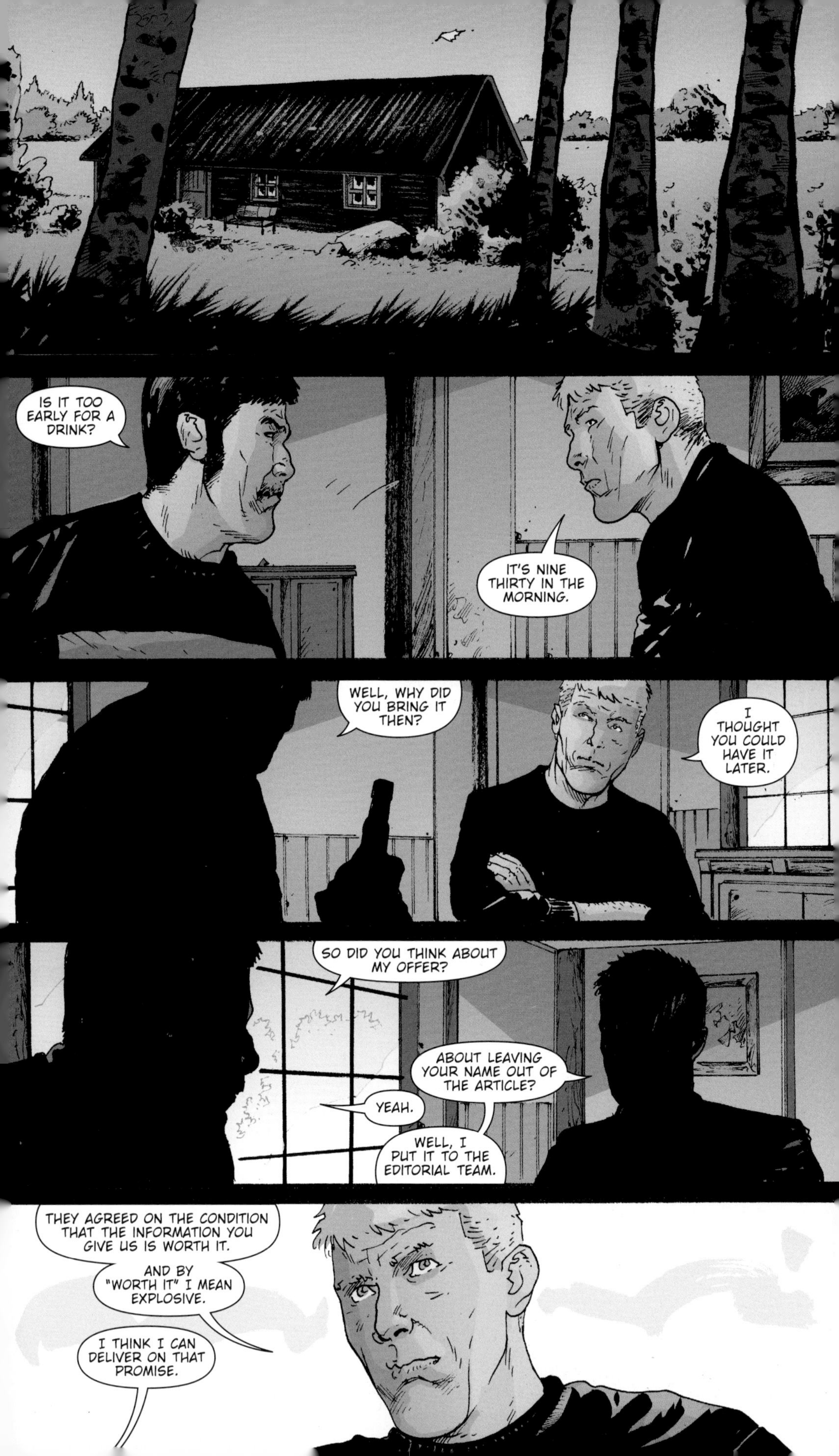
IS IT TOO EARLY FOR A DRINK?
IT'S NINE THIRTY IN THE MORNING.
WELL, WHY DID YOU BRING IT THEN?
I THOUGHT YOU COULD HAVE IT LATER.
SO DID YOU THINK ABOUT MY OFFER?
ABOUT LEAVING YOUR NAME OUT OF THE ARTICLE?
YEAH.
WELL, I PUT IT TO THE EDITORIAL TEAM.
THEY AGREED ON THE CONDITION THAT THE INFORMATION YOU GIVE US IS WORTH IT.
AND BY "WORTH IT" I MEAN EXPLOSIVE.
I THINK I CAN DELIVER ON THAT PROMISE.

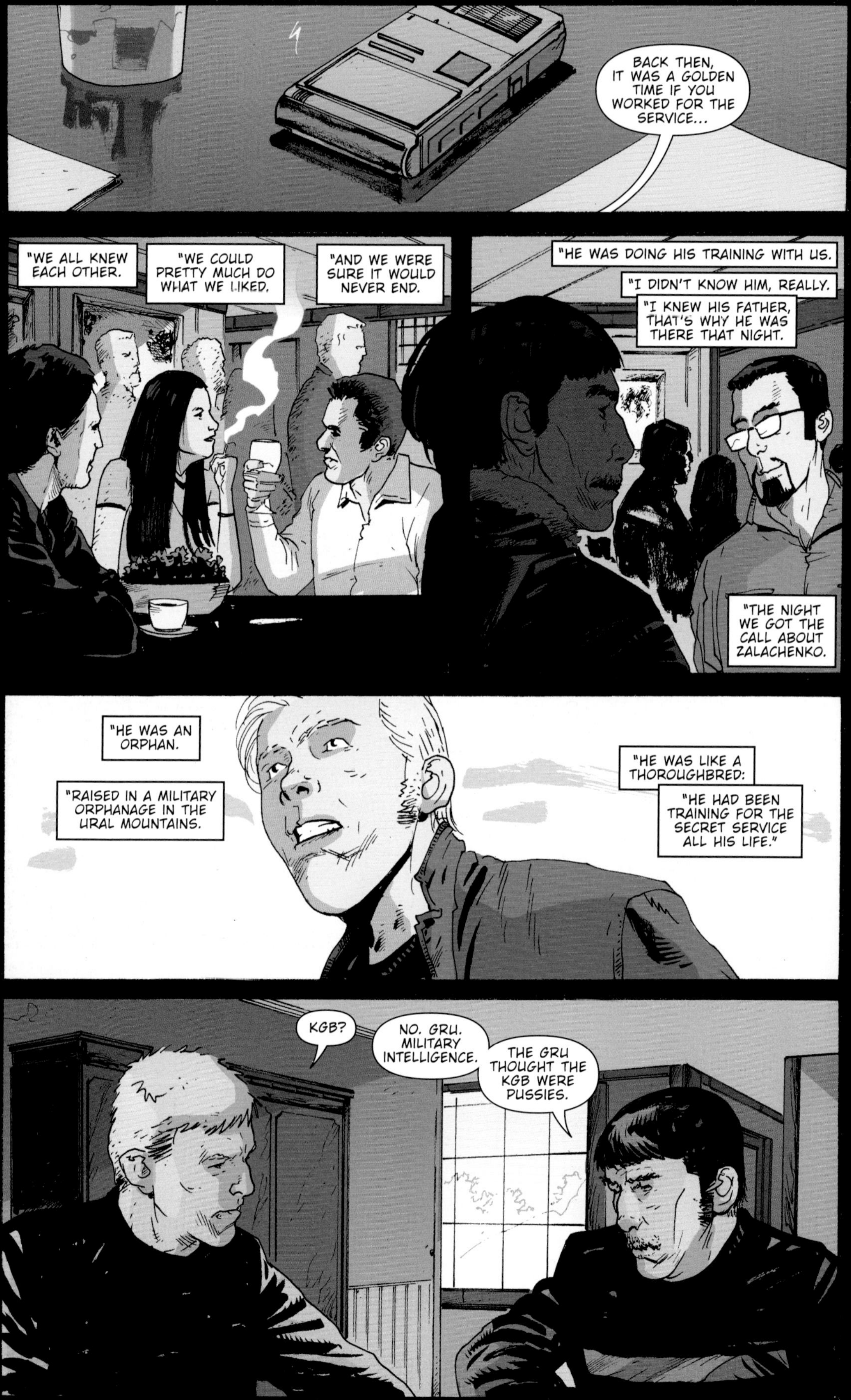
BACK THEN, IT WAS A GOLDEN TIME IF YOU WORKED FOR THE SERVICE...
"WE ALL KNEW EACH OTHER.
"WE COULD PRETTY MUCH DO WHAT WE LIKED.
"AND WE WERE SURE IT WOULD NEVER END.
"HE WAS DOING HIS TRAINING WITH US.
"I DIDN'T KNOW HIM, REALLY.
"I KNEW HIS FATHER, THAT'S WHY HE WAS THERE THAT NIGHT.
"THE NIGHT WE GOT THE CALL ABOUT ZALACHENKO.
"HE WAS AN ORPHAN.
"RAISED IN A MILITARY ORPHANAGE IN THE URAL MOUNTAINS.
"HE WAS LIKE A THOROUGHBRED:
"HE HAD BEEN TRAINING FOR THE SECRET SERVICE ALL HIS LIFE."
KGB?
NO. GRU. MILITARY INTELLIGENCE.
THE GRU THOUGHT THE KGB WERE PUSSIES.

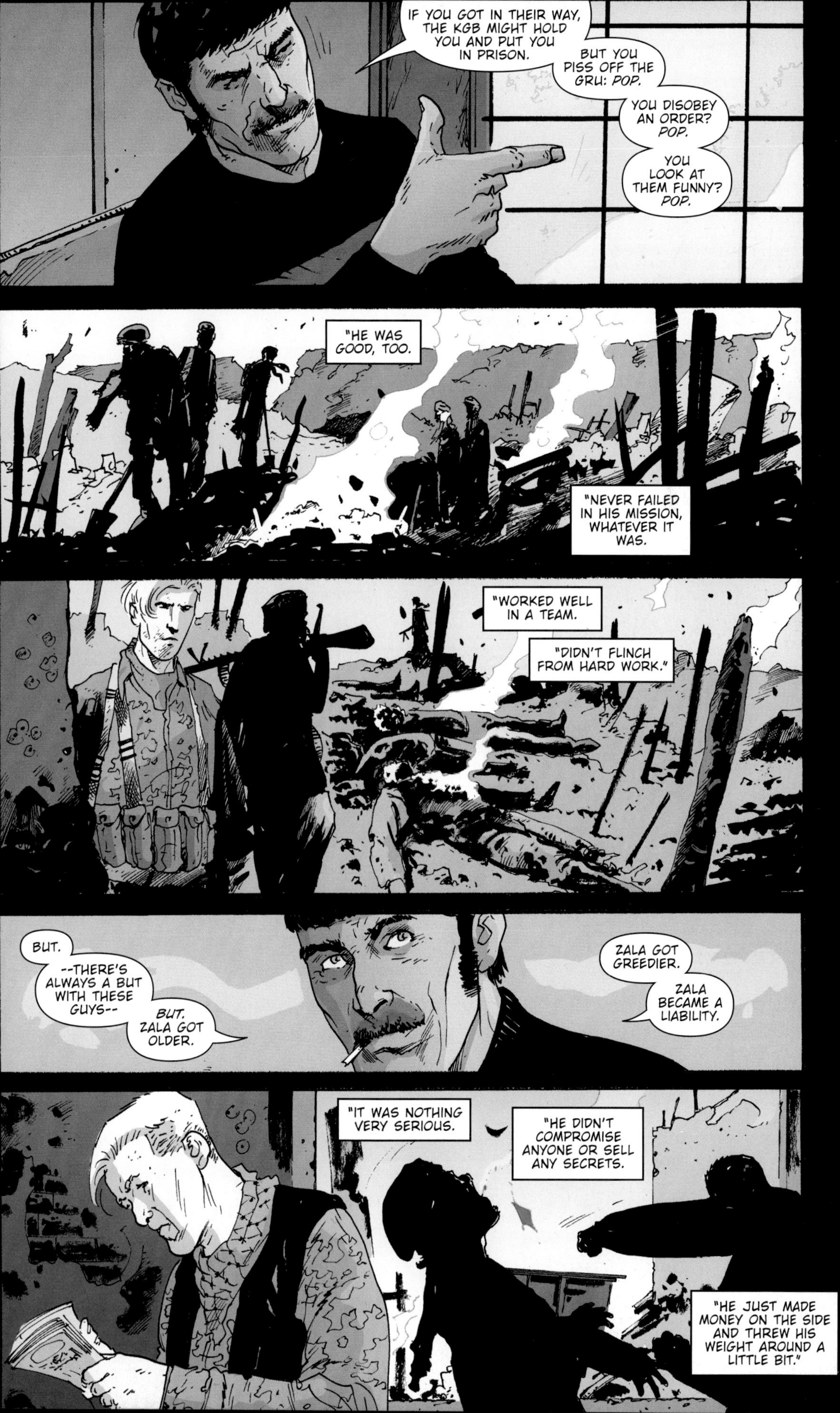
IF YOU GOT IN THEIR WAY, THE KGB MIGHT HOLD YOU AND PUT YOU IN PRISON.
BUT YOU PISS OFF THE GRU: POP.
YOU DISOBEY AN ORDER? POP.
YOU LOOK AT THEM FUNNY? POP.
"HE WAS GOOD, TOO.
"NEVER FAILED IN HIS MISSION, WHATEVER IT WAS.
"WORKED WELL IN A TEAM.
"DIDN'T FLINCH FROM HARD WORK."
BUT.
--THERE'S ALWAYS A BUT WITH THESE GUYS--
BUT. ZALA GOT OLDER.
ZALA GOT GREEDIER.
ZALA BECAME A LIABILITY.
"IT WAS NOTHING VERY SERIOUS.
"HE DIDN'T COMPROMISE ANYONE OR SELL ANY SECRETS.
"HE JUST MADE MONEY ON THE SIDE AND THREW HIS WEIGHT AROUND A LITTLE BIT."

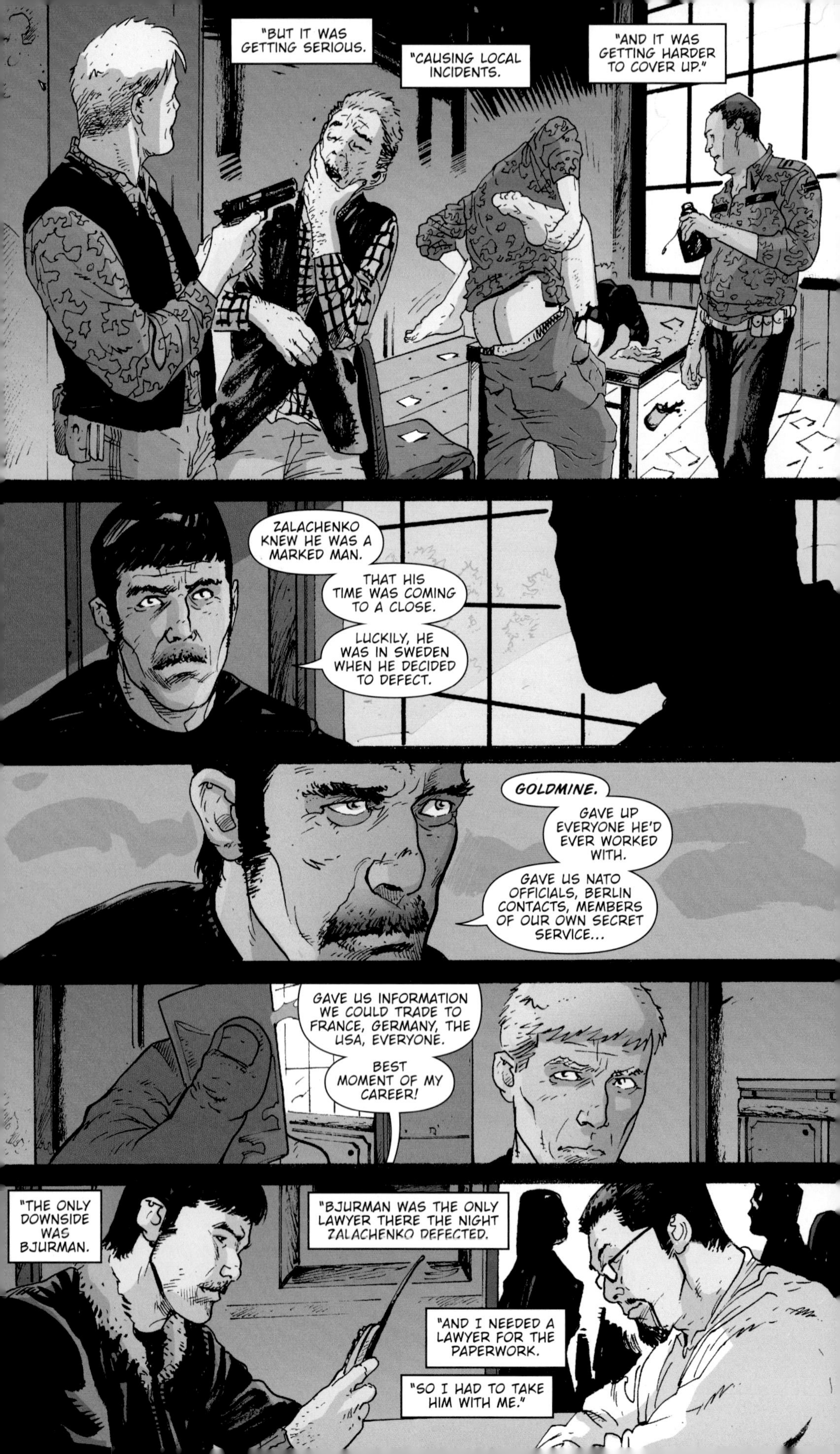

"BUT IT WAS GETTING SERIOUS.
"CAUSING LOCAL INCIDENTS.
"AND IT WAS GETTING HARDER TO COVER UP."
ZALACHENKO KNEW HE WAS A MARKED MAN.
THAT HIS TIME WAS COMING TO A CLOSE.
LUCKILY, HE WAS IN SWEDEN WHEN HE DECIDED TO DEFECT.
GOLDMINE.
GAVE UP EVERYONE HE'D EVER WORKED WITH.
GAVE US NATO OFFICIALS, BERLIN CONTACTS, MEMBERS OF OUR OWN SECRET SERVICE...
GAVE US INFORMATION WE COULD TRADE TO FRANCE, GERMANY, THE USA, EVERYONE.
BEST MOMENT OF MY CAREER!
"THE ONLY DOWNSIDE WAS BJURMAN.
"BJURMAN WAS THE ONLY LAWYER THERE THE NIGHT ZALACHENKO DEFECTED.
"AND I NEEDED A LAWYER FOR THE PAPERWORK.
"SO I HAD TO TAKE HIM WITH ME."

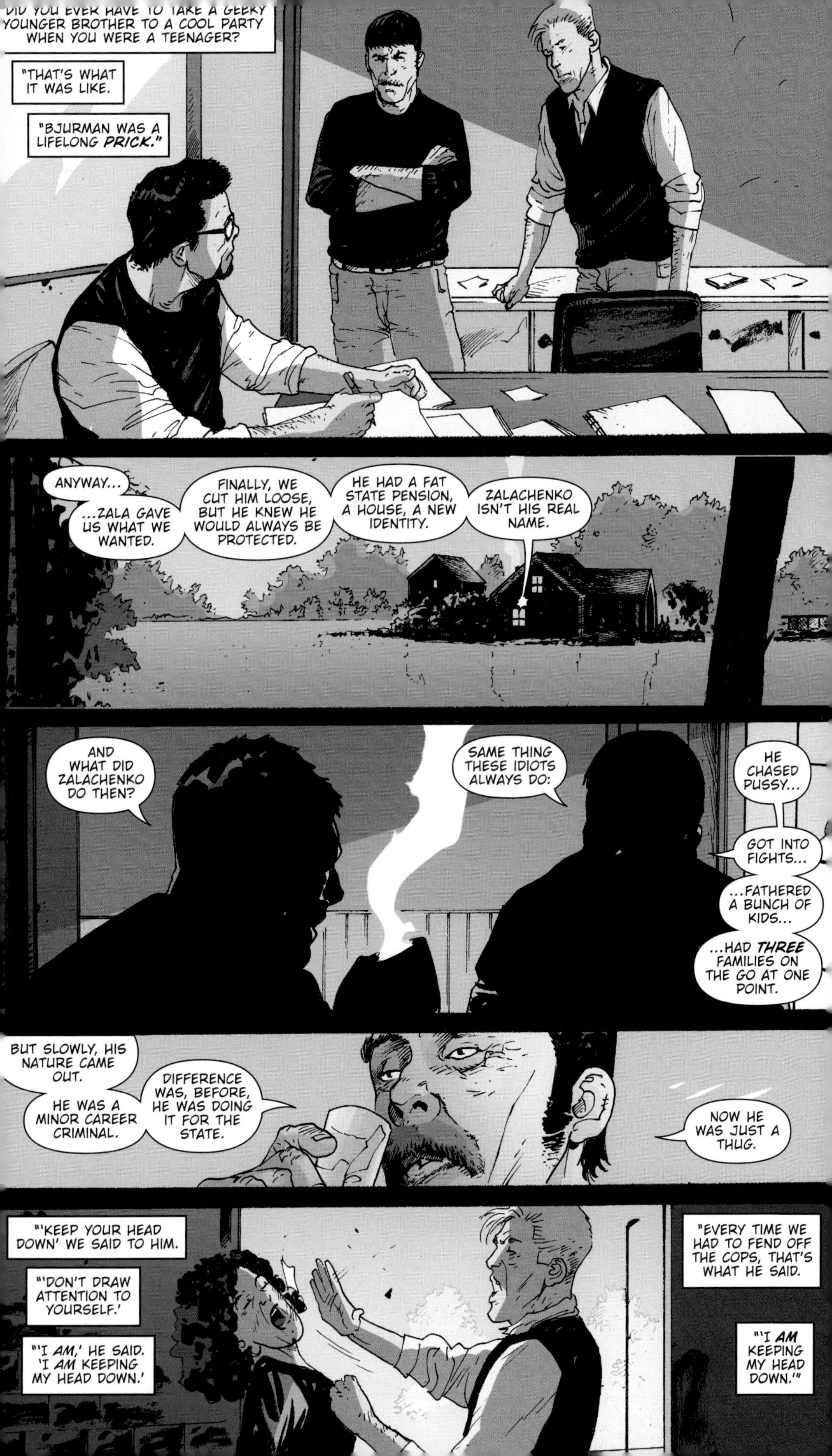
DID YOU EVER HAVE TO TAKE A GEEKY YOUNGER BROTHER TO A COOL PARTY WHEN YOU WERE A TEENAGER?
"THAT'S WHAT IT WAS LIKE.
"BJURMAN WAS A LIFELONG PRICK."
ANYWAY...
...ZALA GAVE US WHAT WE WANTED.
FINALLY, WE CUT HIM LOOSE, BUT HE KNEW HE WOULD ALWAYS BE PROTECTED.
HE HAD A FAT STATE PENSION, A HOUSE, A NEW IDENTITY.
ZALACHENKO ISN'T HIS REAL NAME.
AND WHAT DID ZALACHENKO DO THEN?
SAME THING THESE IDIOTS ALWAYS DO:
HE CHASED PUSSY...
GOT INTO FIGHTS...
...FATHERED A BUNCH OF KIDS...
...HAD THREE FAMILIES ON THE GO AT ONE POINT.
BUT SLOWLY, HIS NATURE CAME OUT.
HE WAS A MINOR CAREER CRIMINAL.
DIFFERENCE WAS, BEFORE, HE WAS DOING IT FOR THE STATE.
NOW HE WAS JUST A THUG.
"'KEEP YOUR HEAD DOWN' WE SAID TO HIM.
"'DON'T DRAW ATTENTION TO YOURSELF.'
"'I AM,' HE SAID. 'I AM KEEPING MY HEAD DOWN.'
"EVERY TIME WE HAD TO FEND OFF THE COPS, THAT'S WHAT HE SAID.
"'I AM KEEPING MY HEAD DOWN.'"

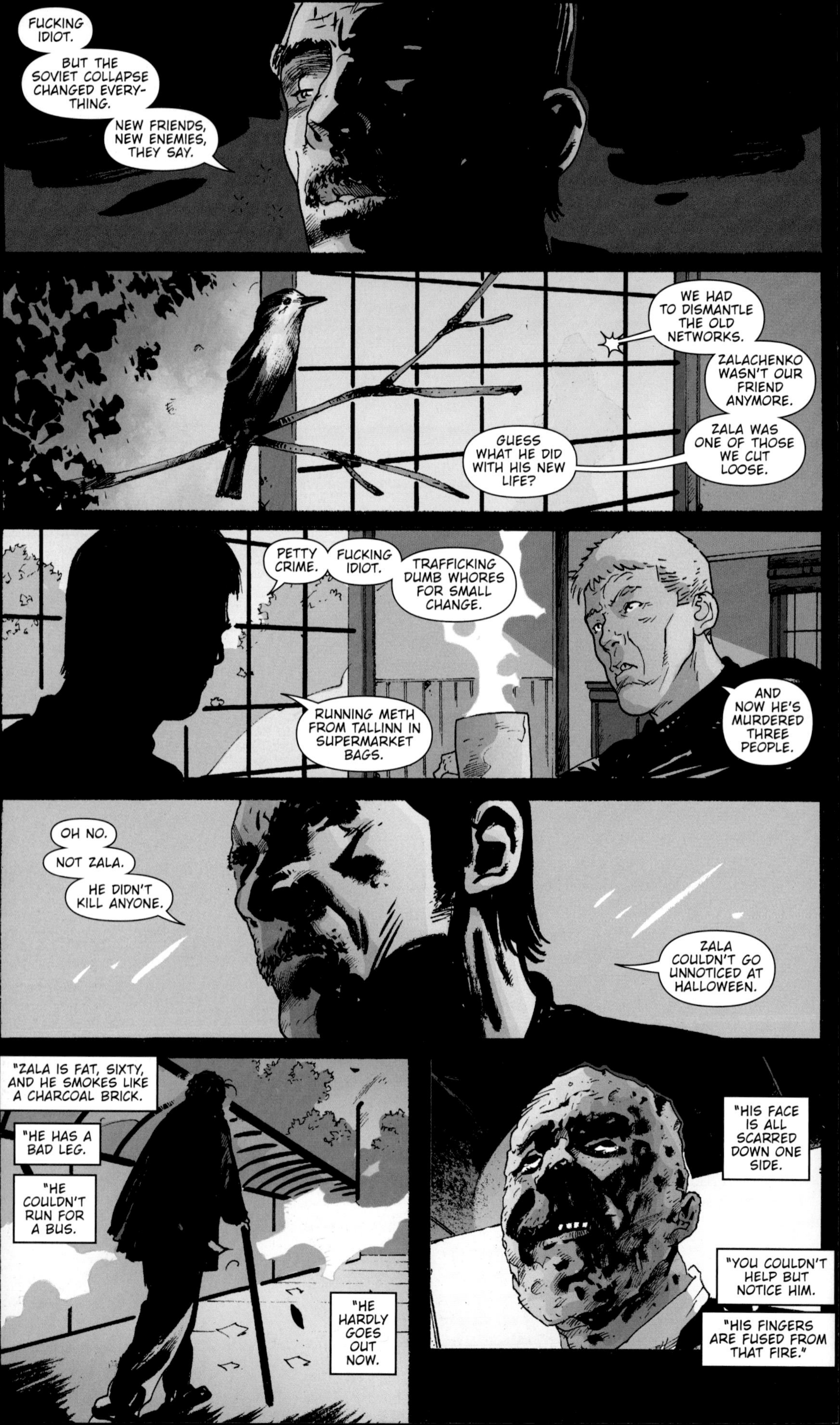
FUCKING IDIOT.
BUT THE SOVIET COLLAPSE CHANGED EVERY-THING.
NEW FRIENDS, NEW ENEMIES, THEY SAY.
WE HAD TO DISMANTLE THE OLD NETWORKS.
ZALACHENKO WASN'T OUR FRIEND ANYMORE.
ZALA WAS ONE OF THOSE WE CUT LOOSE.
GUESS WHAT HE DID WITH HIS NEW LIFE?
PETTY CRIME.
FUCKING IDIOT.
TRAFFICKING DUMB WHORES FOR SMALL CHANGE.
RUNNING METH FROM TALLINN IN SUPERMARKET BAGS.
AND NOW HE'S MURDERED THREE PEOPLE.
OH NO.
NOT ZALA.
HE DIDN'T KILL ANYONE.
ZALA COULDN'T GO UNNOTICED AT HALLOWEEN.
"ZALA IS FAT, SIXTY, AND HE SMOKES LIKE A CHARCOAL BRICK.
"HE HAS A BAD LEG.
"HE COULDN'T RUN FOR A BUS.
"HE HARDLY GOES OUT NOW.
"HIS FACE IS ALL SCARRED DOWN ONE SIDE.
"YOU COULDN'T HELP BUT NOTICE HIM.
"HIS FINGERS ARE FUSED FROM THAT FIRE."

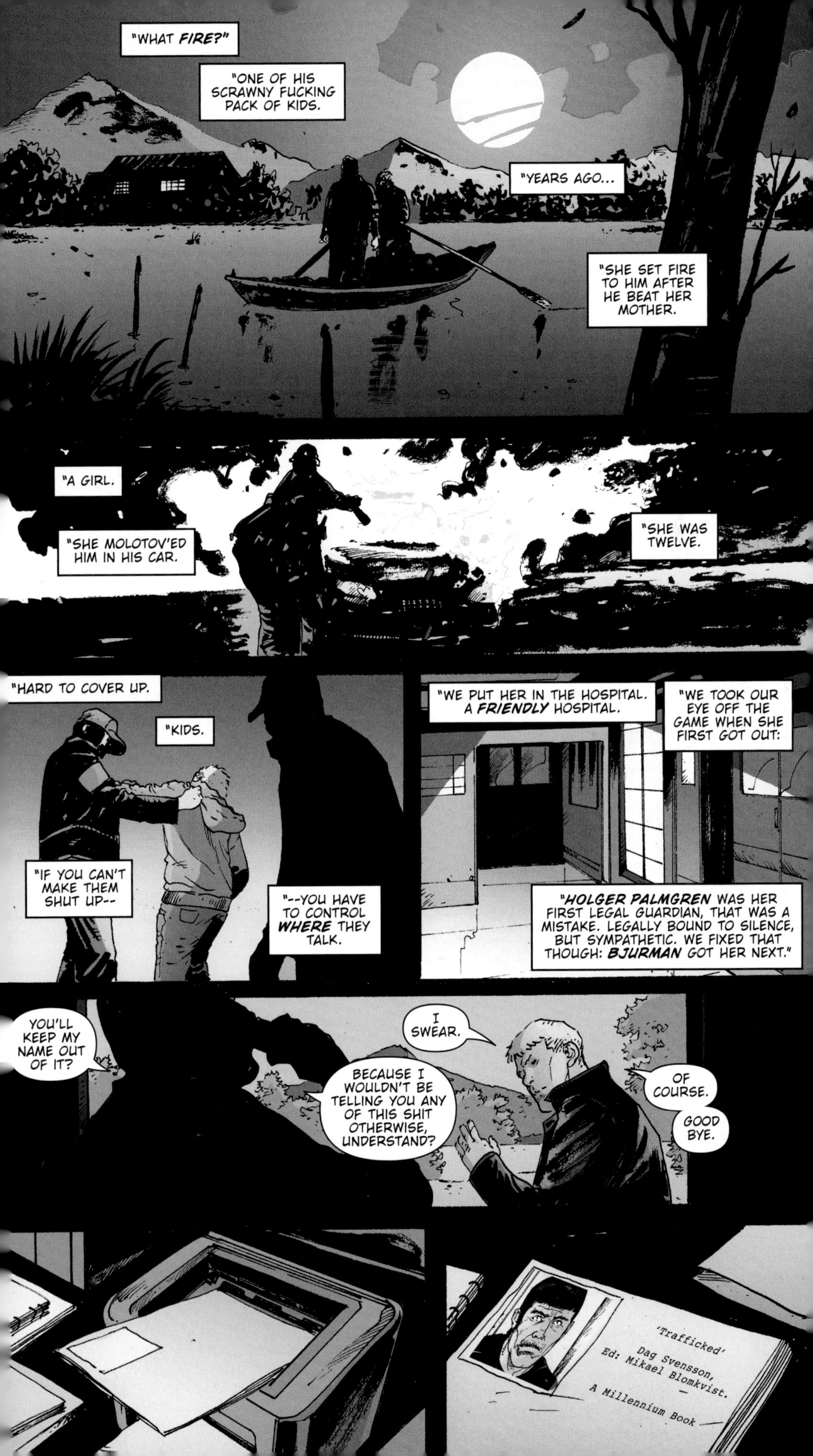
"WHAT FIRE?"
"ONE OF HIS SCRAWNY FUCKING PACK OF KIDS.
"YEARS AGO...
"SHE SET FIRE TO HIM AFTER HE BEAT HER MOTHER.
"A GIRL.
"SHE MOLOTOV'ED HIM IN HIS CAR.
"SHE WAS TWELVE.
"HARD TO COVER UP.
"KIDS.
"IF YOU CAN'T MAKE THEM SHUT UP--
"--YOU HAVE TO CONTROL WHERE THEY TALK.
"WE PUT HER IN THE HOSPITAL. A FRIENDLY HOSPITAL.
"WE TOOK OUR EYE OFF THE GAME WHEN SHE FIRST GOT OUT:
"HOLGER PALMGREN WAS HER FIRST LEGAL GUARDIAN, THAT WAS A MISTAKE. LEGALLY BOUND TO SILENCE, BUT SYMPATHETIC. WE FIXED THAT THOUGH: BJURMAN GOT HER NEXT."
YOU'LL KEEP MY NAME OUT OF IT?
BECAUSE I WOULDN'T BE TELLING YOU ANY OF THIS SHIT OTHERWISE, UNDERSTAND?
I SWEAR.
OF COURSE.
GOOD BYE.
'Trafficked'
Dag Svensson,
Ed: Mikael Blomkvist.
A Millennium Book

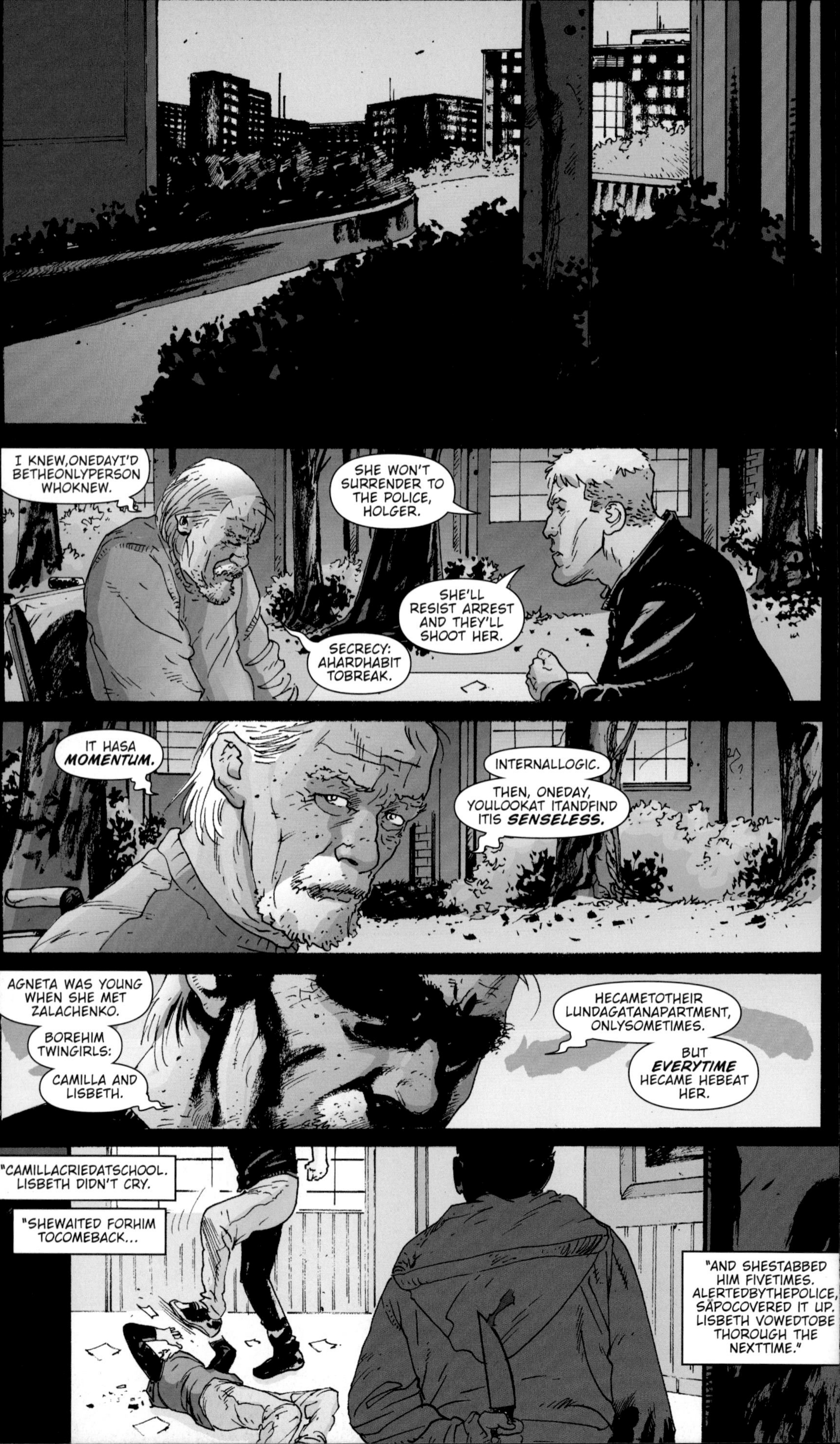
I KNEW, ONE DAY I'D BE THE ONLY PERSON WHO KNEW.
SHE WON'T SURRENDER TO THE POLICE, HOLGER.
SHE'LL RESIST ARREST AND THEY'LL SHOOT HER.
SECRECY: A HARD HABIT TO BREAK.
IT HAS A **MOMENTUM.**
INTERNAL LOGIC.
THEN, ONE DAY, YOU LOOK AT IT AND FIND IT IS **SENSELESS.**
AGNETA WAS YOUNG WHEN SHE MET ZALACHENKO.
BORE HIM TWIN GIRLS:
CAMILLA AND LISBETH.
HE CAME TO THEIR LUNDAGATAN APARTMENT, ONLY SOMETIMES.
BUT ***EVERY TIME*** HE CAME HE BEAT HER.
"CAMILLA CRIED AT SCHOOL. LISBETH DIDN'T CRY.
"SHE WAITED FOR HIM TO COME BACK...
"AND SHE STABBED HIM FIVE TIMES. ALERTED BY THE POLICE, SÄPO COVERED IT UP. LISBETH VOWED TO BE THOROUGH THE NEXT TIME."

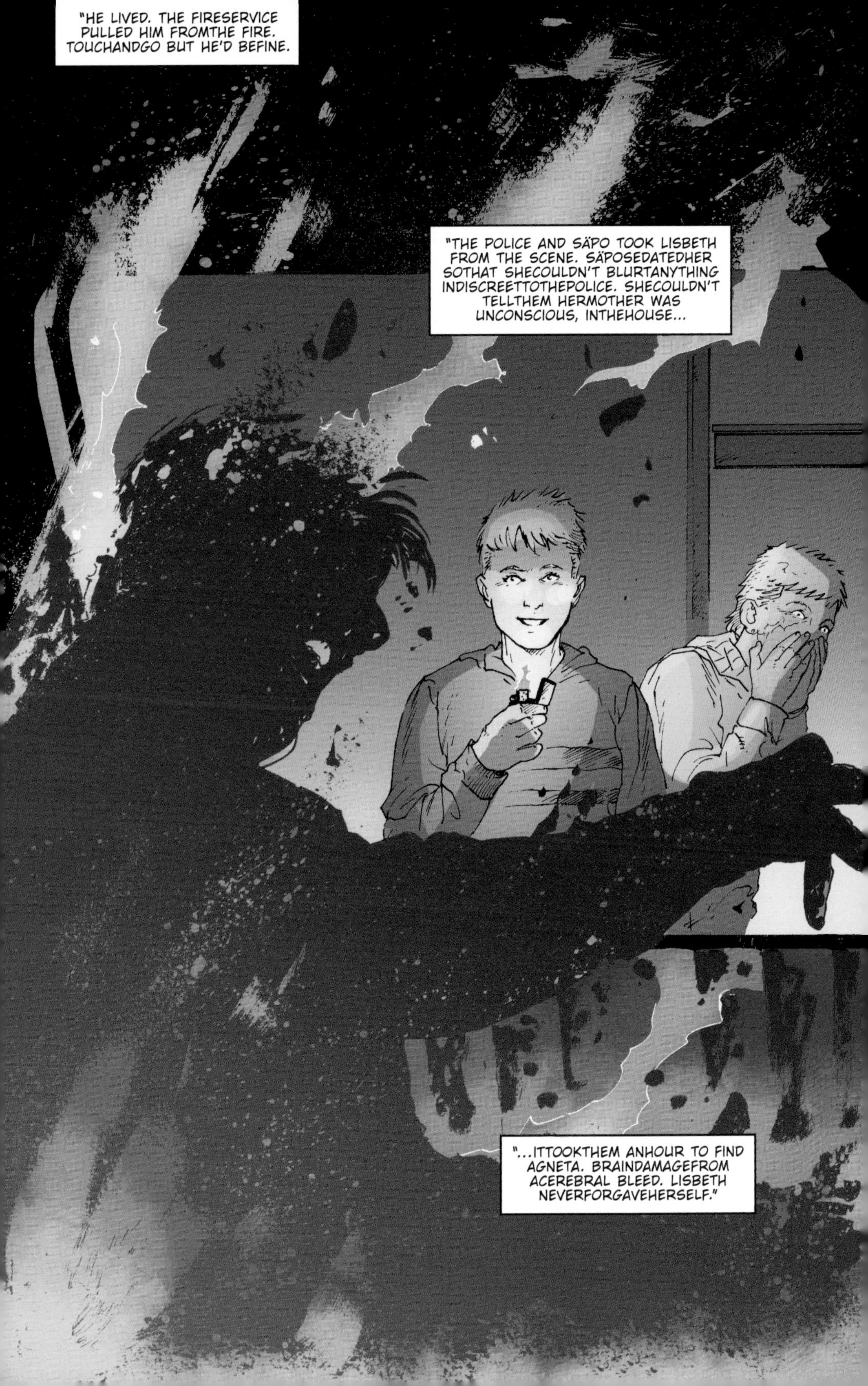
"HE LIVED. THE FIRESERVICE PULLED HIM FROMTHE FIRE. TOUCHANDGO BUT HE'D BEFINE.
"THE POLICE AND SÄPO TOOK LISBETH FROM THE SCENE. SÄPOSEDATEDHER SOTHAT SHECOULDN'T BLURTANYTHING INDISCREETTOTHEPOLICE. SHECOULDN'T TELLTHEM HERMOTHER WAS UNCONSCIOUS, INTHEHOUSE...
"...ITTOOKTHEM ANHOUR TO FIND AGNETA. BRAINDAMAGEFROM ACEREBRAL BLEED. LISBETH NEVERFORGAVEHERSELF."

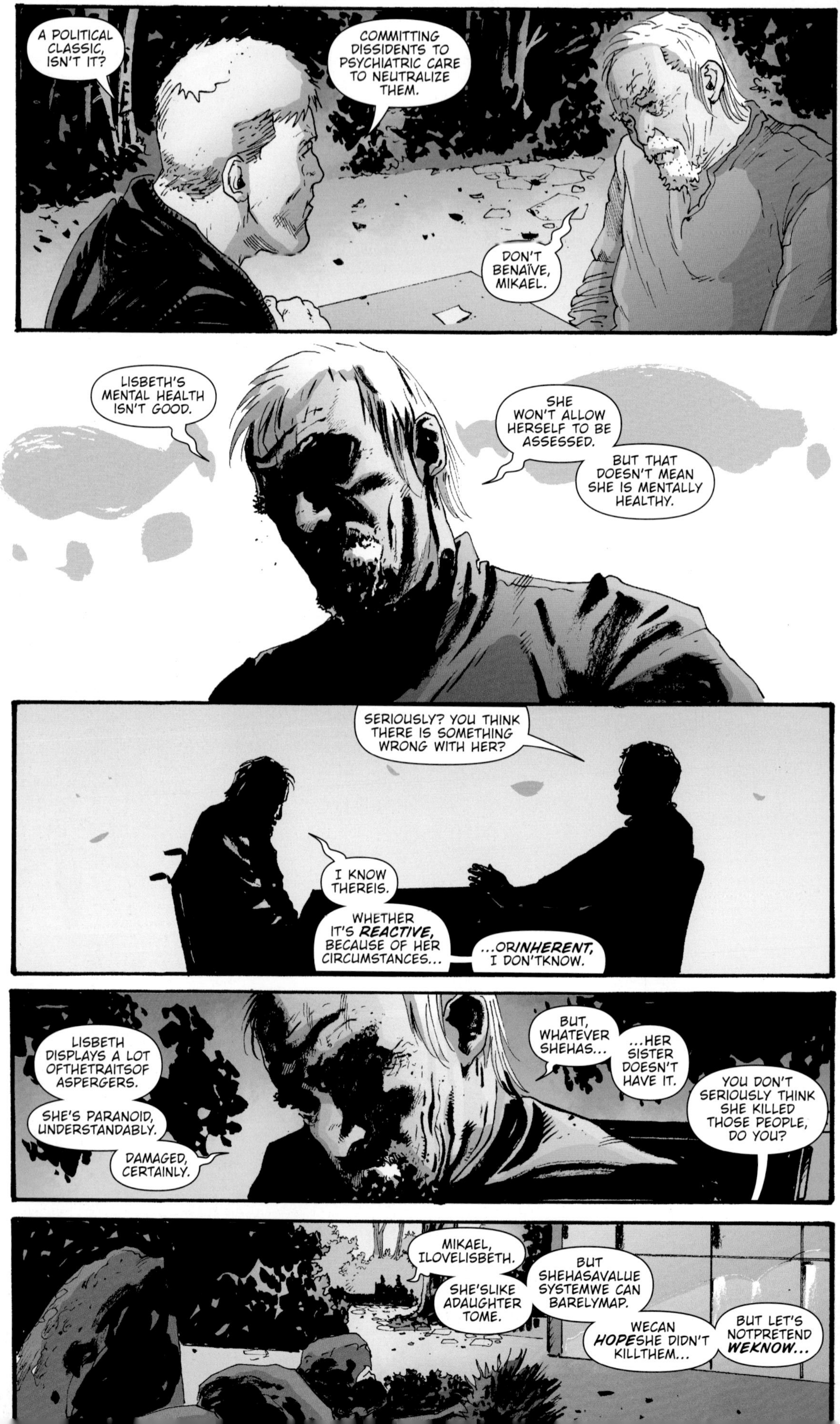
A POLITICAL CLASSIC, ISN'T IT?
COMMITTING DISSIDENTS TO PSYCHIATRIC CARE TO NEUTRALIZE THEM.
DON'T BENAÏVE, MIKAEL.
LISBETH'S MENTAL HEALTH ISN'T GOOD.
SHE WON'T ALLOW HERSELF TO BE ASSESSED.
BUT THAT DOESN'T MEAN SHE IS MENTALLY HEALTHY.
SERIOUSLY? YOU THINK THERE IS SOMETHING WRONG WITH HER?
I KNOW THEREIS.
WHETHER IT'S REACTIVE, BECAUSE OF HER CIRCUMSTANCES...
...ORINHERENT, I DON'TKNOW.
LISBETH DISPLAYS A LOT OFTHETRAITSOF ASPERGERS.
SHE'S PARANOID, UNDERSTANDABLY.
DAMAGED, CERTAINLY.
BUT, WHATEVER SHEHAS...
...HER SISTER DOESN'T HAVE IT.
YOU DON'T SERIOUSLY THINK SHE KILLED THOSE PEOPLE, DO YOU?
MIKAEL, ILOVELISBETH.
SHE'SLIKE ADAUGHTER TOME.
BUT SHEHASAVALUE SYSTEMWE CAN BARELYMAP.
WECAN HOPESHE DIDN'T KILLTHEM...
BUT LET'S NOTPRETEND WEKNOW...

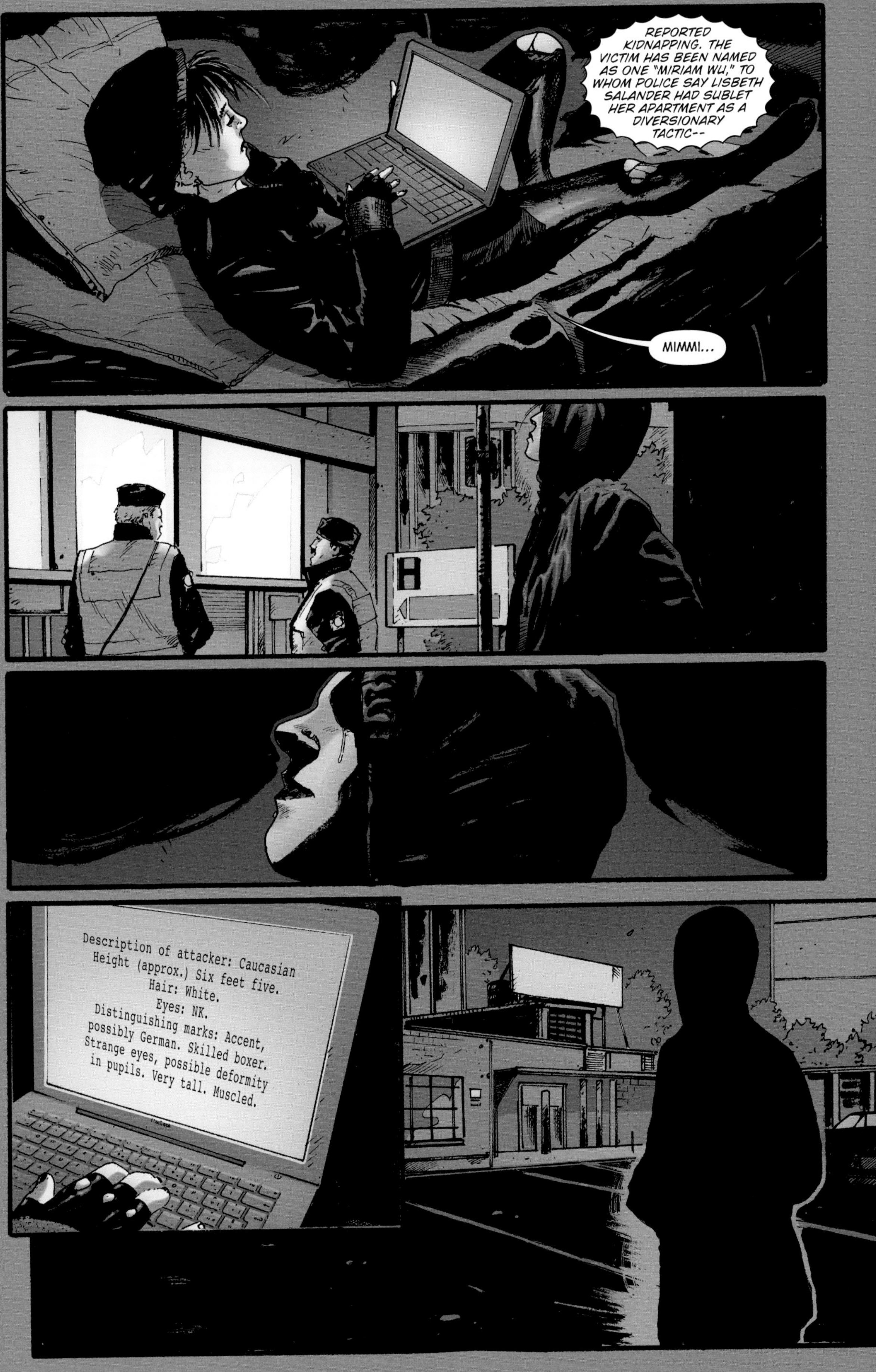
REPORTED KIDNAPPING. THE VICTIM HAS BEEN NAMED AS ONE "MIRIAM WU," TO WHOM POLICE SAY LISBETH SALANDER HAD SUBLET HER APARTMENT AS A DIVERSIONARY TACTIC--
MIMMI...
Description of attacker: Caucasian
Height (approx.) Six feet five.
Hair: White.
Eyes: NK.
Distinguishing marks: Accent, possibly German. Skilled boxer. Strange eyes, possible deformity in pupils. Very tall. Muscled.

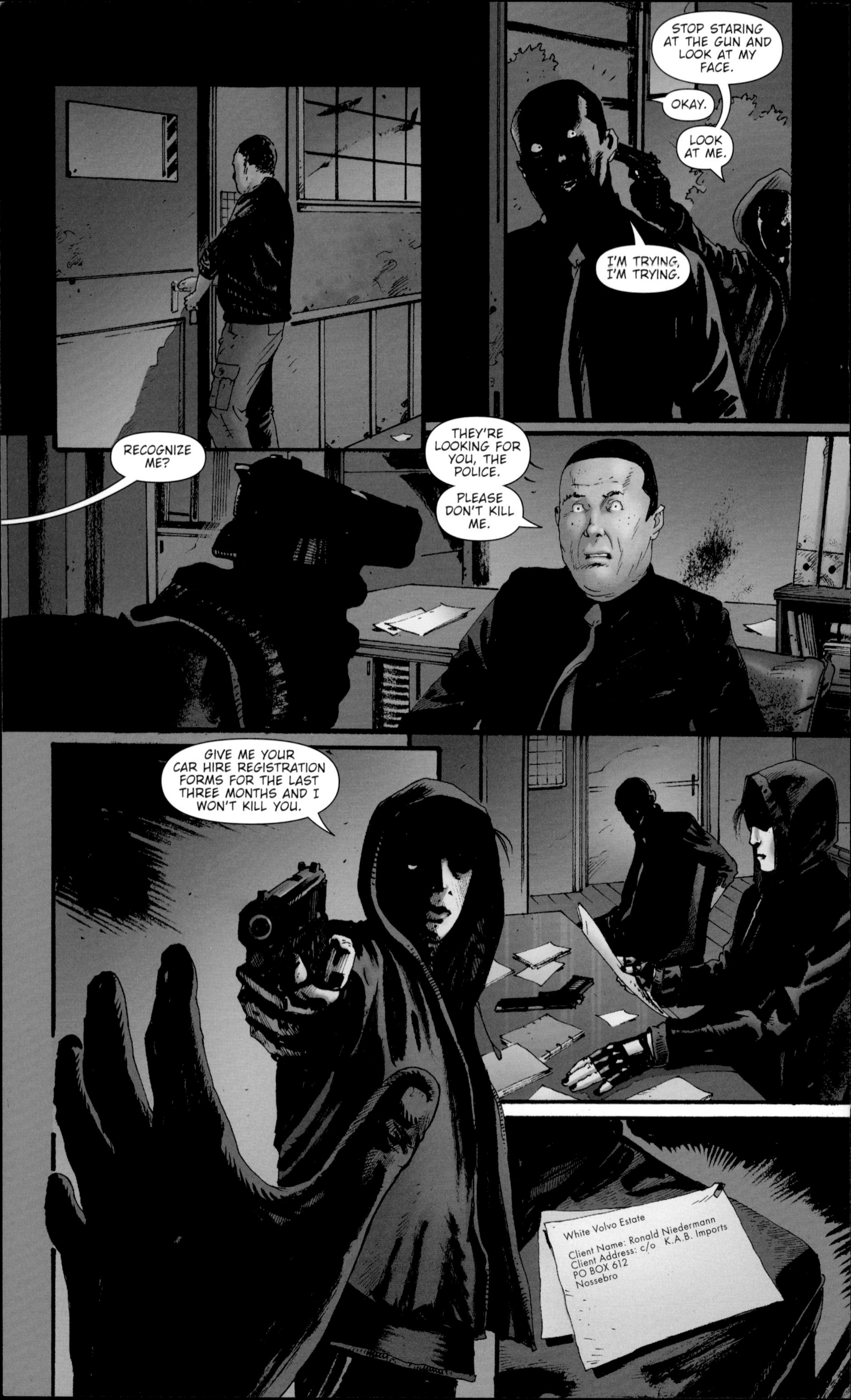

STOP STARING AT THE GUN AND LOOK AT MY FACE.
OKAY.
LOOK AT ME.
I'M TRYING, I'M TRYING.
RECOGNIZE ME?
THEY'RE LOOKING FOR YOU, THE POLICE.
PLEASE DON'T KILL ME.
GIVE ME YOUR CAR HIRE REGISTRATION FORMS FOR THE LAST THREE MONTHS AND I WON'T KILL YOU.
White Volvo Estate
Client Name: Ronald Niedermann
Client Address: c/o K.A.B. Imports
PO BOX 612
Nossebro

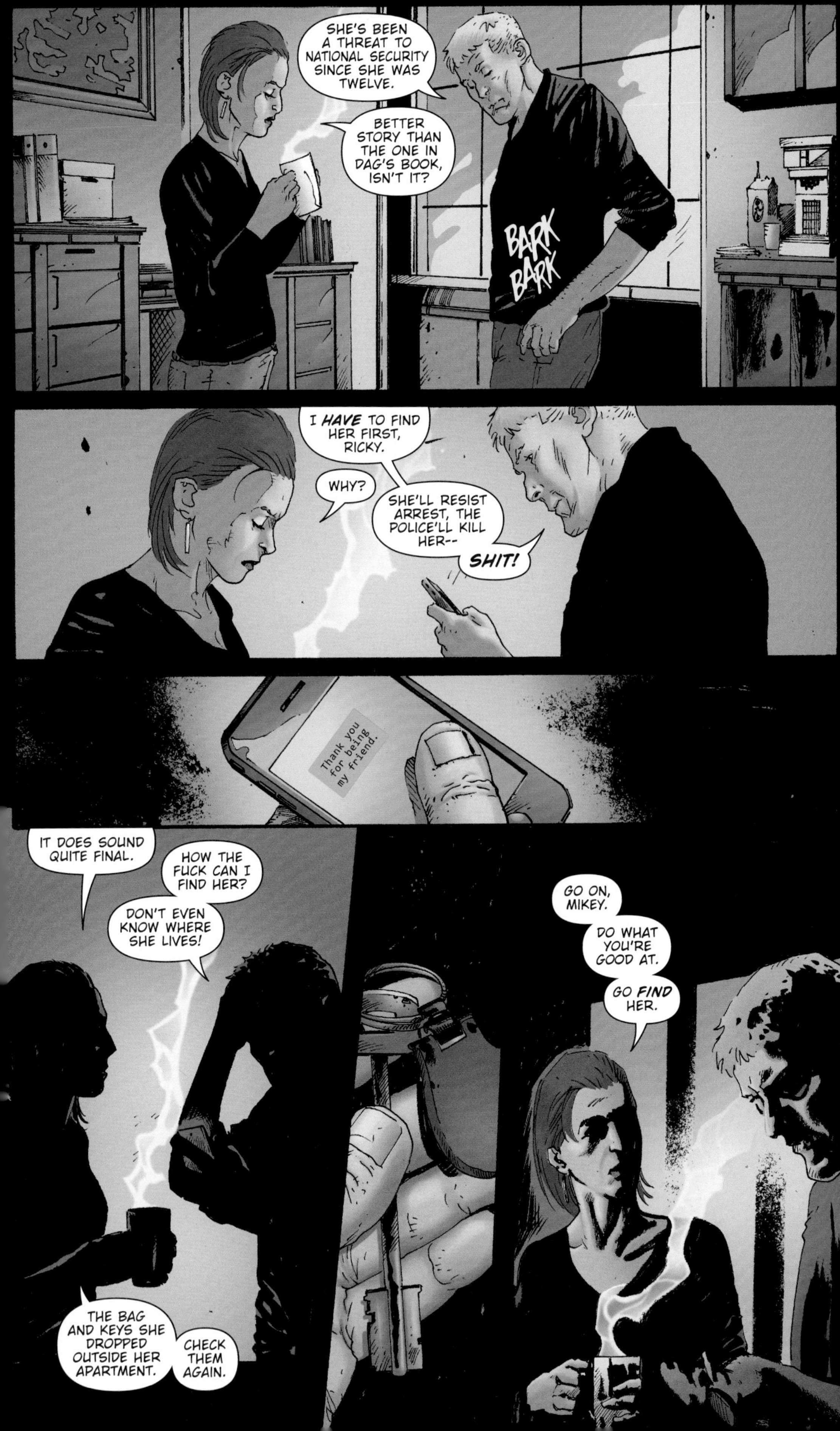
SHE'S BEEN A THREAT TO NATIONAL SECURITY SINCE SHE WAS TWELVE.
BETTER STORY THAN THE ONE IN DAG'S BOOK, ISN'T IT?
BARK BARK
I *HAVE* TO FIND HER FIRST, RICKY.
WHY?
SHE'LL RESIST ARREST, THE POLICE'LL KILL HER--
SHIT!
Thank you for being my friend.
IT DOES SOUND QUITE FINAL.
HOW THE FUCK CAN I FIND HER?
DON'T EVEN KNOW WHERE SHE LIVES!
THE BAG AND KEYS SHE DROPPED OUTSIDE HER APARTMENT.
CHECK THEM AGAIN.
GO ON, MIKEY.
DO WHAT YOU'RE GOOD AT.
GO *FIND* HER.

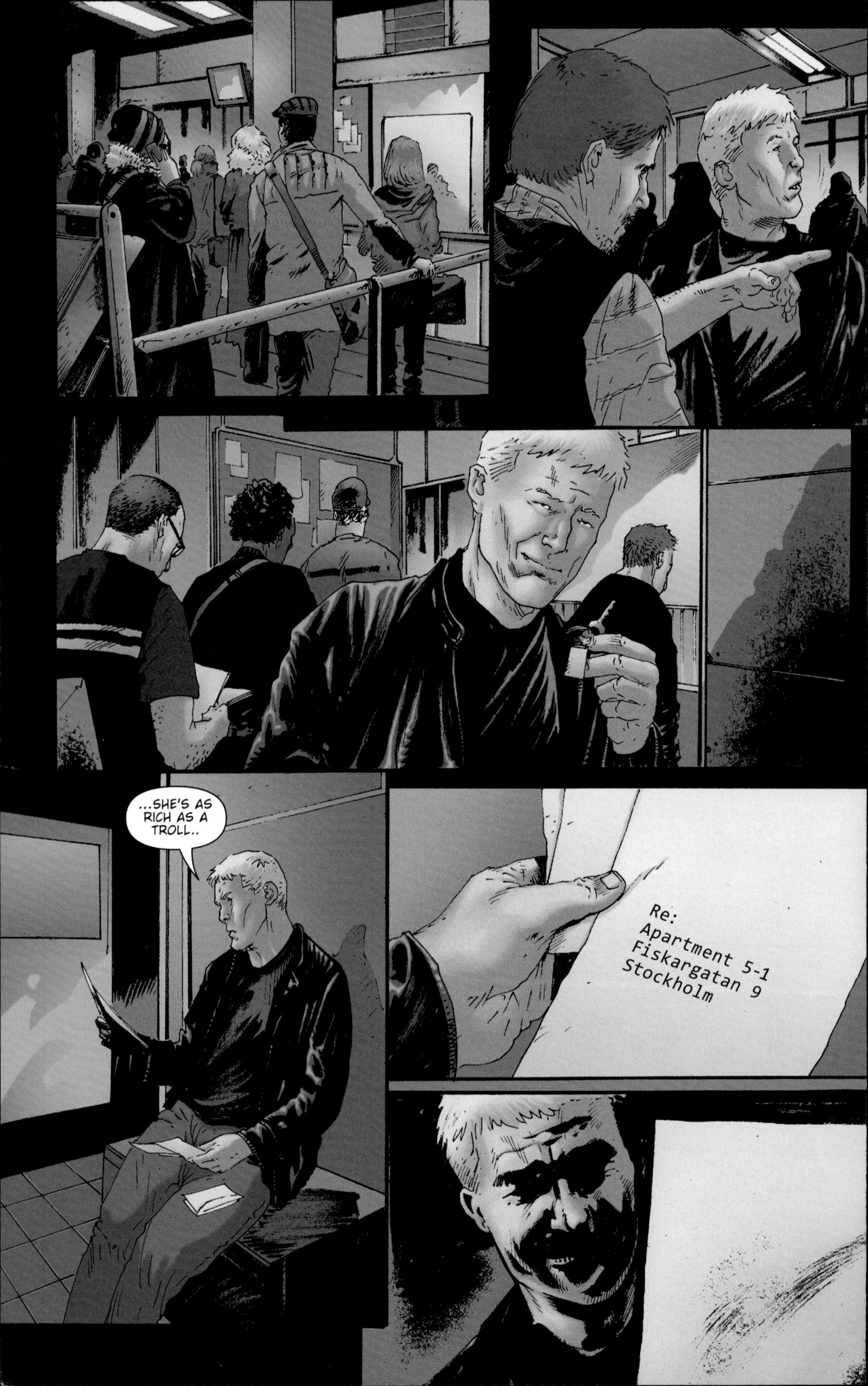
...SHE'S AS RICH AS A TROLL..
Re:
Apartment 5-1
Fiskargatan 9
Stockholm

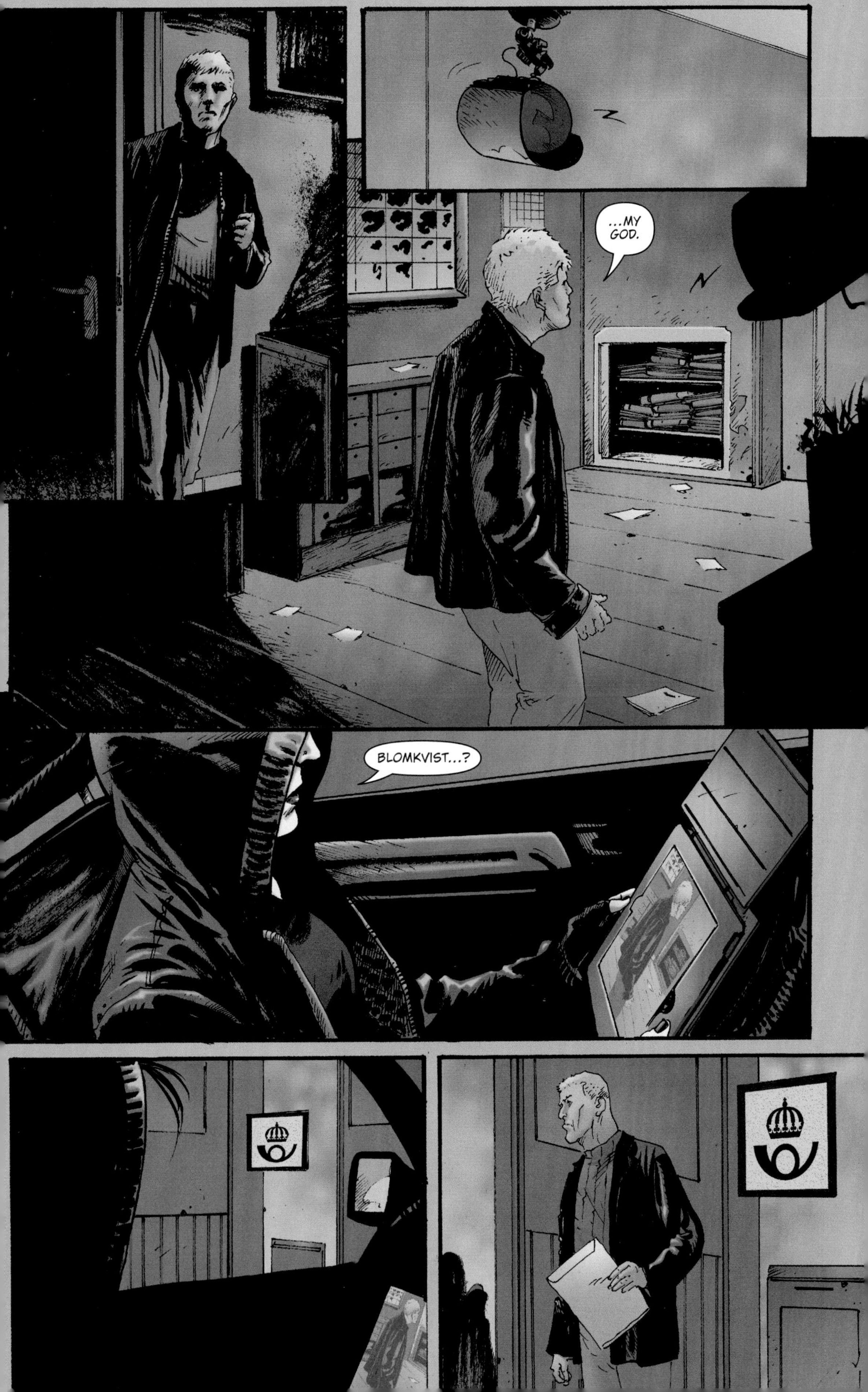
...MY GOD.
BLOMKVIST...?

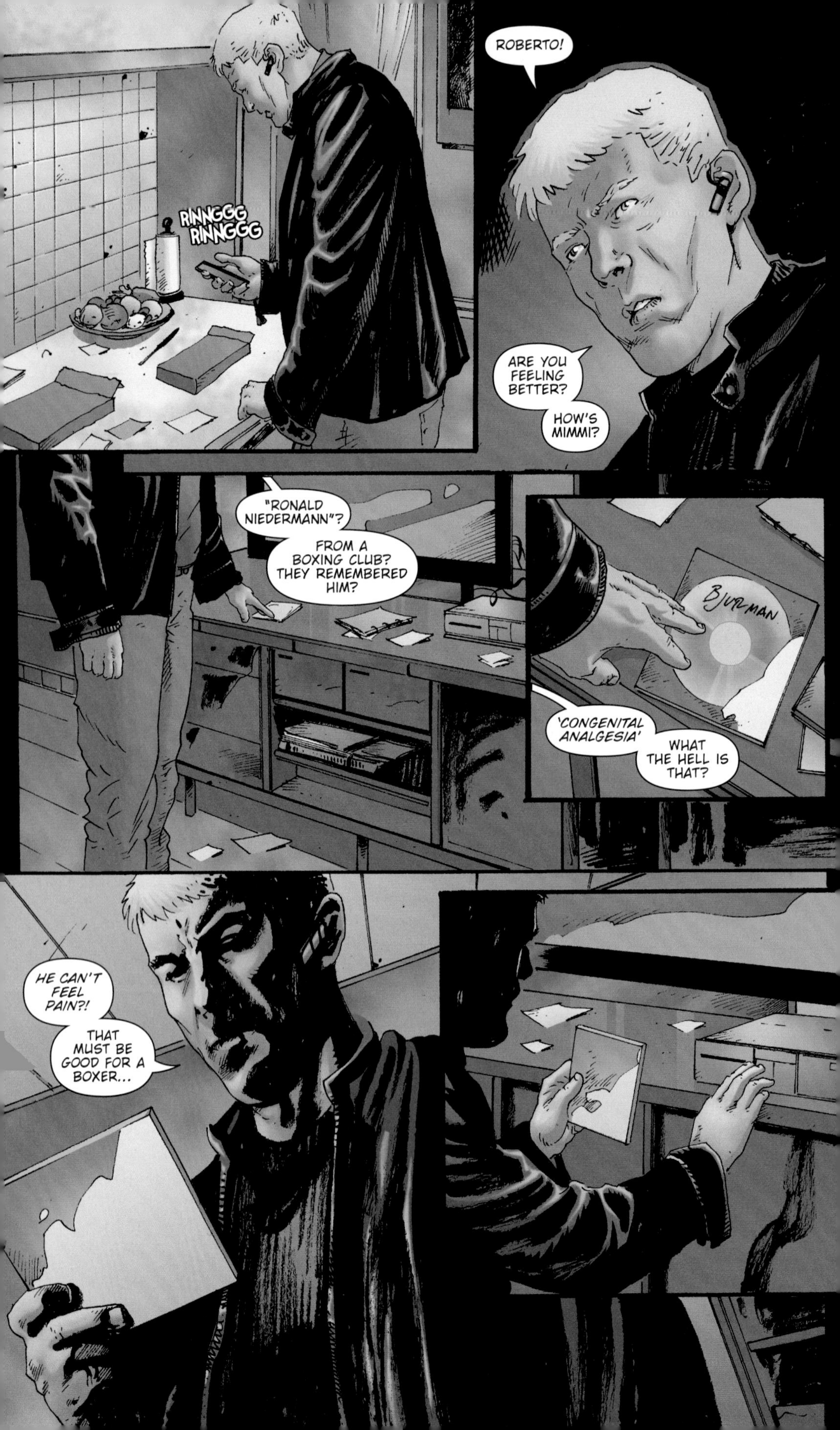
RINNGGG
RINNGGG
ROBERTO!
ARE YOU FEELING BETTER?
HOW'S MIMMI?
"RONALD NIEDERMANN"?
FROM A BOXING CLUB? THEY REMEMBERED HIM?
BJURMAN
'CONGENITAL ANALGESIA'
WHAT THE HELL IS THAT?
HE CAN'T FEEL PAIN?!
THAT MUST BE GOOD FOR A BOXER...

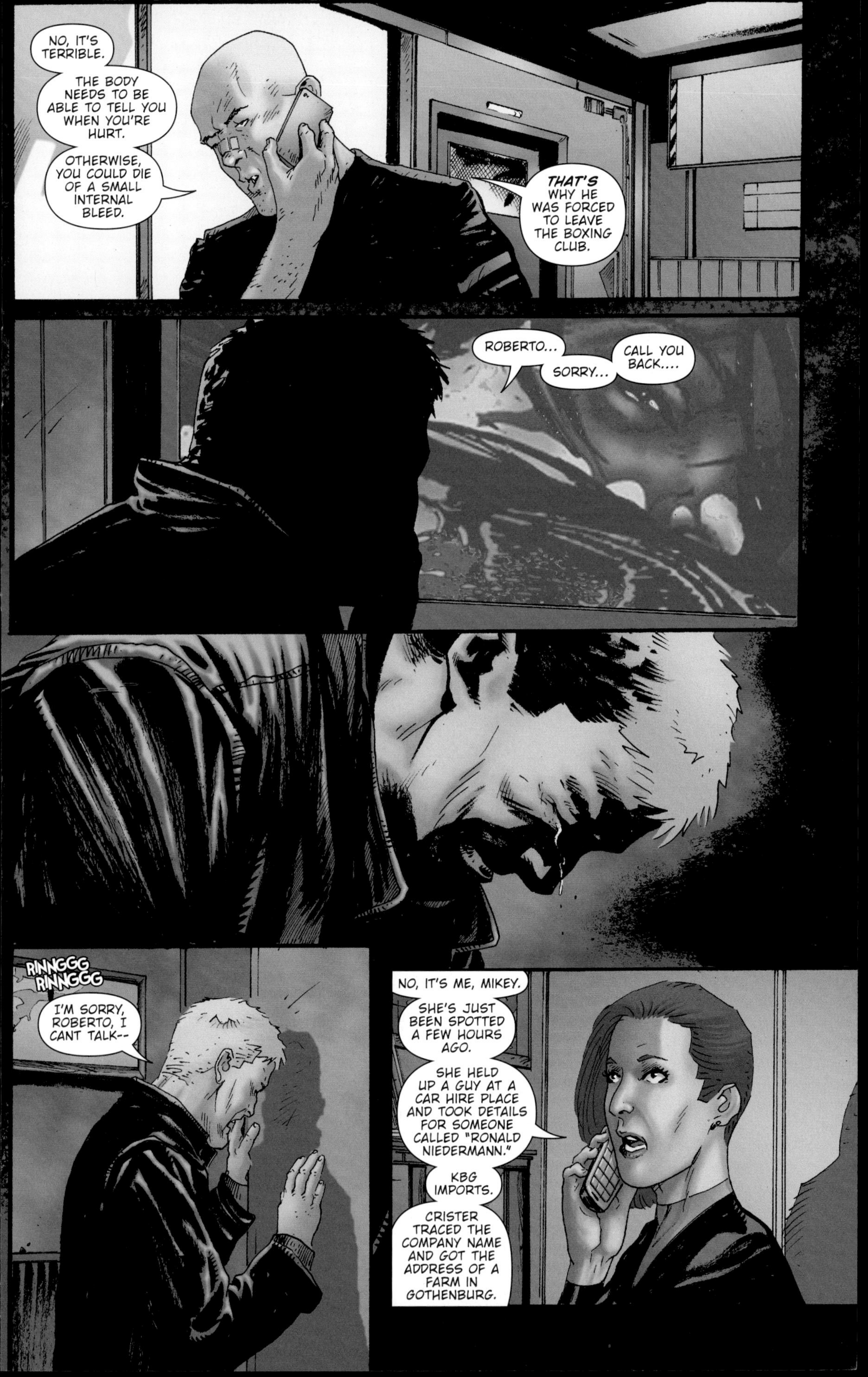
NO, IT'S TERRIBLE.
THE BODY NEEDS TO BE ABLE TO TELL YOU WHEN YOU'RE HURT.
OTHERWISE, YOU COULD DIE OF A SMALL INTERNAL BLEED.
THAT'S WHY HE WAS FORCED TO LEAVE THE BOXING CLUB.
ROBERTO...
SORRY...
CALL YOU BACK....
RINNGGG RINNGGG
I'M SORRY, ROBERTO, I CANT TALK--
NO, IT'S ME, MIKEY.
SHE'S JUST BEEN SPOTTED A FEW HOURS AGO.
SHE HELD UP A GUY AT A CAR HIRE PLACE AND TOOK DETAILS FOR SOMEONE CALLED "RONALD NIEDERMANN."
KBG IMPORTS.
CRISTER TRACED THE COMPANY NAME AND GOT THE ADDRESS OF A FARM IN GOTHENBURG.

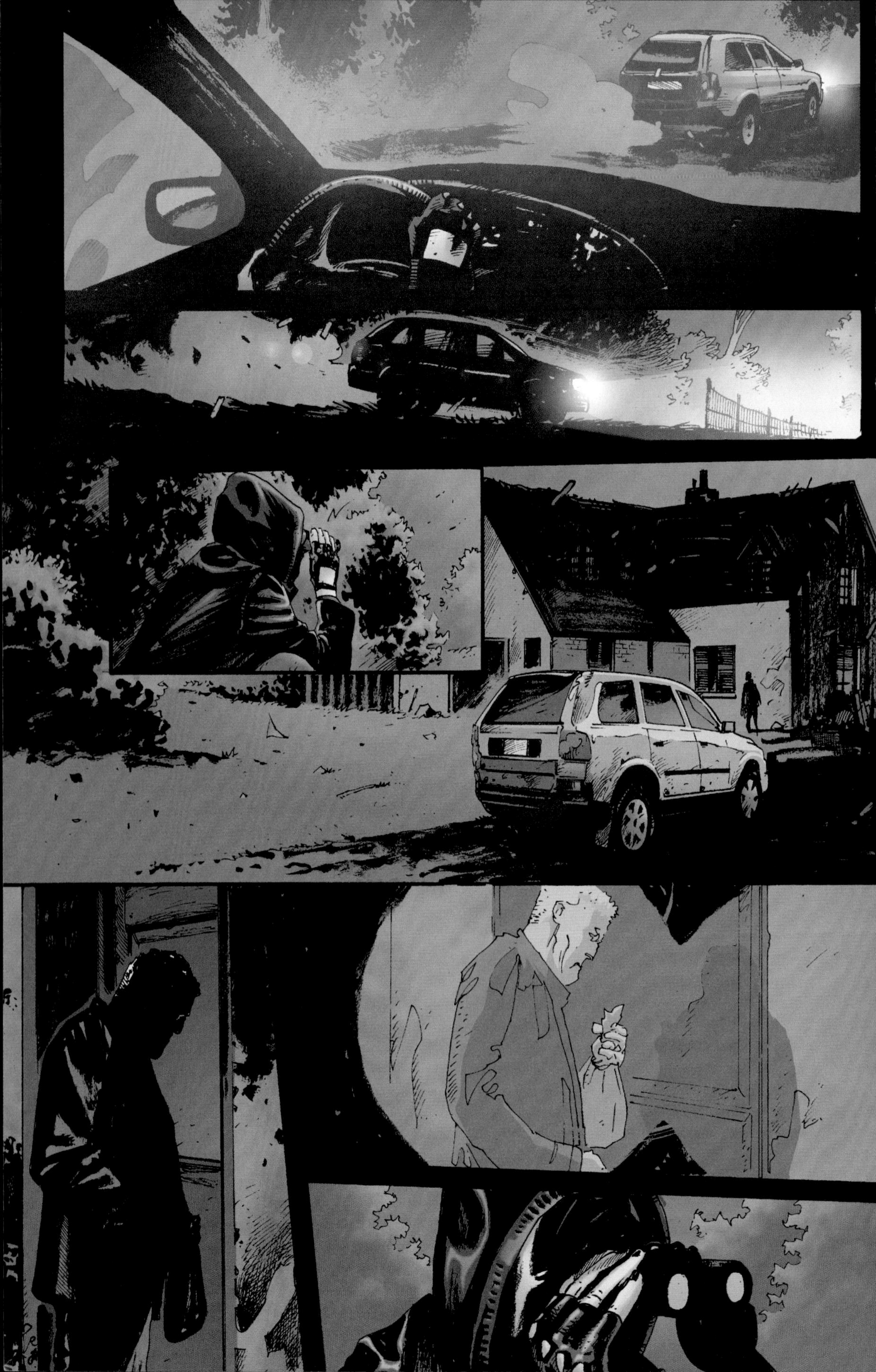

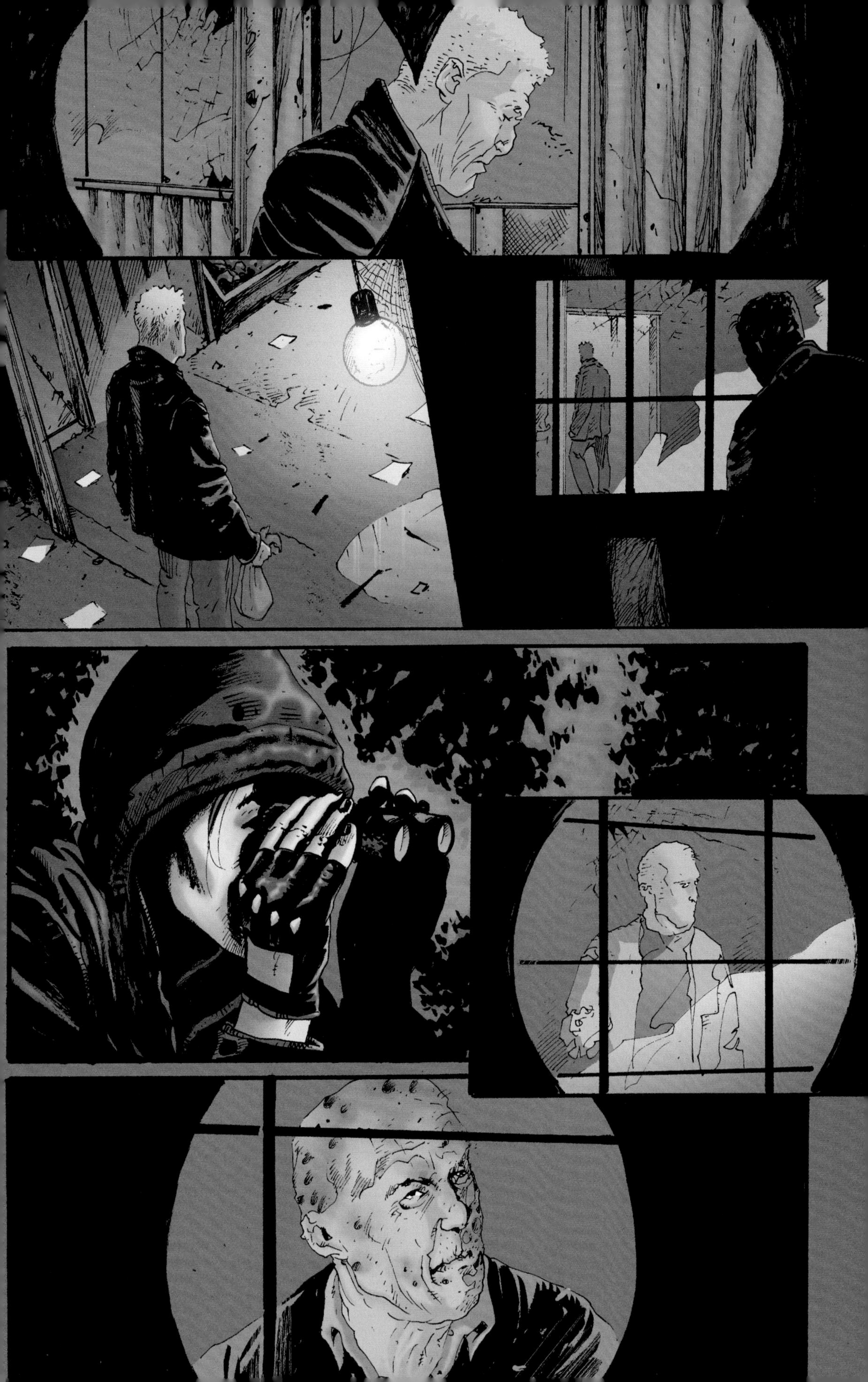

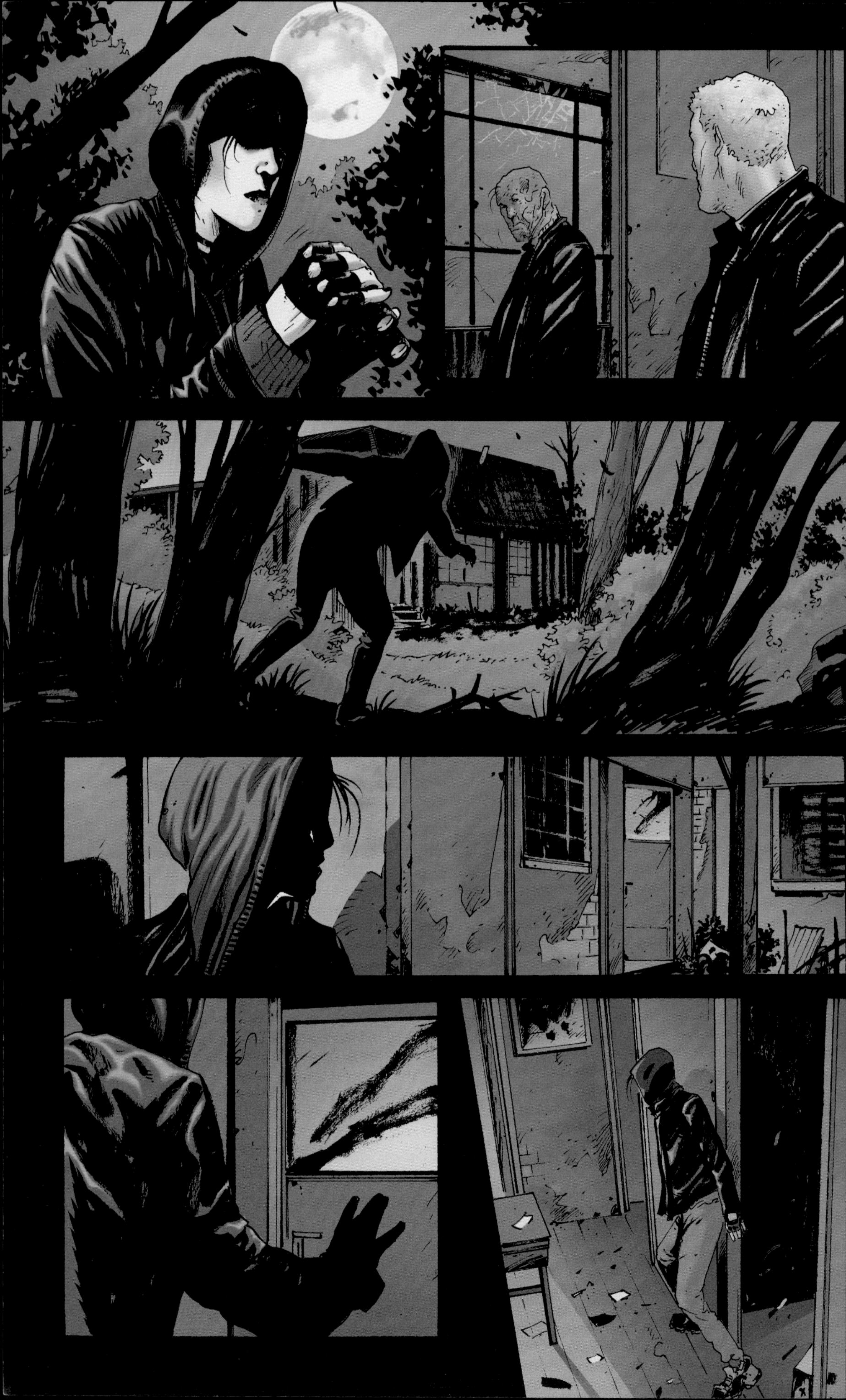

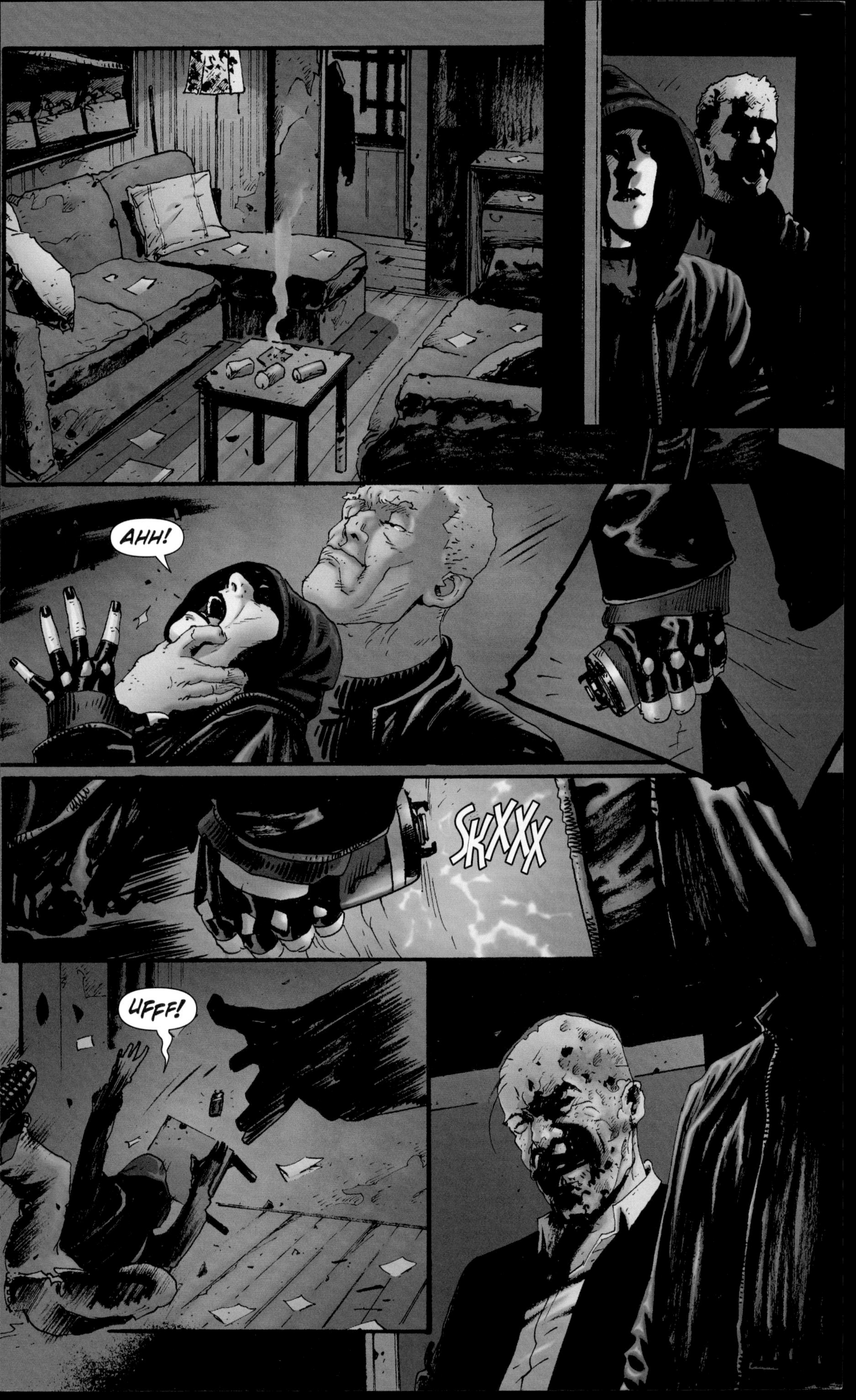
AHH!
SKXXX
UFFF!

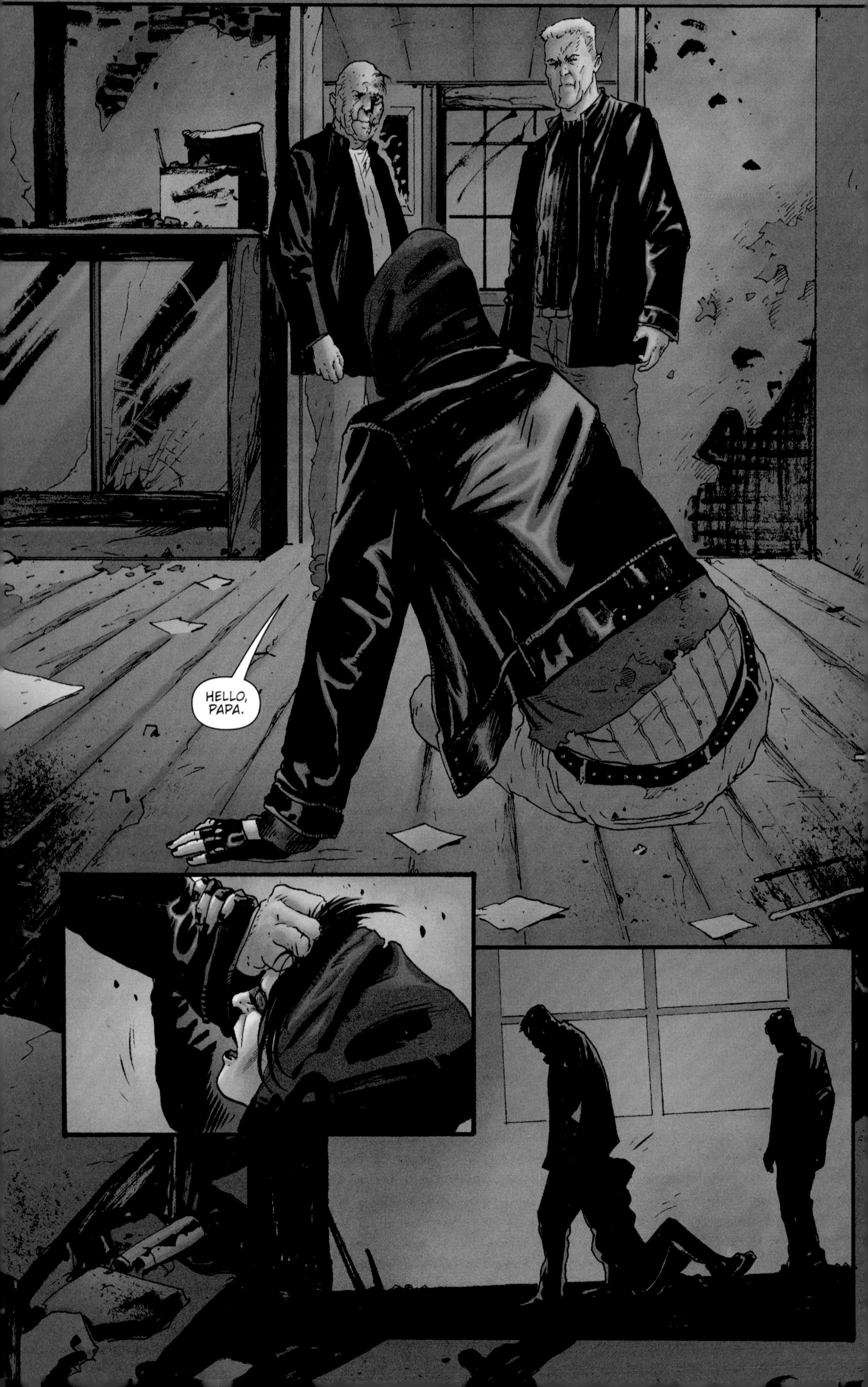
HELLO, PAPA.

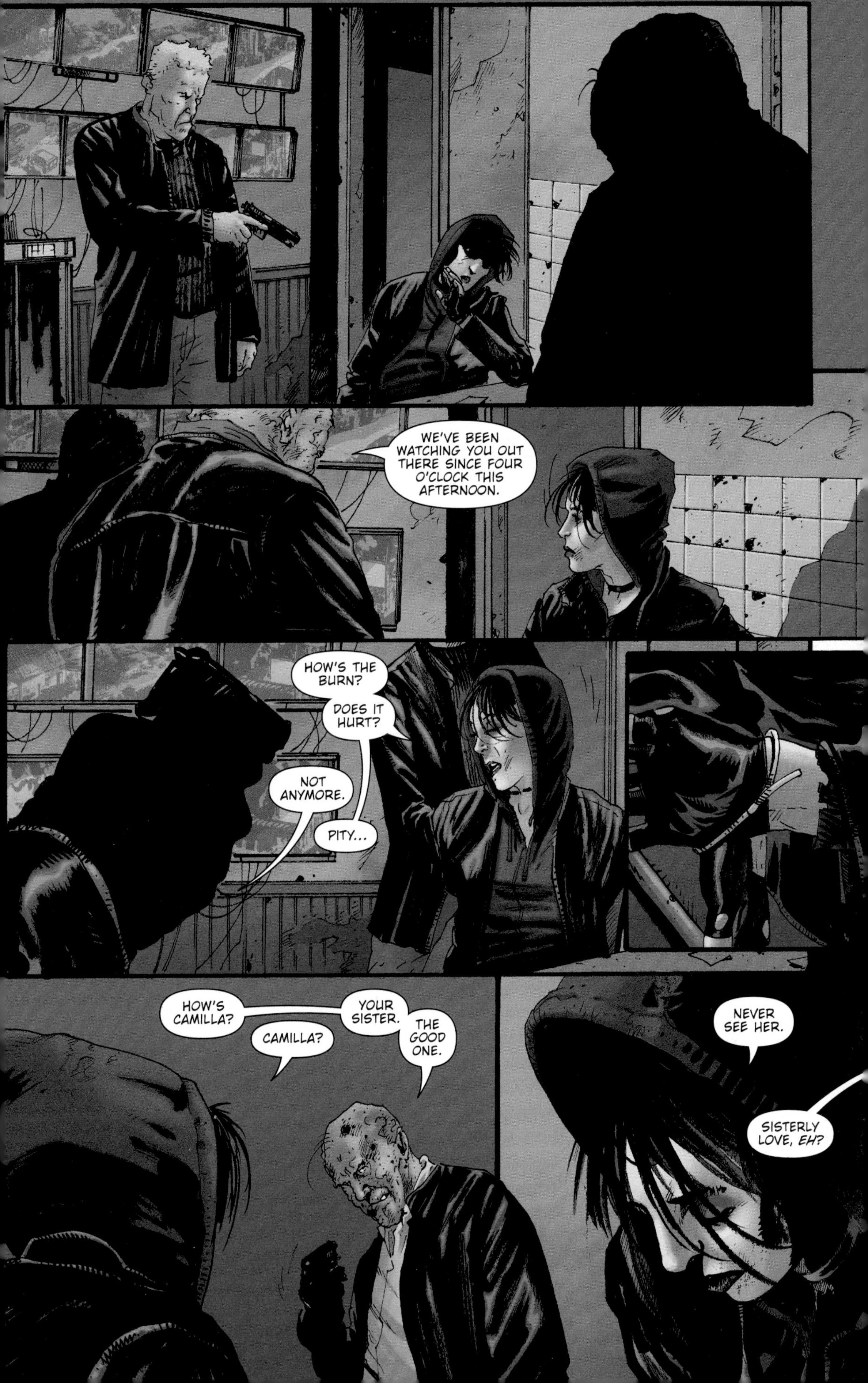
WE'VE BEEN WATCHING YOU OUT THERE SINCE FOUR O'CLOCK THIS AFTERNOON.
HOW'S THE BURN?
DOES IT HURT?
NOT ANYMORE.
PITY...
HOW'S CAMILLA?
CAMILLA?
YOUR SISTER.
THE GOOD ONE.
NEVER SEE HER.
SISTERLY LOVE, *EH?*

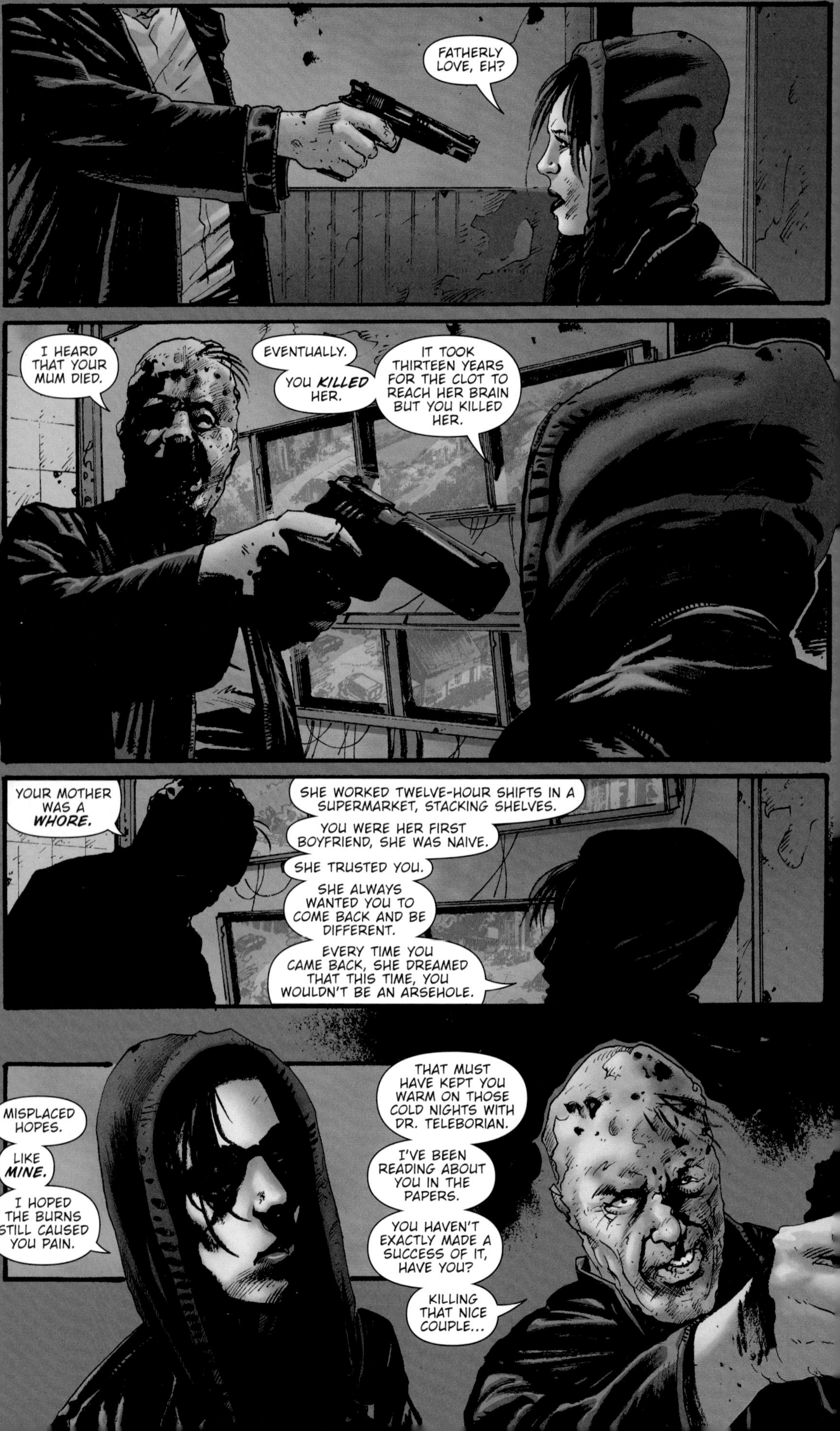
FATHERLY LOVE, EH?
I HEARD THAT YOUR MUM DIED.
EVENTUALLY.
YOU *KILLED* HER.
IT TOOK THIRTEEN YEARS FOR THE CLOT TO REACH HER BRAIN BUT YOU KILLED HER.
YOUR MOTHER WAS A *WHORE.*
SHE WORKED TWELVE-HOUR SHIFTS IN A SUPERMARKET, STACKING SHELVES.
YOU WERE HER FIRST BOYFRIEND, SHE WAS NAIVE.
SHE TRUSTED YOU.
SHE ALWAYS WANTED YOU TO COME BACK AND BE DIFFERENT.
EVERY TIME YOU CAME BACK, SHE DREAMED THAT THIS TIME, YOU WOULDN'T BE AN ARSEHOLE.
MISPLACED HOPES.
LIKE *MINE.*
I HOPED THE BURNS STILL CAUSED YOU PAIN.
THAT MUST HAVE KEPT YOU WARM ON THOSE COLD NIGHTS WITH DR. TELEBORIAN.
I'VE BEEN READING ABOUT YOU IN THE PAPERS.
YOU HAVEN'T EXACTLY MADE A SUCCESS OF IT, HAVE YOU?
KILLING THAT NICE COUPLE...

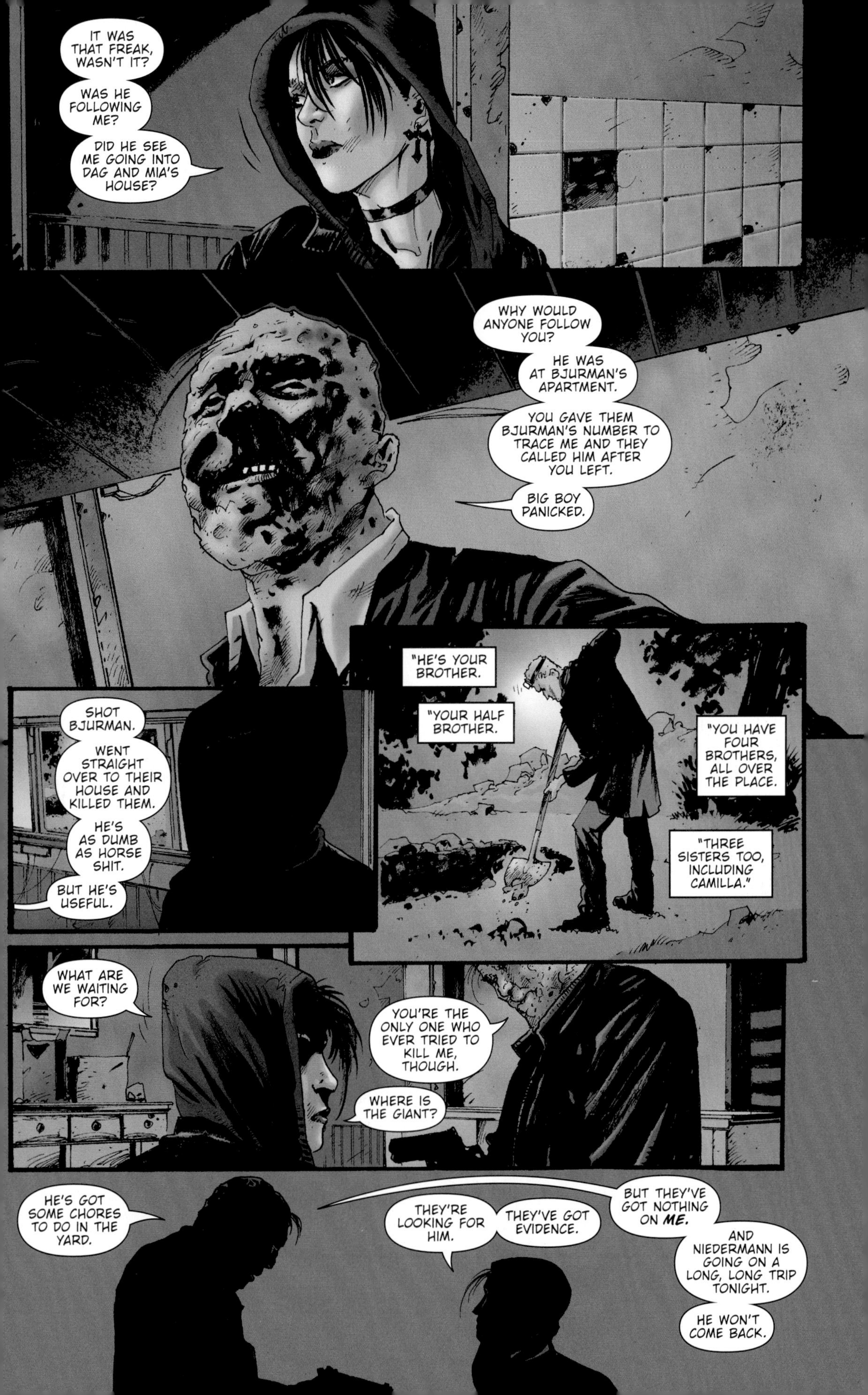
IT WAS THAT FREAK, WASN'T IT?
WAS HE FOLLOWING ME?
DID HE SEE ME GOING INTO DAG AND MIA'S HOUSE?
WHY WOULD ANYONE FOLLOW YOU?
HE WAS AT BJURMAN'S APARTMENT.
YOU GAVE THEM BJURMAN'S NUMBER TO TRACE ME AND THEY CALLED HIM AFTER YOU LEFT.
BIG BOY PANICKED.
SHOT BJURMAN.
WENT STRAIGHT OVER TO THEIR HOUSE AND KILLED THEM.
HE'S AS DUMB AS HORSE SHIT.
BUT HE'S USEFUL.
"HE'S YOUR BROTHER.
"YOUR HALF BROTHER.
"YOU HAVE FOUR BROTHERS, ALL OVER THE PLACE.
"THREE SISTERS TOO, INCLUDING CAMILLA."
WHAT ARE WE WAITING FOR?
YOU'RE THE ONLY ONE WHO EVER TRIED TO KILL ME, THOUGH.
WHERE IS THE GIANT?
HE'S GOT SOME CHORES TO DO IN THE YARD.
THEY'RE LOOKING FOR HIM.
THEY'VE GOT EVIDENCE.
BUT THEY'VE GOT NOTHING ON *ME.*
AND NIEDERMANN IS GOING ON A LONG, LONG TRIP TONIGHT.
HE WON'T COME BACK.

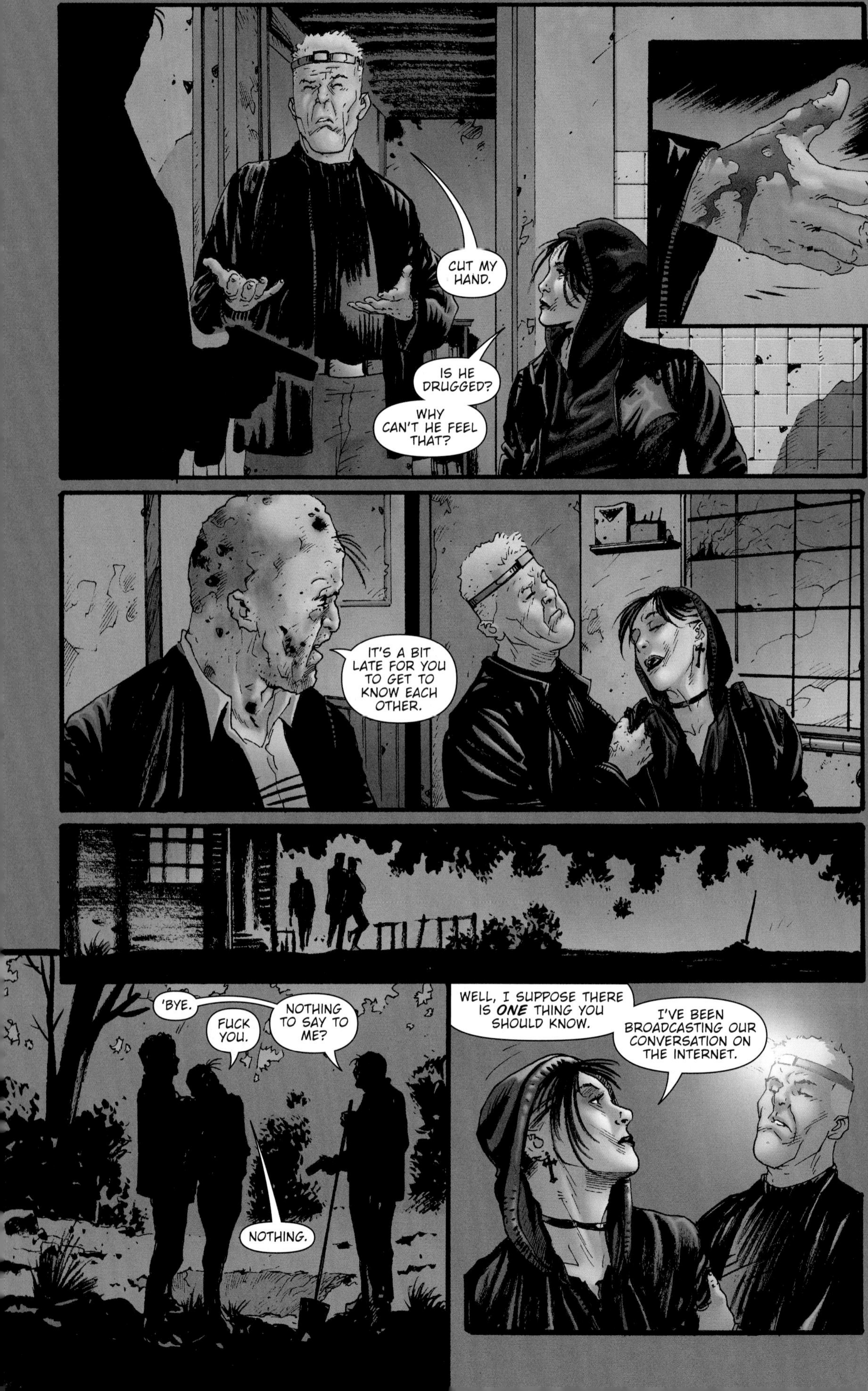
CUT MY HAND.
IS HE DRUGGED?
WHY CAN'T HE FEEL THAT?
IT'S A BIT LATE FOR YOU TO GET TO KNOW EACH OTHER.
'BYE.
NOTHING TO SAY TO ME?
FUCK YOU.
NOTHING.
WELL, I SUPPOSE THERE IS *ONE* THING YOU SHOULD KNOW.
I'VE BEEN BROADCASTING OUR CONVERSATION ON THE INTERNET.

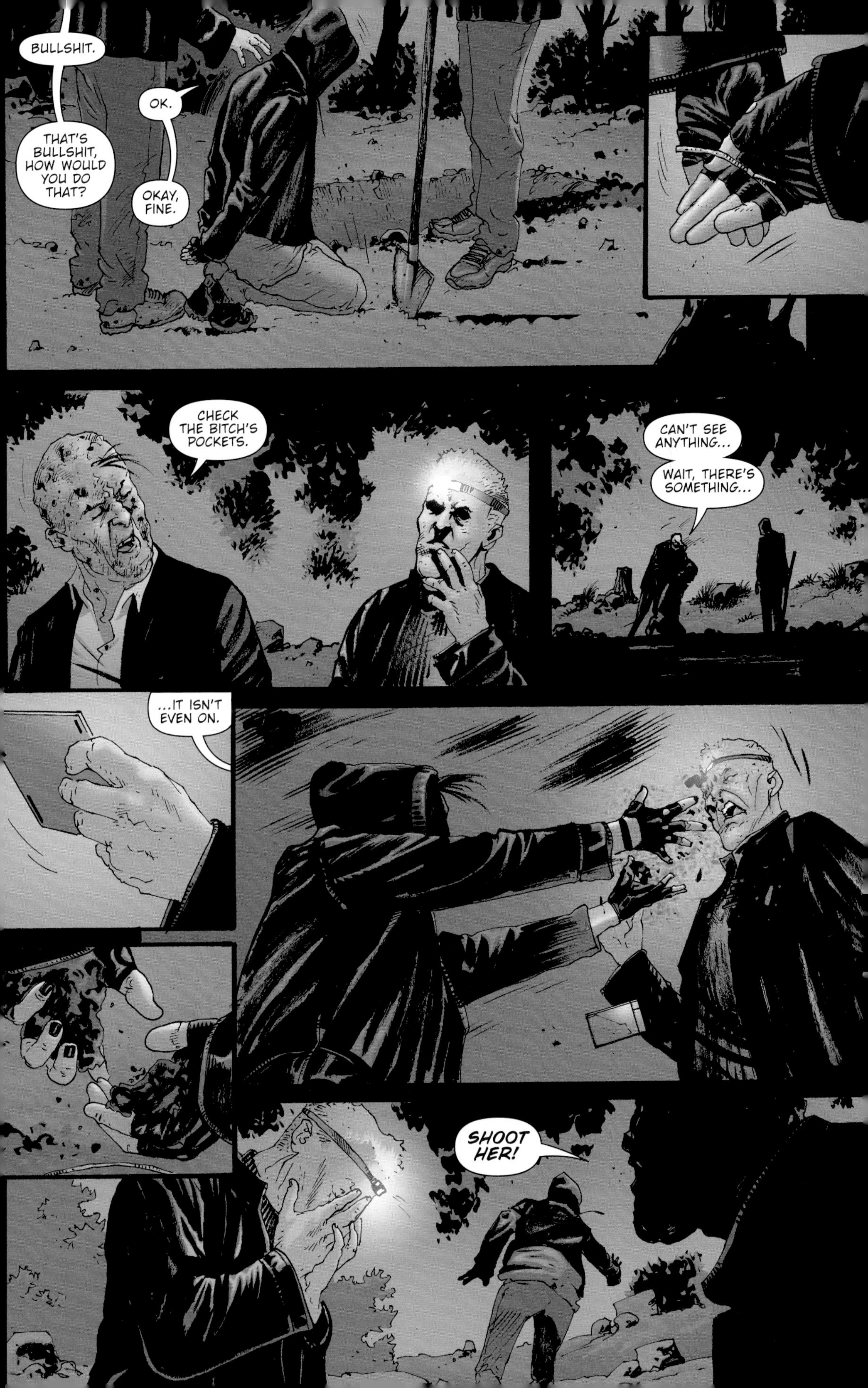
BULLSHIT.
OK.
THAT'S BULLSHIT, HOW WOULD YOU DO THAT?
OKAY, FINE.
CHECK THE BITCH'S POCKETS.
CAN'T SEE ANYTHING...
WAIT, THERE'S SOMETHING...
...IT ISN'T EVEN ON.
SHOOT HER!

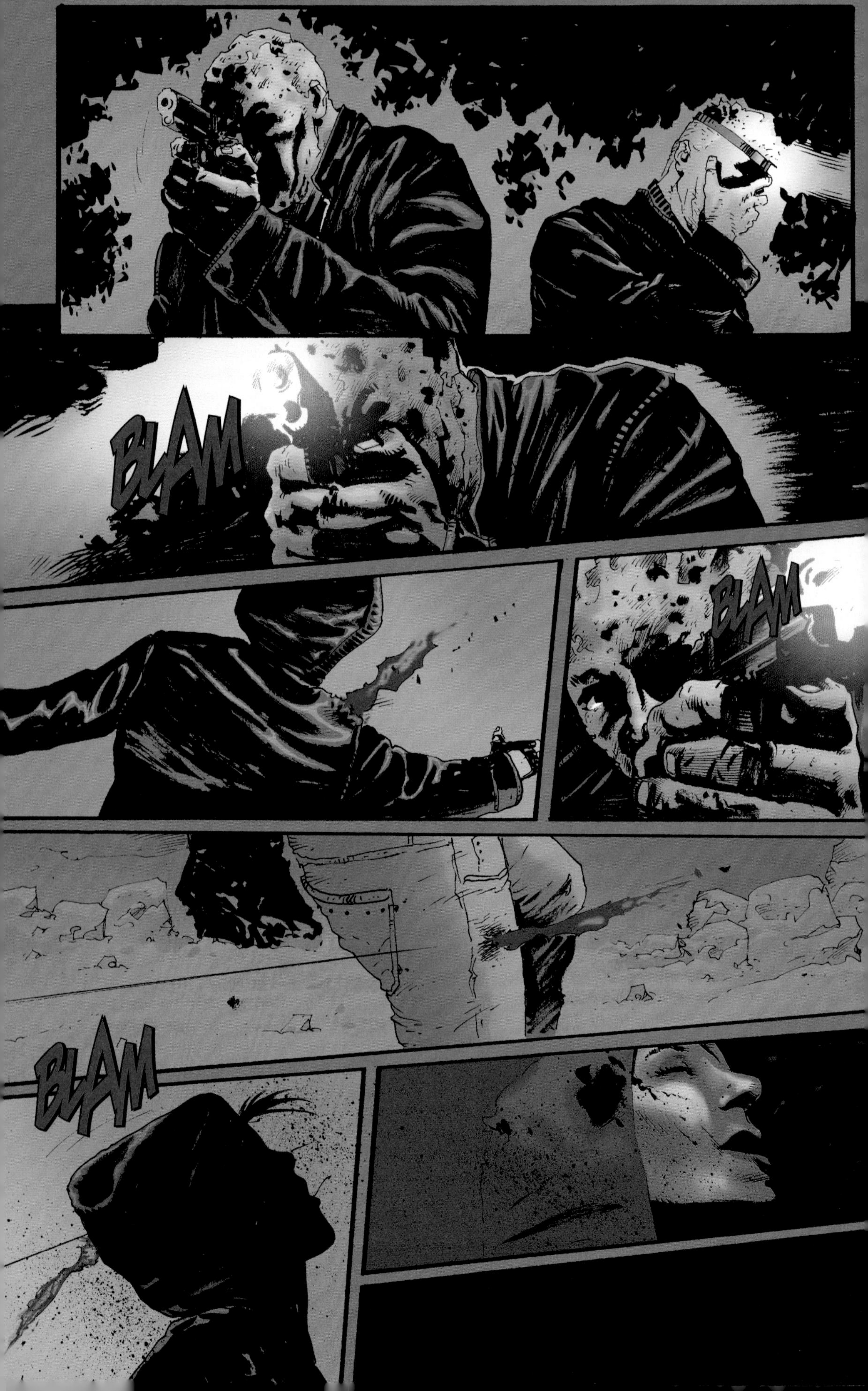
BLAM
BLAM
BLAM

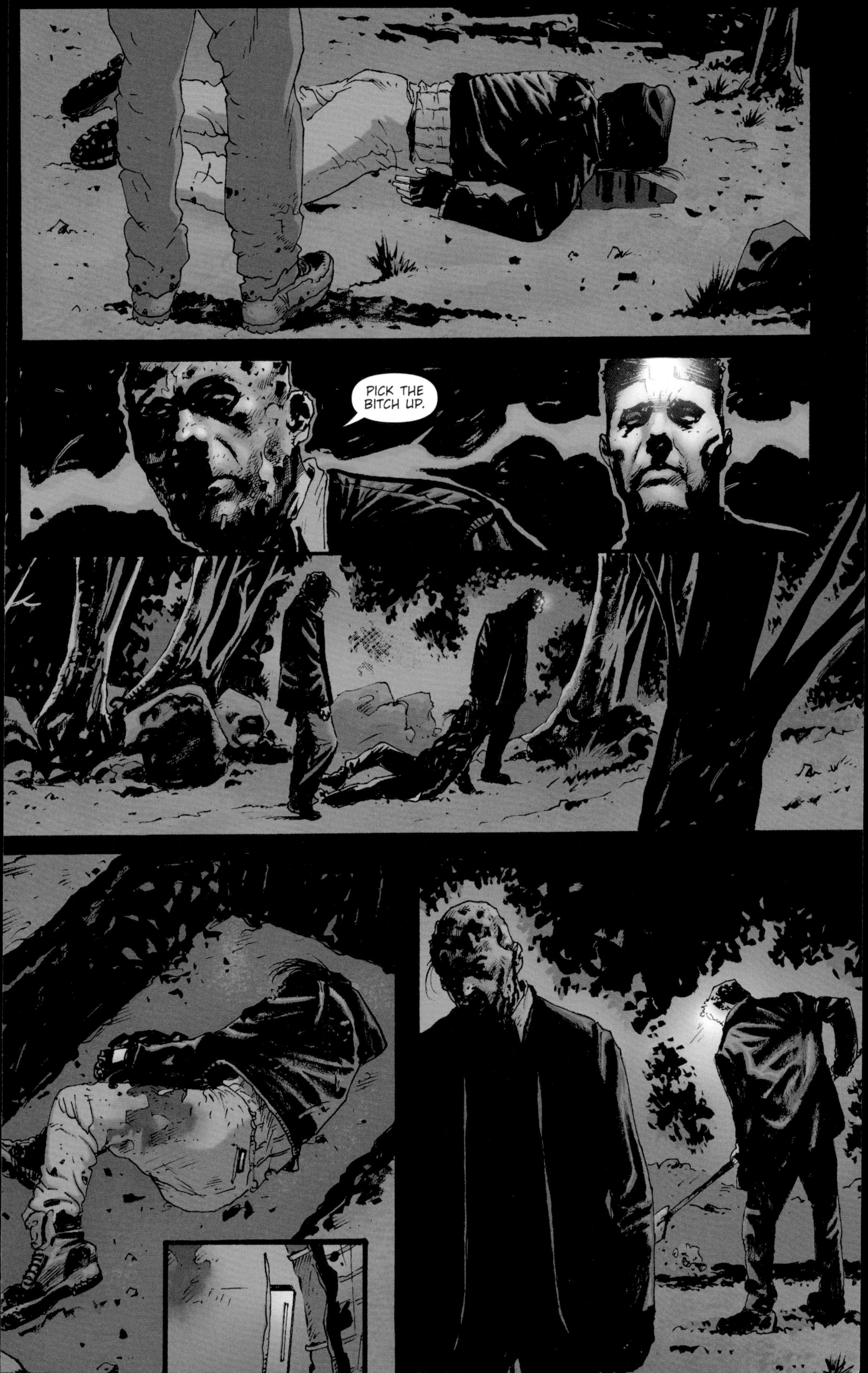
PICK THE BITCH UP.

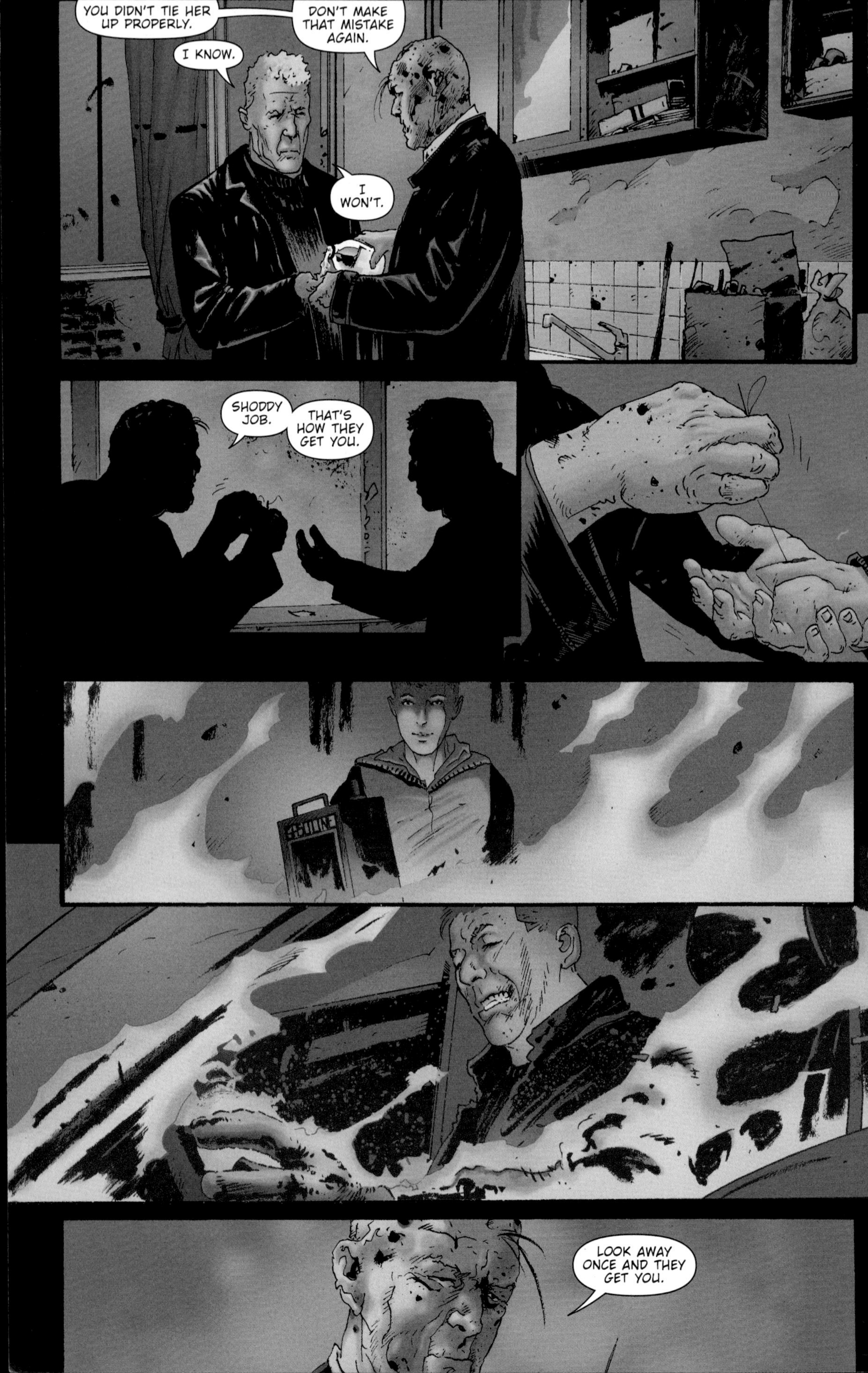

YOU DIDN'T TIE HER UP PROPERLY.
DON'T MAKE THAT MISTAKE AGAIN.
I KNOW.
I WON'T.
SHODDY JOB.
THAT'S HOW THEY GET YOU.
LOOK AWAY ONCE AND THEY GET YOU.

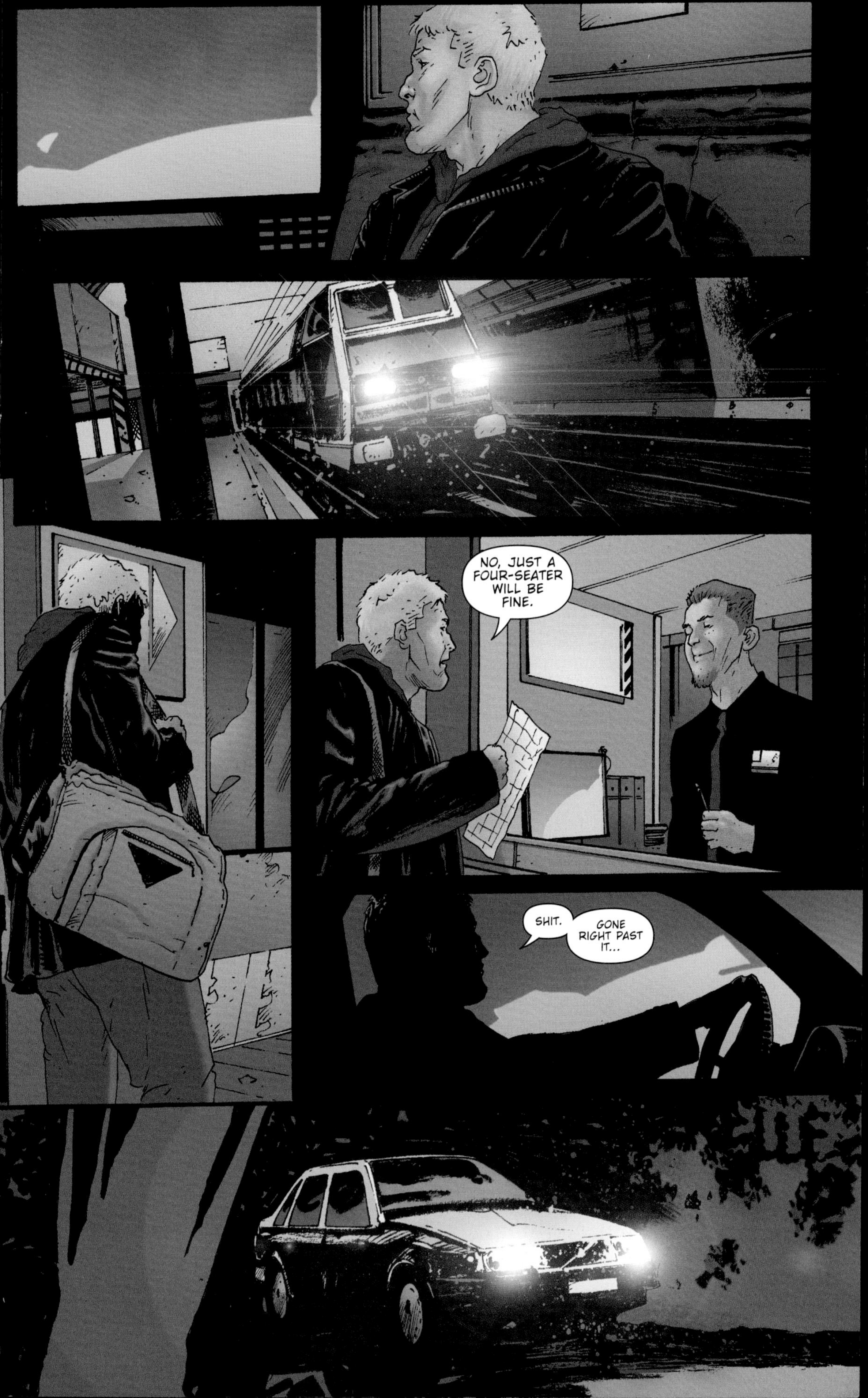
NO, JUST A FOUR-SEATER WILL BE FINE.
SHIT.
GONE RIGHT PAST IT...

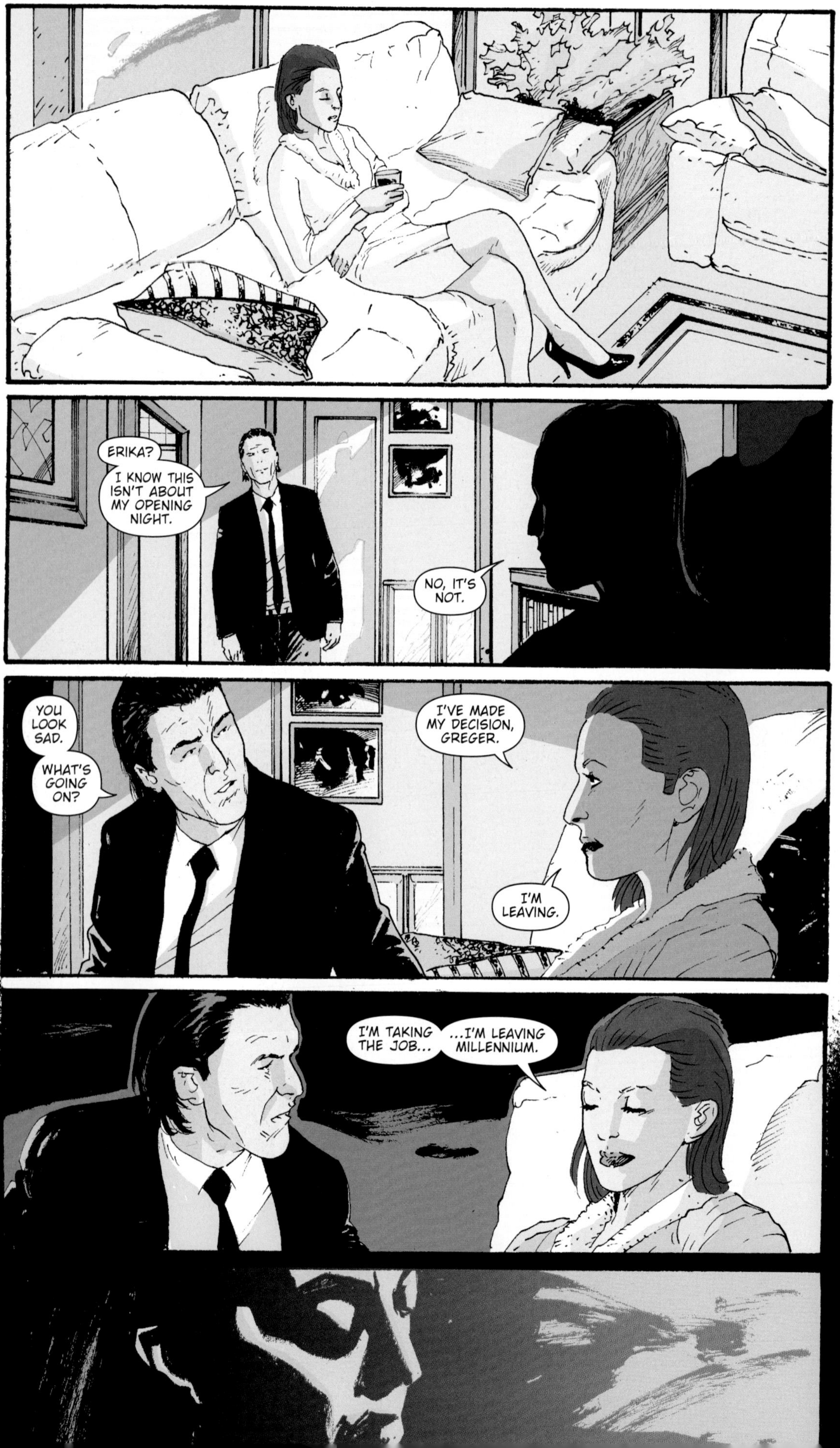
ERIKA?
I KNOW THIS ISN'T ABOUT MY OPENING NIGHT.
NO, IT'S NOT.
YOU LOOK SAD.
WHAT'S GOING ON?
I'VE MADE MY DECISION, GREGER.
I'M LEAVING.
I'M TAKING THE JOB...
...I'M LEAVING MILLENNIUM.

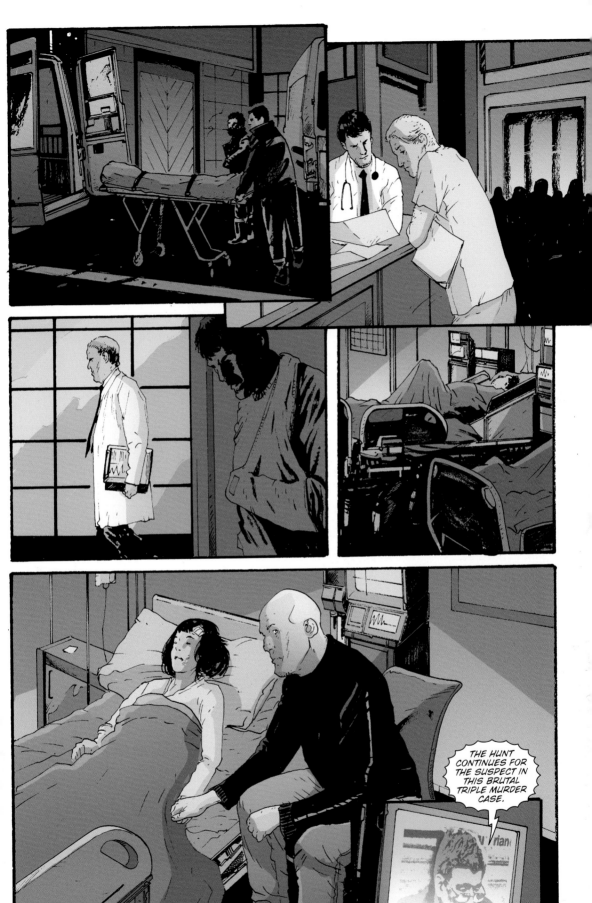

THE HUNT CONTINUES FOR THE SUSPECT IN THIS BRUTAL TRIPLE MURDER CASE.

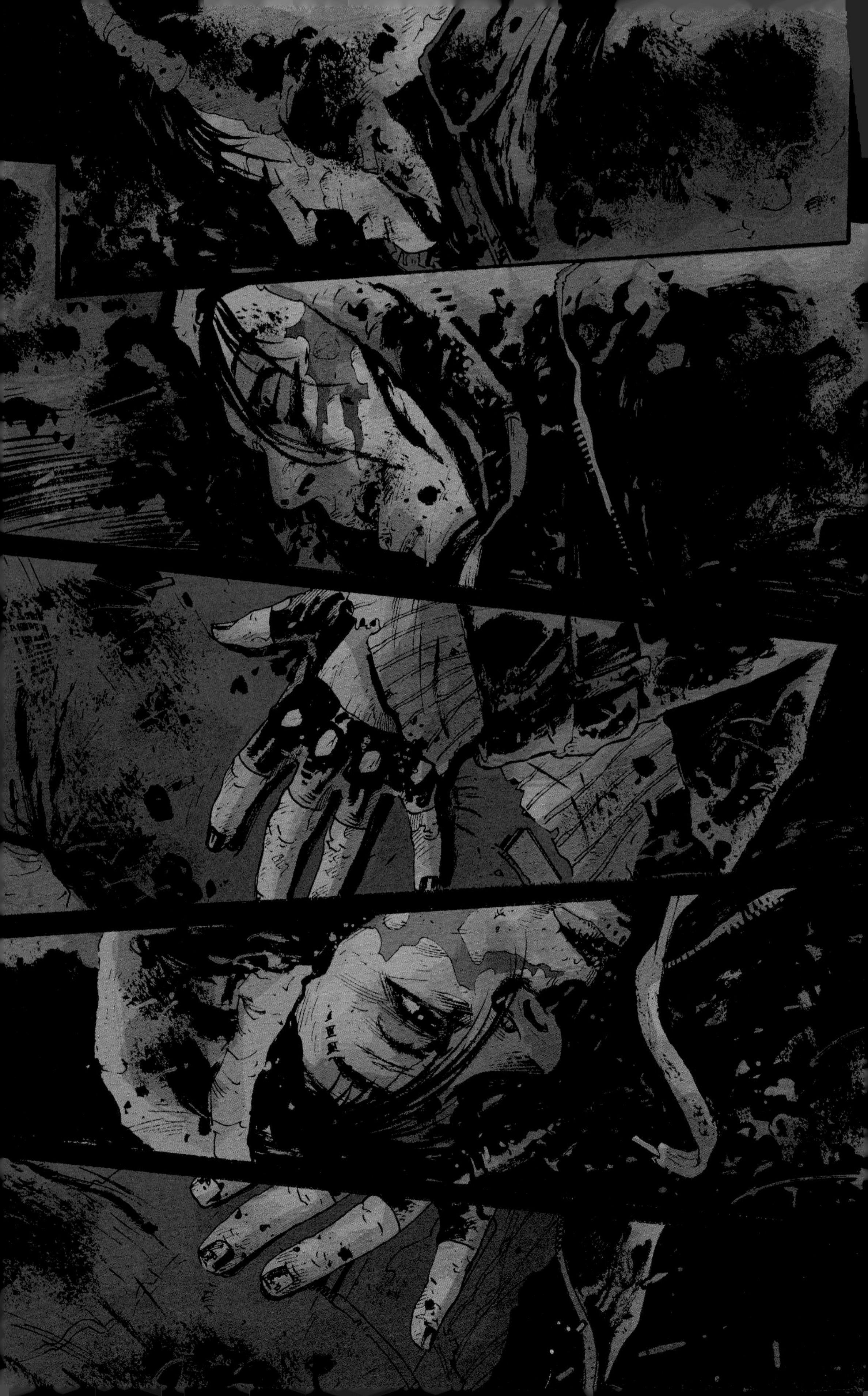

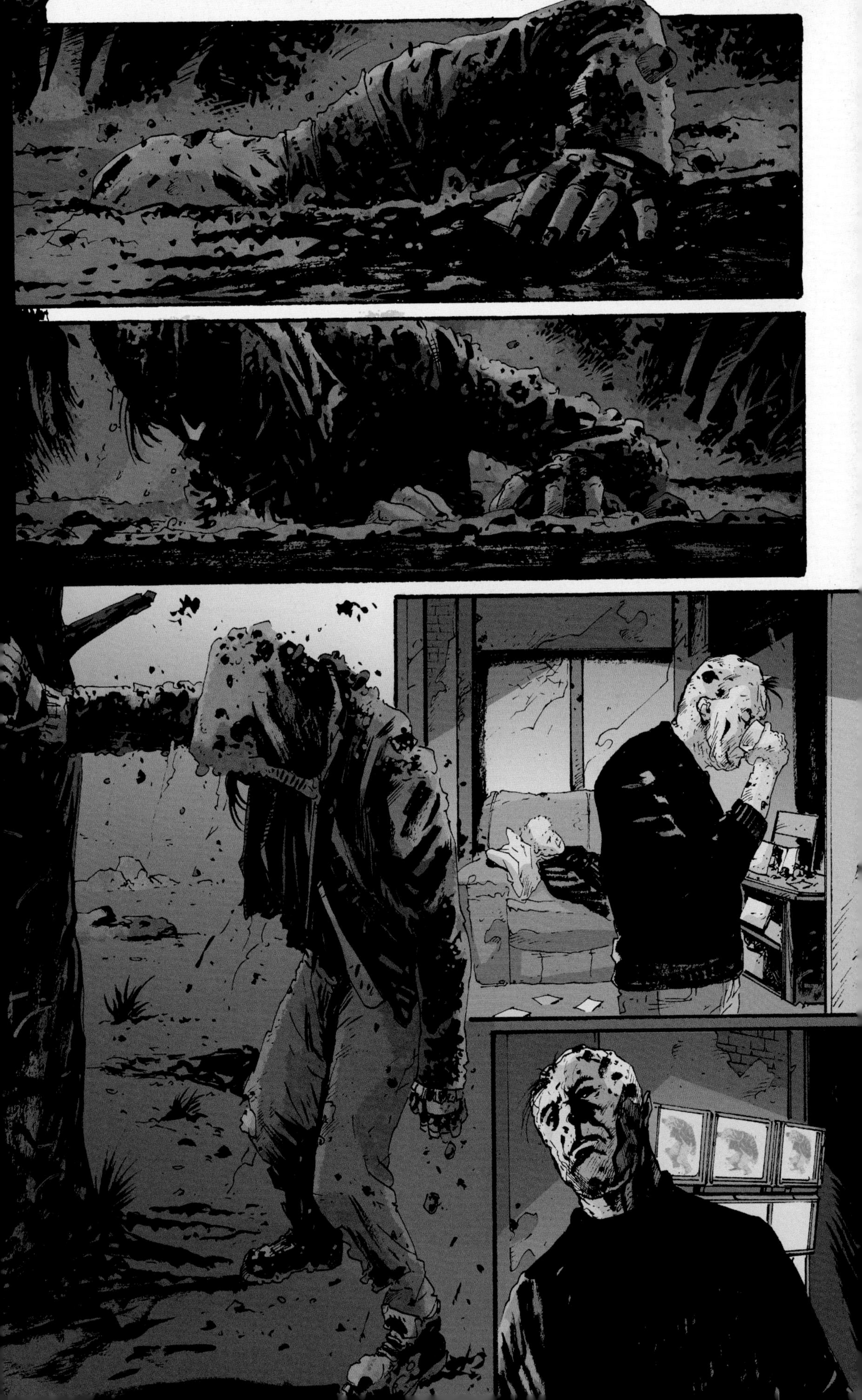

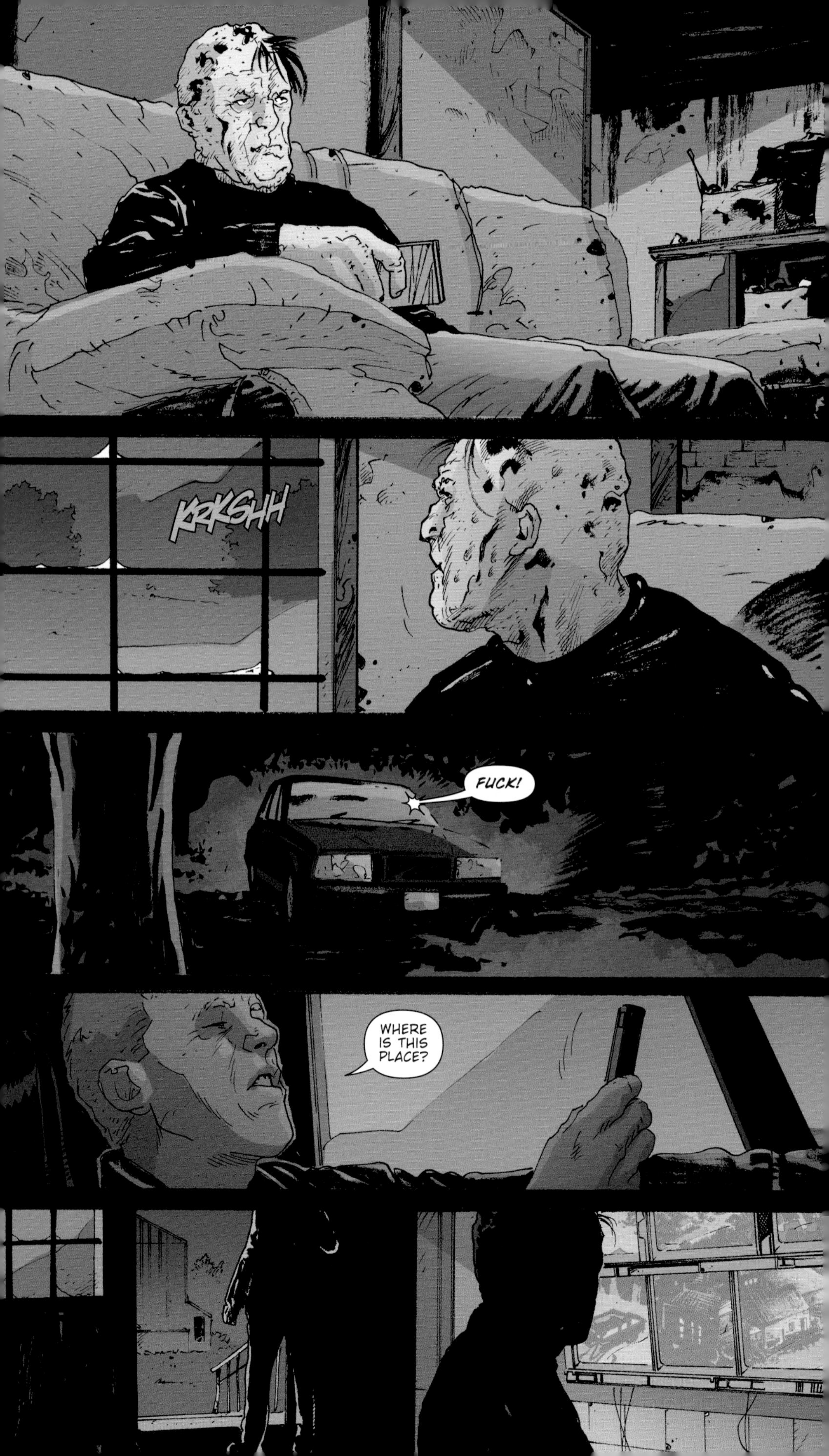
KRKSHH
FUCK!
WHERE IS THIS PLACE?

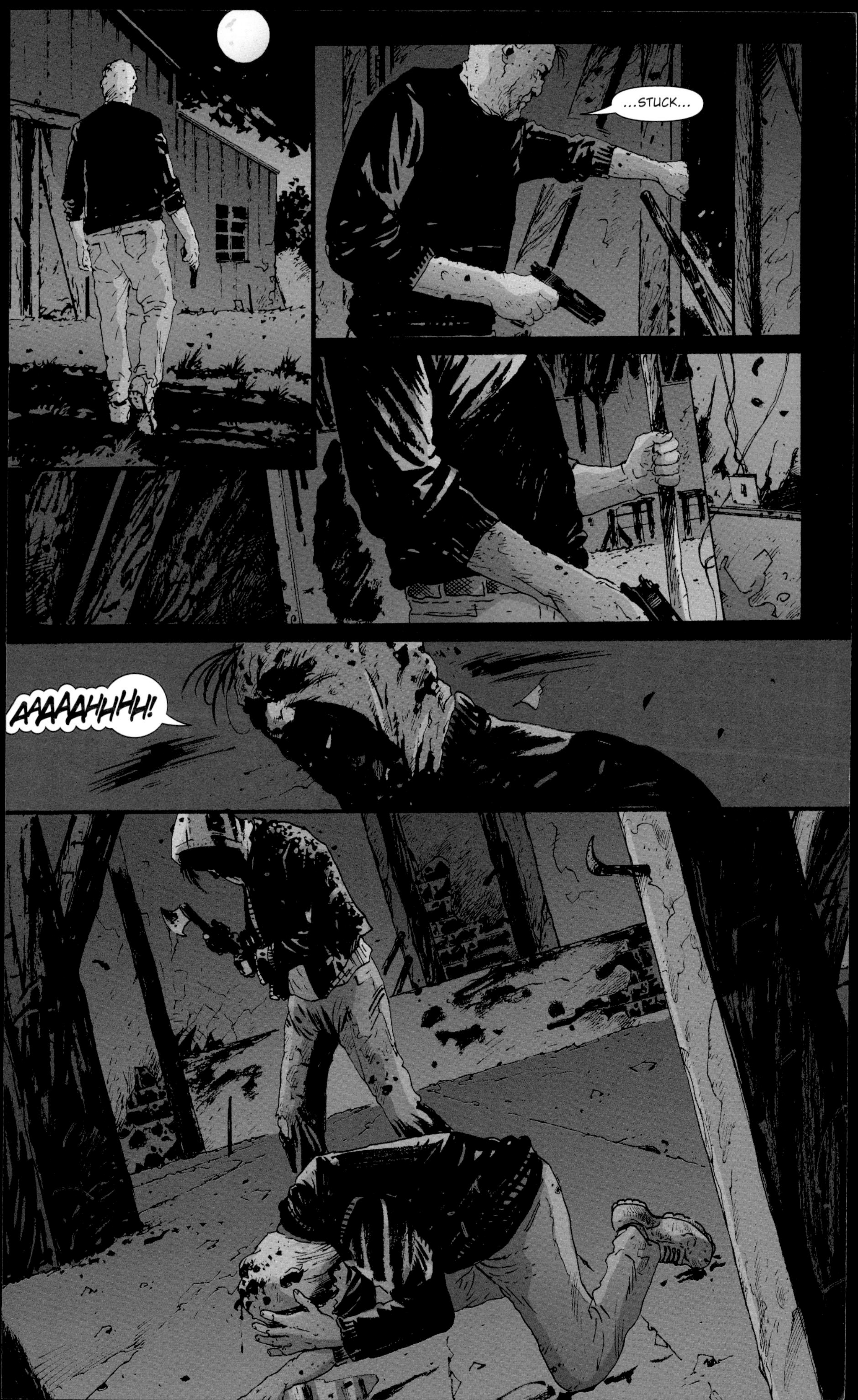
...STUCK...
AAAAAHHHH!

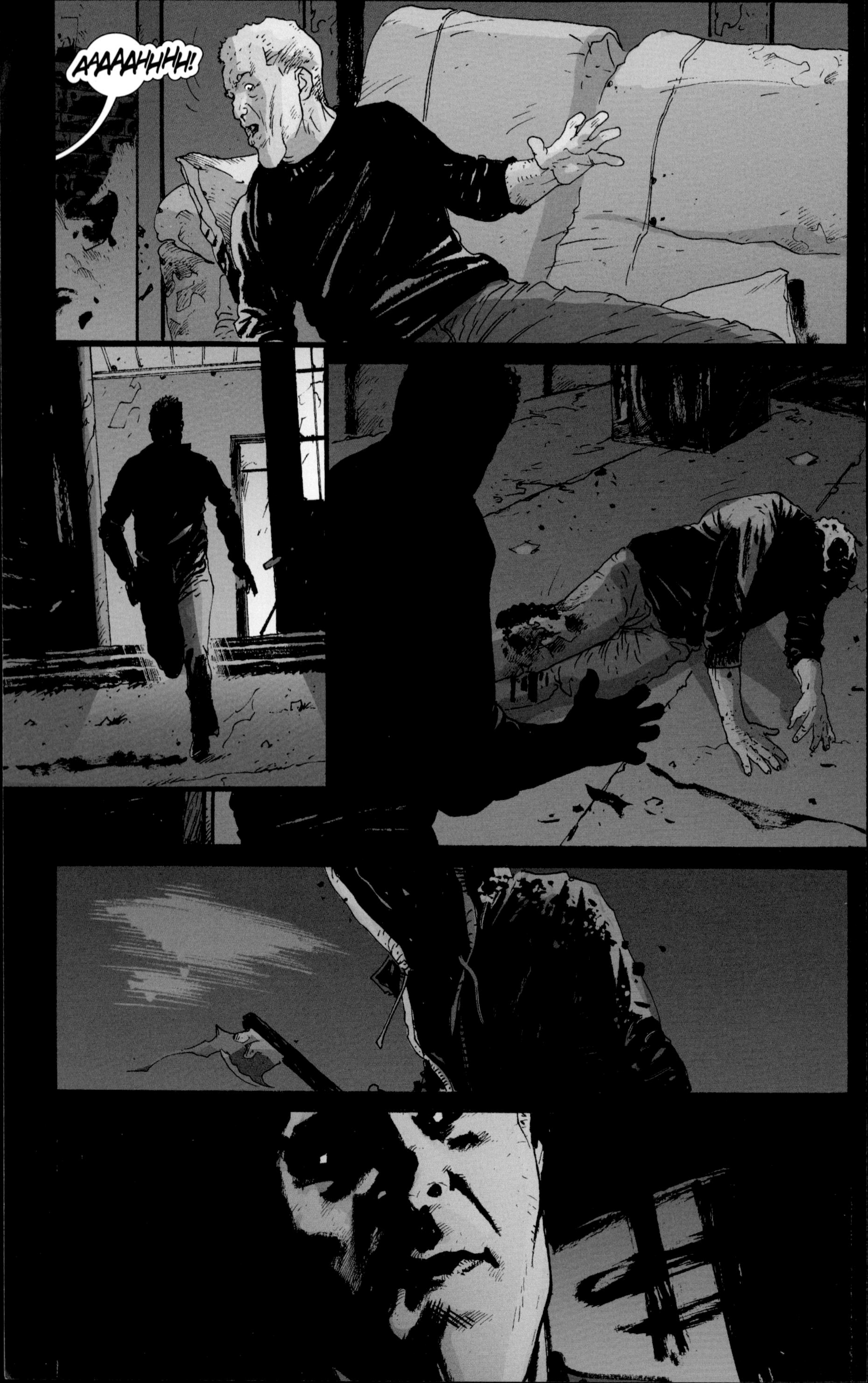
AAAAAHHHH!

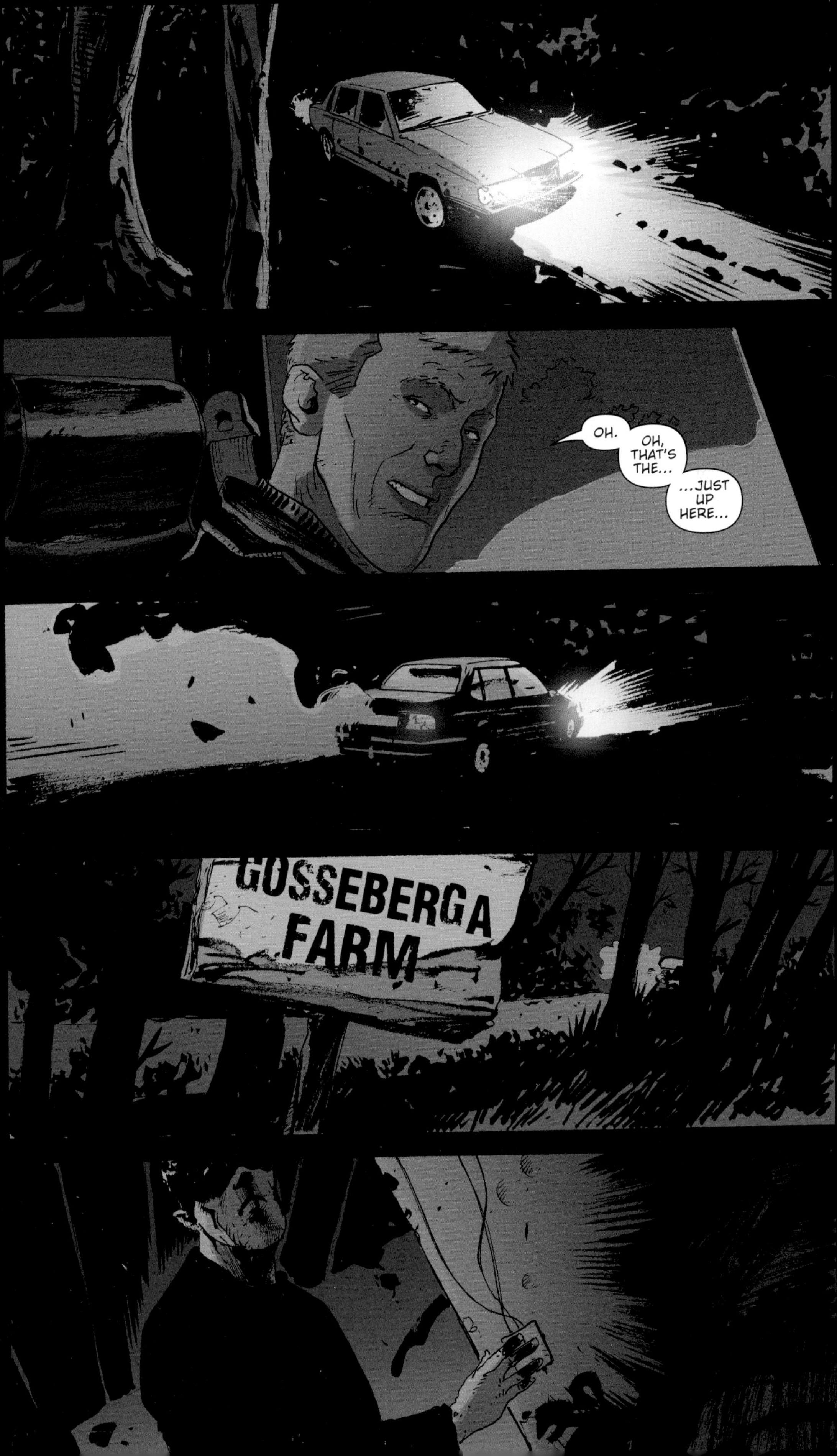
OH.
OH, THAT'S THE...
...JUST UP HERE...
GOSSEBERGA FARM

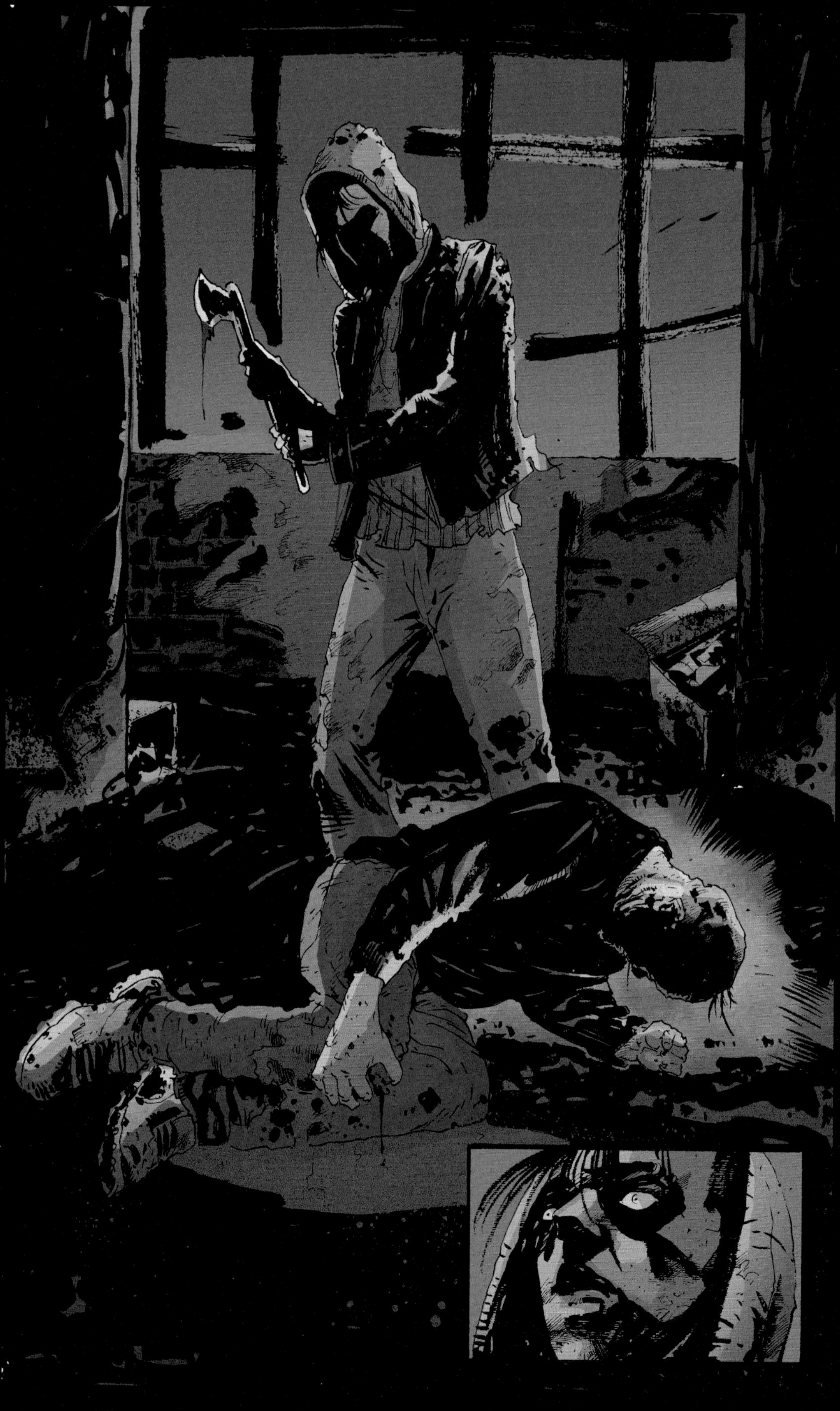

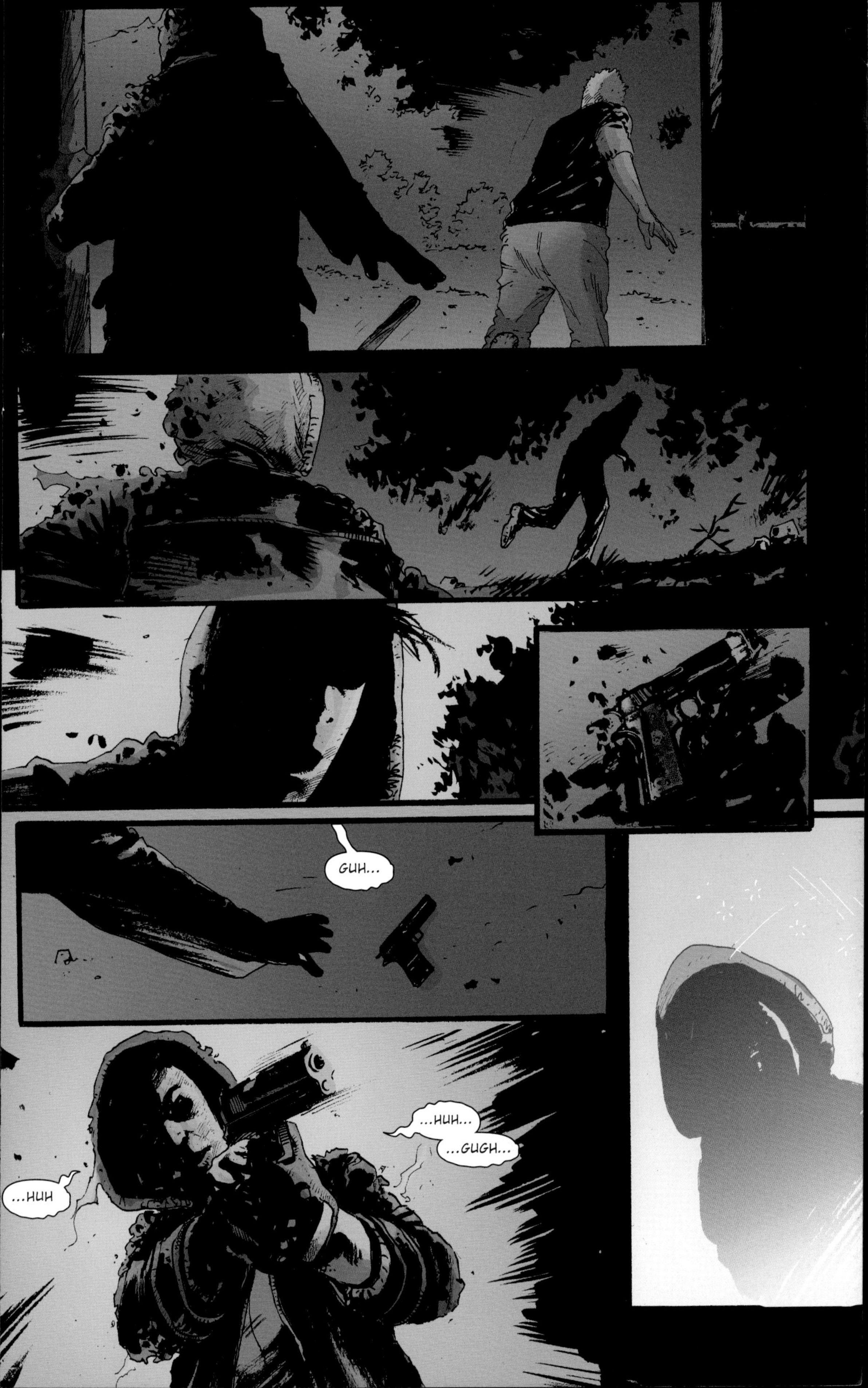
GUH...
...HUH...
...GUGH...
...HUH

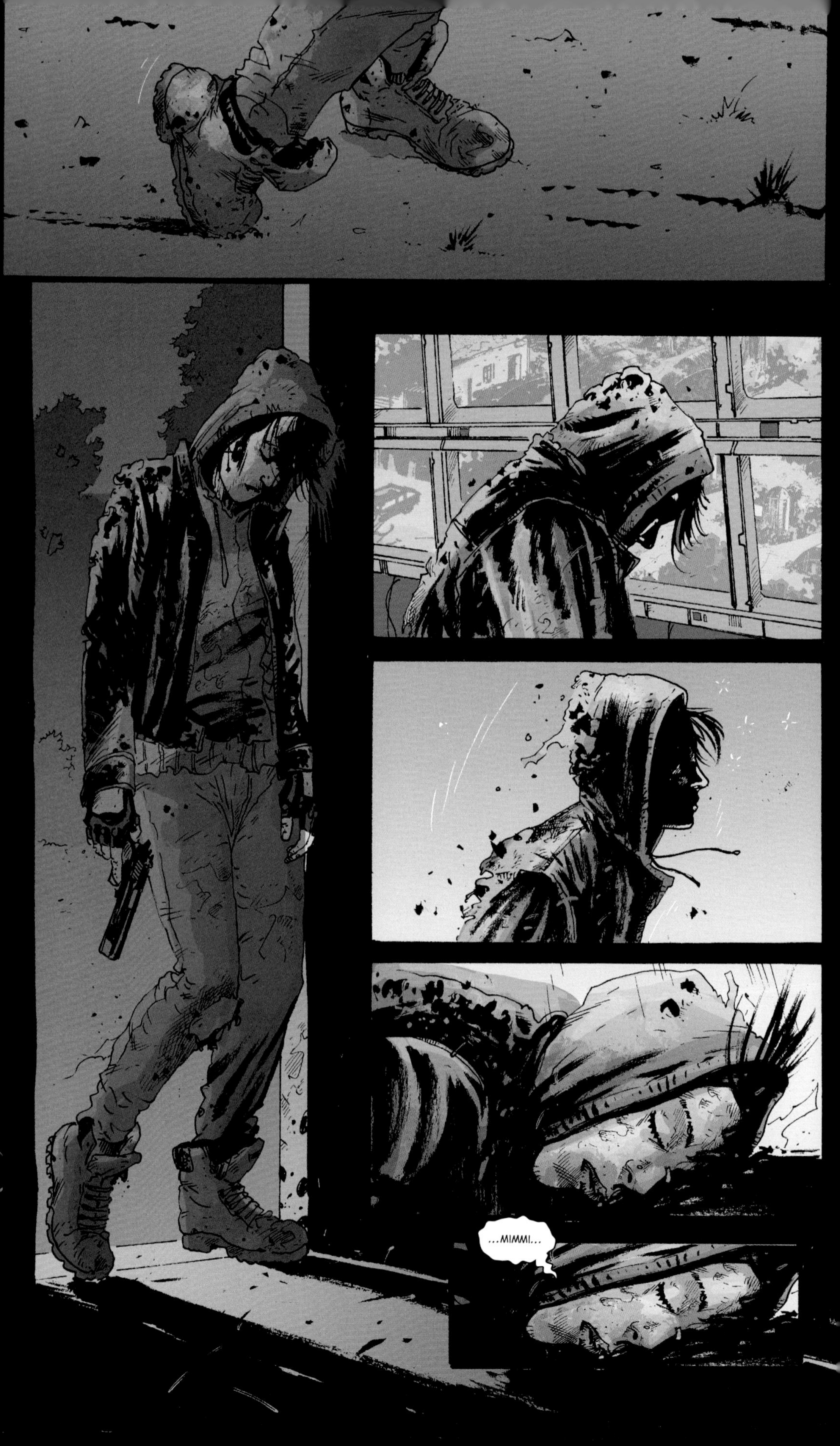
...MIMMI...

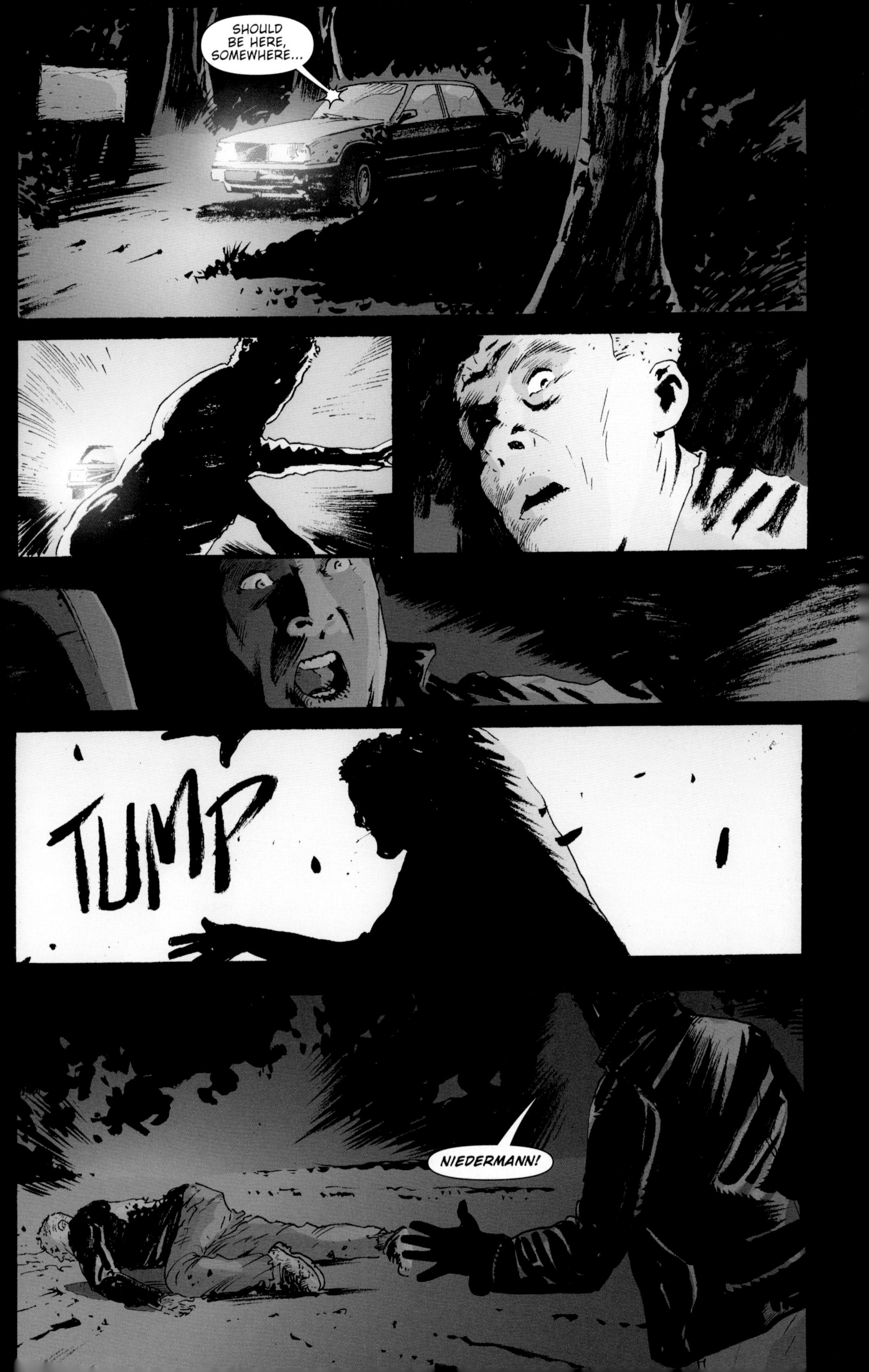
SHOULD BE HERE, SOMEWHERE...
TUMP
NIEDERMANN!

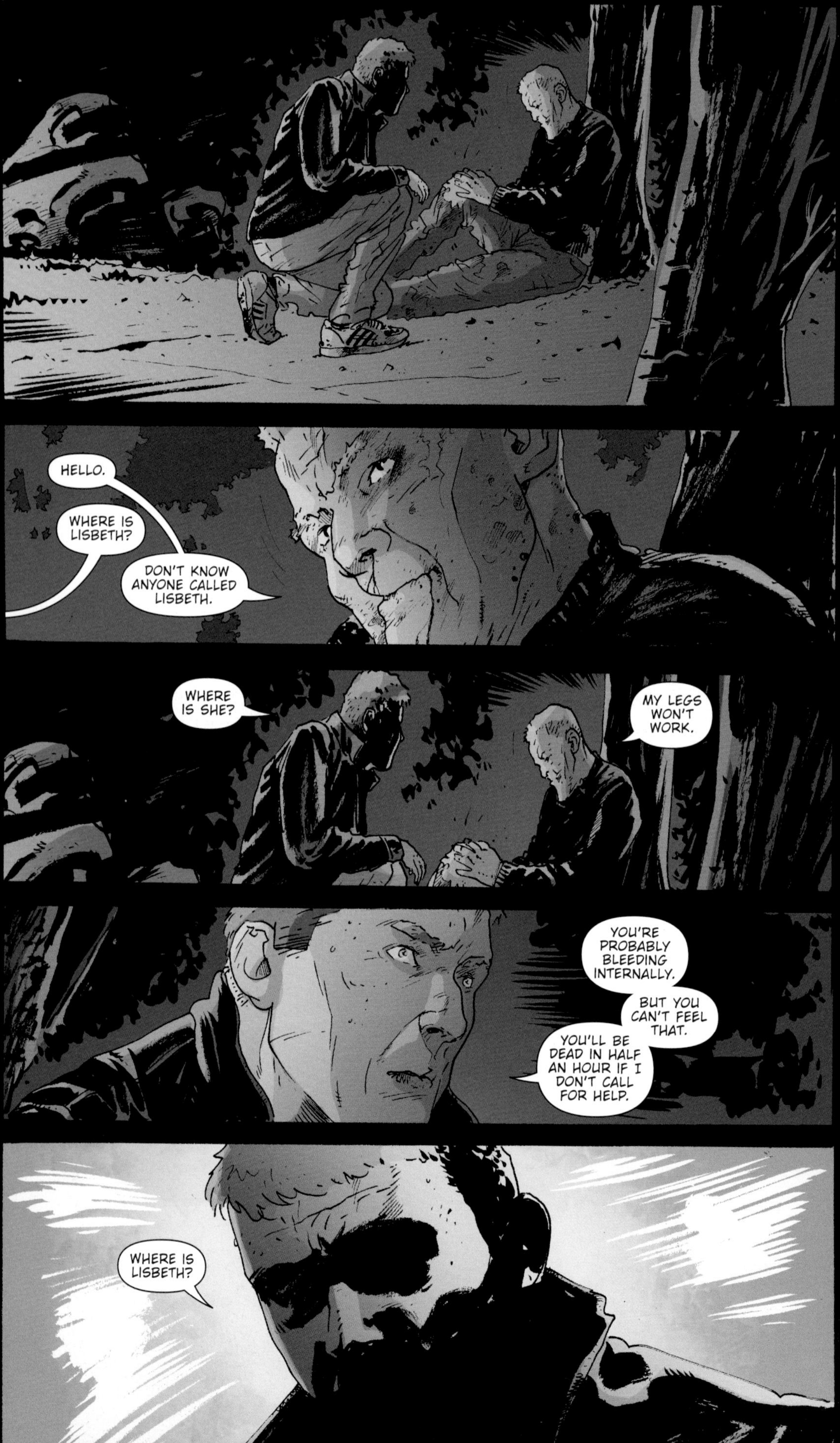
HELLO.
WHERE IS LISBETH?
DON'T KNOW ANYONE CALLED LISBETH.
WHERE IS SHE?
MY LEGS WON'T WORK.
YOU'RE PROBABLY BLEEDING INTERNALLY.
BUT YOU CAN'T FEEL THAT.
YOU'LL BE DEAD IN HALF AN HOUR IF I DON'T CALL FOR HELP.
WHERE IS LISBETH?

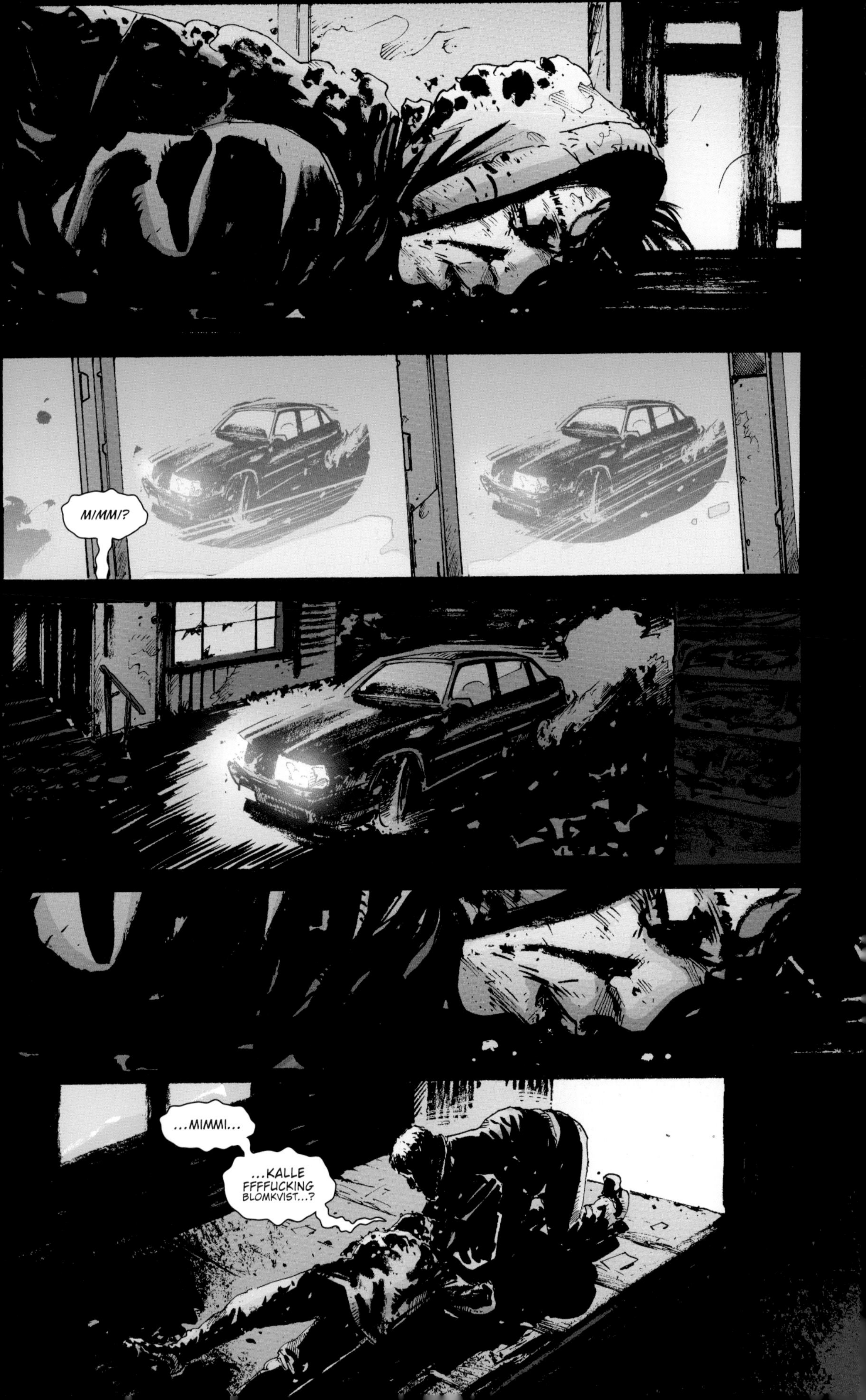
MIMMI?
...MIMMI...
...KALLE FFFFUCKING BLOMKVIST...?

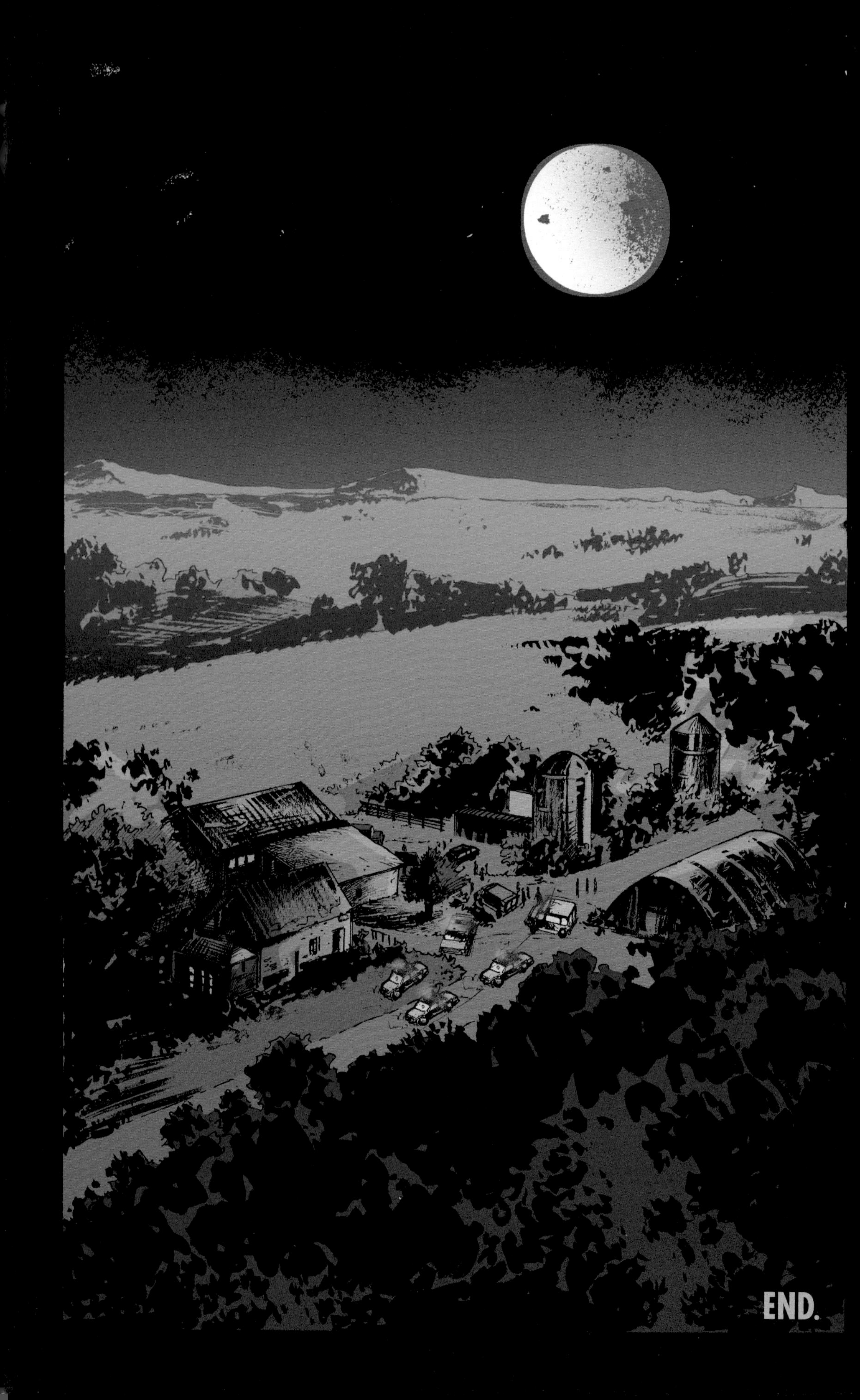
END.

DENISE MINA is a Scottish crime writer and playwright. Her first novel, Garnethill, won the Crime Writers' Association John Creasey Dagger for the best first crime novel. She is also known for writing the DC Comics series HELLBLAZER and the graphic novel A SICKNESS IN THE FAMILY.

ANTONIO FUSO is a comic book artist and illustrator known for his sharp and frenetic style. Works include the VERTIGO graphic novel A SICKNESS IN THE FAMILY (with Denise Mina) and GI Joe: Cobra. He lives and works in Rome, Italy, and is addicted to caffeine.

LEONARDO MANCO is an Argentine comic book artist and penciller best known for his dark and gritty style. Titles include Blaze of Glory, Apache Skies, Deathlok, and HELLBLAZER.

ANDREA MUTTI attended the International School of Comics in Brescia. He has worked extensively for the French market and is known for his work on the DC/Vertigo series DMZ and THE EXECUTOR.

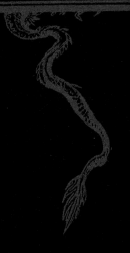

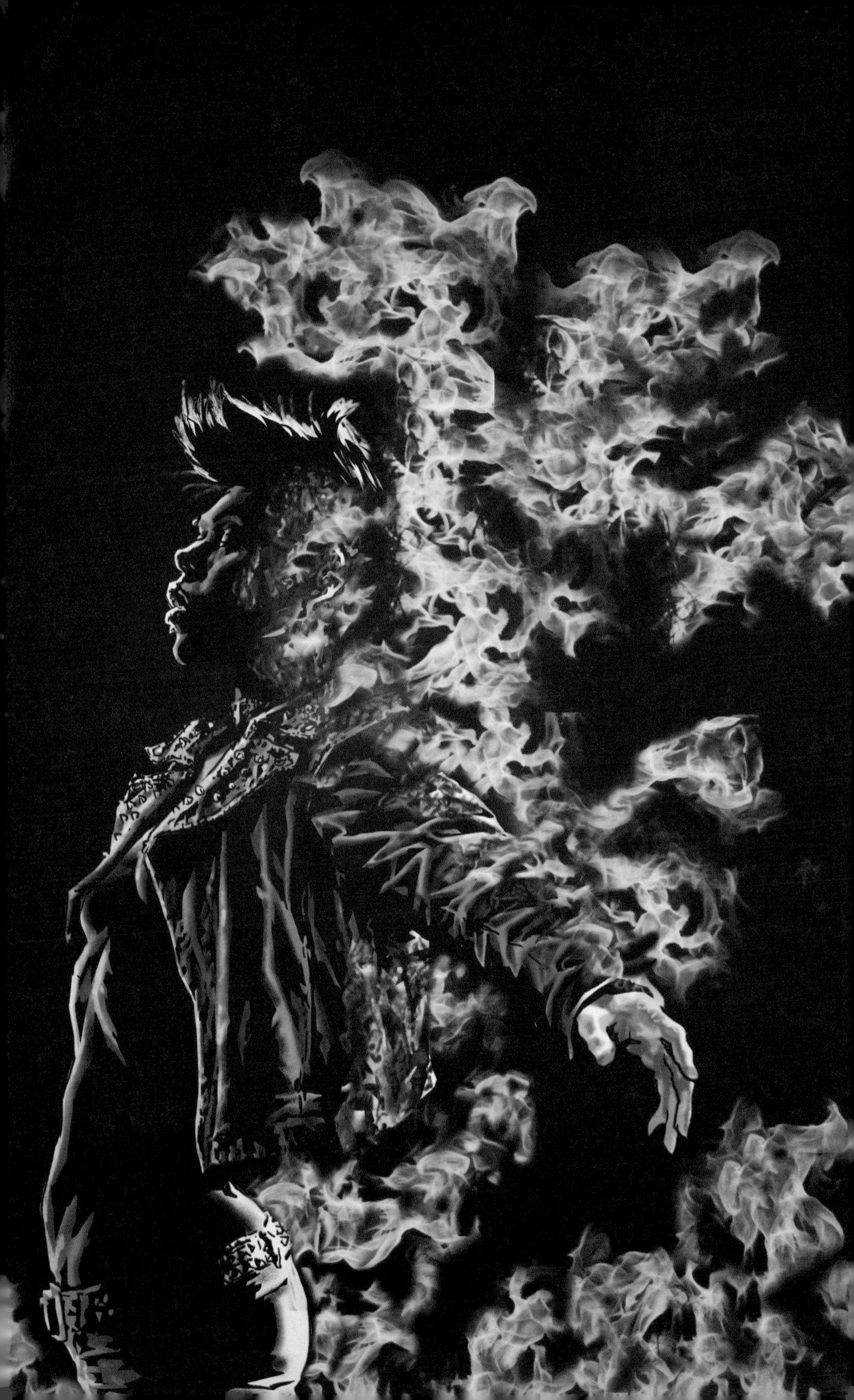

GALLERY ON FIRE

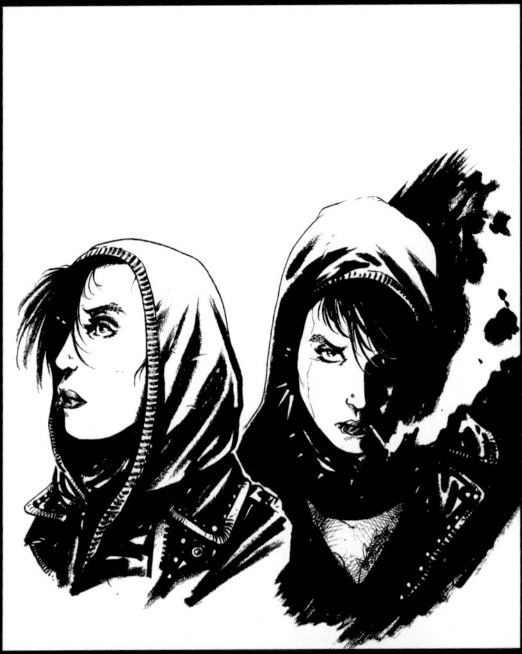

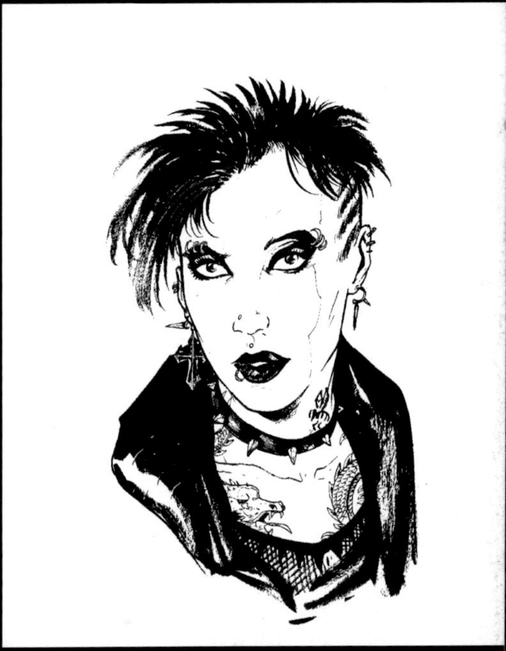

Above and below right: Character sketches by Andrea Mutti

Opposite and below left: Cover comp by Lee Bermejo

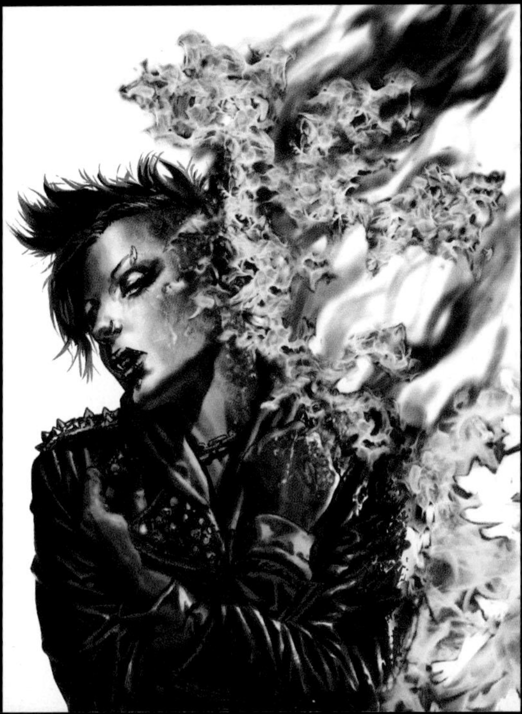

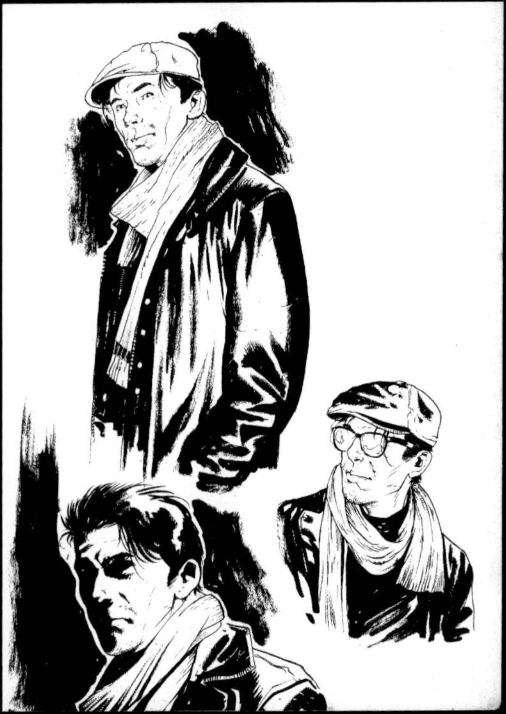

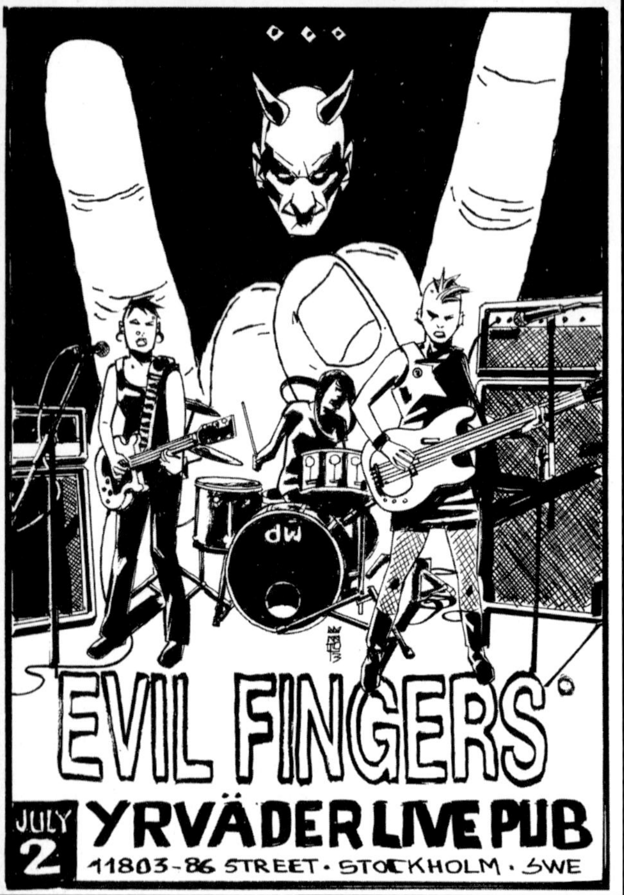
dw
EVIL FINGERS
JULY 2
YRVÄDER LIVE PUB
11803-86 STREET · STOCKHOLM · SWE

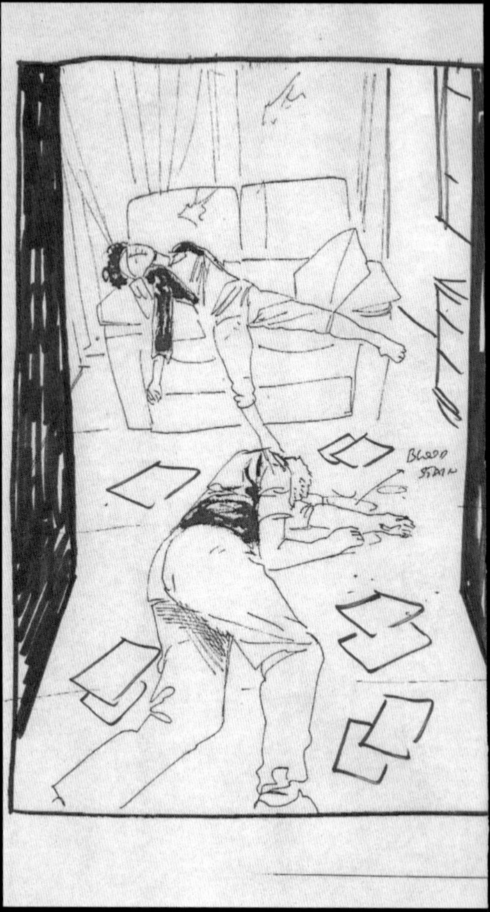
BLOOD STAIN

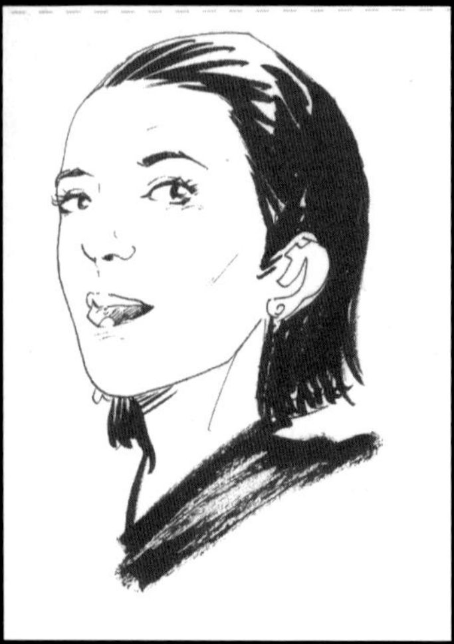

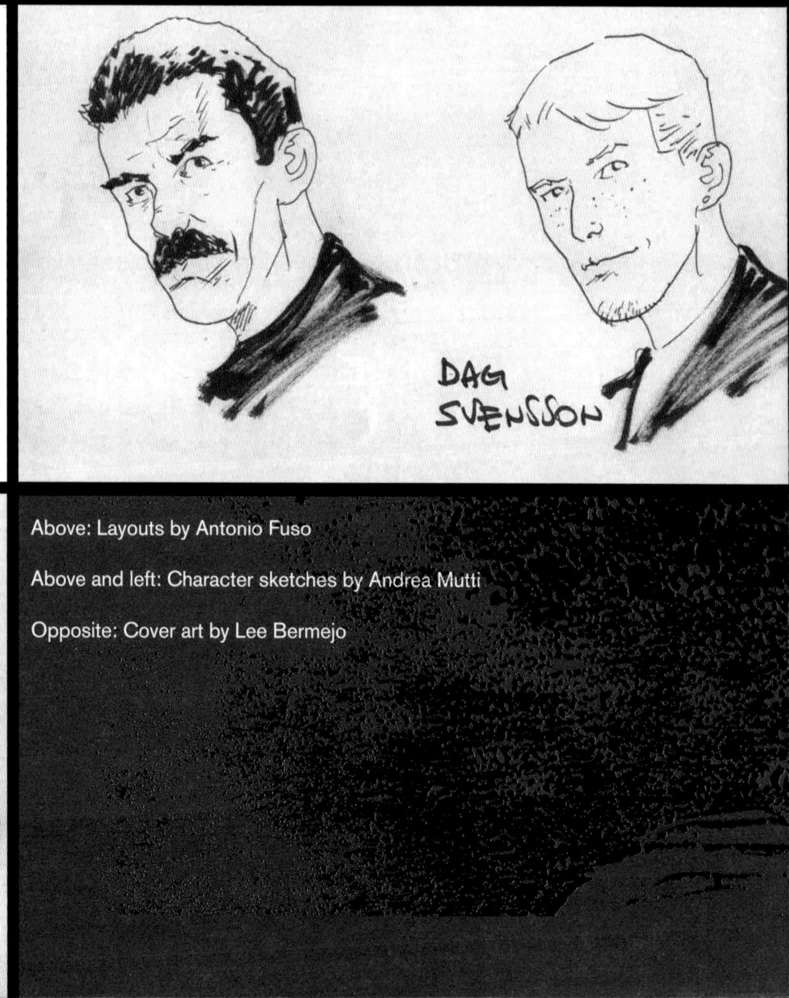
DAG SVENSSON

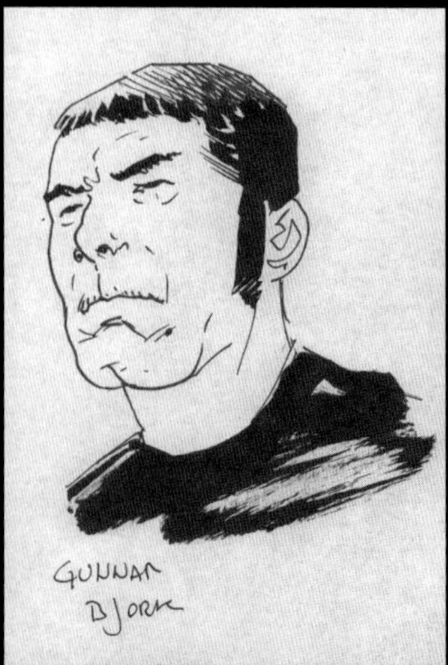
GUNNAR BJORK

Above: Layouts by Antonio Fuso

Above and left: Character sketches by Andrea Mutti

Opposite: Cover art by Lee Bermejo

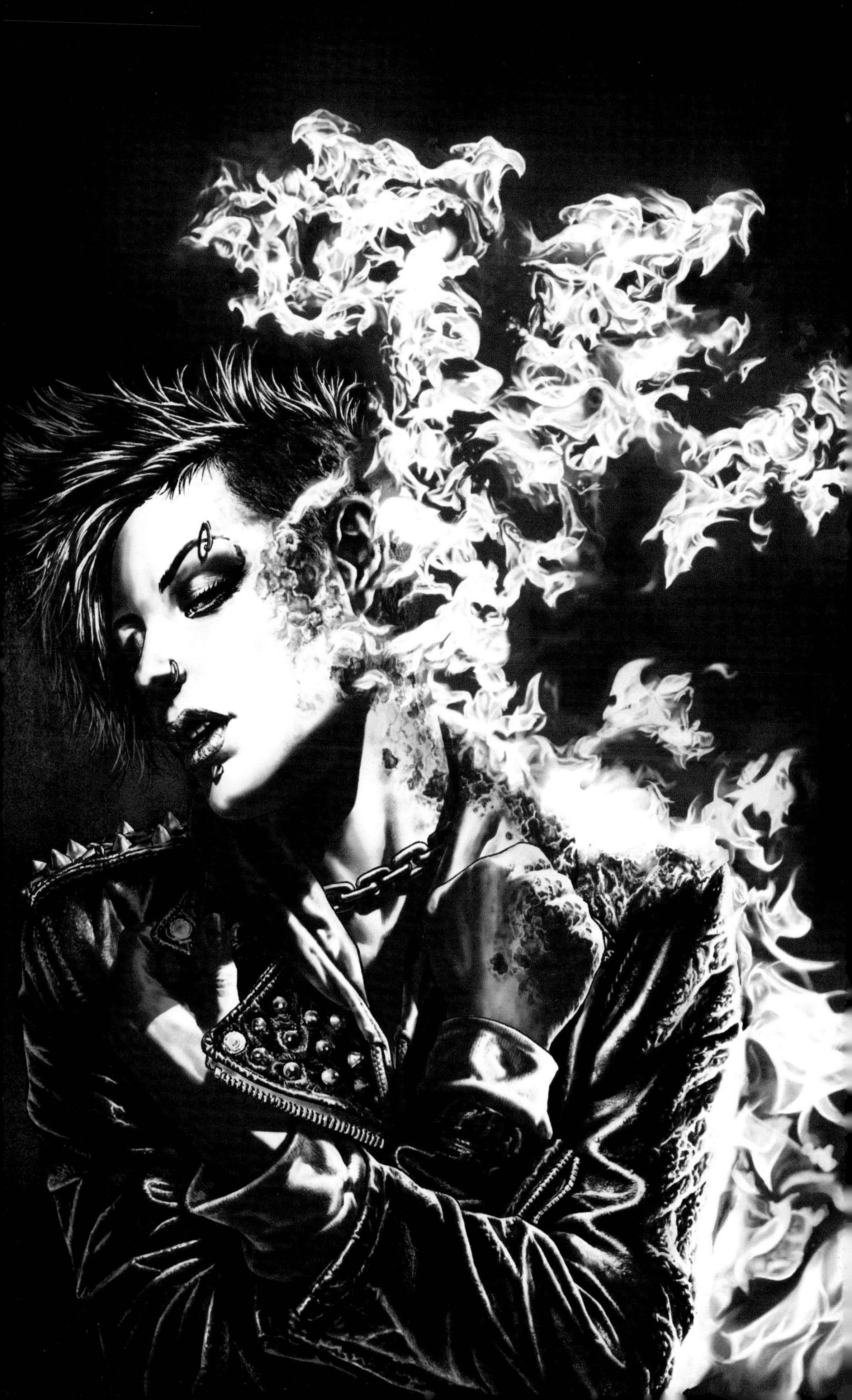